NATIONAL GEOGRAPHIC

Concise
Atlas of the World

FOURTH EDITION

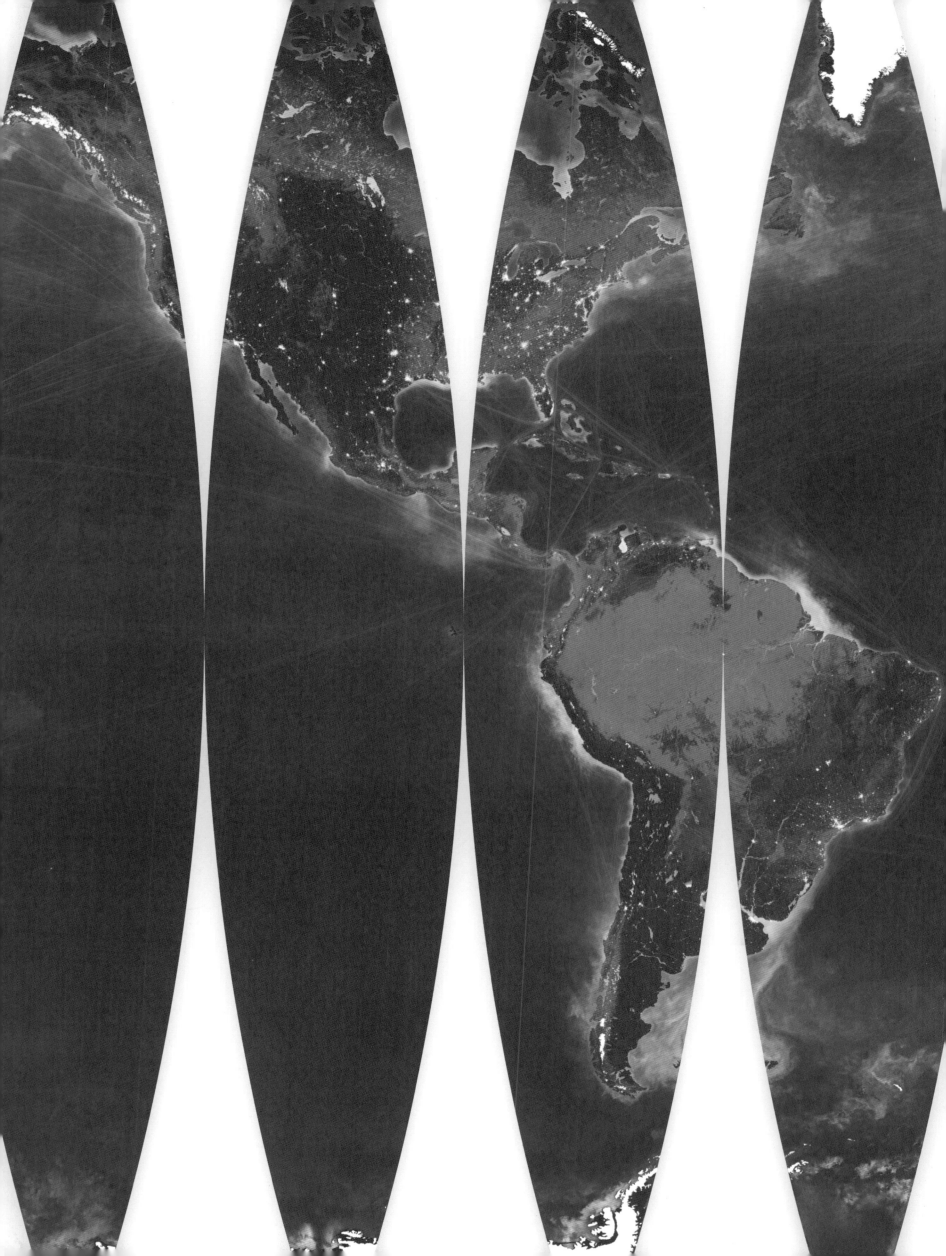

NATIONAL GEOGRAPHIC

Concise
Atlas of the World

FOURTH EDITION

National Geographic
Washington, D.C.

Introduction

"A map is the greatest of all epic poems. Its lines and colors show the realization of great dreams." — Gilbert H. Grosvenor

In October 1888 the first issue of *National Geographic* magazine was mailed from Washington, D.C., to its 200 charter members. This edition of the now iconic magazine contained no photographs. It did, however, contain maps. The future of mapping and its vital importance at National Geographic was established in that very first issue.

Other mapping firsts followed. The first National Geographic Society–sponsored expedition was launched in 1890 to the Mount St. Elias region in Alaska. Its purpose? To map the terrain. Mount Logan was discovered and recognized as Canada's highest peak during that map-driven expedition. Cartographic innovation accelerated in future decades. Albert H. Bumstead, the Society's first official chief cartographer, invented a sun compass, which was used by Richard E. Byrd during his 1926 flight to the North Pole. In the 1960s National Geographic hired painter Heinrich Berann, who partnered with oceanographic cartographer Marie Tharp and geologist Bruce Heezen to create the world's most accurate global maps of the ocean floor. For many readers it was the first time that the topography of the ocean, complete with its peaks and valleys, was revealed.

Maps remain key to National Geographic. They fill the pages of our magazines, books, websites, and mobile applications. They orient us, explain complex phenomena, and show us our place in our world. Mapping is also a thriving and growing science in 2016. The National Geographic Society continues to value excellence in the field of mapping and will expand its support for cartographic innovation and education in the future. We will fund the world's most promising cartographers and gather the brightest mapping minds to visualize the geographic challenges of today.

And why is mapping so key to our lives in 2016? The need for accurate and accessible information about our planet has never been greater. This *Concise Atlas of the World* that you hold gives you just that. You will find the most up-to-date information was used to create this publication. It will orient you and help you understand geographic relationships between towns, mountains, and rivers. Its rich thematic pages will also illuminate and explain some of the most relevant topics of today. Tectonics, climate, and biodiversity are just some of the themes that are explained in a stunning mix of maps, information graphics, and illustrations. Our maps will also take you off planet Earth and into our solar system. New to this version of the atlas is a section of maps dedicated entirely to space. You'll find brand-new maps of the near and far sides of the moon, among others. Absorb these pages and you'll be struck by the diverse yet connected state of our world and universe.

As National Geographic continues to expand our innovative mapping efforts, please enjoy this atlas. Keep it close and consult it often. You'll be amazed at how often you return to its pages to find a town or province mentioned in the news, to plan a trip, or to see what the flag of a particular country looks like.

Most of us won't make many maps for publication or be sent on mapping expeditions to Alaska, but we can all explore and map in our own lives. May you find that the *Concise Atlas of the World* guides you and informs you in your own adventures.

KAITLIN YARNALL
DEPUTY DIRECTOR, CENTERS OF EXCELLENCE
NATIONAL GEOGRAPHIC SOCIETY

Table of Contents

Key to Atlas Maps

RUSSIA

Alaska
see United States
80–85

GREENLAND

ICELAND

CANADA

**NORTH
AMERICA**
72–85

UNITED
KINGDOM

IRELAND

FRA

UNITED STATES
80–85

PORTUGAL

SP

MOROCC

MEXICO

BAHAMAS

Hawai'i
see United States
80–85

WESTERN
SAHARA

CUBA

DOMINICAN
REPUBLIC

MAURITANIA

JAMAICA

HAITI

ST. KITTS AND NEVIS
ANTIGUA AND BARBUDA

BELIZE

PUERTO
RICO

DOMINICA

CABO VERDE

HONDURAS

SENEGAL

GUATEMALA
EL SALVADOR

NICARAGUA

ST. LUCIA

BARBADOS

GAMBIA

GRENADA

ST. VINCENT AND THE GRENADINES

GUINEA-BISSAU

GUINEA

TRINIDAD AND TOBAGO

COSTA RICA

VENEZUELA

GUYANA

SIERRA LEONE

CÔTE
D'IVO

PANAMA

SURINAME

FRENCH GUIANA

LIBERIA

COLOMBIA

KIRIBATI

ECUADOR

B R A Z I L

**AUSTRALIA and
OCEANIA**
136–145

AMERICAN
SAMOA

PERU

**SOUTH
AMERICA**
90–97

SAMOA

BOLIVIA

FRENCH POLYNESIA

PARAGUAY

TONGA

CHILE

URUGUAY

ARGENTINA

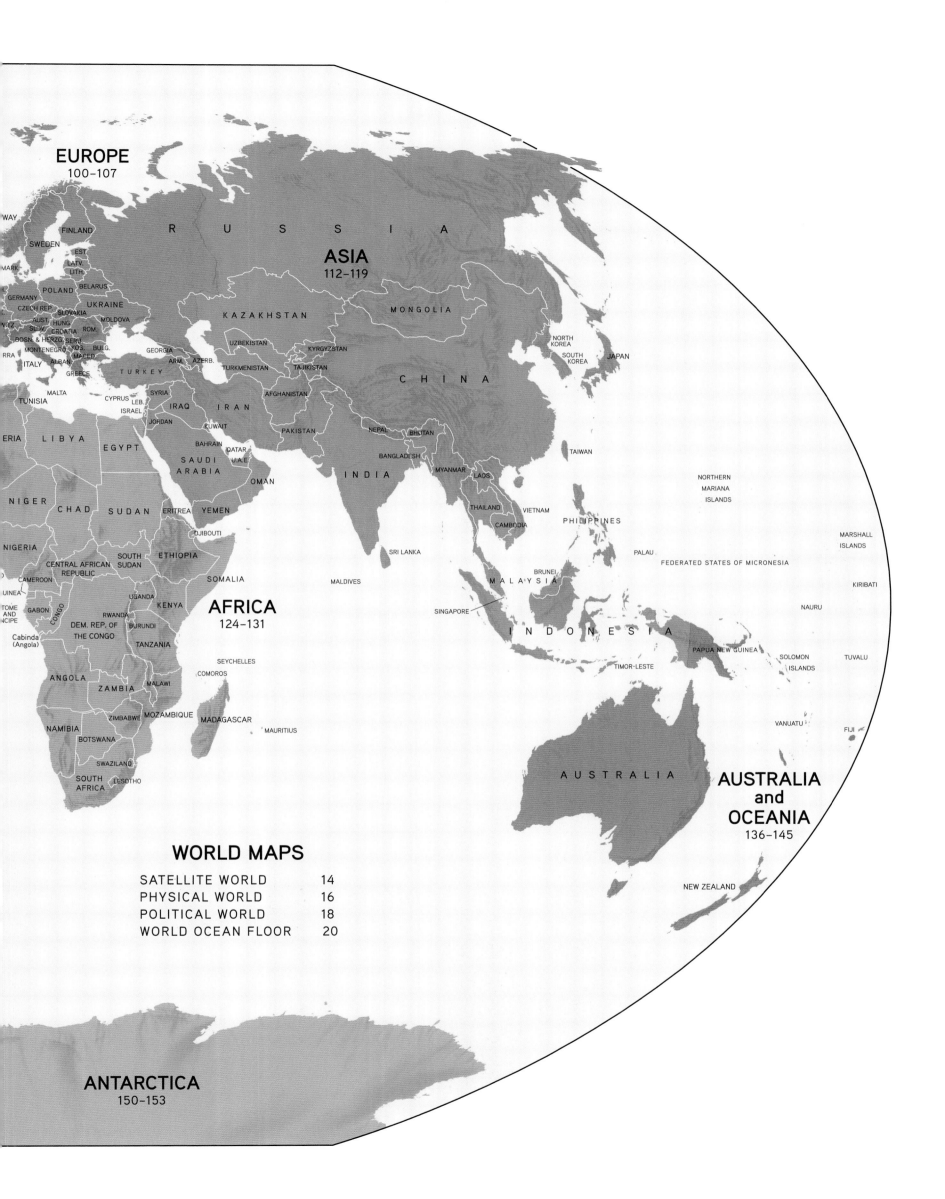

EUROPE
100–107

ASIA
112–119

AFRICA
124–131

AUSTRALIA
and
OCEANIA
136–145

ANTARCTICA
150–153

WORLD MAPS

WAY
FINLAND
SWEDEN
MARK
EST.
LATV.
LITH.
GERMANY
POLAND
BELARUS
CZECH REP
SLOVAKIA
UKRAINE
AUST.
HUNG
SLOV.
MOLDOVA
ROM.
CROATIA
BOSN. & HERZG. SERB.
MONTENEGRO KOS.
BULG.
RRA
ITALY
ALBAN. MACED.
GREECE
MALTA
TUNISIA
CYPRUS
LEB.
ISRAEL
ERIA
LIBYA
EGYPT
NIGER
CHAD
SUDAN
ERITREA
YEMEN
DJIBOUTI
NIGERIA
SOUTH
SUDAN
ETHIOPIA
CENTRAL AFRICAN
REPUBLIC
SOMALIA
CAMEROON
UINEA
TOME
AND
NCIPE
GABON
CONGO
DEM. REP. OF
THE CONGO
RWANDA
BURUNDI
UGANDA
KENYA
TANZANIA
Cabinda
(Angola)
ANGOLA
ZAMBIA
MALAWI
NAMIBIA
ZIMBABWE
MOZAMBIQUE
BOTSWANA
SWAZILAND
SOUTH
AFRICA
LESOTHO
MADAGASCAR
SEYCHELLES
COMOROS
MAURITIUS

RUSSIA
KAZAKHSTAN
MONGOLIA
GEORGIA
ARM.
AZERB.
UZBEKISTAN
KYRGYZSTAN
TURKEY
TURKMENISTAN
TAJIKISTAN
SYRIA
IRAQ
IRAN
AFGHANISTAN
CHINA
NORTH
KOREA
SOUTH
KOREA
JAPAN
JORDAN
KUWAIT
PAKISTAN
NEPAL
BHUTAN
BAHRAIN
QATAR
SAUDI
ARABIA
U.A.E.
OMAN
INDIA
BANGLADESH
MYANMAR
LAOS
TAIWAN
THAILAND
VIETNAM
CAMBODIA
PHILIPPINES
SRI LANKA
MALDIVES
MALAYSIA
SINGAPORE
BRUNEI
INDONESIA
TIMOR-LESTE
NORTHERN
MARIANA
ISLANDS
PALAU
FEDERATED STATES OF MICRONESIA
MARSHALL
ISLANDS
KIRIBATI
NAURU
PAPUA NEW GUINEA
SOLOMON
ISLANDS
TUVALU
VANUATU
FIJI
AUSTRALIA
NEW ZEALAND

Using This Atlas

MAP POLICIES

Maps are a rich, useful, and—to the extent humanly possible—accurate means of depicting the world. Yet maps inevitably make the world seem a little simpler than it really is. A neatly drawn boundary may in reality be a hotly contested war zone. The government-sanctioned, "official" name of a provincial city in an ethnically diverse region may bear little resemblance to the name its citizens routinely use. These cartographic issues often seem obscure and academic. But maps arouse passions. Despite our carefully reasoned map policies, users of National Geographic maps write us strongly worded letters when our maps are at odds with their worldviews.

How do National Geographic cartographers deal with these realities? With constant scrutiny, considerable discussion, and help from many outside experts.

EXAMPLES

Nations: Issues of national sovereignty and contested borders often boil down to "de facto versus de jure" discussions. Governments and international agencies frequently make official rulings about contested regions. These de jure decisions, no matter how legitimate, are often at odds with the wishes of individuals and groups, and they often stand in stark contrast to real-world situations. The inevitable conclusion: It is simplest and best to show the world as it is—de facto—rather than as we or others wish it to be.

Africa's Western Sahara, for example, was divided by Morocco and Mauritania after the Spanish government withdrew in 1976. Although Morocco now controls the entire territory, the United Nations does not recognize Morocco's sovereignty over this still disputed area. This atlas shows the de facto Moroccan rule.

Place-names: Ride a barge down the Danube, and you'll hear the river called Donau, Duna, Dunaj, Dunărea, Dunav, Dunay. These are local names. This atlas uses the conventional name, "Danube," on physical maps. On political maps, local names are used, with the conventional name in parentheses where space permits. Usage conventions for both foreign and domestic place-names are established by the U.S. Board on Geographic Names, a group with representatives from several federal agencies.

Physical Maps

Physical maps of the world, the continents, and the ocean floor reveal landforms and vegetation in stunning detail. Detailed digital relief is rendered and combined with prevailing land cover based on global satellite data.

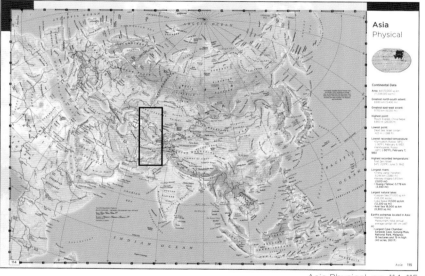

Asia Physical, pp. 114–115

Physical features: Colors and shading illustrate variations in elevation, landforms, and vegetation. Patterns indicate specific landscape features, such as sand, glaciers, and swamps.

Water features: Blue lines indicate rivers; other water bodies are shown as areas of blue.

Boundaries and political divisions are shown in red. Dashed lines indicate disputed or uncertain boundaries.

Political Maps

Political maps portray features such as international boundaries, the locations of cities, population density, and other important elements of the world's human geography. Most index entries are keyed to the political maps, listing the page numbers and then the specific locations on the pages. (See page 171 for details on how to use the index.)

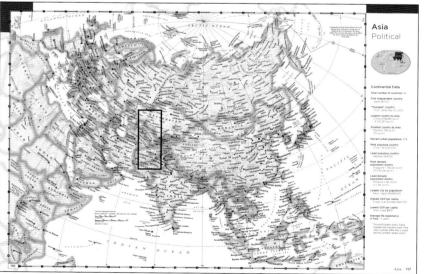

Asia Political, pp. 116–117

Physical features: Gray relief shading depicts surface features such as mountains and valleys.

Water features are shown in blue. Solid lines and filled-in areas indicate perennial water features; dashed lines and patterns indicate intermittent features.

Boundaries and political divisions are defined with both lines and colored bands; they vary according to whether a boundary is internal or international.

Cities: The regional political maps that form the bulk of this atlas depict four categories of cities or towns. The largest cities are shown in all capital letters (e.g., LONDON).

World Thematic Maps

Thematic maps reveal the rich patchwork and infinite interrelationships of our changing planet. The thematic section at the beginning of the atlas focuses on physical and biological topics such as geology, landforms, land cover, freshwater, and biodiversity. It also charts human patterns, with information on population, languages, religions, food, trade, and the world economy. In this section, maps are coupled with charts, diagrams, photographs, and tabular information, which together create a very useful framework for studying geographic patterns.

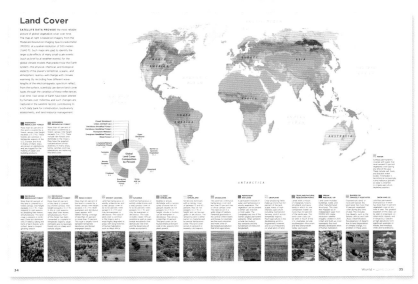

World Land Cover, pp. 34-35

Flags and Facts

This atlas recognizes 195 independent nations. All of these countries, along with dependencies and U.S. states, are profiled in the continental sections of the atlas. Accompanying each entry are highlights of geographic, demographic, and economic data. These details provide a brief overview of each country, state, or territory; they are not intended to be comprehensive. A detailed description of the sources and policies used in compiling the listings is included in the Key to Flags and Facts on page 199.

Brazil
FEDERATIVE REPUBLIC OF BRAZIL

AREA	8,515,770 sq km (3,287,957 sq mi)
POPULATION	204,260,000
CAPITAL	Brasilia 4,155,000
RELIGION	Roman Catholic, Protestant
LANGUAGE	Portuguese
LITERACY	93%
LIFE EXPECTANCY	74 years
GDP PER CAPITA	$16,200
ECONOMY	**IND:** textiles, shoes, chemicals, cement, lumber, iron ore, tin, steel, aircraft, motor vehicles and parts, other machinery and equipment **AGR:** coffee, soybeans, wheat, rice, corn, sugarcane, cocoa, citrus, beef **EXP:** transport equipment, iron ore, soybeans, footwear, coffee, autos

Index and Grid

Beginning on page 171 is a full index of place-names found in this atlas. The edge of each map is marked with letters (in rows) and numbers (in columns), to which the index entries are referenced. As an example, "Cartagena, Col. 94 A2" (see inset below) refers to the grid section on page 94 where row A and column 2 meet. More examples and additional details about the index are included on page 171.

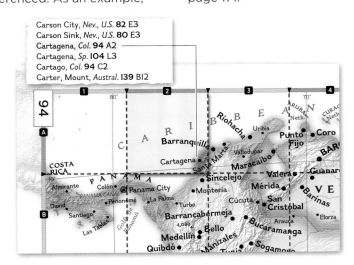

Map Symbols

BOUNDARIES

	Defined
	Undefined or disputed
	Offshore line of separation
	International boundary (Physical Maps)
	Disputed or undefined boundary (Physical Maps)

CITIES

⊛ ⊛ ◎ ◎	Capitals
● ● • ·	Towns
○	Farmstead or homestead

WATER FEATURES

	Drainage
	Intermittent drainage
	Intermittent lake
	Dry salt lake
	Swamp
	Falls or rapids

PHYSICAL FEATURES

	Relief
	Lava and volcanic debris
+8,850 (29,035 ft)	Elevation in meters (feet in United States)
•-86	Elevation in meters below sea level
⇌	Pass
	Sand
	Salt desert
	Below sea level
	Ice shelf
	Glacier

CULTURAL FEATURES

	Canal
▫	Site

MAP SCALE (Sample)

SCALE 1:81,657,000   1 CENTIMETER = 817 KILOMETERS; 1 INCH = 1,289 MILES AT THE EQUATOR

KILOMETERS: 0 500 1000 1500 2000 2500

STATUTE MILES: 0 500 1000 1500 2000 2500

World

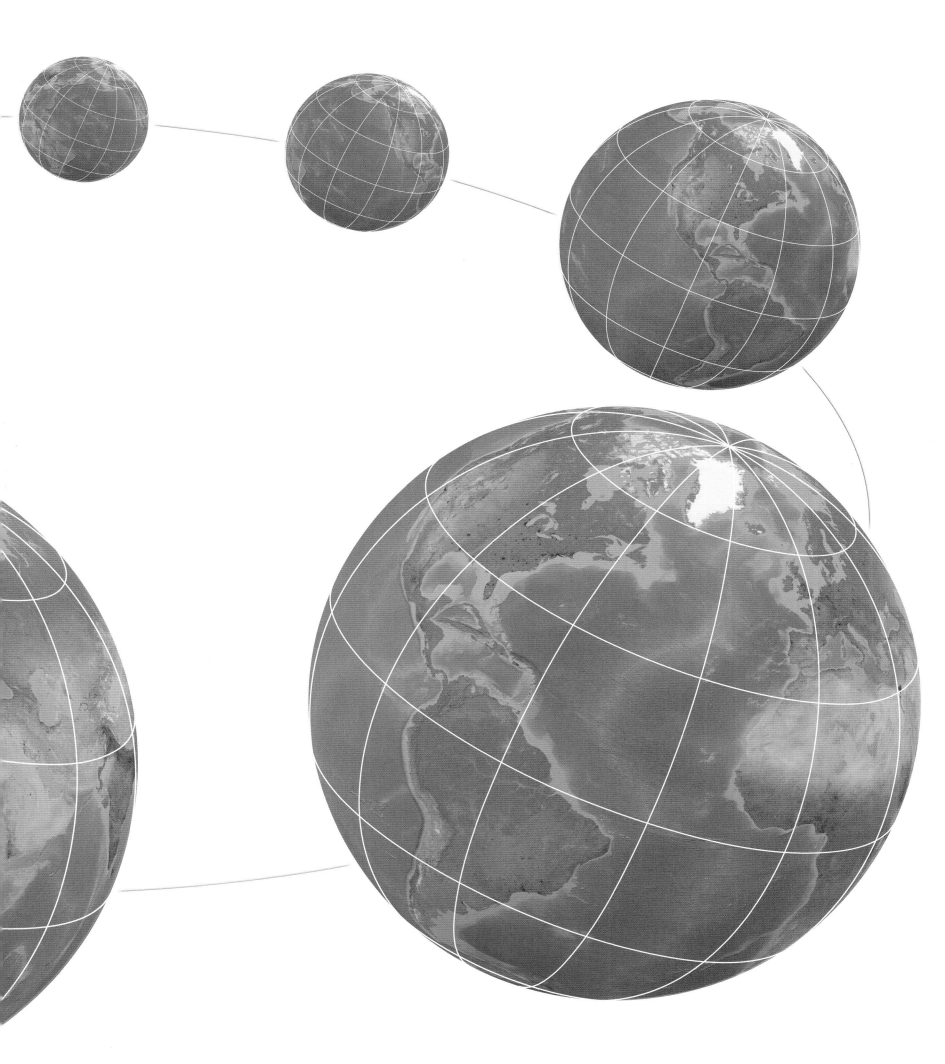

Satellite World

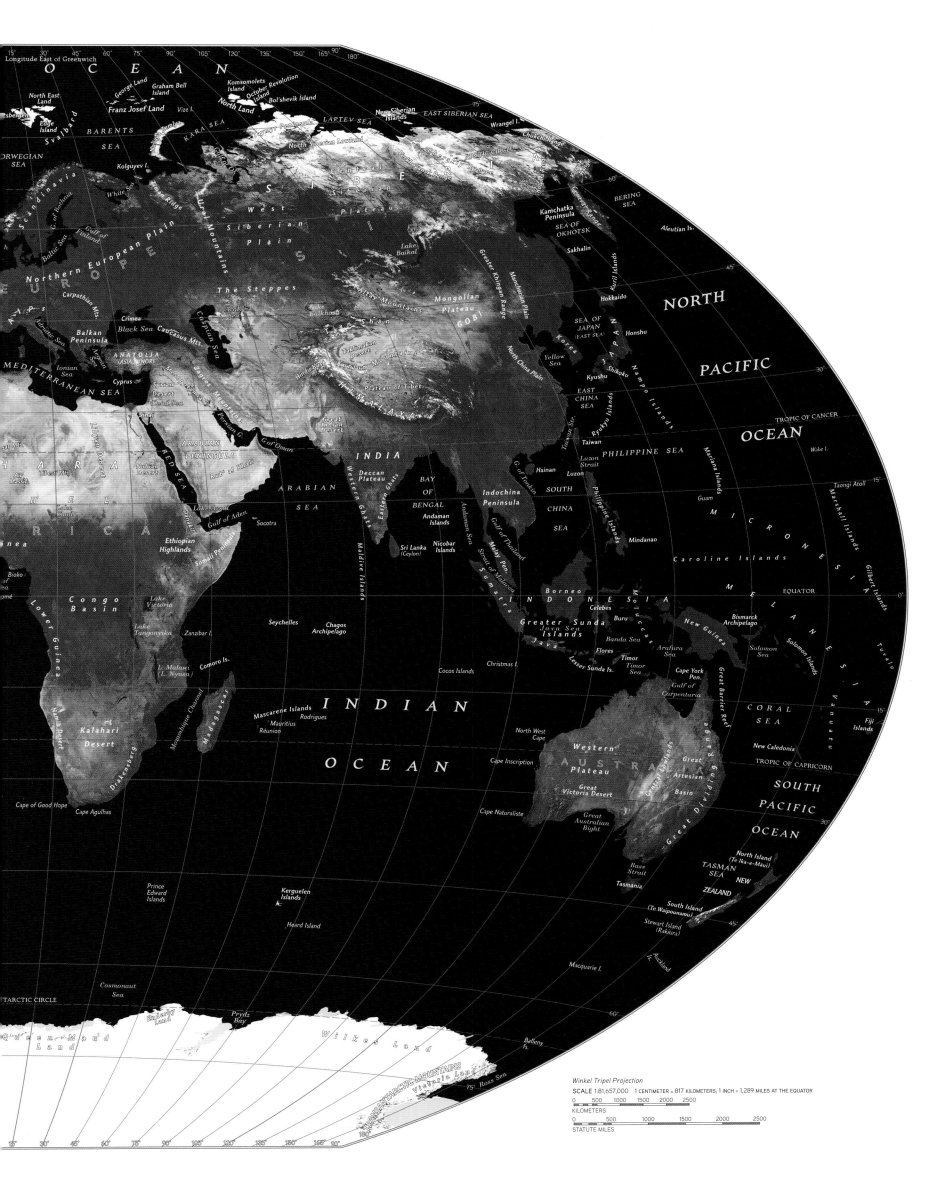

Physical World

ARCTIC

Longitude West of Greenwich

North Magnetic Pole, 2015

QUEEN ELIZABETH ISLANDS

Axel Heiberg 2,012
Prince Patrick I.
Melville I.
Banks Island
Ellesmere Island
Hayes Peninsula
Knud Rasmussen Land
Lincoln Sea
Wandel

GREENLAND

Point Barrow
Wrangel I.
Chukchi Sea
North Slope
SIBERIA
Chukchi Pen.
Bering Strait
Brooks Range
Seward Pen.
ALASKA
Yukon
Alaska Range
Denali (Mt. McKinley) 6,190
Keele Peak 2,952
Highest point in North America

McClure Strait
Parry Is.
Victoria Island 503
Boothia Pen.
Melville Pen.
Devon I.
BAFFIN BAY

Ice thickness 3,366
3,200
Gunnbjørn Fjeld 3,694

Southampton I.
Mackenzie
Great Bear Lake
Mt. Roosevelt
Peace
Great Slave Lake
Back
Thelon
Mt. Robson 3,959
4,016

Hudson Bay
Baffin Island 2,591
Hudson Strait
Davis Strait
Iceland 2,119
Denmark Strait
Faroe Is.

Vancouver Island
ROCKY MOUNTAINS
NORTH AMERICA
Canadian Shield
Nelson
James Bay
Ungava Bay
Mont D'Iberville 1,652
LABRADOR
Cape Farewell
LABRADOR SEA
NORTH
Celtic Sea
Ireland
Br.

Mount Rainier 4,392
Haida Gwaii (Queen Charlotte Is.)
Alexander Archipelago
Gulf of Alaska 4,663
Aleutian Islands 2,857
Alaska Pen.
BERING SEA

L. Winnipeg
L. Superior
Source of the Mississippi
L. Huron
L. Ontario
Gulf of St. Lawrence
Island of Newfoundland
Anticosti I.
Nova Scotia
Gulf of Maine
Bay of Fundy
Cape Cod
Long Island
Point St.-Mathie
Cape Finisterre

NORTH

Cape Mendocino
Mount Shasta 4,317
Sierra Nevada
Great Basin 4,418
Great Salt Lake
3,658
Missouri
Ozark Plateau
Appalachian Mountains
Ohio
Chesapeake Bay
Bermuda Islands
Azores
Cape St. Vincent
Str. of Gibraltar
Madeira Is.
Jebel Toubkal 4,165

PACIFIC
Midway Is.
NORTH
Death Valley -86 (-282 ft) Lowest point in North America
Guadalupe I.
Baja California
TROPIC OF CANCER
Gulf of California
Sierra Madre Occidental
Sierra Madre Oriental
Mississippi R. Delta
Florida
Cape Hatteras
Coastal Plain
GULF OF MEXICO
ATLANTIC
Canary Islands

Hawaiian Islands
Kaua'i
O'ahu
Maui
Hawai'i 4,169
Mauna Loa
Johnston Atoll
False Cape
Pico de Orizaba 5,747
Isthmus of Tehuantepec
Yucatán Peninsula
Bahama Is.
Cuba
Hispaniola
Greater Antilles
Puerto Rico
Jamaica
WEST INDIES
OCEAN
Cape Verde Islands
Cape Verde
Senegal

OCEAN
Palmyra Atoll
Kiritimati (Christmas I.)
Line Islands
CENTRAL AMERICA
Lake Nicaragua
CARIBBEAN SEA
Lesser Antilles
Pt. Gallinas
Trinidad
Orinoco R. Delta

Howland I.
Baker I.
EQUATOR
Jarvis I.
Phoenix Islands
Clipperton
Cocos Island
Azuero Pen.
Isthmus of Panama 3,819
L. Maracaibo
Orinoco
Llanos
Guiana Highlands
Mt. Roraima 2,810
Cerro Marahuaca 2,579
Pico da Neblina 2,994
Mouths of the Amazon
Cape

Galápagos Islands
Chimborazo 6,310
Gulf of Guayaquil
Pariñas Point
Amazon Basin
Amazon
Marajó
Point Calcahar
Point Coqueiros
Ascension

Atafu
Tokelau
Marquesas Islands
Caroline I. (Millennium I.)
Flint I.
Nassau
Swains I.
Savai'i Samoa
Upolu
Manua'e
Nevado Huascarán
SOUTH
Brazilian
St. Helena

Wallis Is.
Rose Atoll
Tuamotu Archipelago
Pukapuka
Mataiva
Society Islands
Tahiti
The Andes
Source of the Amazon
Lake Titicaca
Nevado Coropuna 6,425
6,542
AMERICA
Highlands
Baleia Point
Martin Vaz Islands

Fiji Is.
Tonga Islands
Niue
Rarotonga
Mangaia
Maria
COOK ISLANDS
Íles Gambier
Morane
Salas y Gómez Island
Atacama Desert
Salar de Uyuni
Gran Chaco
Pico da Bandeira 2,890
Cabo Frio
SOUTH

TROPIC OF CAPRICORN
Austral Islands
Pitcairn I.
Easter Island
Cerro Ojos del Salado 6,880
San Félix I.
San Ambrosio I.
Cerro del Toro 6,380
Volcán Llullaillaco 6,723
Cape Santa Marta Grande
Paraná
Patos Lagoon
ATLANTIC

Kermadec Islands
Rapa
Marotiri
Juan Fernández Islands
Salinas Grandes
Cerro Aconcagua 6,959 (22,831 ft) Highest point in South America
Pampas
River Plate
Blanca Bay

Chatham Islands
Isla Grande de Chiloé
San Matías Gulf
Valdés Peninsula
Corcovado Gulf
Taitao Peninsula 4,035
Patagonia
Gulf of San Jorge
Lowest point in South America
Laguna del Carbón -105 (-344 ft)
Falkland Islands
OCEAN

PACIFIC
Wellington I.
Strait of Magellan
Tierra del Fuego
Cape Horn
South Georgia
SCOTIA SEA
South Sandwich Islands

OCEAN
Drake Passage
South Orkney Islands
South Shetland Islands
ANTARCTIC PENINSULA
WEDDELL SEA
Cape Norvegia

ANTARCTIC CIRCLE
Peter I I.
Bellingshausen Sea
Thurston I.
Adelaide Island
Alexander Island

Siple Island
Carney I.
Amundsen Sea
935 Mt. Tuve
Highest point in Antarctica
Ellsworth Land
Vinson Massif 4,897 (16,067 ft)
Berkner Island
Ronne Ice Shelf
Filchner Ice Shelf

Wrigley Gulf
Sulzberger Bay
Mount Giles
Ross Sea
Edward VII Pen.
Marie Byrd Land
Ellsworth Mountains
TRANSANTARCTIC MOUNTAINS
ANTAR

Roosevelt I.
Ross Ice Shelf

16

Political World

World Ocean Floor

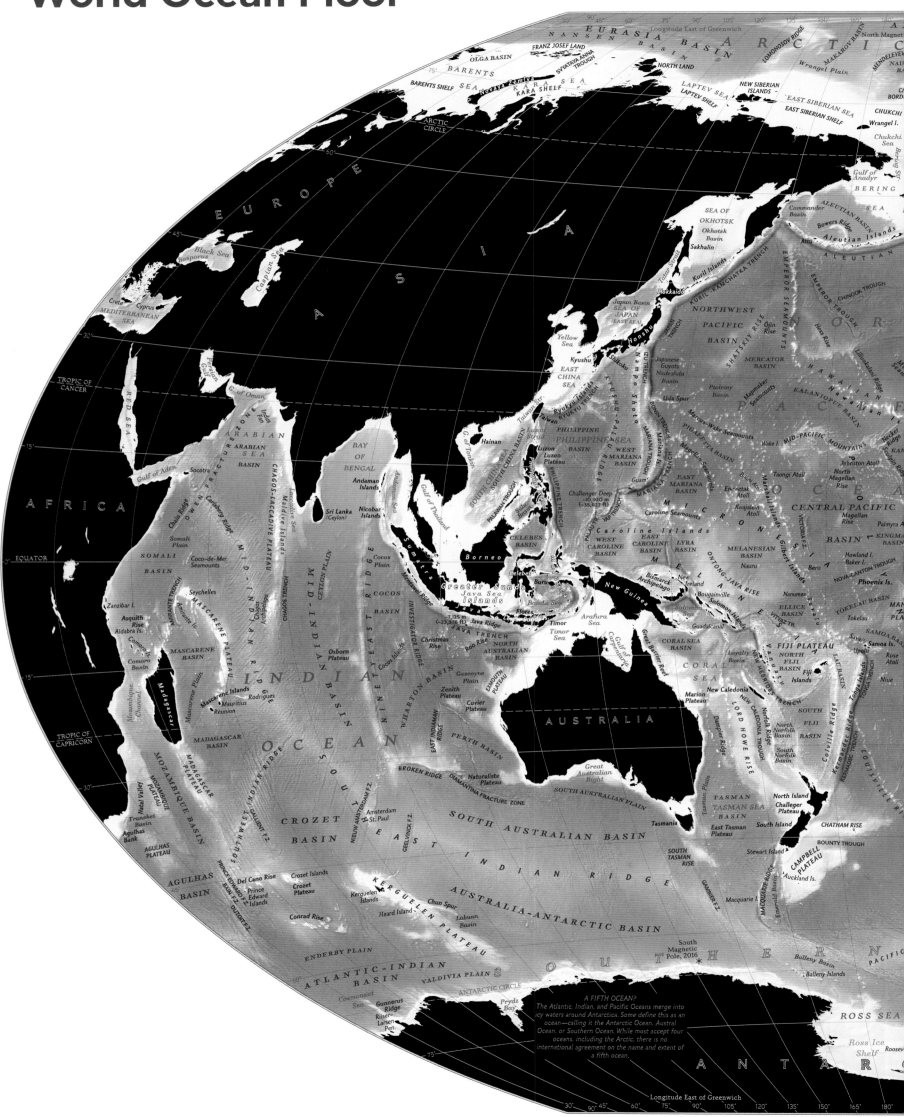

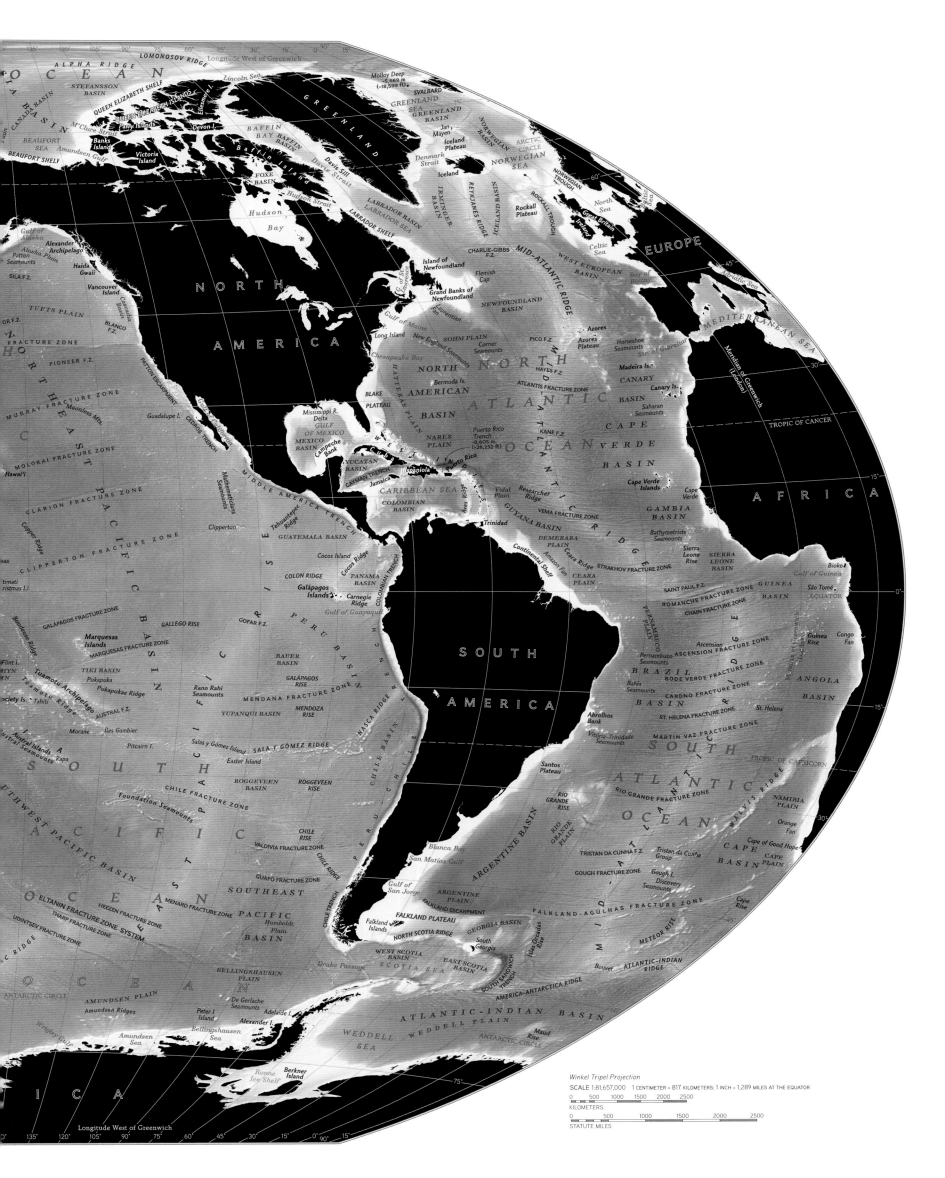

Limits of the Oceans and Seas

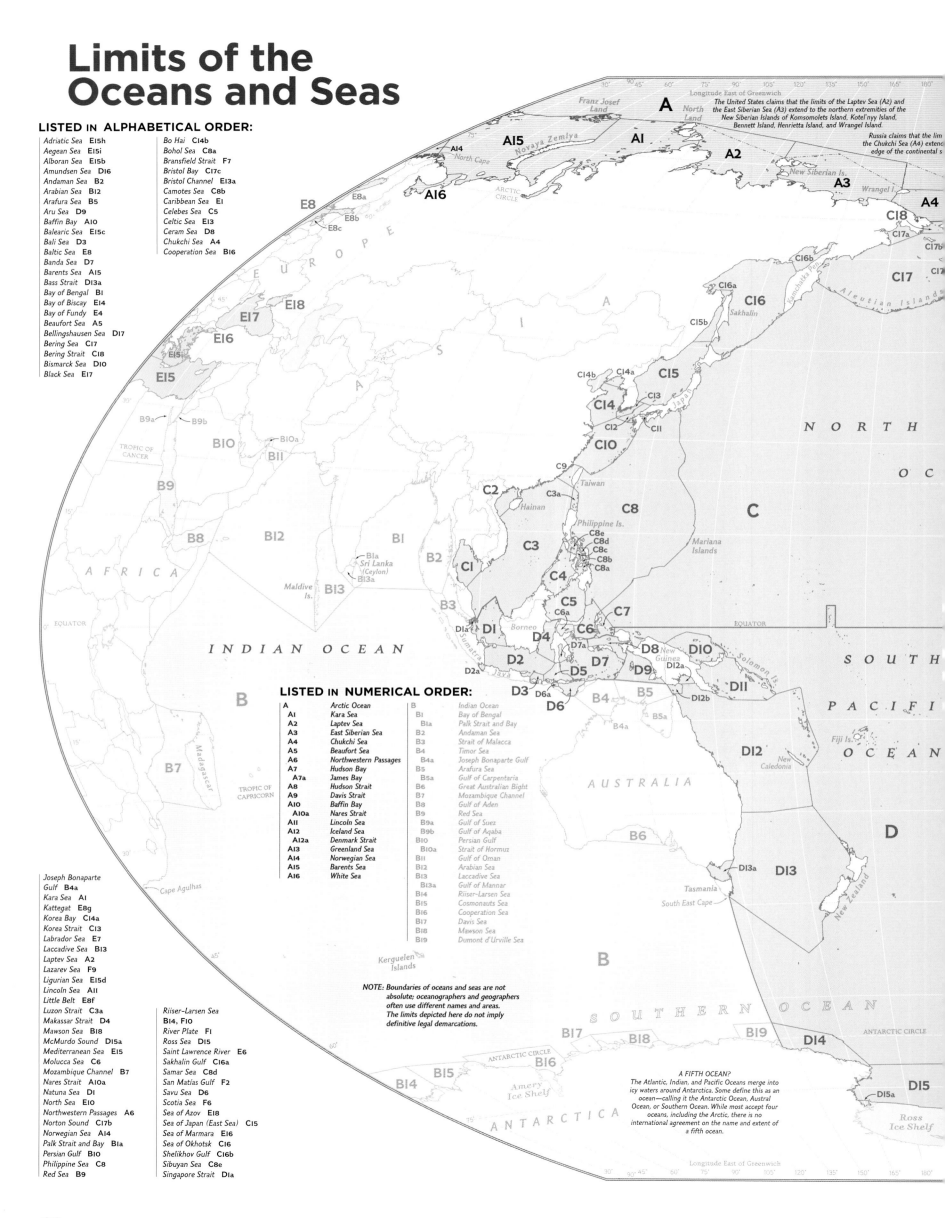

NOTE: Boundaries of oceans and seas are not absolute; oceanographers and geographers often use different names and areas. The limits depicted here do not imply definitive legal demarcations.

The United States claims that the limits of the Laptev Sea (A2) and the East Siberian Sea (A3) extend to the northern extremities of the New Siberian Islands of Komsomolets Island, Kotel'nyy Island, Bennett Island, Henrietta Island, and Wrangel Island.

Russia claims that the lim the Chukchi Sea (A4) exten edge of the continental s

A FIFTH OCEAN?
The Atlantic, Indian, and Pacific Oceans merge into icy waters around Antarctica. Some define this as an ocean—calling it the Antarctic Ocean, Austral Ocean, or Southern Ocean. While most accept four oceans, including the Arctic, there is no international agreement on the name and extent of a fifth ocean.

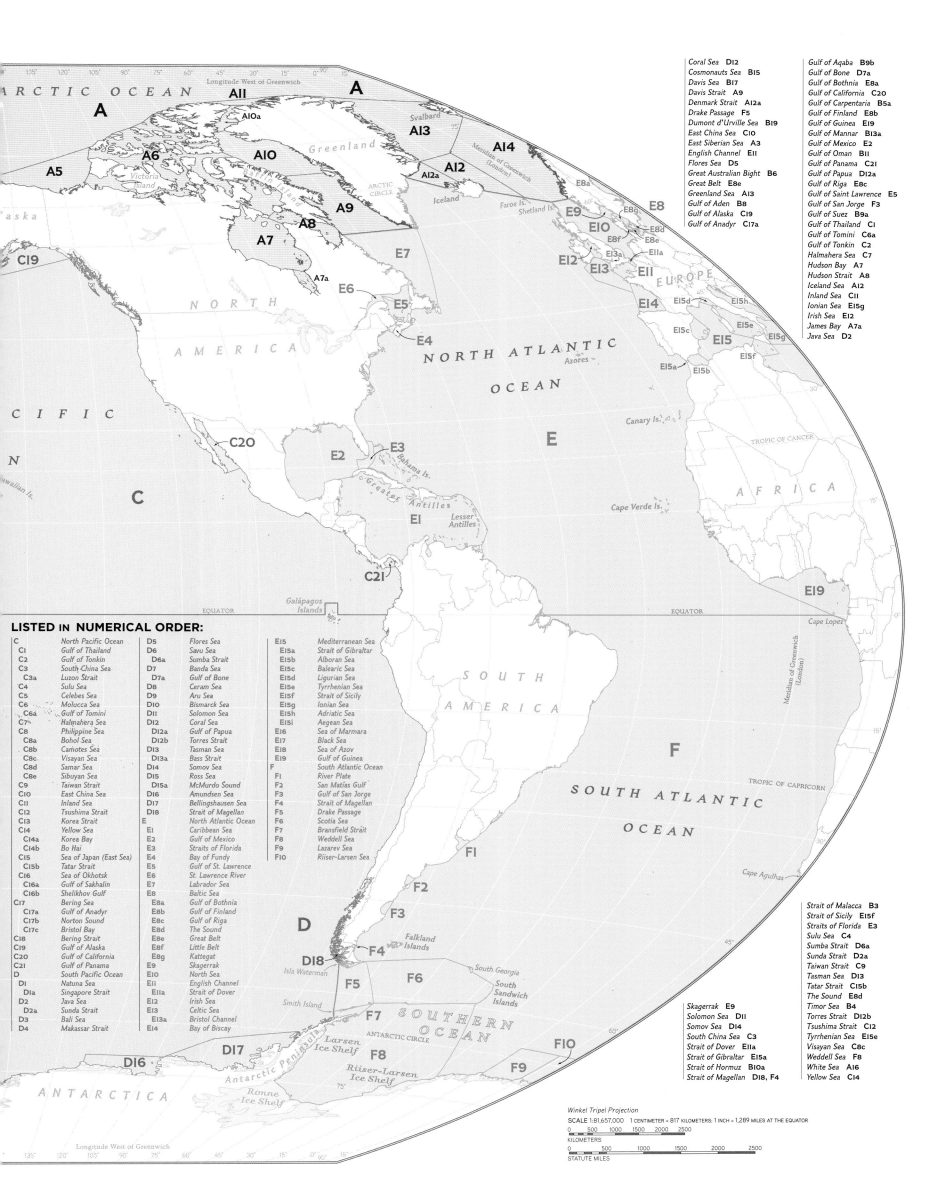

LISTED IN NUMERICAL ORDER:

Winkel Tripel Projection
SCALE 1:81,657,000   1 CENTIMETER = 817 KILOMETERS; 1 INCH = 1,289 MILES AT THE EQUATOR

KILOMETERS 0 500 1000 1500 2000 2500

STATUTE MILES 0 500 1000 1500 2000 2500

The Poles

North Pole

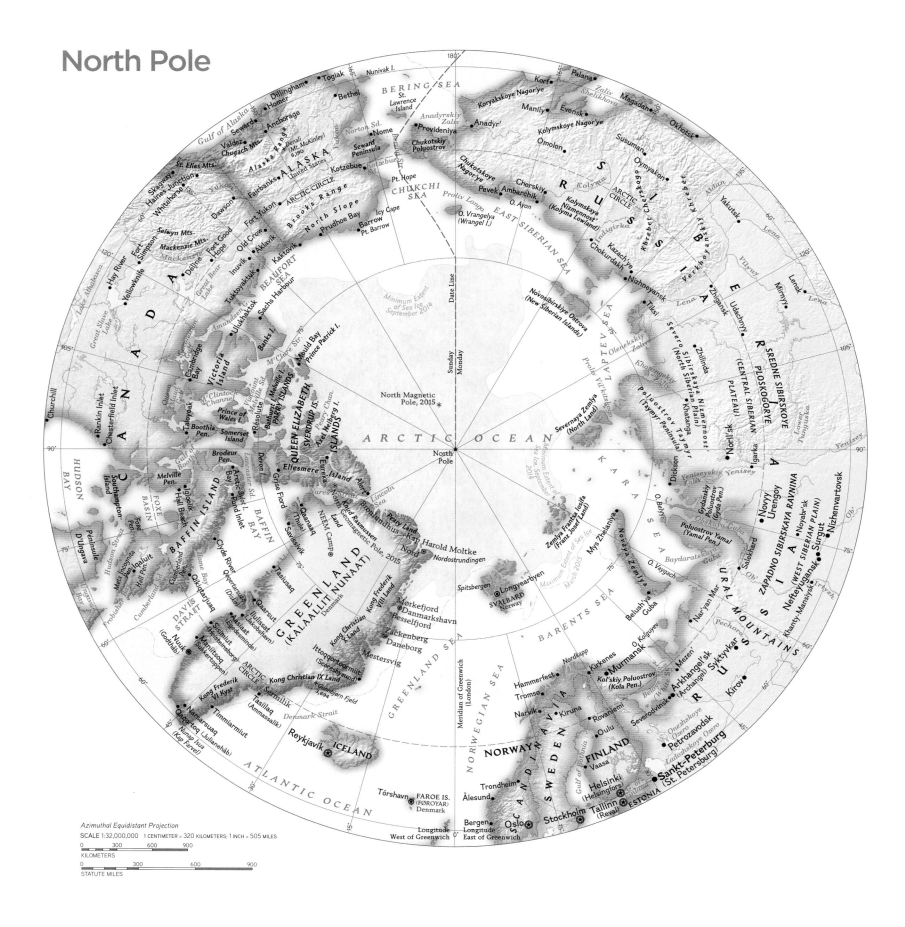

Azimuthal Equidistant Projection
SCALE 1:32,000,000   1 CENTIMETER = 320 KILOMETERS; 1 INCH = 505 MILES

0   300   600   900
KILOMETERS

0   300   600   900
STATUTE MILES

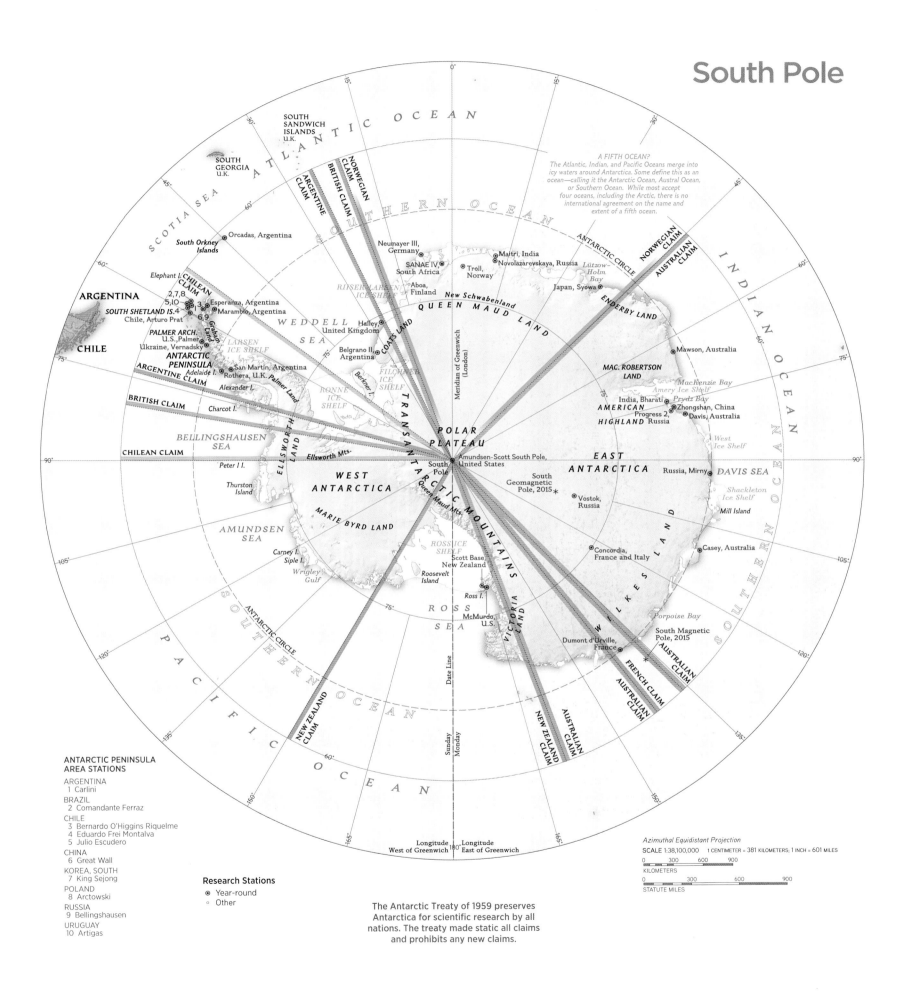

A FIFTH OCEAN?
The Atlantic, Indian, and Pacific Oceans merge into icy waters around Antarctica. Some define this as an ocean—calling it the Antarctic Ocean, Austral Ocean, or Southern Ocean. While most accept four oceans, including the Arctic, there is no international agreement on the name and extent of a fifth ocean.

ANTARCTIC PENINSULA AREA STATIONS

ARGENTINA
1 Carlini

BRAZIL
2 Comandante Ferraz

CHILE
3 Bernardo O'Higgins Riquelme
4 Eduardo Frei Montalva
5 Julio Escudero

CHINA
6 Great Wall

KOREA, SOUTH
7 King Sejong

POLAND
8 Arctowski

RUSSIA
9 Bellingshausen

URUGUAY
10 Artigas

Research Stations
◉ Year-round
○ Other

The Antarctic Treaty of 1959 preserves Antarctica for scientific research by all nations. The treaty made static all claims and prohibits any new claims.

Azimuthal Equidistant Projection
SCALE 1:38,100,000   1 CENTIMETER = 381 KILOMETERS; 1 INCH = 601 MILES

KILOMETERS
0   300   600   900

STATUTE MILES
0   300   600   900

Paleogeography

WITH UNCEASING MOVEMENT of Earth's tectonic plates, continents "drift" over geologic time—breaking apart, reassembling, and again fragmenting to repeat the process. Three times during the past billion years, Earth's drifting landmasses have merged to form so-called supercontinents. Rodinia, a supercontinent in the late Precambrian, began breaking apart about 750 million years ago. In time, its pieces reassembled to form another supercontinent, which in turn split into smaller landmasses during the Paleozoic. The largest of these were called Euramerica (ancestral Europe and North America) and Gondwana (ancestral Africa, Antarctica, Arabia, India, and Australia). More than 250 million years ago, these two landmasses recombined, forming Pangaea. In the Mesozoic era, Pangaea split and the Atlantic and Indian Oceans began forming. Though the Atlantic is still widening today, scientists predict it will close as the seafloor recycles back into Earth's mantle. A new supercontinent, Pangaea Ultima, will eventually form.

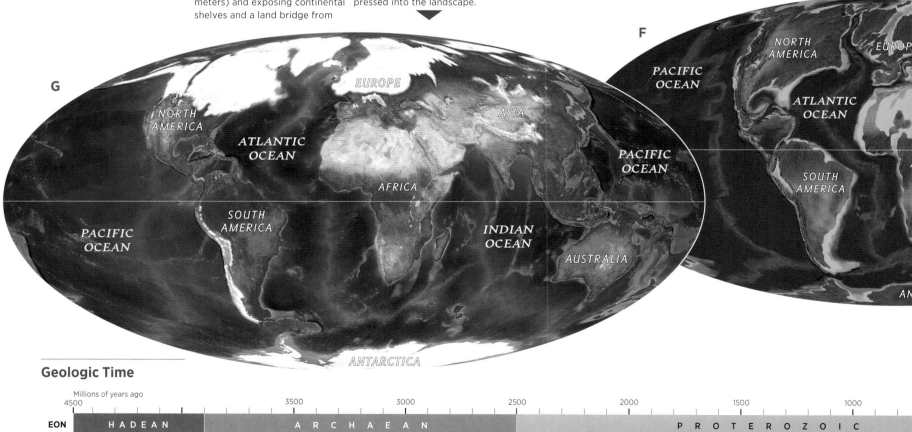

600 Million Years Ago (Late Proterozoic)

After the earliest known supercontinent, Rodinia, began to split apart 750 million years ago, spreading centers opened huge ocean basins, pushing one group of pieces north and the other south over the Pole. Mountains rose and glaciers grew on high peaks, even at the Equator, as the northern fragments collided with what is now Africa. By 600 million years ago all the fragments had reunited, forming another supercontinent, Pannotia.

Continents Adrift in Time

Paleogeographic Map Features

 Seafloor spreading ridge   Continental shelf

Subduction zone   Glacier/ice cap

Landmass

50 Million Years Ago (Eocene)

Pangaea's breakup ended and a new cycle of continental collisions began. Africa hit Europe and India rammed into Asia, thrusting up the Alps and Himalaya. Continental compression led to widening ocean basins, which lowered sea level. Migration routes emerged, and land animals flourished. But greater expanses of heat-reflecting land helped cool Earth and allowed ice to remain year-round in Antarctica.

18,000 Years Ago (Last Glacial Maximum)

At the peak of the last great ice age, glaciers frosted northern Europe, northern North America, and Antarctica. Water locked in ice transformed familiar continental outlines, lowering sea level 300 to 500 feet (91 to 152 meters) and exposing continental shelves and a land bridge from Asia to the Americas. Within the next 8,000 years the glaciers receded, the oceans rose, and the climate turned warmer and wetter. Along its farthest margins the retreating ice left signs of its passage, such as the Great Lakes, pressed into the landscape.

Geologic Time

Millions of years ago											
EON	HADEAN	ARCHAEAN				PROTEROZOIC					
ERA		EOARCHAEAN	PALEOARCHAEAN	MESOARCHAEAN	NEOARCHAEAN	PALEOPROTEROZOIC		MESOPROTEROZOIC		NEO- PROTERO
PERIOD						SIDERIAN / RHYACIAN / OROSIRIAN / STATHERIAN	CALYMMIAN / ECTASIAN / STENIAN			TONIAN / CRYOGENIAN

PRECAMBRIAN

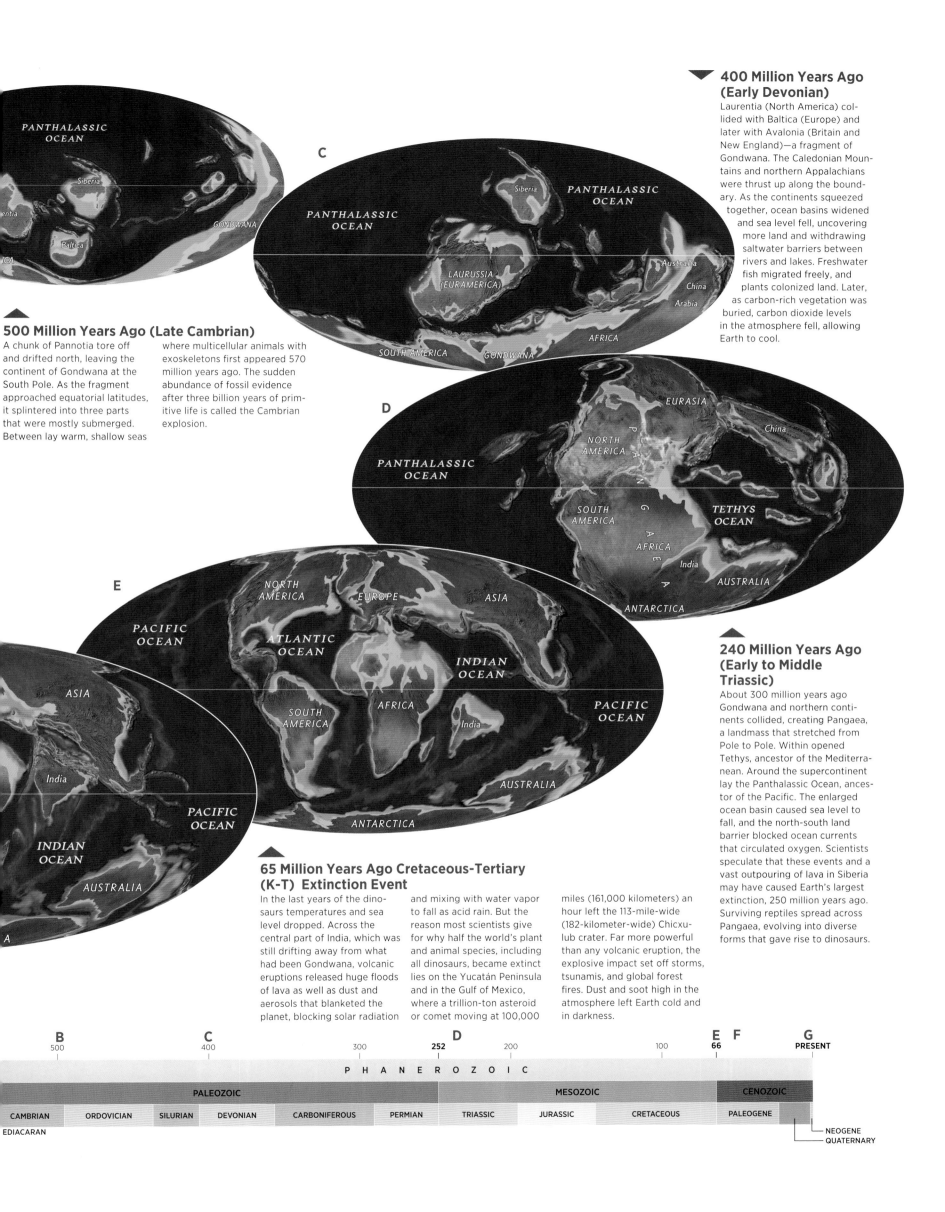

400 Million Years Ago (Early Devonian)

Laurentia (North America) collided with Baltica (Europe) and later with Avalonia (Britain and New England)—a fragment of Gondwana. The Caledonian Mountains and northern Appalachians were thrust up along the boundary. As the continents squeezed together, ocean basins widened and sea level fell, uncovering more land and withdrawing saltwater barriers between rivers and lakes. Freshwater fish migrated freely, and plants colonized land. Later, as carbon-rich vegetation was buried, carbon dioxide levels in the atmosphere fell, allowing Earth to cool.

500 Million Years Ago (Late Cambrian)

A chunk of Pannotia tore off and drifted north, leaving the continent of Gondwana at the South Pole. As the fragment approached equatorial latitudes, it splintered into three parts that were mostly submerged. Between lay warm, shallow seas where multicellular animals with exoskeletons first appeared 570 million years ago. The sudden abundance of fossil evidence after three billion years of primitive life is called the Cambrian explosion.

240 Million Years Ago (Early to Middle Triassic)

About 300 million years ago Gondwana and northern continents collided, creating Pangaea, a landmass that stretched from Pole to Pole. Within opened Tethys, ancestor of the Mediterranean. Around the supercontinent lay the Panthalassic Ocean, ancestor of the Pacific. The enlarged ocean basin caused sea level to fall, and the north-south land barrier blocked ocean currents that circulated oxygen. Scientists speculate that these events and a vast outpouring of lava in Siberia may have caused Earth's largest extinction, 250 million years ago. Surviving reptiles spread across Pangaea, evolving into diverse forms that gave rise to dinosaurs.

65 Million Years Ago Cretaceous-Tertiary (K-T) Extinction Event

In the last years of the dinosaurs temperatures and sea level dropped. Across the central part of India, which was still drifting away from what had been Gondwana, volcanic eruptions released huge floods of lava as well as dust and aerosols that blanketed the planet, blocking solar radiation and mixing with water vapor to fall as acid rain. But the reason most scientists give for why half the world's plant and animal species, including all dinosaurs, became extinct lies on the Yucatán Peninsula and in the Gulf of Mexico, where a trillion-ton asteroid or comet moving at 100,000 miles (161,000 kilometers) an hour left the 113-mile-wide (182-kilometer-wide) Chicxulub crater. Far more powerful than any volcanic eruption, the explosive impact set off storms, tsunamis, and global forest fires. Dust and soot high in the atmosphere left Earth cold and in darkness.

Structure of the Earth

LIKE ICE ON A GREAT LAKE, Earth's crust, or the lithosphere, floats over the planet's molten innards, is cracked in many places, and is in slow but constant movement. Earth's surface is broken into 16 enormous slabs of rock, called plates, averaging thousands of miles wide and having a thickness of several miles. As they move and grind against each other, they push up mountains, spawn volcanoes, and generate earthquakes.

Although these often cataclysmic events capture our attention, the movements that cause them are imperceptible—a slow waltz of rafted rock that continues over eons. How slow? The Mid-Atlantic Ridge (see "spreading" diagram, opposite) is being built by magma oozing between two plates, separating North America and Africa at the speed of a growing human fingernail.

The dividing lines between plates often mark areas of high volcanic and earthquake activity as plates strain against each other or one dives beneath another. In the Ring of Fire around the Pacific Basin, disastrous earthquakes have occurred in Kobe, Japan, and in Los Angeles and San Francisco, California. Volcanic eruptions have taken place at Pinatubo in the Philippines and Mount St. Helens in Washington State.

Interior of the Earth

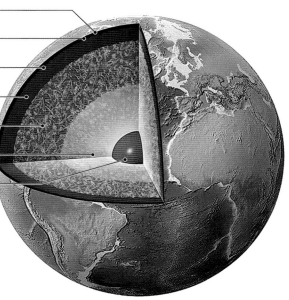

Crust
2 to 45 miles (3 to 72 km) thick

Lithosphere
1 to 120 miles (2 to 193 km) thick

Asthenosphere
60 to 400 miles (97 to 644 km) thick

Upper Mantle
400 miles (644 km) thick

Lower Mantle
1,400 miles (2,253 km) thick

Outer Core
1,400 miles (2,253 km) thick

Inner Core
1,500 miles (2,414 km) in diameter

Plate Boundaries

Convergent boundary

Subduction zone
(triangles indicate direction of subduction)

Divergent boundary

Oceanic spreading boundary

Transform fault

Diffuse plate boundary
(may be more than 100 mi [161 km] across)

Geologic Forces Change the Face of the Planet

ACCRETION
As ocean plates move toward the edges of continents or island arcs and slide under them, seamounts are skimmed off and piled up in submarine trenches. The resulting buildup can cause continents to grow.

FAULTING
Enormous crustal plates do not slide smoothly. Strain built up along their edges may release in a series of small jumps, felt as minor tremors on land. Extended buildup can cause a sudden jump, producing an earthquake.

COLLISION
When two continental plates converge, the result can be the most dramatic mountain-building process on Earth. The Himalaya mountain range rose when the Indian subcontinent collided with Eurasia, driving the land upward.

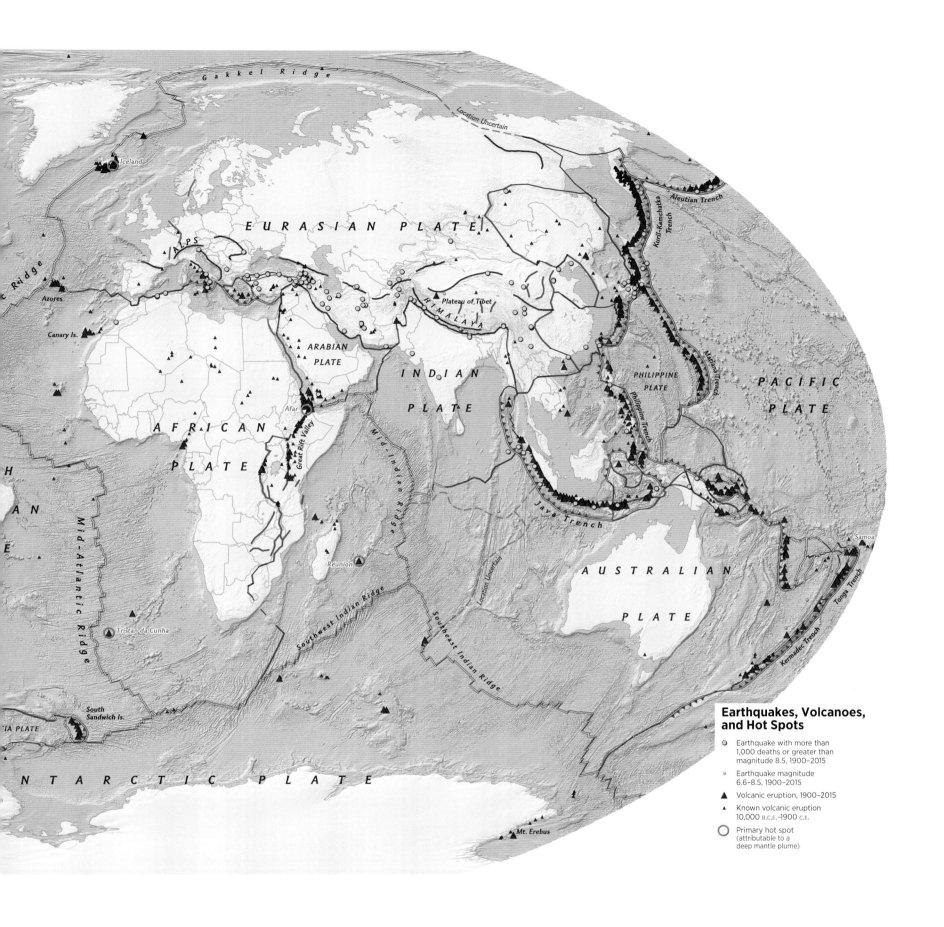

G a k k e l   R i d g e

Location Uncertain

Iceland

Azores

Canary Is.

Mid-Atlantic Ridge

Tristan da Cunha

South Sandwich Is.

IA PLATE

E U R A S I A N   P L A T E

ALPS

ARABIAN PLATE

Afar

Great Rift Valley

A F R I C A N   P L A T E

Plateau of Tibet

HIMALAYA

I N D I A N   P L A T E

Mid-Indian Ridge

Réunion

Southwest Indian Ridge

Southeast Indian Ridge

Location Uncertain

PHILIPPINE PLATE

Philippine Trench

Kuril-Kamchatka Trench

Aleutian Trench

Mariana Trench

Java Trench

P A C I F I C   P L A T E

A U S T R A L I A N   P L A T E

Samoa

Kermadec Trench

Tonga Trench

N T A R C T I C   P L A T E

Mt. Erebus

Earthquakes, Volcanoes, and Hot Spots

- ⊙ Earthquake with more than 1,000 deaths or greater than magnitude 8.5, 1900–2015
- ∘ Earthquake magnitude 6.6–8.5, 1900–2015
- ▲ Volcanic eruption, 1900–2015
- ▴ Known volcanic eruption 10,000 B.C.E.–1900 C.E.
- ◯ Primary hot spot (attributable to a deep mantle plume)

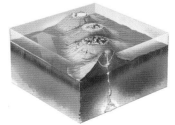

HOT SPOTS

In the cauldron of inner Earth, some areas burn hotter than others and periodically blast through their crustal covering as volcanoes. Such a "hot spot" built the Hawaiian Islands, leaving a string of oceanic protuberances.

SPREADING

At the divergent boundary known as the Mid-Atlantic Ridge, oozing magma forces two plates apart by as much as eight inches (20 cm) a year. If that rate had been constant, the ocean could have reached its current width in 30 million years.

SUBDUCTION

When an oceanic plate and a continental plate converge, the older and heavier sea plate takes a dive. Plunging back into the interior of Earth, it is transformed into molten material, only to rise again as magma.

Landforms

SIX MAJOR LANDFORM TYPES are found on Earth's surface (see map). Except for ice caps, landforms result from tectonic movements, volcanic activity, and weathering and are mapped as areas of distinct slope, elevation, and amount of flat terrain in uplands.

Mountains, the loftiest landforms, are defined as areas with steep slope and high relief. Where continental plates converge, the buckling of the Earth's crust produces mountains. Strong uplifting of land can produce high mountains, such as the Himalaya, whereas weaker uplifts result in low mountains, such as the mountains of the Basin and Range Province of the western United States.

Extensive, relatively flat lands that are higher than surrounding areas are called tablelands. Characterized by an abundance of gently sloping areas in uplands, they include the Guiana Highlands of South America.

Hills and irregular plains are rounded or sculpted landscapes with noticeable local relief but lesser elevation and slope than mountains. The Canadian Shield and Ozarks of North America provide good examples.

Flat plains are extensive areas of very low local relief often dominated by gently sloping areas. Examples include the steppes of Eurasia, the Ganges River plains, and the outback of Australia.

Major Landforms

- High mountains
- Low mountains
- Tablelands
- Hills
- Irregular plains
- Flat plains
- No data

Endogenic Landforms

LANDFORMS THAT RESULT FROM INTERNAL PROCESSES

Forces deep within the Earth give rise to mountains and other endogenic landforms. Some mountains were born when continental plates collided (e.g., the Himalaya). Others rose in the form of volcanoes as sea plates subducted beneath continental plates (e.g., the Cascades of North America, Mount Fuji of Japan) or as plates moved over hot spots in Earth's mantle (e.g., Hawaii). Still others were thrust up by tectonic uplift (parts of the western United States). Rifting and faulting along plate boundaries and within the plates themselves also generate vertical tectonic landforms; these can be seen in Africa's Great Rift Valley and along the San Andreas Fault of California. Magma released by spreading plates on the Mid-Atlantic seafloor created Iceland.

Clockwise from above: the San Andreas Fault in California, a fracture in Earth's crust marking a plate boundary; Mount Fuji in Japan, a volcanic peak; Crater Lake in Oregon, a deep lake inside the caldera of Mount Mazama

Exogenic Landforms

LANDFORMS THAT RESULT FROM EXTERNAL PROCESSES

External agents create exogenic landforms. Weathering by rain, groundwater, and other natural elements slowly breaks down rocks, such as the limestone in karst landscapes or the granite in an exfoliation dome. Erosion removes weathered material and transports it from place to place; collections of such debris at mountain bases are called talus deposits. In the American Southwest, erosion continues to shape the spires of Bryce Canyon and the walls of slot canyons.

ARCTIC OCEAN

Iceland

Central Siberian Plateau

West Siberian Plain

Northern European Plain

EUROPE

Eurasian Steppes

ASIA

Alps

Caucasus Mts.

Ural Mts.

Tian Shan

Tarim Basin

Kunlun Mts.

Zagros Mts.

Hindu Kush

Himalaya

Ganges Plain

Atlas Mts.

PACIFIC OCEAN

AFRICA

Ethiopian Highlands

Deccan Plateau

Western Ghats

Congo Basin

Great Rift Valley

ATLANTIC OCEAN

INDIAN OCEAN

AUSTRALIA

Nullarbor Plain

Great Dividing Range

ANTARCTICA

Left to right: Bryce Canyon in Utah, eroded sedimentary rocks in arid climate; Half Dome in Yosemite, California, weathered granite batholith; slot canyon in the American Southwest, sedimentary rock eroded by water

Other Landforms

Some landforms are the impact sites (or craters) of asteroids, comets, and meteorites. The most readily observable are Meteor Crater in Arizona and New Quebec Crater in eastern Canada. Other landforms include constructed dams, open-pit and mountaintop removal mines, hillslope terraces, and canals. Coral reefs made by coral polyps and giant termite mounds are known as biogenic features.

Left to right: Meteor Crater, Arizona; termite mound, Australia

Landforms

All of Earth's features are created and continually reshaped by such factors as wind, water, ice, tectonics, and humans. This illustration brings together 41 natural and man-made features to show typical locations and relationships of landforms; it does not depict an actual region. Definitions of most landforms can be found in the glossary.

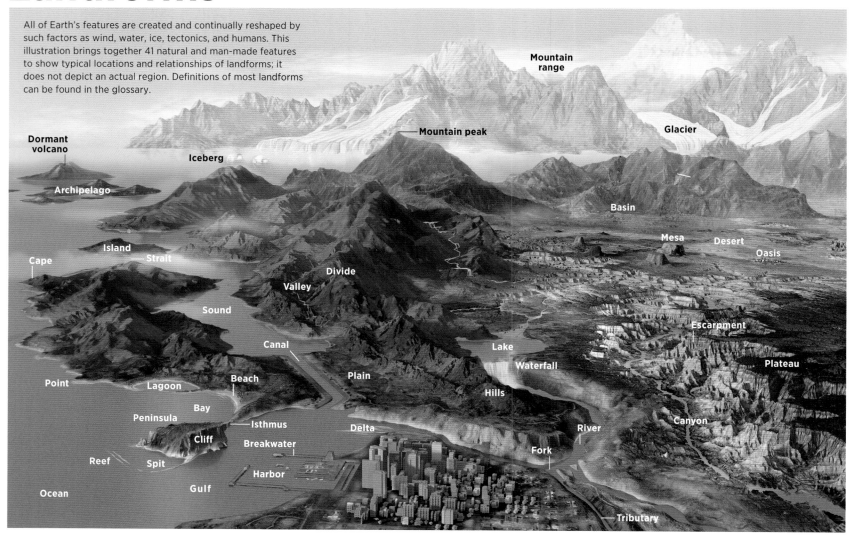

Mountain range

Mountain peak

Glacier

Dormant volcano

Iceberg

Archipelago

Basin

Island

Mesa

Desert

Oasis

Cape

Strait

Divide

Valley

Sound

Escarpment

Canal

Lake

Waterfall

Plateau

Point

Lagoon

Beach

Plain

Hills

Bay

Peninsula

Isthmus

Cliff

Delta

Canyon

Reef

Spit

Breakwater

River

Fork

Harbor

Ocean

Gulf

Tributary

Landforms Created by Wind

The term "eolian" (from Aeolus, the Greek god of the winds) describes landforms shaped by the wind. The erosive action of wind is characterized by deflation, or the removal of dust and sand from dry soil; sandblasting, the erosion of rock by wind-borne sand; and deposition, the laying down of sediments. The effects of wind erosion are evident in many parts of the world (see map), particularly where there are large deposits of sand or loess (dust and silt dropped by wind). Among desert landforms, sand dunes may be the most spectacular. They come in several types (below): Barchan dunes are crescents with arms pointing downwind; transverse dunes are "waves," with crests perpendicular to the wind; star dunes have curving ridges radiating from their centers; longitudinal, or Seif, dunes lie parallel to the wind; and parabolic dunes are crescents with arms that point upwind.

NORTH AMERICA

EUROPE

ASIA

AFRICA

SOUTH AMERICA

AUSTRALIA

Desert

Loess deposit

ANTARCTICA

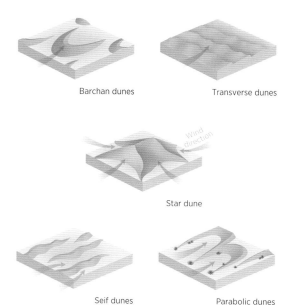

Barchan dunes

Transverse dunes

Wind direction

Star dune

Seif dunes

Parabolic dunes

EOLIAN LANDFORMS

Desert dunes, which actually cover only a small portion of desert areas, range in height from just a few feet to more than a thousand feet. Coastal dunes form when wind and waves deposit sediments along the shores of oceans and other large bodies of water. Loess hills are large deposits of wind-borne silt, the most extensive of which are found in North America and Asia.

Desert dunes: Death Valley National Park, California

Coastal dunes: Magdalen Islands, Quebec

Loess deposits: Palouse Hills, Washington

Landforms Created by Water

Highlighted on the map at right are Earth's major watersheds. These are drainage basins for rivers, which create fluvial (from a Latin word meaning "river") landforms. Wave action and groundwater also produce characteristic landforms.

RIVERS
Some rivers form broad loops (called meanders) as faster currents erode their outer banks and slower currents deposit materials along inner banks. When a river breaks through the narrow neck of a meander, the abandoned curve becomes an oxbow lake.

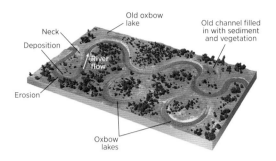

RIVER DELTAS
Sediment deposited at a river's mouth builds a delta, a term first used by the ancient Greeks to describe the Nile Delta; its triangular shape resembles the fourth letter of the Greek alphabet. Not all deltas have that classic shape: The Mississippi River forms a bird's-foot delta.

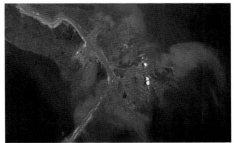

Mississippi River Delta: Louisiana, United States

COASTAL AREAS
Through erosion and deposition, tides and wave action continually reshape the coastlines of the world. Ocean currents transport sand and gravel from one part of a shore to another, sometimes building beach extensions called spits, long ridges that project into open water. Relentless waves undercut coastal cliffs, eroding volumes of material and leaving behind sea stacks and sea arches, remnants made of more resistant rock. As ocean levels rise, narrow arms of the sea (fjords) may reach inland for miles, filling deep valleys once occupied by glaciers flowing to the sea.

Limestone sea stacks: Victoria, Australia

GROUNDWATER
Water in the ground slowly dissolves limestone, a highly soluble rock. Over time, caves form and underground streams flow through the rock; sinkholes develop at the surface as underlying rock gives way. Karst landscapes, named for the rugged Karst region of the former Yugoslavia, are large areas of unusual landforms created by weathered and eroded limestone.

Karst hills: Guangxi Zhuang, China

The world's ten largest watersheds
Other major watersheds

Mackenzie-Peace
Ob-Irtysh
Yenisey-Angara
Lena
Amur
Mississippi-Missouri
Nile
Amazon
Congo
Paraná

Landforms Created by Ice

Among the legacies of Earth's most recent ice age (see map) are landforms shaped by glaciers. There are two kinds of glaciers: valley, or alpine, and continental ice sheets. These large, slow-moving masses of ice can crush or topple anything in their paths; they can even stop rivers in their tracks, creating ice-dammed lakes. Glaciers are also powerful agents of erosion, grinding against the ground and picking up and carrying huge amounts of rock and soil, which they deposit at their margins when they begin to melt; these deposits are called lateral and terminal moraines. The illustrations below show how an ice sheet (upper) leaves a lasting imprint on the land (lower).

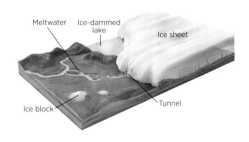

BEFORE AND AFTER
Meltwater deposits material in long, narrow ridges (eskers, lower left). Ice embedded in the ground melts and forms lakes (kettles). Ice overruns unconsolidated materials and shapes them into hills (drumlins).

Greatest extent of ice during last ice age

NORTH AMERICA
EUROPE
ASIA
AFRICA
SOUTH AMERICA
AUSTRALIA
ANTARCTICA

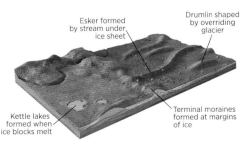

U-shaped glacial valley: Yosemite National Park, California

POSTGLACIAL LANDFORMS
As they move, alpine glaciers widen their V-shaped valleys, often leaving behind U-shaped ones when they withdraw. Ice sheets leave an even larger legacy simply because they cover more territory. Among their creations are drumlin fields and lake basins, including the ones now filled by the Great Lakes of North America.

Glacial lake: Spitsbergen, Svalbard, Norway

Land Cover

SATELLITE DATA PROVIDE the most reliable picture of global vegetative cover over time. The map at right is based on imagery from the Moderate Resolution Imaging Spectroradiometer (MODIS), at a spatial resolution of 500 meters (1,640 ft). Such maps are used to identify the large-scale effects of many small-scale events (such as brief local weather events) for the global climate models that predict how the Earth system—the physical, chemical, and biological aspects of the planet's terrestrial, oceanic, and atmospheric realms—will change with climate warming. By recording how different wavelengths of the electromagnetic spectrum reflect from the surface, scientists can derive land-cover types through the variation of these reflectances over time. Vast areas of Earth have been altered by humans over millennia, and such changes are captured in the satellite record, contributing to a rich data bank for conservation, biodiversity assessments, and land resource management.

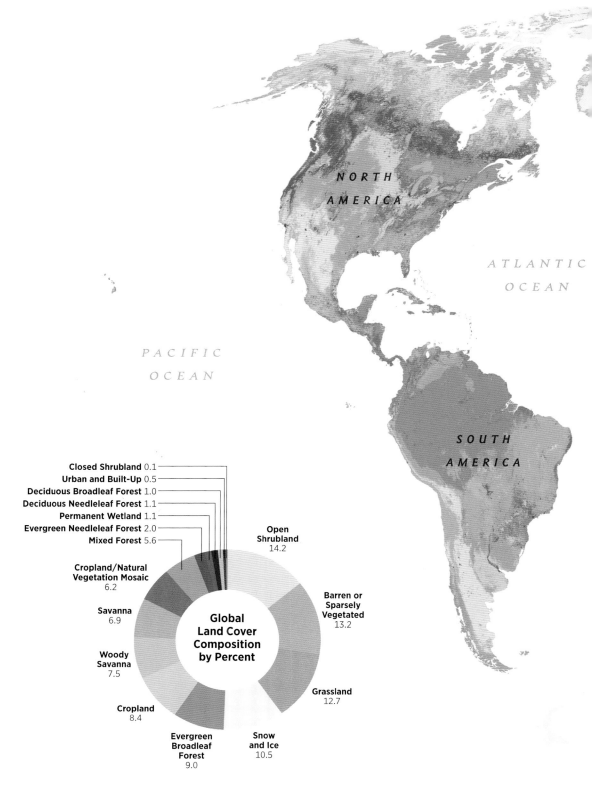

NORTH AMERICA

ATLANTIC OCEAN

PACIFIC OCEAN

SOUTH AMERICA

EVERGREEN NEEDLELEAF FOREST

More than 60 percent of this land is covered by a forest canopy; tree height exceeds 2 m (7 ft). These forests are common in temperate regions of the U.S., Europe, and Asia. In many of them, trees are grown on plantations and are logged for the making of paper and building products.

EVERGREEN BROADLEAF FOREST

More than 60 percent of this land is covered by a forest canopy; tree height exceeds 2 m (7 ft). These include rain forests and dominate in the tropics; they have the greatest concentrations of biodiversity. In many areas, farms, ranches, and tree plantations are replacing this land cover.

Global Land Cover Composition by Percent

- Closed Shrubland 0.1
- Urban and Built-Up 0.5
- Deciduous Broadleaf Forest 1.0
- Deciduous Needleleaf Forest 1.1
- Permanent Wetland 1.1
- Evergreen Needleleaf Forest 2.0
- Mixed Forest 5.6
- Cropland/Natural Vegetation Mosaic 6.2
- Savanna 6.9
- Woody Savanna 7.5
- Cropland 8.4
- Evergreen Broadleaf Forest 9.0
- Snow and Ice 10.5
- Grassland 12.7
- Barren or Sparsely Vegetated 13.2
- Open Shrubland 14.2

DECIDUOUS NEEDLELEAF FOREST

More than 60 percent of this land is covered by a forest canopy; tree height exceeds 2 m (7 ft). Trees respond to cold seasons by shedding their leaves simultaneously. This land cover is present in northeast China but dominant only in Siberia, taking the form of larch forests with a short June-to-August growing season.

DECIDUOUS BROADLEAF FOREST

More than 60 percent of this land is covered by a forest canopy; tree height exceeds 2 m (7 ft). In dry or cold seasons, trees shed their leaves simultaneously. Much of this forest has been converted to cropland in temperate regions; large remnants are increasingly found only on steep and remote slopes.

MIXED FOREST

More than 60 percent of this land is covered by a forest canopy; tree height exceeds 2 m (7 ft). Both evergreen and deciduous types appear, with neither having coverage of less than 25 percent or more than 75 percent. This type is largely found between temperate deciduous and boreal evergreen forests.

WOODY SAVANNA

Land has herbaceous or woody understories and a tree canopy cover of 30 to 60 percent; trees exceed 2 m (7 ft) and may be evergreen or deciduous. This type of land cover is common in the tropics and is most highly degraded in areas with long histories of human habitation, such as West Africa.

SAVANNA

Land has herbaceous or woody understories and a tree canopy cover of 10 to 30 percent; trees exceed 2 m (7 ft) and may be evergreen or deciduous. This type includes classic African savanna as well as open boreal woodlands that demarcate tree lines and the beginning of tundra ecosystems.

CLOSED SHRUBLAND

Bushes or shrubs dominate, with a canopy cover of more than 60 percent. Bushes do not exceed 2 m (7 ft) in height; shrubs or bushes can be evergreen or deciduous. Tree canopy is less than 10 percent. This land cover can be found where prolonged cold or dry seasons limit plant growth.

OPEN SHRUBLAND

Shrubs are dominant, with a canopy cover of between 10 and 60 percent; they do not exceed 2 m (7 ft) in height and can be evergreen or deciduous. The remaining land is either barren or characterized by annual herbaceous cover. This land cover occurs in semiarid or severely cold regions.

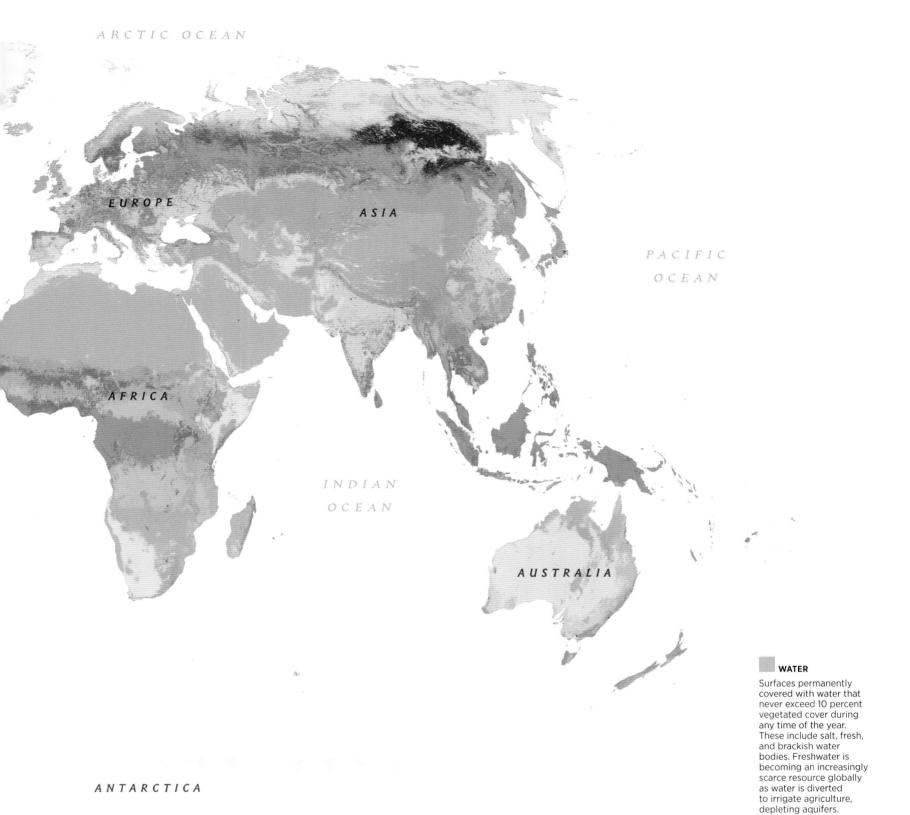

ARCTIC OCEAN

EUROPE

ASIA

PACIFIC OCEAN

AFRICA

INDIAN OCEAN

AUSTRALIA

ANTARCTICA

WATER

Surfaces permanently covered with water that never exceed 10 percent vegetated cover during any time of the year. These include salt, fresh, and brackish water bodies. Freshwater is becoming an increasingly scarce resource globally as water is diverted to irrigate agriculture, depleting aquifers.

GRASSLAND

This land has continuous herbaceous cover and less than 10 percent tree or shrub canopy cover. This type occurs in a wide range of habitats. Perennial grasslands in the central United States and Russia, for example, are the most extensive and mark a line of decreased precipitation that limits agriculture.

PERMANENT WETLAND

A permanent mixture of water and herbaceous or woody vegetation. The vegetation can be present in either salt, brackish, or fresh water. The Everglades are one of the world's largest permanent wetlands. Other wetlands include the Hudson Bay lowlands and the Sundarbans of India and Bangladesh.

CROPLAND

Crop-producing fields make up more than 60 percent of the land-scape. Areas of high-intensity agriculture, including mechanized farming, stretch across temperate regions. Much agriculture in the developing world is fragmented, however, and occurs frequently on small plots of land.

CROPLAND/NATURAL VEGETATION MOSAIC

Lands with a mosaic of croplands, forests, shrubland, and grass-lands in which no one component makes up more than 60 percent of the landscape. This land-cover class can be seen in much of the U.S.; examples include southwestern Wisconsin and the Shenandoah Valley (pictured).

URBAN AND BUILT-UP

Land cover includes buildings, roads, and other manufactured structures. This class was mapped as an independent layer from MODIS 500-meter-resolution satellite imagery created in 2010. Urban and built-up cover represents the most densely developed areas of human habitation.

BARREN OR SPARSELY VEGETATED

Exposed soil, sand, or rocks are typical; the land never has more than 10 percent vegetated cover during any time of year. This includes true deserts, such as the Sahara (Africa) and Gobi (Asia). Desertification, the expansion of deserts due to land degradation or climate change, is a problem in these areas.

SNOW AND ICE

Land has permanent snow and ice; it never has more than 10 percent vegetated cover at any time of year. The greatest expanses of this class can be seen in Greenland, on other Arctic islands, and in Antarctica. Glaciers at high elevations form significant examples in Alaska, the Himalaya, Chile, and Scandinavia.

Freshwater

ON AVERAGE, HUMAN BEINGS EACH USE TEN GALLONS

(37.8 L) of freshwater a day for drinking, cooking, and cleaning. It seems like so little, and yet more than one billion people around the world lack access to or sufficient supplies of freshwater. In part, that's due to inadequate infrastructure. But freshwater is also naturally distributed unevenly across the globe—in some cases, tragically out of step with the location and need of human populations. In water-rich nations, potable water is sprayed on lawns while rain-water washes down storm drains; in desert regions, every drop is precious.

Agriculture is the main use of freshwater around the world, and some of its applications are shocking. For instance, it takes over 925 gallons (3,500 L) of water to grow and prepare two pounds (900 g) of rice and almost 4,000 gallons (15,140 L) to produce a single pound (450 g) of beef. Awareness of water shortages has spurred interest in foods that have low water inputs and has focused new attention on bringing irrigation to areas where appropriate rivers and lakes already exist.

Worldwide, industry consumes less than a third of agriculture's take. Regional withdrawals vary widely: In South Asia, this sector accounts for 2 percent of the region's consumption; in Western Europe, it claims 77 percent. Freshwater is used not only as a raw material itself, but also for steam, for cleaning and removing waste, and for heating and cooling equipment.

Municipal use currently accounts for 11 percent of global withdrawals, but its share is increasing as urban populations swell. In cities where even present demand is not being met, crises are sure to arise. In a few cases, typically high-consumption, affluent communities are reducing withdrawals as a result of household conservation, improved infrastructure, and consumer awareness. In New York City, for example, consumption in 2010 was 127 gallons (481 L) per capita per day, down from 213 gallons (806 L) in 1980.

Water is usually considered a renewable resource because there is an expectation that what we use will cycle back to us through land, sea, cloud, and rain. For many millennia, the natural recycling of freshwater has been a fair assumption. But climate change is affecting the hydrologic cycle, and weather patterns are shifting in sometimes devastating ways—soaking some formerly dry areas and pushing once wet zones into persistent drought. The warming climate is also melting annual snowpack and ancient glaciers, releasing spring floods for now but threatening downstream areas with chronic water shortages once the frozen reserves are gone.

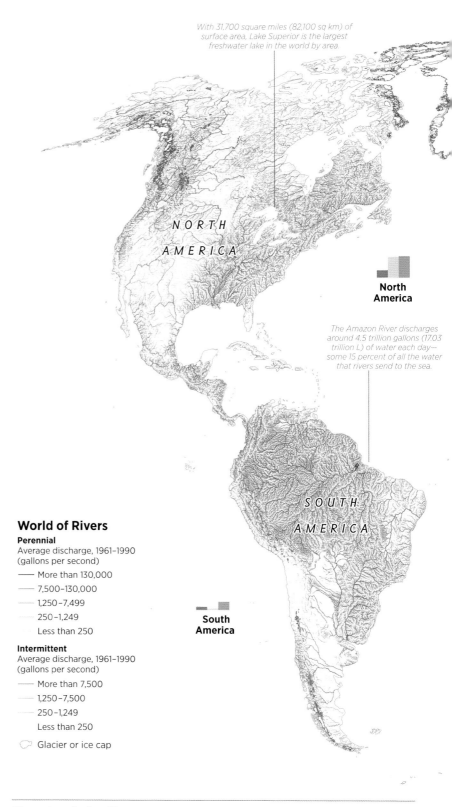

With 31,700 square miles (82,100 sq km) of surface area, Lake Superior is the largest freshwater lake in the world by area.

North America

The Amazon River discharges around 4.5 trillion gallons (17.03 trillion L) of water each day—some 15 percent of all the water that rivers send to the sea.

South America

World of Rivers

Perennial
Average discharge, 1961–1990
(gallons per second)
— More than 130,000
— 7,500–130,000
— 1,250–7,499
— 250–1,249
— Less than 250

Intermittent
Average discharge, 1961–1990
(gallons per second)
— More than 7,500
— 1,250–7,500
— 250–1,249
— Less than 250

🗘 Glacier or ice cap

Water Availability

Precious little of Earth's water is suitable for most human use. Of the 2.5 percent of the planet's water that doesn't reside in the salty oceans, most is locked up in the massive ice caps of Antarctica and Greenland, leaving less than one percent that is exploitable for human use. Making seawater safe for human consumption is possible but energy intensive.

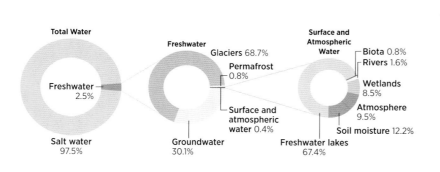

Total Water
- Freshwater 2.5%
- Salt water 97.5%

Freshwater
- Glaciers 68.7%
- Permafrost 0.8%
- Surface and atmospheric water 0.4%
- Groundwater 30.1%

Surface and Atmospheric Water
- Biota 0.8%
- Rivers 1.6%
- Wetlands 8.5%
- Atmosphere 9.5%
- Soil moisture 12.2%
- Freshwater lakes 67.4%

Mapping Irrigation

In many parts of the world, agriculture is impossible without irrigation. While irrigation needs and methods vary regionally, the need for water to grow food is a constant. From California's Central Valley to the coffee farms in Ethiopia's highlands, and from India's Ganges River Valley to the rice paddies of China, irrigation means food for billions of mouths.

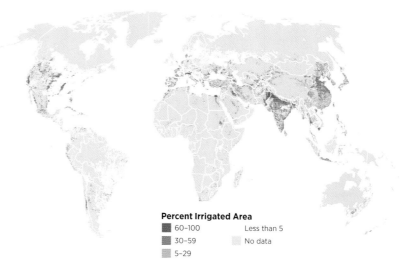

Percent Irrigated Area
- 60–100
- 30–59
- 5–29
- Less than 5
- No data

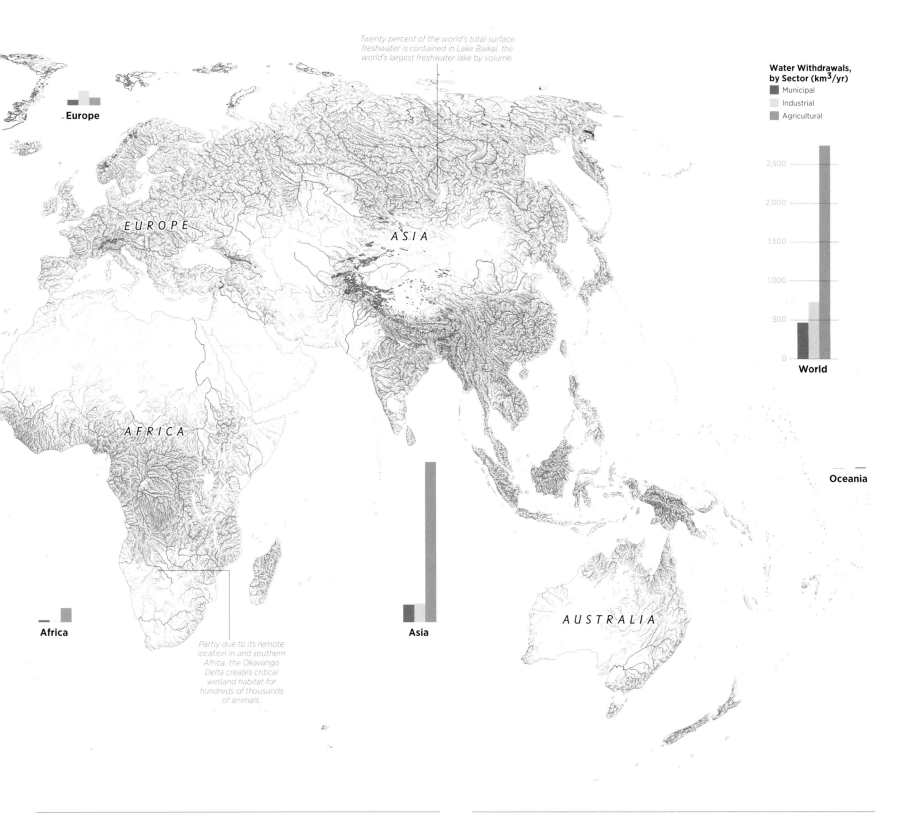

Twenty percent of the world's total surface freshwater is contained in Lake Baikal, the world's largest freshwater lake by volume.

Europe

ASIA

EUROPE

Water Withdrawals, by Sector (km³/yr)
■ Municipal
■ Industrial
■ Agricultural

2,500

2,000

1,500

1,000

500

World

AFRICA

Oceania

Africa

Partly due to its remote location in arid southern Africa, the Okavango Delta creates critical wetland habitat for hundreds of thousands of animals.

Asia

AUSTRALIA

Renewable Freshwater Resources

The average annual flow of rivers and recharge of aquifers from precipitation over a 30-year period is referred to as the total actual renewable water resources (TARWR).

A country with more than 1,700 cubic meters annually per inhabitant is said to be water-rich; places where that figure is below 1,000 cubic meters are labeled water-scarce.

Safe Drinking Water

Water quality is as important as quantity. The 1.1 billion people lacking clean drinking water must often resort to using water contaminated with pathogens, disease vectors, and chemicals. Waterborne diseases—from cholera to dysentery to salmonella-caused illnesses—claim an estimated 2.2 million lives a year; young children are the most vulnerable.

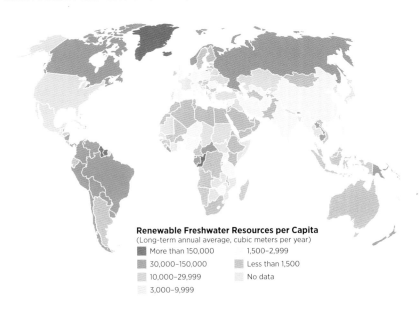

Renewable Freshwater Resources per Capita
(Long-term annual average, cubic meters per year)
■ More than 150,000
■ 30,000–150,000
■ 10,000–29,999
■ 3,000–9,999
1,500–2,999
Less than 1,500
No data

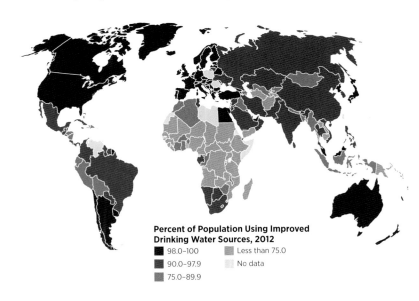

Percent of Population Using Improved Drinking Water Sources, 2012
■ 98.0–100
■ 90.0–97.9
■ 75.0–89.9
Less than 75.0
No data

World • Freshwater 37

Climate

THE TERM "CLIMATE" describes the average weather conditions, as measured over many years, that prevail at any given point around the world at a given time of the year. Daily weather may differ dramatically from that expected on the basis of climatic statistics.

Energy from the sun drives the global climate system. Much of this incoming energy is absorbed in the tropics. Outgoing heat radiation, much of which exits at high latitudes, balances the absorbed incoming solar energy. To achieve a balance across the globe, huge amounts of heat are moved from the tropics to polar regions by both the atmosphere and the oceans.

The tilt of Earth's axis leads to shifting patterns of incoming solar energy throughout the year. More energy is transported to higher latitudes in winter than in summer, and hence the contrast in temperatures between the tropics and polar regions is greatest at this time of year—especially in the Northern Hemisphere. Scientists present this data in many ways, using climographs (see page 40), which show information about specific places. Alternatively, they produce maps that show regional and worldwide data.

The effects of the climatic contrasts are seen in the distribution of Earth's life-forms. Temperature, precipitation, and the amount of sunlight all determine both what plants can grow in a region and the animals that live there. People are more adaptable, but climate still exerts powerful constraints on where we live. Climatic conditions affect our planning decisions, such as how much heating oil is needed for the winter and how to irrigate crops given the anticipated summer rainfall. Fluctuations from year to year (e.g., unusually cold winters or summer droughts) make planning more difficult.

In the longer term, continued global warming is changing climatic conditions around the world, which could dramatically alter temperature and precipitation patterns and lead to more frequent heat waves, floods, and droughts. An increase in temperature means more disease-spreading mosquitoes; droughts and floods will lead to more famine. In addition, rising sea levels put much of the world's population at risk, as many of the most densely populated areas are coastal.

JANUARY SOLAR ENERGY*

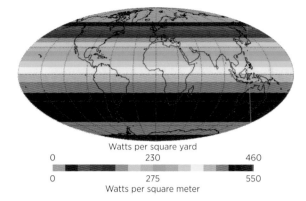

Watts per square yard
0   230   460

0   275   550
Watts per square meter

JULY SOLAR ENERGY*

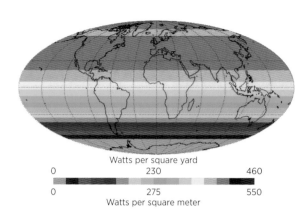

Watts per square yard
0   230   460

0   275   550
Watts per square meter

*Amount of solar energy reaching the upper atmosphere

JANUARY AVERAGE TEMPERATURE

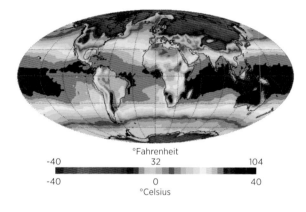

°Fahrenheit
-40   32   104

-40   0   40
°Celsius

JULY AVERAGE TEMPERATURE

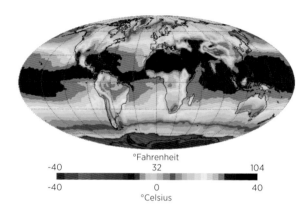

°Fahrenheit
-40   32   104

-40   0   40
°Celsius

JANUARY CLOUD COVER

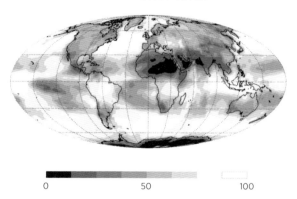

0   50   100

JULY CLOUD COVER

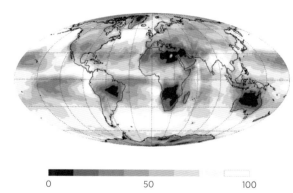

0   50   100

JANUARY PRECIPITATION

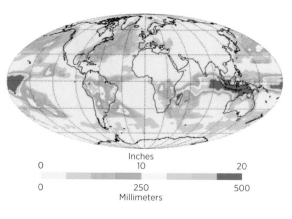

Inches
0   10   20

0   250   500
Millimeters

JULY PRECIPITATION

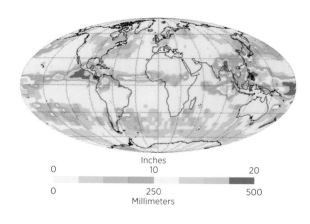

Inches
0   10   20

0   250   500
Millimeters

Climate Change

The scientific evidence is clear: Earth is warming at a pace that signals an unprecedented shift in the global climate. Such epochal changes have occurred in the past, but they were set in motion by the natural variations in Earth's orbit that affect the amount of sunlight warming the planet. Those cycles of cooling and warming unfolded slowly, over the course of millennia. In fact, only recently did the 10,000-year period of climate stability that helped human civilization flourish come to an end. Now, though, the climate is changing more rapidly than it has for 650,000 years, and humans' burning of fossil fuels—and the attendant rise in greenhouse gases—is the main cause. Scientists believe that unless greenhouse gas emissions are reduced by 50 percent by 2050, the damage to Earth will be irreversible. Already impacts include altered precipitation patterns, melting glaciers and permafrost, more intense weather events, and a rise in sea level. Particularly hard hit will be people in the tropics and poorer countries without the resources to adapt.

Left: As global temperatures rise, drought is becoming more frequent and lasting longer, as evident in the dry bed of a reservoir in California (2015). Right: In some areas where extreme downpours were not common, severe flooding has become more frequent, as was the case in the United Kingdom (2015).

TAKING THE PLANET'S RISING TEMPERATURE

The temperature is rising across the planet. The Arctic has seen the greatest change, largely because of its lower albedo rates (how much solar radiation is reflected back into space). Heat waves are becoming more common, often with deadly consequences. Landmasses warm faster than oceans—one reason most heating is observed in the land-dominant Northern Hemisphere—but oceans are also warming. In some areas where oceans are cooling, changing currents are bringing up cold water from the deep.

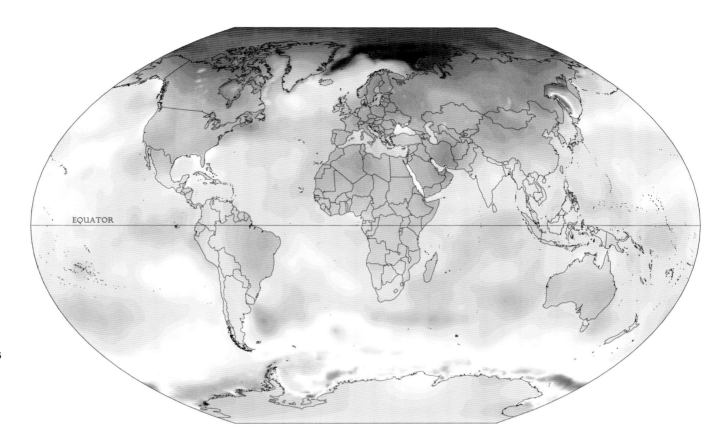

Temperature Trends, 1960–2015
Change in degrees

-20°C   -15°   -12°   -9°
-5°F   No change   5°   10°   15°

RISING TEMPERATURES AND CO_2

When graphed together, the rise in the global average temperature—an increase of about 1.4°F (0.8°C) since the early 20th century—and the exponential rise in carbon dioxide (CO_2) concentrations track each other closely over the past half century. And the trend is only getting more severe: The ten warmest years on record have all occurred since 1998. This climb is expected to continue, given our unabated appetite for oil, gas, and coal, initiated by the industrial revolution.

SHRINKING POLAR ICE

Often referred to as the "canary in the coal mine" of global climate change, the Arctic is exhibiting change faster than any other part of the world. Sea ice is shrinking at a rapid rate, influencing global climate as it affects ocean circulation. Rapid melting is compounded by a climatic feedback loop: Areas covered by ice, which are light in color, are getting smaller, so less solar radiation is bounced back into the atmosphere; instead, more radiation is being absorbed by the darker ocean waters—which then results in a further reduction of sea ice.

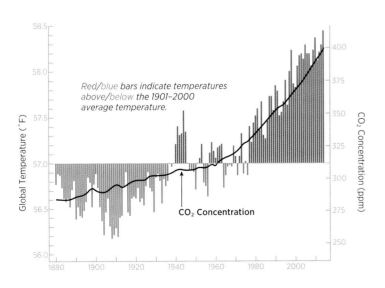

Climate

CLIMATE ZONES ARE PRIMARILY CONTROLLED by latitude—which governs the prevailing winds, the angle of the sun's rays, and the length of day throughout the year—and by geographical location with respect to mountains and oceans. Elevation, surface attributes, and other variables modify the primary controlling factors. Latitudinal banding of climate zones is most pronounced over Africa and Asia, where fewer north-south mountain ranges mean less disruption of prevailing winds. In the Western Hemisphere, the high, almost continuous mountain range that extends from western Canada to southern South America helps create dry regions on its leeward slopes. Over the United States, where westerly winds prevail, areas to the east of the range lie in a "rain shadow" and are therefore drier. In northern parts of South America, where easterly trade winds prevail, the rain shadow lies west of the mountains. Ocean effects dominate much of western Europe and southern parts of Australia.

Climographs

The map at right shows the global distribution of climate zones, while the following 12 climographs (graphs of monthly temperature and precipitation) provide snapshots of the climate at specific places. Each place has a different climate type, which is described in general terms. Rainfall is shown in a bar graph format (scale on right side of the graph); temperature is expressed with a line graph (scale on left side). Places with highland and upland climates were not included because local changes in elevation can produce significant variations in local conditions.

Climate Zones
(based on modified Köppen system)

Tropical
- Tropical wet
- Tropical wet & dry

Dry
- Semiarid
- Arid

Mild
- Marine west coast
- Mediterranean
- Humid subtropical

Continental
- Warm summer
- Cool summer
- Subarctic

Polar
- Tundra
- Ice sheet

High elevations
- Highlands
- Uplands

→ Warm ocean current
→ Cool ocean current

In 1884, Wladimir Köppen initially developed a system for describing Earth's climate regions that is still widely used today. Based on the idea that natural vegetation regions are best at defining climate boundaries, the system relies on monthly and annual temperature and precipitation data to help delineate climate types.

TROPICAL WET

This climate type has the most predictable conditions. Warm and rainy year-round, regions with a tropical wet climate experience little variation from month to month. This type is mainly found within a zone extending about 10 degrees on either side of the Equator. With as much as 60 inches (152 cm) of rain each year, the tropical wet climate supports lush vegetation.

TROPICAL WET AND DRY

Because of seasonal reversals in wind direction (monsoons), this climate type is characterized by a slightly cooler dry season and a warmer, extremely moist wet season. The highest temperatures usually occur just before the wet season. Although average annual conditions may be similar to a tropical wet climate, the rainy season brings much more rain.

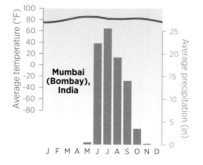

ARID

Centered between 20 and 30 degrees north and south latitude, this climate type is the result of a persistent high-pressure area and, along the western margins of continents, a cold ocean current. Rainfall amounts in regions with this climate type are negligible, and there is some seasonal variation in temperature. Desert vegetation is typically sparse.

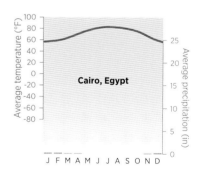

SEMIARID

Regions with a semiarid climate lie poleward of areas with a desert (arid) climate; they have a much greater range in monthly temperatures and receive significantly more rainfall than deserts. This climate type is often found in inland regions, in the rain shadow of mountain ranges. Annual rainfall amounts support mainly grasses and small shrubs.

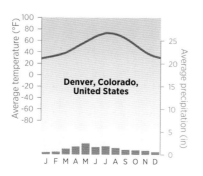

MARINE WEST COAST

This climate type is primarily found between 40 and 60 degrees latitude; it occurs on the west coasts of continents and across much of Europe. Prevailing westerly winds bring milder ocean air ashore, but sunny days are limited and precipitation is frequent. Except in the highest elevations, most precipitation falls as rain. This climate supports extensive forests.

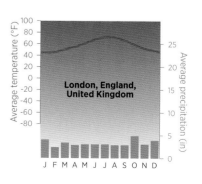

CONTINENTAL WARM SUMMER

Regions with this climate type have warmer year-round temperatures and more rainfall than regions with cool summers. This type is found from about 40 to 50 degrees north (except in Europe, where it extends to about 60 degrees north) and is marked by large variations in average monthly temperature. Summer averages can exceed 70°F (21°C); winter averages can be in the 20s (-7°C).

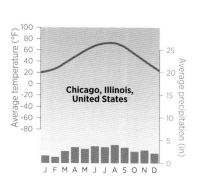

CONTINENTAL COOL SUMMER

Found only from about 40 to 60 degrees north, this type is marked by temperature extremes. Summers are cool (around 60°F/15°C as a monthly average); winter months may have below-freezing average temperatures. Rainfall is moderate to abundant.

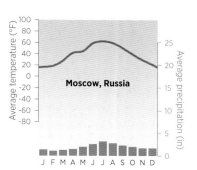

SUBARCTIC

This climate type is found along and just south of the Arctic Circle; it is driven by large seasonal swings in the amount of daylight a region receives. Winter tends to be cold with light snow and little melting. Summer months are quite warm for the latitude, with temperatures 70° or 80°F (39° or 44°C) higher than monthly averages in winter; summer has significant rainfall.

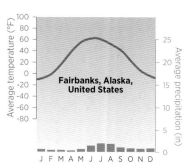

MEDITERRANEAN

This term describes the climate of much of the Mediterranean region. Such a climate is also found in narrow bands along the west coasts of continents that lie around 30 to 35 degrees poleward from the Equator. Summer months are typically warm to hot with dry conditions, while winter months are cool (but not cold) and provide modest precipitation.

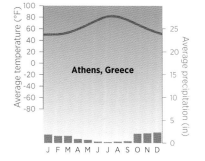

TUNDRA

Along the southern boundary of this climatic zone, ground-hugging plants meet the northernmost trees (the tree line). Here, the warmest average monthly temperature is below 50°F (10°C), with only one to four months having an average monthly temperature that is above freezing. Precipitation amounts are low, typically about 10 inches (25 cm) or less annually.

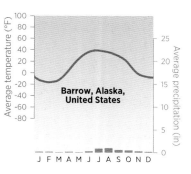

HUMID SUBTROPICAL

This climate type dominates eastern regions of continents at 30 to 35 degrees latitude. Here, warm ocean waters lead to warm and humid summers. Rainfall is greatest near the coast, supporting forest growth; precipitation is less farther west, supporting grasslands. Winter can bring cold waves and snowy periods, except in areas right on the coast.

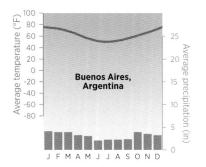

ICE SHEET

This climate type is found at high latitudes in interior Greenland and across most of Antarctica; average monthly temperatures are around zero degrees Fahrenheit (-18°C) and below. Snow defines the landscape, but precipitation is only about 5 inches (13 cm) or less annually. The combined effects of cold and dryness produce desertlike conditions.

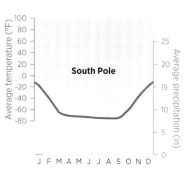

Biodiversity

BIODIVERSITY REFERS TO THREE MEASURES of Earth's intricate web of life: the number of different species, the genetic diversity within a species, and the variety of ecosystems in which species live. Greatest in the wet tropics, biodiversity is important for many reasons, including helping to provide food and medicine, breathable air, drinkable water, livable climates, protection from pests and diseases, and ecosystem stability.

Humankind is only one species in a vast array of life-forms. It is, however, an especially influential and increasingly disruptive actor in the huge cast of characters on the stage of planet Earth. Estimates of the total number of plant and animal species range from a few million to a hundred million; of these, only 1.7 million have been described. Yet, a substantial number of those species may be gone before we even have a chance to understand their value.

For most of human history, people have often looked at plants and animals simply as resources for meeting their own basic needs. Scientists today can count over 300,000 plant species, of which just 9 provide three-quarters of all our food; in that respect, biodiversity has been an unimaginable luxury. It is ironic that even as humankind's power to destroy other species grows, so does our ingenuity in finding new and beneficial uses for them.

Sometimes the benefits of preserving a species may have nothing to do with food or medicine. Before a worldwide ban on exports of elephant ivory, the estimated value of such exports was $40 million a year for all of Africa. Now, some wildlife experts estimate that elephants generate more money for ecotourism than their tusks are worth on the black market.

The Natural World
Labeled for their natural vegetation, biomes are defined by their distinctive mix of plants and animals.

1. Tundra
2. Northern coniferous forest (also called boreal forest or taiga)
3. Temperate coniferous forest
4. Temperate broadleaf forest (includes rain forest)
5. Temperate grassland
6. Desert and dry shrub
7. Mediterranean scrub
8. Mountain grassland
9. Flooded grassland and savanna
10. Tropical grassland and savanna
11. Tropical dry forest
12. Tropical coniferous forest
13. Tropical moist broadleaf (includes rain forest)
14. Mangrove
15. Permanent ice cover

Species Diversity

Among fauna and flora, insects make up the largest classification in terms of sheer number of species, with fungi ranked a distant second. At the other extreme, the categories with the smallest numbers—mammals, birds, and mollusks—also happen to be the classes with the greatest percentage of threatened species (see Threatened Species graph, below right). This is not just a matter of proportion: These groups include the most at-risk species in terms of absolute numbers as well.

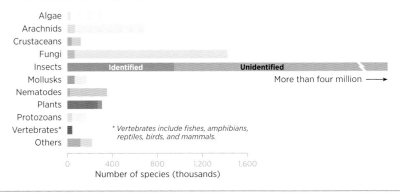

Algae
Arachnids
Crustaceans
Fungi
Insects — Identified — Unidentified
Mollusks — More than four million ⟶
Nematodes
Plants
Protozoans
Vertebrates*
Others

Vertebrates include fishes, amphibians, reptiles, birds, and mammals.

0   400   800   1,200   1,600
Number of species (thousands)

Biodiversity Hotspots

British ecologist Norman Myers defined the "biodiversity hotspot" concept in 1988 to help address the dilemma of identifying conservation priorities. The biodiversity hotspots hold especially high numbers of endemic species, yet their combined area of remaining habitat covers only 2.3 percent of Earth's land surface. Each hotspot faces extreme threats, and collectively they have lost 85 percent of their original natural vegetation. Of particular concern to scientists is that 69 percent of all threatened terrestrial vertebrates occur only in the hotspots.

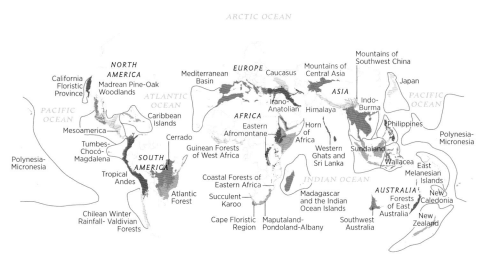

Biodiversity Hotspots, 2013
▬ Hotspot areas
— Hotspot outer limit

Threatened Species

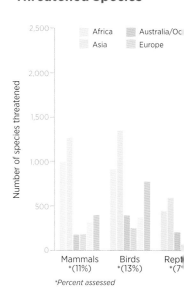

Africa   Australia/Oc
Asia   Europe

2,500
2,000
1,500
1,000
500
0

Number of species threatened

Mammals *(11%)*   Birds *(13%)*   Rept *(7*

*Percent assessed

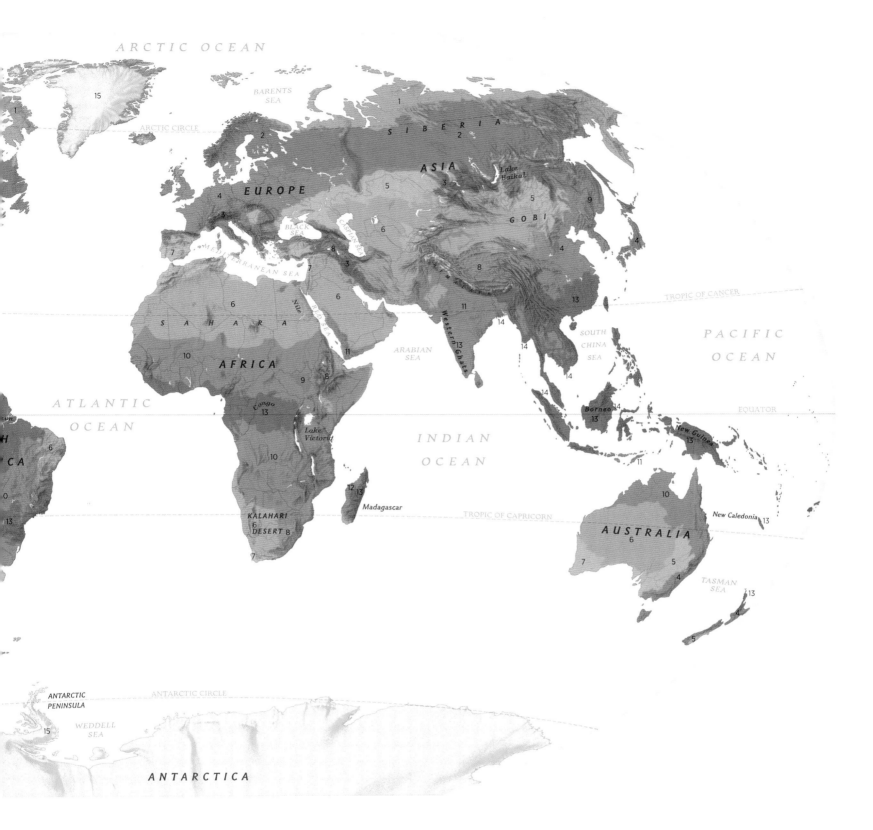

Conservation Status of Terrestrial Ecoregions

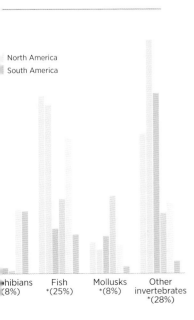

Biodiversity is decreasing at a rapidly increasing rate. According to scientists, current extinction rates are a hundred to a thousand times greater than the normal rate of extinction; furthermore, the number of species threatened with extinction continues to increase (with, for example, one in three amphibians and one in four mammals at risk in the wild). Species are not being killed off directly: The two leading causes of extinction are loss of habitat and the impact of invasive species, although other threats include over-exploitation, pollution, disease, and climate change.

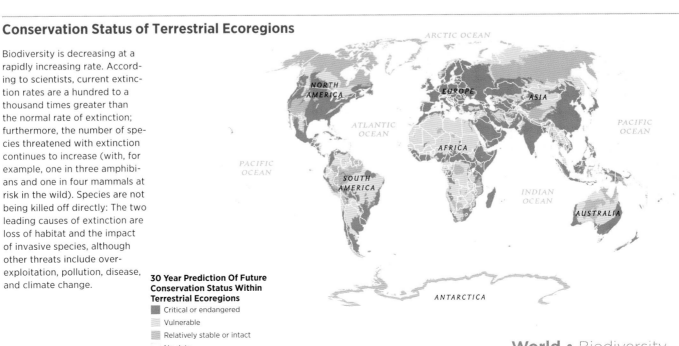

30 Year Prediction Of Future Conservation Status Within Terrestrial Ecoregions

- ▪ Critical or endangered
- ▪ Vulnerable
- ▪ Relatively stable or intact
- No data

Human Influences

EARTH'S 4.5-BILLION-YEAR HISTORY has been characterized by epochs—periods of time that leave a clear record in the planet's rock layers. Each geologic epoch lasts from a few million to tens of millions of years, but the most recent one, the Holocene, which began when the glaciers last receded, may have come to a sudden end after only 11,500 years. Some scientists now believe a new and entirely different phase in Earth's history has begun, and they're calling it the Anthropocene, or "human epoch"—an age in which humans are radically changing the planet.

Humans first began altering Earth's ecology long ago with their use of fire and by hunting large animal species to extinction. Clearing lands for agriculture generated even greater changes in ecology and allowed human populations to grow larger than ever before. Yet, the most rapid and unprecedented changes caused by humans date to the 1800s and the industrial revolution, when humans suddenly acquired an unprecedented ability to exploit energy, especially fossil fuels, and thereby manipulate the environment. These later changes are what are most widely referred to as the origins of the Anthropocene. Now human impacts—habitat conversion for land use, environmental pollution, and plant and animal extinctions—are leaving a record in the rock, the very definition of an epoch.

At the beginning of the industrial revolution, almost half of Earth's land had not yet received the impression of significant human populations or land use; most of the other half, too, was still seminatural, bearing only a light footprint of agriculture or small settlements. But with industrialization, humans' influences on the biosphere began to change dramatically. As urban centers attracted more and more workers, nearby intensive agricultural and forestry techniques altered more and more of the terrestrial biosphere, from its rock layers to its ocean waters to its atmosphere—changing the very nature of planet Earth.

Anthromes

Dense Settlements
- Urban
- Mixed settlements

Villages
- Rice villages
- Irrigated villages
- Rainfed villages
- Pastoral villages

Croplands
- Residential irrigated croplands
- Residential rainfed croplands
- Populated croplands
- Remote croplands

Rangelands
- Residential rangelands
- Populated rangelands
- Remote rangelands

Seminatural
- Residential woodlands
- Populated woodlands
- Remote woodlands
- Inhabited treeless and barren lands

Wildlands
- Wild woodlands
- Wild treeless and barren lands

Human Influence Index

Based on the Human Influence Index created by the Wildlife Conservation Society and Columbia University's Center for International Earth Science Information Network, this map combines data on settlements, transportation infrastructure, landscape transformation, and electric power infrastructure. Such an overview of human influence provides a useful tool for wildlife conservation planning, natural resource management, and research on human-environment interactions.

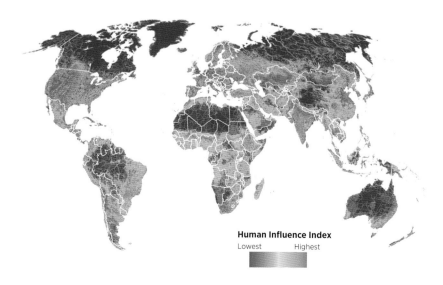

Human Influence Index

Lowest   Highest

Last of the Wild

Essentially an inverse of the Human Influence Index map at left (and made by the same researchers), the Last of the Wild map is a tool for finding the best places to preserve wildlife. To help identify priority areas, the scientists looked at the world in terms of biomes. The areas colored in on the map below contain fewer people, less infrastructure, less human land use, and less power—and less human conflict. As such, these places provide the most practical opportunities for conservation efforts.

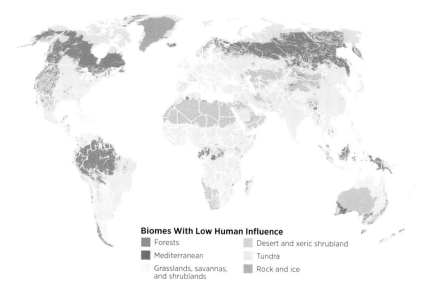

Biomes With Low Human Influence
- Forests
- Mediterranean
- Grasslands, savannas, and shrublands
- Desert and xeric shrubland
- Tundra
- Rock and ice

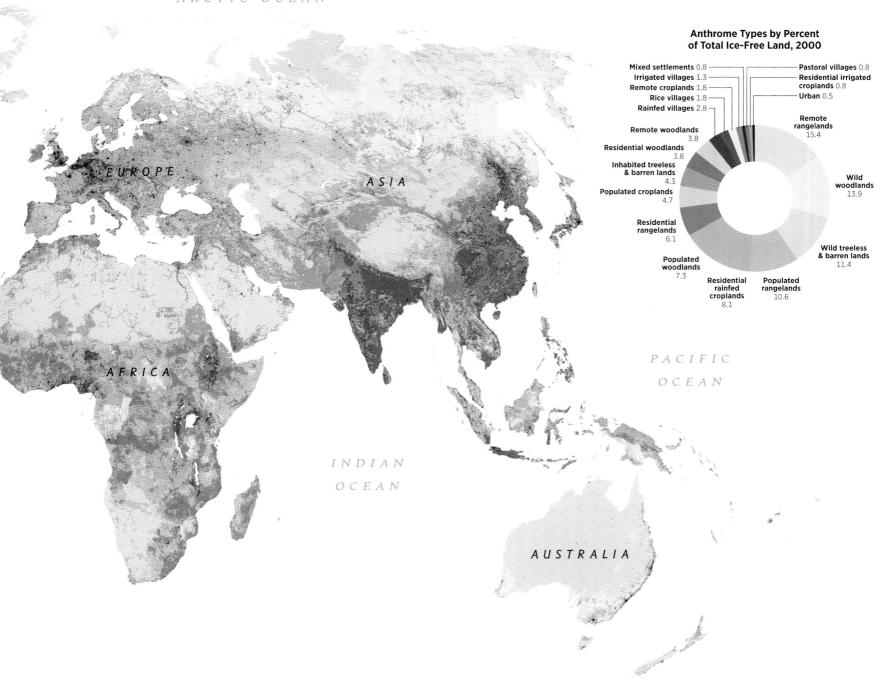

Anthrome Types by Percent of Total Ice-Free Land, 2000

- Mixed settlements 0.8
- Irrigated villages 1.3
- Remote croplands 1.8
- Rice villages 1.8
- Rainfed villages 2.8
- Remote woodlands 3.8
- Residential woodlands 3.8
- Inhabited treeless & barren lands 4.3
- Populated croplands 4.7
- Residential rangelands 6.1
- Populated woodlands 7.3
- Residential rainfed croplands 8.1
- Populated rangelands 10.6
- Wild treeless & barren lands 11.4
- Wild woodlands 13.9
- Remote rangelands 15.4
- Urban 0.5
- Residential irrigated croplands 0.8
- Pastoral villages 0.8

Human Influences Over Time

In 1700, 95 percent of the planet's ice-free land was in wildlands and seminatural anthromes, the latter of which supported about half of the human population. The other half of the population at that time lived in croplands and villages. Over the next 300 years, dramatic shifts in land use took place. Humans transformed 55 percent of Earth's ice-free land into rangelands, croplands, villages, and densely settled anthromes. Settlement patterns changed as well: In 2000, seminatural anthromes were home to just 4 percent of Earth's six billion inhabitants; 51 percent were living in villages. Now extensive wildlands mostly remain in the cold or dry biomes where humans prefer not to live.

Planetary Stewardship

We can and should make every effort to preserve areas only lightly touched by humans, but we cannot undo what has been done. People are, as the researchers who coined the term anthrome have said, "in the map." To effect lasting change, conservation efforts need to begin with the mind-set of humans *and* Earth, not humans *versus* Earth. By recognizing that the biosphere is now being reshaped more dramatically by human systems than by biophysical processes alone, we can take on the mantle of stewards instead of invaders or exploiters. In approaching issues such as urbanization and agricultural expansion from this paradigm, we can work toward solutions that address both environmental and human needs.

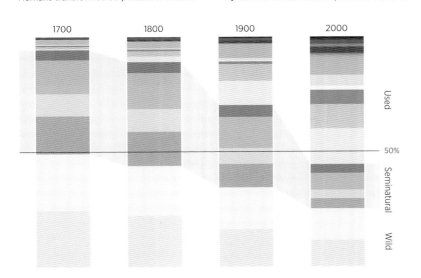

1700   1800   1900   2000

Used   50%   Seminatural   Wild

Dense settlement, China

Mixed settlement, Greece

Barren land, Canada

Rice village, Thailand

Cropland, United Kingdom

Rangeland, Australia

Population

WHILE POPULATIONS IN MANY PARTS of the world are expanding, some other rich industrial areas such as Japan show little to no growth or may actually be shrinking. Many such countries must bring in immigrant workers to keep their economies thriving. A clear correlation exists between wealth and low fertility: The higher the incomes and educational levels, the lower the rates of reproduction.

Many governments keep vital statistics, recording births and deaths, and count their populations regularly to try to plan ahead. The United States has taken a census every ten years since 1790, recording the ages, the occupations, and other important facts about its people. The United Nations helps less developed countries carry out censuses and improve their demographic information.

Governments of some poor countries may find that half their populations are under the age of 20. They are faced with the overwhelming tasks of providing adequate education and jobs while encouraging better family-planning programs. Governments of nations with low birthrates find themselves with growing numbers of elderly people who need health care and pension disbursements but fewer workers able to contribute to the tax base that funds such programs and accounts.

In a mere 150 years, the world population has grown fivefold, at an ever increasing pace. The industrial revolution helped bring about improvements in food supplies and advances in both medicine and public health, which allowed people to live longer and to have more healthy babies. Today, 15,000 people are born into the world every hour, and nearly all of them are in poor African, Asian, and South American nations. This situation concerns planners, who look to demographers (professionals who study all aspects of population) for important data.

People per Square Mile
- More than 500
- 150–500
- 25–149
- 1–24
- Less than 1

People per Square Kilometer
- More than 195
- 60–195
- 10–59
- 1–9
- Less than 1

Urban Area Population
(in millions)
- ■ More than 20
- ▲ 15–20
- • 10–14

Population Density

A country's population density is estimated by figuring out how many people would occupy one square kilometer (0.39 square miles) if they were all spread out evenly. In reality, people live together most closely in cities, on seacoasts, and in river valleys. Singapore, a tiny country largely composed of a single city, has a high population density—more than 7,800 people per square kilometer (0.39 square miles).

Greenland, by comparison, has less than one person per square kilometer (0.39 square miles) because it is mostly covered by ice. Its people mainly fish for a living and dwell in small groups near the shore.

Population Pyramids

A population pyramid shows the number of males and females in every age group of a population. A pyramid for Nigeria reveals that over half—about 55 percent—of the population is under 20, while only 19 percent of Italy's population is younger than 20.

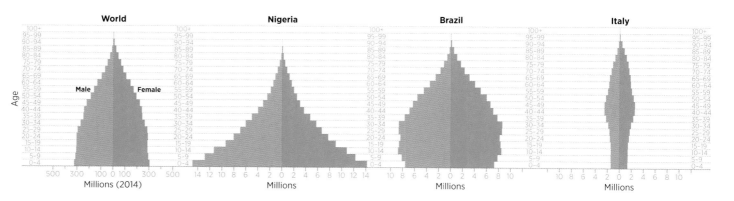

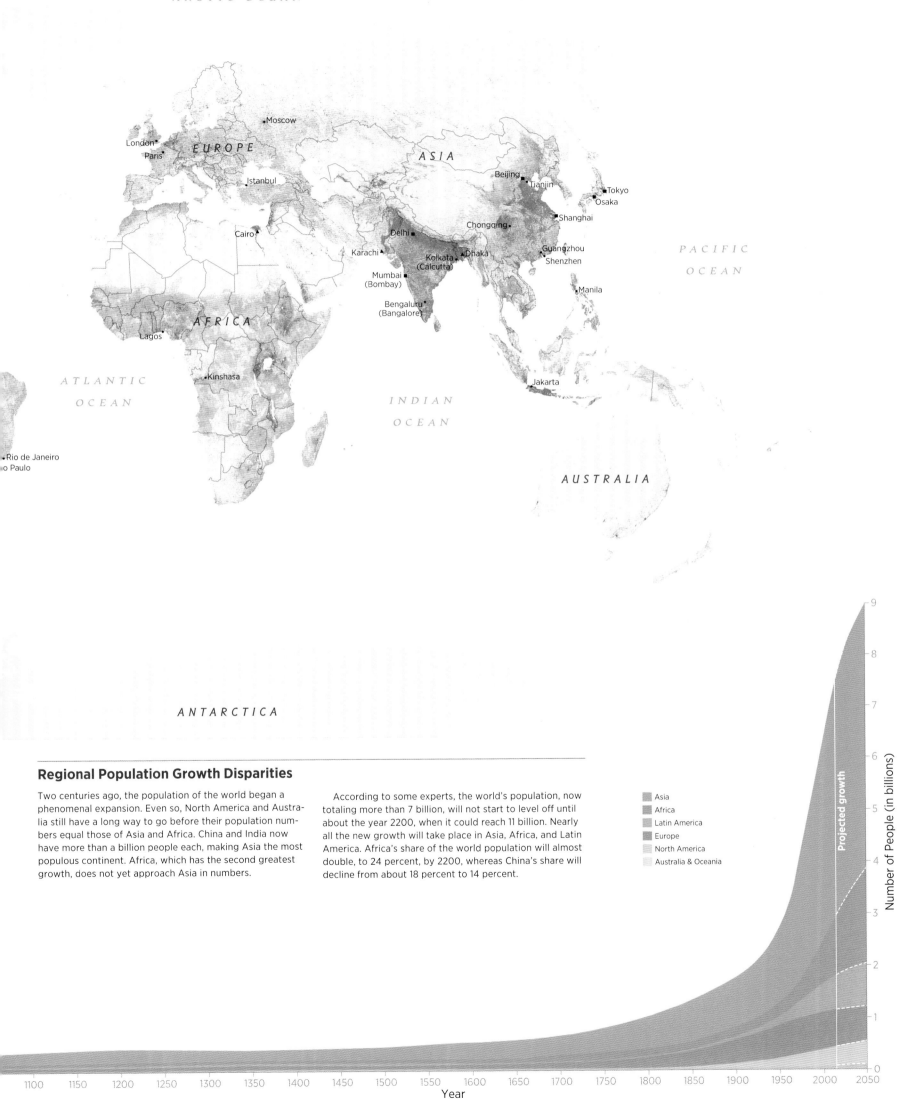

ARCTIC OCEAN

EUROPE
•Moscow
London•
Paris•
Istanbul

ASIA
Beijing•
•Tianjin
•Tokyo
•Osaka
•Shanghai
Chongqing•
Delhi•
Karachi•
Kolkata•
(Calcutta)
•Dhaka
Guangzhou•
Shenzhen•
Mumbai•
(Bombay)
Bengaluru
(Bangalore)

PACIFIC

OCEAN

Cairo•

AFRICA

Lagos•

ATLANTIC

OCEAN

•Kinshasa

INDIAN

OCEAN

•Manila

•Jakarta

AUSTRALIA

•Rio de Janeiro
o Paulo

ANTARCTICA

Regional Population Growth Disparities

Two centuries ago, the population of the world began a phenomenal expansion. Even so, North America and Australia still have a long way to go before their population numbers equal those of Asia and Africa. China and India now have more than a billion people each, making Asia the most populous continent. Africa, which has the second greatest growth, does not yet approach Asia in numbers.

According to some experts, the world's population, now totaling more than 7 billion, will not start to level off until about the year 2200, when it could reach 11 billion. Nearly all the new growth will take place in Asia, Africa, and Latin America. Africa's share of the world population will almost double, to 24 percent, by 2200, whereas China's share will decline from about 18 percent to 14 percent.

Asia
Africa
Latin America
Europe
North America
Australia & Oceania

Number of People (in billions)

Projected growth

9
8
7
6
5
4
3
2
1
0

1100 1150 1200 1250 1300 1350 1400 1450 1500 1550 1600 1650 1700 1750 1800 1850 1900 1950 2000 2050
Year

Population

Fertility

Fertility, or birthrate, measures the average number of children born to women in a given population. It can also be expressed as the number of live births per thousand people in a population per year. In low-income countries with limited educational opportunities for girls and women, fertility is often highest.

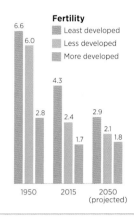

Fertility
- Least developed
- Less developed
- More developed

1950	2015	2050 (projected)
6.6 6.0 2.8	4.3 2.4 1.7	2.9 2.1 1.8

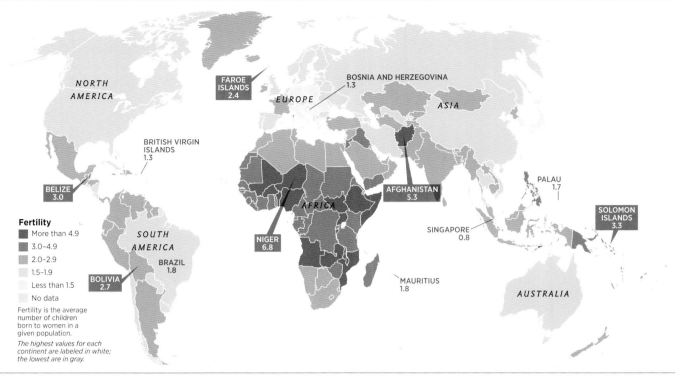

NORTH AMERICA

EUROPE

FAROE ISLANDS 2.4

BOSNIA AND HERZEGOVINA 1.3

ASIA

BRITISH VIRGIN ISLANDS 1.3

BELIZE 3.0

AFRICA

AFGHANISTAN 5.3

PALAU 1.7

SOLOMON ISLANDS 3.3

SINGAPORE 0.8

SOUTH AMERICA

BRAZIL 1.8

NIGER 6.8

BOLIVIA 2.7

MAURITIUS 1.8

AUSTRALIA

Fertility
- More than 4.9
- 3.0–4.9
- 2.0–2.9
- 1.5–1.9
- Less than 1.5
- No data

Fertility is the average number of children born to women in a given population.

The highest values for each continent are labeled in white; the lowest are in gray.

Urban Population Densities

People around the world are leaving farms and moving to cities, where jobs and opportunities are better. By 2008, half the world's people lived in towns or cities. The shift of population from the countryside to urban centers will probably continue in less developed countries for many years to come.

Population in Urban Areas
(as a percentage of total population)
- Least developed
- Less developed
- More developed

1950	2015	2050 (projected)
8 19 55	31 52 78	50 67 85

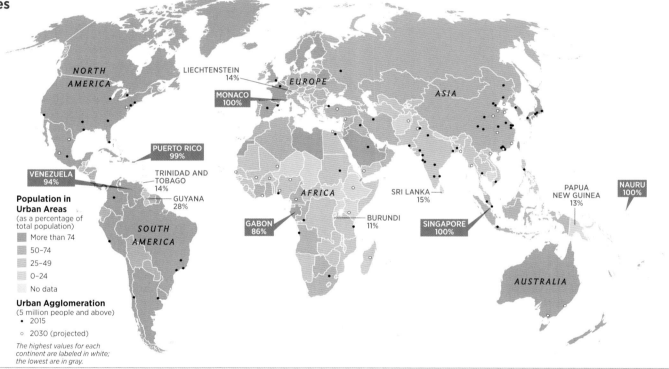

NORTH AMERICA

LIECHTENSTEIN 14%

EUROPE

MONACO 100%

ASIA

PUERTO RICO 99%

VENEZUELA 94%

TRINIDAD AND TOBAGO 14%

GUYANA 28%

SRI LANKA 15%

PAPUA NEW GUINEA 13%

NAURU 100%

SOUTH AMERICA

AFRICA

BURUNDI 11%

SINGAPORE 100%

GABON 86%

AUSTRALIA

Population in Urban Areas
(as a percentage of total population)
- More than 74
- 50–74
- 25–49
- 0–24
- No data

Urban Agglomeration
(5 million people and above)
- 2015
- 2030 (projected)

The highest values for each continent are labeled in white; the lowest are in gray.

Urban Population Growth

In general, urban populations are growing more than twice as fast as populations as a whole. The world's city dwellers now outnumber its rural inhabitants as towns have become cities and cities have merged into megacities with more than ten million people. Globalization speeds the process. Although cities generate wealth and provide better health care along with benefits such as electricity, clean water, and sewage treatment, they can also cause great ecological damage. Squatter settlements and slums may develop if cities cannot accommodate millions of new arrivals. Smog, congestion, pollution, and crime are other dangers. Good city management is a key to future prosperity.

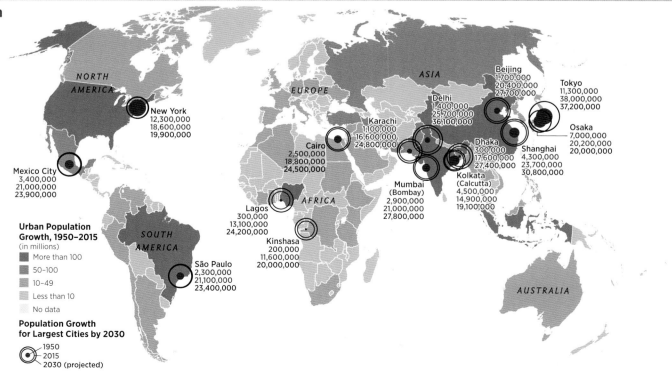

NORTH AMERICA

New York 12,300,000 18,600,000 19,900,000

EUROPE

ASIA

Beijing 1,700,000 20,400,000 27,700,000

Tokyo 11,300,000 38,000,000 37,200,000

Delhi 1,400,000 25,700,000 36,100,000

Karachi 1,100,000 16,600,000 24,800,000

Osaka 7,000,000 20,200,000 20,000,000

Dhaka 300,000 17,600,000 27,400,000

Shanghai 4,300,000 23,700,000 30,800,000

Cairo 2,500,000 18,800,000 24,500,000

Mexico City 3,400,000 21,000,000 23,900,000

Mumbai (Bombay) 2,900,000 21,000,000 27,800,000

Kolkata (Calcutta) 4,500,000 14,900,000 19,100,000

Lagos 300,000 13,100,000 24,200,000

AFRICA

Kinshasa 200,000 11,600,000 20,000,000

SOUTH AMERICA

São Paulo 2,300,000 21,100,000 23,400,000

AUSTRALIA

Urban Population Growth, 1950–2015
(in millions)
- More than 100
- 50–100
- 10–49
- Less than 10
- No data

Population Growth for Largest Cities by 2030
- 1950
- 2015
- 2030 (projected)

Life Expectancy

Life expectancy for population groups does not mean that all people die by a certain age. It is an average of death statistics. High infant mortality results in low life expectancy: People who live to adulthood will probably reach old age; there are just fewer of them.

Life Expectancy
- Least developed
- Less developed
- More developed

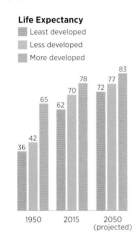

1950   2015   2050 (projected)

36 42
62 65 70 78
72 77 83

Life Expectancy (years)
- More than 79
- 75–79
- 65–74
- 55–64
- Less than 55
- No data

The highest values for each continent are labeled in white; the lowest are in gray.

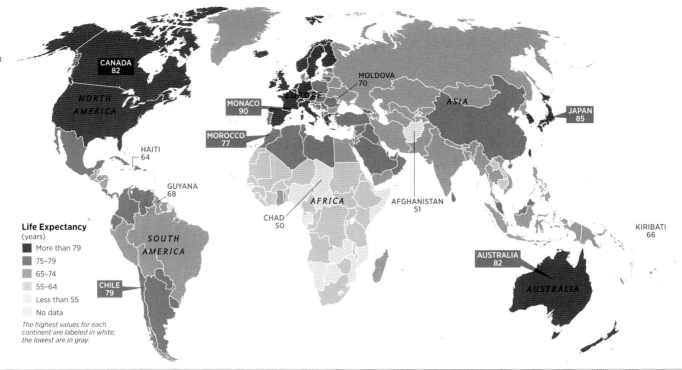

CANADA 82
NORTH AMERICA
HAITI 64
GUYANA 68
SOUTH AMERICA
CHILE 79
MONACO 90
MOROCCO 77
EUROPE
MOLDOVA 70
ASIA
AFRICA
CHAD 50
AFGHANISTAN 51
JAPAN 85
KIRIBATI 66
AUSTRALIA 82
AUSTRALIA

Migration

International migration has reached its highest level, with foreign workers now providing the labor in several Middle Eastern countries and immigrant workers proving essential to rich countries with low birthrates. Refugees continue to escape grim political and environmental conditions, while businesspeople and tourists keep many economies spinning.

Migrant Population
(percentage of regional population)

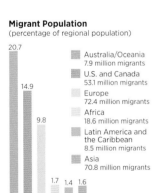

20.7
14.9
9.8
1.7 1.4 1.6

- Australia/Oceania 7.9 million migrants
- U.S. and Canada 53.1 million migrants
- Europe 72.4 million migrants
- Africa 18.6 million migrants
- Latin America and the Caribbean 8.5 million migrants
- Asia 70.8 million migrants

Migrant Population (as a percentage of total population)
- More than 19.9
- 10.0–19.9
- 5.0–9.9
- 1.0–4.9
- 0–0.9
- No data

Migrant population based on place of birth (2013 data)

The highest values for each continent are labeled in white; the lowest are in gray.

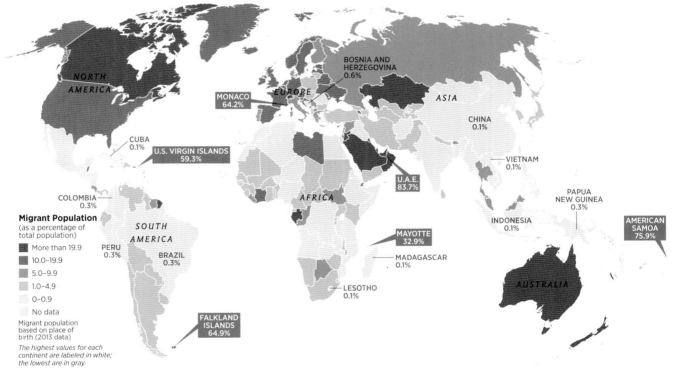

NORTH AMERICA
CUBA 0.1%
U.S. VIRGIN ISLANDS 59.3%
COLOMBIA 0.3%
PERU 0.3%
SOUTH AMERICA
BRAZIL 0.3%
FALKLAND ISLANDS 64.9%
MONACO 64.2%
EUROPE
BOSNIA AND HERZEGOVINA 0.6%
ASIA
CHINA 0.1%
AFRICA
U.A.E. 83.7%
MAYOTTE 32.9%
LESOTHO 0.1%
MADAGASCAR 0.1%
VIETNAM 0.1%
INDONESIA 0.1%
PAPUA NEW GUINEA 0.3%
AMERICAN SAMOA 75.9%
AUSTRALIA

Population Growth

The population of the world is not distributed evenly. In this cartogram, Canada is almost invisible, while India looks enormous because its population is 35 times as large as Canada's. In reality, Canada's area is three times as large as India's. The shape of almost every country looks distorted when populations are compared in this way.

Population sizes are constantly changing, however. In countries that are experiencing many more births than deaths, population totals are ballooning. In others, too few babies are born to replace the number of people who die, and populations are shrinking. A cartogram devoted solely to growth rates around the world would look quite different from this one.

Population and Growth Rates
- More than 2.9%
- 2.0–2.9%
- 1.0–1.9%
- 0–0.9%
- Population decline

Each square represents one million people (mid-2014 data).

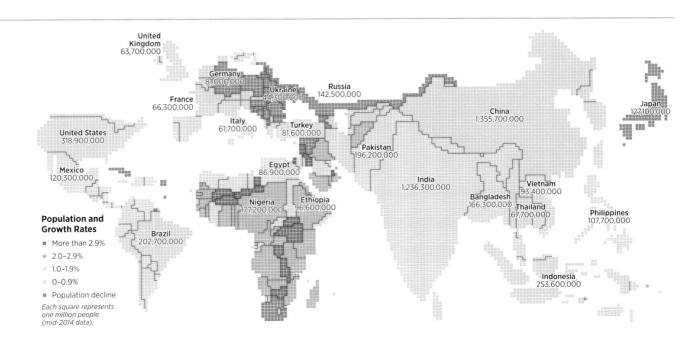

United Kingdom 63,700,000
Germany 81,000,000
France 66,300,000
United States 318,900,000
Mexico 120,300,000
Italy 61,700,000
Ukraine 44,300,000
Russia 142,500,000
Turkey 81,600,000
Egypt 86,900,000
Nigeria 177,200,000
Ethiopia 96,600,000
Brazil 202,700,000
Pakistan 196,200,000
China 1,355,700,000
India 1,236,300,000
Bangladesh 166,300,000
Vietnam 93,400,000
Thailand 67,700,000
Japan 127,100,000
Philippines 107,700,000
Indonesia 253,600,000

Languages

LANGUAGE MAY EASILY BE RANKED as one of humankind's most distinctive and versatile adaptations. Though its exact origins are lost in the recesses of prehistory, spoken language has allowed humans to communicate and develop in ways inconceivable without it. Written language came much later, and even in recent history, many languages were without a written component. Yet today, the written word has a profound impact on daily life, global communications, and human development. It's virtually impossible to imagine a world without it.

As living, organic entities, languages easily morph over time and place to fit cultural and geographical circumstances. In an often cited example of this, Arctic peoples have many different words for snow—words that reflect different qualities, because those qualities can be critical to human survival in a harsh environment. By studying subtle variations in sounds and concepts embedded in languages, linguists have devised systems to classify them into broad families.

Today, Earth's 7 billion people speak some 7,000 languages, but these languages are not equally distributed among the globe's inhabitants. Roughly 78 percent of the world's population, well over 5 billion people, speaks only 85 of the largest languages, while some 3,500 of the smallest languages have only 8.25 million speakers in all. Often speakers of these smaller languages are the elder members of cultural groups that have been marginalized over time by a more dominant culture. As they die out, so too do the languages only they kept alive. Globalization has only exacerbated this trend, but some small cultures, aware of the fragility of their own languages, are working hard to preserve linguistic traditions.

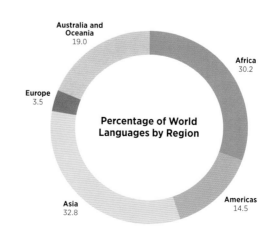

A variety of indigenous languages exist in the Americas, but because their distribution is fairly sparse, many are not shown on this generalized map.

Evolution of Languages

Even as many languages have disappeared, a few dominant linguistic groups have spawned numerous related tongues. Thus, the Germanic language, which derived from Proto-Indo-European and was spoken by tribes that settled in northern and western Europe, has diversified into several major languages today.

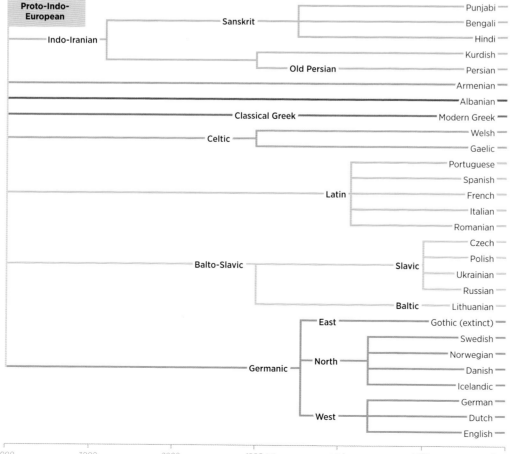

How Many Speak What?

Languages can paint vivid historical pictures of migration and colonization. The languages of a few small European countries are spoken by over a billion people worldwide. In contrast, Australia and Oceania, a constellation of isolated islands in the Pacific, have just 0.5 percent of the world's total population but 19 percent of the world's languages.

Percentage of World Languages by Region

- Australia and Oceania 19.0
- Africa 30.2
- Europe 3.5
- Americas 14.5
- Asia 32.8

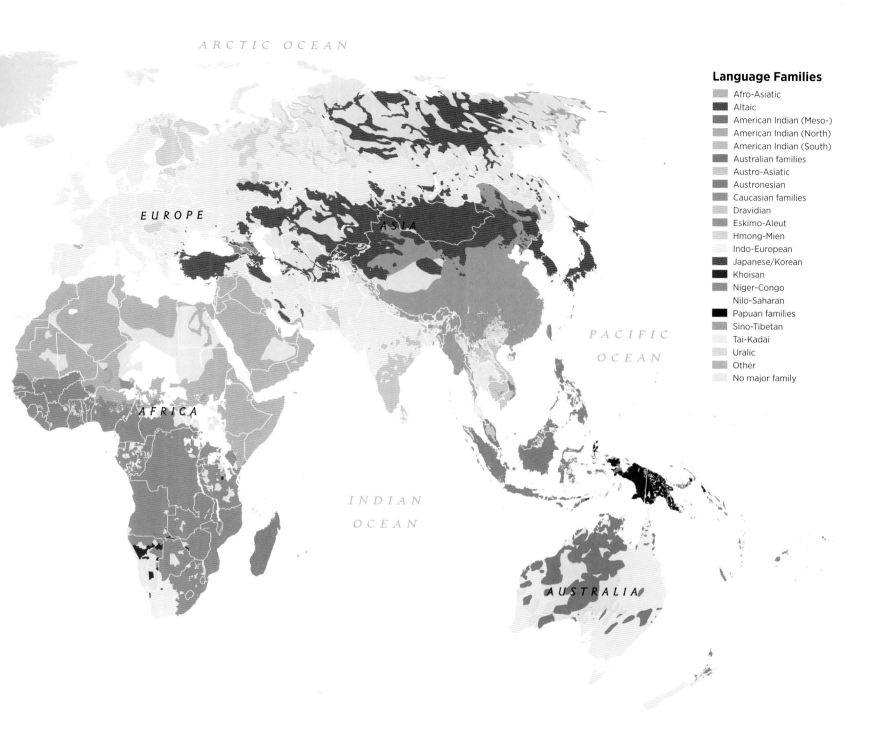

Language Families

- Afro-Asiatic
- Altaic
- American Indian (Meso-)
- American Indian (North)
- American Indian (South)
- Australian families
- Austro-Asiatic
- Austronesian
- Caucasian families
- Dravidian
- Eskimo-Aleut
- Hmong-Mien
- Indo-European
- Japanese/Korean
- Khoisan
- Niger-Congo
- Nilo-Saharan
- Papuan families
- Sino-Tibetan
- Tai-Kadai
- Uralic
- Other
- No major family

Mapping Language Diversity

Measuring language diversity often provides insight into the multicultural nature of countries. Some have high language diversity because of their position in areas of trade or cultural exchange, as seen in Kazakhstan, which was part of the Silk Road. Other countries have high diversity because of multiple surviving ethnic groups, as seen in Bolivia, India, and Chad. Countries with low levels of linguistic diversity, such as Japan and Norway, are often culturally homogeneous.

Vanishing Languages

Every 14 days, another endangered language somewhere in the world dies with its last speaker. These languages tend to be concentrated in hot spots scattered across the world. Linguists fear that by 2100, over half of the 7,000 languages now spoken (many with no recordings for posterity) will be lost forever. Languages become threatened when speakers are past childbearing age and parent-child transmission is unlikely. They are lost when the language is no longer associated with an ethnic identity.

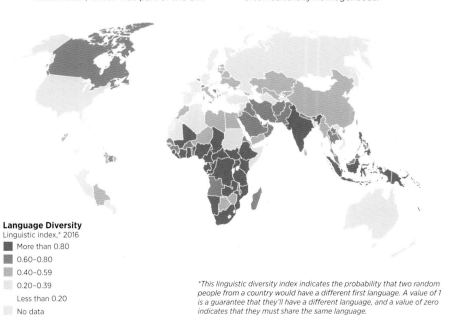

Language Diversity
Linguistic index,* 2016

- More than 0.80
- 0.60–0.80
- 0.40–0.59
- 0.20–0.39
- Less than 0.20
- No data

*This linguistic diversity index indicates the probability that two random people from a country would have a different first language. A value of 1 is a guarantee that they'll have a different language, and a value of zero indicates that they must share the same language.

Threat Level

- Severe
- High
- Medium
- Low

Religions

THE GREAT POWER OF RELIGION comes from its ability to speak to the heart and longings of individuals and societies. Since humankind's earliest times, some combination of rituals that acknowledged the mysteries of life and death, practices that honored nature spirits, and beliefs in supreme beings has been part of community life.

In time, an untold number of local religious practices yielded to just a few widespread traditions. Now billions of people are adherents of Hinduism, Buddhism, Judaism, Christianity, and Islam, all of which began in Asia or the Middle East. Universal elements of these faiths include worship, sacred sites, saints and martyrs, ritual clothing, dietary laws and fasting, festivals and holy days, and special ceremonies for life's major moments. Each of these religions gives its followers ways to relate to the spiritual realm as well as moral guidelines that attempt to make life better on Earth. Their tenets and goals are taught not only at the church, synagogue, mosque, or temple, but also through schools, storytelling, and artistic creations.

The world's major religions blossomed from the teachings and revelations of individuals who transmitted the voice of God or discovered a way to salvation that could be understood by others. Abraham and Moses for Jews, the Buddha for Buddhists, Jesus Christ for Christians, and the Prophet Muhammad for Muslims—these individuals fulfilled the roles of divine teachers who experienced essential truths of existence. Leadership was passed to priests, rabbis, ministers, and imams, who have continued to pass down their words, and those found in sacred texts, to faithful followers.

NORTH AMERICA

SOUTH AMERICA

Dominant Religion

90.0% and above
70.0%–89.9%
50.0%–69.9%
Below 50.0%

Christianity · Islam · Unaffiliated · Hinduism · Buddhism · Ethno-Religionism · Judaism

Christianity

Christian belief in eternal life is based on the preaching and example of Jesus Christ, a Jew born some 2,000 years ago. The New Testament tells of his teaching, persecution, Crucifixion and resurrection, and of the early church. Today Christianity is found around the world in three main forms: Roman Catholicism, Eastern Orthodoxy, and Protestantism.

Islam

Muslims believe that the Koran, Islam's sacred book, accurately records the spoken word of God (Allah) as revealed to the Prophet Muhammad, born in Mecca around A.D. 570. Strict adherents pray five times a day, fast during the holy month of Ramadan, and make at least one pilgrimage to Mecca, Islam's holiest city—a trip known as a hajj.

Hinduism

Hinduism began in India more than 4,000 years ago and is still flourishing. Sacred texts known as the Vedas form the basis of Hindu faith and ritual. The main trinity of gods comprises Brahma the creator, Vishnu the preserver, and Shiva the destroyer. Hindus believe in reincarnation and hold that actions in this life affect circumstances of the next (karma).

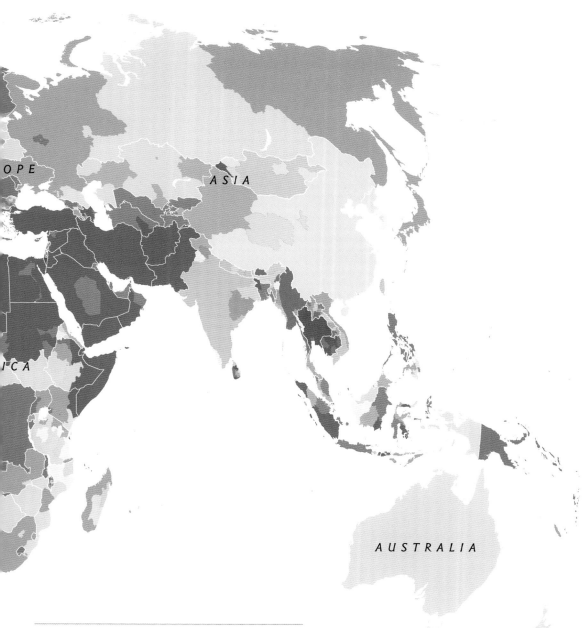

Buddhism

Founded about 2,500 years ago by Shakyamuni Buddha (or Gautama Buddha), Buddhism teaches liberation from suffering through the threefold cultivation of morality, meditation, and wisdom. Buddhists revere the Three Jewels: Buddha (the Awakened One), Dharma (the Truth), and Sangha (the community of monks and nuns).

Ethno-Religionism

As the term implies, ethno-religious traditions combine ethnic and religious identities. Indeed, each of the major faiths are universalized ethno-religions. Some ethno-religions, such as Haitian voodoo, incorporate one of the major faiths; others, such as Sikhism, have branched off. Still more, such as Shinto, are expressions of indigenous and folk religions.

Judaism

The 4,000-year-old religion of the world's 14 million Jews stands as the oldest of the major faiths that believe in a single god (monotheism). Judaism's traditions, customs, laws, and beliefs date back to Abraham, the founder, and to the Torah, the first five books of the Old Testament, believed to have been handed down to Moses on Mount Sinai.

By the Numbers

The world's largest religion is Christianity, in its varying forms. The three largest concentrations of Christians are found in the Western Hemisphere, making Christianity the dominant religion of the West because of European colonization. The second largest religion is Islam, which is spreading at a faster rate. All of the leading Islamic nations are in Asia and North Africa, with Indonesia being the most populous Muslim country. Hinduism, the dominant religion of India, also has large concentrations of adherents in other Asian countries, such as Bangladesh and Indonesia. Harder to define as a group are the roughly 1.1 billion people who identify themselves as unaffiliated and are spread throughout the world, with high numbers in Asia and Europe.

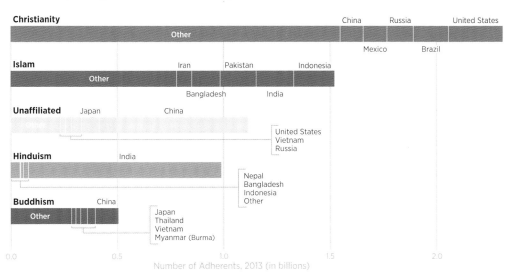

Health and Education

IN THE PAST 50 YEARS, health conditions have improved dramatically. With better economic and living conditions and access to immunization and other basic health services, global life expectancy has risen from 53 to 70 years; the death rate for children under five years old has fallen by half in the past 25 years; and many infectious and parasitic diseases that once killed and disabled millions have been eradicated, eliminated, or greatly reduced in impact.

Despite major strides, however, infant and child mortality from infectious diseases remains relatively high in many of the poorest countries. Each year, more than six million children under five years old die; about four out of every ten of those deaths occur in sub-Saharan Africa and three in South Asia. Undernutrition is a major contributor to half of child deaths, hitting poor families the hardest.

The age-old link between social inequality and ill health is also manifested in the emergence of new health threats. The HIV/AIDS pandemic has erased decades of steady improvements in sub-Saharan Africa, where almost 70 percent of all people living with the disease reside. The death toll in some southern African countries, where adult prevalence exceeds 15 percent, contributed to reversals in life expectancy in the 1990s. Life expectancy is now on the rise again, thanks in part to HIV/AIDS prevention and treatment protocols. At the end of 2013, 36 percent of people living with HIV in low- and middle-income countries were receiving antiretroviral therapy.

Increasingly, lifestyle diseases are also afflicting low-income countries, coming with demographic changes, urbanization, changes in eating habits and physical activity, and environmental degradation. Traffic accidents account for more than a million deaths and upward of 50 million injuries annually; with the rapid increase of automobile use, observers expect that by 2020 the number of traffic deaths will have increased by more than 80 percent in developing countries.

While many international leaders focus on high-profile infectious diseases, the looming challenges of chronic diseases may be even greater. In many high- and middle-income countries, chronic lifestyle-related diseases such as cardiovascular disease and diabetes are becoming the predominant cause of disability and death. In developed countries, smoking is the cause of more than one-third of male deaths in middle age and about one in eight female deaths. Because the focus of policymakers has been on treatment rather than prevention, the costs of dealing with these ailments contributes to high (and increasing) health care spending.

Income Levels: Indicators of Health and Literacy

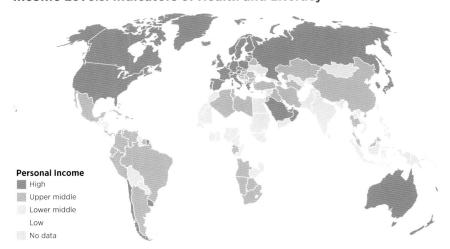

Personal Income
- High
- Upper middle
- Lower middle
- Low
- No data

Access to Improved Sanitation

Population Using Improved Sanitation
(as a percentage of total population)
- 90-100
- 75-89
- 50-74
- Less than 50
- No data

Nutrition

Undernourishment
(as a percentage of population)
- More than 30
- 15-30
- 10-14
- 5-9
- Less than 5
- No data

Health Care Availability

Regional differences in health care resources are striking. While countries in Europe and the Americas have relatively large numbers of physicians and nurses, nations with far higher burdens of disease (particularly African countries) are experiencing severe deficits in both health workers and health facilities.

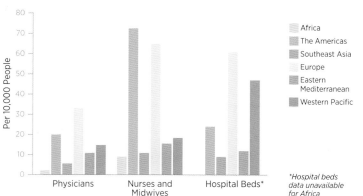

Per 10,000 People

- Africa
- The Americas
- Southeast Asia
- Europe
- Eastern Mediterranean
- Western Pacific

Physicians | Nurses and Midwives | Hospital Beds*

*Hospital beds data unavailable for Africa

HIV

HIV
(percentage of adults ages 15-49 living with HIV)
- More than 15
- 10-15
- 3-9
- 1-2
- Less than 1
- No data

Global Disease Burden

While infectious and parasitic diseases account for nearly one-quarter of total deaths in developing countries, they result in relatively few deaths in wealthier countries. In contrast, cardiovascular diseases and cancer are more significant causes of death in industrialized countries. Over time, as fertility rates fall, social and living conditions improve, the population ages, and further advances are made against infectious diseases in poorer countries, the differences in causes of death between high-income and low-income countries may converge.

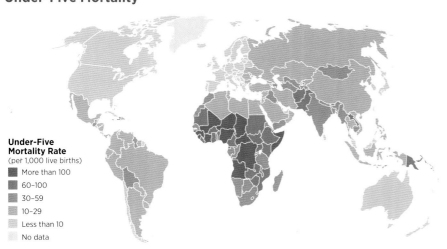

Disease Burden
(percentage of deaths attributable to communicable disease or maternal, perinatal, or nutritional conditions)

- 65–100
- 55–64
- 40–54
- 25–39
- 0–24
- No data

Causes of Death
- Infectious & parasitic diseases
- Cardiovascular diseases
- Respiratory infections
- Perinatal conditions
- Unintentional injuries
- Cancers
- Respiratory diseases
- Digestive diseases
- Intentional injuries
- Maternal conditions
- Neuropsychiatric disorders
- Other

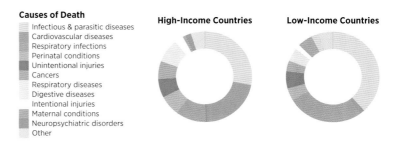

High-Income Countries   **Low-Income Countries**

Under-Five Mortality

Under-Five Mortality Rate
(per 1,000 live births)
- More than 100
- 60–100
- 30–59
- 10–29
- Less than 10
- No data

Maternal Mortality

MATERNAL MORTALITY RATIO PER 100,000 LIVE BIRTHS*

COUNTRIES WITH THE HIGHEST MATERNAL MORTALITY RATES		COUNTRIES WITH THE LOWEST MATERNAL MORTALITY RATES	
1. Sierra Leone	1,360	1. Finland	3
2. Central African Rep.	882	Greece	3
3. Chad	856	Iceland	3
4. Nigeria	814	Poland	3
5. South Sudan	789	2. Austria	4
6. Somalia	732	Belarus	4
7. Liberia	725	Czech Republic	4
8. Burundi	712	Italy	4
9. Gambia	706	Kuwait	4
10. Dem. Rep. of the Congo	693	Sweden	4

*Adjusted for underreporting and misclassification

Education and Literacy

Basic education is an investment for the long-term prosperity of a country, generating individual, household, and social benefits. Some countries (e.g., Eastern and Western Europe, the United States) have long traditions of high educational attainment among both genders and now have well-educated populations of all ages. In contrast, many low-income countries have only recently expanded access to primary education; girls still lag behind boys in enrollment and completion of primary school and then in making the transition to secondary school. These countries will have to wait many years before most individuals in the productive ages have even minimal levels of reading, writing, and basic arithmetic skills.

The expansion of secondary schooling tends to lag even further behind, so countries with low educational attainment will likely be at a disadvantage for at least a generation. While no one doubts that the key to long-term economic growth and poverty reduction lies in greater education opportunities for all, many poor countries face the tremendous challenge of paying for schools and teachers today while having to wait 20 years for the economic returns to those investments.

Adult Literacy
(as a percentage of population)
- More than 98
- 90–98
- 75–89
- 60–74
- Less than 60
- No data

School Enrollment for Girls

Primary Education Enrollment of Girls
(as a percentage of primary school-age girls)
- More than 97
- 95–97
- 90–94
- 80–89
- Less than 80
- No data

Developing Human Capital

In the pyramids below, more orange and blue in the bars indicates a higher level of educational attainment, or "human capital," which contributes greatly to a country's ability for future economic growth. These two countries are similar in population size, but their human capital measures are significantly different.

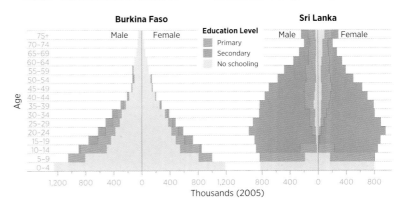

Burkina Faso   **Sri Lanka**

Education Level
- Primary
- Secondary
- No schooling

Thousands (2005)

Economy

A GLOBAL ECONOMIC ACTIVITY MAP (right) reveals striking differences between the composition of output in advanced economies and that in less developed economies. The services sector tends to dominate the former, whereas the latter are likely driven by agriculture and industry.

Although countries rich in natural resources can be notable exceptions, economies have generally followed a common trajectory. The majority of an undeveloped economy's employment has been in agriculture. Then, a period of industrialization emerged in which agricultural production became more efficient and less expensive, the market for industrial goods grew in response to demand from customers no longer spending most of their income on food, and those once employed in the shrinking agriculture sector moved on to jobs in the other sectors. As industrial production expanded, both mineral mining and natural resource consumption became more vigorous.

This process now continues to postindustrialization, marked by an evolution in consumer demand—from material goods to services such as health care, education, and entertainment. The number of jobs and proportion of GDP held by the other sectors continue to shrink as efficiency and technological advances increase; however, because in the services sector workers are not easily replaced by machines, employment is relatively stable and costly, raising the sector's share of GDP.

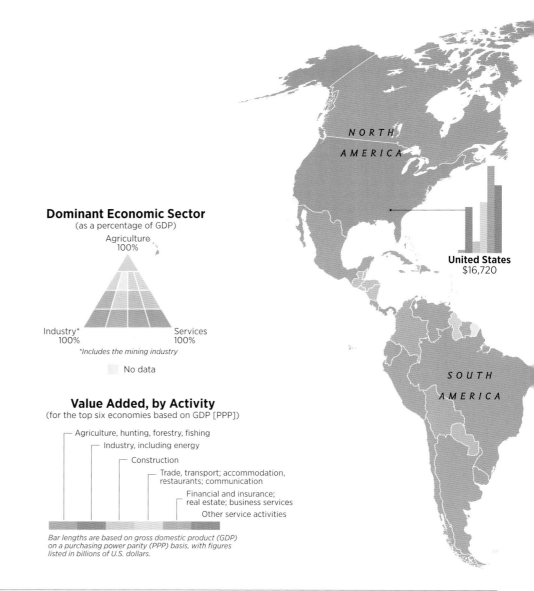

Dominant Economic Sector
(as a percentage of GDP)

Agriculture 100%

Industry* 100%

Services 100%

*Includes the mining industry

No data

Value Added, by Activity
(for the top six economies based on GDP [PPP])

Agriculture, hunting, forestry, fishing
Industry, including energy
Construction
Trade, transport; accommodation, restaurants; communication
Financial and insurance; real estate; business services
Other service activities

Bar lengths are based on gross domestic product (GDP) on a purchasing power parity (PPP) basis, with figures listed in billions of U.S. dollars.

United States $16,720

Human Development Index

Since the UN's first Human Development Index in 1970, quality of life has increased globally. Most gains have been in health, education, and income per capita, which has doubled in the past four decades. But for some countries, especially those in sub-Saharan Africa, the national HDI has been a roller-coaster ride of ups and downs. The current aggregated HDI is influenced by China and India, the most populous nations. In the past 20 years, both have doubled their output per capita, creating an economic maelstrom impacting more humans than did the industrial revolution. Economists predict that by 2050, China, India, and Brazil will control 40 percent of global purchasing power.

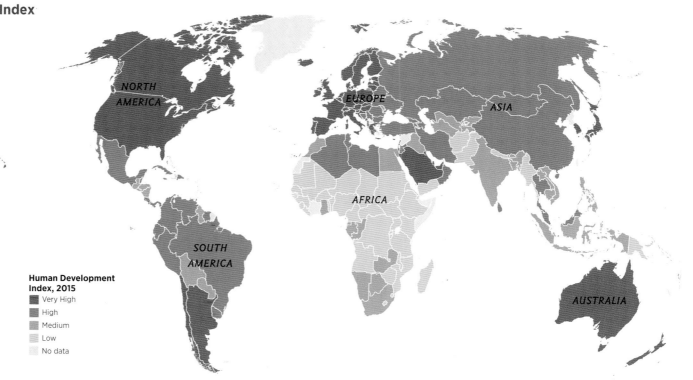

Human Development Index, 2015
- Very High
- High
- Medium
- Low
- No data

Top GDP Growth Rates
(based on PPP, or purchasing power parity)

2010–2014 AVERAGE
1.	Turkmenistan	11.1%
	Mongolia	11.1%
2.	Ethiopia	10.6%
3.	Sierra Leone	10.1%
4.	Qatar	9.3%
5.	China	8.6%
6.	Ghana	8.5%
7.	Zimbabwe	8.4%
	Myanmar	8.4%
8.	Panama	8.2%

The World's Richest and Poorest Countries (2015 figures, listed in U.S. dollars)

	RICHEST	GDP PER CAPITA (PPP)
1.	Qatar	$145,000
2.	Luxembourg	$102,900
3.	Liechtenstein	$89,400
4.	Singapore	$85,700
5.	Brunei	$79,700
6.	Monaco	$78,700
7.	Kuwait	$72,200
8.	Norway	$68,400
9.	United Arab Emirates	$67,000
10.	Australia	$65,400

	POOREST	GDP PER CAPITA (PPP)
1.	Somalia	$400
2.	Central African Republic	$600
3.	Democratic Republic of the Congo	$800
4.	Burundi	$900
	Liberia	$900
6.	Niger	$1,000
7.	Eritrea	$1,200
	Malawi	$1,200
9.	Guinea	$1,300
	Mozambique	$1,300

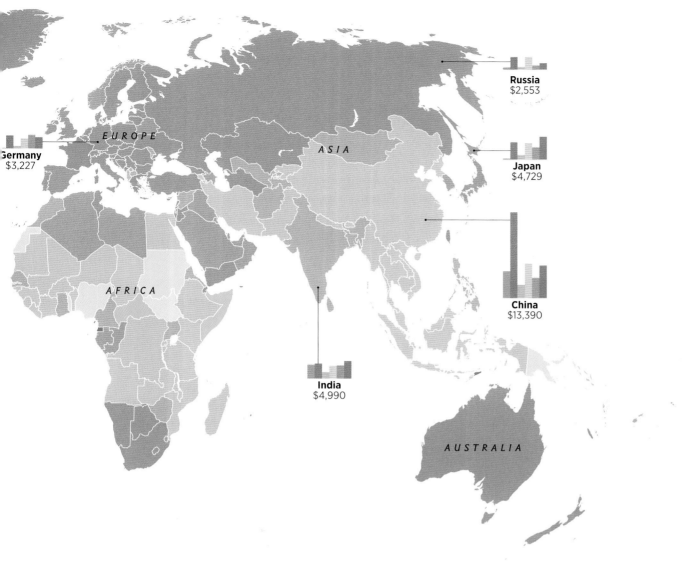

Russia
$2,553

Germany
$3,227

EUROPE

ASIA

Japan
$4,729

AFRICA

China
$13,390

India
$4,990

AUSTRALIA

Major Exporters
(value of total exports in billions of U.S. dollars, 2014)

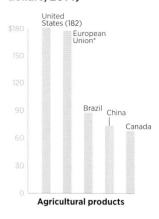

United States (182)
European Union*
Brazil
China
Canada

Agricultural products

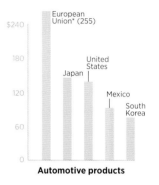

European Union* (255)
Japan
United States
Mexico
South Korea

Automotive products

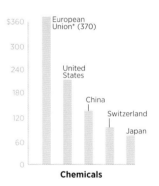

European Union* (370)
United States
China
Switzerland
Japan

Chemicals

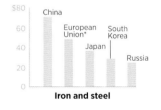

China
European Union*
Japan
South Korea
Russia

Iron and steel

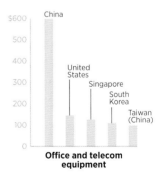

China
United States
Singapore
South Korea
Taiwan (China)

Office and telecom equipment

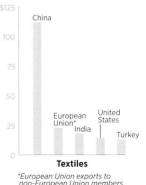

China
European Union*
India
United States
Turkey

Textiles

European Union exports to non-European Union members.

Gross Domestic Product

The gross domestic product (GDP) is the total market value of goods and services produced by a nation's economy in a given year using global currency exchange rates. It is a convenient way of calculating the level of a nation's international purchasing power and economic strength, but it does not show average wealth of individuals or measure standard of living. For example, a country could have high exports in products but still have a low standard of living.

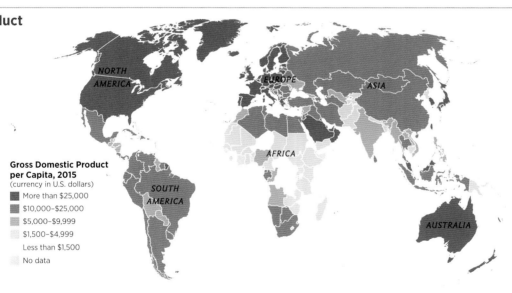

NORTH AMERICA

EUROPE

ASIA

AFRICA

SOUTH AMERICA

AUSTRALIA

Gross Domestic Product per Capita, 2015
(currency in U.S. dollars)
- More than $25,000
- $10,000–$25,000
- $5,000–$9,999
- $1,500–$4,999
- Less than $1,500
- No data

Global Innovation Index

The Global Innovation Index weighs a country's institutions and infrastructure, human capital and research, and business and market sophistication against its knowledge, technology, and creative outputs to determine world leaders in innovation. While innovation thrives where quality education is available and infrastructure and institutions are strong—as this map shows—creative and critical thinking, openness to risk, and entrepreneurial drive can be found in every country.

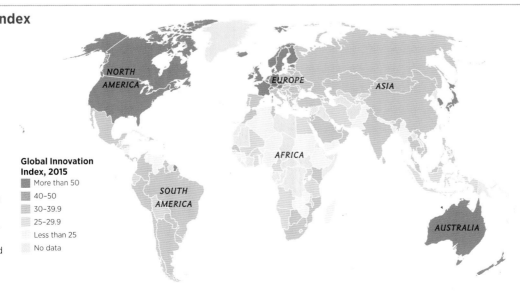

NORTH AMERICA

EUROPE

ASIA

AFRICA

SOUTH AMERICA

AUSTRALIA

Global Innovation Index, 2015
- More than 50
- 40–50
- 30–39.9
- 25–29.9
- Less than 25
- No data

Trade

WORLD TRADE EXPANDED at a dizzying pace in the half century following World War II. The dollar value of world merchandise exports rose from $61 billion in 1950 to $18.3 trillion in 2013. Adjusted for price changes, world trade grew more than 30 times over the last six decades, much faster than world output. Trade in manufactured goods expanded much faster than that in mining products (including fuels) and agricultural products. In the last decades, many developing countries (e.g., China, South Korea, Mexico) have become important exporters of manufactures. However, there are still many less developed countries—primarily in Africa and the Middle East—that are dependent on a few primary commodities for their export earnings. Commercial services exports have expanded rapidly over the past few decades and amounted to

$4.6 trillion in 2013. While developed countries account for more than two-thirds of world services trade, some developing countries now gain most of their export earnings from services exports. Earnings from tourism in the Caribbean and that from software exports in India are prominent examples of developing countries' dynamic services exports.

Capital flows and worker remittances have gained in importance worldwide and are another important aspect of globalization. The stock of worldwide foreign direct investment was estimated to be $23 trillion at the end of 2012, $13.2 trillion of which was invested in G-20 countries (those with major economies). Capital markets in many developing countries remain small, fragile, and underdeveloped, which hampers household savings and the funding of local enterprises.

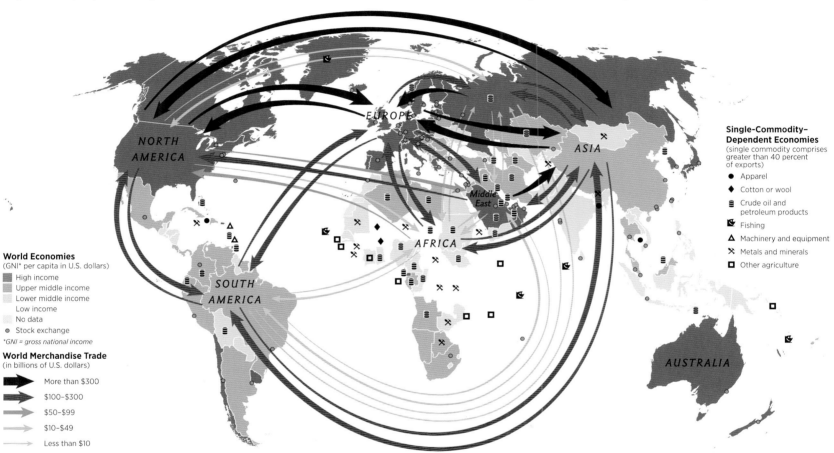

Growth of World Trade

After World War II, the export growth of manufactured goods greatly outstripped other exports. This graph shows the volume growth on a semi-log scale (a straight line represents constant growth) rather than a standard scale (a straight line indicates a constant increase in the absolute values in each year).

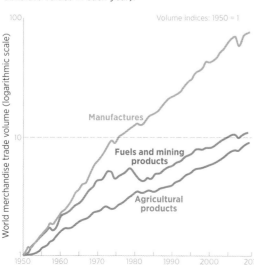

Merchandise Exports

Fuels, because of their heavy concentration in relatively few areas, are the leading category of exports, having increased their share of world exports from 9 percent in 2000 to 19 percent in 2012. Meanwhile, export values for ores and other minerals, raw materials, and iron and steel saw heavy declines from 2011.

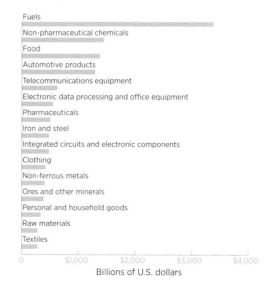

Main Trading Nations

The United States, China, and Germany account for nearly 30 percent of total world merchandise trade. Ongoing negotiations among the 160 member nations of the World Trade Organization are tackling market-access barriers in agriculture, textiles, and clothing—areas where many developing countries hope to compete.

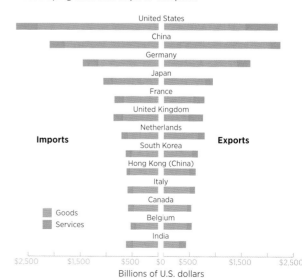

World Debt

Measuring a country's outstanding foreign debt in relation to its GDP indicates the size of future income needed to pay back the debt; it also shows how much a country has relied in the past on foreign savings to finance investment and consumption expenditures. A high external debt ratio can pose a financial risk if debt service payments are not assured.

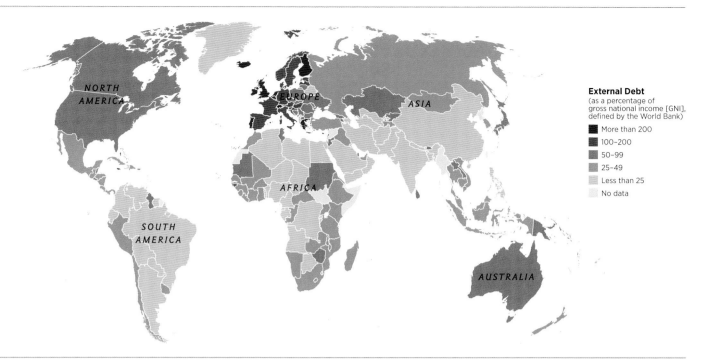

External Debt
(as a percentage of gross national income [GNI], defined by the World Bank)

- More than 200
- 100–200
- 50–99
- 25–49
- Less than 25
- No data

Trade Blocs

Regional trade is on the rise. Agreements between neighboring countries to offer each other trade benefits can create larger markets and improve the economy of the region as a whole. But they can also lead to discrimination, especially when more efficient suppliers outside the regional agreements are prevented from supplying their goods and services.

Major Regional Trade Agreements

- **APEC:** Asia-Pacific Economic Cooperation
- **ASEAN:** Association of Southeast Asian Nations
- **APEC & ASEAN**
- **COMESA:** Common Market for Eastern and Southern Africa
- **ECOWAS:** Economic Community of West African States
- **EU:** European Union
- **MERCOSUR:** Southern Common Market
- **NAFTA & APEC:** North American Free Trade Agreement
- **SAFTA:** South Asian Free Trade Area

Trade Flow: Fuels

The leading exporters of fuel products are countries in the Middle East, Africa, Russia, and central and western Asia; all export more fuel than they consume. But intra-regional energy trade is growing, with some of the key producers—Canada, Indonesia, Norway, and the United Kingdom, for example—located in regions that are net energy importers.

Intra-Region Fuel Trade
(in billions of U.S. dollars)

Africa
$27

Middle East
$33

CIS*
$49

South/Central America
$71

North America
$229

Asia/Australia/Oceania
$575

Europe
$656

*Commonwealth of Independent States

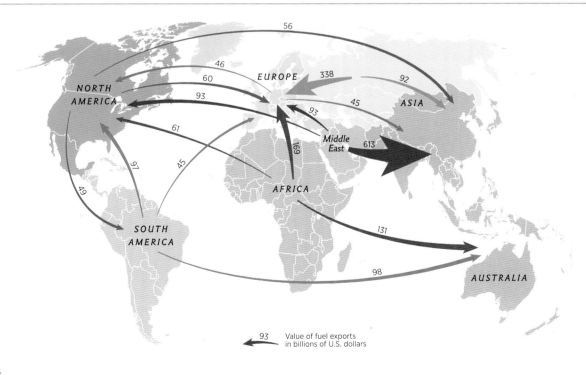

→ 93 Value of fuel exports in billions of U.S. dollars

Food

THE POPULATION OF THE PLANET, which already exceeds seven billion, will grow to nine billion by 2050. To provide everyone with a diet like that available in developed countries by mid-century, food production will need to double.

Yet, food insecurity is already an urgent concern at current population levels. For although the Food and Agriculture Organization of the United Nations reports that 100 million fewer people are chronically undernourished today than a decade ago, over 800 million people (one in nine) still do not have access to the daily recommended minimum of 2,000–2,500 calories per person. The majority of the undernourished live in developing countries; of greatest concern are communities in sub-Saharan Africa and southern Asia. In striking contrast, patterns of consumption in developed countries reveal that changing diets, which incorporate more fat, sugar, and salt, are leading to both undernourishment and widespread obesity.

Feeding an additional two billion people is not only an issue of logistics, however. It is also one of environmental stewardship. The problematic greenhouse gases emitted by agricultural enterprises exceed emissions from automobiles, trains, and airplanes. Water sources are both consumed and polluted by agriculture. Wildlife habitat and biodiversity are lost when undeveloped land is converted for agricultural purposes.

A group of scientists wrestling with the issue of how to make agriculture both more productive and less destructive have created a five-step plan: We must freeze agriculture's footprint, grow more on existing farms, use resources more efficiently, shift our diets, and reduce waste.

Agriculture's Footprint

Almost 40 percent of Earth's ice-free land, and more than 70 percent of land developed by humankind, is used to raise crops or livestock. But even as these practices sustain us, they jeopardize our quality of life and the health of our environment by polluting the ground and waterways, degrading the wildlife habitats around us, and contributing to climate change.

Of the 19.4 million square miles (50.25 million sq km) we already use for agriculture, land with an area about the size of South America supports crops. Even more

land, equal to the size of Africa, is committed to livestock.

So although the obvious approach to increasing food production would be to expand the amount of land under cultivation, this would lead to plowing more grasslands or clearing more forests, the latter likely in tropical areas—far from areas where food security is a pressing concern. This destruction would endanger more species in order to make space for noncritical livestock, soybeans, and palm oil.

Crop Allocation

100% area / Pasture — 50% — 100% / Cropland

Where Crop Yields Could Improve

Crop production worldwide has tripled in the last five decades. Gains are largely the result not of expanding the area under cultivation but of increasing yields from existing acreage. Greater yields may indicate that land lay fallow less often, that multiple crops were raised simultaneously, or that planting and growing techniques were improved. They may also be attributable to different inputs—such as more productive crop varieties, better fertilizer, and improved irrigation—or to the introduction of machines. Similar gains were seen in Asia and Latin America in the second half of the 20th century during the so-called green revolution.

Current efforts to apply best practices from both industrial and organic agriculture are focusing on less productive farmland in Africa, Latin America, and Eastern Europe.

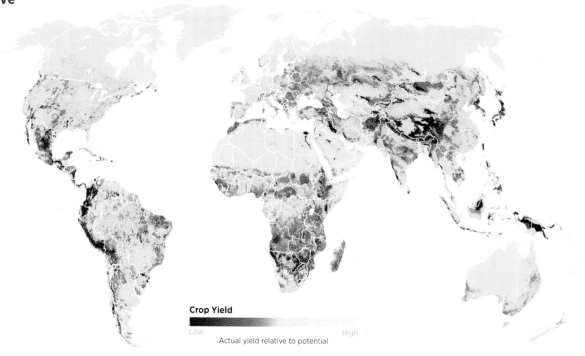

Crop Yield

Low — High
Actual yield relative to potential

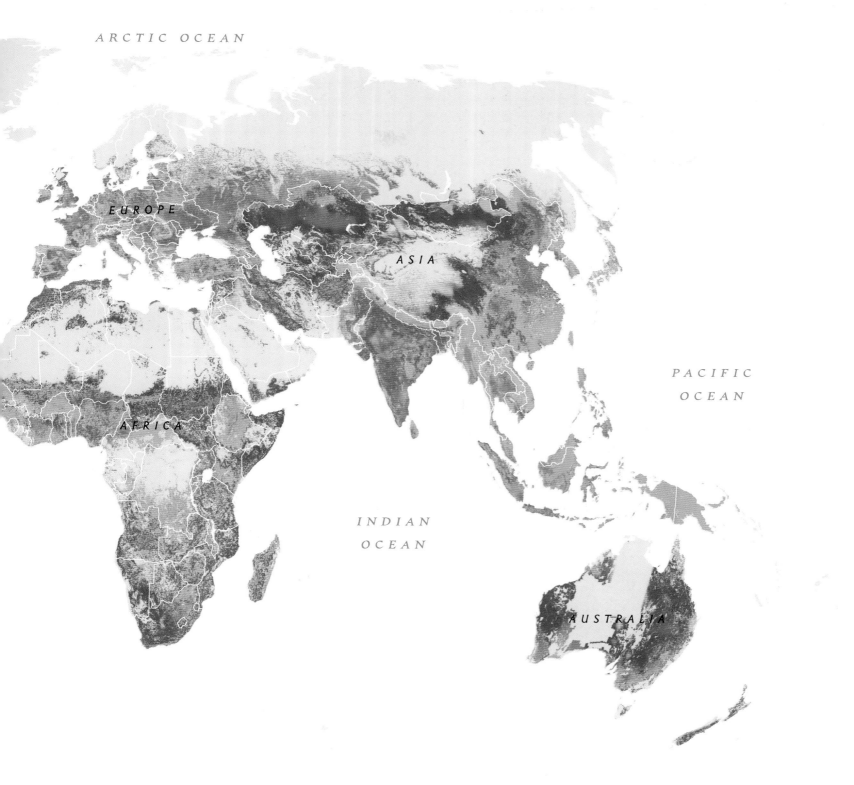

How Our Crops Are Used

Just over half of the calories raised are consumed by humans; the balance are used for biofuels or fed to livestock. However, meat, dairy, and eggs contain only a fraction of the calories that were directed to the animals. For instance, 100 calories of grain fed to cattle produces just 3 calories of beef. Reducing the amount of grain-fed meat in our diet would decrease diverted crops.

How Global Crop Calories Are Used by Percent

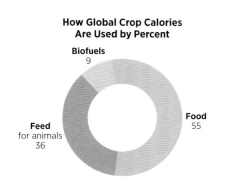

Biofuels
9

Food
55

Feed
for animals
36

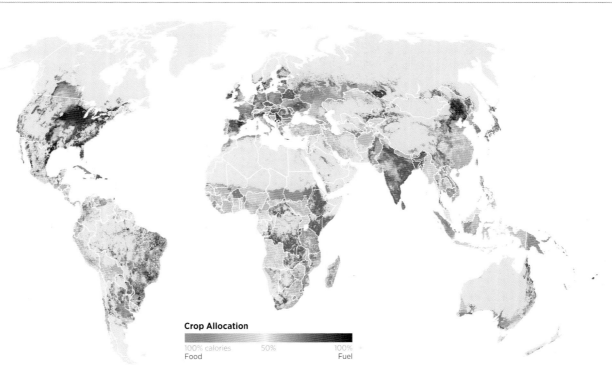

Crop Allocation

100% calories 50% 100%
Food Fuel

Food

Distribution of Major Crops and Livestock

Humans rely on plant sources for carbohydrates, with grains (the edible parts of cereal plants) providing 80 percent of the food energy (calorie) supply. This means that the major grains—corn, wheat, and rice—are the foods that fuel humanity. Most cereal grains are grown in the Northern Hemisphere, with the United States and France producing enough to be the largest exporters.

In many parts of the world, cereal grains cannot be grown because of the lack of productive farmland or the absence of necessary technology. Again and again throughout history, the actions of countries have been shaped by disparities in the supply and demand of grains as well as by the knowledge that grains equal survival. As food historian Waverley Root once wrote: "Possession of wheat or lack of it sways the destinies of nations; nor is it rare to find wheat being used as a political weapon . . . It is difficult to foresee any future in which it will not still exert a powerful influence on human history."

Recently, rising standards of living in developing countries have increased the worldwide appetite for meat and other animal products, such as eggs and dairy, further increasing demand for grains that are used in livestock feed. The rapidly expanding livestock sector will soon provide about half of the global agricultural GDP.

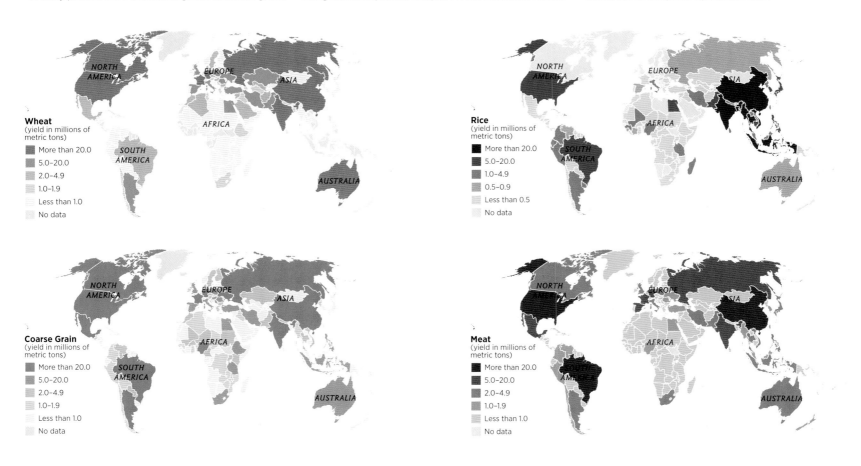

Wheat
(yield in millions of metric tons)
- More than 20.0
- 5.0–20.0
- 2.0–4.9
- 1.0–1.9
- Less than 1.0
- No data

Rice
(yield in millions of metric tons)
- More than 20.0
- 5.0–20.0
- 1.0–4.9
- 0.5–0.9
- Less than 0.5
- No data

Coarse Grain
(yield in millions of metric tons)
- More than 20.0
- 5.0–20.0
- 2.0–4.9
- 1.0–1.9
- Less than 1.0
- No data

Meat
(yield in millions of metric tons)
- More than 20.0
- 5.0–20.0
- 2.0–4.9
- 1.0–1.9
- Less than 1.0
- No data

Fishing and Aquaculture

Marine fisheries are vital for food security in developing countries and are a heavily subsidized industry in developed countries. Today, no parts of the world's oceans are unaffected by our appetite for seafood. Most fish are caught in coastal waters, with the most intense fishing in northern Europe and off China and Southeast Asia. The world's reported catch has more than quadrupled since 1950, but it peaked in the late 1980s and has leveled off since. Fish farming, called aquaculture, is one of the fastest-growing areas of food production. The bulk of marine aquaculture occurs in developing countries, with China accounting for around two-thirds of the total output. Of the 148 million metric tons of fish, crustaceans, and mollusks supplied by marine fisheries and fish farms in 2010, 20 million were used as fishmeal, oil, and animal feed. The other 128 million were for human consumption. On average, fish provides about 17 percent of the animal protein eaten per person per year.

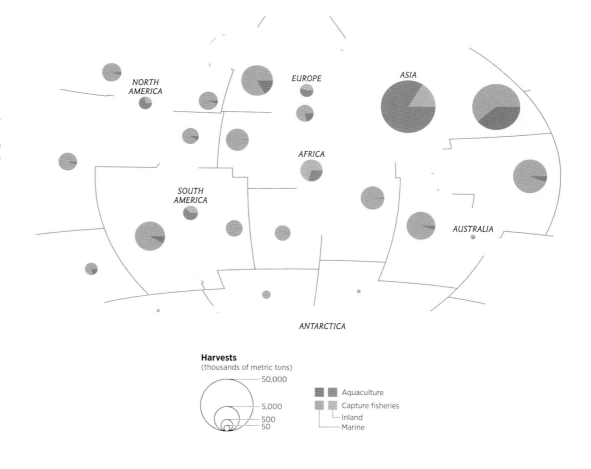

Harvests
(thousands of metric tons)
- 50,000
- 5,000
- 500
- 50

- Aquaculture
- Capture fisheries
- Inland
- Marine

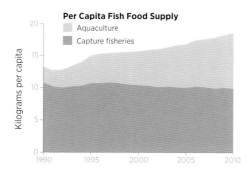

Per Capita Fish Food Supply
- Aquaculture
- Capture fisheries

Kilograms per capita

1990 1995 2000 2005 2010

World Food Production

In the past few decades, world food production has more than kept pace with the burgeoning global population. Meat and cereals account for the most dramatic increases. New high-yield crops, additional irrigated land, and fertilizers have contributed to the rise in production. But there are related problems: Scientists warn that overuse of fertilizers causes nitrogen overload in Earth's waters; on the other hand, the insufficient use of fertilizers, particularly in Africa, has long-term adverse consequences for food security. It is also still the case that farmable land is distributed unequally and is not always available near growing population centers.

Per Capita Food Production Index

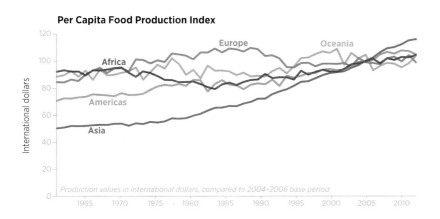

Production values in international dollars, compared to 2004-2006 base period

Food Security

Food security is a complex and multifaceted issue. While populations facing food shortages can be said to lack food security, the same is true for those who are unable to afford the plentiful food around them or those who are kept from it because of political instability, for example. Even in wealthy countries where food is abundant, like the United States, pockets of the population live in areas where nutritional food is not accessible—places called food deserts. For these reasons, researchers evaluating food security need to consider both causes, such as insufficient supply, poverty, and vulnerability (whether from human or natural causes), and effects, including undernourishment.

Prevalence of Food Inadequacy
- More than 35%
- 25%–35%
- 15%–24.9%
- 5%–14.9%
- Less than 5%
- No data

Genetically Modified Crops

Though it can be said that humans have been manipulating plant and animal species for thousands of years through breeding and hybridization, genetic engineering is a modern practice. In 2013, 12 percent of total crops were genetically modified. Proponents cite benefits such as increased yield, pest resistance without pesticides, improved nutrition, ability to withstand extreme weather, and longer shelf life. Critics emphasize unexpected distribution, unanticipated harmful mutations, unknown effects on wildlife, and farmers' restricted access to patented plant material.

Hectares of Land Planted With Genetically Modified Crops

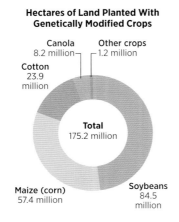

Canola 8.2 million
Other crops 1.2 million
Cotton 23.9 million
Total 175.2 million
Maize (corn) 57.4 million
Soybeans 84.5 million

Area of Biotech Crops
(millions of hectares)
- More than 40.0
- 10.0–40.0
- 1.0–9.9
- 0.1–0.9
- Less than 0.1
- None

Caloric Supply

Changes in diet are largely tied to changes in economic status and urbanization. Low-income and rural populations are often restricted to a diet of roots, tubers, and cereals, which may not provide the minimum daily threshold of 2,000–2,500 calories per person. As communities gain wealth and access to diverse food items, consumption of meat and dairy products as well as of wheat, rice, sugar, and vegetable oils increases. The world now faces a good news–bad news scenario: Many efforts to eradicate undernourishment have been successful; per person daily food availability in recently at-risk countries is nearly 3,000 calories. But in developed countries, where lifestyles are increasingly sedentary and people are eating more saturated fats, salt, and sugar, overnutrition and obesity are more prevalent.

Legend:
- Cereals
- Fruits
- Meat
- Milk
- Pulses
- Starchy roots
- Sugar and sweeteners
- Vegetable oils
- Vegetables
- Fish and seafood
- Other

Regional Caloric Supply
(calories per capita per day)

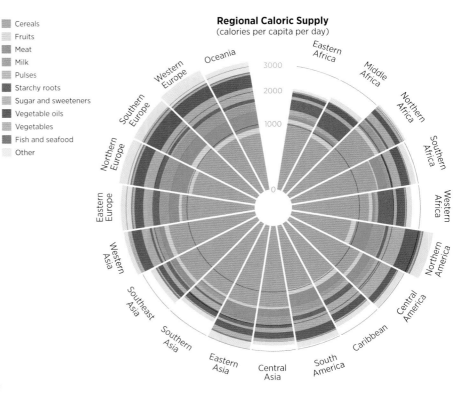

Food Supply
(calories per capita per day)
- 3,500 and above
- 3,000–3,499
- 2,500–2,999
- 2,000–2,499
- Less than 2,000
- No data

Energy

THE WORLD RUNS ON ENERGY, and in the industrialized world that typically means burning oil, natural gas, or coal. Our modern life is built on the idea that energy is cheap and plentiful, powering heavy industry and our homes, our global transportation networks, and even the billions of electronic devices vital to business and communications in the 21st century. Access to fuel is more than a luxury: It can mean the difference between edible food or indigestible grain, and it makes it possible to survive frigid nights and sweltering days. Most energy is consumed in the wealthiest nations or in recently industrialized China and India; in the poorer nations, the fuel likely to be available for everyday life may still be animal dung or gathered firewood. North America, with less than one-tenth of the world's population, consumes about one-quarter of the energy used; Africa, with twice the population, uses five times less than that.

Worldwide, oil accounts for more than 40 percent of energy usage. But as oil supplies dwindle and prices rise, new energy sources are being explored and exploited—from natural gas (obtained by fracking) to renewable energy from the sun, wind, and tides. Not only are these renewable sources inexhaustible, but they are also environmentally neutral, unlike fossil fuels—such as natural gas, petroleum, and coal—whose burning releases greenhouse gases. Those gases, particularly CO_2, are a major cause of the climate change that is now proving so damaging to life and the future of the planet.

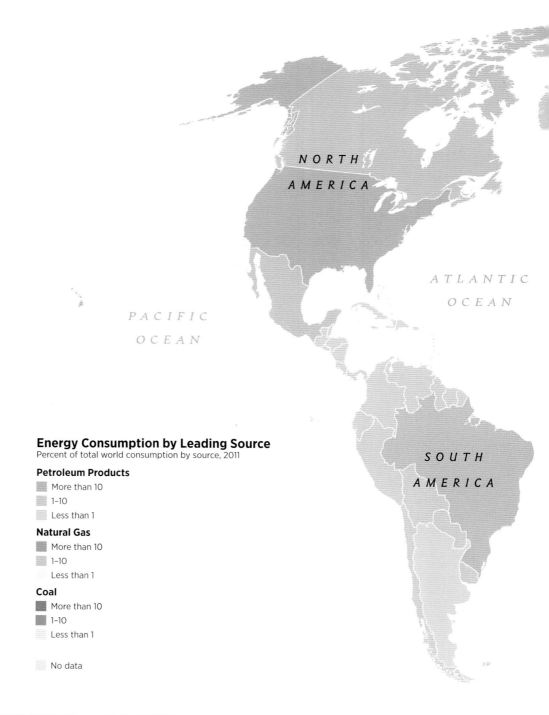

Energy Consumption by Leading Source
Percent of total world consumption by source, 2011

Petroleum Products
- More than 10
- 1–10
- Less than 1

Natural Gas
- More than 10
- 1–10
- Less than 1

Coal
- More than 10
- 1–10
- Less than 1

- No data

Energy Production by Fuel Type

The production of energy grows yearly to meet the demands of an ever more populous, affluent, and industrialized world. Even the demand for coal, the least clean-burning fuel, has climbed in recent years, but like all fossil fuels, coal's reserves are limited and nonrenewable. Natural gas production is also likely to increase worldwide as previously inaccessible shale gas is recovered via hydraulic fracturing. Geothermal, solar, and wind energies are included in the graph under "other."

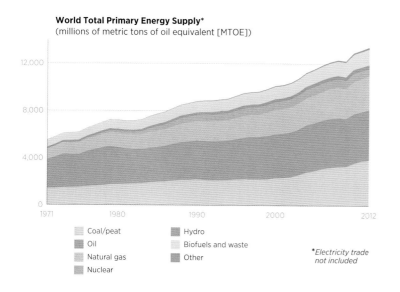

World Total Primary Energy Supply*
(millions of metric tons of oil equivalent [MTOE])

- Coal/peat
- Oil
- Natural gas
- Nuclear
- Hydro
- Biofuels and waste
- Other

*Electricity trade not included

Energy Production by Region

The global energy market both influences economic conditions and is influenced by them. For example, the energy crises of the 1970s led to a general downturn in oil consumption in the 1980s, and Asian producers (specifically those in the Middle East) reacted with a drop in production. Yet even with the Great Recession, production between 2000 and 2013 grew in Russia and Saudi Arabia by about 30 percent. China more than doubled its production during that time, from about 1,100 to 2,500 MTOE.

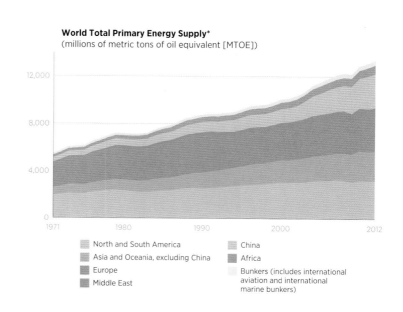

World Total Primary Energy Supply*
(millions of metric tons of oil equivalent [MTOE])

- North and South America
- Asia and Oceania, excluding China
- Europe
- Middle East
- China
- Africa
- Bunkers (includes international aviation and international marine bunkers)

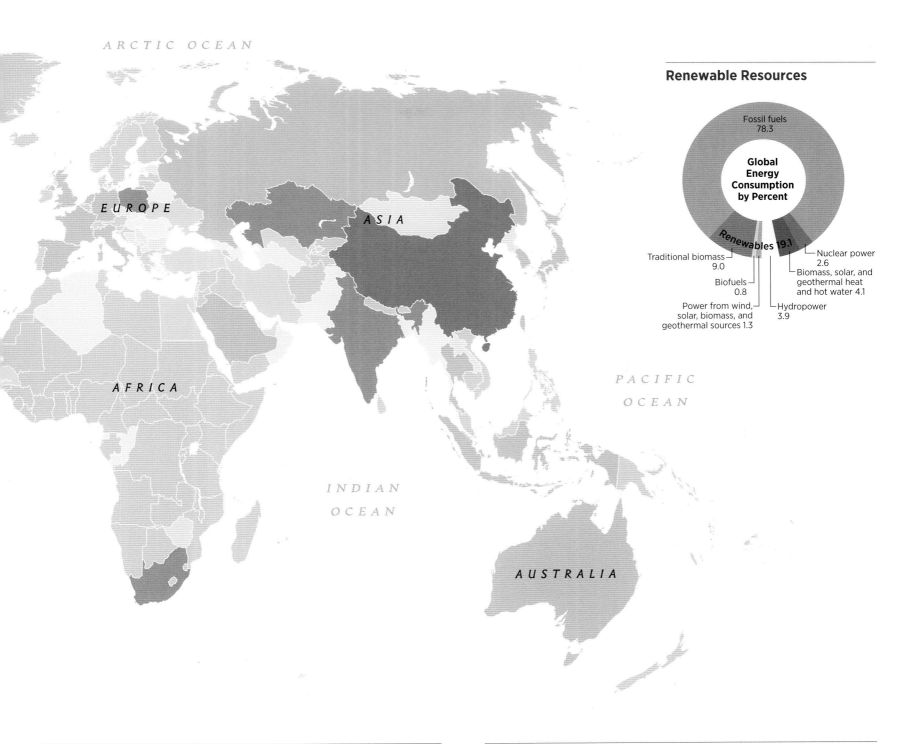

Renewable Resources

Global Energy Consumption by Percent

Fossil fuels 78.3

Renewables 19.1

Traditional biomass 9.0

Biofuels 0.8

Power from wind, solar, biomass, and geothermal sources 1.3

Nuclear power 2.6

Biomass, solar, and geothermal heat and hot water 4.1

Hydropower 3.9

Balancing Consumption and Production

Few nations have a perfect balance between energy consumption and production. Countries with few energy resources or high consumer populations often have a balance that tips toward net consumption. The United States, followed by Japan and China, has the highest positive consumption balance. Countries rich in energy resources or with small populations often are net energy producers. Russia has the highest production balance, followed by Saudi Arabia.

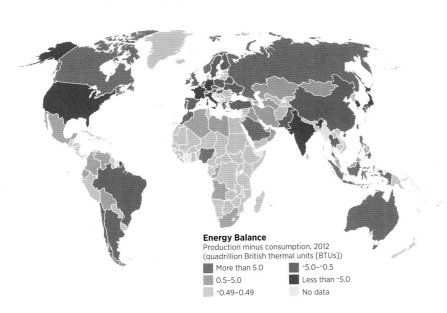

Energy Balance
Production minus consumption, 2012 (quadrillion British thermal units [BTUs])

- More than 5.0
- 0.5–5.0
- -0.49–0.49
- -5.0–-0.5
- Less than -5.0
- No data

Renewable Leaders

Changes in global consumption are visible as much of the world weans itself off fossil fuels. Large economies such as China, the U.S., and Brazil lead in terms of total renewable power capacity. As of 2014, policies in support of renewable energy sources were in place in 144 countries, two-thirds of which are developing or emerging economies.

Renewable Energy, 2014
Countries ranked by capacity

- Total renewable power
- Hydroelectric
- Geothermal
- Wind
- Solar photovoltaics
- Biomass and waste

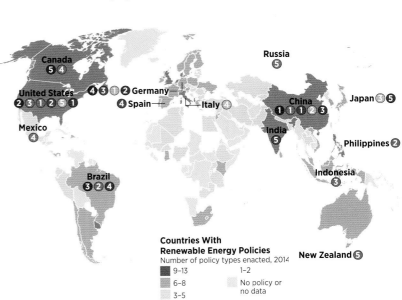

Canada 5 4

United States 2 3 1 2 5 1

Mexico 4

Germany 4 3 1 2

Spain 4

Italy 4

Russia 5

China 1 1 1 2 3

Japan 3 5

Philippines 2

India 5

Indonesia 3

Brazil 3 2 4

New Zealand 5

Countries With Renewable Energy Policies
Number of policy types enacted, 2014

- 9–13
- 6–8
- 3–5
- 1–2
- No policy or no data

Environmental Stresses

LIKE ALL LIFEFORMS ON EARTH, humans need natural systems—from deserts to forests to riverine biosystems to oceans—to thrive. Yet, through pollution and exploitation, these systems have been degraded and compromised. The negative consequences of this are already playing out and will continue to do so into the future.

Many types of environmental stresses are interrelated and have far-reaching consequences. For example, the thinning of the protective ozone layer, resulting from the release of chlorofluorocarbons (CFCs) into the atmosphere through aerosol sprays and refrigeration equipment, has already led to more ultraviolet light penetrating the atmosphere, which affects plant growth on land and in the sea as well as the health of humans. And in the coming decades, global warming caused by the burning of fossil fuels will likely increase water scarcity, desertification, deforestation, and sea-level increase, all of which will create significant problems for humans in both the developed and developing worlds.

Although socioeconomic indicators can reveal a great deal about long-term trends in human impact on the environment, this kind of data is not collected routinely in many countries. But the rapid conversion of countryside to built-up areas is one indicator that change is occurring at a fast pace. While scientists work to develop products and technologies with few or no adverse effects on the environment, their efforts will be nullified if humans' population and consumption of resources continue to increase.

Land Degradation and Desertification

Dryland systems

Land degradation in drylands

Land Degradation and Desertification

Deserts exist where rainfall is too little and too erratic to support life except in a few favored localities. Even in these "oases," occasional sandstorms may inhibit agricultural activity. In semiarid zones, lands can easily become degraded or desertlike if they are overused or subject to long or frequent drought. The Sahel of Africa faced this situation in the 1970s and early 1980s, but rainfall subsequently returned to normal, and some of the land recovered.

Often, an extended drought over a wide area can trigger desertification if the land has already been degraded by human actions. Causes of degradation include overgrazing, deforestation, overcultivation, overconsumption of groundwater, and the salinization or waterlogging of irrigated lands.

An emerging issue is the effect of climate change on desertification: Warming will probably lead to more drought in more parts of the world. As glaciers begin to disappear, the meltwater flowing through semiarid downstream areas diminishes as a consequence.

Deforestation

In the latter part of the 20th century, headlines alerted the world to the crisis facing the planet's forests. International agencies and governments responded with efforts to improve the situation through education, restoration, and land protection—efforts that continue today. Yet, while the rate of deforestation is slowing, the decrease is slight.

Deforestation also results in changes in rainfall patterns, soil erosion, and soil nutrient losses. The main cause of biodiversity loss is the widespread conversion of forest to agricultural use in the wet tropics, home to more than half of the world's species.

Pollution

In the months leading up to the 2008 Olympics in Beijing, horrendous smog threatened not only residents but also athletes competing in the games. As a temporary solution, the Chinese government halted work at construction sites; closed factories, chemical plants, and mines; and kept more than a million vehicles off the roads. The number of particulates in the air dropped and the games were held, but just a few years later, a 750-mile (1,207 km) band of smog was visible from space. This is more than an issue of appearances. Worldwide, 3.7 million deaths are attributed to ambient air pollution annually.

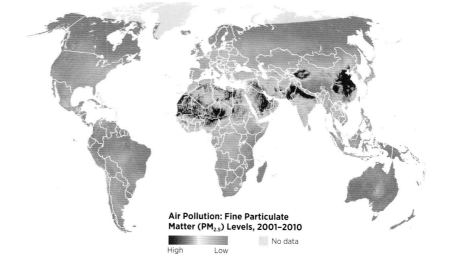

Deforestation Hot Spots
- Net loss of forest
- Current forest cover
- Net gain of forest

Air Pollution: Fine Particulate Matter (PM$_{2.5}$) Levels, 2001–2010
High — Low   No data

EUROPE

ASIA

AFRICA

AUSTRALIA

Water Scarcity

Shortages of drinking water are increasing in many parts of the world, and the United Nations' Global Environment Outlook (GEO-4) predicts that by 2025, if present trends continue, 1.8 billion people will be living in countries or regions with absolute water scarcity and that two-thirds of the world population could be subject to water stress.

Some countries are pumping groundwater more rapidly than it can be replaced, an activity that will lead to even greater water shortages. In river basins where water is shared among jurisdictions, political tensions are likely to increase.

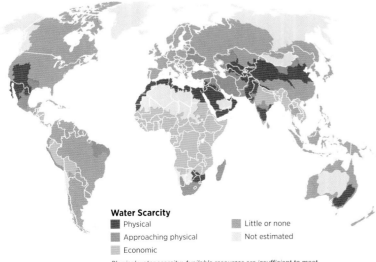

Water Scarcity

- Physical
- Approaching physical
- Economic
- Little or none
- Not estimated

Physical water scarcity: Available resources are insufficient to meet all demands, including minimum environmental flow requirements.
Economic water scarcity: insufficient investment or human capacity is available to keep up with growing water demands.

Depletion of the Ozone Layer

The ozone layer in the stratosphere has long shielded the biosphere from harmful solar ultraviolet radiation. In the 1970s, however, the layer began thinning over Antarctica. This grew into a hole that reached its largest point in September 2006, stretching across nearly the entire area below the 60th parallel south—over 11 million square miles (28.49 million sq km). Fortunately, as a result of the 1987 Montreal Protocol—which called for discontinuing production and consumption of specific chlorine compounds that deplete ozone, including chlorofluorocarbons (CFCs)—progress is being made. From 1986 to 2008, consumption of ozone-depleting substances (ODSs) dropped 98 percent. However, it will take decades to reverse the damage caused by ODSs. The hole grew in size again in 2011 and reached the tip of South America in 2014. And because the area is still saturated in chlorine, experts say it won't really be on the path to total recovery until about 2070.

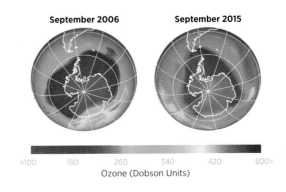

September 2006   September 2015

<100   180   260   340   420   500>
Ozone (Dobson Units)

Geographic Comparisons

EARTH

Planet Facts

Age: Formed 4.54 billion years ago. Life appeared on its surface within a billion years.

Interior: Remains active, with a thick layer of relatively solid mantle, a liquid outer core that generates a magnetic field, and a solid iron inner core.

Mass: 5,973,600,000,000,000,000,000,000—5.9736 sextillion—metric tons (6.5848 sextillion short tons)

Total Area: 510,072,000 sq km (196,940,000 sq mi)

Surface: About 71% of the surface is covered with a saltwater ocean, the remainder consisting of continents and islands.

Land Area: 148,940,000 sq km (57,506,000 sq mi), 29.1% of total

Water Area: 361,132,000 sq km (139,434,000 sq mi), 70.9% of total

Atmosphere Composition: Dry air is 78.08% Nitrogen (N_2), 20.95% Oxygen (O_2), 0.93% Argon (Ar), 0.038% Carbon dioxide (CO_2), and 0.002% other gases. Water vapor is variable and typically about 1%.

Orbit: Earth moves around the sun once for every 366.26 times it rotates about its axis. This time period is a sidereal year, which equals 365.26 solar days.

Equatorial Diameter: 12,756 km (7,926 mi)

Polar Diameter: 12,714 km (7,900 mi)

Planetary Extremes

Hottest Place: Dalol, Danakil Depression, Ethiopia, annual average temperature 34°C (93°F)

Coldest Place: Ridge A, Antarctica, annual average temperature -70°C (-94°F)

Hottest Recorded Air Temperature: Furnace Creek Ranch (Death Valley), California, U.S., 56.7°C (134°F), October 7, 1913

Coldest Recorded Air Temperature: Antarctica, -93.2°C (-135.8°F), August 10, 2010

Wettest Place: Mawsynram, Meghalaya, India, annual average rainfall 1,187 cm (467 in)

Driest Place: Arica, Atacama Desert, Chile, rainfall barely measurable

Largest Hot Desert: Sahara, Africa, 9,000,000 sq km (3,475,000 sq mi)

Largest Ice Desert: Antarctica, 13,209,000 sq km (5,100,000 sq mi)

Largest Canyon: Grand Canyon, Colorado River, Arizona, U.S., 446 km (277 mi) long along river, 180 m (600 ft) to 29 km (18 mi) wide, about 1.6 km (1 mi) deep

Largest Coral Reef Ecosystem: Great Barrier Reef, Australia, 348,300 sq km (134,000 sq mi)

Greatest Tidal Range: Bay of Fundy, Canadian Atlantic Coast, 16 m (53 ft)

Tallest Waterfall: Angel Falls, Venezuela, 979 m (3,212 ft)

Deepest and Oldest Lake: Lake Baikal, Russia, -1,642 m (-5,387 ft), about 25 million years old

Strongest Recorded Wind Gust: Barrow Island, Australia, 408 km/h (254 mph)

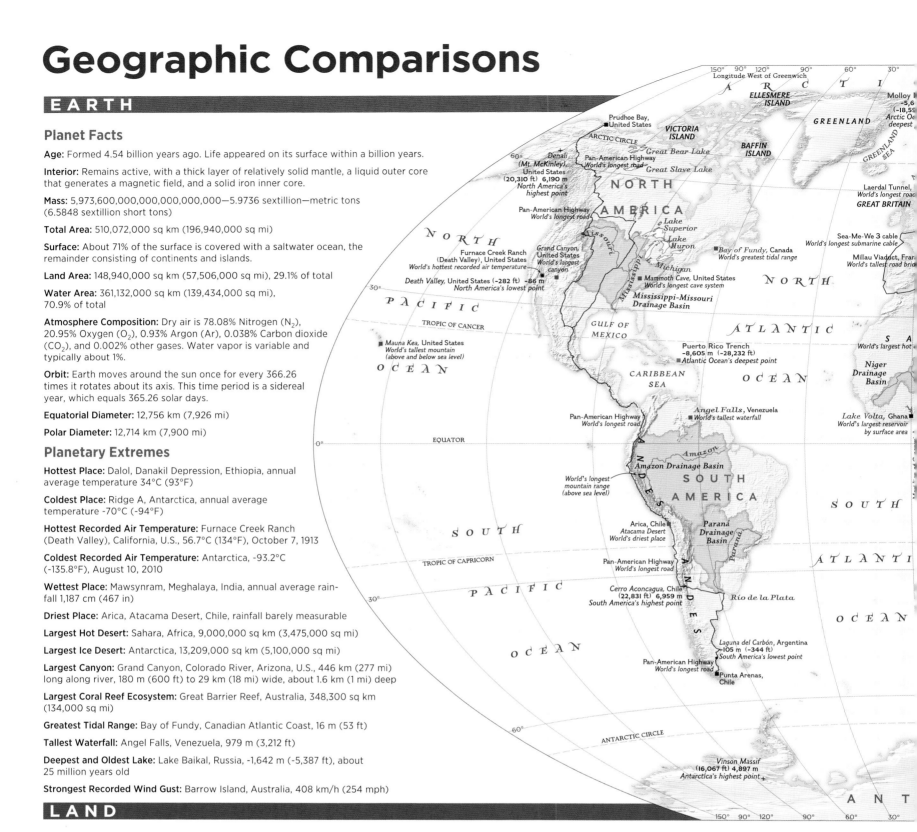

LAND

Area of Each Continent

	sq km	sq mi	% of land
Asia	44,570,000	17,208,000	30.0
Africa	30,065,000	11,608,000	20.2
North America	24,474,000	9,449,000	16.5
South America	17,819,000	6,880,000	12.0
Antarctica	13,209,000	5,100,000	8.9
Europe	9,947,000	3,841,000	6.7
Australia	7,692,000	2,970,000	5.2

Largest Islands by Area

		sq km	sq mi
1	Greenland	2,166,000	836,000
2	New Guinea	792,500	306,000
3	Borneo	725,500	280,100
4	Madagascar	587,000	226,600
5	Baffin Island	507,500	196,000
6	Sumatra	427,300	165,000
7	Honshu	227,400	87,800
8	Great Britain	218,100	84,200
9	Victoria Island	217,300	83,900
10	Ellesmere Island	196,200	75,800

Lowest Surface Point on Each Continent

	meters	feet
Dead Sea, Asia	-423	-1,388
Lake Assal, Africa	-155	-509
Laguna del Carbón, South America	-105	-344
Death Valley, North America	-86	-282
Caspian Sea, Europe	-28	-92
Lake Eyre, Australia	-15	-49
Byrd Glacier (depression), Antarctica	-2,870	-9,416

Highest Point on Each Continent

	meters	feet
Mount Everest, Asia	8,850	29,035
Cerro Aconcagua, South America	6,959	22,831
Denali (Mount McKinley), N. America	6,190	20,310
Kilimanjaro, Africa	5,895	19,340
El'brus, Europe	5,642	18,510
Vinson Massif, Antarctica	4,897	16,067
Mount Kosciuszko, Australia	2,228	7,310

Mountains and Caves

Tallest Mountain (above and below sea level): Mauna Kea, Hawai'i, U.S., 9,966 m (32,696 ft) above the seafloor and 4,205 m (13,796 ft) above sea level

Highest Mountain (above sea level): Mount Everest, China and Nepal border, 8,850 m (29,035 ft) above sea level

Longest Mountain Range (above sea level): Andes, South America, 7,600 km (4,700 mi)

Longest Mountain Range (above and below sea level): Mid-Ocean Ridge, 60,000 km (37,000 mi), encircles the Earth mostly along the seafloor

Largest Cave Chamber: Sarawak Chamber, Gunung Mulu National Park, Malaysia, 16 hectares and 80 meters high (40.2 acres and 260 feet)

Longest Cave System: Mammoth Cave, Kentucky, U.S., more than 627 km (390 mi) of passageways mapped

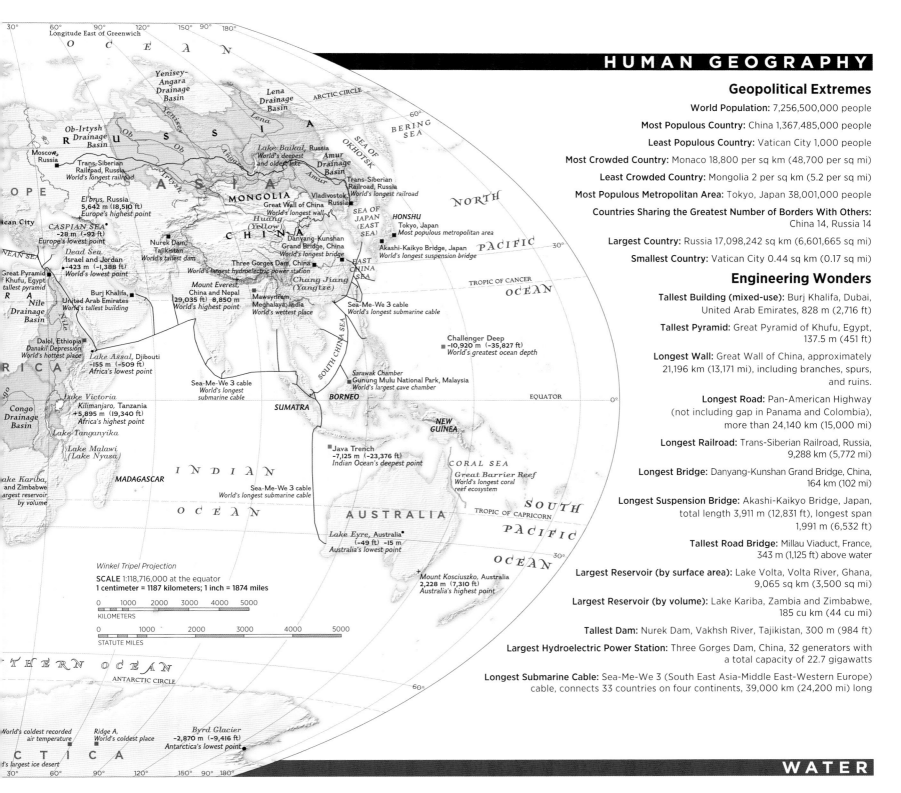

Geopolitical Extremes

World Population: 7,256,500,000 people

Most Populous Country: China 1,367,485,000 people

Least Populous Country: Vatican City 1,000 people

Most Crowded Country: Monaco 18,800 per sq km (48,700 per sq mi)

Least Crowded Country: Mongolia 2 per sq km (5.2 per sq mi)

Most Populous Metropolitan Area: Tokyo, Japan 38,001,000 people

Countries Sharing the Greatest Number of Borders With Others:
China 14, Russia 14

Largest Country: Russia 17,098,242 sq km (6,601,665 sq mi)

Smallest Country: Vatican City 0.44 sq km (0.17 sq mi)

Engineering Wonders

Tallest Building (mixed-use): Burj Khalifa, Dubai, United Arab Emirates, 828 m (2,716 ft)

Tallest Pyramid: Great Pyramid of Khufu, Egypt, 137.5 m (451 ft)

Longest Wall: Great Wall of China, approximately 21,196 km (13,171 mi), including branches, spurs, and ruins.

Longest Road: Pan-American Highway (not including gap in Panama and Colombia), more than 24,140 km (15,000 mi)

Longest Railroad: Trans-Siberian Railroad, Russia, 9,288 km (5,772 mi)

Longest Bridge: Danyang-Kunshan Grand Bridge, China, 164 km (102 mi)

Longest Suspension Bridge: Akashi-Kaikyo Bridge, Japan, total length 3,911 m (12,831 ft), longest span 1,991 m (6,532 ft)

Tallest Road Bridge: Millau Viaduct, France, 343 m (1,125 ft) above water

Largest Reservoir (by surface area): Lake Volta, Volta River, Ghana, 9,065 sq km (3,500 sq mi)

Largest Reservoir (by volume): Lake Kariba, Zambia and Zimbabwe, 185 cu km (44 cu mi)

Tallest Dam: Nurek Dam, Vakhsh River, Tajikistan, 300 m (984 ft)

Largest Hydroelectric Power Station: Three Gorges Dam, China, 32 generators with a total capacity of 22.7 gigawatts

Longest Submarine Cable: Sea-Me-We 3 (South East Asia-Middle East-Western Europe) cable, connects 33 countries on four continents, 39,000 km (24,200 mi) long

Winkel Tripel Projection

SCALE 1:118,716,000 at the equator
1 centimeter = 1187 kilometers; 1 inch = 1874 miles

KILOMETERS
0 1000 2000 3000 4000 5000

STATUTE MILES
0 1000 2000 3000 4000 5000

Deepest Point in Each Ocean

	meters	feet
Challenger Deep, Pacific Ocean	-10,920	-35,827
Puerto Rico Trench, Atlantic Ocean	-8,605	-28,232
Java Trench, Indian Ocean	-7,125	-23,376
Molloy Deep, Arctic Ocean	-5,669	-18,599

Area of Each Ocean

	sq km	sq mi	% ocean area
Pacific	178,800,000	69,000,000	49.5
Atlantic	91,700,000	35,400,000	25.4
Indian	76,200,000	29,400,000	21.0
Arctic	14,700,000	5,600,000	4.1

The Atlantic, Indian, and Pacific Oceans merge into icy waters around Antarctica. Some define this as an ocean— calling it the Antarctic Ocean, Austral Ocean, or Southern Ocean. While most accept four oceans, including the Arctic, there is no international agreement on the name and extent of a fifth ocean. The "Southern Ocean" extends from the Antarctic coast to 60° south latitude and includes portions of the Atlantic, Indian, and Pacific Oceans (estimated area: 20,327,000 sq km, 7,848,000 sq mi).

Largest Seas by Area

		area		avg. depth	
		sq km	sq mi	meters	feet
1	Coral Sea	4,184,000	1,615,500	2,471	8,107
2	South China Sea	3,596,000	1,388,400	1,180	3,871
3	Caribbean Sea	2,834,000	1,094,200	2,596	8,517
4	Bering Sea	2,520,000	973,000	1,832	6,010
5	Mediterranean Sea	2,469,000	953,300	1,572	5,157
6	Sea of Okhotsk	1,625,000	627,400	814	2,671
7	Gulf of Mexico	1,532,000	591,500	1,544	5,066
8	Norwegian Sea	1,425,000	550,200	1,768	5,801
9	Greenland Sea	1,158,000	447,100	1,443	4,734
10	Sea of Japan (East Sea)	1,008,000	389,200	1,647	5,404

Largest Lakes by Area (with maximum depth)

		sq km	sq mi	meters	feet
1	Caspian Sea	371,000	143,200	1,025	3,363
2	Lake Superior	82,100	31,700	406	1,332
3	Lake Victoria	69,500	26,800	82	269
4	Lake Huron	59,600	23,000	229	751
5	Lake Michigan	57,800	22,300	281	922
6	Lake Tanganyika	32,600	12,600	1,470	4,823
7	Lake Baikal	31,500	12,200	1,642	5,387
8	Great Bear Lake	31,300	12,100	446	1,463
9	Lake Malawi (L. Nyasa)	28,900	11,200	695	2,280
10	Great Slave Lake	28,600	11,000	614	2,014

Longest Rivers

		kilometers	miles
1	Nile, Africa	7,081	4,400
2	Amazon, South America	6,679	4,150
3	Chang Jiang (Yangtze), Asia	6,244	3,880
4	Mississippi-Missouri, N. America	6,083	3,780
5	Yenisey-Angara, Asia	5,810	3,610
6	Huang (Yellow), Asia	5,778	3,590
7	Ob-Irtysh, Asia	5,520	3,430
8	Amur, Asia	5,504	3,420
9	Lena, Asia	5,150	3,200
10	Congo, Africa	5,118	3,180

Largest River Drainage Basins by Area

		sq km	sq mi
1	Amazon, South America	6,145,186	2,372,670
2	Congo, Africa	3,730,881	1,440,500
3	Nile, Africa	3,254,853	1,256,706
4	Mississippi-Missouri, N. Amer.	3,202,185	1,236,370
5	Ob-Irtysh, Asia	2,972,493	1,147,686
6	Paraná, South America	2,582,704	997,188
7	Yenisey-Angara, Asia	2,554,388	986,255
8	Lena, Asia	2,306,743	890,638
9	Niger, Africa	2,261,741	873,263
10	Amur, Asia	1,929,955	745,160

Time Zones

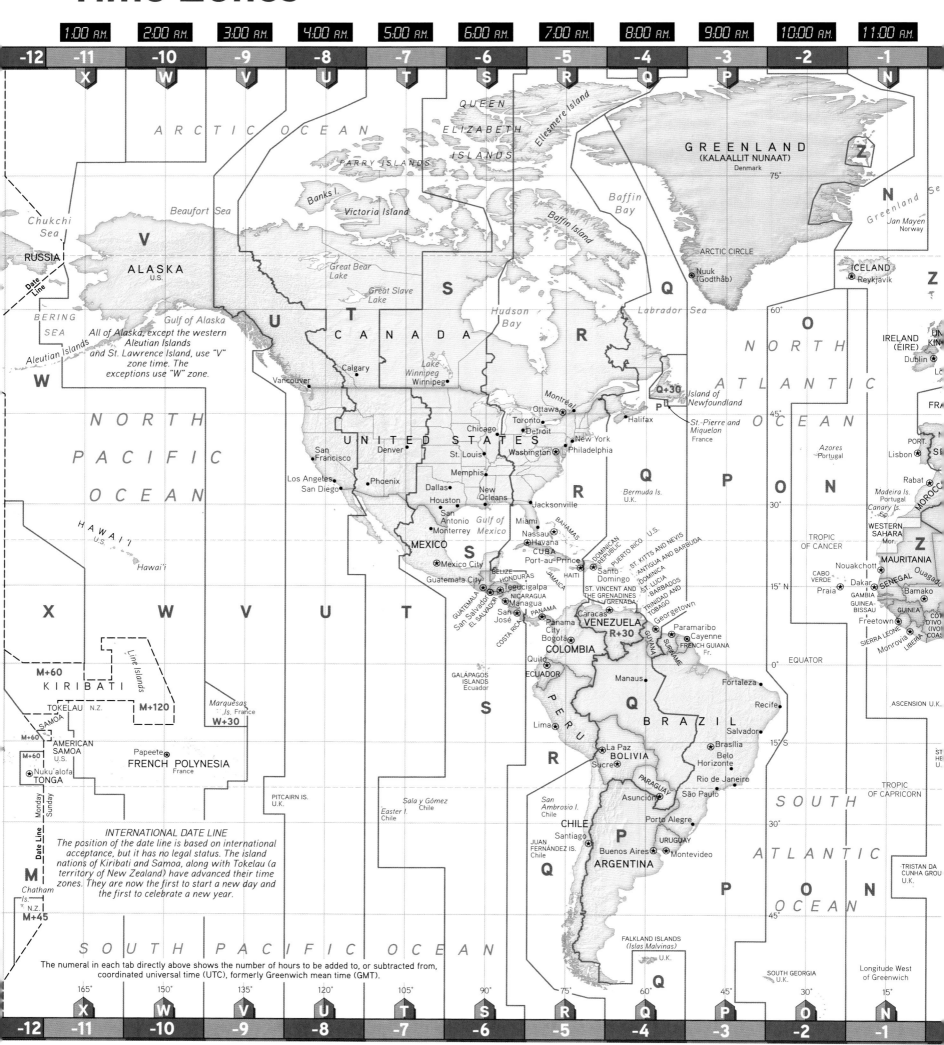

1:00 A.M.	2:00 A.M.	3:00 A.M.	4:00 A.M.	5:00 A.M.	6:00 A.M.	7:00 A.M.	8:00 A.M.	9:00 A.M.	10:00 A.M.	11:00 A.M.
-12	-11	-10	-9	-8	-7	-6	-5	-4	-3	-2	-1
X	W	V	U	T	S	R	Q	P	N

All of Alaska, except the western Aleutian Islands and St. Lawrence Island, use "V" zone time. The exceptions use "W" zone.

The numeral in each tab directly above shows the number of hours to be added to, or subtracted from, coordinated universal time (UTC), formerly Greenwich mean time (GMT).

INTERNATIONAL DATE LINE
The position of the date line is based on international acceptance, but it has no legal status. The island nations of Kiribati and Samoa, along with Tokelau (a territory of New Zealand) have advanced their time zones. They are now the first to start a new day and the first to celebrate a new year.

165°	150°	135°	120°	105°	90°	75°	60°	45°	30°	15°
X	W	V	U	T	S	R	Q	P	O	N
-12	-11	-10	-9	-8	-7	-6	-5	-4	-3	-2	-1

Longitude West of Greenwich

LEGEND

The map outlines the Earth's 24 time zones with purple lines, with each time zone covering 15° longitude—the distance the Earth rotates in 1 hour in a 24-hour day.

Time zones are measured in reference to the Meridian of Greenwich (0° longitude) in England, sometimes called the prime meridian. Time at Greenwich is known as Greenwich mean time (GMT) or coordinated universal time (UTC) and is the starting point in determining time worldwide. Letters on the map label each time zone,

and the corresponding numbers (with plus or minus signs) indicate the time difference from GMT/UTC. For example, the C time zone is +3. This means that when it is noon in the Greenwich Z zone, it is 3 p.m. standard time in the C zone—the time shown on the clock face (along the top of the map). Daylight savings time, normally one hour ahead of local standard time, is not shown on this map.

Most time zones differ in one-hour increments, but some countries choose to offset time zones by a fraction of an hour. For

example, India (E time zone, +5) shows the label E+30, which means that it is 5 hours and 30 minutes ahead of GMT/UTC time. Nepal is E+45, making it 5 hours and 45 minutes ahead of GMT/UTC.

Many governments choose to have their entire country in one time zone. China is the largest country with only one time zone; normally, it would be divided by five time zones. Other examples of countries in one time zone include India, Iran, and Norway.

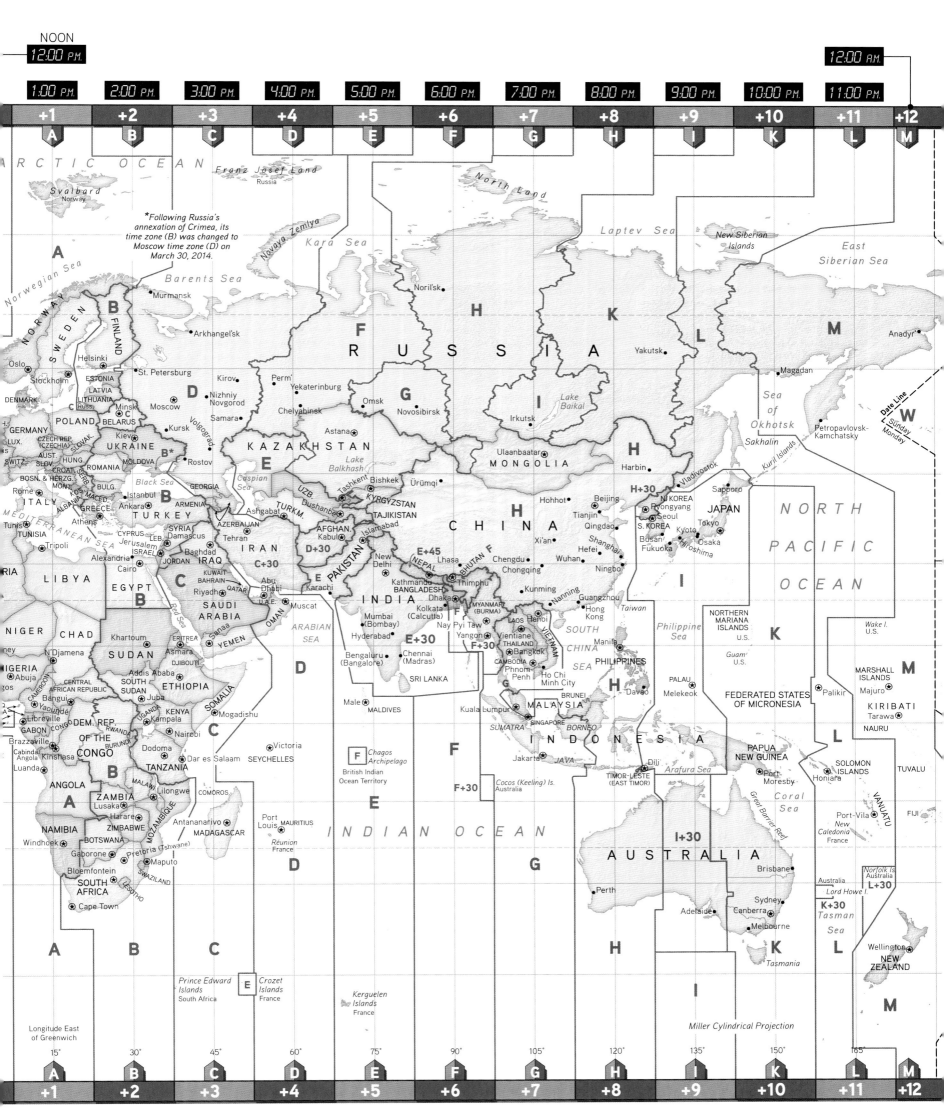

MERIDIAN OF GREENWICH

Britain's Royal Observatory at Greenwich (London) is the home of Greenwich mean time and the "prime meridian of the world" (0° longitude). In 1884, an international conference in Washington, D.C., decided on Greenwich as the location for the prime meridian. At that time, most of the world's commerce depended on sea charts, which already used Greenwich as the prime meridian.

DATE LINE

The international date line, or date line, is an imaginary line located on or near the 180° meridian in the middle of the Pacific Ocean, shown on this map by a dashed black line. The date changes when planes or ships cross it, thus the name date line. A person traveling west across the date line would add a day, but a person traveling east would subtract a day. The position of the date line is based on international acceptance, but it has no legal status. Island countries near the line can choose which date they will observe.

North America

LOCATED BETWEEN THE ATLANTIC, Pacific, and Arctic Oceans, North America is almost an island unto itself, connected to the rest of the world only by the tenuous thread running through the Isthmus of Panama. Geologically old in some places, young in others, and diverse throughout, the continent sweeps from Arctic tundra in the north through the plains, prairies, and deserts of the interior to the tropical rain forests of Central America. Its eastern coastal plain is furrowed by broad rivers that drain worn and ancient mountain ranges, while in the West younger and more robust ranges thrust their still growing high peaks skyward. Though humans have peopled the continent for perhaps as long as 40,000 years, political boundaries were unknown there until some 400 years ago when European settlers imprinted the land with their ideas of ownership. Despite, or perhaps because of, its relative youth—and its geographic location—most of North America has remained remarkably stable. In the past century, when country borders throughout much of the rest of the world have altered dramatically, they have changed little in North America, while the system of government by democratic rule, first rooted in this continent's soil in the 18th century, has spread to many corners of the globe.

Third largest of the Earth's continents, North America seems made for human habitation. Its waterways—the inland seas of Hudson Bay and the Great Lakes, the enormous Mississippi system draining its midsection, and the countless navigable rivers of the East—have long provided natural corridors for human commerce. In its vast interior, the nurturing soils of plains and prairies have offered up bountiful harvests, while rich deposits of oil and gas have fueled industrial growth, making this continent's mainland one of the world's economic powerhouses.

Just in the past couple of centuries, North America has experienced dramatic changes in its population, landscapes, and environment, an incredible transformation brought about by waves of immigration, booming economies, and relentless development. During the 20th century, the United States and Canada managed to propel themselves into the ranks of the world's richest nations. But success has brought a host of concerns, not least of which is the continued exploitation of natural resources. North America is home to roughly 8 percent of the planet's people, yet its per capita consumption of energy is almost six times as great as the average for all other continents.

The United States ended the 20th century as the only true superpower, with a military presence and political, economic, and cultural influences that extend around the globe. But the rest of the continent south of the U.S. failed to keep pace, plagued by poverty, despotic governments, and social unrest. Poverty has spurred millions of Mexicans, Central Americans, and Caribbean islanders to migrate northward (legally and illegally) in search of better lives. Finding ways to integrate these disenfranchised masses into the continent's economic miracle is one of the greatest challenges facing North America in the 21st century.

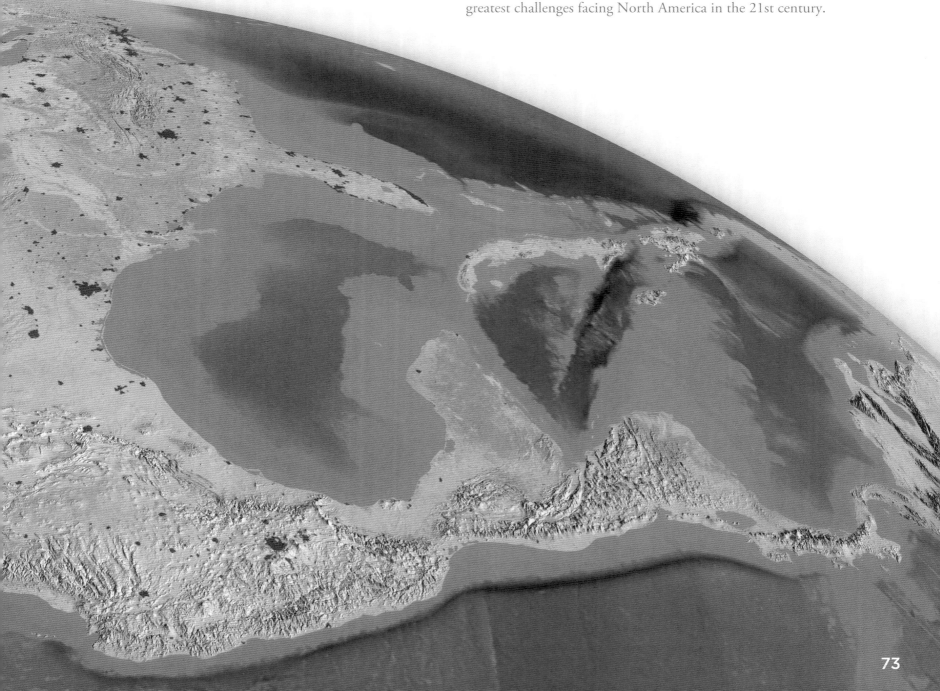

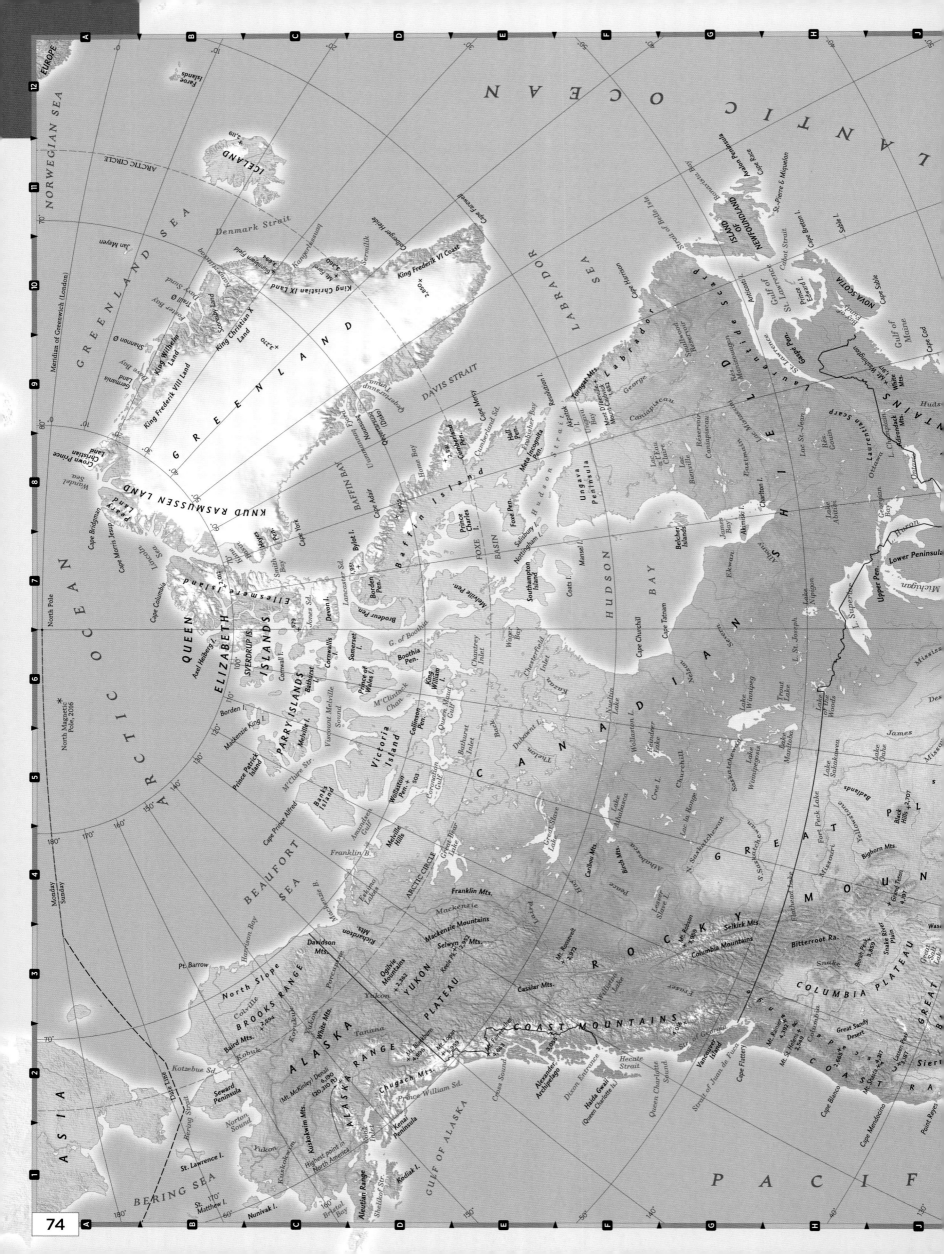

North America
Physical

Continental Data

Area:
24,474,000 sq km
(9,449,000 sq mi)

Greatest north-south extent:
7,200 km (4,470 mi)

Greatest east-west extent:
6,400 km (3,980 mi)

Highest point:
Denali (Mount McKinley),
Alaska, United States
6,190 m (20,310 ft)

Lowest point:
Death Valley, California,
United States -86 m (-282 ft)

Lowest recorded temperature:
Snag, Yukon Territory, Canada
-63°C (-81.4°F), February 3, 1947

Highest recorded temperature:
Death Valley, California,
United States
56.6°C (134°F), July 10, 1913

Longest rivers:
• Mississippi-Missouri
5,970 km (3,710 mi)
• Mackenzie-Peace
4,241 km (2,635 mi)
• Yukon
3,220 km (2,000 mi)

Largest natural lakes:
• Lake Superior
82,100 sq km (31,700 sq mi)
• Lake Huron
59,600 sq km (23,000 sq mi)
• Lake Michigan
57,800 sq km (22,300 sq mi)

**Earth's extremes located
in North America:**
• Largest Cave System:
Mammoth Cave, Kentucky,
United States; over
530 km (330 mi)
of mapped passageways

• Most Predictable Geyser:
Old Faithful, Wyoming, United
States; annual average interval
75 to 79 minutes

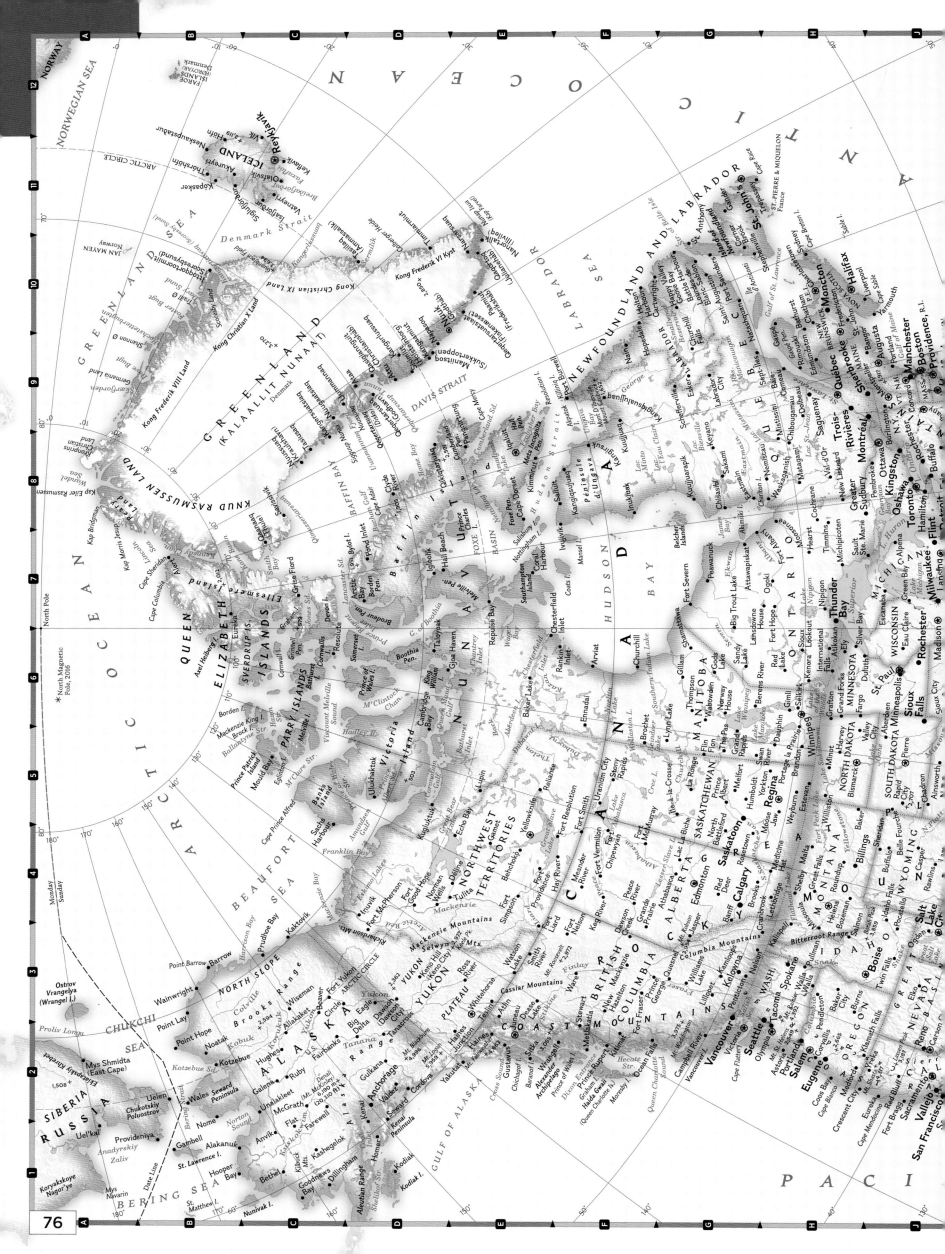

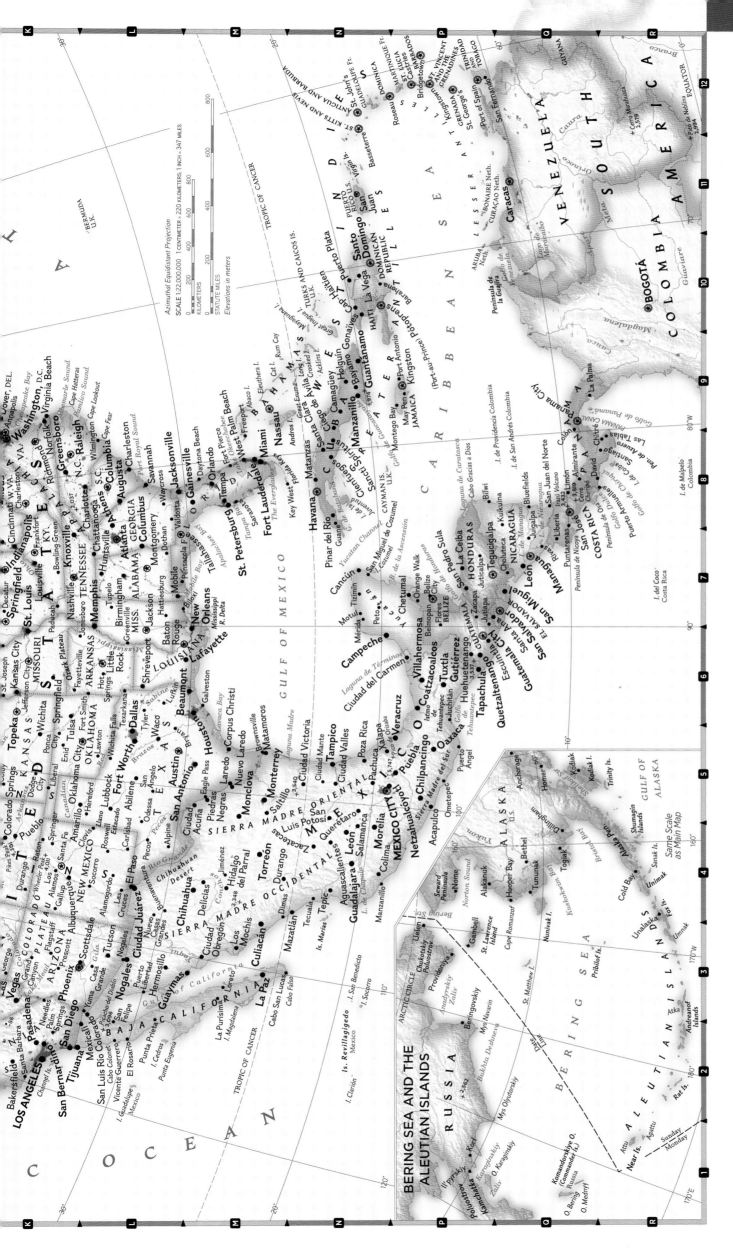

North America
Political

Continental Data

Total number of countries: 23

First independent country:
United States, July 4, 1776

"Youngest" country:
St. Kitts and Nevis, Sept. 19, 1983

Largest country by area:
Canada 9,984,670 sq km
(3,855,101 sq mi)

Smallest country by area:
St. Kitts and Nevis 261 sq km
(101 sq mi)

Percent urban population: 84%

Most populous country:
United States 322,560,000

Least populous country:
St. Kitts and Nevis 52,000

**Most densely
populated country:**
Barbados 676 per sq km
(1,750 per sq mi)

**Least densely
populated country:**
Canada 4 per sq km
(10 per sq mi)

Largest city by population:
Mexico City, Mexico 20,999,000

Highest GDP per capita:
United States $56,300

Lowest GDP per capita:
Haiti $1,800

Average life expectancy: 77 years

Human and Natural Themes

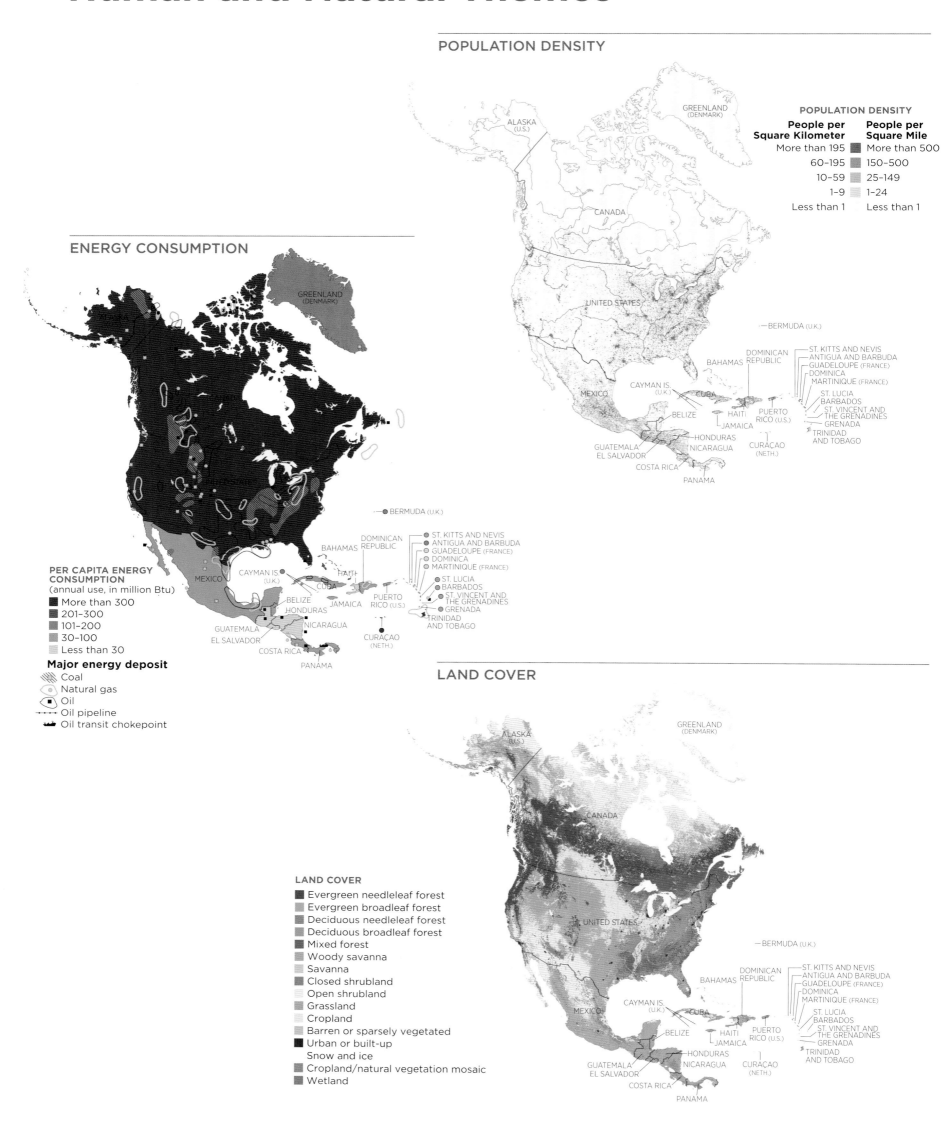

POPULATION DENSITY

POPULATION DENSITY

People per Square Kilometer	People per Square Mile
More than 195	More than 500
60–195	150–500
10–59	25–149
1–9	1–24
Less than 1	Less than 1

ENERGY CONSUMPTION

PER CAPITA ENERGY CONSUMPTION
(annual use, in million Btu)

- More than 300
- 201–300
- 101–200
- 30–100
- Less than 30

Major energy deposit
- Coal
- Natural gas
- Oil
- Oil pipeline
- Oil transit chokepoint

LAND COVER

LAND COVER
- Evergreen needleleaf forest
- Evergreen broadleaf forest
- Deciduous needleleaf forest
- Deciduous broadleaf forest
- Mixed forest
- Woody savanna
- Savanna
- Closed shrubland
- Open shrubland
- Grassland
- Cropland
- Barren or sparsely vegetated
- Urban or built-up
- Snow and ice
- Cropland/natural vegetation mosaic
- Wetland

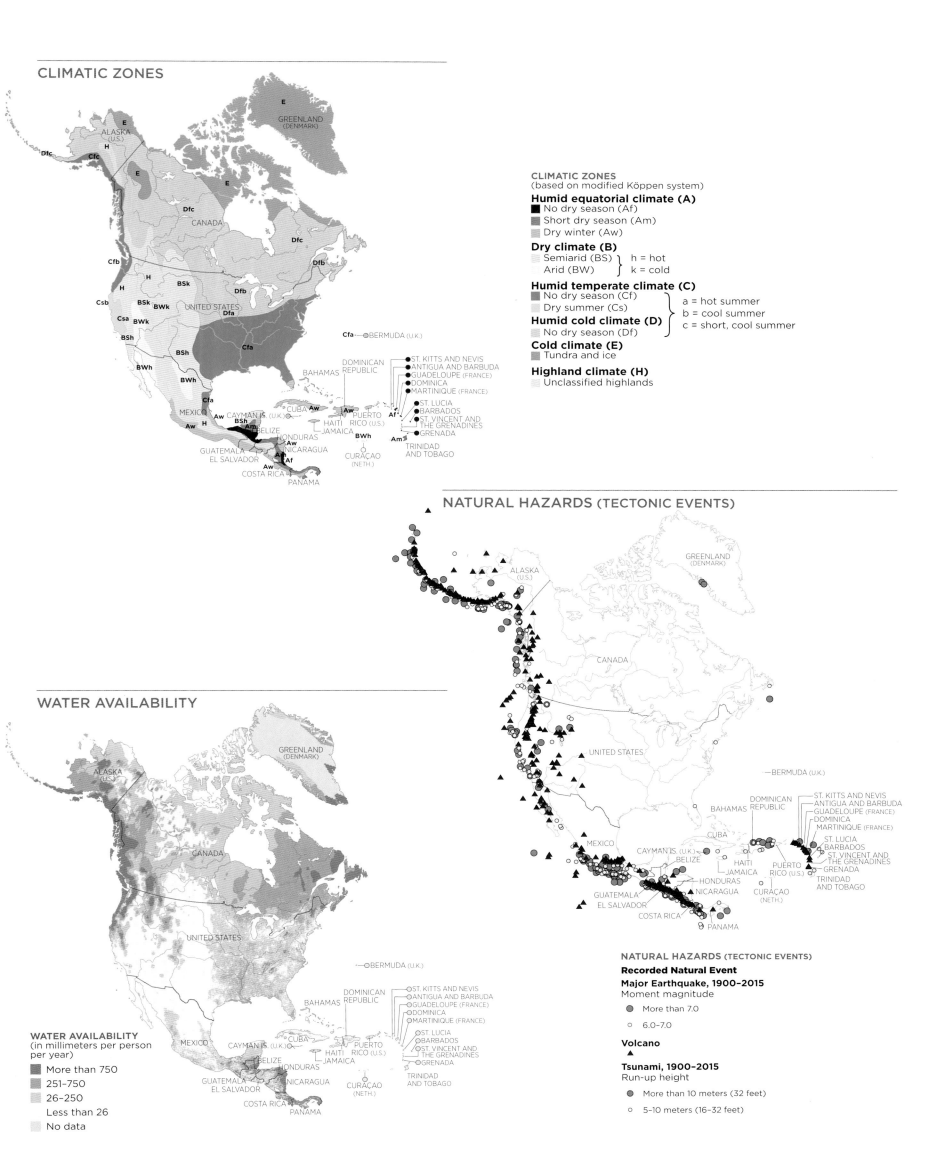

CLIMATIC ZONES

CLIMATIC ZONES
(based on modified Köppen system)

Humid equatorial climate (A)
- No dry season (Af)
- Short dry season (Am)
- Dry winter (Aw)

Dry climate (B)
- Semiarid (BS)   h = hot
- Arid (BW)   k = cold

Humid temperate climate (C)
- No dry season (Cf)
- Dry summer (Cs)

a = hot summer
b = cool summer
c = short, cool summer

Humid cold climate (D)
- No dry season (Df)

Cold climate (E)
- Tundra and ice

Highland climate (H)
- Unclassified highlands

NATURAL HAZARDS (TECTONIC EVENTS)

NATURAL HAZARDS (TECTONIC EVENTS)
Recorded Natural Event
Major Earthquake, 1900–2015
Moment magnitude
- ● More than 7.0
- ○ 6.0–7.0

Volcano
- ▲

Tsunami, 1900–2015
Run-up height
- ● More than 10 meters (32 feet)
- ○ 5–10 meters (16–32 feet)

WATER AVAILABILITY

WATER AVAILABILITY
(in millimeters per person per year)
- More than 750
- 251–750
- 26–250
- Less than 26
- No data

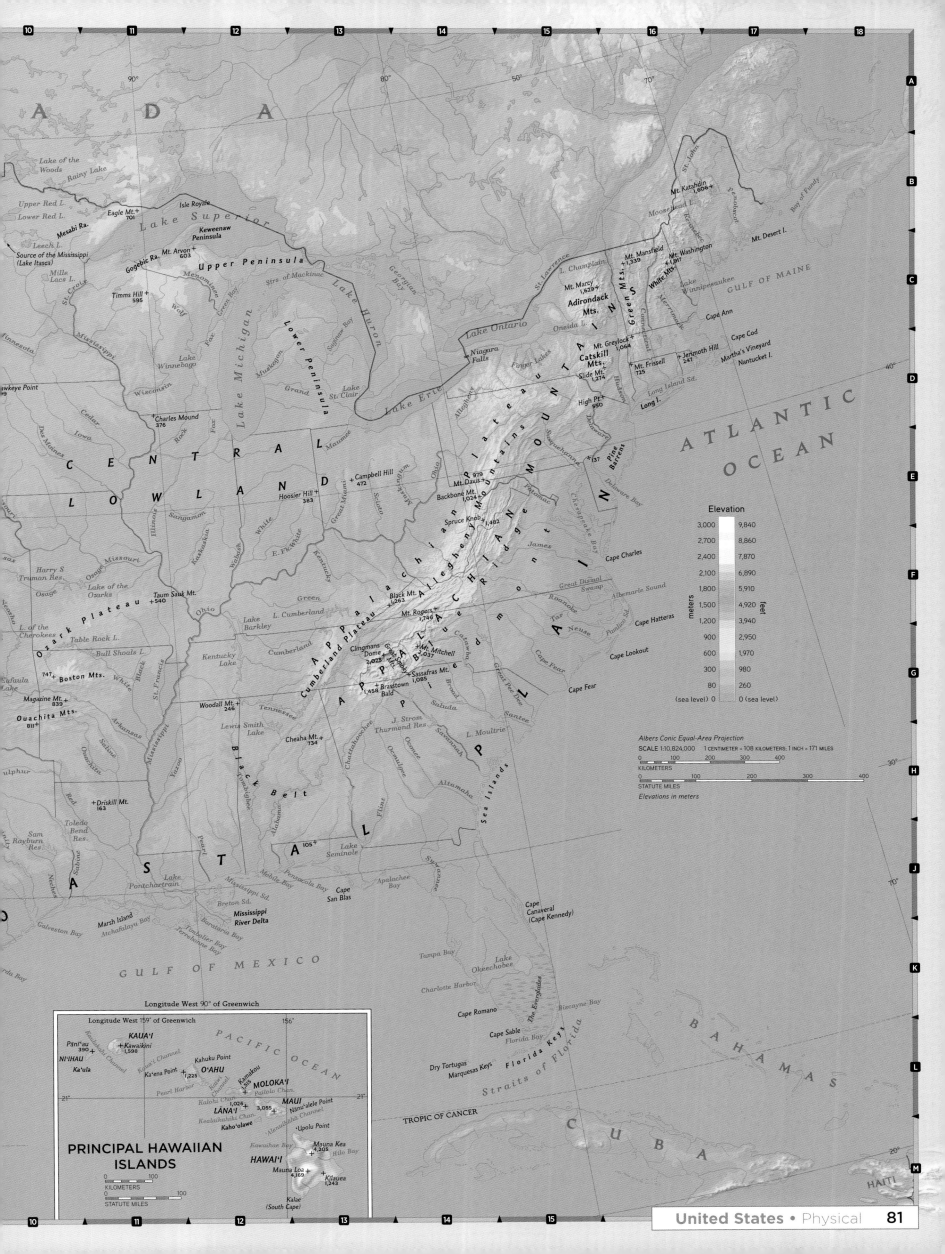

United States
Political

Human and Natural United States

TEMPERATURE AND PRECIPITATION

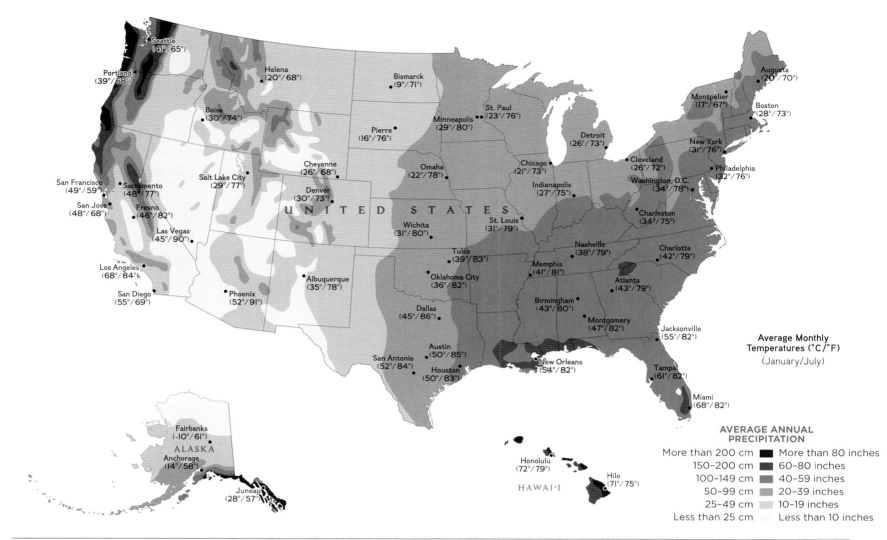

Seattle (41°/65°)
Portland (39°/68°)
Helena (20°/68°)
Bismarck (9°/71°)
Augusta (20°/70°)
Montpelier (17°/67°)
Boston (28°/73°)
Boise (30°/74°)
St. Paul (23°/76°)
Minneapolis (29°/80°)
Detroit (26°/73°)
New York (31°/76°)
Pierre (16°/76°)
Cheyenne (26°/68°)
Omaha (22°/78°)
Chicago (21°/73°)
Cleveland (26°/72°)
Philadelphia (32°/76°)
San Francisco (49°/59°)
Sacramento (48°/77°)
Salt Lake City (29°/77°)
Denver (30°/73°)
Indianapolis (27°/75°)
Washington, D.C. (34°/78°)
UNITED STATES
San Jose (48°/68°)
Fresno (46°/82°)
Wichita (31°/80°)
St. Louis (31°/79°)
Charleston (34°/75°)
Las Vegas (45°/90°)
Nashville (38°/79°)
Charlotte (42°/79°)
Los Angeles (68°/84°)
Albuquerque (35°/78°)
Tulsa (39°/83°)
Memphis (41°/81°)
Atlanta (43°/79°)
San Diego (55°/69°)
Phoenix (52°/91°)
Oklahoma City (36°/82°)
Birmingham (43°/80°)
Dallas (45°/86°)
Montgomery (47°/82°)
Jacksonville (55°/82°)
Austin (50°/85°)
San Antonio (52°/84°)
New Orleans (54°/82°)
Houston (50°/83°)
Tampa (61°/82°)
Miami (68°/82°)

Fairbanks (-10°/61°)
ALASKA
Anchorage (14°/58°)
Juneau (28°/57°)

Honolulu (72°/79°)
Hilo (71°/75°)
HAWAI'I

Average Monthly Temperatures (°C/°F)
(January/July)

AVERAGE ANNUAL PRECIPITATION

More than 200 cm	More than 80 inches
150–200 cm	60–80 inches
100–149 cm	40–59 inches
50–99 cm	20–39 inches
25–49 cm	10–19 inches
Less than 25 cm	Less than 10 inches

LAND USE AND LAND COVER

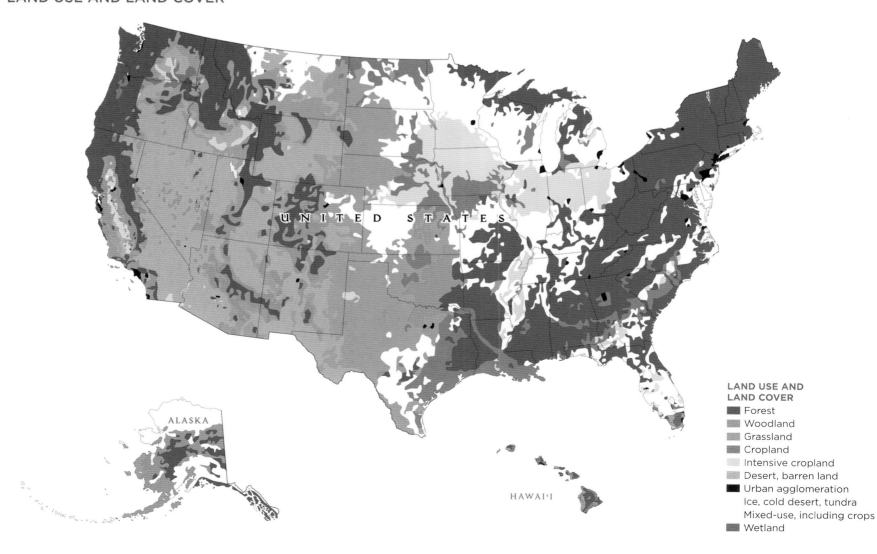

UNITED STATES
ALASKA
HAWAI'I

LAND USE AND LAND COVER

- Forest
- Woodland
- Grassland
- Cropland
- Intensive cropland
- Desert, barren land
- Urban agglomeration
- Ice, cold desert, tundra
- Mixed-use, including crops
- Wetland

POPULATION

URBAN AREA POPULATION
- ■ 5 million and greater
- ▲ 1 million–4,999,999
- • 750,000–999,999
- ○ 500,000–749,999

POPULATION DENSITY

People per Square Kilometer	People per Square Mile
More than 195	More than 500
60-195	150-500
10-59	25-149
1-9	1-24
Less than 1	Less than 1

NATIONAL PARK SERVICE LANDS

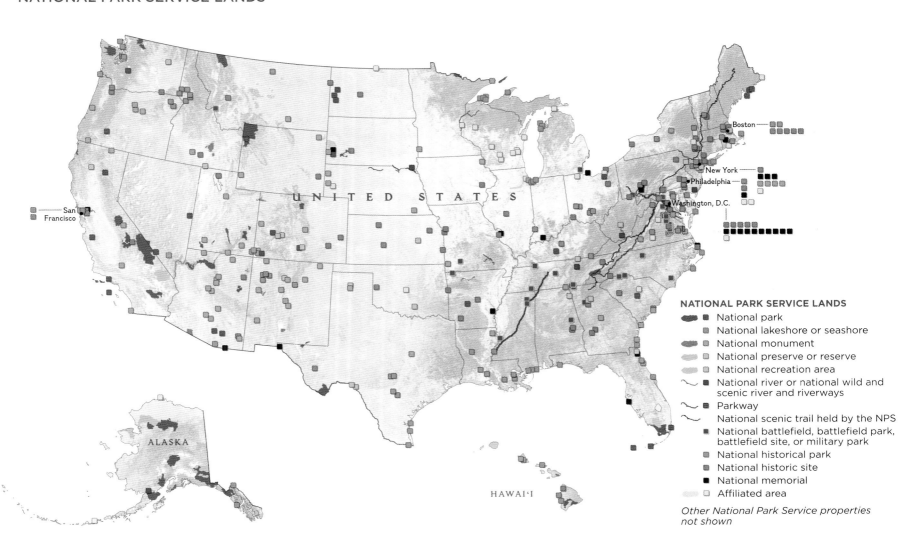

NATIONAL PARK SERVICE LANDS
- ■ National park
- ■ National lakeshore or seashore
- ■ National monument
- ■ National preserve or reserve
- ■ National recreation area
- 〜 National river or national wild and scenic river and riverways
- 〜 ■ Parkway
- 〜 National scenic trail held by the NPS
- ■ National battlefield, battlefield park, battlefield site, or military park
- ■ National historical park
- ■ National historic site
- ■ National memorial
- □ Affiliated area

Other National Park Service properties not shown

Flags and Facts

COUNTRIES

Antigua and Barbuda
ANTIGUA AND BARBUDA

AREA	443 sq km (171 sq mi)
POPULATION	92,000
CAPITAL	Saint John's 22,000
RELIGION	Protestant, Roman Catholic
LANGUAGE	English, Antiguan creole
LITERACY	99%
LIFE EXPECTANCY	76 years
GDP PER CAPITA	$23,700

ECONOMY IND: tourism, construction, light manufacturing (clothing, alcohol, household appliances) AGR: cotton, fruits, vegetables, bananas, coconuts, cucumbers, mangoes, sugarcane, livestock EXP: petroleum products, bedding, handicrafts, electronic components, transport equipment, food and live animals

Bahamas
COMMONWEALTH OF THE BAHAMAS

AREA	13,880 sq km (5,359 sq mi)
POPULATION	325,000
CAPITAL	Nassau 267,000
RELIGION	Protestant, Roman Catholic, other Christian
LANGUAGE	English, Creole
LITERACY	96%
LIFE EXPECTANCY	72 years
GDP PER CAPITA	$25,600

ECONOMY IND: tourism, banking, oil bunkering, maritime industries, pharmaceuticals AGR: citrus, vegetables, poultry EXP: crawfish, aragonite, crude salt, polystyrene products

Barbados
BARBADOS

AREA	430 sq km (166 sq mi)
POPULATION	291,000
CAPITAL	Bridgetown 90,000
RELIGION	Protestant, other Pentecostal, Adventist, Methodist
LANGUAGE	English, Bajan
LITERACY	100%
LIFE EXPECTANCY	75 years
GDP PER CAPITA	$16,700

ECONOMY IND: tourism, sugar, light manufacturing, component assembly for export AGR: sugarcane, vegetables, cotton EXP: manufactures, sugar, molasses, rum, other foods and beverages, chemicals

Belize
BELIZE

AREA	22,966 sq km (8,867 sq mi)
POPULATION	347,000
CAPITAL	Belmopan 17,000
RELIGION	Roman Catholic, Protestant, Jehovah's Witness
LANGUAGE	English, Spanish, Creole
LITERACY	77%
LIFE EXPECTANCY	69 years
GDP PER CAPITA	$8,600

ECONOMY IND: garment production, food processing, tourism, construction, oil AGR: bananas, cacao, citrus, sugar, fish, cultured shrimp, lumber EXP: sugar, bananas, citrus, clothing, fish products, molasses, wood, crude oil

Canada
CANADA

AREA	9,984,670 sq km (3,855,101 sq mi)
POPULATION	35,100,000
CAPITAL	Ottawa 1,326,000
RELIGION	Catholic, Roman Catholic, Protestant
LANGUAGE	English, French
LITERACY	99%
LIFE EXPECTANCY	82 years
GDP PER CAPITA	$45,900

ECONOMY IND: transportation equipment, chemicals, processed and unprocessed minerals, food products, wood and paper products, fish products, petroleum and natural gas AGR: wheat, barley, oilseed, tobacco, fruits, vegetables, dairy products, forest products, fish EXP: motor vehicles and parts, industrial machinery, aircraft, telecommunications equipment, chemicals, plastics, fertilizers, wood pulp, timber, crude petroleum, natural gas, electricity, aluminum

Costa Rica
REPUBLIC OF COSTA RICA

AREA	51,100 sq km (19,730 sq mi)
POPULATION	4,814,000
CAPITAL	San José 1,170,000
RELIGION	Roman Catholic, Evangelical
LANGUAGE	Spanish, English
LITERACY	98%
LIFE EXPECTANCY	78 years
GDP PER CAPITA	$15,500

ECONOMY IND: medical equipment, food processing, textiles and clothing, construction materials, fertilizer, plastic products AGR: bananas, pineapples, coffee, melons, ornamental plants, sugar, corn, rice, beans, potatoes, beef, poultry, dairy, timber EXP: bananas, pineapples, coffee, melons, ornamental plants, sugar, beef, seafood, electronic components, medical equipment

Cuba
REPUBLIC OF CUBA

AREA	110,860 sq km (42,803 sq mi)
POPULATION	11,031,000
CAPITAL	Havana 2,137,000
RELIGION	Roman Catholic
LANGUAGE	Spanish
LITERACY	100%
LIFE EXPECTANCY	78 years
GDP PER CAPITA	$10,200

ECONOMY IND: petroleum, nickel, cobalt, pharmaceuticals, tobacco, construction, steel, cement, agricultural machinery, sugar AGR: sugar, tobacco, citrus, coffee, rice, potatoes, beans, livestock EXP: petroleum, nickel, medical products, sugar, tobacco, fish, citrus, coffee

Dominica
COMMONWEALTH OF DOMINICA

AREA	751 sq km (290 sq mi)
POPULATION	74,000
CAPITAL	Roseau 15,000
RELIGION	Roman Catholic, Protestant
LANGUAGE	English, French patois
LITERACY	94%
LIFE EXPECTANCY	76 years
GDP PER CAPITA	$11,600

ECONOMY IND: soap, coconut oil, tourism, copra, furniture, cement blocks, shoes AGR: bananas, citrus, mangos, root crops, coconuts, cocoa EXP: bananas, soap, bay oil, vegetables, grapefruit, oranges

Dominican Republic
DOMINICAN REPUBLIC

AREA	48,670 sq km (18,791 sq mi)
POPULATION	10,479,000
CAPITAL	Santo Domingo 2,945,000
RELIGION	Roman Catholic
LANGUAGE	Spanish
LITERACY	92%
LIFE EXPECTANCY	78 years
GDP PER CAPITA	$14,900

ECONOMY IND: tourism, sugar processing, gold mining, textiles, cement, tobacco AGR: cocoa, tobacco, sugarcane, coffee, cotton, rice, beans, potatoes, corn, bananas, cattle, pigs, dairy products, beef, eggs EXP: gold, silver, cocoa, sugar, coffee, tobacco meats, consumer goods

El Salvador
REPUBLIC OF EL SALVADOR

AREA	21,041 sq km (8,124 sq mi)
POPULATION	6,141,000
CAPITAL	San Salvador 1,098,000
RELIGION	Roman Catholic, Protestant
LANGUAGE	Spanish, Nawat
LITERACY	88%
LIFE EXPECTANCY	74 years
GDP PER CAPITA	$8,300

ECONOMY IND: food processing, beverages, petroleum, chemicals, fertilizer, textiles, furniture, light metals AGR: coffee, sugar, corn, rice, beans, oilseed, cotton, sorghum, beef, dairy products EXP: offshore assembly exports, coffee, sugar, textiles and apparel, gold, ethanol, chemicals, electricity, iron and steel manufactures

Grenada
GRENADA

AREA	344 sq km (133 sq mi)
POPULATION	111,000
CAPITAL	Saint George's 38,000
RELIGION	Roman Catholic, Protestant, Jehovah's Witness
LANGUAGE	English, French patois
LITERACY	96%
LIFE EXPECTANCY	74 years
GDP PER CAPITA	$13,000

ECONOMY IND: food and beverages, textiles, light assembly operations, tourism, construction AGR: bananas, cocoa, nutmeg, mace, citrus, avocados, root crops, sugarcane, corn, vegetables EXP: nutmeg, bananas, cocoa, fruit and vegetables, clothing, mace

Guatemala
REPUBLIC OF GUATEMALA

AREA	108,889 sq km (42,042 sq mi)
POPULATION	14,919,000
CAPITAL	Guatemala City 2,918,000
RELIGION	Roman Catholic, Protestant, indigenous Mayan beliefs
LANGUAGE	Spanish, Amerindian languages
LITERACY	82%
LIFE EXPECTANCY	72 years
GDP PER CAPITA	$7,900

ECONOMY IND: sugar, textiles and clothing, furniture, chemicals, petroleum, metals, rubber, tourism AGR: sugarcane, corn, bananas, coffee, beans, cardamom, cattle, sheep, pigs, chickens EXP: sugar, coffee, petroleum, apparel, bananas, fruits and vegetables, cardamom, manufacturing products, precious stones and metals, electricity

Haiti
REPUBLIC OF HAITI

AREA	27,750 sq km (10,714 sq mi)
POPULATION	10,110,000
CAPITAL	Port-au-Prince 2,440,000
RELIGION	Roman Catholic, Protestant
LANGUAGE	French, Creole
LITERACY	61%
LIFE EXPECTANCY	64 years
GDP PER CAPITA	$1,800

ECONOMY IND: textiles, sugar refining, flour milling, cement, light assembly based on imported parts AGR: coffee, mangoes, cocoa, sugarcane, rice, corn, sorghum, wood, vetiver EXP: apparel, manufactures, oils, cocoa, mangoes, coffee

Honduras
REPUBLIC OF HONDURAS

AREA	112,090 sq km (43,278 sq mi)
POPULATION	8,747,000
CAPITAL	Tegucigalpa 1,123,000
RELIGION	Roman Catholic, Protestant
LANGUAGE	Spanish, Amerindian dialects
LITERACY	89%
LIFE EXPECTANCY	71 years
GDP PER CAPITA	$5,000

ECONOMY IND: sugar, coffee, woven and knit apparel, wood products, cigars AGR: bananas, coffee, citrus, corn, African palm, beef, timber, shrimp, tilapia, lobster, sugar EXP: coffee, apparel, shrimp, wire harnesses, cigars, bananas, gold, palm oil, fruit, lobster, lumber

Jamaica
JAMAICA

AREA	10,991 sq km (4,244 sq mi)
POPULATION	2,950,000
CAPITAL	Kingston 588,000
RELIGION	Protestant, none
LANGUAGE	English, English patois
LITERACY	89%
LIFE EXPECTANCY	74 years
GDP PER CAPITA	$8,800

ECONOMY IND: tourism, bauxite/alumina, agro processing, light manufactures, rum, cement, metal, paper, chemical products, telecommunications AGR: sugarcane, bananas, coffee, citrus, yams, ackees, vegetables, poultry, goats, milk, crustaceans, mollusks EXP: alumina, bauxite, sugar, rum, coffee, yams, beverages, chemicals, apparel, mineral fuels

Mexico
UNITED MEXICAN STATES

AREA	1,964,375 sq km (758,445 sq mi)
POPULATION	121,737,000
CAPITAL	Mexico City 20,999,000
RELIGION	Roman Catholic
LANGUAGE	Spanish
LITERACY	95%
LIFE EXPECTANCY	76 years
GDP PER CAPITA	$18,500

ECONOMY IND: food and beverages, tobacco, chemicals, iron and steel, petroleum, mining, textiles, clothing, motor vehicles, consumer durables, tourism AGR: corn, wheat, soybeans, rice, beans, cotton, coffee, fruit, tomatoes, beef, poultry, dairy products, wood products EXP: manufactured goods, oil and oil products, silver, fruits, vegetables, coffee, cotton

Nicaragua

REPUBLIC OF NICARAGUA

AREA	130,370 sq km (50,336 sq mi)
POPULATION	5,908,000
CAPITAL	Managua 956,000
RELIGION	Roman Catholic, Protestant
LANGUAGE	Spanish, Miskito
LITERACY	83%
LIFE EXPECTANCY	73 years
GDP PER CAPITA	$5,000

ECONOMY **IND**: food processing, chemicals, machinery and metal products, knit and woven apparel, petroleum refining and distribution, beverages, footwear, wood **AGR**: coffee, bananas, sugarcane, rice, corn, tobacco, cotton, sesame, soya, beans, beef, veal, pork, poultry, dairy products, shrimp, lobsters **EXP**: coffee, beef, gold, sugar, peanuts, shrimp and lobster, tobacco, cigars, textiles and apparel

Panama

REPUBLIC OF PANAMA

AREA	75,420 sq km (29,120 sq mi)
POPULATION	3,657,000
CAPITAL	Panama City 1,673,000
RELIGION	Roman Catholic, Protestant
LANGUAGE	Spanish, English
LITERACY	95%
LIFE EXPECTANCY	78 years
GDP PER CAPITA	$20,900

ECONOMY **IND**: construction, brewing, cement and other construction materials, sugar milling **AGR**: bananas, rice, corn, coffee, sugarcane, vegetables, livestock, shrimp **EXP**: fruits and nuts, fish, iron and steel waste, wood

St. Kitts and Nevis

FEDERATION OF SAINT KITTS AND NEVIS

AREA	261 sq km (101 sq mi)
POPULATION	52,000
CAPITAL	Basseterre 14,000
RELIGION	Anglican, other Protestant, Roman Catholic
LANGUAGE	English
LITERACY	98%
LIFE EXPECTANCY	76 years
GDP PER CAPITA	$22,800

ECONOMY **IND**: tourism, cotton, salt, copra, clothing, footwear, beverages **AGR**: sugarcane, rice, yams, vegetables, bananas, fish **EXP**: machinery, food, electronics, beverages, tobacco

St. Lucia

SAINT LUCIA

AREA	616 sq km (238 sq mi)
POPULATION	164,000
CAPITAL	Castries 22,000
RELIGION	Roman Catholic, Protestant
LANGUAGE	English, French patois
LITERACY	90%
LIFE EXPECTANCY	78 years
GDP PER CAPITA	$12,000

ECONOMY **IND**: tourism, clothing, assembly of electronic components, beverages, corrugated cardboard boxes, lime processing, coconut processing **AGR**: bananas, coconuts, vegetables, citrus, root crops, cocoa **EXP**: bananas, clothing, cocoa, avocados, mangoes coconut oil

St. Vincent and the Grenadines

SAINT VINCENT AND THE GRENADINES

AREA	389 sq km (150 sq mi)
POPULATION	103,000
CAPITAL	Kingstown 27,000
RELIGION	Protestant, Roman Catholic
LANGUAGE	English, French patois
LITERACY	96%
LIFE EXPECTANCY	75 years
GDP PER CAPITA	$11,000

ECONOMY **IND**: tourism, food processing, cement, furniture, clothing **AGR**: bananas, coconuts, sweet potatoes, spices, fish **EXP**: bananas, taro, arrowroot, rice

Trinidad and Tobago

REPUBLIC OF TRINIDAD AND TOBAGO

AREA	5,128 sq km (1,980 sq mi)
POPULATION	1,222,000
CAPITAL	Port of Spain 34,000
RELIGION	Protestant, Roman Catholic, Hindu
LANGUAGE	English, Caribbean Hindustani, French, Spanish
LITERACY	99%
LIFE EXPECTANCY	73 years
GDP PER CAPITA	$32,800

ECONOMY **IND**: petroleum and petroleum products, liquefied natural gas (LNG), methanol, ammonia, urea, steel products, beverages, food processing, cement, cotton textiles **AGR**: cocoa, rice, citrus, coffee, vegetables, poultry **EXP**: petroleum and petroleum products, liquefied natural gas (LNG), methanol, ammonia, urea, steel products, beverages, cereal and cereal products, sugar, cocoa, coffee, citrus fruit, vegetables, flowers

United States

UNITED STATES OF AMERICA

AREA	9,826,675 sq km (3,794,079 sq mi)
POPULATION	322,560,000
CAPITAL	Washington, D.C. 4,995,000
RELIGION	Protestant, Roman Catholic, unaffiliated
LANGUAGE	English, Spanish
LITERACY	99%
LIFE EXPECTANCY	80 years
GDP PER CAPITA	$56,300

ECONOMY **IND**: petroleum, steel, motor vehicles, aerospace, telecommunications, chemicals, electronics, food processing, consumer goods, lumber, mining **AGR**: wheat, corn, other grains, fruits, vegetables, cotton, beef, pork, poultry, dairy products, fish, forest products **EXP**: agricultural products, industrial supplies, capital goods, consumer goods

DEPENDENCIES

Anguilla

(U.K.)
ANGUILLA

AREA	91 sq km (35 sq mi)
POPULATION	16,400
CAPITAL	The Valley 1,000
RELIGION	Protestant, Roman Catholic
LANGUAGE	English
LITERACY	95%
LIFE EXPECTANCY	81 years
GDP PER CAPITA	NA

ECONOMY **IND**: tourism, boat building, offshore financial services **AGR**: small quantities of tobacco, vegetables, cattle raising **EXP**: lobster, fish, livestock, salt, concrete blocks, rum

Aruba

(NETHERLANDS)
ARUBA

AREA	180 sq km (69 sq mi)
POPULATION	112,000
CAPITAL	Oranjestad 29,000
RELIGION	Roman Catholic, Protestant
LANGUAGE	Papiamento, Spanish, English, Dutch
LITERACY	98%
LIFE EXPECTANCY	77 years
GDP PER CAPITA	$25,300

ECONOMY **IND**: tourism, transshipment facilities, banking **AGR**: aloes, livestock, fish **EXP**: live animals and animal products, art and collectibles, machinery and electrical equipment, transport equipment

Bermuda

(U.K.)
BERMUDA

AREA	54 sq km (21 sq mi)
POPULATION	70,000
CAPITAL	Hamilton 10,000
RELIGION	Protestant, Roman Catholic, none
LANGUAGE	English, Portuguese
LITERACY	98%
LIFE EXPECTANCY	81 years
GDP PER CAPITA	$85,700

ECONOMY **IND**: international business, tourism, light manufacturing **AGR**: bananas, vegetables, citrus, flowers, dairy products, honey **EXP**: reexports of pharmaceuticals

British Virgin Islands

(U.K.)
BRITISH VIRGIN ISLANDS

AREA	151 sq km (58 sq mi)
POPULATION	33,000
CAPITAL	Road Town 13,000
RELIGION	Protestant, Roman Catholic
LANGUAGE	English
LITERACY	98%
LIFE EXPECTANCY	78 years
GDP PER CAPITA	$42,300

ECONOMY **IND**: tourism, light industry, construction, rum, concrete block, offshore financial center **AGR**: fruits, vegetables, livestock, poultry, fish **EXP**: rum, fresh fish, fruits, animals, gravel, sand

Cayman Islands

(U.K.)
CAYMAN ISLANDS

AREA	264 sq km (102 sq mi)
POPULATION	56,000
CAPITAL	George Town 31,000
RELIGION	Protestant, Roman Catholic
LANGUAGE	English
LITERACY	99%
LIFE EXPECTANCY	81 years
GDP PER CAPITA	$43,800

ECONOMY **IND**: tourism, banking, insurance and finance, construction, construction materials **AGR**: vegetables, fruit, livestock, turtle farming **EXP**: turtle products, manufactured consumer goods

Curaçao
(NETHERLANDS)
CURAÇAO

AREA	444 sq km (171 sq mi)
POPULATION	147,000
CAPITAL	Willemstad 145,000
RELIGION	Roman Catholic, Pentecostal, Protestant
LANGUAGE	Papiamento, Dutch
LITERACY	NA
LIFE EXPECTANCY	78
GDP PER CAPITA	$15,000

ECONOMY **IND**: tourism, petroleum refining, petroleum transshipment facilities, light manufacturing, financial and business services **AGR**: aloe, sorghum, peanuts, vegetables, tropical fruit **EXP**: petroleum products

Greenland

(DENMARK)
GREENLAND

AREA	2,166,086 sq km (836,326 sq mi)
POPULATION	58,000
CAPITAL	Nuuk (Godthåb) 17,000
RELIGION	Evangelical Lutheran, traditional Inuit spiritual beliefs
LANGUAGE	Greenlandic, Danish, English
LITERACY	100%
LIFE EXPECTANCY	72 years
GDP PER CAPITA	$37,900

ECONOMY **IND**: fish processing, gold, niobium, tantalite, uranium, iron and diamond mining, handicrafts, hides and skins, small shipyards **AGR**: sheep, cow, reindeer, fish **EXP**: fish and fish products, metals

Guadeloupe, Martinique
(FRANCE)

Guadeloupe and Martinique are French overseas departments, having equal status to the 13 metropolitan regions that make up European France. Please see "France" for facts about Guadeloupe and Martinique.

Montserrat

(U.K.)
MONTSERRAT

AREA	102 sq km (39 sq mi)
POPULATION	5,240
CAPITAL	Brades (interim) 1,000 Plymouth (abandoned)
RELIGION	Protestant, Roman Catholic
LANGUAGE	English
LITERACY	97%
LIFE EXPECTANCY	74 years
GDP PER CAPITA	$8,500

ECONOMY **IND**: tourism, rum, textiles, electronic appliances **AGR**: cabbages, carrots, cucumbers, tomatoes, onions, peppers, livestock products **EXP**: electronic components, plastic bags, apparel, hot peppers, limes, live plants, cattle

Puerto Rico

(U.S.)
COMMONWEALTH OF PUERTO RICO

AREA	13,790 sq km (5,324 sq mi)
POPULATION	3,474,000
CAPITAL	San Juan 2,463,000
RELIGION	Roman Catholic, Protestant
LANGUAGE	Spanish, English
LITERACY	93%
LIFE EXPECTANCY	79 years
GDP PER CAPITA	$28,500

ECONOMY **IND**: pharmaceuticals, electronics, apparel, food products, tourism **AGR**: sugarcane, coffee, pineapples, plantains, bananas, livestock products, chickens **EXP**: chemicals, electronics, apparel, canned tuna, rum, beverage concentrates, medical equipment

St.-Barthélemy
(FRANCE)
SAINT-BARTHÉLEMY

AREA	21 sq km (8 sq mi)
POPULATION	7,200
CAPITAL	Gustavia 2,000
RELIGION	Roman Catholic, Protestant, Jehovah's Witnesses
LANGUAGE	French, English
LITERACY	NA
LIFE EXPECTANCY	NA
GDP PER CAPITA	NA

ECONOMY **IND**: NA **AGR**: NA **EXP**: NA

Flags and Facts

St.-Martin
(FRANCE)
SAINT-MARTIN

AREA	54 sq km (21 sq mi)
POPULATION	32,000
CAPITAL	Marigot 6,000
RELIGION	Roman Catholic, Jehovah's Witnesses, Protestant
LANGUAGE	French, English, Dutch, French patois, Spanish, Papiamento
LITERACY	NA
LIFE EXPECTANCY	NA
GDP PER CAPITA	19,300
ECONOMY	IND: tourism, light industry and manufacturing, heavy industry AGR: NA EXP: NA

St.-Pierre and Miquelon
(FRANCE)
TERRITORIAL COLLECTIVITY OF SAINT-PIERRE AND MIQUELON

AREA	242 sq km (93 sq mi)
POPULATION	5,700
CAPITAL	Saint-Pierre 5,000
RELIGION	Roman Catholic
LANGUAGE	French
LITERACY	99%
LIFE EXPECTANCY	80 years
GDP PER CAPITA	$34,900
ECONOMY	IND: fish processing and supply base for fishing fleets, tourism AGR: vegetables, poultry, cattle, sheep, pigs, fish EXP: meat, clothing, fuel, electrical equipment, machinery, building materials

Sint Maarten
(NETHERLANDS)
COUNTRY OF SINT MAARTEN

AREA	34 sq km (13 sq mi)
POPULATION	38,000
CAPITAL	Philipsburg 1,300
RELIGION	Protestant, Roman Catholic
LANGUAGE	English, Spanish, Dutch, Papiamento
LITERACY	NA
LIFE EXPECTANCY	78
GDP PER CAPITA	$66,800
ECONOMY	IND: tourism, light industry AGR: sugar EXP: sugar

Turks and Caicos Islands
(U.K.)
TURKS AND CAICOS ISLANDS

AREA	948 sq km (366 sq mi)
POPULATION	50,000
CAPITAL	Cockburn Town 5,000
RELIGION	Protestant, Roman Catholic
LANGUAGE	English
LITERACY	98%
LIFE EXPECTANCY	79 years
GDP PER CAPITA	$29,100
ECONOMY	IND: tourism, offshore financial services AGR: corn, beans, cassava (tapioca), citrus fruits, fish EXP: lobster, dried and fresh conch, conch shells

Virgin Islands
(U.S.)
UNITED STATES VIRGIN ISLANDS

AREA	1,910 sq km (737 sq mi)
POPULATION	104,000
CAPITAL	Charlotte Amalie 52,000
RELIGION	Protestant, Roman Catholic
LANGUAGE	English, Spanish, Spanish Creole
LITERACY	90-95%
LIFE EXPECTANCY	80 years
GDP PER CAPITA	$36,100
ECONOMY	IND: tourism, watch assembly, rum distilling, construction, pharmaceuticals, electronics AGR: fruit, vegetables, sorghum, Senepol cattle EXP: rum

UNITED STATES' STATE FLAGS

Alabama
POPULATION 4,859,000
CAPITAL Montgomery

Hawai'i
POPULATION 1,432,000
CAPITAL Honolulu

Massachusetts
POPULATION 6,794,000
CAPITAL Boston

New Mexico
POPULATION 2,085,000
CAPITAL Santa Fe

South Dakota
POPULATION 858,000
CAPITAL Pierre

Alaska
POPULATION 738,000
CAPITAL Juneau

Idaho
POPULATION 1,655,000
CAPITAL Boise

Michigan
POPULATION 9,923,000
CAPITAL Lansing

New York
POPULATION 19,796,000
CAPITAL Albany

Tennessee
POPULATION 6,600,000
CAPITAL Nashville

Arizona
POPULATION 6,828,000
CAPITAL Phoenix

Illinois
POPULATION 12,860,000
CAPITAL Springfield

Minnesota
POPULATION 5,490,000
CAPITAL St. Paul

North Carolina
POPULATION 10,043,000
CAPITAL Raleigh

Texas
POPULATION 27,469,000
CAPITAL Austin

Arkansas
POPULATION 2,978,000
CAPITAL Little Rock

Indiana
POPULATION 6,620,000
CAPITAL Indianapolis

Mississippi
POPULATION 2,992,000
CAPITAL Jackson

North Dakota
POPULATION 757,000
CAPITAL Bismarck

Utah
POPULATION 2,996,000
CAPITAL Salt Lake City

California
POPULATION 39,145,000
CAPITAL Sacramento

Iowa
POPULATION 3,124,000
CAPITAL Des Moines

Missouri
POPULATION 6,084,000
CAPITAL Jefferson City

Ohio
POPULATION 11,613,000
CAPITAL Columbus

Vermont
POPULATION 626,000
CAPITAL Montpelier

Colorado
POPULATION 5,457,000
CAPITAL Denver

Kansas
POPULATION 2,912,000
CAPITAL Topeka

Montana
POPULATION 1,033,000
CAPITAL Helena

Oklahoma
POPULATION 3,911,000
CAPITAL Oklahoma City

Virginia
POPULATION 8,383,000
CAPITAL Richmond

Connecticut
POPULATION 3,591,000
CAPITAL Hartford

Kentucky
POPULATION 4,425,000
CAPITAL Frankfort

Nebraska
POPULATION 1,896,000
CAPITAL Lincoln

Oregon
POPULATION 4,028,000
CAPITAL Salem

Washington
POPULATION 7,170,000
CAPITAL Olympia

Delaware
POPULATION 946,000
CAPITAL Dover

Louisiana
POPULATION 4,671,000
CAPITAL Baton Rouge

Nevada
POPULATION 2,891,000
CAPITAL Carson City

Pennsylvania
POPULATION 12,803,000
CAPITAL Harrisburg

West Virginia
POPULATION 1,844,000
CAPITAL Charleston

Florida
POPULATION 20,271,000
CAPITAL Tallahassee

Maine
POPULATION 1,329,000
CAPITAL Augusta

New Hampshire
POPULATION 1,331,000
CAPITAL Concord

Rhode Island
POPULATION 1,056,000
CAPITAL Providence

Wisconsin
POPULATION 5,771,000
CAPITAL Madison

Georgia
POPULATION 10,215,000
CAPITAL Atlanta

Maryland
POPULATION 6,006,000
CAPITAL Annapolis

New Jersey
POPULATION 8,958,000
CAPITAL Trenton

South Carolina
POPULATION 4,896,000
CAPITAL Columbia

Wyoming
POPULATION 586,000
CAPITAL Cheyenne

District of Columbia
POPULATION 672,000
United States capital

Protected Areas

ARCTIC OCEAN

GREENLAND
(Denmark)

UNITED STATES

LABRADOR SEA

HUDSON BAY

CANADA

PACIFIC OCEAN

ST.-PIERRE AND MIQUELON
(France)

ATLANTIC OCEAN

UNITED STATES

BERMUDA
(U.K.)

ANGUILLA
(U.K.)

ST. MAARTEN
(Netherlands)

ST.-MARTIN
(France)

VIRGIN ISLANDS
(U.S. and U.K.)

ST.-BARTHÉLEMY
(France)

ST. KITTS AND
NEVIS

ANTIGUA AND
BARBUDA

BAHAMAS

MONTSERRAT
(U.K.)

TURKS AND
CAICOS ISLANDS
(U.K.)

CUBA

DOMINICAN
REPUBLIC

GUADELOUPE
(France)

GULF OF MEXICO

DOMINICA

CAYMAN ISLANDS
(U.K.)

PUERTO RICO
(U.S.)

MARTINIQUE
(France)

MEXICO

HAITI

ST. LUCIA

BELIZE

JAMAICA

CURAÇAO
(Netherlands)

ST. VINCENT AND
THE GRENADINES

BARBADOS

HONDURAS

GRENADA

C A R I B B E A N   S E A

GUATEMALA

ARUBA
(Netherlands)

TRINIDAD
AND
TOBAGO

EL SALVADOR

NICARAGUA

COSTA RICA

PANAMA

Cocos Island
(Costa Rica)

Protected Areas
- Terrestrial
- Marine

*Protected areas as defined by the
International Union for Conservation
of Nature (IUCN). The degree of
protection and governing body varies
by protected area.*

Azimuthal Equidistant Projection
SCALE 1:36,050,000

0 km   300   600
0 mi   300   600
1 CENTIMETER = 361 KILOMETERS; 1 INCH = 569 MILES

South America

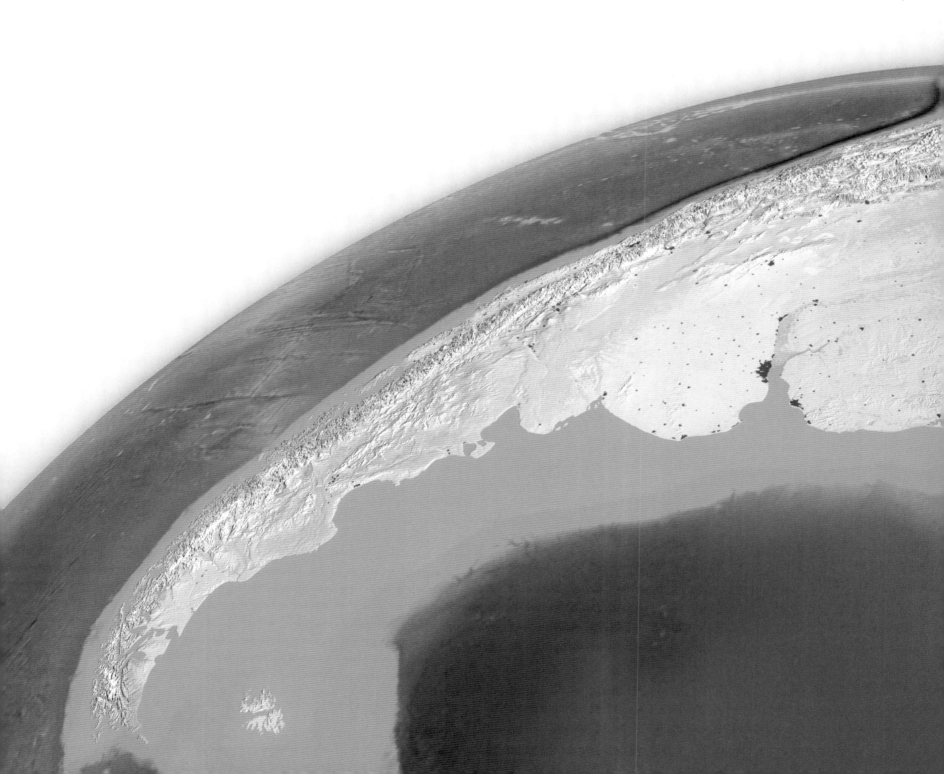

CONTINENT OF EXTREMES, South America extends from the Isthmus of Panama, in the Northern Hemisphere, to a ragged tail less than 700 miles (1,130 kilometers) from Antarctica. There the Andes, a continuous continental rampart that forms the world's second highest range, finally dives undersea to continue as a submarine ridge. Occupying nearly half the continent, the world's largest and biologically richest rain forest spans the Equator, drained by the Amazon River, second longest river in the world but largest by volume anywhere.

These formidable natural barriers shaped lopsided patterns of settlement in South America, the fourth largest continent. As early as 1531, when Spaniard Francisco Pizarro began his conquest of the Inca Empire, Iberians were pouring into coastal settlements that now hold most of the continent's burgeoning population. Meanwhile, Portuguese planters imported millions of African slaves to work vast sugar estates on Brazil's littoral. There and elsewhere, wealth and power coalesced in family oligarchies and in the Roman Catholic Church, building a system that 19th-century liberal revolutions failed to dismantle.

Independence did not necessarily bring regional unity: Boundary wars dragged on into the 20th century before yielding the present-day borders of 12 nations. French Guiana remains an overseas department of France; the Falkland Islands a dependency of the United Kingdom.

Natural riches still dominate economies, in the form of processed agricultural goods and minerals, as manufacturing matures. Privatization of nationalized industries in the 1990s followed free-market policies instituted by military regimes in the '70s and '80s, sometimes adding tumult to nations troubled by debt and inflation. By the end of the century; however, democracy had flowered across the continent, spurring an era of relative prosperity.

A rich blend of Iberian, African, and Amerindian traditions, South America has one of the world's liveliest and most distinctive cultures. Although the majority of people can still trace their ancestors back to Spain or Portugal, waves of immigration have transformed South America into an ethnic smorgasbord. This blend has produced a vibrant modern culture with influence far beyond the bounds of its South American cradle.

The vast majority of South Americans live in cities rather than the rain forest or mountains. A massive rural exodus since the 1950s has transformed South America into the second most urbanized continent (after Australia), a region that now boasts 3 of the world's 15 largest cities—São Paulo, Buenos Aires, and Rio de Janeiro. Ninety percent of the people live within 200 miles (320 kilometers) of the coast, leaving huge expanses of the interior virtually unpopulated. Despite protests from indigenous tribes and environmental groups, South American governments have tried to spur growth by opening up the Amazon region to economic exploitation, thereby wreaking ecological havoc. The Amazon could very well be the key to the region's economic future—not by the exploitation of the world's richest forest, but by the sustainable management and commercial development of its largely untapped biodiversity into medical, chemical, and nutritional products.

ATLANTIC OCEAN

CARIBBEAN SEA

LESSER ANTILLES

EQUATOR

Mouths of the Amazon.

GUIANA HIGHLANDS

World's highest waterfall
Angel Falls
Total drop 970 meters
(3212 ft)

AMAZON

BASIN

LA MONTAÑA

CORDILLERA OCCIDENTAL

ANDES

Atacama Desert

BRAZILIAN HIGHLANDS

Serra do Espinhaço

Espigão Mestre

Chapada dos Parecis

Chaco Boreal

Chaco Central

Pantanal

TROPIC OF CAPRICORN

Sechura Desert

Santa Elena Peninsula

Altiplano

Cordillera Central
Cordillera Oriental

Yungas

Maracaibo Basin

Guajira Peninsula

PANAMA CANAL
Isthmus of Panama

South America
Physical

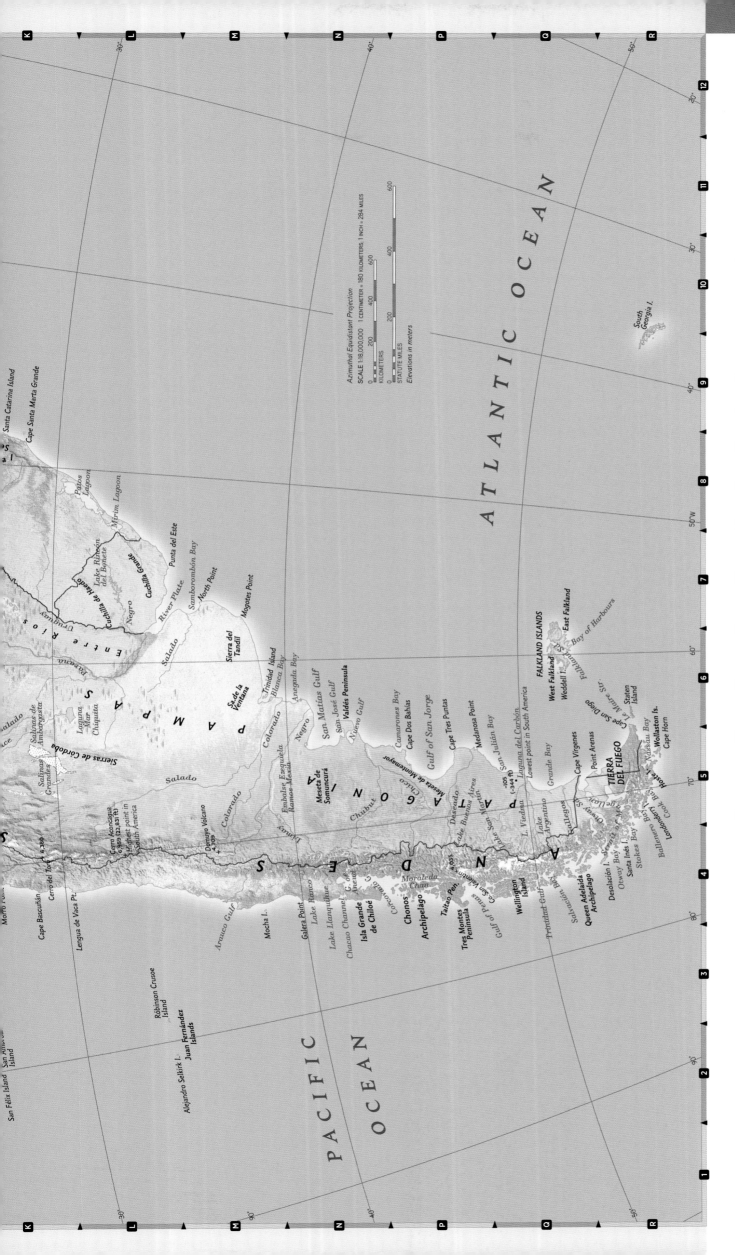

Continental Data

Area: 17,819,000 sq km
(6,880,000 sq mi)

Greatest north-south extent:
7,645 km (4,750 mi)

Greatest east-west extent:
5,150 km (3,200 mi)

Highest point:
Cerro Aconcagua, Argentina
6,959 m (22,831 ft)

Lowest point:
Laguna del Carbón, Argentina
-105 m (-344 ft)

Lowest recorded temperature:
Sarmiento, Argentina -33°C
(-27°F), June 1, 1907

Highest recorded temperature:
Rivadavia, Argentina
49°C (120°F), December 11, 1905

Longest rivers:
• Amazon 6,437 km (4,000 mi)
• Paraná-Río de la Plata
4,000 km (2,485 mi)
• Purus 3,380 km (2,100 mi)

Largest natural lakes:
• Lake Maracaibo (recognized by
some as a lake) 13,280 sq km
(5,127 sq mi)
• Lake Titicaca 8,372 sq km
(3,232 sq mi)
• Lake Poopó, 2,499 sq km
(965 sq mi)

**Earth's extremes located
in South America:**
• Driest Place:
Arica, Atacama Desert, Chile;
rainfall barely measurable
• Highest Waterfall:
Angel Falls, Venezuela
979 m (3,212 ft)

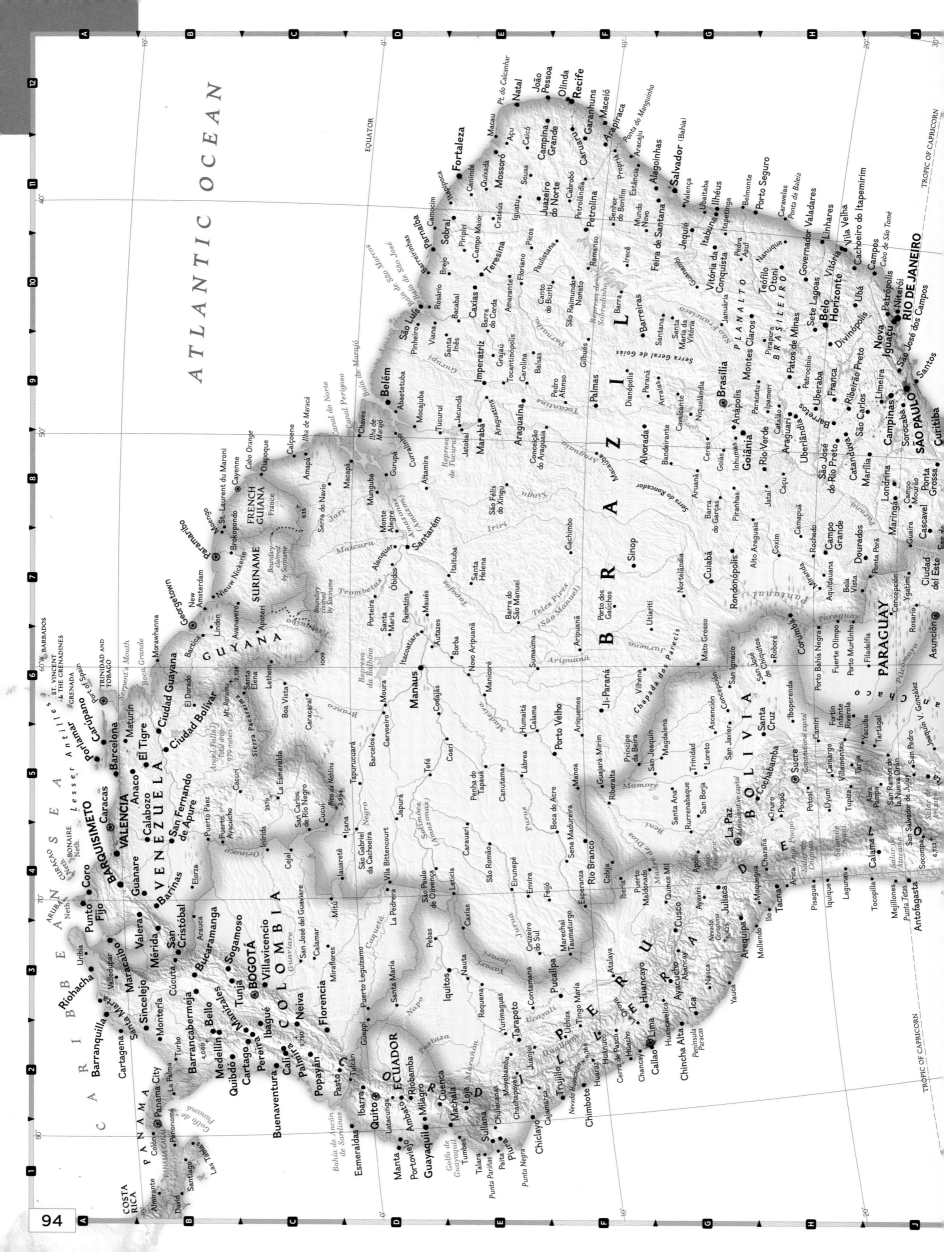

ATLANTIC OCEAN

EQUATOR

Continental Data

Total number of countries: 12

First independent country:
Colombia, July 20, 1810

"Youngest" country:
Suriname, Nov. 25, 1975

Largest country by area:
Brazil 8,515,770 sq km
(3,287,956 sq mi)

Smallest country by area:
Suriname 163,820 sq km
(63,251 sq mi)

Percent urban population: 84%

Most populous country:
Brazil 204,260,000

Least populous country:
Suriname 580,000

**Most densely
populated country:**
Ecuador 56 per sq km
(145 per sq mi)

**Least densely
populated country:**
Guyana 3 per sq km
(8 per sq mi)

Largest city by population:
São Paulo, Brazil 21,066,000

Highest GDP per capita:
Chile $23,800

Lowest GDP per capita:
Bolivia $6,500

Average life expectancy: 75 years

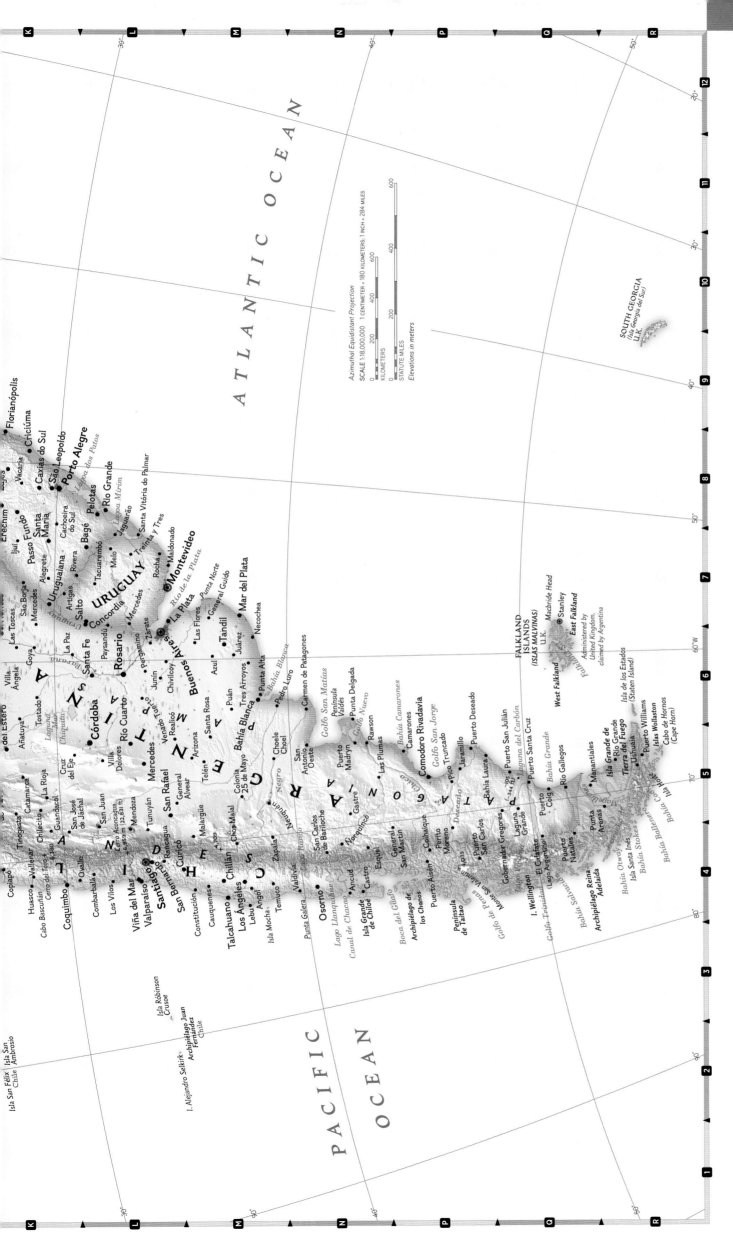

Human and Natural Themes

POPULATION DENSITY

VENEZUELA
GUYANA
SURINAME
FRENCH GUIANA (FRANCE)
COLOMBIA
ECUADOR
GALÁPAGOS ISLANDS (ECUADOR)
PERU
BRAZIL
BOLIVIA
PARAGUAY
CHILE
ARGENTINA
URUGUAY
FALKLAND ISLANDS (U.K.)
POPULATION DENSITY
People per Square Kilometer
People per Square Mile
More than 195 — More than 500
60–195 — 150–500
10–59 — 25–149
1–9 — 1–24
Less than 1 — Less than 1

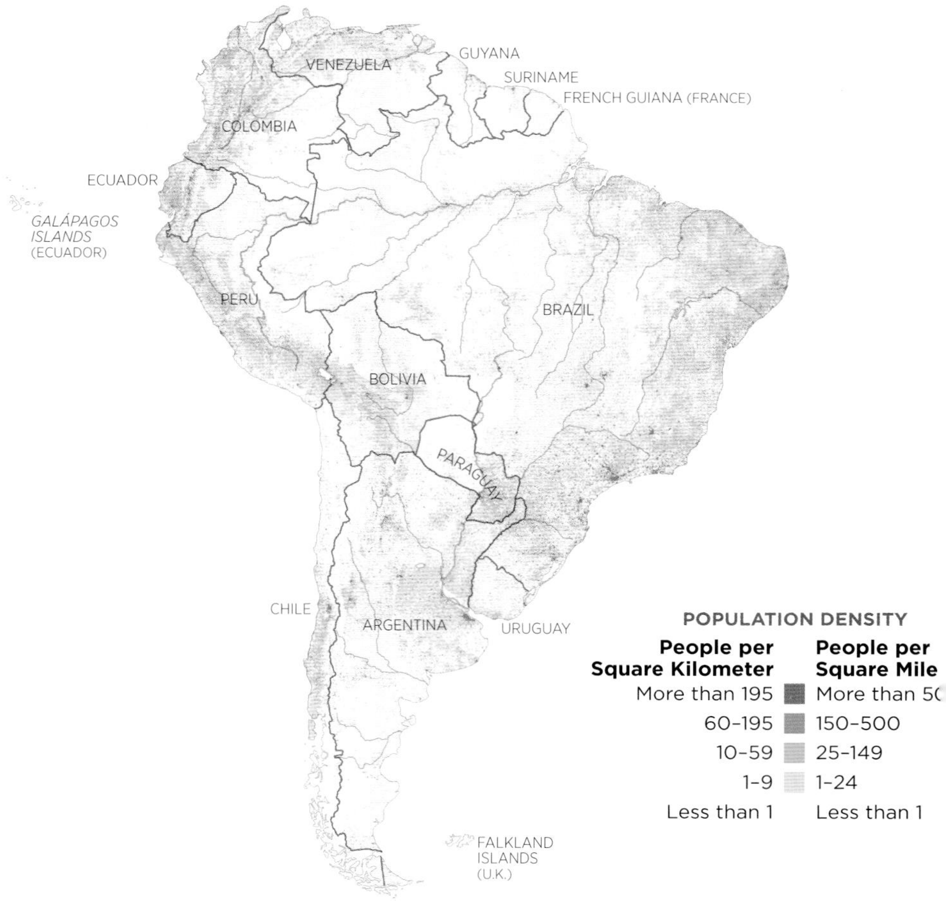

ENERGY CONSUMPTION

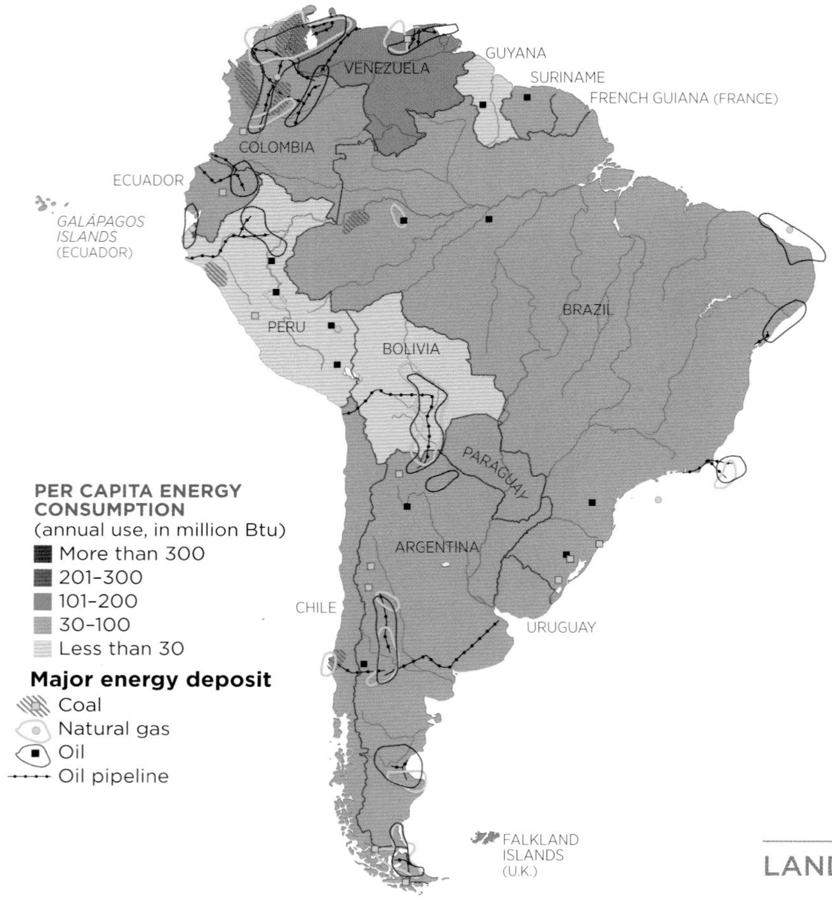

VENEZUELA
GUYANA
SURINAME
FRENCH GUIANA (FRANCE)
COLOMBIA
ECUADOR
GALÁPAGOS ISLANDS (ECUADOR)
PERU
BRAZIL
BOLIVIA
PARAGUAY
ARGENTINA
CHILE
URUGUAY
FALKLAND ISLANDS (U.K.)
PER CAPITA ENERGY CONSUMPTION
(annual use, in million Btu)
More than 300
201–300
101–200
30–100
Less than 30
Major energy deposit
Coal
Natural gas
Oil
Oil pipeline

LAND COVER

VENEZUELA
GUYANA
SURINAME
FRENCH GUIANA (FRANCE)
COLOMBIA
ECUADOR
GALÁPAGOS ISLANDS (ECUADOR)
PERU
BRAZIL
BOLIVIA
PARAGUAY
ARGENTINA
CHILE
URUGUAY
FALKLAND ISLANDS (U.K.)
LAND COVER
Evergreen needleleaf forest
Evergreen broadleaf forest
Deciduous needleleaf forest
Deciduous broadleaf forest
Mixed forest
Woody savanna
Savanna
Closed shrubland
Open shrubland
Grassland
Cropland
Barren or sparsely vegetated
Urban or built-up
Snow and ice
Cropland/natural vegetation mosaic
Wetland

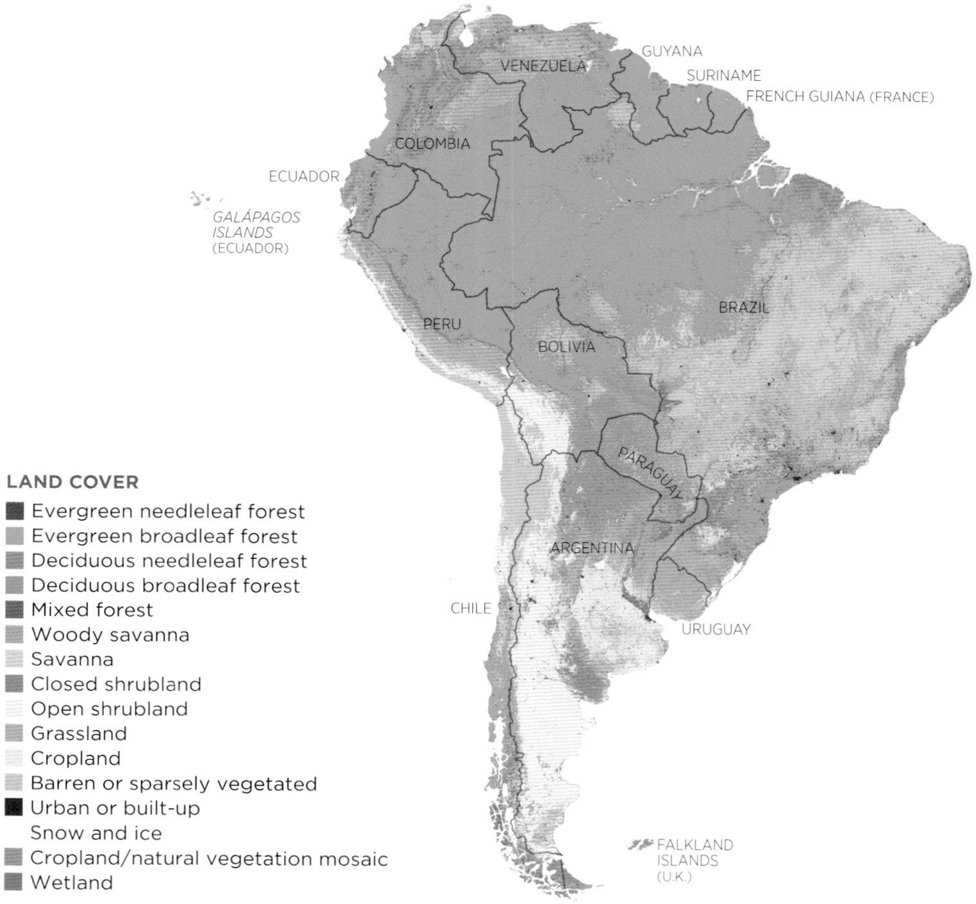

CLIMATIC ZONES

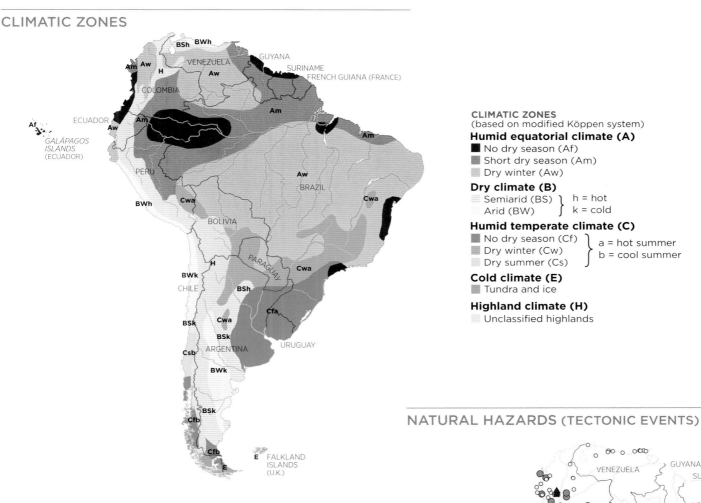

CLIMATIC ZONES
(based on modified Köppen system)
Humid equatorial climate (A)
■ No dry season (Af)
■ Short dry season (Am)
□ Dry winter (Aw)
Dry climate (B)
Semiarid (BS)   } h = hot
Arid (BW)   } k = cold
Humid temperate climate (C)
■ No dry season (Cf) } a = hot summer
■ Dry winter (Cw)   } b = cool summer
□ Dry summer (Cs)
Cold climate (E)
■ Tundra and ice
Highland climate (H)
□ Unclassified highlands

NATURAL HAZARDS (TECTONIC EVENTS)

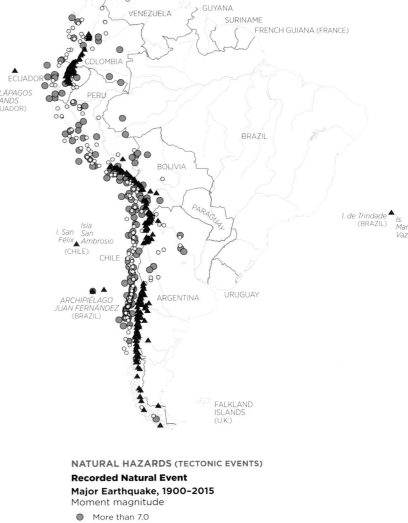

NATURAL HAZARDS (TECTONIC EVENTS)
Recorded Natural Event
Major Earthquake, 1900–2015
Moment magnitude
● More than 7.0
○ 6.0–7.0

Volcano
▲

Tsunami, 1900–2015
Run-up height
● More than 10 meters (32 feet)
○ 5–10 meters (16–32 feet)

WATER AVAILABILITY

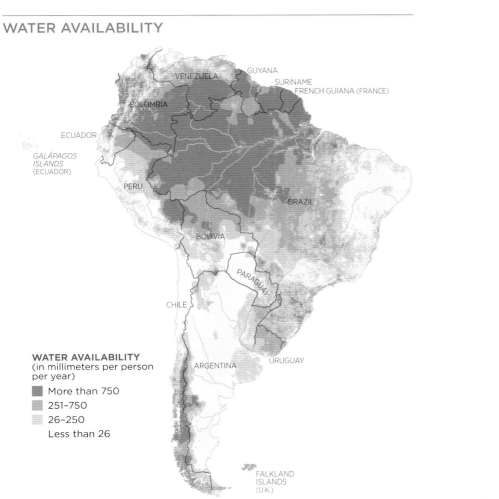

WATER AVAILABILITY
(in millimeters per person
per year)
■ More than 750
■ 251–750
□ 26–250
□ Less than 26

Flags and Facts

COUNTRIES

Argentina
ARGENTINE REPUBLIC

AREA	2,780,400 sq km
	(1,073,512 sq mi)
POPULATION	43,432,000
CAPITAL	Buenos Aires 15,180,000
RELIGION	Roman Catholic
LANGUAGE	Spanish, Italian, English, German, French
LITERACY	98%
LIFE EXPECTANCY	78 years
GDP PER CAPITA	$22,400

ECONOMY IND: food processing, motor vehicles, consumer durables, textiles, chemicals and petrochemicals, printing, metallurgy, steel **AGR:** sunflower seeds, lemons, soybeans, grapes, corn, tobacco, peanuts, tea, wheat, livestock **EXP:** soybeans and derivatives, petroleum and gas, vehicles, corn, wheat

Bolivia
PLURINATIONAL STATE OF BOLIVIA

AREA	1,098,581 sq km
	(424,164 sq mi)
POPULATION	10,801,000
CAPITAL	La Paz (administrative) 1,816,000, Sucre (constitutional) 372,000
RELIGION	Roman Catholic
LANGUAGE	Spanish, Quechua, Aymara
LITERACY	96%
LIFE EXPECTANCY	69 years
GDP PER CAPITA	$6,500

ECONOMY IND: mining, smelting, petroleum, food and beverages, tobacco, handicrafts, clothing **AGR:** soybeans, quinoa, Brazil nuts, sugarcane, coffee, corn, rice, potatoes, chia, coca **EXP:** natural gas, mineral ores, gold, soybeans and soy products, tin

Brazil
FEDERATIVE REPUBLIC OF BRAZIL

AREA	8,515,770 sq km
	(3,287,956 sq mi)
POPULATION	204,260,000
CAPITAL	Brasília 4,155,000
RELIGION	Roman Catholic, Protestant
LANGUAGE	Portuguese
LITERACY	93%
LIFE EXPECTANCY	74 years
GDP PER CAPITA	$15,800

ECONOMY IND: textiles, shoes, chemicals, cement, lumber, iron ore, tin, steel, aircraft, motor vehicles and parts, other machinery and equipment **AGR:** coffee, soybeans, wheat, rice, corn, sugarcane, cocoa, citrus, beef **EXP:** transport equipment, iron ore, soybeans, footwear, coffee, autos

Chile
REPUBLIC OF CHILE

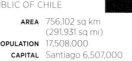

AREA	756,102 sq km
	(291,931 sq mi)
POPULATION	17,508,000
CAPITAL	Santiago 6,507,000
RELIGION	Roman Catholic, Evangelical
LANGUAGE	Spanish, English, Indigenous
LITERACY	98%
LIFE EXPECTANCY	79 years
GDP PER CAPITA	$23,800

ECONOMY IND: copper, lithium, other minerals, foodstuffs, fish processing, iron and steel, wood and wood products, transport equipment **AGR:** grapes, apples, pears, onions, wheat, corn, oats, peaches, garlic, asparagus, beans, beef, poultry, wool, fish, timber **EXP:** copper, fruit, fish products, paper and pulp, chemicals, wine

Colombia
REPUBLIC OF COLOMBIA

AREA	1,138,910 sq km
	(439,733 sq mi)
POPULATION	46,737,000
CAPITAL	Bogotá 9,765,000
RELIGION	Roman Catholic
LANGUAGE	Spanish
LITERACY	95%
LIFE EXPECTANCY	75 years
GDP PER CAPITA	$14,000

ECONOMY IND: textiles, food processing, oil, clothing and footwear, beverages, chemicals, cement, gold, coal, emeralds **AGR:** coffee, cut flowers, bananas, rice, tobacco, corn, sugarcane, cocoa beans, oilseed, vegetables, shrimp, forest products **EXP:** petroleum, coal, emeralds, coffee nickel, cut flowers, bananas, apparel

Ecuador
REPUBLIC OF ECUADOR

AREA	283,561 sq km
	(109,483 sq mi)
POPULATION	15,868,000
CAPITAL	Quito 1,726,000
RELIGION	Roman Catholic
LANGUAGE	Spanish, Quechua
LITERACY	96%
LIFE EXPECTANCY	77 years
GDP PER CAPITA	$11,300

ECONOMY IND: petroleum, food processing, textiles, wood products, chemicals **AGR:** bananas, coffee, cocoa, rice, potatoes, cassava (tapioca), plantains, sugarcane, cattle, sheep, pigs, beef, pork, dairy products, fish, shrimp balsa wood **EXP:** petroleum, bananas, cut flowers, shrimp, cacao, coffee, wood, fish

Guyana
CO-OPERATIVE REPUBLIC OF GUYANA

AREA	214,969 sq km
	(83,000 sq mi)
POPULATION	735,000
CAPITAL	Georgetown 124,000
RELIGION	Protestant, Hindu
LANGUAGE	English, Guyanese Creole, Amerinidian dialects, Indian languages
LITERACY	89%
LIFE EXPECTANCY	68 years
GDP PER CAPITA	$7,200

ECONOMY IND: bauxite, sugar, rice milling, timber, textiles, gold mining **AGR:** sugarcane, rice, edible oils, beef, pork, poultry, shrimp, fish **EXP:** sugar, gold, bauxite, alumina, rice, shrimp, molasses, rum, timber

Paraguay
REPUBLIC OF PARAGUAY

AREA	406,752 sq km
	(157,047 sq mi)
POPULATION	6,783,000
CAPITAL	Asunción 2,356,000
RELIGION	Roman Catholic
LANGUAGE	Spanish, Guarani
LITERACY	94%
LIFE EXPECTANCY	77 years
GDP PER CAPITA	$8,800

ECONOMY IND: sugar, cement, textiles, beverages, wood products, steel, metallurgy, electric power **AGR:** cotton, sugarcane, soybeans, corn, wheat, tobacco, cassava (tapioca), fruits, vegetables, beef, pork, eggs, milk, timber **EXP:** soybeans, feed, cotton, meat, edible oils, wood, leather

Peru
REPUBLIC OF PERU

AREA	1,285,216 sq km
	(496,222 sq mi)
POPULATION	30,445,000
CAPITAL	Lima 9,897,000
RELIGION	Roman Catholic, Evangelical
LANGUAGE	Spanish, Quechua, Aymara, Ashaninka
LITERACY	95%
LIFE EXPECTANCY	73 years
GDP PER CAPITA	$12,300

ECONOMY IND: mining and refining of minerals, steel, metal fabrication, petroleum extraction and refining, natural gas and natural gas liquefaction, fishing and fish processing, cement, glass, textiles, clothing, food processing **AGR:** artichokes, asparagus, avocados, blueberries, coffee, cocoa, cotton, sugarcane, rice, potatoes, corn, plantains, grapes, oranges, pineapples, guavas, bananas, apples, lemons, pears, coca, tomatoes, mango, barley, medicinal plants, quinioa, palm oil, marigolds, onions, wheat, dry beans, poultry, beef, dairy products **EXP:** copper, gold, lead, zinc, tin, iron ore, molybdenum, crude petroleum and petroleum products, natural gas, coffee, asparagus and other vegetables, fruit, apparel and textiles, fishmeal

Suriname
REPUBLIC OF SURINAME

AREA	163,820 sq km
	(63,251 sq mi)
POPULATION	580,000
CAPITAL	Paramaribo 234,000
RELIGION	Hindu, Protestant, Roman Catholic, Muslim
LANGUAGE	Dutch, English, Sranang Tongo, Caribbean Hindustani, Javanese
LITERACY	96%
LIFE EXPECTANCY	72 years
GDP PER CAPITA	$16,700

ECONOMY IND: bauxite and gold mining, alumina production, oil, lumbering, food processing, fishing **AGR:** rice, bananas, palm kernels, coconuts, plantains, peanuts, beef, chickens, shrimp, forest products **EXP:** alumina, gold, crude oil, lumber, shrimp and fish, rice, bananas

Uruguay
ORIENTAL REPUBLIC OF URUGUAY

AREA	176,215 sq km
	(68,037 sq mi)
POPULATION	3,342,000
CAPITAL	Montevideo 1,707,000
RELIGION	Roman Catholic, none
LANGUAGE	Spanish, Portunol, Brazilero
LITERACY	99%
LIFE EXPECTANCY	77 years
GDP PER CAPITA	$21,800

ECONOMY IND: food processing, electrical machinery, transportation equipment, petroleum products, textiles, chemicals, beverages **AGR:** soybeans, rice, wheat, beef, dairy products, fish, lumber, cellulose **EXP:** beef, soybeans, cellulose, rice, wheat, wood, dairy products, wool

GALÁPAGOS ISLANDS
(Ecuador)

Venezuela
BOLIVARIAN REPUBLIC OF VENEZUELA

AREA	912,050 sq km
	(352,143 sq mi)
POPULATION	29,275,000
CAPITAL	Caracas 2,916,000
RELIGION	Roman Catholic
LANGUAGE	Spanish
LITERACY	96%
LIFE EXPECTANCY	75 years
GDP PER CAPITA	$16,100

ECONOMY IND: agricultural products, livestock, raw materials, machinery and equipment, transport equipment, construction materials, medical equipment, pharmetceuticals, chemicals, icon and steel products Agr: corn, sorghum, sugarcane, rice, bananas, vegetables, coffee, beef, pork, milk, eggs, fish Exp: petroleum and petroleum products, bauxite and aluminum, minerals, chemicals, agricultural products

DEPENDENCIES

Falkland Islands
(U.K.)
FALKLAND ISLANDS

AREA	12,173 sq km
	(4,700 sq mi)
POPULATION	2,900
CAPITAL	Stanley 2,000
RELIGION	Christian, none
LANGUAGE	English, Spanish
LITERACY	NA
LIFE EXPECTANCY	78
GDP PER CAPITA	$55,400

ECONOMY IND: fish and wool processing, tourism **AGR:** fodder and vegetable crops, venison, sheep, dairy products, fish, squid **EXP:** wool, hides, meat, venison, fish, squid

French Guiana
(FRANCE)

French Guiana is a French overseas department, having equal status to the 13 metropolitan regions that make up European France. Please see "France" for facts about French Guiana.

Protected Areas

CARIBBEAN SEA

VENEZUELA

GUYANA

SURINAME

FRENCH GUIANA
(France)

COLOMBIA

ECUADOR

Atol das Rocas
(Brazil)

Fernando de
Noronha
(Brazil)

PERU

BRAZIL

BOLIVIA

PACIFIC

OCEAN

PARAGUAY

ATLANTIC

OCEAN

URUGUAY

CHILE

ARGENTINA

Protected Areas

Terrestrial

Marine

*Protected areas as defined by the
International Union for Conservation
of Nature (IUCN). The degree of
protection and governing body varies
by protected area.

Azimuthal Equidistant Projection
SCALE 1:27,225,000

0 km 200 400
0 mi 200 400

1 CENTIMETER = 272 KILOMETERS; 1 INCH = 430 MILES

FALKLAND ISLANDS
(ISLAS MALVINAS)
(U.K.)

Europe

EUROPE APPEARS FROM SPACE as a cluster of peninsulas and islands thrusting westward from Asia into the Atlantic Ocean. The smallest continent except Australia, Europe nonetheless has a population density second only to Asia's. Colliding tectonic plates and retreating Ice Age glaciers continue to shape Europe's fertile plains and rugged mountains, and the North Atlantic's Gulf Stream tempers the continent's climate. Europe's highly irregular coastline measures more than one and a half times the length of the Equator, leaving only 14 out of 45 counties landlocked.

Europe has been inhabited for some 40,000 years. During the last millennium Europeans explored the planet and established far-flung empires, leaving their imprint on every corner of the Earth. Europe led the world in science and invention, and launched the industrial revolution. Great periods of creativity in the arts have occurred at various times all over the continent and shape its collective culture. By the end of the 19th century Europe dominated world commerce, spreading ideas, languages, legal systems, and political patterns around the globe. But the Europeans who explored, colonized, and knitted together the world's regions knew themselves only as Portuguese, Spanish, Dutch, British, French, German, and Russian. After centuries of rivalry and war the two devastating world wars launched from its soil in the

20th century ended Europe's world dominance. By the 1960s nearly all its colonial possessions had gained independence.

European countries divided into two blocs, playing out the new superpowers' Cold War—the west allied to North America and the east bound to the Soviet Union, with Germany split between them. From small beginnings in the 1950s, Western Europe began to unify. Germany's unification and the Soviet Union's unexpected breakup in the early 1990s sped the movement. Led by former enemies France and Germany, 25 countries of Western Europe now form the European Union (EU), with common European citizenship. Several Eastern European countries clamor to join. In 1999, 12 of the EU members adopted a common currency, the euro, creating a single economic market, one of the largest in the world.

Scores of distinct ethnic groups, speaking some 40 languages, inhabit more than 40 countries, which vary in size from European Russia to tiny Luxembourg, each with its own history and traditions. Yet Europe has a more uniform culture than any other continent. Its population is overwhelmingly of one race, Caucasian, despite the recent arrival of immigrants from Africa and Asia. Most of its languages fall into three groups with Indo-European roots: Germanic, Romance, or Slavic. One religion, Christianity, predominates in various forms, and social structures nearly everywhere are based on economic classes. However, immigrant groups established as legitimate and illegal workers, refugees, and asylum seekers cling to their own habits, religions, and languages. Every European society is becoming more multicultural, with political as well as cultural consequences.

A commonly accepted division between Europe and Asia—here marked by an orange line—is formed by the Ural Mountains, Ural River, Caspian Sea, Caucasus Mountains, and the Black Sea with its outlets, the Bosporus and Dardanelles.

NORWEGIAN SEA

ICELAND
North Cape
Bjargtangar
Breiðafjörður   Húnaflói
Paxaflói   Eyjafjörður
Reykjanes   Rifstangi
Hekla   Thistilfjörður
1,491   Langanes
Surtsey Westman Islands   Gerpir
+2,119
Vatnajökull
+ Hvannadalshnúkur
925

ATLANTIC OCEAN

BRITISH ISLES
Outer Hebrides
Lewis
Inner Hebrides
Malin Head
Erris Head
Donegal Bay
L. Neagh
IRELAND
Dingle Bay
Shannon
+ Carrauntoohil
1,041
Bristol Chan.
St. George's Channel
CELTIC SEA
Land's End

Shetland Islands

Faroe Islands

Orkney Is.
Moray Firth
Highlands
Ben Nevis
1,344
Grampian Mts.
Rattray Head
Southern Uplands
Firth of Forth
GREAT BRITAIN
Isle of Man
The Pennines
IRISH SEA
Snowdon
1,085
Cambrian Mts.
The Wolds
Spurn Head
The Wash
Thames

NORTH SEA

ENGLISH CHANNEL
Strait of Dover
Point St-Mathieu
Channel Is.
Normandy
Brittany
Armorican Massif
+917
Seine
PARIS BASIN
Loire
Sologne
Berry
Poitou
Limousin
Puy de Sancy +1,886
MASSIF CENTRAL
Guienne
Garonne
Landes
AQUITAINE BASIN
Gascony
Navarre
Dordogne
+1,753
Languedoc
Rhône
Provence

BAY OF BISCAY

Cape Ortegal
Cape Peñas
Cape Finisterre
Cape Matxitxako
Cantabrian Mountains
2,648
Cape Mondego
Cape Roca
Douro
León
Old Castile
Iberian Mountains
+2,313
Ebro
Aragon
PYRENEES
Pico de Aneto
3,404
Catalonia
Cape Tortosa
Valencia
Cape Nao
475
Iviza
Balearic Islands
Majorca
Minorca
1,445   357
BALEARIC SEA

PENINSULA IBERIAN
Extremadura
Tagus
New Castile
La Mancha
+1,323
Guadiana
Guadalquivir
Murcia
Andalusia
Baetic Mountains
Mulhacén
+3,481
Cape Gata
Cape Palos
ALBORAN SEA
Strait of Gibraltar
St. Vincent
Cape
Rif

CELTIC SEA
Flanders
Artois
Picardy
Brabant
Holland
IJsselmeer
Rhine
Ems
Weser
Westphalia
NORTHERN
Ardennes
Eifel
Moselle
Champagne
Lorraine
Meuse
Vosges
Jura Mts.
1,424
Black Forest
+1,493
Source of the Danube
Saône
Burgundy
Dauphine
Mont Blanc
4,810
Matterhorn
Lake Geneva
Lake Como
Mont Cenis
ALPS
Grossglockner
3,798
Lake Constance
Bohemian Forest
Main
Thuringia
+1,141
Harz
Brandenburg
Saxony
Ore Mts.
1,244
Sudeten
1,602
Silesia
Bohemian Forest
Moravia
Neusiedler Lake

Frisian Islands
Helgoländer Bay
Lüneburger Heide
Holstein
Schleswig
Elbe
JUTLAND
Blåvands Pt.
Fyn
Zealand
Lolland
Rügen
Pomeranian Bay
Pomerania
Oder
246

SKAGERRAK
Lindesnes
Boknafjorden
Hardangerfjorden
Sognefjorden
Nordfjord
Trondheimsfjorden
Folda
1,796
Galdhøpiggen 2,469
Jotunheimen
Telemark
Mjøsa
Österdalen
Glåma
Klarälven
Svealand
Götaland
Vänern
Vättern
Öland
Skåne
Bornholm
Gotland
KATTEGAT
The Sound
The Skaw
The Great Belt
Lim Fjord

SCANDINAVIA
Norrland
North Cape
Sørøya
Finnmark Plateau
Kebnekaise +2,111
Vesterålen
Lofoten
Vestfjorden
Andfjorden
Storavan
GULF OF BOTHNIA
Indalsälven
Oulu
384
Suomen Ridge
Näsijärvi
Lappajärvi
Lake Region
Saimaa
GULF OF FINLAND
Åland Is.
Hiiumaa
Saaremaa
Gulf of Riga
Livonia
L. Peipus
BALTIC SEA
Courland
224
Neman
East Prussia
Masuria
Gulf of Gdańsk
Białowieża Forest
Vistula
Bug
Oder
NORTHERN EU
+246

CARPATHIAN MOUNTAINS
Gerlach
2,655
Mátra
Bakony
2,303
Great Hungarian Plain
Balaton
Drava
Sava
Danube
Tisza
Mureș
Transylvania
+2,543
Transylvanian Alps
Iron Gate
Banat
BALKAN
Balkan Mountains
2,925
2,376
Macedonia
Rhodope
BALKAN PENINSULA
2,637
Mt. Olympus
2,917
Thessaly
Pindus Mts.
Parnassus
2,457
Peloponnesus
Euboea
Northern Sporades
IONIAN SEA

DINARIC ALPS
Durmitor
2,522
Dalmatia
Kapela
ADRIATIC SEA
Istria
Gulf of Venice
Veneto
Plain of Lombardy
Piedmont
Po
Garda
Riviera
Genoa
LIGURIAN SEA
Cape Corse
CORSICA
2,710
Strait of Bonifacio
Gulf of Cagliari
SARDINIA
1,834
Cape Teulada
Cape San Vito
Strait of Sicily
SICILY
Etna
3,330
Cape Passero
Malta
Maltese Islands
Gulf of Hamamet

APENNINES
Tuscany
Umbria
Latium
Corno Grande
2,912
Campania
Vesuvius
1,281
Gulf of Salerno
Apulia
Gulf of Taranto
Gulf of Policastro
Calabria
3,330
Gulf of Squillace
Cape Spartivento
Strait of Messina

MEDITERRANEAN SEA
TYRRHENIAN SEA

AFRICA

Gulf of Lion
Gulf of Venice

Azimuthal Equidistant Projection
SCALE 1:13,000,000 1 CENTIMETER = 130 KILOMETERS; 1 INCH = 205 MILES
KILOMETERS
0   100   200   300   400   500
STATUTE MILES
0   100   200   300   400   500
Elevations in meters

102

Europe
Physical

Continental Data

Area: 9,947,000 sq km
(3,841,000 sq mi)

Greatest north-south extent:
4,800 km (2,980 mi)

Greatest east-west extent:
6,400 km (3,980 mi)

Highest point: El'brus, Russia
5,642 m (18,510 ft)

Lowest point: Caspian Sea
-28 m (-92 ft)

Lowest recorded temperature:
Ust'Shchugor, Russia -55°C
(-67°F), Date unknown

Highest recorded temperature:
Seville, Spain 50°C (122°F),
August 4, 1881

Longest rivers:
- Volga 3,685 km (2,290 mi)
- Danube 2,848 km (1,770 mi)
- Dnieper 2,285 km (1,420 mi)

Largest natural lakes:
- Caspian Sea 371,000 sq km
(143,200 sq mi)
- Lake Ladoga 17,872 sq km
(6,900 sq mi)
- Lake Onega 9,842 sq km
(3,800 sq mi)

A commonly accepted division between Asia and Europe—here marked by an orange line—is formed by the Ural Mountains, Ural River, Caspian Sea, Caucasus Mountains, and the Black Sea with its outlets, the Bosporus and Dardanelles.

NORWEGIAN SEA

NORTH SEA

ATLANTIC OCEAN

CELTIC SEA

BAY OF BISCAY

ENGLISH CHANNEL

SKAGERRAK

KATTEGAT

BALTIC SEA

GULF OF BOTHNIA

GULF OF FINLAND

ADRIATIC SEA

LIGURIAN SEA

TYRRHENIAN SEA

MEDITERRANEAN SEA

IONIAN SEA

ALBORAN SEA

Strait of Gibraltar

ICELAND
Reykjavík
Keflavík
Akranes
Ólafsvík
Blönduós
Ísafjörður
Vatneyri
Siglufjörður
Sauðárkrókur
Raufarhöfn
Vopnafjörður
Þórshöfn
Seyðisfjörður
Egilsstaðir
Höfn
Vík
2,119
Faxaflói
Húnaflói
Thistilfjörður

FAROE ISLANDS (FØROYAR) Denmark
Tórshavn

Shetland Islands
Lerwick

Orkney Is.
Kirkwall
Wick

Outer Hebrides
Inner Hebrides

SCOTLAND
Inverness
Aberdeen
Dundee
Ben Nevis 1,344
Glasgow
Edinburgh
GREAT BRITAIN
Newcastle
Middlesbrough
Kingston upon Hull
Sheffield
Manchester
Liverpool
ENGLAND
Norwich
Birmingham
LONDON
Bristol
Cardiff (Caerdydd)
WALES (CYMRU)
Exeter
Plymouth
Portsmouth
Dover
Land's End

NORTHERN IRELAND
Belfast
(Derry) Londonderry
Malin Head
Donegal Bay
Erris Head
(ÉIRE) IRELAND
DUBLIN (Baile Átha Cliath)
Shannon (Sionainn)
Limerick (Luimneach)
Cork (Corcaigh)
1,041
ISLE OF MAN
Douglas
IRISH SEA
St. George's Channel
Bristol Chan.
N. Chan.

NORWAY
SWEDEN
FINLAND
Hammerfest
Vardø
Vadsø
Kirkenes
Pechenga
Alta
Ivalo
Tromsø
Narvik
Kiruna
Muonio
Svolvær
Bodø
Gällivare
Mo i Rana
Haparanda
Kemi
Rovaniemi
Mosjøen
Brønnøysund
Luleå
Piteå
Oulu
Namsos
Vilhelmina
Steinkjer
Strömsund
Umeå
Vaasa
Kokkola
Suomenselkä
Trondheim
Åre
Östersund
Kuopio
Savonlinna
Kristiansund
Ålesund
Andalsnes
Sundsvall
Pori
Tampere
Jyväskylä
Flora
Galdhøpiggen 2,469
Jotunheimen
Søderhamn
Lahti
Salpausselkä
Høyanger
Hamar
Falun
Gävle
Turku
Helsinki (Helsingfors)
Sognefjorden
Bergen
Haugesund
Drammen
Oslo
Uppsala
Västerås
Hiiumaa
TALLINN (Reval)
ESTONIA
L. Pi
Chud
Boknafjorden
Skien
Larvik
Stockholm
Saaremaa
Pärnu
Tartu
Stavanger
Flekkefjord
Arendal
Norrköping
Visby
Gotland
Ventspils
Gulf of Riga
RĪGA
LATVIA
Kristiansand
Jönköping
Öland
Liepāja
Jelgava
Daugav
Göteborg
Växjö
Klaipėda
Panevėžys
LITHUANIA
DENMARK
Ålborg
Halmstad
Karlskrona
Bornholm
Kaliningrad
Russia
Kaunas
Vilni
JUTLAND
Aarhus
Malmö
EAST PRUSSIA
Chernyakhovsk
Esbjerg
KØBENHAVN (Copenhagen)
Gdańsk
Hrodna
BE
Odense
Viborg
Kołobrzeg
Białystok
Helgoländer Bucht
Kiel
Rostock
Szczecin
Bydgoszcz
Lübeck
Gorzów Wielkopolski
Brest
Frisian Is.
Hamburg
Elbe
Berlin
Poznań
Włocławek
Warszawa (Warsaw)
Groningen
Bremen
Braunschweig (Brunswick)
Łódź
Lublin
NETHERLANDS
Amsterdam
Hannover
Bielefeld
Leszno
POLAND
Den Haag (The Hague)
Münster
Essen
GERMANY
Leipzig
Wrocław
Kielce
Khmel'nyts
Eindhoven
Köln
Düsseldorf
Erfurt
Dresden
Kraków
Rzeszów
L'viv
BRUXELLES (Brussels, Brüssel, Brussel)
BELGIUM
Liège
Wiesbaden
Frankfurt
Praha (Prague)
Hradec Králové
Olomouc
Nowy Sącz
Luxembourg
LUX.
Heidelberg
Nürnberg
CZECH REPUBLIC (CZECHIA)
Brno
CARPATHIAN MO
Calais
Amiens
Reims
Stuttgart
München (Munich)
SLOVAKIA
Košice
Satu Mare
Cherbourg-Octeville
Le Havre
Nancy
Strasbourg
Augsburg
Freiburg
Salzburg
Wien (Vienna)
Bratislava
Zvolen
Pointe de Saint-Mathieu
St.-Brieuc
Paris
Luzern
Zürich
LIECH.
AUSTRIA
Linz
Budapest
Debrecen
Brest
Rennes
Vannes
Orléans
Dijon
Bern
SWITZERLAND
Innsbruck
Leoben
Graz
HUNGARY
Oradea
Cluj-Napoca
ROMAN
Le Mans
Tours
Besançon?
Lausanne
Genève (Geneva)
Belluno
Belluno
Ljubljana
Szeged
Timişoara
Nantes
FRANCE
Vichy
Lyon
Mt. Blanc
Torino (Turin)
Milano (Milan)
Verona
SLOVENIA
Zagreb
Novi Sad
Sibiu
2,543
La Rochelle
Limoges
Brive
Valence
Piacenza
Venezia (Venice)
Rijeka
CROATIA
Osijek
MASSIF CENTRAL
Genova (Genoa)
Bologna
Banja Luka
Beograd (Belgrade)
Bucure
(Bucharest)
Bordeaux
Avignon
Nîmes
La Spezia
SAN MARINO
BOSN. & HERZG.
Craiova
Nice
MONACO
Livorno
Sarajevo
Valjevo
Santiago de Compostela
Toulouse
Narbonne
Marseille
Toulon
Firenze (Florence)
Pesaro
Mostar
Dubrovnik
Niš
Giu
A Coruña
PYRENEES
Perpignan
CORSICA France
Perugia
SERBIA
BUL
Oviedo
Gijón
Santander
Donostia-San Sebastián
Biarritz
ANDORRA
Ajaccio
Bastia
Niksić
Vigo
Bilbao
Logroño
Golfe du Lion
ITALY
VATICAN CITY
ROMA (Rome)
KOSOVO
Sofiya (Sofia)
Star
Braga
Burgos
Pristina
Zagor
Ourense
Valladolid
Zaragoza
Lleida
Barcelona
Porto-Vecchio
Pescara
Podgorica
Prizren
Porto (Oporto)
Cap de Tortosa
Duero
MONTENEGRO
ALBANIA
Skopje
Coimbra
Salamanca
Castellón de la Plana (Castelló de la Plana)
Foggia
Tiranë (Tirana)
MACEDONIA
PORTUGAL
Madrid
Tortosa
Cuenca
Sassari
Napoli (Naples)
Bari
Korçë
Bitola
Sérres
Lisboa (Lisbon)
Cáceres
SPAIN
Valencia
Olbia
Salerno
Vesuvio
Taranto
Véroia
Thessaloni
Setúbal
Badajoz
Albacete
Palma de Mallorca
Mahón (Minorca)
Menorca
SARDINIA Italy
Sapri
Golfo di Taranto
2,917
Olympos
Sierra Morena
Murcia
Ibiza (Iviza)
Mallorca (Majorca)
Nuoro
GREECE
Huelva
Córdoba
Granada
Linares
Alicante (Alacant)
Balearic Islands
Oristano
Cosenza
Pátra
Lárisa
Cádiz
Sevilla
Málaga
Almería
Cartagena
Cagliari
Catanzaro
Reggio di Calabria
Messina
Ioánnina
Pýrgos
Volos
Lamía
Agrínio
GIBRALTAR U.K.
Ceuta Sp.
Alger (Algiers)
Palermo
Etna 3,330
SICILY
Strait of Messina
Stretto di Messina
Peiraiás
Athi (Athens)
Pelopónnisos
Kalamáta
Kyk
MOROCCO
Melilla
Sp.
Tunis
Catania
Siracusa
Gulf of Hamamet
MALTA
Valletta
Chanía
Kríti (Crete)
CR
ALGERIA
TUNISIA

Azimuthal Equidistant Projection
SCALE 1:13,000,000   1 CENTIMETER = 130 KILOMETERS; 1 INCH = 205 MILES
KILOMETERS
0 100 200 300 400 500
STATUTE MILES
0 100 200 300 400 500
Elevations in meters

Continental Data

Total number of countries: 46

First independent country:
San Marino, September 3, 301

"Youngest" country:
Kosovo, February 17, 2008

Largest country by area:
*Ukraine 603,550 sq km
(233,032 sq mi)

Smallest country by area:
Vatican City
0.4 sq km (0.2 sq mi)

Percent urban population: 73%

Most populous country:
Russia 142,424,000

Least populous country:
Vatican City 1,000

**Most densely
populated country:**
Monaco 15,268 per sq km
(39,543 per sq mi)

**Least densely
populated country:**
Iceland 3 per sq km
(8 per sq mi)

Largest city by population:
Moscow, Russia 12,166,000

Highest GDP per capita:
Luxembourg $102,900

Lowest GDP per capita:
Moldova $5,000

Average life expectancy: 78 years

*Ukraine, whose territory lies entirely
within Europe, is considered the continent's largest country. Both France and
Russia are larger but have significant
territory outside of Europe.

Human and Natural Themes

ENERGY CONSUMPTION

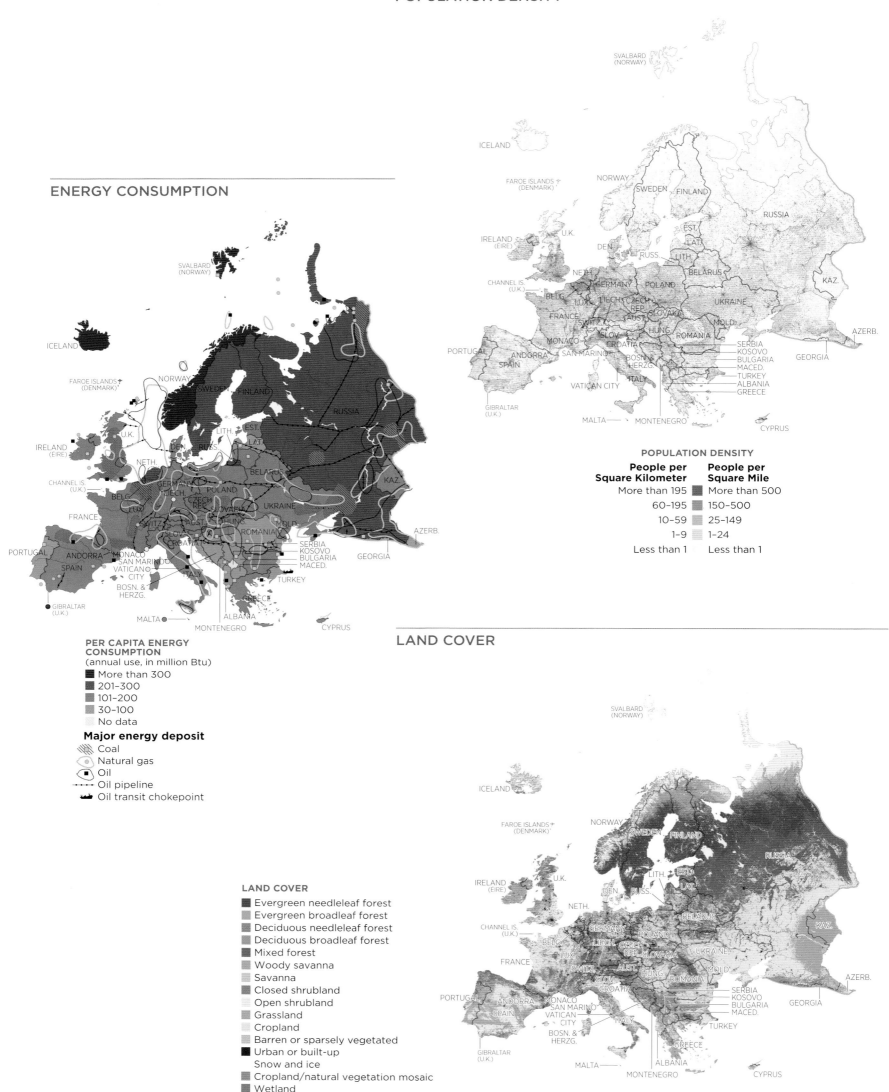

PER CAPITA ENERGY CONSUMPTION
(annual use, in million Btu)
- More than 300
- 201–300
- 101–200
- 30–100
- No data

Major energy deposit
- Coal
- Natural gas
- Oil
- Oil pipeline
- Oil transit chokepoint

POPULATION DENSITY

People per Square Kilometer	People per Square Mile
More than 195	More than 500
60–195	150–500
10–59	25–149
1–9	1–24
Less than 1	Less than 1

LAND COVER

LAND COVER
- Evergreen needleleaf forest
- Evergreen broadleaf forest
- Deciduous needleleaf forest
- Deciduous broadleaf forest
- Mixed forest
- Woody savanna
- Savanna
- Closed shrubland
- Open shrubland
- Grassland
- Cropland
- Barren or sparsely vegetated
- Urban or built-up
- Snow and ice
- Cropland/natural vegetation mosaic
- Wetland

CLIMATIC ZONES

CLIMATIC ZONES
(based on modified Köppen system)

Dry climate (B)
- Semiarid (BS)
- Arid (BW) } k = cold

Humid temperate climate (C)
- No dry season (Cf)
- Dry summer (Cs) } a = hot summer

Humid cold climate (D)
- No dry season (Df) } b = cool summer
c = short, cool summer

Cold climate (E)
- Tundra and ice

Highland climate (H)
- Unclassified highlands

NATURAL HAZARDS (TECTONIC EVENTS)

WATER AVAILABILITY

WATER AVAILABILITY
(in millimeters per person per year)
- More than 750
- 251–750
- 26–250
- Less than 26
- No data

NATURAL HAZARDS (TECTONIC EVENTS)

Recorded Natural Event

Major Earthquake, 1900–2015
Moment magnitude
- More than 7.0
- 6.0–7.0

Volcano
▲

Tsunami, 1900–2015
Run-up height
- More than 10 meters (32 feet)
- 5–10 meters (16–32 feet)

Flags and Facts

COUNTRIES

Albania
REPUBLIC OF ALBANIA

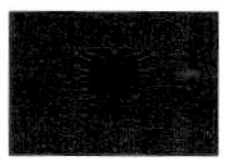

AREA 28,748 sq km (11,100 sq mi)
POPULATION 3,029,000
CAPITAL Tirana 454,000
RELIGION Muslim, Roman Catholic, Orthodox
LANGUAGE Albanian, Greek, Vlach, Romani, Slavic dialects
LITERACY 98%
LIFE EXPECTANCY 78 years
GDP PER CAPITA $11,900
ECONOMY **IND:** food and tobacco products, textiles and clothing, lumber, oil, cement, chemicals, mining **AGR:** wheat, corn, potatoes, vegetables, fruits, sugar beets, grapes, meat, dairy products **EXP:** textiles and footwear, asphalt, metals and metallic ores, crude oil

Andorra
PRINCIPALITY OF ANDORRA

AREA 468 sq km (181 sq mi)
POPULATION 86,000
CAPITAL Andorra la Vella 23,000
RELIGION Roman Catholic
LANGUAGE Catalan, French, Castilian, Portuguese
LITERACY 100%
LIFE EXPECTANCY 83 years
GDP PER CAPITA $37,200
ECONOMY **IND:** tourism (skiing), timber, banking, furniture **AGR:** rye, wheat, barley, oats, sheep **EXP:** tobacco products, furniture

Austria
REPUBLIC OF AUSTRIA

AREA 83,871 sq km (32,383 sq mi)
POPULATION 8,666,000
CAPITAL Vienna 1,753,000
RELIGION Roman Catholic
LANGUAGE German
LITERACY 98%
LIFE EXPECTANCY 81 years
GDP PER CAPITA $47,500
ECONOMY **IND:** construction, machinery, vehicles and parts, tourism **AGR:** grains, potatoes, wine, fruit, dairy products, cattle **EXP:** machinery and equipment, motor vehicles and parts, paper and paperboard, metal goods

Belarus
REPUBLIC OF BELARUS

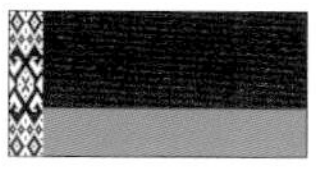

AREA 207,600 sq km (80,154 sq mi)
POPULATION 9,590,000
CAPITAL Minsk 1,915,000
RELIGION Eastern Orthodox
LANGUAGE Russian, Belarusian
LITERACY 100%
LIFE EXPECTANCY 72 years
GDP PER CAPITA $17,800
ECONOMY **IND:** metal-cutting machine tools, tractors, trucks, earthmovers, motorcycles, televisions **AGR:** grain, potatoes, vegetables, sugar beets, beef **EXP:** machinery and equipment, mineral products, chemicals, metals, textiles

Belgium
KINGDOM OF BELGIUM

AREA 30,528 sq km (11,787 sq mi)
POPULATION 11,324,000
CAPITAL Brussels 2,045,000
RELIGION Roman Catholic
LANGUAGE Dutch, French
LITERACY 99%
LIFE EXPECTANCY 81 years
GDP PER CAPITA $44,100
ECONOMY **IND:** engineering and metal products, motor vehicle assembly, transportation equipment, scientific instruments **AGR:** sugar beets, fresh vegetables, fruits, grain, beef, veal **EXP:** chemicals, machinery and equipment, finished diamonds, metals and metal products, foodstuffs

Bosnia and Herzegovina
BOSNIA AND HERZEGOVINA

AREA 51,197 sq km (19,767 sq mi)
POPULATION 3,867,000
CAPITAL Sarajevo 318,000
RELIGION Muslim, Orthodox, Roman Catholic
LANGUAGE Bosnian, Croatian, Serbian
LITERACY 99%
LIFE EXPECTANCY 77 years
GDP PER CAPITA $10,200
ECONOMY **IND:** steel, coal, iron ore, lead, bauxite, aluminum, textiles **AGR:** wheat, corn, fruits, vegetables, livestock **EXP:** metals, clothing, wood products

Bulgaria
REPUBLIC OF BULGARIA

AREA 110,879 sq km (42,810 sq mi)
POPULATION 7,187,000
CAPITAL Sofia 1,226,000
RELIGION Bulgarian Orthodox, Muslim
LANGUAGE Bulgarian, Turkish
LITERACY 98%
LIFE EXPECTANCY 74 years
GDP PER CAPITA $18,400
ECONOMY **IND:** machinery and equipment, base metals, chemical products, refined petroleum **AGR:** vegetables, fruits, tobacco, wine, wheat, barley, livestock **EXP:** clothing, footwear, iron and steel, machinery and equipment, fuels

Croatia
REPUBLIC OF CROATIA

AREA 56,594 sq km (21,851 sq mi)
POPULATION 4,465,000
CAPITAL Zagreb 687,000
RELIGION Roman Catholic
LANGUAGE Croatian
LITERACY 99%
LIFE EXPECTANCY 77 years
GDP PER CAPITA $21,300
ECONOMY **IND:** chemicals and plastics, machine tools, fabricated metal, electronics, tourism **AGR:** wheat, corn, barley, vegetables, fruits, livestock, dairy products **EXP:** transportation equipment, machinery, textiles, chemicals, fuels

Cyprus
REPUBLIC OF CYPRUS

AREA 9,251 sq km (3,572 sq mi)
POPULATION 1,189,000
CAPITAL Nicosia 251,000
RELIGION Orthodox Christian
LANGUAGE Greek, Turkish, English
LITERACY 99%
LIFE EXPECTANCY 79 years
GDP PER CAPITA $31,000
ECONOMY **IND:** tourism, food and beverage processing, ship repair and refurbishment, textiles **AGR:** citrus, vegetables, barley, grapes, olives **EXP:** citrus, potatoes, pharmaceuticals, cement, clothing

Czech Republic (Czechia)
CZECH REPUBLIC

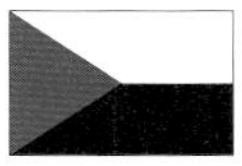

AREA 78,867 sq km (30,451 sq mi)
POPULATION 10,645,000
CAPITAL Prague 1,314,000
RELIGION Roman Catholic
LANGUAGE Czech
LITERACY 99%
LIFE EXPECTANCY 78 years
GDP PER CAPITA $31,500
ECONOMY **IND:** motor vehicles, metallurgy, machinery and equipment, armaments **AGR:** wheat, potatoes, sugar beets, hops, pigs **EXP:** machinery and transport equipment, raw materials and fuel, chemicals

Denmark
KINGDOM OF DENMARK

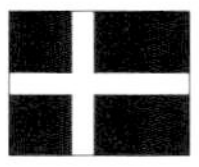

AREA 43,094 sq km (16,639 sq mi)
POPULATION 5,582,000
CAPITAL Copenhagen 1,268,000
RELIGION Evangelical Lutheran
LANGUAGE Danish, English
LITERACY 99%
LIFE EXPECTANCY 79 years
GDP PER CAPITA $45,800
ECONOMY **IND:** iron, steel, food processing, machinery, fuel, textiles and clothing, electronics, **AGR:** barley, wheat, potatoes, sugar beets, pork, fish **EXP:** machinery and instruments, pharmaceuticals, wind turbines

Estonia
REPUBLIC OF ESTONIA

AREA 45,228 sq km (17,463 sq mi)
POPULATION 1,265,000
CAPITAL Tallinn 391,000
RELIGION Lutheran, Orthodox
LANGUAGE Estonian, Russian
LITERACY 100%
LIFE EXPECTANCY 76 years
GDP PER CAPITA $28,700
ECONOMY **IND:** engineering, electronics, wood and wood products, textiles **AGR:** grain, potatoes, vegetables, livestock and dairy products, fish **EXP:** machinery and electrical equipment, mineral fuels, wood and wood products, metals

Finland
REPUBLIC OF FINLAND

AREA 338,145 sq km (130,558 sq mi)
POPULATION 5,477,000
CAPITAL Helsinki 1,180,000
RELIGION Lutheran
LANGUAGE Finnish, Swedish
LITERACY 100%
LIFE EXPECTANCY 81 years
GDP PER CAPITA $41,200
ECONOMY **IND:** metals and metal products, electronics, machinery and scientific instruments, shipbuilding **AGR:** barley, wheat, sugar beets, potatoes, dairy cattle, fish **EXP:** electrical and optical equipment, machinery, paper and pulp, metals

France
FRENCH REPUBLIC

AREA 643,801 sq km (248,572 sq mi)
POPULATION 66,554,000
CAPITAL Paris 10,843,000
RELIGION Roman Catholic, Muslim
LANGUAGE French
LITERACY 99%
LIFE EXPECTANCY 82 years
GDP PER CAPITA $41,400
ECONOMY **IND:** machinery, chemicals, automobiles, aircraft, tourism **AGR:** wheat, cereals, sugar beets, potatoes, wine grapes, beef, dairy products, fish **EXP:** machinery and transportation equipment, aircraft, plastics

Germany
FEDERAL REPUBLIC OF GERMANY

AREA 357,022 sq km (137,846 sq mi)
POPULATION 80,854,000
CAPITAL Berlin 3,563,000
RELIGION Protestant, Roman Catholic
LANGUAGE German
LITERACY 99%
LIFE EXPECTANCY 81 years
GDP PER CAPITA $47,400
ECONOMY **IND:** steel, coal, vehicles, machine tools, electronics **AGR:** potatoes, wheat, barley, sugar beets, cattle, pigs **EXP:** motor vehicles, machinery, chemicals, computer and electronic products, electrical equipment, pharmaceuticals

Greece
HELLENIC REPUBLIC

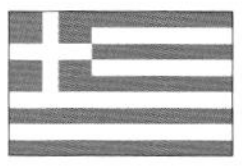

AREA 131,957 sq km (50,949 sq mi)
POPULATION 10,776,000
CAPITAL Athens 3,052,000
RELIGION Greek Orthodox
LANGUAGE Greek
LITERACY 98%
LIFE EXPECTANCY 80 years
GDP PER CAPITA $25,600
ECONOMY **IND:** tourism, food and tobacco processing, textiles **AGR:** wheat, corn, barley, sugar beets, olives, wine, beef, fish **EXP:** food and beverages, manufactured goods, petroleum products, chemicals

Hungary
HUNGARY

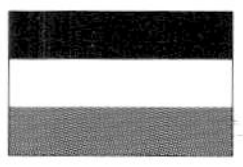

AREA 93,028 sq km (35,918 sq mi)
POPULATION 9,898,000
CAPITAL Budapest 1,714,000
RELIGION Roman Catholic, Calvinist
LANGUAGE Hungarian
LITERACY 99%
LIFE EXPECTANCY 76 years
GDP PER CAPITA $26,000
ECONOMY **IND:** metallurgy, construction materials, pharmaceuticals, motor vehicles **AGR:** wheat, corn, sunflower seed, potatoes, sugar beets, pigs, cattle, poultry **EXP:** machinery and equipment, manufacturing, raw materials, food products

Iceland
REPUBLIC OF ICELAND

AREA 103,000 sq km (39,768 sq mi)
POPULATION 332,000
CAPITAL Reykjavík 184,000
RELIGION Lutheran Church of Iceland
LANGUAGE Icelandic, English, Nordic languages
LITERACY 99%
LIFE EXPECTANCY 83 years
GDP PER CAPITA $46,600
ECONOMY **IND:** fish processing, aluminum smelting, geothermal power, hydropower, tourism **AGR:** potatoes, vegetables, mutton, chicken, fish **EXP:** fish and fish products, aluminum, animal products, ferroalloys

Ireland (Éire)
IRELAND

AREA 70,273 sq km (27,132 sq mi)
POPULATION 4,892,000
CAPITAL Dublin 1,169,000
RELIGION Roman Catholic
LANGUAGE English, Irish
LITERACY 99%
LIFE EXPECTANCY 81 years
GDP PER CAPITA $54,300
ECONOMY **IND:** pharmaceuticals, chemicals, food products, beverages and brewing **AGR:** barley, potatoes, wheat, beef **EXP:** machinery and equipment, chemicals, pharmaceuticals

Italy
ITALIAN REPUBLIC

AREA 301,340 sq km (116,347 sq mi)
POPULATION 61,855,000
CAPITAL Rome 3,718,000
RELIGION Roman Catholic
LANGUAGE Italian, German, French, Slovene
LITERACY 98%
LIFE EXPECTANCY 82 years
GDP PER CAPITA $35,800
ECONOMY **IND:** tourism, machinery, chemicals, food processing, textiles, motor vehicles, clothing, footwear **AGR:** fruits, vegetables, wine, grapes, potatoes, sugar beets, olives, fish **EXP:** refined petroleum, textiles and clothing, motor vehicles, transport equipment, chemicals, food

Kosovo
REPUBLIC OF KOSOVO

AREA 10,887 sq km (4,203 sq mi)
POPULATION 1,871,000
CAPITAL Pristina 207,000
RELIGION Muslim, Serbian Orthodox, Roman Catholic
LANGUAGE Albanian, Serbian, Bosnian, Turkish, Roma
LITERACY 92%
LIFE EXPECTANCY 70 years
GDP PER CAPITA NA
ECONOMY **IND:** mineral mining, construction materials, base metals, leather, machinery, appliances **AGR:** wheat, corn, grapes, berries, potatoes, peppers **EXP:** mining and processed metal products, scrap metals, leather products, machinery

Latvia
REPUBLIC OF LATVIA

AREA 64,589 sq km (24,938 sq mi)
POPULATION 1,987,000
CAPITAL Riga 621,000
RELIGION Lutheran, Orthodox
LANGUAGE Latvian, Russian
LITERACY 100%
LIFE EXPECTANCY 73 years
GDP PER CAPITA $24,500
ECONOMY **IND:** petroleum, processed wood products, textiles, processed metals, pharmaceuticals **AGR:** grain, rapeseed, potatoes, vegetables, pork, fish **EXP:** food products, wood and wood products, metals, machinery and equipment, textiles

Liechtenstein
PRINCIPALITY OF LIECHTENSTEIN

AREA 160 sq km (62 sq mi)
POPULATION 38,000
CAPITAL Vaduz 5,000
RELIGION Roman Catholic
LANGUAGE German, Alemannic dialect
LITERACY 100%
LIFE EXPECTANCY 82 years
GDP PER CAPITA $89,400
ECONOMY **IND:** electronics, metal manufacturing, dental products, ceramics, pharmaceuticals, food products, precision instruments **AGR:** wheat, barley, corn, potatoes, livestock **EXP:** machine and tool engineering, connectors for audio and video, parts for motor vehicles, dental products

Lithuania
REPUBLIC OF LITHUANIA

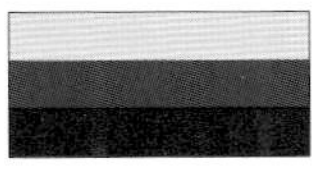

AREA 65,300 sq km (25,212 sq mi)
POPULATION 2,884,000
CAPITAL Vilnius 517,000
RELIGION Roman Catholic
LANGUAGE Lithuanian
LITERACY 100%
LIFE EXPECTANCY 76 years
GDP PER CAPITA $28,000
ECONOMY **IND:** petroleum refining, mineral products, machinery, food processing, tobacco, furniture making **AGR:** grain, potatoes, sugar beets, flax, vegetables, beef, fish **EXP:** mineral products, machinery and equipment, chemicals, wood products

Luxembourg
GRAND DUCHY OF LUXEMBOURG

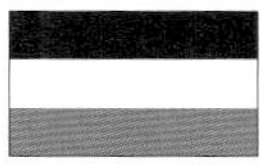

AREA 2,586 sq km (998 sq mi)
POPULATION 570,000
CAPITAL Luxembourg 107,000
RELIGION Roman Catholic
LANGUAGE Luxembourgish, German, French
LITERACY 100%
LIFE EXPECTANCY 80 years
GDP PER CAPITA $102,900
ECONOMY **IND:** banking and financial services, iron and steel, information technology, telecommunications **AGR:** wine, grapes, barley, oats, potatoes, wheat, dairy and livestock products **EXP:** machinery, steel products, chemicals, rubber products, glass

Macedonia
REPUBLIC OF MACEDONIA

AREA 25,713 sq km (9,928 sq mi)
POPULATION 2,096,000
CAPITAL Skopje 503,000
RELIGION Macedonian Orthodox, Muslim
LANGUAGE Macedonian, Albanian
LITERACY 96%
LIFE EXPECTANCY 75 years
GDP PER CAPITA $14,000
ECONOMY **IND:** food processing, textiles, chemicals, iron, steel, cement, energy, pharmaceuticals **AGR:** grapes, tobacco, vegetables, fruits, milk **EXP:** textiles, manufactured goods

Malta
REPUBLIC OF MALTA

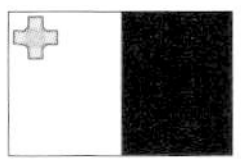

AREA 316 sq km (122 sq mi)
POPULATION 414,000
CAPITAL Valletta 197,000
RELIGION Roman Catholic
LANGUAGE Maltese
LITERACY 93%
LIFE EXPECTANCY 80 years
GDP PER CAPITA $34,700
ECONOMY **IND:** tourism, electronics, ship building and repair, pharmaceuticals, footwear, clothing **AGR:** potatoes, cauliflower, grapes, wheat, pork **EXP:** refined petroleum, pharmaceutical products, electronics

Moldova
REPUBLIC OF MOLDOVA

AREA 33,851 sq km (13,070 sq mi)
POPULATION 3,547,000
CAPITAL Chişinău 725,000
RELIGION Eastern Orthodox
LANGUAGE Moldovan, Russian, Gagauz
LITERACY 99%
LIFE EXPECTANCY 70 years
GDP PER CAPITA $5,000
ECONOMY **IND:** sugar, vegetable oil, food processing, agricultural machinery, foundry equipment, refrigerators and freezers, washing machines **AGR:** vegetables, fruits, grapes, wine, grain, sugar beets, beef **EXP:** foodstuffs, wine, insulated wire

Monaco
PRINCIPALITY OF MONACO

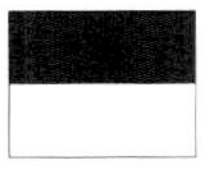

AREA 2 sq km (1 sq mi)
POPULATION 38,000
CAPITAL Monaco 38,000
RELIGION Roman Catholic
LANGUAGE French, English, Italian, Monegasque
LITERACY 99%
LIFE EXPECTANCY 90 years
GDP PER CAPITA $78,700
ECONOMY **IND:** tourism, construction, small-scale industrial and consumer products **AGR:** NA **EXP:** NA

Montenegro
MONTENEGRO

AREA 13,812 sq km (5,333 sq mi)
POPULATION 647,000
CAPITAL Podgorica 165,000
RELIGION Orthodox, Muslim
LANGUAGE Serbian, Montenegrin
LITERACY 96%
LIFE EXPECTANCY 74 years
GDP PER CAPITA $15,700
ECONOMY **IND:** steelmaking, aluminum, agricultural processing, consumer goods, tourism **AGR:** tobacco, potatoes, fruits, olives, grapes, sheep **EXP:** aluminium, ships, wine, metals

Netherlands
KINGDOM OF THE NETHERLANDS

AREA 41,543 sq km (16,040 sq mi)
POPULATION 16,948,000
CAPITAL Amsterdam 1,091,000 (seat of government is The Hague)
RELIGION Roman Catholic, Protestant
LANGUAGE Dutch, Frisian
LITERACY 99%
LIFE EXPECTANCY 81 years
GDP PER CAPITA $49,300
ECONOMY **IND:** agro-industries, metal and engineering products, electrical machinery and equipment, petroleum **AGR:** tulips, grains, potatoes, sugar beets, fruits, livestock **EXP:** refined petroleum, machinery and equipment, chemicals, foodstuffs

Norway
KINGDOM OF NORWAY

AREA 323,802 sq km (125,020 sq mi)
POPULATION 5,208,000
CAPITAL Oslo 986,000
RELIGION Church of Norway
LANGUAGE Norwegian, Sami
LITERACY 100%
LIFE EXPECTANCY 80 years
GDP PER CAPITA $68,400
ECONOMY **IND:** petroleum and gas, food processing, shipbuilding, pulp and paper products, metals, chemicals, timber, fishing **AGR:** barley, wheat, potatoes, pork, beef, fish **EXP:** petroleum, petroleum products, machinery and equipment, metals, ships, fish

Poland
REPUBLIC OF POLAND

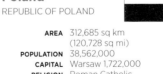

AREA 312,685 sq km (120,728 sq mi)
POPULATION 38,562,000
CAPITAL Warsaw 1,722,000
RELIGION Roman Catholic
LANGUAGE Polish
LITERACY 100%
LIFE EXPECTANCY 76 years
GDP PER CAPITA $26,400
ECONOMY **IND:** machine building, iron and steel, coal mining, chemicals, shipbuilding, food processing, glass **AGR:** potatoes, fruits, vegetables, wheat, poultry, eggs, pork **EXP:** machinery and transport equipment, refined petroleum, textiles, electronics

Portugal
PORTUGUESE REPUBLIC

AREA 92,090 sq km (35,556 sq mi)
POPULATION 10,825,000
CAPITAL Lisbon 2,884,000
RELIGION Roman Catholic
LANGUAGE Portuguese, Mirandese
LITERACY 93%
LIFE EXPECTANCY 79 years
GDP PER CAPITA $27,800
ECONOMY **IND:** textiles, clothing, footwear, wood and cork, paper, chemicals, auto-parts manufacturing, tourism **AGR:** grain, potatoes, tomatoes, olives, wine, grapes, sheep, cattle, fish **EXP:** agricultural products, oil products, chemical products, vehicles and parts, wood pulp and paper

Romania
ROMANIA

AREA 238,391 sq km (92,043 sq mi)
POPULATION 21,666,000
CAPITAL Bucharest 1,868,000
RELIGION Eastern Orthodox
LANGUAGE Romanian
LITERACY 97%
LIFE EXPECTANCY 74 years
GDP PER CAPITA $20,600
ECONOMY **IND:** electric machinery and equipment, textiles and footwear, vehicle assembly, mining, timber, construction materials **AGR:** wheat, corn, barley, sugar beets, grapes, eggs, sheep **EXP:** machinery, metals and metal products, textiles and footwear, chemicals

Russia
RUSSIAN FEDERATION

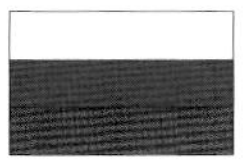

AREA 17,098,242 sq km (6,601,631 sq mi)
POPULATION 142,424,000
CAPITAL Moscow 12,166,000
RELIGION Russian Orthodox, Muslim
LANGUAGE Russian
LITERACY 99%
LIFE EXPECTANCY 66 years
GDP PER CAPITA $23,700
ECONOMY **IND:** coal, oil, natural gas, chemicals, metals, aircraft and space vehicles, defense industries, shipbuilding, road and rail transportation equipment, communications equipment **AGR:** grain, sugar beets, sunflower seed, vegetables, fruits, beef, milk **EXP:** petroleum and petroleum products, natural gas, metals, wood and wood products, chemicals, military manufactures

San Marino
REPUBLIC OF SAN MARINO

AREA 61 sq km (24 sq mi)
POPULATION 33,000
CAPITAL San Marino 4,000
RELIGION Roman Catholic
LANGUAGE Italian
LITERACY 96%
LIFE EXPECTANCY 83 years
GDP PER CAPITA $62,100
ECONOMY **IND:** tourism, banking, textiles, electronics, ceramics **AGR:** wheat, grapes, corn, olives, cattle **EXP:** machinery, pharmaceuticals, textiles

Serbia
REPUBLIC OF SERBIA

AREA 77,474 sq km (29,913 sq mi)
POPULATION 7,177,000
CAPITAL Belgrade 1,182,000
RELIGION Serbian Orthodox
LANGUAGE Serbian
LITERACY 96%
LIFE EXPECTANCY 75 years
GDP PER CAPITA $13,600
ECONOMY **IND:** base metals, food processing, machinery, tires, clothes **AGR:** wheat, maize, sugar beets, sunflower seeds, beef **EXP:** corn, metal products, vehicles, rubber tires, fruits and nuts

Slovakia
SLOVAK REPUBLIC

AREA 49,035 sq km (18,932 sq mi)
POPULATION 5,445,000
CAPITAL Bratislava 401,000
RELIGION Roman Catholic, Protestant
LANGUAGE Slovak, Hungarian
LITERACY 100%
LIFE EXPECTANCY 76 years
GDP PER CAPITA $29,500
ECONOMY **IND:** metal and metal products, food and beverages, electricity, gas **AGR:** grains, potatoes, sugar beets, hops, fruit, pigs, cattle **EXP:** vehicles, machinery and electrical equipment, base metals, refined petroleum

Flags and Facts

Slovenia
REPUBLIC OF SLOVENIA

AREA	20,273 sq km (7,827 sq mi)
POPULATION	1,983,000
CAPITAL	Ljubljana 279,000
RELIGION	Catholic, Muslim, Orthodox
LANGUAGE	Slovenian
LITERACY	100%
LIFE EXPECTANCY	78 years
GDP PER CAPITA	$30,900

ECONOMY **IND:** ferrous metallurgy and aluminum products, electronics, vehicles and parts **AGR:** potatoes, hops, wheat, sugar beets, corn, cattle, sheep **EXP:** manufactured goods, machinery and transportation equipment, chemicals, pharmaceuticals

Spain
KINGDOM OF SPAIN

AREA	505,370 sq km (195,123 sq mi)
POPULATION	48,146,000
CAPITAL	Madrid 6,199,000
RELIGION	Roman Catholic
LANGUAGE	Castilian Spanish, Catalan
LITERACY	98%
LIFE EXPECTANCY	82 years
GDP PER CAPITA	$35,200

ECONOMY **IND:** textiles and apparel (including footwear), food and beverages, metals and metal manufactures, chemicals, shipbuilding, automobiles, tourism **AGR:** grain, vegetables, olives, wine grapes, sugar beets, fish **EXP:** machinery, motor vehicles, foodstuffs, pharmaceuticals

Sweden
KINGDOM OF SWEDEN

AREA	450,295 sq km (173,859 sq mi)
POPULATION	9,802,000
CAPITAL	Stockholm 1,486,000
RELIGION	Lutheran
LANGUAGE	Swedish
LITERACY	99%
LIFE EXPECTANCY	82 years
GDP PER CAPITA	$48,000

ECONOMY **IND:** iron and steel, precision equipment (bearings, radio and telephone parts, armaments), wood pulp and paper products **AGR:** barley, wheat, sugar beets, meat, milk **EXP:** machinery, motor vehicles, pharmaceuticals, paper products, iron and steel products, chemicals

Switzerland
SWISS CONFEDERATION

AREA	41,277 sq km (15,937 sq mi)
POPULATION	8,122,000
CAPITAL	Bern 358,000
RELIGION	Roman Catholic, Protestant
LANGUAGE	German, French
LITERACY	99%
LIFE EXPECTANCY	83 years
GDP PER CAPITA	$59,300

ECONOMY **IND:** machinery, watches, textiles, precision instruments, tourism, banking **AGR:** grains, fruits, vegetables, meat, eggs **EXP:** machinery, chemicals, metals, watches, agricultural productseuticals, watches

Ukraine
UKRAINE

AREA	603,550 sq km (233,031 sq mi)
POPULATION	44,429,000
CAPITAL	Kiev 2,942,000
RELIGION	Ukrainian Orthodox
LANGUAGE	Ukrainian, Russian
LITERACY	100%
LIFE EXPECTANCY	72 years
GDP PER CAPITA	$8,000

ECONOMY **IND:** coal, ferrous and non-ferrous metals, machinery and transportation equipment, food processing **AGR:** grain, sugar beets, sunflower seeds, vegetables, beef **EXP:** ferrous and nonferrous metals, fuel and petroleum products, chemicals, foodstuffs, machinery

United Kingdom
UNITED KINGDOM OF GREAT BRITAIN AND NORTHERN IRELAND

AREA	243,610 sq km (94,058 sq mi)
POPULATION	64,088,000
CAPITAL	London 10,313,000
RELIGION	Christian
LANGUAGE	English
LITERACY	99%
LIFE EXPECTANCY	81 years
GDP PER CAPITA	$41,200

ECONOMY **IND:** machine tools, electric power equipment, aircraft, motor vehicles and parts, petroleum **AGR:** cereals, oilseed, potatoes, vegetables, cattle, sheep, fish **EXP:** manufactured goods, fuels, chemicals, food, beverages, tobacco

Vatican City
STATE OF THE VATICAN CITY

AREA	0.4 sq km (0.2 sq mi)
POPULATION	1,000
CAPITAL	Vatican City 1,000
RELIGION	Roman Catholic
LANGUAGE	Italian, Latin, French
LITERACY	100%
LIFE EXPECTANCY	NA
GDP PER CAPITA	NA

ECONOMY **IND:** tourism, printing, banking, production of coins, medals, postage stamps **AGR:** NA **EXP:** paintings, stamps, brochures

DEPENDENCIES

Faroe Islands
(DENMARK)
FAROE ISLANDS

SOVEREIGN
LOCAL

AREA	1,393 sq km (538 sq mi)
POPULATION	50,000
CAPITAL	Tórshavn 21,000
RELIGION	Evangelical Lutheran
LANGUAGE	Faroese, Danish
LITERACY	99%
LIFE EXPECTANCY	80 years
GDP PER CAPITA	$30,500

ECONOMY **IND:** fishing, fish processing, small ship repair and refurbishment, handicrafts **AGR:** milk, potatoes, vegetables, sheep, fish **EXP:** fish and fish products, stamps, ships

Gibraltar
(UNITED KINGDOM)
GIBRALTAR

SOVEREIGN
LOCAL

AREA	7 sq km (3 sq mi)
POPULATION	29,000
CAPITAL	Gibraltar 29,000
RELIGION	Roman Catholic
LANGUAGE	English, Spanish, Italian, Portuguese
LITERACY	80%
LIFE EXPECTANCY	79 years
GDP PER CAPITA	$43,000

ECONOMY **IND:** tourism, banking and finance, ship repair, tobacco **AGR:** NA **EXP:** refined petroleum, manufactured goods

Guernsey
(UNITED KINGDOM)
BAILIWICK OF GUERNSEY

SOVEREIGN
LOCAL

AREA	78 sq km (30 sq mi)
POPULATION	63,000
CAPITAL	Saint Peter Port 19,000
RELIGION	Protestant, Roman Catholic
LANGUAGE	English, French, Norman
LITERACY	NA
LIFE EXPECTANCY	82 years
GDP PER CAPITA	$52,300

ECONOMY **IND:** tourism, banking **AGR:** tomatoes, greenhouse flowers, sweet peppers, eggplant, fruit, Guernsey cattle **EXP:** tomatoes, flowers and ferns, sweet peppers, eggplant, other vegetables

Isle of Man
(UNITED KINGDOM)
ISLE OF MAN

SOVEREIGN
LOCAL

AREA	572 sq km (221 sq mi)
POPULATION	88,000
CAPITAL	Douglas 29,000
RELIGION	Protestant, Roman Catholic
LANGUAGE	English, Manx Gaelic
LITERACY	NA
LIFE EXPECTANCY	81 years
GDP PER CAPITA	$83,100

ECONOMY **IND:** financial services, light manufacturing, tourism **AGR:** cereals, vegetables, cattle, sheep, pigs, poultry **EXP:** tweeds, herring, processed shellfish, beef, lamb

Jersey
(UNITED KINGDOM)
BAILIWICK OF JERSEY

SOVEREIGN
LOCAL

AREA	116 sq km (45 sq mi)
POPULATION	101,000
CAPITAL	Saint Helier 34,000
RELIGION	Protestant, Roman Catholic
LANGUAGE	English
LITERACY	NA
LIFE EXPECTANCY	82 years
GDP PER CAPITA	$57,000

ECONOMY **IND:** tourism, banking, dairy, electronics **AGR:** potatoes, cauliflower, tomatoes, beef, dairy products **EXP:** light industrial and electrical goods, dairy cattle, foodstuffs, textiles, flowers

Svalbard
(NORWAY)
SVALBARD

AREA	62,045 sq km (23,956 sq mi)
POPULATION	2,700
CAPITAL	Longyearbyen 2,000
RELIGION	NA
LANGUAGE	Norwegian, Russian
LITERACY	NA
LIFE EXPECTANCY	NA
GDP PER CAPITA	NA

ECONOMY **IND:** NA **AGR:** NA **EXP:** NA

ICELAND

FAROE ISLA
(Den

ISLE OF MAN

IRELAND
(EIRE)

UNITE
KINGDO

CHANNEL IS.
(U.K.)

A T L A N T I C

O C E A N

PORTUGAL

ANDORR

S P A I N

GIBRALTAR
(U.K.)

Protected Areas

ARCTIC OCEAN

SVALBARD
(Norway)

KARA SEA

BARENTS SEA

NORWEGIAN SEA

NORTH SEA

BALTIC SEA

FINLAND

NORWAY

SWEDEN

DENMARK

ESTONIA

LATVIA

KALIN.
(Russia)

LITHUANIA

BELARUS

RUSSIA

ASIA
EUROPE

NETH.

BELG.

LUX.

GERMANY

POLAND

UKRAINE

CASPIAN SEA

RANCE

CZECH REP.
(CZECHIA)

SLOVAKIA

LIECH.

AUSTRIA

SWITZ.

HUNGARY

MOLDOVA

SLOV.

ROMANIA

SAN MARINO

CROATIA

MONACO

BOSN. &
HERZG.

SERBIA

BLACK SEA

ITALY

MONTEN.

KOS.

BULGARIA

VATICAN
CITY

ALBANIA

MACED.

GREECE

MALTA

MEDITERRANEAN SEA

Protected Areas

◼ Terrestrial

◼ Marine

*Protected areas as defined by the
International Union for Conservation
of Nature (IUCN). The degree of
protection and governing body varies
by protected area.*

Azimuthal Equidistant Projection
SCALE 1:17,000,000

0 km   150   300
0 mi   150   300

1 CENTIMETER = 170 KILOMETERS; 1 INCH = 268 MILES

Asia

THE CONTINENT OF ASIA, occupying four-fifths of the giant Eurasian landmass, stretches across ten time zones, from the Pacific Ocean in the east to the Ural Mountains and Black Sea in the west. It is the largest of the continents, with dazzling geographic diversity and 30 percent of the Earth's land surface. Asia includes numerous island nations, such as Japan, the Philippines, Indonesia, and Sri Lanka, as well as many of the world's major islands: Borneo, Sumatra, Honshu, Celebes, Java, and half of New Guinea. Siberia, the huge Asian section of Russia, reaches deep inside the Arctic Circle and fills the continent's northern quarter. Within its 46 countries, Asia holds 60 percent of humanity, yet deserts, mountains, jungles, and inhospitable zones render much of the continent empty or underpopulated.

Great river systems allowed the growth of the world's first civilizations in the Middle East, the Indian subcontinent, and northern China. Numerous cultural forces, each linked to these broad geographical areas, have formed and influenced Asia's rich civilizations and hundreds of ethnic groups. The two oldest are the cultural milieus of India and China. India's culture still reverberates throughout countries as varied as Sri Lanka, Pakistan, Nepal, Myanmar, Cambodia, and Indonesia. The world religions of Hinduism and Buddhism originated in India and spread as traders, scholars, and priests

sought distant footholds. China's ancient civilization has profoundly influenced the development of all of East Asia, much of Southeast Asia, and parts of Central Asia. Most influential of all Chinese institutions were the Chinese written language, a complex script with thousands of characters, and Confucianism, an ethical worldview that affected philosophy, politics, and relations within society. Islam, a third great influence in Asia, proved formidable in its energy and creative genius. Arabs from the seventh century onward, spurred on by faith, moved rapidly into Southwest Asia. Their religion and culture, particularly Arabic writing, spread through Iran and Afghanistan to the Indian subcontinent.

Today nearly all of Asia's people continue to live beside rivers or along coastal zones. Dense concentrations of population fill Japan, China's eastern half, Java, parts of Southeast Asia, and much of the Indian subcontinent. China and India, acting as demographic, political, and cultural counterweights, hold nearly half of Asia's population. India, with a billion people, expects to surpass China as the world's most populous nation by 2050. As China seeks to take center stage, flexing economic muscle and pushing steadily into the oil-rich South China Sea, many Asian neighbors grow concerned. The development of nuclear weapons by India and Pakistan complicates international relations. Religious, ethnic, and territorial conflicts continue to beset the continent, from the Middle East to Korea, from Cambodia to Uzbekistan. Asians also face the threats of overpopulation, resource depletion, pollution, and the growth of megacities. If vibrant Asia meets the challenges of rebuilding and reconciliation, overcoming age-old habits of rivalry, corruption, and cronyism, it may yet fulfill the promise to claim the first hundred years of the new millennium as Asia's century.

Asia
Physical

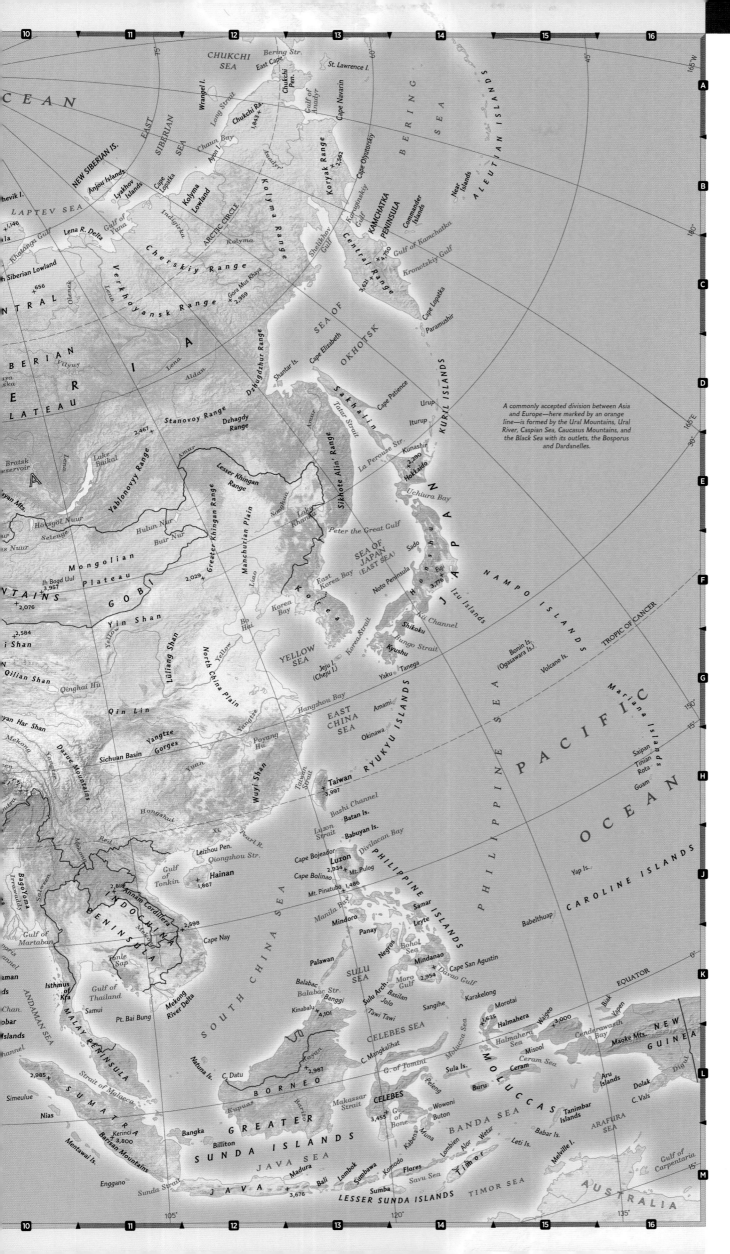

Continental Data

Area: 44,570,000 sq km (17,208,000 sq mi)

Greatest north-south extent: 8,690 km (5,400 mi)

Greatest east-west extent: 9,700 km (6,030 mi)

Highest point: Mount Everest, China-Nepal 8,850 m (29,035 ft)

Lowest point: Dead Sea, Israel-Jordan -423 m (-1,388 ft)

Lowest recorded temperature:
•Oymyakon, Russia -68°C (-90°F), February 6, 1933
•Verkhoyansk, Russia -68°C (-90°F), February 7, 1892

Highest recorded temperature: Tirat Zevi, Israel 54°C (129°F), June 21, 1942

Longest rivers:
•Chang Jiang (Yangtze) 6,244 km (3,880 mi)
•Yenisey-Angara 5,810 km (3,610 mi)
•Huang (Yellow) 5,778 km (3,590 mi)

Largest natural lakes:
•Caspian Sea 371,000 sq km (143,200 sq mi)
•Lake Baikal 31,500 sq km (12,200 sq mi)
•Aral Sea 18,000 sq km (6,900 sq mi)

Earth's extremes located in Asia:
•Wettest Place: Mawsynram, India; annual average rainfall 1,187 cm (467 in)
•Largest Cave Chamber: Sarawak Cave, Gunung Mulu National Park, Malaysia; 16 hectares and 79 m high (40 acres, 260 ft)

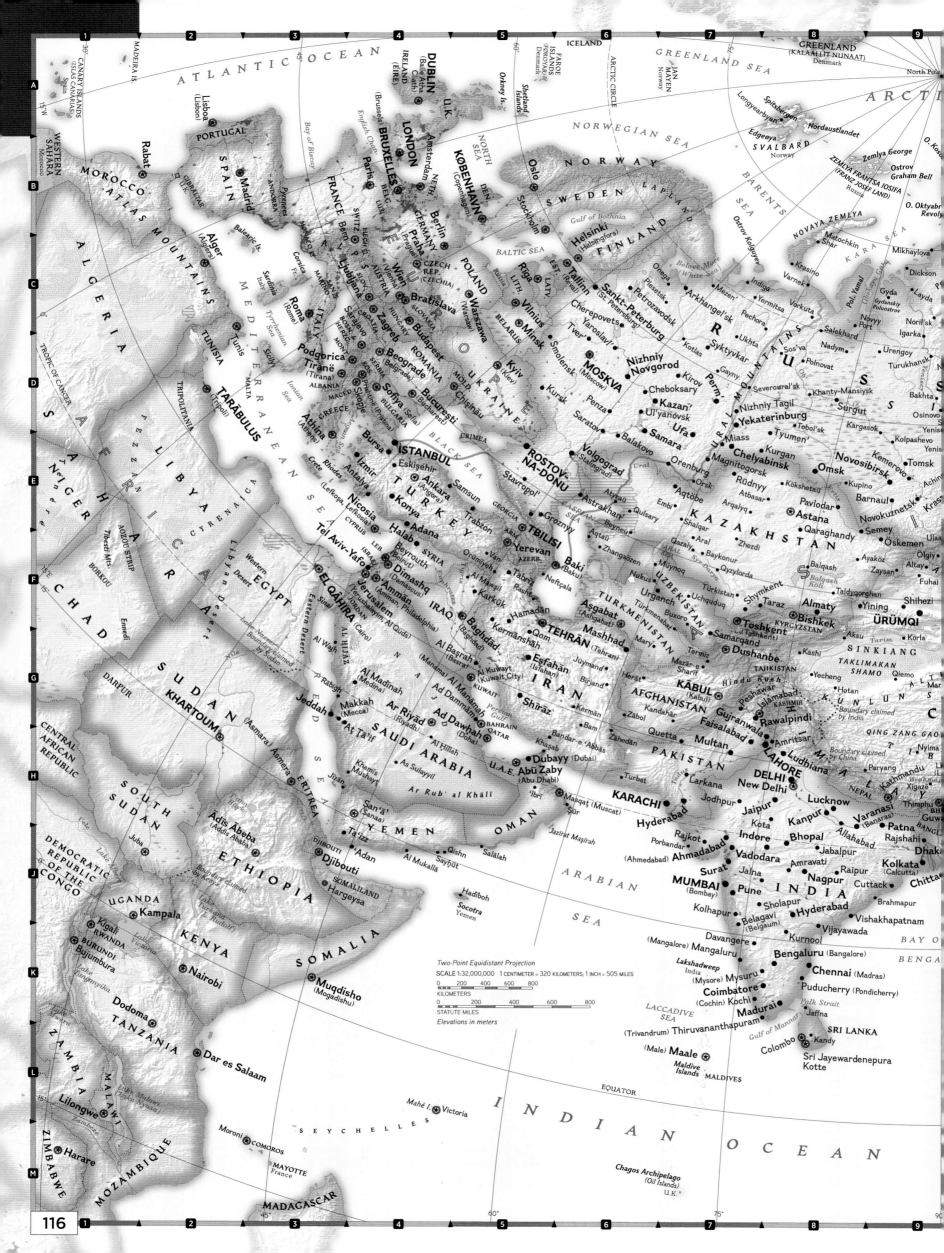

Asia
Political

A commonly accepted division between Asia and Europe—here marked by an orange line—is formed by the Ural Mountains, Ural River, Caspian Sea, Caucasus Mountains, and the Black Sea with its outlets, the Bosporus and Dardanelles.

Continental Data

Total number of countries: 46

First independent country:
Japan, 660 B.C.

"Youngest" country:
Timor-Leste (East Timor), May 20, 2002

Largest country by area:
*China 9,596,960 sq km (3,705,405 sq mi)

Smallest country by area:
Maldives 298 sq km (115 sq mi)

Percent urban population: 47%

Most populous country:
China 1,367,485,000

Least populous country:
Maldives 393,000

Most densely populated country:
Singapore 8,141 per sq km (21,086 per sq mi)

Least densely populated country:
Mongolia 2 per sq km (5 per sq mi)

Largest city by population:
Tokyo, Japan 38,001,000

Highest GDP per capita:
Qatar $145,000

Lowest GDP per capita:
North Korea $1,800

Average life expectancy: 72 years

*The world's largest country, Russia, straddles both Asia and Europe. China, which is entirely within Asia, is considered the continent's largest country.

Human and Natural Themes

POPULATION DENSITY

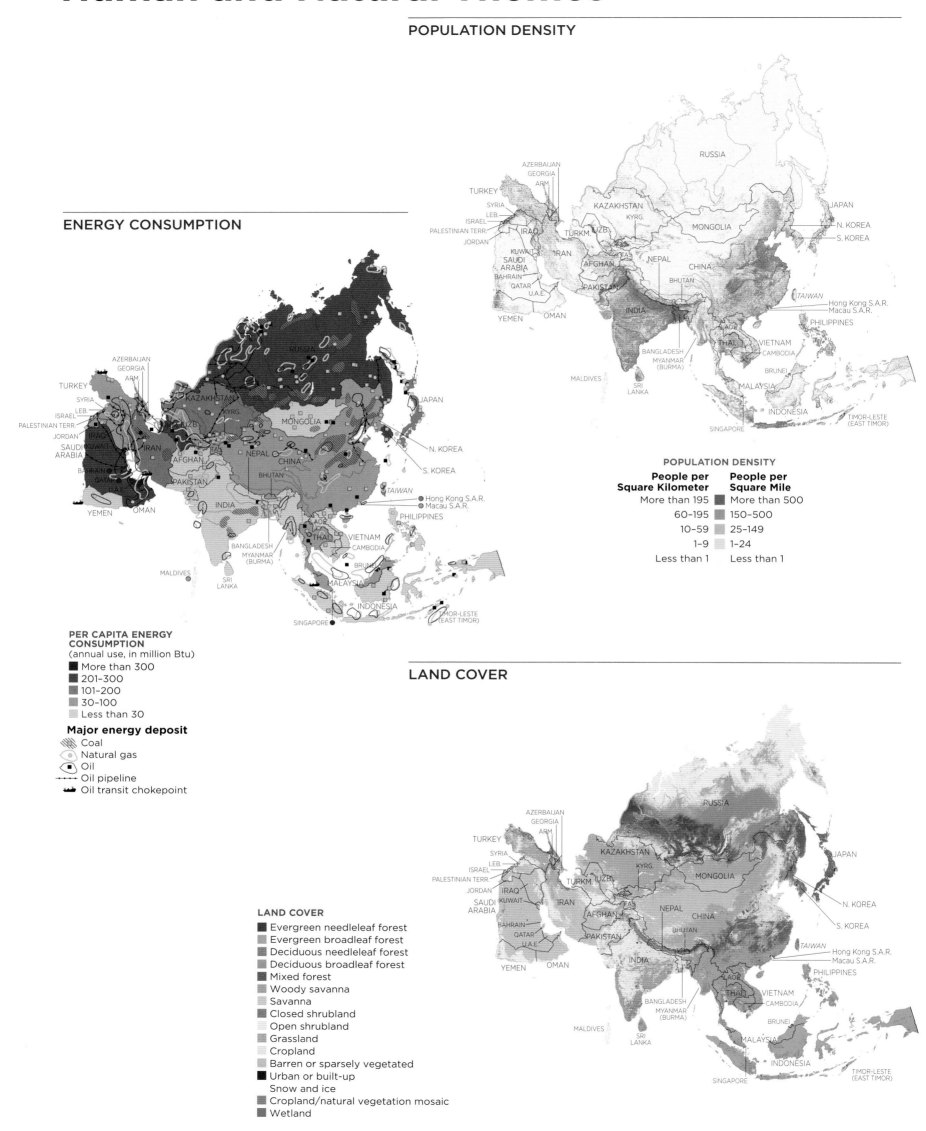

ENERGY CONSUMPTION

PER CAPITA ENERGY CONSUMPTION
(annual use, in million Btu)
- More than 300
- 201–300
- 101–200
- 30–100
- Less than 30

Major energy deposit
- Coal
- Natural gas
- Oil
- Oil pipeline
- Oil transit chokepoint

POPULATION DENSITY

People per Square Kilometer	People per Square Mile
More than 195	More than 500
60–195	150–500
10–59	25–149
1–9	1–24
Less than 1	Less than 1

LAND COVER

LAND COVER
- Evergreen needleleaf forest
- Evergreen broadleaf forest
- Deciduous needleleaf forest
- Deciduous broadleaf forest
- Mixed forest
- Woody savanna
- Savanna
- Closed shrubland
- Open shrubland
- Grassland
- Cropland
- Barren or sparsely vegetated
- Urban or built-up
- Snow and ice
- Cropland/natural vegetation mosaic
- Wetland

CLIMATIC ZONES

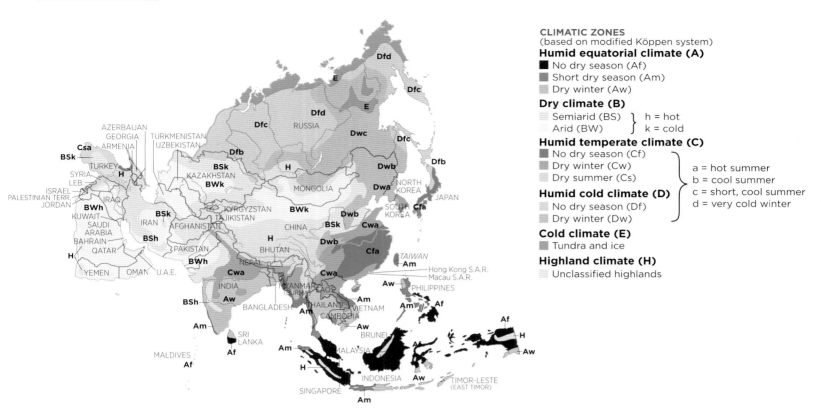

CLIMATIC ZONES
(based on modified Köppen system)

Humud equatorial climate (A)
- No dry season (Af)
- Short dry season (Am)
- Dry winter (Aw)

Dry climate (B)
- Semiarid (BS) } h = hot
- Arid (BW) } k = cold

Humid temperate climate (C)
- No dry season (Cf)
- Dry winter (Cw) } a = hot summer
- Dry summer (Cs) } b = cool summer
                   } c = short, cool summer
Humid cold climate (D) } d = very cold winter
- No dry season (Df)
- Dry winter (Dw)

Cold climate (E)
- Tundra and ice

Highland climate (H)
- Unclassified highlands

NATURAL HAZARDS (TECTONIC EVENTS)

WATER AVAILABILITY

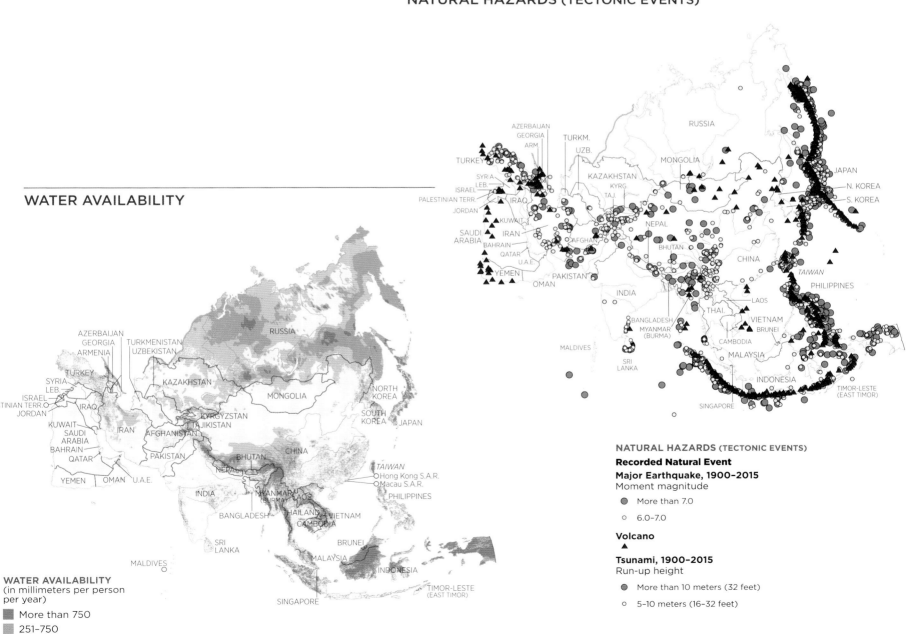

NATURAL HAZARDS (TECTONIC EVENTS)

Recorded Natural Event

Major Earthquake, 1900–2015
Moment magnitude
- ● More than 7.0
- ○ 6.0–7.0

Volcano
- ▲

Tsunami, 1900–2015
Run-up height
- ● More than 10 meters (32 feet)
- ○ 5–10 meters (16–32 feet)

WATER AVAILABILITY
(in millimeters per person
per year)
- More than 750
- 251–750
- 26–250
- Less than 26

Flags and Facts

COUNTRIES

Afghanistan
ISLAMIC REPUBLIC OF
AFGHANISTAN

AREA 652,230 sq km
(251,826 sq mi)
POPULATION 32,564,000
CAPITAL Kabul 4,635,000
RELIGION Sunni Muslim, Shia Muslim
LANGUAGE Afghan Persian or Dari,
Pashto, Turkic languages
LITERACY 38%
LIFE EXPECTANCY 51 years
GDP PER CAPITA $2,000
ECONOMY IND: small-scale production
of textiles, furniture, apparel, food-products,
handwoven carpets, natural gas, coal, copper
AGR: opium, wheat, fruits, nuts, wool, mutton,
sheepskins, lambskins EXP: opium, fruits and
nuts, handwoven carpets, wool, cotton, hides
and pelts, precious and semi-precious gems

Armenia
REPUBLIC OF ARMENIA

AREA 29,743 sq km (11,484 sq mi)
POPULATION 3,056,000
CAPITAL Yerevan 1,044,000
RELIGION Armenian Apostolic
LANGUAGE Armenian
LITERACY 100%
LIFE EXPECTANCY 74 years
GDP PER CAPITA $8,400
ECONOMY IND: diamond-processing,
metal-cutting machine tools, forging-
pressing machines, electric motors, knitted
wear, hosiery, shoes, software development,
food processing, brandy, mining AGR: fruit
(especially grapes), vegetables, livestock
EXP: pig iron, unwrought copper, nonferrous
metals, gold, diamonds, mineral products,
foodstuffs, energy

Azerbaijan
REPUBLIC OF
AZERBAIJAN

AREA 86,600 sq km
(33,436 sq mi)
POPULATION 9,781,000
CAPITAL Baku 2,374,000
RELIGION Muslim
LANGUAGE Azerbaijani (Azeri)
LITERACY 100%
LIFE EXPECTANCY 72 years
GDP PER CAPITA $18,700
ECONOMY IND: petroleum and natural
gas, petroleum products, oilfield equip-
ment, steel, iron ore, cement, chemicals and
petrochemicals, textiles AGR: cotton, grain,
rice, grapes, fruit, vegetables, tea, tobacco,
cattle, pigs, sheep, goats EXP: oil and gas,
machinery, cotton, foodstuffs

Bahrain
KINGDOM OF BAHRAIN

AREA 760 sq km (293 sq mi)
POPULATION 1,347,000
CAPITAL Manama 411,000
RELIGION Muslim, Christian
LANGUAGE Arabic, English, Farsi, Urdu
LITERACY 96%
LIFE EXPECTANCY 79 years
GDP PER CAPITA $51,200
ECONOMY IND: petroleum process-
ing and refining, aluminum smelting, iron
pelletization, fertilizers, Islamic and offshore
banking, insurance, ship repairing, tourism
AGR: fruit, vegetables, poultry, dairy products,
shrimp, fish EXP: petroleum and petroleum
products, aluminum, textiles

Bangladesh
PEOPLE'S REPUBLIC OF
BANGLADESH

AREA 143,998 sq km
(55,598 sq mi)
POPULATION 168,958,000
CAPITAL Dhaka 17,598,000
RELIGION Muslim, Hindu
LANGUAGE Bangla (Bengali)
LITERACY 62%
LIFE EXPECTANCY 71 years
GDP PER CAPITA $3,600
ECONOMY IND: jute, cotton, garments,
paper, leather, cement, chemical fertil-
izer, sugar, natural gas AGR: rice, jute, tea,
wheat, sugarcane, potatoes, tobacco, pulses,
oilseeds, spices, fruit, beef, milk, poultry EXP:
garments, frozen fish and seafood, jute and
jute goods, leather

Bhutan
KINGDOM OF BHUTAN

AREA 38,394 sq km
(14,824 sq mi)
POPULATION 742,000
CAPITAL Thimphu 152,000
RELIGION Lamaistic Buddhist, Indian-
and Nepalese-influenced
Hinduism
LANGUAGE Sharchhopka, Dzongkha,
Lhotshamkha
LITERACY 65%
LIFE EXPECTANCY 70 years
GDP PER CAPITA $8,200
ECONOMY IND: cement, wood products,
processed fruits, alcoholic beverages, calcium
carbide, tourism AGR: rice, corn, root crops,
citrus, foodgrains, dairy products, eggs EXP:
electricity (to India), ferrosilicon, cement,
calcium carbide, copper wire, manganese,
vegetable oil

Brunei
BRUNEI DARUSSALAM

AREA 5,765 sq km (2,226 sq mi)
POPULATION 430,000
CAPITAL Bandar Seri Begawan
241,000
RELIGION Muslim, Christian, Buddhist
LANGUAGE Malay, English, Chinese
LITERACY 96%
LIFE EXPECTANCY 77 years
GDP PER CAPITA $79,700
ECONOMY IND: petroleum, petroleum
refining, liquefied natural gas, construction
AGR: rice, vegetables, fruits, chickens, water
buffalo, cattle, goats, eggs EXP: crude oil,
natural gas, garments

Cambodia
KINGDOM OF CAMBODIA

AREA 181,035 sq km
(69,898 sq mi)
POPULATION 15,709,000
CAPITAL Phnom Penh 1,731,000
RELIGION Buddhist
LANGUAGE Khmer, other
LITERACY 77%
LIFE EXPECTANCY 64 years
GDP PER CAPITA $3,500
ECONOMY IND: tourism, garments,
construction, rice milling, fishing, wood and
wood products, rubber, cement, gem mining,
textiles AGR: rice, rubber, corn, vegetables,
cashews, tapioca, silk EXP: clothing, timber,
rubber, rice, fish, tobacco, footwear

China
PEOPLE'S REPUBLIC
OF CHINA

AREA 9,596,960 sq km
(3,705,405 sq mi)
POPULATION 1,367,485,000
CAPITAL Beijing 20,384,000
RELIGION Buddhist, folk religion
LANGUAGE Mandarin, Yue, Wu, Minbei,
Minnan, Xiang, Gan, Hakka
LITERACY 96%
LIFE EXPECTANCY 75 years
GDP PER CAPITA $14,300
ECONOMY IND: mining and ore processing, iron, steel, aluminum, and other metals,
coal, machine building, armaments, textiles
and apparel, petroleum, cement, chemicals,
fertilizers, consumer products, footwear, toys,
and electronics, food processing, transportation equipment, automobiles, rail cars and
locomotives, ships, aircraft, telecommunications equipment, commercial space launch
vehicles, satellites AGR: rice, wheat, potatoes,
corn, peanuts, tea, millet, barley, apples,
cotton, oilseed, pork, fish EXP: electrical and
other machinery, data processing equipment,
apparel, furniture, textiles, integrated circuits

Georgia
GEORGIA

AREA 69,700 sq km
(26,911 sq mi)
POPULATION 4,931,000
CAPITAL Tbilisi 1,147,000
RELIGION Orthodox Christian, Muslim
LANGUAGE Georgian, Russian
LITERACY 100%
LIFE EXPECTANCY 76 years
GDP PER CAPITA $9,500
ECONOMY IND: steel, aircraft, machine
tools, electrical appliances, mining (man-
ganese, copper, gold), chemicals, wood
products, wine AGR: citrus, grapes, tea,
hazelnuts, vegetables, livestock EXP: vehicles,
ferroalloys, fertilizer, nuts, gold, copper ore

India
REPUBLIC OF INDIA

AREA 3,287,263 sq km
(1,269,212 sq mi)
POPULATION 1,251,696,000
CAPITAL New Delhi 25,703,000
RELIGION Hindu, Muslim
LANGUAGE Hindi, Bengali, English,
13 other official languages
LITERACY 71%
LIFE EXPECTANCY 68 years
GDP PER CAPITA $6,300
ECONOMY IND: textiles, chemicals, food
processing, steel, transportation equipment,
cement, mining, petroleum, machinery,
software, pharmaceuticals AGR: rice, wheat,
oilseed, cotton, jute, tea, sugarcane, lentils,
onions, potatoes, dairy products, sheep,
goats, poultry, fish EXP: petroleum products,
precious stones, machinery, iron and steel,
chemicals, vehicles, apparel

Indonesia
REPUBLIC OF INDONESIA

AREA 1,904,569 sq km
(735,354 sq mi)
POPULATION 255,994,000
CAPITAL Jakarta 10,323,000
RELIGION Muslim, Christian
LANGUAGE Bahasa Indonesia, English,
Dutch, Javanese
LITERACY 94%
LIFE EXPECTANCY 72 years
GDP PER CAPITA $11,300
ECONOMY IND: petroleum and natural
gas, textiles, apparel, footwear, mining, ce-
ment, chemical fertilizers, plywood, rubber,
food, tourism AGR: rubber, palm oil, poultry,
beef, shrimp, cocoa, coffee medicinal herbs,
essential oils, fish, spices EXP: palm oil, oil
and gas, ores and slags, electrical appliances,
plywood, textiles, rubber

Iran
ISLAMIC REPUBLIC
OF IRAN

AREA 1,648,195 sq km
(636,368 sq mi)
POPULATION 81,824,000
CAPITAL Tehran 8,432,000
RELIGION Shia Muslim, Sunni Muslim
LANGUAGE Persian, Azeri Turkic,
Kurdish
LITERACY 87%
LIFE EXPECTANCY 71 years
GDP PER CAPITA $17,800
ECONOMY IND: petroleum, petrochemicals, fertilizers, caustic soda, textiles,
cement and other construction materials,
food processing (particularly sugar refining
and vegetable oil production), ferrous and
non-ferrous metal fabrication, armaments
AGR: wheat, rice, other grains, sugar beets,
sugar cane, fruits, nuts, cotton, dairy products, wool, caviar EXP: petroleum, chemical
and petrochemical products, fruits and nuts,
carpets, cement, ore

Iraq
REPUBLIC OF IRAQ

AREA 438,317 sq km
(169,234 sq mi)
POPULATION 37,056,000
CAPITAL Baghdad 6,643,000
RELIGION Shia Muslim, Sunni Muslim
LANGUAGE Arabic, Kurdish, Turkoman,
Assyrian, Armenian
LITERACY 80%
LIFE EXPECTANCY 75 years
GDP PER CAPITA $15,500
ECONOMY IND: petroleum, chemicals,
textiles, leather, construction materials, food
processing, fertilizer, metal fabrication/pro-
cessing AGR: wheat, barley, rice, vegetables,
dates, cotton, cattle, sheep, poultry
EXP: crude oil, crude materials excluding
fuels, food and live animals

Israel
STATE OF ISRAEL

AREA 20,770 sq km
(8,019 sq mi)
POPULATION 8,049,000
CAPITAL Jerusalem 839,000
RELIGION Jewish, Muslim, Christian
LANGUAGE Hebrew, Arabic, English
LITERACY 98%
LIFE EXPECTANCY 82 years
GDP PER CAPITA $34,300
ECONOMY IND: high-technology products, wood and paper products, potash and
phosphates, food, beverages, and tobacco,
caustic soda, construction, metals products,
chemical products, plastics, cut diamonds,
textiles, footwear AGR: citrus, vegetables,
cotton, beef, poultry, dairy products EXP:
machinery and equipment, software, cut
diamonds, agricultural products, chemicals,
textiles and apparel

Japan
JAPAN

AREA 377,915 sq km
(145,913 sq mi)
POPULATION 126,920,000
CAPITAL Tokyo 38,001,000
RELIGION Shintoism, Buddhism
LANGUAGE Japanese
LITERACY 99%
LIFE EXPECTANCY 85 years
GDP PER CAPITA $38,200
ECONOMY IND: motor vehicles, electronic equipment, machine tools, steel and
nonferrous metals, ships, chemicals, textiles,
processed foods AGR: rice, sugar beets, vegetables, fruit, pork, poultry, dairy products,
eggs, fish EXP: motor vehicles, electronic
equipment, machine tools, iron and steel
products, ships, chemicals, processed foods

Jordan

HASHEMITE KINGDOM OF JORDAN

AREA 89,342 sq km (34,495 sq mi)
POPULATION 8,118,000
CAPITAL Amman 1,155,000
RELIGION Sunni Muslim
LANGUAGE Arabic, English
LITERACY 98%
LIFE EXPECTANCY 74 years
GDP PER CAPITA $12,400
ECONOMY **Ind:** tourism, information technology, clothing, fertilizers, potash, phophate mining, pharmaceuticals, petroleum refining, cement, inorganic chemicals **Agr:** citrus, tomatoes, cucumbers, olives, strawberries, stone fruits, sheep, poultry, dairy **Exp:** clothing, fertilizers, potash, phosphates, vegetables, pharmaceuticals

Kazakhstan

REPUBLIC OF KAZAKHSTAN

AREA 2,724,900 sq km (1,052,084 sq mi)
POPULATION 18,157,000
CAPITAL Astana 759,000
RELIGION Muslim, Russian Orthodox
LANGUAGE Kazakh, Russian
LITERACY 100%
LIFE EXPECTANCY 71 years
GDP PER CAPITA $24,700
ECONOMY **Ind:** oil, coal, iron ore, manganese, chromite, lead, zinc, copper, titanium, bauxite, gold, silver, phosphates, sulfur, uranium, iron and steel, tractors and other agricultural machinery, electric motors, construction materials **Agr:** grain (mostly spring wheat), cotton, livestock **Exp:** oil and oil products, ferrous metals, chemicals, machinery, grain, wool, meat, coal

Kuwait

STATE OF KUWAIT

AREA 17,818 sq km (6,880 sq mi)
POPULATION 2,789,000
CAPITAL Kuwait City 2,779,000
RELIGION Muslim, Christian
LANGUAGE Arabic, English
LITERACY 96%
LIFE EXPECTANCY 78 years
GDP PER CAPITA $72,200
ECONOMY **Ind:** petroleum, petrochemicals, cement, shipbuilding and repair, water desalination, food processing, construction materials **Agr:** fish **Exp:** oil and refined products, fertilizers

Kyrgyzstan

KYRGYZ REPUBLIC

AREA 199,951 sq km (77,201 sq mi)
POPULATION 5,665,000
CAPITAL Bishkek 865,000
RELIGION Muslim, Russian Orthodox
LANGUAGE Kyrgyz, Uzbek, Russian
LITERACY 100%
LIFE EXPECTANCY 70 years
GDP PER CAPITA $3,400
ECONOMY **Ind:** small machinery, textiles, food processing, cement, shoes, sawn logs, refrigerators, furniture, electric motors, gold, rare earth metals **Agr:** tobacco, cotton, potatoes, vegetables, grapes, fruits and berries, sheep, goats, cattle, wool **Exp:** gold, cotton, wool, garments, meat, tobacco, mercury, uranium, hydropower, machinery, shoes

Laos
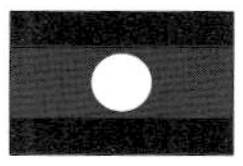

LAO PEOPLE'S DEMOCRATIC REPUBLIC

AREA 236,800 sq km (91,428 sq mi)
POPULATION 6,912,000
CAPITAL Vientiane 997,000
RELIGION Buddhist, other
LANGUAGE Lao, French, English
LITERACY 80%
LIFE EXPECTANCY 64 years
GDP PER CAPITA $5,400
ECONOMY **Ind:** copper, tin, gold, and gypsum mining, timber, electric power, agricultural processing, construction, garments, cement, tourism **Agr:** sweet potatoes, vegetables, corn, coffee, sugarcane, tobacco, cotton, tea, peanuts, rice, water buffalo, pigs, cattle, poultry **Exp:** wood products, coffee, electricity, tin, copper, gold, cassava

Lebanon

LEBANESE REPUBLIC

AREA 10,400 sq km (4,015 sq mi)
POPULATION 6,185,000
CAPITAL Beirut 2,226,000
RELIGION Muslim, Christian
LANGUAGE Arabic, French, English, Armenian
LITERACY 94%
LIFE EXPECTANCY 77 years
GDP PER CAPITA $18,600
ECONOMY **Ind:** banking, tourism, food processing, wine, jewelry, cement, textiles, mineral and chemical products, wood and furniture products, oil refining, metal fabricating **Agr:** citrus, grapes, tomatoes, apples, vegetables, potatoes, olives, tobacco, sheep, goats **Exp:** jewelry, base metals, chemicals, miscellaneous consumer goods, fruit and vegetables, tobacco, construction minerals, textile fibers, paper

Malaysia

MALAYSIA

AREA 329,847 sq km (127,354 sq mi)
POPULATION 30,514,000
CAPITAL Kuala Lumpur 6,837,000
RELIGION Muslim, Buddhist, Christian
LANGUAGE Bahasa Malaysia, English, Chinese, Tamil, Telugu, Malayalam, Panjabi, Thai
LITERACY 95%
LIFE EXPECTANCY 75 years
GDP PER CAPITA $26,600
ECONOMY **Ind:** rubber and oil palm processing and manufacturing, light manufacturing, pharmaceuticals, medical technology, electronics, logging, timber processing, petroleum production, agriculture processing **Agr:** palm oil, rubber, cocoa, rice, subsistence crops, timber, pepper **Exp:** electronic equipment, petroleum and liquefied natural gas, wood and wood products, rubber, textiles, chemicals, solar panels

Maldives

REPUBLIC OF MALDIVES

AREA 298 sq km (115 sq mi)
POPULATION 393,000
CAPITAL Male 156,000
RELIGION Sunni Muslim
LANGUAGE Dhivehi, English
LITERACY 94%
LIFE EXPECTANCY 75 years
GDP PER CAPITA $13,600
ECONOMY **Ind:** tourism, fish processing, shipping, boat building, coconut processing, garments, woven mats, rope, handicrafts, coral and sand mining **Agr:** coconuts, corn, sweet potatoes, fish **Exp:** fish

Mongolia

MONGOLIA

AREA 1,564,116 sq km (603,905 sq mi)
POPULATION 2,993,000
CAPITAL Ulaanbaatar 1,377,000
RELIGION Buddhist, Muslim, Christian
LANGUAGE Khalkha Mongol, Turkic, Russian
LITERACY 98%
LIFE EXPECTANCY 69 years
GDP PER CAPITA $12,500
ECONOMY **Ind:** construction and construction materials, mining (coal, copper, molybdenum, fluorspar, tin, tungsten, and gold), oil, food and beverages, cashmere and natural fiber manufacturing **Agr:** wheat, barley, vegetables, forage crops, sheep, goats, cattle, camels, horses **Exp:** copper, apparel, livestock, animal products, cashmere, wool, hides, fluorspar, other nonferrous metals, coal, crude oil

Myanmar (Burma)

REPUBLIC OF THE UNION OF MYANMAR

AREA 676,578 sq km (261,227 sq mi)
POPULATION 56,320,000
CAPITAL Yangon (legislative) 4,802,000, Nay Pyi Taw (administrative) 1,030,000
RELIGION Buddhist
LANGUAGE Burmese
LITERACY 93%
LIFE EXPECTANCY 66 years
GDP PER CAPITA $5,200
ECONOMY **Ind:** agricultural processing, wood and wood products, copper, tin, tungsten, iron, cement, construction materials, pharmaceuticals, fertilizer, oil and natural gas, garments, jade and gems **Agr:** rice, pulses, beans, sesame, groundnuts, sugarcane, hardwood, fish and fish products **Exp:** natural gas, wood products, pulses, beans, fish, rice, clothing, jade and gems

Nepal

FEDERAL DEMOCRATIC REPUBLIC OF NEPAL

AREA 147,181 sq km (56,827 sq mi)
POPULATION 31,551,000
CAPITAL Kathmandu 1,183,000
RELIGION Hindu, Buddhist
LANGUAGE Nepali, Maithali
LITERACY 64%
LIFE EXPECTANCY 68 years
GDP PER CAPITA $2,500
ECONOMY **Ind:** tourism, carpets, textiles, small rice, jute, sugar, and oilseed mills, cigarettes, cement and brick production **Agr:** pulses, rice, corn, wheat, sugarcane, jute, root crops, milk, water buffalo meat **Exp:** clothing, pulses, carpets, textiles, juice, pashima, jute goods

North Korea

DEMOCRATIC PEOPLE'S REPUBLIC OF KOREA

AREA 120,538 sq km (46,540 sq mi)
POPULATION 24,983,000
CAPITAL Pyongyang 2,863,000
RELIGION None, Buddhist, Confucianist
LANGUAGE Korean
LITERACY 100%
LIFE EXPECTANCY 70 years
GDP PER CAPITA $1,800
ECONOMY **Ind:** military products, machine building, electric power, chemicals, mining (coal, iron ore, limestone, magnesite, graphite, copper, zinc, lead, and precious metals), metallurgy, textiles, food processing, tourism **Agr:** rice, corn, potatoes, soybeans, pulses, cattle, pigs, pork, eggs **Exp:** minerals, metallurgical products, textiles, agricultural and fishery products

Oman

SULTANATE OF OMAN

AREA 309,500 sq km (119,498 sq mi)
POPULATION 3,287,000
CAPITAL Muscat 838,000
RELIGION Ibadhi Muslim
LANGUAGE Arabic, English, Baluchi, Urdu
LITERACY 91%
LIFE EXPECTANCY 75 years
GDP PER CAPITA $46,200
ECONOMY **Ind:** crude oil production and refining, natural and liquefied natural gas production, construction, cement, copper, steel, chemicals, optic fiber **Agr:** dates, limes, bananas, alfalfa, vegetables, camels, cattle, fish **Exp:** petroleum, reexports, fish, metals, textiles

Pakistan

ISLAMIC REPUBLIC OF PAKISTAN

AREA 796,095 sq km (307,372 sq mi)
POPULATION 199,086,000
CAPITAL Islamabad 1,365,000
RELIGION Sunni Muslim, Shia Muslim
LANGUAGE Punjabi, Sindhi, Saraiki, English, Urdu
LITERACY 58%
LIFE EXPECTANCY 67 years
GDP PER CAPITA $4,900
ECONOMY **Ind:** textiles and apparel, food processing, pharmaceuticals, construction materials, paper products, fertilizer, shrimp **Agr:** cotton, wheat, rice, sugarcane, fruits, vegetables, milk, beef, mutton, eggs **Exp:** textiles (garments, bed linen, cotton cloth, yarn), rice, leather goods, sports goods, chemicals, manufactures, carpets and rugs

Philippines

REPUBLIC OF THE PHILIPPINES

AREA 300,000 sq km (115,830 sq mi)
POPULATION 100,998,000
CAPITAL Manila 12,946,000
RELIGION Catholic
LANGUAGE Filipino, English, Tagalog
LITERACY 96%
LIFE EXPECTANCY 69 years
GDP PER CAPITA $7,500
ECONOMY **Ind:** electronics assembly, garments, footwear, pharmaceuticals, chemicals, wood products, petroleum refining, fishing **Agr:** sugarcane, coconuts, rice, corn, bananas, cassavas, pineapples, mangoes, beef, fish **Exp:** semiconductors and electronic products, transport equipment, garments, petroleum products, coconut oil, fruits

Qatar
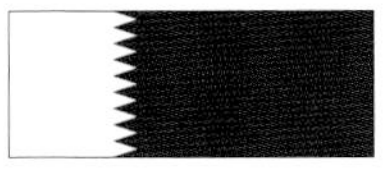

STATE OF QATAR

AREA 11,586 sq km (4,473 sq mi)
POPULATION 2,195,000
CAPITAL Doha 718,000
RELIGION Muslim, Christian
LANGUAGE Arabic, English
LITERACY 97%
LIFE EXPECTANCY 79 years
GDP PER CAPITA $145,000
ECONOMY **Ind:** liquefied natural gas, crude oil production and refining, ammonia, fertilizers, petrochemicals, steel reinforcing bars, cement, commercial ship repair **Agr:** fruits, vegetables, poultry, dairy products, beef, fish **Exp:** liquefied natural gas, petroleum products, fertilizers, steel

Flags and Facts

Saudi Arabia
KINGDOM OF SAUDI ARABIA

AREA	2,149,690 sq km (829,995 sq mi)
POPULATION	27,752,000
CAPITAL	Riyadh 6,195,000
RELIGION	Muslim
LANGUAGE	Arabic
LITERACY	95%
LIFE EXPECTANCY	75 years
GDP PER CAPITA	$54,600

ECONOMY IND: crude oil production, petroleum refining, basic petrochemicals, ammonia, industrial gases, sodium hydroxide (caustic soda), cement, fertilizer, plastics, metals, commercial aircraft repair, construction **AGR:** wheat, barley, tomatoes, melons, dates, citrus, mutton, chickens, eggs, milk **EXP:** petroleum and petroleum products

Singapore
REPUBLIC OF SINGAPORE

AREA	697 sq km (269 sq mi)
POPULATION	5,674,000
CAPITAL	Singapore 5,619,000
RELIGION	Buddhist, Muslim, Taoist
LANGUAGE	Mandarin, English, Malay, Hokkien, Tamil
LITERACY	97%
LIFE EXPECTANCY	85 years
GDP PER CAPITA	$85,700

ECONOMY IND: electronics, chemicals, financial services, oil drilling equipment, petroleum refining, rubber products, processed food and beverages, ship repair, offshore platform construction, life sciences, entrepot trade **AGR:** orchids, vegetables, poultry, eggs, fish, ornamental fish **EXP:** machinery and electronic equipment, pharmaceuticals and other chemicals, refined petroleum products

South Korea
REPUBLIC OF KOREA

AREA	99,720 sq km (38,502 sq mi)
POPULATION	49,115,000
CAPITAL	Seoul 9,774,000
RELIGION	None, Christian, Buddhist
LANGUAGE	Korean, English
LITERACY	98%
LIFE EXPECTANCY	80 years
GDP PER CAPITA	$36,700

ECONOMY IND: electronics, telecommunications, automobile production, chemicals, shipbuilding, steel **AGR:** rice, root crops, barley, vegetables, fruit, cattle, pigs, chickens, milk, eggs, fish **EXP:** semiconductors, petrochemicals, automobile/auto parts, wireless telecommunications equipment, computers, steel, ships

Sri Lanka
DEMOCRATIC SOCIALIST REPUBLIC OF SRI LANKA

AREA	65,610 sq km (25,332 sq mi)
POPULATION	22,053,000
CAPITAL	Colombo (administrative) 707,000, Sri Jayewardenepura Kotte (legislative) 128,000
RELIGION	Buddhist, Hindu
LANGUAGE	Sinhala, Tamil, English
LITERACY	93%
LIFE EXPECTANCY	77 years
GDP PER CAPITA	$11,200

ECONOMY IND: processing of rubber, tea, coconuts, tobacco and other agricultural commodities, banking, tourism, shipping, clothing, textiles, cement, petroleum refining, information technology services, construction **AGR:** rice, sugarcane, grains, pulses, oilseed, spices, vegetables, fruit, tea, rubber, coconuts, milk, eggs, hides, beef, fish **EXP:** textiles and apparel, tea and spices, rubber manufactures, precious stones, coconut products, fish

Syria
SYRIAN ARAB REPUBLIC

AREA	185,180 sq km (71,498 sq mi)
POPULATION	17,065,000
CAPITAL	Damascus 2,566,000
RELIGION	Sunni Muslim, other Muslim, Christian
LANGUAGE	Arabic, Kurdish, Armenian, Aramaic, Circassian, French, English
LITERACY	86%
LIFE EXPECTANCY	75 years
GDP PER CAPITA	$5,100

ECONOMY IND: petroleum, textiles, food processing, beverages, tobacco, phosphate rock mining, cement, oil seeds crushing, car assembly **AGR:** wheat, barley, cotton, lentils, chickpeas, olives, sugar beets, beef, mutton, eggs, poultry, milk **EXP:** crude oil, minerals, petroleum products, fruits and vegetables, cotton fiber, textiles, clothing, meat and live animals, wheat

Tajikistan
REPUBLIC OF TAJIKISTAN

AREA	143,100 sq km (55,251 sq mi)
POPULATION	8,192,000
CAPITAL	Dushanbe 822,000
RELIGION	Sunni Muslim, Shia Muslim
LANGUAGE	Tajik, Russian
LITERACY	100%
LIFE EXPECTANCY	67 years
GDP PER CAPITA	$2,800

ECONOMY IND: aluminum, cement, vegetable oil **AGR:** cotton, grain, fruits, grapes, vegetables, cattle, sheep, goats **EXP:** aluminum, electricity, cotton, fruits, vegetable oil, textiles

Thailand
KINGDOM OF THAILAND

AREA	513,120 sq km (198,116 sq mi)
POPULATION	67,976,000
CAPITAL	Bangkok 9,270,000
RELIGION	Buddhist
LANGUAGE	Thai, English
LITERACY	97%
LIFE EXPECTANCY	74 years
GDP PER CAPITA	$16,100

ECONOMY IND: tourism, textiles and garments, agricultural processing, beverages, tobacco, cement, light manufacturing such as jewelry and electric appliances, computers and parts, integrated circuits, plastics, tungsten, tin **AGR:** rice, cassava (tapioca), rubber, corn, sugarcane, coconuts, fish products **EXP:** automobiles and parts, chemical products, rice, rubber, jewelry, automobiles, machinery and parts

Timor-Leste (East Timor)
DEMOCRATIC REPUBLIC OF TIMOR-LESTE

AREA	14,874 sq km (5,743 sq mi)
POPULATION	1,231,000
CAPITAL	Dili 228,000
RELIGION	Roman Catholic
LANGUAGE	Tetum, Portuguese, Indonesian, English
LITERACY	68%
LIFE EXPECTANCY	68 years
GDP PER CAPITA	$5,800

ECONOMY IND: printing, soap manufacturing, handicrafts, woven cloth **AGR:** coffee, rice, corn, cassava, sweet potatoes, soybeans, cabbage, mangoes, bananas, vanilla **EXP:** coffee, sandalwood, marble

Turkey
REPUBLIC OF TURKEY

AREA	783,562 sq km (302,533 sq mi)
POPULATION	79,414,000
CAPITAL	Ankara 4,750,000
RELIGION	Sunni Muslim
LANGUAGE	Turkish, Kurdish
LITERACY	95%
LIFE EXPECTANCY	75 years
GDP PER CAPITA	$20,500

ECONOMY IND: textiles, food processing, autos, electronics, mining (coal, chromate, copper, boron), steel, petroleum, construction, lumber, paper **AGR:** tobacco, cotton, grain, olives, sugar beets, hazelnuts, pulse, citrus, livestock **EXP:** apparel, foodstuffs, textiles, metal manufactures, transport equipment

Turkmenistan
TURKMENISTAN

AREA	488,100 sq km (188,455 sq mi)
POPULATION	5,231,000
CAPITAL	Ashgabat 746,000
RELIGION	Muslim
LANGUAGE	Turkmen, Russian, Uzbek
LITERACY	100%
LIFE EXPECTANCY	70 years
GDP PER CAPITA	$15,600

ECONOMY IND: natural gas, oil, petroleum products, textiles, food processing **AGR:** cotton, grain, melons livestock **EXP:** gas, crude oil, petrochemicals, textiles, cotton fiber

United Arab Emirates
UNITED ARAB EMIRATES

AREA	83,600 sq km (32,278 sq mi)
POPULATION	5,780,000
CAPITAL	Abu Dhabi 1,145,000
RELIGION	Muslim, Christian
LANGUAGE	Arabic, Persian, English, Hindi, Urdu
LITERACY	94%
LIFE EXPECTANCY	77 years
GDP PER CAPITA	$67,000

ECONOMY IND: petroleum and petrochemicals, fishing, aluminum, cement, fertilizers, commercial ship repair, construction materials, some boat building, handicrafts, textiles **AGR:** dates, vegetables, watermelons, poultry, eggs, dairy products, fish **EXP:** crude oil, natural gas, reexports, dried fish, dates

Uzbekistan
REPUBLIC OF UZBEKISTAN

AREA	447,400 sq km (172,741 sq mi)
POPULATION	29,200,000
CAPITAL	Tashkent 2,251,000
RELIGION	Sunni Muslim
LANGUAGE	Uzbek, Russian
LITERACY	100%
LIFE EXPECTANCY	74 years
GDP PER CAPITA	$6,100

ECONOMY IND: textiles, food processing, machine building, metallurgy, mining, hydrocarbon extraction, chemicals **AGR:** cotton, vegetables, fruits, grain, livestock **EXP:** energy products, cotton, gold, mineral fertilizers, ferrous and nonferrous metals, textiles, food products, machinery, automobiles

Vietnam
SOCIALIST REPUBLIC OF VIETNAM

AREA	331,210 sq km (127,880 sq mi)
POPULATION	94,349,000
CAPITAL	Hanoi 3,629,000
RELIGION	None, Buddhist
LANGUAGE	Vietnamese, English
LITERACY	95%
LIFE EXPECTANCY	73 years
GDP PER CAPITA	$6,100

ECONOMY IND: food processing, garments, shoes, machine-building, mining, coal, steel, cement, chemical fertilizer, glass, tires, oil, mobile phones **AGR:** rice, coffee, rubber, tea, pepper, soybeans, cashews, sugar cane, peanuts, bananas, poultry, fish, seafood **EXP:** food processing, garmets, shoes, machine-building; mining, coal, steel, cement, chemical fertilizer, glass, tires, oil, mobile phones

Protected Areas

Yemen
REPUBLIC OF YEMEN

AREA	527,968 sq km (203,848 sq mi)
POPULATION	26,737,000
CAPITAL	Sanaa 2,962,000
RELIGION	Muslim
LANGUAGE	Arabic
LITERACY	70%
LIFE EXPECTANCY	65 years
GDP PER CAPITA	$2,800

ECONOMY **IND:** crude oil production and petroleum refining, small-scale production of cotton textiles and leather goods, food processing, handicrafts, small aluminum products factory, cement, commercial ship repair, natural gas production **AGR:** grain, fruits, vegetables, pulses, qat, coffee, cotton, dairy products, livestock (sheep, goats, cattle, camels), poultry, fish **EXP:** crude oil, coffee, dried and salted fish, liquefied natural gas

DISPUTED TERRITORIES

Gaza Strip
GAZA STRIP

AREA	360 sq km (139 sq mi)
POPULATION	1,869,000
CAPITAL	none
RELIGION	Sunni Muslim
LANGUAGE	Arabic, Hebrew, English
LITERACY	97%
LIFE EXPECTANCY	75 years
GDP PER CAPITA	NA

ECONOMY **IND:** textiles, food processing, furniture **AGR:** olives, fruit, vegetables, flowers, beef, dairy products **EXP:** strawberries, carnations, vegetables, fish

Taiwan
REPUBLIC OF CHINA, CHINA

AREA	35,980 sq km (13,892 sq mi)
POPULATION	23,415,000
CAPITAL	Taipei 2,666,000
RELIGION	mixture of Buddhist and Taoist
LANGUAGE	Mandarin, Taiwanese, Hakka
LITERACY	99%
LIFE EXPECTANCY	80 years
GDP PER CAPITA	$47,500

ECONOMY **IND:** electronics, communications and information technology products, petroleum refining, textiles, iron and steel, machinery, food processing, vehicles, consumer products, pharmaceuticals **AGR:** rice, vegetables, fruit, tea, flowers, pigs, poultry, fish **EXP:** semiconductors, petrochemicals, ships, wireless communication equipment, flat display displays, electronics, computers

West Bank
WEST BANK

AREA	5,860 sq km (2,263 sq mi)
POPULATION	2,785,000
CAPITAL	none
RELIGION	Muslim, Jewish
LANGUAGE	Arabic, Hebrew, English
LITERACY	97%
LIFE EXPECTANCY	76 years
GDP PER CAPITA	$4,300

ECONOMY **IND:** small-scale manufacturing, quarrying, textiles, soap, olive-wood carvings, and mother-of-pearl souvenirs **AGR:** olives, citrus fruit, vegetables, beef, dairy products **EXP:** stone, olives, fruit, vegetables, limestone

Protected Areas
- Terrestrial
- Marine

Protected areas as defined by the International Union for Conservation of Nature (IUCN). The degree of protection and governing body varies by protected area.

Two-Point Equidistant Projection
SCALE 1:42,845,000

0 km 400
0 mi 300 600

1 CENTIMETER = 428 KILOMETERS; 1 INCH = 676 MILES

Africa

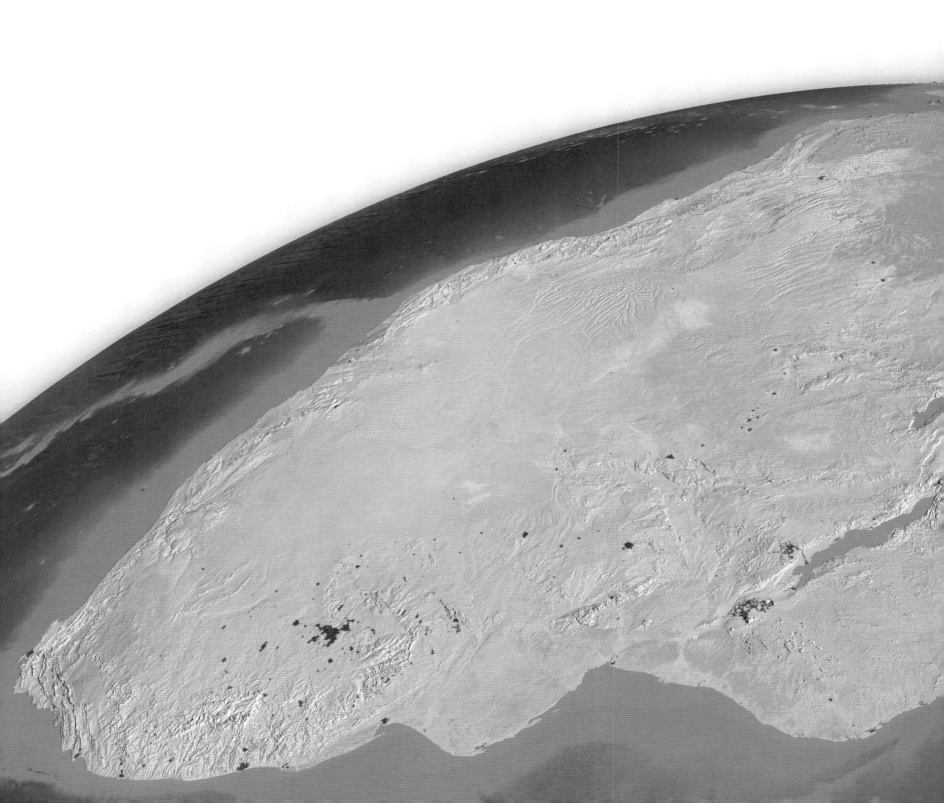

ELEMENTAL AND UNCONQUERABLE, Africa remains something of a paradox among continents. Birthplace of humankind and of the great early civilizations of Egypt and Kush, also called Nubia, the continent has since thwarted human efforts to exploit many of its resources. The forbidding sweep of the Sahara, largest desert in the world, holds the northern third of Africa in thrall, while the bordering Sahel sands alternately advance and recede in unpredictable, drought-invoking rhythms. In contrast to the long, life-giving thread of the Nile, the lake district in the east, and the Congo drainage in central Africa, few major waterways provide irrigation and commercial navigation to large, arid segments of the continent.

Africa's unforgettable form, bulging to the west, lies surrounded by oceans and seas. The East African Rift System is the continent's most dramatic geologic feature. This great rent actually begins in the Red Sea, then cuts southward to form the stunning landscape of lakes, volcanoes, and deep valleys that finally ends near the mouth of the Zambezi River. Caused by the Earth's crust pulling apart, the rift may one day separate East Africa from the rest of the continent.

Most of Africa is made up of savanna—high, rolling, grassy plains. These savannas have been home since earliest times to people often called

Bantu, a reference both to social groupings and to their languages. Other distinct physical types exist around the continent as well: BaMbuti (Pygmies), San (Bushmen), Nilo-Saharans, and Hamito-Semitics (Berbers and Cushites). Africa's astonishing 1,600 spoken languages—more than any other continent—reflect the great diversity of ethnic and social groups.

Africa ranks among the richest regions in the world in natural resources; it contains vast reserves of fossil fuels and precious metals, ores, and gems, including almost all of the world's chromium, much uranium, copper, enormous underground gold reserves, and diamonds. Yet Africa accounts for a mere one percent of world economic output. South Africa's economy alone nearly equals those of all other sub-Saharan countries. Many obstacles complicate the way forward. Lack of clean water and the spread of diseases—malaria, tuberculosis, cholera, and AIDS—undermine people's health. AIDS has shortened life expectancy to 47 years in parts of Africa, destroyed families, and erased decades of social progress and economic activity by killing people in their prime working years. In addition, war and huge concentrations of refugees displaced by fighting, persecution, and famine deter any chance of growth and stability.

Africa's undeveloped natural beauty—along with its wealth of animal life, despite a vast diminution in their numbers due to poaching and habitat loss—has engendered a booming tourist industry. Names such as Serengeti Plain, Kalahari Desert, and Okavango Delta still evoke images of an Africa unspoiled, unconquerable, and, throughout the Earth, unsurpassed.

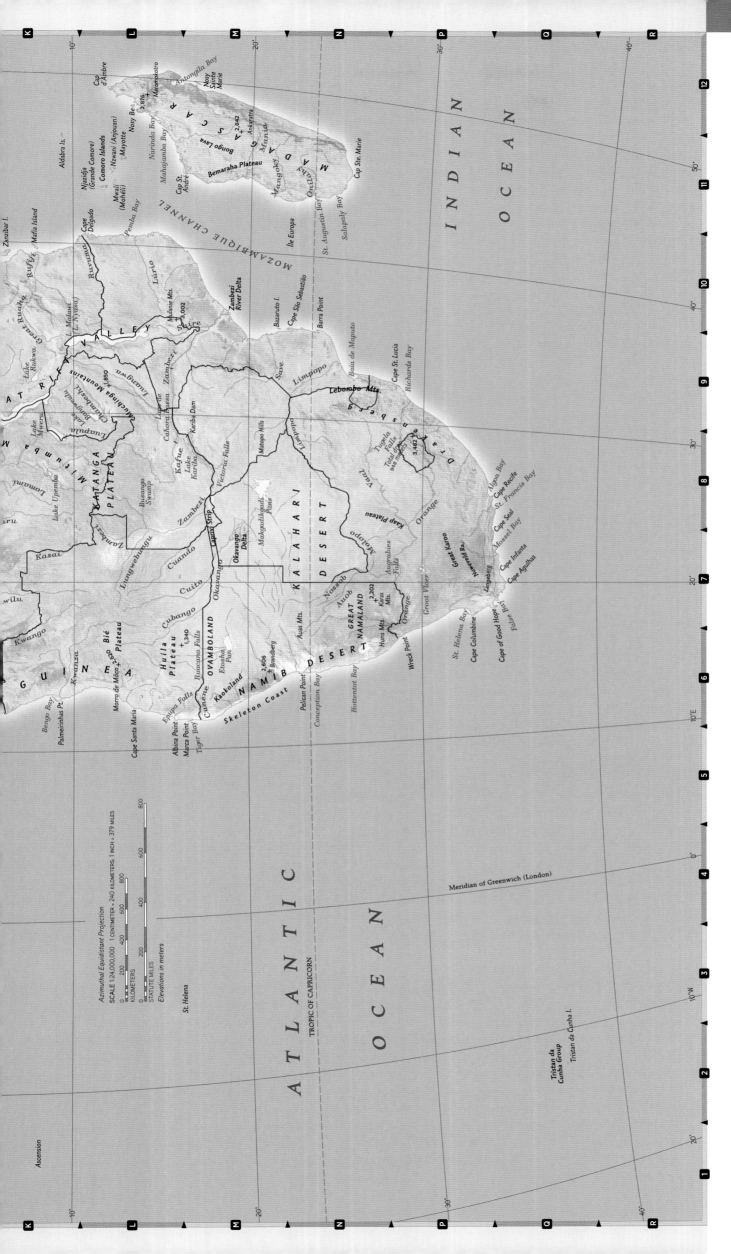

Africa
Physical

Continental Data

Area: 30,065,000 sq km
(11,608,000 sq mi)

Greatest north-south extent:
8,047 km (5,000 mi)

Greatest east-west extent:
7,564 km (4,700 mi)

Highest point:
Kilimanjaro, Tanzania
5,895 m (19,340 ft)

Lowest point:
Lake Assal, Djibouti
-156 m (-512 ft)

Lowest recorded temperature:
Ifrane, Morocco -24°C (-11°F),
February 11, 1935

Highest recorded temperature:
Al Aziziyah, Libya 58°C (136.4°F),
September 13, 1922

Longest rivers:
• Nile 6,695 km (4,160 mi)
• Congo 4,700 km (2,900 mi)
• Niger 4,170 km (2,591 mi)

Largest natural lakes:
• Lake Victoria 69,500 sq km
  (26,800 sq mi)
• Lake Tanganyika 32,600 sq km
  (12,600 sq mi)
• Lake Malawi (Lake Nyasa)
  28,900 sq km
  (11,200 sq mi)

Earth's extremes in Africa:
• Largest Desert on Earth:
  Sahara 9,000,000 sq km
  (3,475,000 sq mi)
• Hottest Place on Earth:
  Dalol, Danakil Desert,
  Ethiopia; annual average
  temperature 34°C (93°F)

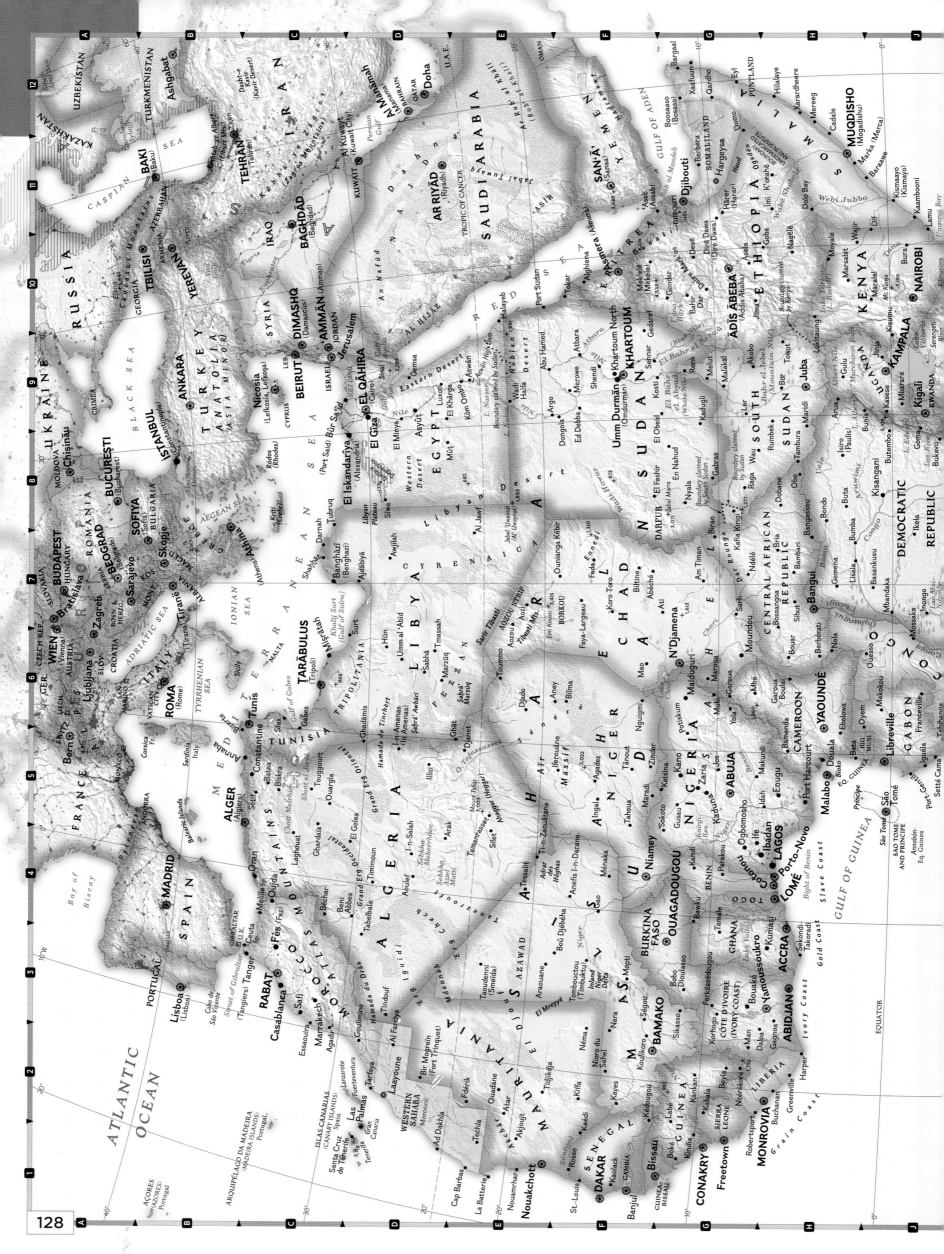

Africa
Political

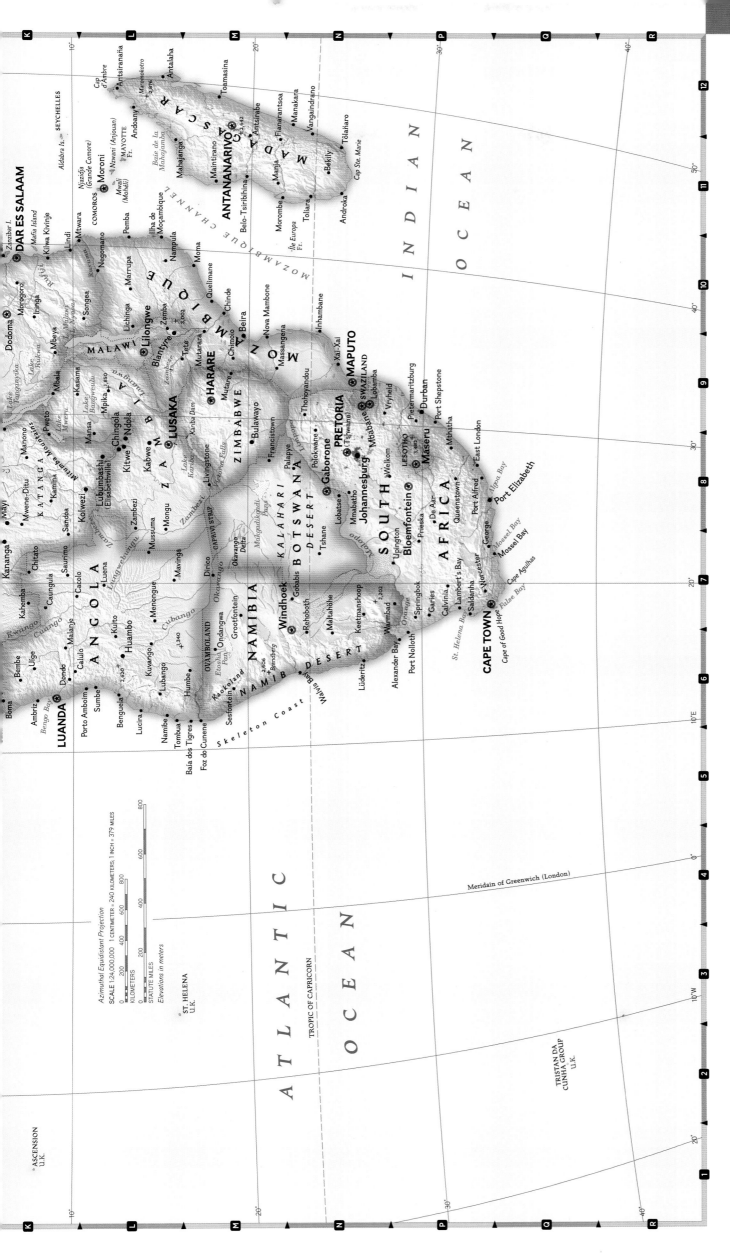

Continental Data

Total number of countries: 54

First independent country:
Ethiopia, over 2,000 years old

"Youngest" country:
South Sudan, July 9, 2011

Largest country in area:
Algeria 2,381,741 sq km
(919,595 sq mi)

Smallest country in area:
Seychelles 455 sq km (176 sq mi)

Percent urban population: 40%

Most populous country:
Nigeria 181,562,000

Least populous country:
Seychelles 92,000

**Most densely
populated country:**
Mauritius 657 per sq km
(1,701 per sq mi)

**Least densely
populated country:**
Namibia 3 per sq km
(8 per sq mi)

Largest city by population:
Cairo, Egypt 18,772,000

Highest GDP per capita:
Equatorial Guinea $33,300

Lowest GDP per capita:
Somalia $400

Average life expectancy:
60 years

Human and Natural Themes

POPULATION DENSITY

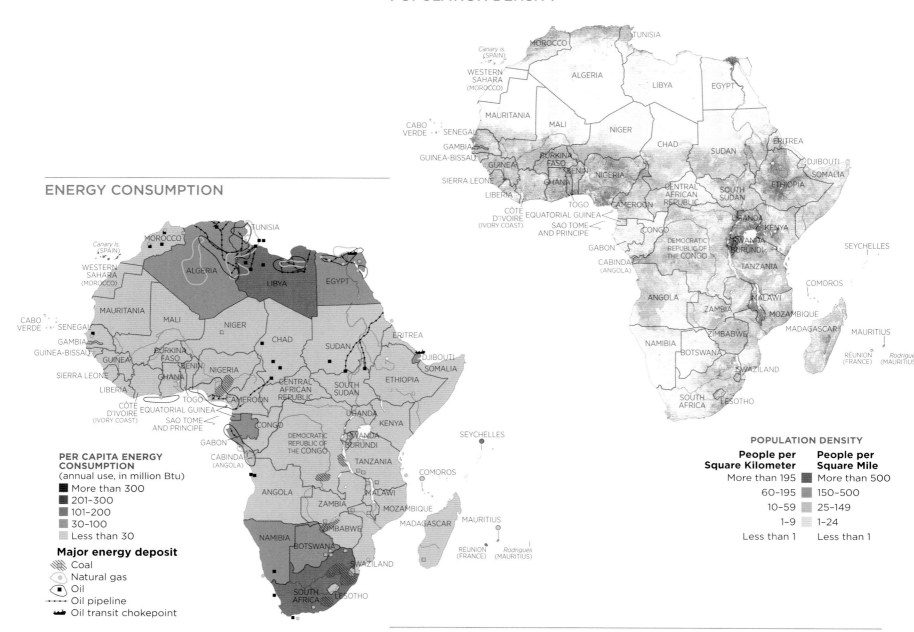

POPULATION DENSITY

People per Square Kilometer	People per Square Mile
More than 195	More than 500
60–195	150–500
10–59	25–149
1–9	1–24
Less than 1	Less than 1

ENERGY CONSUMPTION

PER CAPITA ENERGY CONSUMPTION
(annual use, in million Btu)

- More than 300
- 201–300
- 101–200
- 30–100
- Less than 30

Major energy deposit

- Coal
- Natural gas
- Oil
- Oil pipeline
- Oil transit chokepoint

LAND COVER

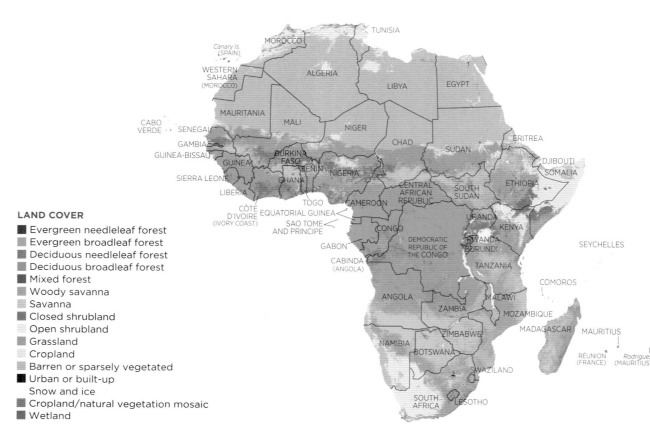

LAND COVER

- Evergreen needleleaf forest
- Evergreen broadleaf forest
- Deciduous needleleaf forest
- Deciduous broadleaf forest
- Mixed forest
- Woody savanna
- Savanna
- Closed shrubland
- Open shrubland
- Grassland
- Cropland
- Barren or sparsely vegetated
- Urban or built-up
- Snow and ice
- Cropland/natural vegetation mosaic
- Wetland

CLIMATIC ZONES

CLIMATIC ZONES
(based on modified Köppen system)
Humid equatorial climate (A)
- No dry season (Af)
- Short dry season (Am)
- Dry winter (Aw)

Dry climate (B)
- Semiarid (BS) } h = hot
- Arid (BW) } k = cold

Humid temperate climate (C)
- No dry season (Cf) } a = hot summer
- Dry winter (Cw) } b = cool summer
- Dry summer (Cs)

Highland climate (H)
- Unclassified highlands

NATURAL HAZARDS (TECTONIC EVENTS)

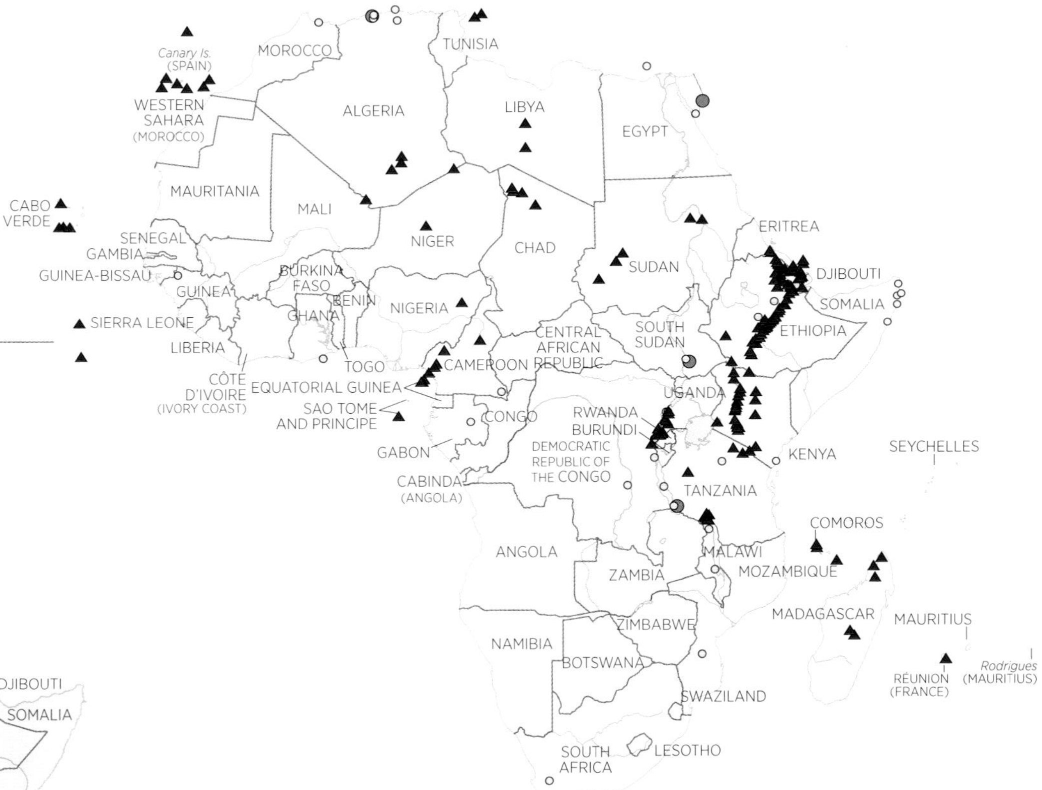

NATURAL HAZARDS (TECTONIC EVENTS)
Recorded Natural Event
Major Earthquake, 1900–2015
Moment magnitude
- ● More than 7.0
- ○ 6.0–7.0

Volcano
- ▲

Tsunami, 1900–2015
Run-up height
- ○ 5–10 meters (16–32 feet)

WATER AVAILABILITY

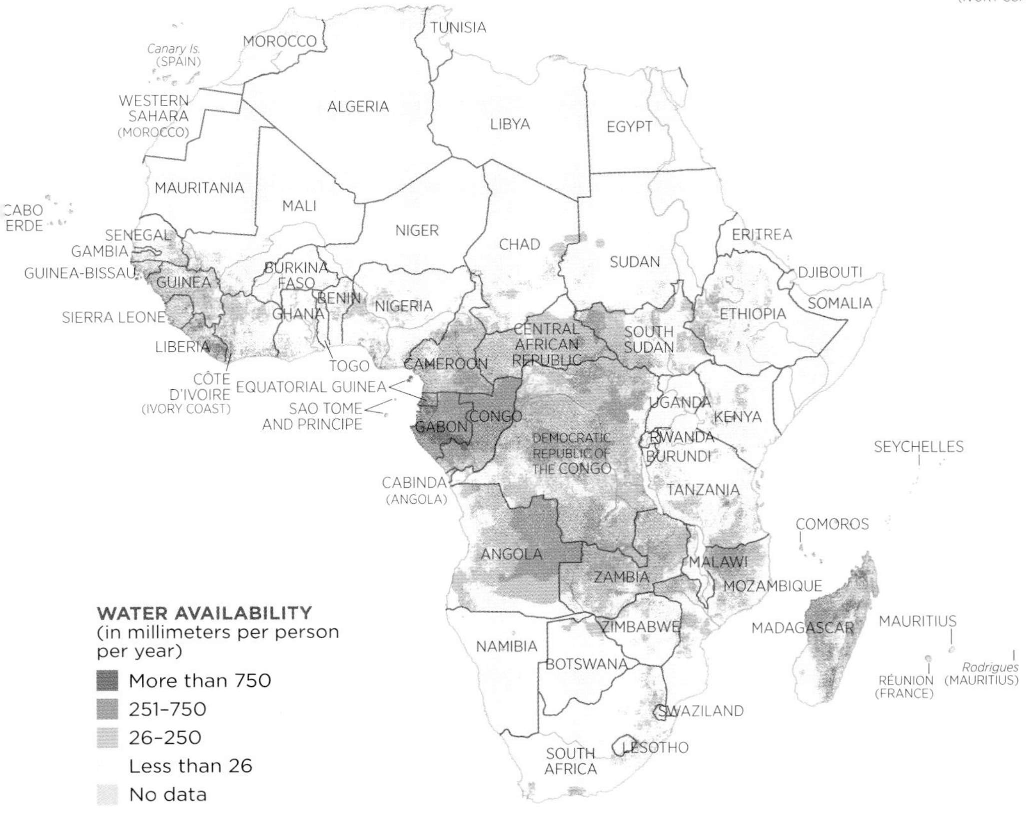

WATER AVAILABILITY
(in millimeters per person per year)
- More than 750
- 251–750
- 26–250
- Less than 26
- No data

Flags and Facts

COUNTRIES

Algeria

PEOPLE'S DEMOCRATIC REPUBLIC OF ALGERIA

AREA 2,381,741 sq km (919,590 sq mi)
POPULATION 39,542,000
CAPITAL Algiers 2,594,000
RELIGION Sunni Muslim
LANGUAGE Arabic, French, Berber dialects
LITERACY 80%
LIFE EXPECTANCY 77 years
GDP PER CAPITA $14,400
ECONOMY **Ind:** petroleum, natural gas, light industries, mining, electrical, petrochemicals, food processing **Agr:** wheat, barley, oats, grapes, olives, citrus, sheep **Exp:** petroleum, natural gas, petroleum products

Angola

REPUBLIC OF ANGOLA

AREA 1,246,700 sq km (481,351 sq mi)
POPULATION 19,625,000
CAPITAL Luanda 5,506,000
RELIGION Indigenous beliefs, Roman Catholic, Protestant
LANGUAGE Portuguese, Bantu, other African languages
LITERACY 71%
LIFE EXPECTANCY 56 years
GDP PER CAPITA $7,600
ECONOMY **Ind:** petroleum, cement, basic metal products, fish processing **Agr:** bananas, sugarcane, coffee, sisal, corn, cotton, cassava (tapioca), fish **Exp:** crude oil, diamonds, refined petroleum, coffee, sisal

Benin

REPUBLIC OF BENIN

AREA 112,622 sq km (43,483 sq mi)
POPULATION 10,449,000
CAPITAL Porto-Novo (official) 268,000, Cotonou (seat of government) 682,000
RELIGION Catholic, Muslim, Vodoun, Protestant
LANGUAGE French, Fon, Yoruba
LITERACY 38%
LIFE EXPECTANCY 61 years
GDP PER CAPITA $2,000
ECONOMY **Ind:** textiles, food processing, construction materials, cement **Agr:** cotton, corn, cassava (tapioca), yams, beans **Exp:** cotton, cashews, shea butter, textiles, palm products

Botswana
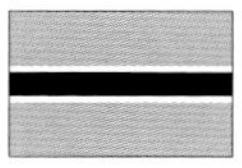

REPUBLIC OF BOTSWANA

AREA 581,730 sq km (224,606 sq mi)
POPULATION 2,183,000
CAPITAL Gaborone 247,000
RELIGION Christian, Badimo
LANGUAGE Setswana, Kalanga, Sekgalagadi, English
LITERACY 89%
LIFE EXPECTANCY 54 years
GDP PER CAPITA $17,700
ECONOMY **Ind:** diamonds, copper, nickel, salt, soda ash, livestock processing **Agr:** livestock, sorghum, maize, millet, beans, sunflowers, groundnuts **Exp:** diamonds, copper, nickel, soda ash, meat, textiles

Burkina Faso

BURKINA FASO

AREA 274,200 sq km (105,869 sq mi)
POPULATION 18,932,000
CAPITAL Ouagadougou 2,741,000
RELIGION Muslim, Catholic, animist
LANGUAGE French, native African languages
LITERACY 36%
LIFE EXPECTANCY 55 years
GDP PER CAPITA $1,800
ECONOMY **Ind:** cotton, beverages, agricultural processing, soap, cigarettes, textiles, gold **Agr:** cotton, peanuts, shea nuts, sesame, sorghum, millet, corn, rice, livestock **Exp:** gold, cotton, livestock

Burundi

REPUBLIC OF BURUNDI

AREA 27,830 sq km (10,745 sq mi)
POPULATION 10,742,000
CAPITAL Bujumbura 751,000
RELIGION Catholic, Protestant
LANGUAGE Kirundi, French
LITERACY 86%
LIFE EXPECTANCY 60 years
GDP PER CAPITA $900
ECONOMY **Ind:** light consumer goods such as blankets, shoes, soap, and beer, assembly of imported components, food processing **Agr:** coffee, cotton, tea, corn, sorghum, bananas, beef **Exp:** coffee, tea, sugar, cotton, hides

Cabo Verde

REPUBLIC OF CABO VERDE

AREA 4,033 sq km (1,557 sq mi)
POPULATION 546,000
CAPITAL Praia 145,000
RELIGION Roman Catholic, Protestant
LANGUAGE Portuguese, Crioulo
LITERACY 88%
LIFE EXPECTANCY 72 years
GDP PER CAPITA $6,700
ECONOMY **Ind:** food and beverages, fish processing, shoes and garments, salt mining, ship repair **Agr:** bananas, corn, beans, sweet potatoes, sugarcane, coffee, peanuts, fish **Exp:** fuel, shoes, garments, fish, hides

Cameroon

REPUBLIC OF CAMEROON

AREA 475,440 sq km (183,567 sq mi)
POPULATION 23,739,000
CAPITAL Yaoundé 3,066,000
RELIGION Indigenous beliefs, Christian, Muslim
LANGUAGE various African languages, English, French
LITERACY 75%
LIFE EXPECTANCY 58 years
GDP PER CAPITA $3,200
ECONOMY **Ind:** petroleum production and refining, aluminum production, food processing, lumber **Agr:** coffee, cocoa, cotton, rubber, bananas, timber **Exp:** crude oil and petroleum products, lumber, cocoa beans, aluminum, coffee, cotton

Central African Republic

CENTRAL AFRICAN REPUBLIC

AREA 622,984 sq km (240,534 sq mi)
POPULATION 5,392,000
CAPITAL Bangui 794,000
RELIGION Indigenous beliefs, Protestant, Roman Catholic, Muslim
LANGUAGE French, Sangho
LITERACY 37%
LIFE EXPECTANCY 52 years
GDP PER CAPITA $600
ECONOMY **Ind:** gold and diamond mining, logging, brewing, sugar refining **Agr:** cotton, coffee, tobacco, cassava (tapioca), yams **Exp:** diamonds, timber, cotton, coffee

Chad

REPUBLIC OF CHAD

AREA 1,284,000 sq km (495,752 sq mi)
POPULATION 11,631,000
CAPITAL N'Djamena 1,260,000
RELIGION Muslim, Catholic, Protestant
LANGUAGE French, Arabic, Sara, more than 120 languages and dialects
LITERACY 40%
LIFE EXPECTANCY 50 years
GDP PER CAPITA $2,800
ECONOMY **Ind:** oil, cotton textiles, brewing, natron, soap **Agr:** cotton, sorghum, millet, peanuts, sesame, corn **Exp:** oil, livestock, cotton, sesame, gum arabic

Comoros

UNION OF THE COMOROS

AREA 2,235 sq km (863 sq mi)
POPULATION 781,000
CAPITAL Moroni 56,000
RELIGION Sunni Muslim
LANGUAGE Arabic, French, Shikomoro
LITERACY 78%
LIFE EXPECTANCY 64 years
GDP PER CAPITA $1,600
ECONOMY **Ind:** fishing, tourism, perfume distillation **Agr:** vanilla, cloves, ylang-ylang (perfume essence), coconuts **Exp:** vanilla, ylang-ylang, cloves

Congo

REPUBLIC OF THE CONGO

AREA 342,000 sq km (132,046 sq mi)
POPULATION 4,755,000
CAPITAL Brazzaville 1,888,000
RELIGION Roman Catholic, Awakening Churches/Christian Revival
LANGUAGE French, Lingala, Monokutuba, Kikongo
LITERACY 79%
LIFE EXPECTANCY 59 years
GDP PER CAPITA $6,800
ECONOMY **Ind:** petroleum, cement, lumber **Agr:** cassava (tapioca), sugar, rice, forest products **Exp:** petroleum, lumber, plywood, sugar, cocoa, coffee, diamonds

Congo, Democratic Republic of the

DEMOCRATIC REPUBLIC OF THE CONGO

AREA 2,344,858 sq km (905,350 sq mi)
POPULATION 79,375,000
CAPITAL Kinshasa 11,587,000
RELIGION Roman Catholic, Protestant, Kimbanguist, Muslim
LANGUAGE French, Lingala, Kingwana, Kikongo, Tshiluba
LITERACY 64%
LIFE EXPECTANCY 57 years
GDP PER CAPITA $800
ECONOMY **Ind:** mining (copper, cobalt, gold, diamonds, coltan, zinc, tin, tungsten) **Agr:** coffee, sugar, palm oil, rubber **Exp:** diamonds, copper, gold, cobalt

Côte d'Ivoire (Ivory Coast)
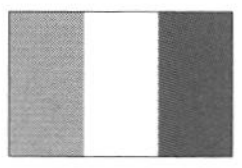

REPUBLIC OF CÔTE D'IVOIRE

AREA 322,463 sq km (124,503 sq mi)
POPULATION 23,295,000
CAPITAL Abidjan (administrative) 4,860,000, Yamoussoukro (legislative) 259,000
RELIGION Muslim, Catholic
LANGUAGE French, Dioula, native dialects
LITERACY 43%
LIFE EXPECTANCY 58 years
GDP PER CAPITA $3,400
ECONOMY **Ind:** foodstuffs, beverages, wood products, petroleum, gold mining, **Agr:** coffee, cocoa beans, bananas, palm kernels **Exp:** cocoa, coffee, petroleum, cotton

Djibouti

REPUBLIC OF DJIBOUTI

AREA 23,200 sq km (8,958 sq mi)
POPULATION 828,000
CAPITAL Djibouti 529,000
RELIGION Muslim, Christian
LANGUAGE French, Arabic, Somali, Afar
LITERACY 68%
LIFE EXPECTANCY 63 years
GDP PER CAPITA $3,300
ECONOMY **Ind:** construction, agricultural processing **Agr:** fruits, vegetables, goats, sheep, camels, animal hides **Exp:** reexports, hides and skins, coffee (in transit)

Egypt

ARAB REPUBLIC OF EGYPT

AREA 1,001,450 sq km (386,660 sq mi)
POPULATION 88,487,000
CAPITAL Cairo 18,772,000
RELIGION Muslim
LANGUAGE Arabic, English, French
LITERACY 74%
LIFE EXPECTANCY 74 years
GDP PER CAPITA $11,500
ECONOMY **Ind:** textiles, food processing, tourism, chemicals **Agr:** cotton, rice, corn, wheat, fruits, cattle **Exp:** crude oil and petroleum products, cotton, textiles, metal products, chemicals

Equatorial Guinea

REPUBLIC OF EQUATORIAL GUINEA

AREA 28,051 sq km (10,830 sq mi)
POPULATION 741,000
CAPITAL Malabo 145,000
RELIGION Roman Catholic
LANGUAGE Spanish, French, Fang, Bubi
LITERACY 95%
LIFE EXPECTANCY 64 years
GDP PER CAPITA $33,300
ECONOMY **Ind:** petroleum, natural gas, sawmilling **Agr:** coffee, cocoa, rice, yams, livestock, timber **Exp:** petroleum products, timber

Eritrea

STATE OF ERITREA

AREA 117,600 sq km (45,405 sq mi)
POPULATION 6,528,000
CAPITAL Asmara 804,000
RELIGION Muslim, Coptic Christian, Roman Catholic, Protestant
LANGUAGE Tigrinya, Arabic, English, Tigre, Kunama, Afar
LITERACY 74%
LIFE EXPECTANCY 64 years
GDP PER CAPITA $1,200
ECONOMY **Ind:** food processing, beverages, clothing and textiles, salt **Agr:** sorghum, lentils, vegetables, corn, livestock **Exp:** gold, livestock, sorghum, textiles

Ethiopia

FEDERAL DEMOCRATIC REPUBLIC OF ETHIOPIA

AREA 1,104,300 sq km (426,370 sq mi)
POPULATION 99,466,000
CAPITAL Addis Ababa 3,238,000
RELIGION Orthodox, Muslim, Protestant
LANGUAGE Oromo, Amharic, Somali, Tigrigna, Sidamo, Wolaytta
LITERACY 49%
LIFE EXPECTANCY 61 years
GDP PER CAPITA $1,700
ECONOMY **Ind:** food processing, beverages, textiles, chemicals **Agr:** cereals, coffee, cotton, oilseeds, cattle, sheep **Exp:** coffee, khat, gold, leather products, live animals, oilseeds

Gabon
GABONESE REPUBLIC

AREA 267,667 sq km (103,346 sq mi)
POPULATION 1,705,000
CAPITAL Libreville 707,000
RELIGION Christian, animist
LANGUAGE French, Fang, Myene, Nzebi, Bapounou/Eschira, Bandjabi
LITERACY 83%
LIFE EXPECTANCY 52 years
GDP PER CAPITA $21,700
ECONOMY **IND:** petroleum extraction and refining, manganese, gold, chemicals, ship repair **AGR:** cocoa, coffee, sugar, palm oil, rubber, cattle, okoume (a tropical softwood) **EXP:** crude oil, timber, manganese, uranium

Gambia
ISLAMIC REPUBLIC OF THE GAMBIA

AREA 11,300 sq km (4,361 sq mi)
POPULATION 1,968,000
CAPITAL Banjul 504,000
RELIGION Muslim, Christian
LANGUAGE English, Mandinka, Wolof, Fula
LITERACY 56%
LIFE EXPECTANCY 65 years
GDP PER CAPITA $1,700
ECONOMY **IND:** peanuts, fish, hides, tourism, beverages, agricultural machinery assembly **AGR:** rice, millet, sorghum, peanuts, cattle **EXP:** peanuts products, fish, cotton lint

Ghana
REPUBLIC OF GHANA

AREA 238,533 sq km (92,098 sq mi)
POPULATION 26,328,000
CAPITAL Accra 2,277,000
RELIGION Christian, Muslim, traditional
LANGUAGE Asante, Ewe, Fante, Boron (Brong), Dagomba, Dangme, Dagarte (Dagaba, Akyern, Ga, Akuapem, English
LITERACY 77%
LIFE EXPECTANCY 66 years
GDP PER CAPITA $4,300
ECONOMY **IND:** mining, lumbering, light manufacturing, aluminum smelting, food processing **AGR:** cocoa, rice, coffee, peanuts, timber, fish **EXP:** oil, gold, cocoa, timber, tuna, bauxite, aluminum, manganese ore

Guinea
REPUBLIC OF GUINEA

AREA 245,857 sq km (94,925 sq mi)
POPULATION 11,780,000
CAPITAL Conakry 1,936,000
RELIGION Muslim, Christian, indigenous beliefs
LANGUAGE French
LITERACY 30%
LIFE EXPECTANCY 60 years
GDP PER CAPITA $1,300
ECONOMY **IND:** bauxite, gold, diamonds, iron ore, light manufacturing **AGR:** rice, coffee, pineapples, palm kernels, cocoa, timber **EXP:** bauxite, gold, diamonds, coffee, fish

Guinea-Bissau
REPUBLIC OF GUINEA-BISSAU

AREA 36,125 sq km (13,948 sq mi)
POPULATION 1,726,000
CAPITAL Bissau 492,000
RELIGION Muslim, Christian, animist
LANGUAGE Crioulo, Portuguese, French
LITERACY 60%
LIFE EXPECTANCY 50 years
GDP PER CAPITA $1,500
ECONOMY **IND:** agricultural products processing, beer, soft drinks **AGR:** rice, corn, cashew nuts, timber, fish **EXP:** fish, shrimp, cashews, peanuts, palm kernels, lumber

Kenya
REPUBLIC OF KENYA

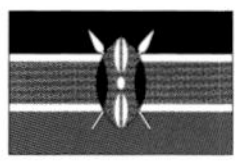

AREA 580,367 sq km (224,080 sq mi)
POPULATION 45,925,000
CAPITAL Nairobi 3,915,000
RELIGION Protestant, Catholic, Muslim
LANGUAGE English, Kiswahili, indigenous languages
LITERACY 78%
LIFE EXPECTANCY 64 years
GDP PER CAPITA $3,300
ECONOMY **IND:** small-scale consumer goods, agricultural products, horticulture, oil refining, tourism **AGR:** tea, coffee, corn, wheat, sugarcane, fruit, vegetables **EXP:** tea, horticultural products, coffee,petroleum products, fish, cement

Lesotho
KINGDOM OF LESOTHO

AREA 30,355 sq km (11,720 sq mi)
POPULATION 1,948,000
CAPITAL Maseru 267,000
RELIGION Christian, indigenous beliefs
LANGUAGE Sesotho, English, Zulu, Xhosa
LITERACY 79%
LIFE EXPECTANCY 53 years
GDP PER CAPITA $3,000
ECONOMY **IND:** food, beverages, textiles, apparel assembly, handicrafts, construction, tourism **AGR:** corn, wheat, pulses, sorghum, barley, livestock **EXP:** manufactures (clothing, footwear), wool and mohair, food and live animals, water

Liberia
REPUBLIC OF LIBERIA

AREA 111,369 sq km (43,000 sq mi)
POPULATION 4,196,000
CAPITAL Monrovia 1,264,000
RELIGION Christian, Muslim
LANGUAGE English, ethnic group languages
LITERACY 48%
LIFE EXPECTANCY 59 years
GDP PER CAPITA $900
ECONOMY **IND:** mining (iron ore), rubber processing, timber, diamonds **AGR:** rubber, coffee, cocoa, rice, sheep, goats, timber **EXP:** rubber, timber, iron, diamonds, cocoa, coffee

Libya
LIBYA

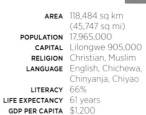

AREA 1,759,540 sq km (679,358 sq mi)
POPULATION 6,412,000
CAPITAL Tripoli 1,126,000
RELIGION Sunni Muslim, Christian
LANGUAGE Arabic, Italian, English, Berber
LITERACY 91%
LIFE EXPECTANCY 76 years
GDP PER CAPITA $15,100
ECONOMY **IND:** petroleum, petrochemicals, aluminum, iron and steel, textiles **AGR:** wheat, barley, olives, dates, citrus, cattle **EXP:** crude oil, petroleum products, natural gas, chemicals

Madagascar
REPUBLIC OF MADAGASCAR

AREA 587,041 sq km (226,657 sq mi)
POPULATION 23,813,000
CAPITAL Antananarivo 2,610,000
RELIGION Indigenous beliefs, Christian, Muslim
LANGUAGE French, Malagasy, English
LITERACY 65%
LIFE EXPECTANCY 66 years
GDP PER CAPITA $1,500
ECONOMY **IND:** meat processing, seafood, soap, beer, leather **AGR:** coffee, vanilla, sugarcane, cloves, livestock products **EXP:** coffee, vanilla, cloves, shellfish, sugar, clothing

Malawi
REPUBLIC OF MALAWI

AREA 118,484 sq km (45,747 sq mi)
POPULATION 17,965,000
CAPITAL Lilongwe 905,000
RELIGION Christian, Muslim
LANGUAGE English, Chichewa, Chinyanja, Chiyao
LITERACY 66%
LIFE EXPECTANCY 61 years
GDP PER CAPITA $1,200
ECONOMY **IND:** tobacco, tea, sugar, sawmill products, cement **AGR:** tobacco, sugarcane, cotton, tea, cattle **EXP:** tobacco, tea, sugar, cotton, coffee, peanuts, apparel

Mali
REPUBLIC OF MALI

AREA 1,240,192 sq km (478,838 sq mi)
POPULATION 16,956,000
CAPITAL Bamako 2,515,000
RELIGION Muslim, Christian
LANGUAGE French, Bambara, various African languages
LITERACY 39%
LIFE EXPECTANCY 55 years
GDP PER CAPITA $1,800
ECONOMY **IND:** food processing, construction, phosphate and gold mining **AGR:** cotton, millet, rice, corn, vegetables, cattle **EXP:** cotton, gold, livestock

Mauritania
ISLAMIC REPUBLIC OF MAURITANIA

AREA 1,030,700 sq km (397,953 sq mi)
POPULATION 3,597,000
CAPITAL Nouakchott 968,000
RELIGION Muslim
LANGUAGE Arabic, Pulaar, Soninke, Wolof, French, Hassaniya
LITERACY 52%
LIFE EXPECTANCY 63 years
GDP PER CAPITA $4,500
ECONOMY **IND:** fish processing, oil production, mining (iron ore, gold, and copper) **AGR:** dates, millet, sorghum, rice **EXP:** iron ore, fish and fish products, gold

Mauritius
REPUBLIC OF MAURITIUS

AREA 2,040 sq km (788 sq mi)
POPULATION 1,340,000
CAPITAL Port Louis 135,000
RELIGION Hindu, Roman Catholic, Muslim, other Christian
LANGUAGE Creole, Bhojpuri, French, English
LITERACY 91%
LIFE EXPECTANCY 75 years
GDP PER CAPITA $19,500
ECONOMY **IND:** food processing (largely sugar milling), textiles, clothing, mining, tourism **AGR:** sugarcane, tea, corn, potatoes, fish **EXP:** clothing and textiles, sugar, cut flowers, molasses, fish

Morocco
KINGDOM OF MOROCCO

AREA 446,550 sq km (172,413 sq mi)
POPULATION 33,323,000
CAPITAL Rabat 1,967,000
RELIGION Muslim (predominantly Sunni)
LANGUAGE Arabic, Berber languages, Tamazight, French
LITERACY 69%
LIFE EXPECTANCY 77 years
GDP PER CAPITA $8,300
ECONOMY **IND:** automotive parts, phosphate mining and processing, food processing, leather goods, textiles, tourism **AGR:** barley, wheat, citrus grapes, wine **EXP:** clothing and textiles, automobiles, electric components, inorganic chemicals, fish

Mozambique
REPUBLIC OF MOZAMBIQUE

AREA 799,380 sq km (308,641 sq mi)
POPULATION 25,303,000
CAPITAL Maputo 1,187,000
RELIGION Roman Catholic, Muslim, Zionist Christian, Protestant
LANGUAGE Emakhuwa, Portuguese, Xichangana, Cisena, Etomwe
LITERACY 59%
LIFE EXPECTANCY 53 years
GDP PER CAPITA $1,300
ECONOMY **IND:** aluminum, petroleum products, chemicals (fertilizer, soap, paints), textiles **AGR:** cotton, cashew nuts, sugarcane, tea, beef, poultry **EXP:** aluminum, petroleum, coal, sugar, bulk electricity

Namibia
REPUBLIC OF NAMIBIA

AREA 824,292 sq km (318,259 sq mi)
POPULATION 2,212,000
CAPITAL Windhoek 368,000
RELIGION Lutheran, indigenous beliefs
LANGUAGE Oshiwambo languages, Nama/Damara, Afrikaans, Otjiherero languages, Kavango languages, Caprivi languages, English
LITERACY 82%
LIFE EXPECTANCY 52 years
GDP PER CAPITA $11,300
ECONOMY **IND:** meatpacking, fish processing, mining (diamonds, lead, zinc, tin, silver, tungsten) **AGR:** millet, sorghum, grapes, fish **EXP:** diamonds, copper, gold, zinc, lead, uranium, cattle, white fish and mollusks

Niger
REPUBLIC OF NIGER

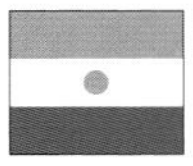

AREA 1,267,000 sq km (489,189 sq mi)
POPULATION 18,046,000
CAPITAL Niamey 1,090,000
RELIGION Muslim, other
LANGUAGE French, Hausa, Djerma
LITERACY 19%
LIFE EXPECTANCY 55 years
GDP PER CAPITA $1,100
ECONOMY **IND:** uranium mining, petroleum, cement, brick **AGR:** cowpeas, cotton, peanuts, cattle, sheep **EXP:** uranium ore, chemicals, petroleum

Nigeria
FEDERAL REPUBLIC OF NIGERIA

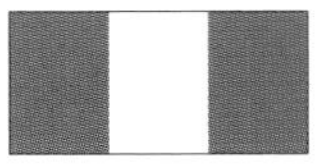

AREA 923,768 sq km (356,667 sq mi)
POPULATION 181,562,000
CAPITAL Abuja 2,440,000
RELIGION Muslim, Christian, indigenous beliefs
LANGUAGE English, Hausa, Yoruba, Igbo, Fulani
LITERACY 59%
LIFE EXPECTANCY 53 years
GDP PER CAPITA $6,400
ECONOMY **IND:** crude oil, coal, tin, columite, rubber products, wood, food products **AGR:** cocoa, peanuts, cotton, rubber, fish **EXP:** petroleum and petroleum products, cocoa, rubber

Rwanda
REPUBLIC OF RWANDA

AREA 26,338 sq km (10,169 sq mi)
POPULATION 12,662,000
CAPITAL Kigali 1,257,000
RELIGION Roman Catholic, Protestant
LANGUAGE Kinyarwandai
LITERACY 71%
LIFE EXPECTANCY 60 years
GDP PER CAPITA $1,800
ECONOMY **IND:** cement, agricultural products, small-scale beverages, soap, cigarettes **AGR:** coffee, tea, pyrethrum (insecticide made from chrysanthemums), bananas, livestock **EXP:** coffee, tea, hides, tin ore

Flags and Facts

Sao Tome and Principe

DEMOCRATIC REPUBLIC OF SAO TOME AND PRINCIPE

AREA 964 sq km (372 sq mi)
POPULATION 194,000
CAPITAL São Tomé 71,000
RELIGION Catholic, Adventist
LANGUAGE Portuguese, Forro
LITERACY 75%
LIFE EXPECTANCY 65 years
GDP PER CAPITA $3,400
ECONOMY **Ind:** light construction, textiles, soap, beer **Agr:** cocoa, coconuts, palm kernels, copra, fish **Exp:** cocoa, copra, coffee, palm oil

Senegal

REPUBLIC OF SENEGAL

AREA 196,722 sq km (75,954 sq mi)
POPULATION 13,976,000
CAPITAL Dakar 3,520,000
RELIGION Muslim, Christian
LANGUAGE French, Wolof, Pulaar, Jola, Mandinka
LITERACY 58%
LIFE EXPECTANCY 61 years
GDP PER CAPITA $2,500
ECONOMY **Ind:** agricultural and fish processing, phosphate mining, fertilizer production, petroleum refining, gold **Agr:** peanuts, millet, corn, sorghum, cattle, fish **Exp:** fish, groundnuts (peanuts), petroleum products, phosphates, cotton

Seychelles

REPUBLIC OF SEYCHELLES

AREA 455 sq km (176 sq mi)
POPULATION 92,000
CAPITAL Victoria 26,000
RELIGION Roman Catholic, Protestant
LANGUAGE Creole, English
LITERACY 92%
LIFE EXPECTANCY 74 years
GDP PER CAPITA $27,000
ECONOMY **Ind:** fishing, tourism, beverages **Agr:** coconuts, cinnamon, vanilla, sweet potatoes, cassava, tuna **Exp:** canned tuna, frozen fish, petroleum products (reexports)

Sierra Leone

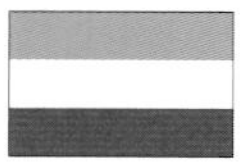

REPUBLIC OF SIERRA LEONE

AREA 71,740 sq km (27,699 sq mi)
POPULATION 5,879,000
CAPITAL Freetown 1,007,000
RELIGION Muslim, indigenous beliefs, Christian
LANGUAGE English, Mende, Temne, Krio
LITERACY 48%
LIFE EXPECTANCY 58 years
GDP PER CAPITA $1,600
ECONOMY **Ind:** mining, small-scale manufacturing (beverages, textiles, cigarettes, footwear), small commercial ship repair **Agr:** rice, coffee, cocoa, palm kernels, fish **Exp:** diamonds, rutile, cocoa, coffee, gold

Somalia

FEDERAL REPUBLIC OF SOMALIA

AREA 637,657 sq km (246,199 sq mi)
POPULATION 10,616,000
CAPITAL Modagishu 2,138,000
RELIGION Sunni Muslim
LANGUAGE Somali, Arabic, Italian, English
LITERACY 38%
LIFE EXPECTANCY 52 years
GDP PER CAPITA $400
ECONOMY **Ind:** light industries including sugar refining, textiles, wireless communication **Agr:** bananas, sorghum, corn, cattle, sheep, fish **Exp:** livestock, bananas, hides, fish, charcoal, scrap metal

South Africa

REPUBLIC OF SOUTH AFRICA

AREA 1,219,090 sq km (470,691 sq mi)
POPULATION 53,676,000
CAPITAL Pretoria (administrative) 2,059,000, Cape Town (legislative) 3,660,000, Bloemfontein (judicial) 496,000
RELIGION Protestant, other Christian
LANGUAGE IsiZulu, IsiXhosa, Afrikaans, Sepedi, English, Setswana, Sesotho, Xitsonga, siSwati, Tshivenda, isiNdebele
LITERACY 74%
LIFE EXPECTANCY 62 years
GDP PER CAPITA $13,400
ECONOMY **Ind:** mining (platinum, gold, chromium), automobile assembly, metalworking, machinery, textiles, iron and steel, chemicals, fertilizer **Agr:** corn, wheat, sugarcane, fruits, vegetables, beef, poultry **Exp:** gold, diamonds, platinum, other metals and minerals, machinery and equipment

South Sudan

REPUBLIC OF SOUTH SUDAN

AREA 644,329 sq km (248,775 sq mi)
POPULATION 12,043,000
CAPITAL Juba 321,000
RELIGION Animist, Christian
LANGUAGE English, Arabic, Dinka, Nuer, Bari, Zande, Shilluk
LITERACY 27%
LIFE EXPECTANCY NA
GDP PER CAPITA $2,000
ECONOMY **Ind:** petroleum, agricultural processing **Agr:** sorghum, maize, rice, millet, wheat, vegetables, cattle, sheep, goats **Exp:** petroleum, vegetables, scrap iron, hides

Sudan

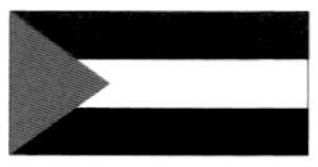

REPUBLIC OF THE SUDAN

AREA 1,861,484 sq km (718,719 sq mi)
POPULATION 36,109,000
CAPITAL Khartoum 5,129,000
RELIGION Sunni Muslim
LANGUAGE Arabic, English, Nubian, Ta Bedawie, Fur
LITERACY 61%
LIFE EXPECTANCY 76 years
GDP PER CAPITA $4,500
ECONOMY **Ind:** cotton ginning, textiles, cement, edible oils, shoes **Agr:** cotton, groundnuts (peanuts), sorghum, millet, sheep **Exp:** gold, oil and petroleum products, cotton, sesame, livestock, gum arabic

Swaziland

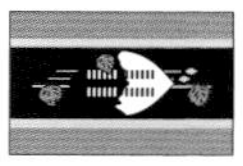

KINGDOM OF SWAZILAND

AREA 17,364 sq km (6,704 sq mi)
POPULATION 1,436,000
CAPITAL Mbabane (administrative) 66,000, Lobamba (royal and legislative) 5,800
RELIGION Zionist, Roman Catholic, Muslim
LANGUAGE English, siSwati
LITERACY 88%
LIFE EXPECTANCY 51 years
GDP PER CAPITA $9,800
ECONOMY **Ind:** coal, forestry, sugar, soft drink concentrates, textiles **Agr:** sugarcane, cotton, corn, tobacco, cattle **Exp:** soft drink concentrates, sugar, timber, cotton yarn, refrigerators

Tanzania

UNITED REPUBLIC OF TANZANIA

AREA 947,300 sq km (365,753 sq mi)
POPULATION 51,046,000
CAPITAL Dar es Salaam (administrative) 5,116,000; Dodoma (legislative) 228,000
RELIGION Muslim, indigenous beliefs, Christian
LANGUAGE Kiswahili, Swahili, English, Arabic
LITERACY 71%
LIFE EXPECTANCY 62 years
GDP PER CAPITA $3,000
ECONOMY **Ind:** agricultural processing (sugar, beer, cigarettes, sisal twine); mining (diamonds, gold, and iron), salt, soda ash **Agr:** coffee, sisal, tea, cotton, pyrethrum (insecticide made from chrysanthemums), cashew nuts, cattle, sheep **Exp:** gold, coffee, cashew nuts, manufacturers, cotton

Togo

TOGOLESE REPUBLIC

AREA 56,785 sq km (21,925 sq mi)
POPULATION 7,552,000
CAPITAL Lomé 956,000
RELIGION indigenous beliefs, Christian, Muslim
LANGUAGE French, Ewe, Mina, Kabye, Dagomba
LITERACY 67%
LIFE EXPECTANCY 65 years
GDP PER CAPITA $1,500
ECONOMY **Ind:** phosphate mining, agricultural processing, cement, handicrafts, textiles **Agr:** coffee, cocoa, cotton, yams, cassava (tapioca), livestock, fish **Exp:** reexports, cotton, phosphates, coffee, cocoa

Tunisia

REPUBLIC OF TUNISIA

AREA 163,610 sq km (63,170 sq mi)
POPULATION 11,037,000
CAPITAL Tunis 1,993,000
RELIGION Muslim
LANGUAGE Arabic, French
LITERACY 82%
LIFE EXPECTANCY 76 years
GDP PER CAPITA $11,600
ECONOMY **Ind:** petroleum, mining (particularly phosphate and iron ore), tourism, textiles **Agr:** olives, olive oil, grain, tomatoes, citrus, beef **Exp:** clothing, semifinished goods and textiles, agricultural products, mechanical goods, phosphates

Uganda

REPUBLIC OF UGANDA

AREA 241,038 sq km (93,065 sq mi)
POPULATION 37,102,000
CAPITAL Kampala 1,936,000
RELIGION Roman Catholic, Protestant, Muslim
LANGUAGE English, Ganda, Luganda, Swahili, Arabic
LITERACY 79%
LIFE EXPECTANCY 55 years
GDP PER CAPITA $2,100
ECONOMY **Ind:** sugar, brewing, tobacco, cotton textiles; cement **Agr:** coffee, tea, cotton, tobacco, poultry **Exp:** coffee, fish and fish products, tea, cotton, flowers, gold

Zambia

REPUBLIC OF ZAMBIA

AREA 752,618 sq km (290,586 sq mi)
POPULATION 15,066,000
CAPITAL Lusaka 2,179,000
RELIGION Protestant, Roman Catholic, other
LANGUAGE Bemba, Nyanja, Tonga, Lozi, Chewa, Nsenga, Tumbuka, English
LITERACY 63%
LIFE EXPECTANCY 52 years
GDP PER CAPITA $4,300
ECONOMY **Ind:** copper mining and processing, construction, foodstuffs, beverages **Agr:** corn, sorghum, rice, peanuts, coffee; cattle **Exp:** copper, cobalt, electricity; tobacco, flowers, cotton

Zimbabwe

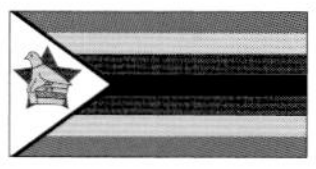

REPUBLIC OF ZIMBABWE

AREA 390,757 sq km (150,871 sq mi)
POPULATION 14,230,000
CAPITAL Harare 1,501,000
RELIGION Protestant, Roman Catholic, indigenous beliefs
LANGUAGE Shona, Ndebele, English
LITERACY 89%
LIFE EXPECTANCY 57 years
GDP PER CAPITA $2,100
ECONOMY **Ind:** mining (diamonds, coal, gold, platinum), steel, wood products, cement **Agr:** tobacco, corn, cotton, wheat, coffee, sugarcane, peanuts; sheep **Exp:** platinum, cotton, tobacco, gold, ferroalloys

DEPENDENCIES

Mayotte, Réunion

(FRANCE)

Mayotte and Réunion are French overseas departments, having equal status to the 13 metropolitan regions that make up European France. Please see "France" for facts about Mayotte and Réunion.

St. Helena

SOVEREIGN

LOCAL

(U.K.)
SAINT HELENA, ASCENSION, AND TRISTAN DA CUNHA

AREA 308 sq km (119 sq mi)
POPULATION 7,800
CAPITAL Jamestown 1,000
RELIGION Protestant, Roman Catholic
LANGUAGE English
LITERACY 97%
LIFE EXPECTANCY 79 years
GDP PER CAPITA $7,800
ECONOMY **Ind:** construction, crafts (furniture, lacework, fancy woodwork), fishing, collectable postage stamps **Agr:** coffee, corn, potatoes, vegetables, fish, lobster **Exp:** fish (frozen, canned, and salt-dried skipjack, tuna), coffee, handicrafts

DISPUTED TERRITORY

Western Sahara

(MOROCCO)
WESTERN SAHARA

AREA 266,000 sq km (102,703 sq mi)
POPULATION 571,000
CAPITAL Laayoune 262,000
RELIGION Muslim
LANGUAGE Arabic
LITERACY NA
LIFE EXPECTANCY 63 years
GDP PER CAPITA $2,500
ECONOMY **Ind:** phosphate mining, handicrafts **Agr:** fruits and vegetables, camels, sheep, goats, fish **Exp:** phosphates

Protected Areas

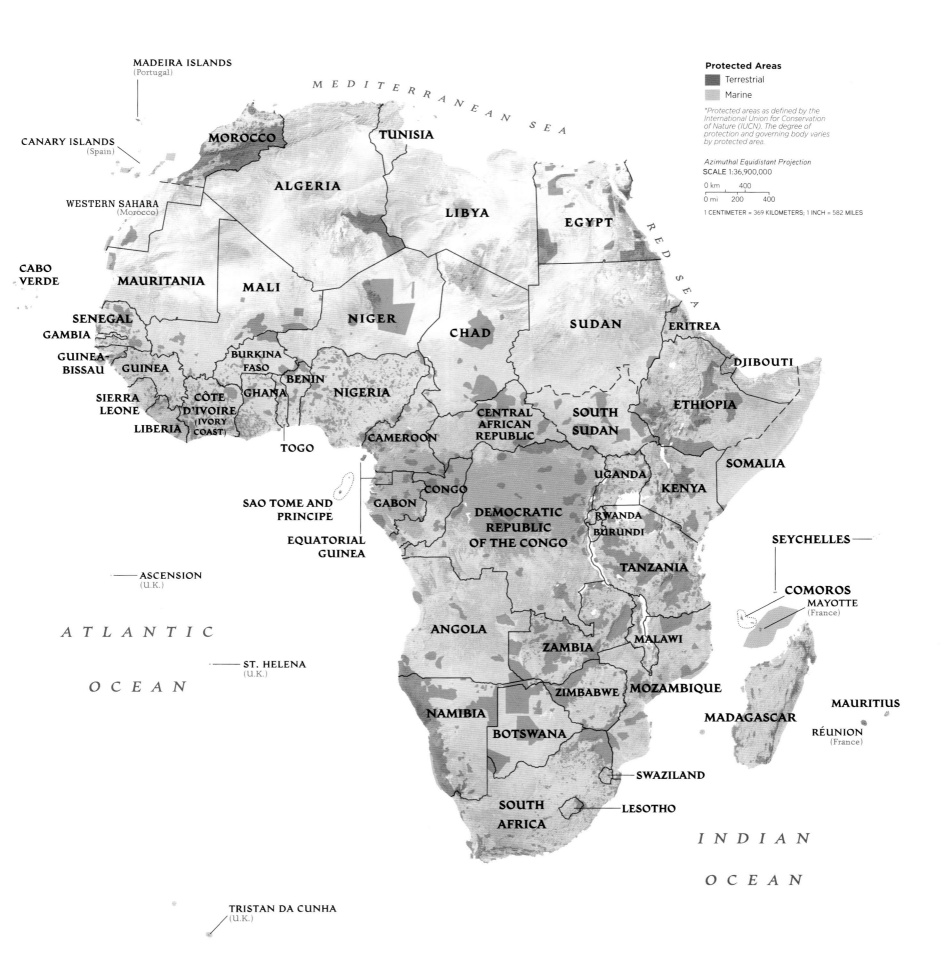

MADEIRA ISLANDS
(Portugal)

M E D I T E R R A N E A N   S E A

CANARY ISLANDS
(Spain)

MOROCCO

TUNISIA

ALGERIA

LIBYA

EGYPT

WESTERN SAHARA
(Morocco)

RED SEA

**CABO
VERDE**

MAURITANIA

MALI

NIGER

CHAD

SUDAN

ERITREA

SENEGAL

GAMBIA

1

DJIBOUTI

**GUINEA-
BISSAU**

GUINEA

**BURKINA
FASO**

BENIN

NIGERIA

**CENTRAL
AFRICAN
REPUBLIC**

**SOUTH
SUDAN**

ETHIOPIA

**SIERRA
LEONE**

**CÔTE
D'IVOIRE
(IVORY
COAST)**

GHANA

LIBERIA

TOGO

CAMEROON

SOMALIA

**SAO TOME AND
PRINCIPE**

GABON

CONGO

UGANDA

KENYA

**EQUATORIAL
GUINEA**

**DEMOCRATIC
REPUBLIC
OF THE CONGO**

RWANDA
BURUNDI

SEYCHELLES

ASCENSION
(U.K.)

TANZANIA

COMOROS
MAYOTTE
(France)

A T L A N T I C

O C E A N

ST. HELENA
(U.K.)

ANGOLA

ZAMBIA

MALAWI

MOZAMBIQUE

MAURITIUS

MADAGASCAR

RÉUNION
(France)

ZIMBABWE

NAMIBIA

BOTSWANA

SWAZILAND

**SOUTH
AFRICA**

LESOTHO

I N D I A N

O C E A N

TRISTAN DA CUNHA
(U.K.)

Protected Areas
Terrestrial
Marine

*Protected areas as defined by the
International Union for Conservation
of Nature (IUCN). The degree of
protection and governing body varies
by protected area.*

Azimuthal Equidistant Projection
SCALE 1:36,900,000

0 km   400
0 mi   200   400

1 CENTIMETER = 369 KILOMETERS; 1 INCH = 582 MILES

Australia
and Oceania

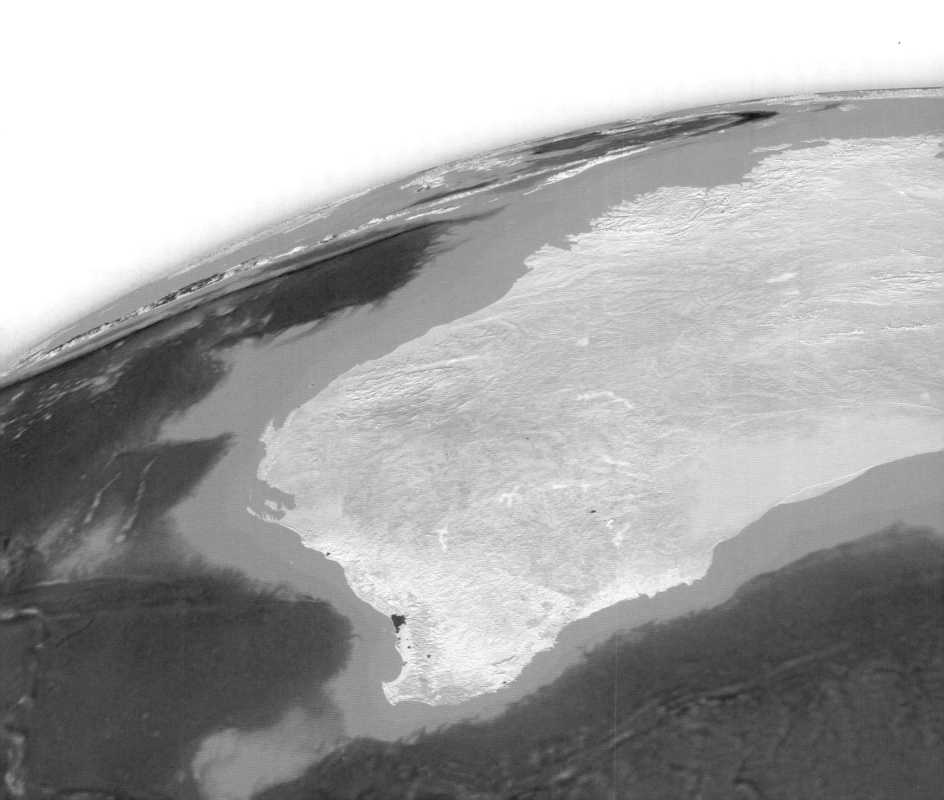

AUSTRALIA IS A CONTINENT OF EXTREMES—smallest and flattest, it's also the only continent-nation, with a landmass equal to that of the lower 48 states of the United States. Yet it is less populous than any other continent except Antarctica. And more than 80 percent of its people inhabit only the 1 percent of the continent that stretches along the southeast and south coasts. The sun-scorched outback that swells across the Australian interior has daunted virtually all comers, except the Aborigines. Traditionally hunter-gatherers, the Aborigines for eons—long before the arrival of Europeans—considered it home, both spiritually and physically.

The continent itself has been on a kind of planetary walkabout since it broke away from the supercontinent of Gondwana about 65 million years ago. Isolated, dry, and scorched by erosion, Australia developed its own unique species. Kangaroos, koalas, and duck-billed platypuses are well-known examples, but it also boasts rare plants, including 600 species of eucalyptus. The land surface has been stable enough to preserve some of the world's oldest rocks and mineral deposits, whereas the two islands of its neighboring nation New Zealand are younger and tell of a more violent geology that raised high volcanic mountains above deep fjords. Both nations share a past as British colonies, but in recent decades each has transformed itself from a ranching-based society into a fully industrialized and service-oriented economy.

Sitting at the southwestern edge of Oceania, Australia is the economic powerhouse in this region. By contrast the islands of Oceania—more than 10,000 of them sprawling across the vast stretches of the central and South Pacific—are in various states of nationhood or dependency, prosperity or poverty. Their diverse populations and cultures are testament to the seafaring peoples who began settling these islands several thousand years ago, again, long before the explorations and exploitations of Europeans in the 16th through the 19th century.

Geographers today divide Oceania into three major ethnographic regions. The largest, Polynesia, or "many islands," composes an immense oceanic triangle, with apexes at Hawai'i in the north, Easter Island in the east, and New Zealand in the southwest. The second Oceanic region, Melanesia, derives its name from the Greek words for "black islands"—either a reference to its dark, lush landscapes or what European explorers described as the dark skin of most of its inhabitants. North and east of Australia, Melanesia encompasses such groups as the Bismarck Archipelago, the Solomon Islands, Vanuatu, the Fiji Islands, and New Caledonia. North of Melanesia, Micronesia contains a widely scattered group of small islands and coral atolls, as well as the world's deepest ocean point—the 35,827-foot-deep (10,920-meter-deep) Challenger Deep—located in the southern Mariana Trench off the southwest coast of Guam. Micronesia stretches across more than 3,000 miles (4,830 kilometers) of the western Pacific, with volcanic peaks that reach 2,500 feet (760 meters). Palau; Nauru; and the Caroline, Mariana, Marshall, and Gilbert Islands all form this third subdivision of Oceania.

INDIAN OCEAN

SAVU SEA

Sumba

Timor

Sawu

Roti

T I M O R

S E A

Ashmore Is.

Cartier I.

ARNHE
LAND

Cape Van Diemen
Cape Don
Port Essington
Croker I.
Dundas Strait
Mountnorris
Cobourg Pen.
Bay
Junction Bay
Bathurst Island
Melville
Island
Skirmish Point
Cape Steep
Cape Fourcroy
Van
Diemen
Gulf
S. Alligator
Fog Bay
Port Darwin
Point Blaze
Anson Bay
Murrenja Hill
135
Parsons Ra.
Cape Ford
Daly
Katherine
Rope

Cape Talbot
Cape Londonderry
Vansittart Bay
Cape Bougainville
Cape Rulhieres
Bonaparte Archipelago
Admiralty Gulf
Cape Voltaire
Joseph
Bonaparte
Gulf
Table Hill
+ 198

Sandy
Islet

Browse I.

York Sound
Prince
Frederick
Harbour
Cambridge
Gulf
Drysdale
Queens Chan.
+ Endeavour Hill
210

St. George Basin
Augustus Island
Doubtful Bay
Collier Bay
Mt. Hann
777 +
Durack
Ord River Dam
Ord

Buccaneer
Archipelago
Cape Leveque
KIMBERLEY
PLATEAU
Lake
Argyle

Pender Bay
Beagle Bay
King
Sd.
Mt. Ord
+ 947
King Leopold Ranges
Ord

Lake Woods
Tarrabool
Lake

Mermaid Reef
Clerke Reef
Imperieuse Reef
Rowley
Shoals
Cape Bertholet
Dampier
Land
Gautheaume Point
Roebuck Bay
Cape Latouche Treville
Lagrange Bay
Cape Bossut
Fitzroy

La
Sylvest

Mount
Frederick
+ 530
Tanami
Desert

Poissonnier Point
Eighty Mile Beach
GREAT

Lewis Range
+ Mt. Tanami
489

Dampier
Archipelago
Nickol Bay
De Grey
SANDY
Southesk
Tablelands
Gregory L.

Davenport Ra.

Monte Bello Is.
Barrow I.
DESERT
Lake
Waukarlycarly
Percival Lakes
Lake White

North West Cape
Exmouth Gulf
NORTH WEST BASIN
Fortescue
Hamersley A Range
Chichester Range
L. Dora
Lake Auld
Lake Mackay
WESTERN
Lake Bennett
Mt. Zeil
+1,531

Point Cloates
Mt. Bruce
1,235 +
RA
Lake George
Lake
Macdonald
Mt. Leisler
897
Macdonnell Ranges

TROPIC OF CAPRICORN

Mt. Meharry +
1,250
Lake
Disappointment
Mt. Madley +
487
Gibson Desert
L. Neale
Lake Hopkins
Amadeus Depression
L. Amadeus
James Range

Lake
Macleod
Ashburton
Ophthalmia Range
Lofty Range
Petermann Ranges
Kata Tjuta
(Mt. Olga)
1,069
Uluru
(Ayers Rock)
868
Mt. Woodroffe
+1,435

Geographe Chan.
Lyons
Mount Augustus
+1,105
Collier Range
Mt. Essendon +
910
L. Burnside
PLATEAU
Mt. Aloysius +
982
Mt. Whinham +
1,228
Musgrave Ranges
Finke

Bernier I.
Dorre I.
C. Inscription
Gascoyne
Robinson Range
Mt. Fraser +
799
Lake
Gregory
Lake Gillen
Lake
Radgo
Mount
+ Sir Thomas
805
Stuart Range

Dirk Hartog I.
Shark Bay
Coor-De-Wandy Hill
519
L. Carnegie
Baker
Lake

Steep Point
Murchison
Lake Way
Lake Wells

Edel Land
Hamelin
Pool
Mt. Luke
+ 519
Nicholson Ra.
L. Austin
Lake Annean
Lake Darlot
Lake Throssell
Yeo Lake
Great Victoria Desert
Lake
Meramangye
Lake Dey Dey

Gantheaume Bay
Bluff Point
+ Dalgaranga Hill
642
Mt. Shenton +
594
Lake Rason
Serpentine
Lakes
Lake
Maurice

Geelvink Channel
Wyemandoo
+ 524
Mt. Redcliffe
553 +
Lake
Carey
Jubilee Lake
Shed
Lakes
Forest
Lakes

Houtman Abrolhos
Canning Hill
535 +
Lake Raeside
Plumridge Lakes
Lake
Nyanga

Mongers
Lake
Lake
Barlee
L. Minigwal
Yarle
Lakes
Lake Harris

Lake
Moore
Lake Ballard
Lake Goongarrie
L. Rebecca
Nullarbor Plain
Lake
Everard

Green Head
Jurien Bay
+ Walyahmoning Rock
484
Lake
Yindarlgooda
EUCLA
BASIN
Head
of Bight
Lake Aeraman

Mt. Grey +
404
L. Lefroy
Hampton Tableland
Cape Adieu
Anxious
Bay

L. Cowan
Red Rocks Point
Fowlers Bay
Pe

Darling Range
L. Johnston
L. Dundas
Point Culver
Twilight Cove
GREAT
AUSTRALIAN BIGHT
Coffin Bay

Mt. Cook
582 +
L. Hope
Mt. Ragged
585 +
Pt. Whidbey

Cape Peron
Swan
Blackwood
Cape Pasley
Cape Carn

Geographe Bay
Cape Naturaliste
Bluff Knoll
1,100 +
Hood Point
Cape Knob
Cape Arid
Archipelago
of the
Recherche

Cape Leeuwin
Stirling Range
Cheyne Bay
Esperance Bay

Point D'Entrecasteaux
West Cape Howe
King George Sound

INDIAN OCEAN

Azimuthal Equidistant Projection
SCALE 1:10,500,000   1 CENTIMETER = 105 KILOMETERS; 1 INCH = 166 MILES
0   200   400
KILOMETERS
0   200   400
STATUTE MILES
Elevations in meters

TASMANIA
Same Scale
as Main Map

145°E
Wilsons Promontory
150°
Bass Strait
King Island
Flinders Island
FURNEAUX
GROUP
Mt. Stanley
+ 213
Hunter Is.
C. Barren I.
Stokes Pt.
Banks Str.
Clarke I.
Cape Grim
Anderson Bay
Sleaford
Great Western Tiers
Legges Tor
+1,572
Mount Ossa
4,617
Great L.
Great Oyster B.
Macquarie Harbour
Lake Gordon
Lake Pedder
Tasman Pen.
Port Davey
Storm Bay
South West
Cape
South Bruny Island
South East Cape

40°

135°

Australia
Physical

Continental Data

Area: 7,687,000 sq km
(2,968,000 sq mi)

Greatest north-south extent:
3,138 km (1,950 mi)

Greatest east-west extent:
3,983 km (2,475 mi)

Highest point:
Mount Kosciuszko,
New South Wales
2,228 m (7,310 ft)

Lowest point:
Lake Eyre -16 m (-52 ft)

Lowest recorded temperature:
Charlotte Pass, New South Wales
-23°C (-9.4°F), June 29, 1994

Highest recorded temperature:
Cloncurry, Queensland 53.3°C
(128°F), January 16, 1889

Longest rivers:
•Murray 2,375 km (1,476 mi)
•Murrumbidgee
 1,485 km (923 mi)
•Darling 1,472 km (915 mi)

Largest natural lakes (Aus.):
•Lake Eyre 0–9,690 sq km
 (0–3,741 sq mi)
•Lake Torrens 0–5,745 sq km
 (0–2,218 sq mi)
•Lake Gairdner 0–4,351 sq km
 (0–1,680 sq mi)

**Earth's extremes
located in Australia:**
•Longest Reef:
 Great Barrier Reef
 2,300 km (1,429 mi)

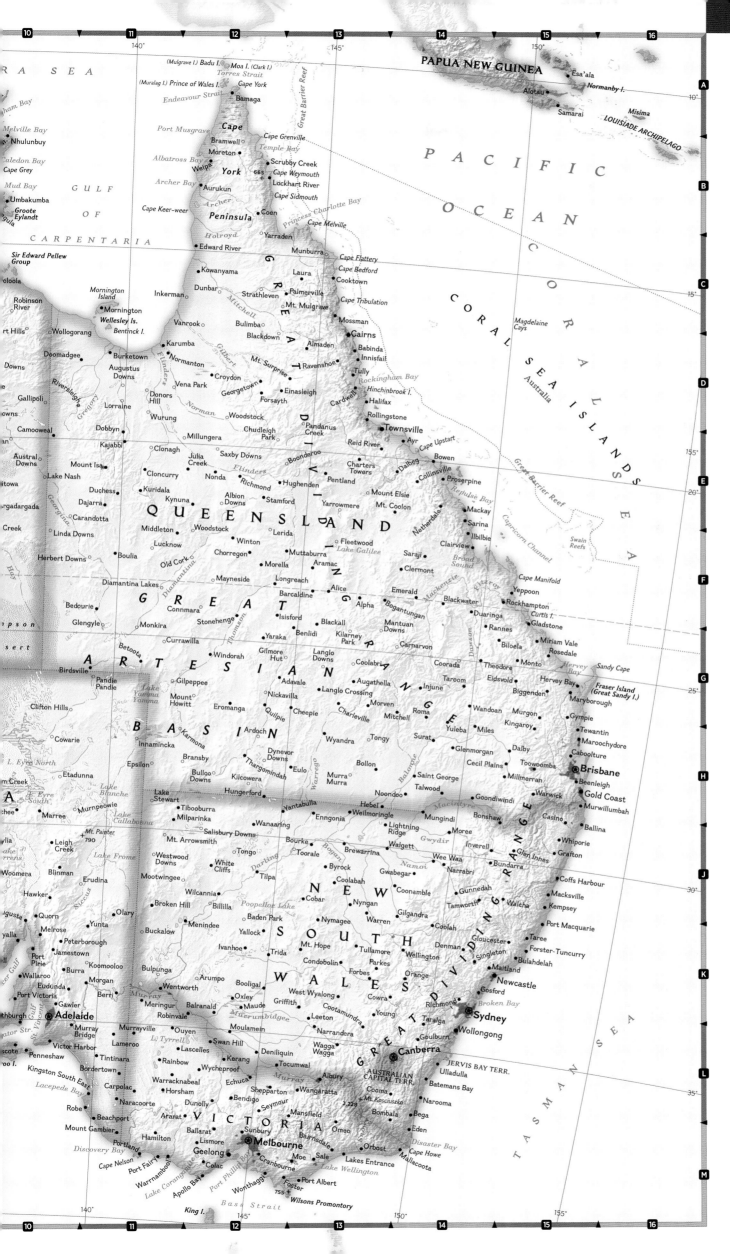

Australia
Political

Continental Data

Total number of countries: 1

Date of independence:
January 1, 1901

Area:
7,741,220 sq km (2,988,885 sq mi)

Percent urban population: 89%

Population: 22,751,000

Population density:
3 per sq km (8 per sq mi)

Largest city by population:
Sydney 4,505,000

GDP per capita:
$65,400

Average life expectancy: 82 years

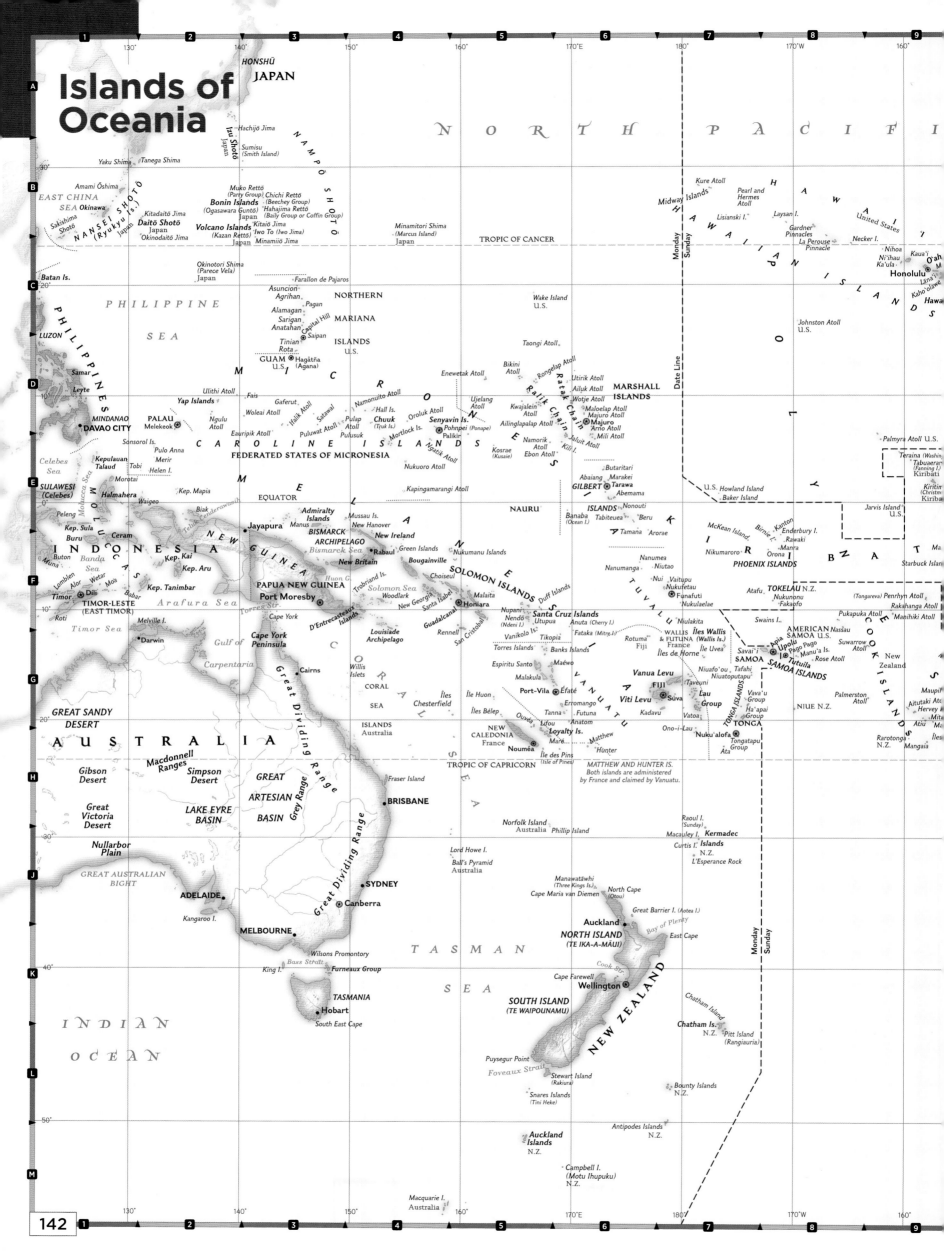

Oceania
Political

Regional Data

Total number of countries: 13

First independent country:
New Zealand, September 26, 1907

"Youngest" country:
Palau, October 1, 1994

Largest country by area:
Papua New Guinea 462,840 sq km (178,703 sq mi)

Smallest country by area:
Nauru 21 sq km (8 sq mi)

Percent urban population: 40%

Most populous country:
Papua New Guinea 6,672,000

Least populous country:
Nauru 9,500

Most densely populated country:
Nauru 454 per sq km (1,177 per sq mi)

Least densely populated country:
Papua New Guinea 14 per sq km (37 per sq mi)

Largest city by population:
Auckland, New Zealand 1,344,000

Highest GDP per capita:
New Zealand $36,400

Lowest GDP per capita:
Soloman Islands $2,000

Average life expectancy: 69 years

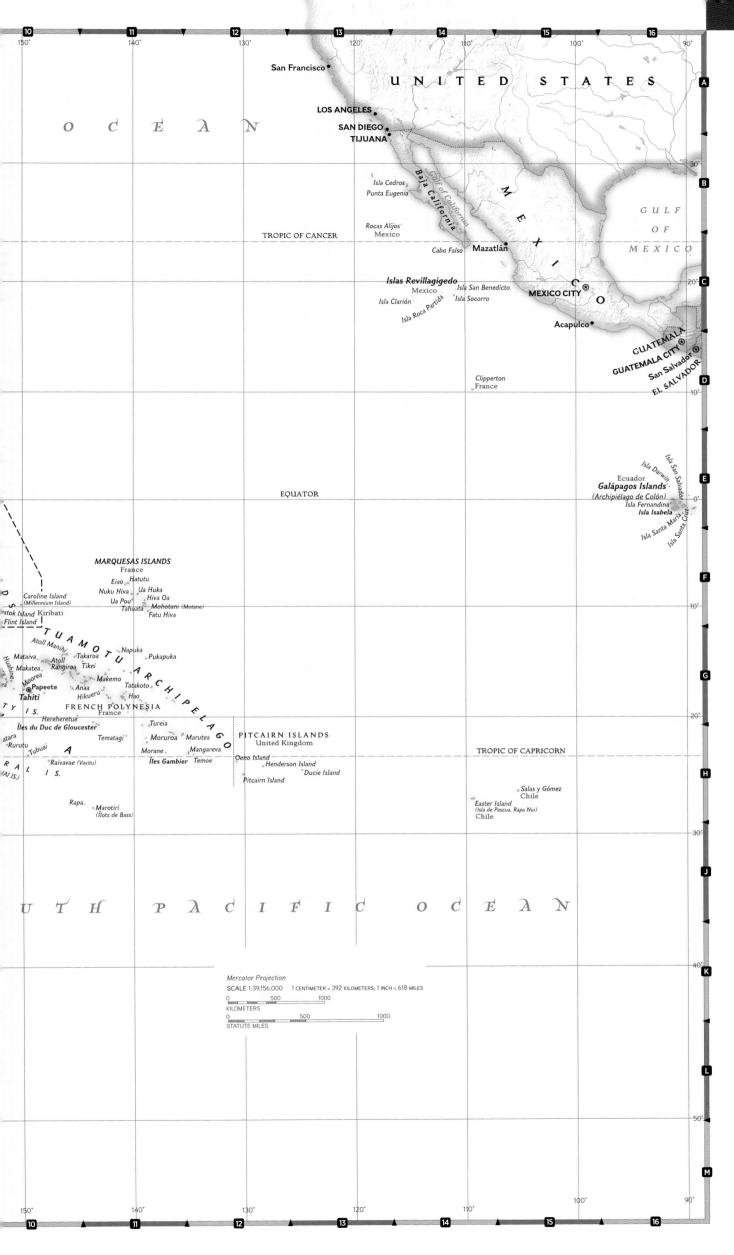

UNITED STATES

OCEAN

San Francisco

LOS ANGELES
SAN DIEGO
TIJUANA

Isla Cedros
Punta Eugenia

MEXICO

Baja California

Gulf of California

Rocas Alijos
Mexico

TROPIC OF CANCER

Cabo Falso · Mazatlán

GULF
OF
MEXICO

Islas Revillagigedo
Mexico

Isla San Benedicto
Isla Clarión · Isla Socorro
Isla Roca Partida

MEXICO CITY

Acapulco

GUATEMALA
GUATEMALA CITY
San Salvador
EL SALVADOR

Clipperton
France

Isla Darwin
Isla San Salvador

Ecuador
Galápagos Islands
(Archipiélago de Colón)
Isla Fernandina
Isla Isabela

EQUATOR

Isla Santa María
Isla Santa Cruz

MARQUESAS ISLANDS
France

Eiao · Hatutu
Nuku Hiva · Ua Huka
Ua Pou · Hiva Oa
Tahuata · Mohotani (Motane)
Fatu Hiva

Caroline Island
(Millennium Island)
stok Island Kiribati
Flint Island

TUAMOTU ARCHIPELAGO

Atoll Manihi
Mataiva · Napuka
Takaroa · Pukapuka
Atoll Rangiroa · Tikei
Makatea
Moorea · Makemo
Papeete · Anaa · Tatakoto
Tahiti · Hikueru · Hao
Huahine
FRENCH POLYNESIA
France

Hereheretue

Îles du Duc de Gloucester

Tureia
Tematagi · Moruroa · Marutea
Morane · Mangareva
Îles Gambier · Temoe

Rurutu
atara
Tubuai
Raivavae (Vavitu)

Rapa · Marotiri
(Îlots de Bass)

PITCAIRN ISLANDS
United Kingdom

Oeno Island
Henderson Island
Ducie Island
Pitcairn Island

TROPIC OF CAPRICORN

Salas y Gómez
Chile
Easter Island
(Isla de Pascua, Rapa Nui)
Chile

SOUTH PACIFIC OCEAN

Mercator Projection
SCALE 1:39,156,000   1 CENTIMETER = 392 KILOMETERS; 1 INCH = 618 MILES

0   500   1000
KILOMETERS

0   500   1000
STATUTE MILES

Human and Natural Themes

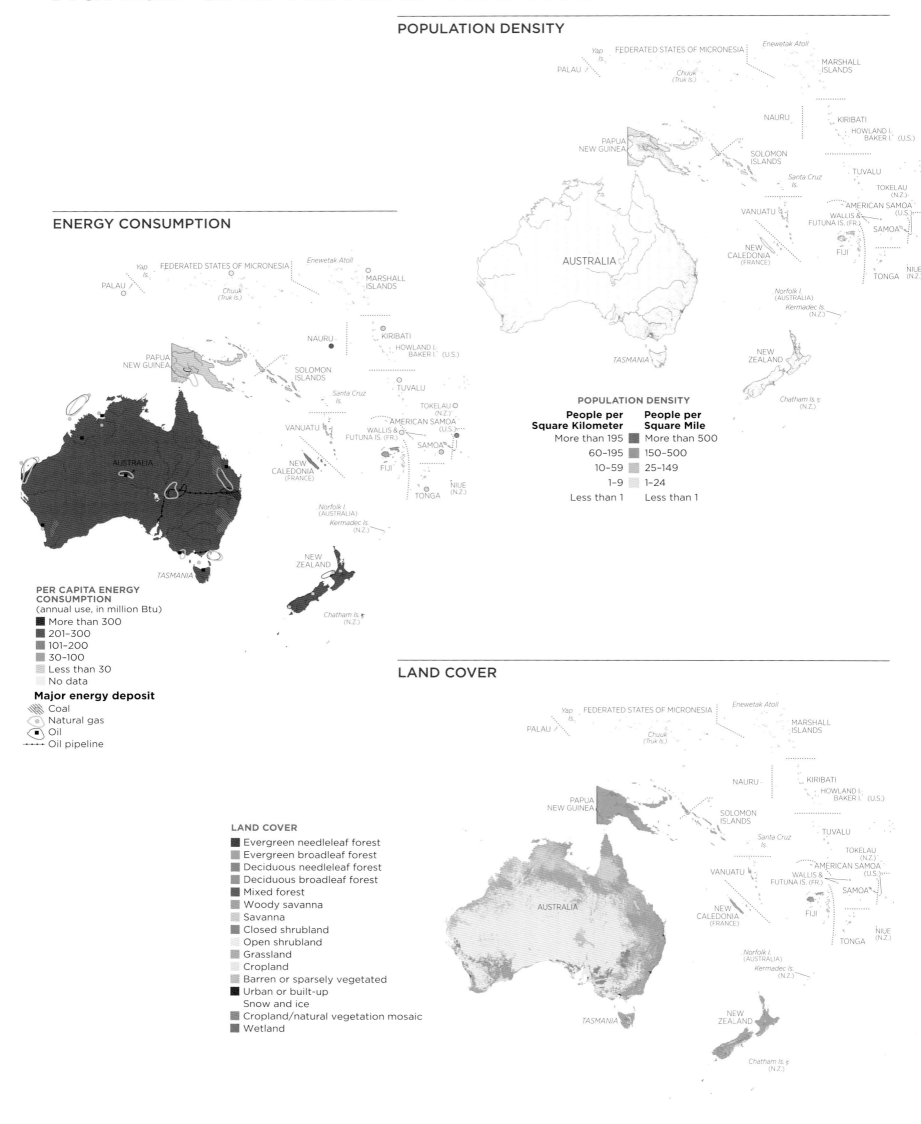

POPULATION DENSITY

POPULATION DENSITY

People per Square Kilometer		People per Square Mile
More than 195	■	More than 500
60–195	■	150–500
10–59	■	25–149
1–9	■	1–24
Less than 1		Less than 1

ENERGY CONSUMPTION

PER CAPITA ENERGY CONSUMPTION
(annual use, in million Btu)
- ■ More than 300
- ■ 201–300
- ■ 101–200
- ■ 30–100
- Less than 30
- No data

Major energy deposit
- Coal
- Natural gas
- Oil
- ‒‒‒ Oil pipeline

LAND COVER

LAND COVER
- ■ Evergreen needleleaf forest
- ■ Evergreen broadleaf forest
- ■ Deciduous needleleaf forest
- ■ Deciduous broadleaf forest
- ■ Mixed forest
- ■ Woody savanna
- ■ Savanna
- ■ Closed shrubland
- Open shrubland
- ■ Grassland
- Cropland
- Barren or sparsely vegetated
- ■ Urban or built-up
- Snow and ice
- ■ Cropland/natural vegetation mosaic
- ■ Wetland

CLIMATIC ZONES

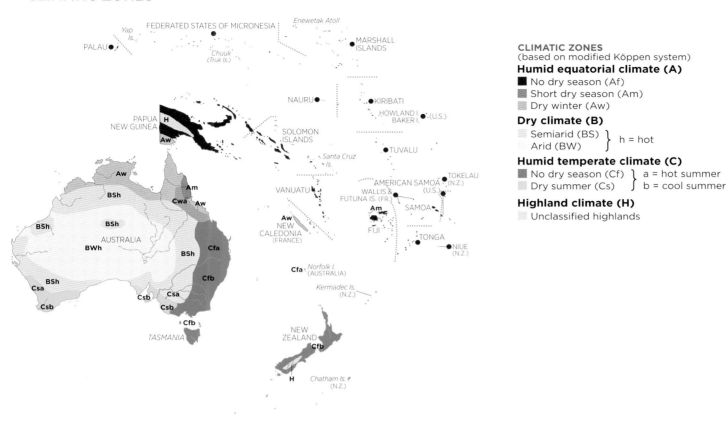

NATURAL HAZARDS (TECTONIC EVENTS)

WATER AVAILABILITY

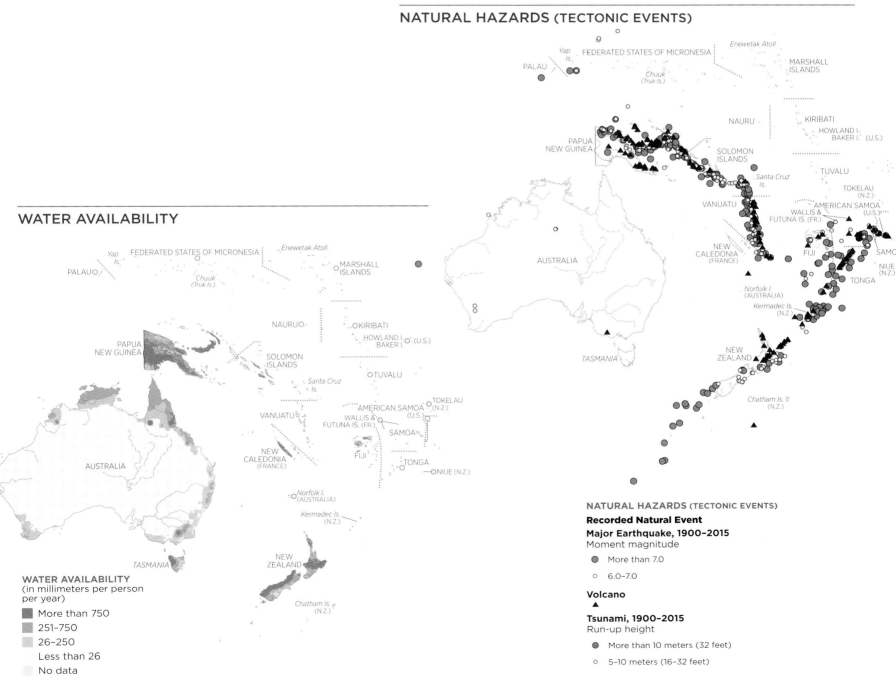

WATER AVAILABILITY
(in millimeters per person
per year)
■ More than 750
▨ 251–750
▨ 26–250
□ Less than 26
□ No data

NATURAL HAZARDS (TECTONIC EVENTS)
Recorded Natural Event
Major Earthquake, 1900–2015
Moment magnitude
● More than 7.0
○ 6.0–7.0

Volcano
▲

Tsunami, 1900–2015
Run-up height
● More than 10 meters (32 feet)
○ 5–10 meters (16–32 feet)

Flags and Facts

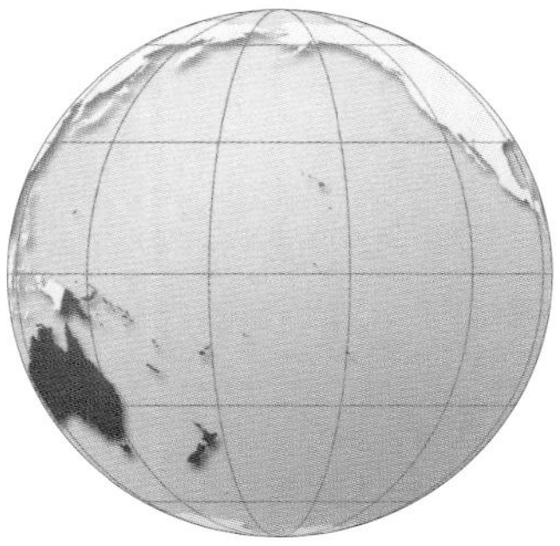

COUNTRIES

Australia

COMMONWEALTH OF AUSTRALIA

AREA 7,741,220 sq km (2,988,885 sq mi)
POPULATION 22,751,000
CAPITAL Canberra 423,000
RELIGION Protestant, Catholic, none
LANGUAGE English, Australian
LITERACY 99%
LIFE EXPECTANCY 82 years
GDP PER CAPITA $65,400
ECONOMY **Ind:** mining, industrial and transportation equipment, food processing, chemicals, steel **Agr:** wheat, barley, sugarcane, fruits, cattle, sheep, poultry **Exp:** coal, iron ore, gold, meat, wool, alumina, wheat, machinery and transport equipment

Fiji

REPUBLIC OF FIJI

AREA 18,274 sq km (7,056 sq mi)
POPULATION 909,000
CAPITAL Suva 176,000
RELIGION Protestant, Hindu
LANGUAGE English, Fijian, Hindustani
LITERACY 94%
LIFE EXPECTANCY 72 years
GDP PER CAPITA $8,800
ECONOMY **Ind:** tourism, sugar, clothing, copra, gold, silver, lumber, small cottage industries **Agr:** sugarcane, coconuts, cassava (tapioca), rice, sweet potatoes, bananas, cattle, pigs, horses, goats, fish **Exp:** sugar, garments, gold, timber, fish, molasses, coconut oil

Kiribati

REPUBLIC OF KIRIBATI

AREA 811 sq km (313 sq mi)
POPULATION 106,000
CAPITAL Tarawa 46,000
RELIGION Roman Catholic, Kempsville Presbyterian Church
LANGUAGE I-Kiribati, English
LITERACY NA
LIFE EXPECTANCY 66 years
GDP PER CAPITA $2,200
ECONOMY **Ind:** fishing, handicrafts **Agr:** copra, taro, breadfruit, fish **Exp:** fish, coconut products

Marshall Islands

REPUBLIC OF THE MARSHALL ISLANDS

AREA 181 sq km (70 sq mi)
POPULATION 72,000
CAPITAL Majuro 31,000
RELIGION Protestant, Assembly of God
LANGUAGE Marshallese, English
LITERACY 94%
LIFE EXPECTANCY 73 years
GDP PER CAPITA $3,400
ECONOMY **Ind:** copra, tuna processing, tourism, craft items (from seashells, wood, and pearls) **Agr:** coconuts, tomatoes, melons, taro, breadfruit, fruits, pigs, chickens **Exp:** copra cake, coconut oil, handicrafts, fish

Micronesia

FEDERATED STATES OF MICRONESIA

AREA 702 sq km (271 sq mi)
POPULATION 105,000
CAPITAL Palikir 7,000
RELIGION Roman Catholic, Protestant
LANGUAGE English, Chuukese, Kosrean, Pohnpeian, Yapese
LITERACY 89%
LIFE EXPECTANCY 73 years
GDP PER CAPITA $3,000
ECONOMY **Ind:** tourism, construction; specialized aquaculture, craft items (shell and wood) **Agr:** taro, yams, coconuts, bananas, cassava (manioc, tapioca), sakau (kava), Kosraen citrus, betel nuts, black pepper, fish, pigs, chickens **Exp:** fish, sakau (kava), betel nuts, black pepper

Nauru

REPUBLIC OF NAURU

AREA 21 sq km (8 sq mi)
POPULATION 9,500
CAPITAL Yaren 750
RELIGION Protestant, Roman Catholic
LANGUAGE Nauruan, English
LITERACY NA
LIFE EXPECTANCY 67 years
GDP PER CAPITA $14,800
ECONOMY **Ind:** phosphate mining, offshore banking, coconut products **Agr:** coconuts **Exp:** phosphates

New Zealand

NEW ZEALAND

AREA 267,710 sq km (103,363 sq mi)
POPULATION 4,438,000
CAPITAL Wellington 383,000
RELIGION Christian
LANGUAGE English, Maori
LITERACY 99%
LIFE EXPECTANCY 81 years
GDP PER CAPITA $36,400
ECONOMY **Ind:** agriculture, forestry, fishing, logs and wood articles, manufacturing, mining, construction, financial services, real estate services, tourism **Agr:** dairy products, sheep, beef, poultry, fruit, vegetables, wine, seafood, wheat and barley **Exp:** dairy products, meat, wood and wood products, wine

Palau

REPUBLIC OF PALAU

AREA 459 sq km (177 sq mi)
POPULATION 21,000
CAPITAL Melekeok 300
RELIGION Roman Catholic, Protestant
LANGUAGE Palauan, Tobi, Anguar
LITERACY 100%
LIFE EXPECTANCY 73 years
GDP PER CAPITA $14,800
ECONOMY **Ind:** tourism, craft items (from shell, wood, pearls), construction, garment making **Agr:** coconuts, copra, cassava (manioc, tapioca), sweet potatoes, fish **Exp:** shellfish, tuna, copra, garments

Papua New Guinea

INDEPENDENT STATE OF PAPUA NEW GUINEA

AREA 462,840 sq km (178,703 sq mi)
POPULATION 6,672,000
CAPITAL Port Moresby 345,000
RELIGION Protestant, Roman Catholic
LANGUAGE Tok Pisin, English, Hiri Motu, 860 indigenous languages
LITERACY 64%
LIFE EXPECTANCY 67 years
GDP PER CAPITA $2,800
ECONOMY **Ind:** copra crushing, palm oil processing, plywood production, wood chip production, gold, silver, copper, crude oil production, petroleum refining, construction, tourism **Agr:** coffee, cocoa, copra, palm kernels, tea, sugar, rubber, sweet potatoes, fruit, vegetables, vanilla, shell fish, poultry, pork **Exp:** oil, gold, copper ore, logs, palm oil, coffee, cocoa, crayfish, prawns

Samoa

INDEPENDENT STATE OF SAMOA

AREA 2,831 sq km (1,093 sq mi)
POPULATION 198,000
CAPITAL Apia 37,000
RELIGION Protestant, Roman Catholic, Mormon
LANGUAGE Samoan, English
LITERACY 100%
LIFE EXPECTANCY 73 years
GDP PER CAPITA $5,400
ECONOMY **Ind:** food processing, building materials, auto parts **Agr:** coconuts, bananas, taro, yams, coffee, cocoa **Exp:** fish, coconut oil and cream, copra, taro, automotive parts, garments, beer

Solomon Islands

SOLOMON ISLANDS

AREA 28,896 sq km (11,157 sq mi)
POPULATION 622,000
CAPITAL Honiara 73,000
RELIGION Protestant, Roman Catholic
LANGUAGE Melanesian pidgin, English
LITERACY 84%
LIFE EXPECTANCY 75 years
GDP PER CAPITA $2,000
ECONOMY **Ind:** fish (tuna), mining, timber **Agr:** cocoa beans, coconuts, palm kernels, rice, potatoes, vegetables, fruit, timber, cattle, pigs, fish **Exp:** timber, fish, copra, palm oil, cocoa

Tonga

KINGDOM OF TONGA

AREA 747 sq km (288 sq mi)
POPULATION 107,000
CAPITAL Nuku'alofa 25,000
RELIGION Christian
LANGUAGE Tongan, English
LITERACY 99%
LIFE EXPECTANCY 76 years
GDP PER CAPITA $5,100
ECONOMY **Ind:** tourism, construction, fishing **Agr:** squash, coconuts, copra, bananas, vanilla beans, cocoa, coffee, sweet potatoes, cassava, taro and kava **Exp:** squash, fish, vanilla beans, root crops

Tuvalu

TUVALU

AREA 26 sq km (10 sq mi)
POPULATION 11,000
CAPITAL Funafuti 6,000
RELIGION Protestant
LANGUAGE Tuvaluan, English, Samoan, Kiribati
LITERACY NA
LIFE EXPECTANCY 66 years
GDP PER CAPITA $3,400
ECONOMY **Ind:** fishing **Agr:** coconuts, fish **Exp:** copra, fish

Vanuatu

REPUBLIC OF VANUATU

AREA 12,189 sq km (4,706 sq mi)
POPULATION 272,000
CAPITAL Port-Vila 53,000
RELIGION Protestant, Roman Catholic
LANGUAGE local languages (more than 100), Bislama, English
LITERACY 85%
LIFE EXPECTANCY 73 years
GDP PER CAPITA $2,600
ECONOMY **Ind:** food and fish freezing, wood processing, meat canning **Agr:** copra, coconuts, cocoa, coffee, taro, yams, fruits, vegetables, beef, fish **Exp:** copra, beef, cocoa, timber, kava, coffee

DEPENDENCIES

American Samoa

SOVEREIGN

LOCAL

(U.S.)
TERRITORY OF AMERICAN SAMOA

AREA 199 sq km (77 sq mi)
POPULATION 54,000
CAPITAL Pago Pago 48,000
RELIGION Christian
LANGUAGE Samoan, English, Tongan
LITERACY 97%
LIFE EXPECTANCY 75 years
GDP PER CAPITA $13,000
ECONOMY **Ind:** tuna canneries (largely supplied by foreign fishing vessels), handicrafts **Agr:** bananas, coconuts, vegetables, taro, breadfruit, yams, copra, pineapples, papayas, dairy products, livestock **Exp:** canned tuna

Cook Islands

SOVEREIGN

LOCAL

(NEW ZEALAND)
COOK ISLANDS

AREA 236 sq km (91 sq mi)
POPULATION 21,000
CAPITAL Avarua NA
RELIGION Protestant, Roman Catholic
LANGUAGE English, Maori
LITERACY 95%
LIFE EXPECTANCY 76 years
GDP PER CAPITA $12,300
ECONOMY **Ind:** fruit processing, tourism, fishing, clothing, handicrafts **Agr:** copra, citrus, pineapples, tomatoes, beans, pawpaws, bananas, yams, taro, coffee, pigs, poultry **Exp:** copra, papayas, fresh and canned citrus fruit, coffee, fish, pearls and pearl shells, clothing

French Polynesia

SOVEREIGN

LOCAL

(FRANCE)
FRENCH POLYNESIA

AREA 4,167 sq km (1,609 sq mi)
POPULATION 283,000
CAPITAL Papeete 133,000
RELIGION Protestant, Roman Catholic
LANGUAGE French, Polynesian
LITERACY 98%
LIFE EXPECTANCY 77 years
GDP PER CAPITA $26,100
ECONOMY **Ind:** tourism, pearls, agricultural processing, handicrafts, phosphates **Agr:** fish, coconuts, vanilla, vegetables, fruits, coffee, poultry, beef, dairy products, fish **Exp:** cultured pearls, coconut products, mother-of-pearl, vanilla, shark meat

Guam

(U.S.)
TERRITORY OF GUAM

AREA	544 sq km
POPULATION	162,000
CAPITAL	Hagåtña 143,000
RELIGION	Roman Catholic
LANGUAGE	English, Filipino, Charmarro, other Pacific island languages
LITERACY	99%
LIFE EXPECTANCY	79 years
GDP PER CAPITA	$30,500

ECONOMY **IND:** national defense, tourism, construction, transshipment services, concrete products, printing and publishing, food processing, textiles **AGR:** fruits, copra, vegetables, eggs, pork, poultry, beef **EXP:** transshipments of refined petroleum products, construction materials, fish, food and beverage products

New Caledonia

(FRANCE)
NEW CALEDONIA

AREA	18,575 sq km (7,172 sq mi)
POPULATION	272,000
CAPITAL	Nouméa 181,000
RELIGION	Roman Catholic, Protestant
LANGUAGE	French, 33 Melanesian-Polynesian dialects
LITERACY	97%
LIFE EXPECTANCY	78 years
GDP PER CAPITA	$38,800

ECONOMY **IND:** nickel mining and smelting **AGR:** vegetables, beef, deer, other livestock products, fish **EXP:** ferronickels, nickel ore, fish

Niue

(NEW ZEALAND)
NIUE

AREA	260 sq km (100 sq mi)
POPULATION	1,200
CAPITAL	Alofi 1,000
RELIGION	Ekalesia Niue
LANGUAGE	English, Niuean
LITERACY	95%
LIFE EXPECTANCY	NA
GDP PER CAPITA	$5,800

ECONOMY **IND:** handicrafts, food processing **AGR:** coconuts, passion fruit, honey, limes, taro, yams, cassava (tapioca), sweet potatoes, pigs, poultry, beef cattle **EXP:** canned coconut cream, copra, honey, vanilla, passion fruit products, pawpaws, root crops, limes, footballs, stamps, handicrafts

Northern Mariana Islands

(U.S.)
COMMONWEALTH OF THE NORTHERN MARIANA ISLANDS

AREA	464 sq km (179 sq mi)
POPULATION	52,000
CAPITAL	Saipan 49,000
RELIGION	Christian
LANGUAGE	Philippine languages, Chinese, Chamorro, English
LITERACY	97%
LIFE EXPECTANCY	78 years
GDP PER CAPITA	$13,300

ECONOMY **IND:** banking, construction, fishing, garment, tourism, handicrafts **AGR:** vegetables and melons, fruits and nuts, ornamental plants, livestock, poultry and eggs, fish and aquaculture products **EXP:** garments

Pitcairn Islands

(U.K.)
PITCAIRN, HENDERSON, DUCIE, AND OENO ISLANDS

AREA	47 sq km (18 sq mi)
POPULATION	48
CAPITAL	Adamstown 48
RELIGION	Seventh-Day Adventist
LANGUAGE	English, Pitkern
LITERACY	NA
LIFE EXPECTANCY	NA
GDP PER CAPITA	NA

ECONOMY **IND:** postage stamps, handicrafts, beekeeping, honey **AGR:** honey, wide variety of fruits and vegetables, goats, chickens, fish **EXP:** fruits, vegetables, curios, stamps

Tokelau

(NEW ZEALAND)
TOKELAU

AREA	12 sq km (5 sq mi)
POPULATION	1,300
CAPITAL	NA
RELIGION	Congregational Christian Church, Roman Catholic
LANGUAGE	Tokelauan, English
LITERACY	NA
LIFE EXPECTANCY	NA
GDP PER CAPITA	$1,000

ECONOMY **IND:** copra production, woodworking, plaited craft goods, stamps, coins, fishing **AGR:** coconuts, copra, breadfruit, papayas, bananas, pigs, poultry, goats, fish **EXP:** stamps, copra, handicrafts

Wallis and Futuna

(FRANCE)
WALLIS AND FUTUNA

AREA	142 sq km (55 sq mi)
POPULATION	16,000
CAPITAL	Mata'Utu 1,100
RELIGION	Roman Catholic
LANGUAGE	Wallisian, Futunian, French
LITERACY	50%
LIFE EXPECTANCY	80 years
GDP PER CAPITA	$3,800

ECONOMY **IND:** copra, handicrafts, fishing, lumber **AGR:** coconuts, breadfruit, yams, taro, bananas, pigs, goats, fish **EXP:** copra, chemicals, construction materials

UNINHABITED DEPENDENCIES

Baker Island
(U.S.)
BAKER ISLAND

AREA 1.4 sq km (0.5 sq mi)

Coral Sea Islands
(AUSTRALIA)
CORAL SEA ISLANDS TERRITORY

AREA less than 3 sq km (1.1 sq mi)

Howland Island
(U.S.)
HOWLAND ISLAND

AREA 1.6 sq km (0.6 sq mi)

Jarvis Island
(U.S.)
JARVIS ISLAND

AREA 4.5 sq km (1.7 sq mi)

Johnston Atoll
(U.S.)
JOHNSTON ATOLL

AREA 2.6 sq km (1.0 sq mi)

Kingman Reef
(U.S.)
KINGMAN REEF

AREA 1.0 sq km (0.4 sq mi)

Midway Islands
(U.S.)
MIDWAY ISLANDS

AREA 6.2 sq km (2.4 sq mi)

Palmyra Atoll
(U.S.)
PALMYRA ATOLL

AREA 11.9 sq km (4.6 sq mi)

Wake Island
(U.S.)
WAKE ISLAND

AREA 6.5 sq km (2.5 sq mi)

Protected Areas

Wake Island
(U.S.)

PHILIPPINE
SEA

NORTHERN
MARIANA
ISLANDS
(U.S.)

GUAM
(U.S.)

MARSHALL ISLANDS

PALAU

FEDERATED STATES
OF MICRONESIA

Howland Island
(U.S.)

Baker Island
(U.S.)

PAPUA
NEW GUINEA

NAURU

K
I
R
I

SOLOMON
ISLANDS

TUVALU

WALLIS AND
FUTUNA
(France)

CORAL
SEA

VANUATU

CORAL SEA ISLANDS
(Australia)

NEW CALEDONIA
(France)

FIJI

TON

AUSTRALIA

Norfolk Island
(Australia)

TASMAN

SEA

INDIAN

OCEAN

NEW ZEALAND

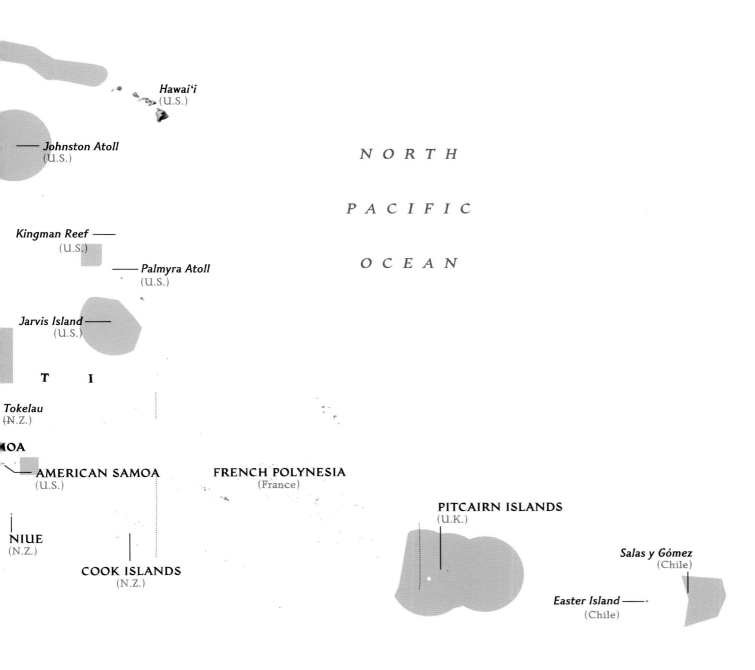

Hawai'i
(U.S.)

Johnston Atoll
(U.S.)

N O R T H

P A C I F I C

O C E A N

Kingman Reef ———
(U.S.)

——— *Palmyra Atoll*
(U.S.)

Jarvis Island ———
(U.S.)

T   **I**

Tokelau
(N.Z.)

MOA

AMERICAN SAMOA
(U.S.)

FRENCH POLYNESIA
(France)

PITCAIRN ISLANDS
(U.K.)

Salas y Gómez
(Chile)

NIUE
(N.Z.)

COOK ISLANDS
(N.Z.)

Easter Island ———
(Chile)

S O U T H

P A C I F I C

O C E A N

Protected Areas

██ Terrestrial

██ Marine

*Protected areas as defined by the
International Union for Conservation
of Nature (IUCN). The degree of
protection and governing body varies
by protected area.*

Azimuthal Equidistant Projection
SCALE 1:40,000,000

0 km   300   600

0 mi   300   600

1 CENTIMETER = 400 KILOMETERS; 1 INCH = 631 MILES

Antarctica

ANTARCTICA, AT THE SOUTHERN extreme of the world, ranks as the coldest, highest, driest, and windiest of Earth's continents. At the South Pole the continent experiences the extremes of day and night, banished from sunlight half the year, bathed in continuous light the other half. As best we know, no indigenous peoples ever lived on this continent. Unlike the Arctic, an ocean surrounded by continents, Antarctica is a continent surrounded by ocean. The only people who live there today, mostly scientists and support staff at research stations, rue-fully call Antarctica "the Ice," and with good reason. All but 2 percent of the continent is covered year-round in ice up to 15,000 feet (4,570 meters) thick.

Not until the early 20th century did men explore the heart of the Antarctic to find an austere beauty and an unmatched hardship. Despite its remoteness, Antarctica has been called the frontier of today's ecological crisis. Temperatures are rising, and a hole in the ozone (caused by atmospheric pollutants) allows harmful ultraviolet radiation to bombard land and sea.

The long tendril of the Antarctic Peninsula reaches to within 700 miles (1,130 kilometers) of South America, separated by the tempestuous Drake Passage, where furious winds build mountainous waves. This "banana belt" of the Antarctic is not nearly so cold as the polar interior, where a great plateau of ice reaches 10,000 feet (3,050 meters) above sea level and winter temperatures can drop lower than -112°F (-80°C). In the Antarctic summer (December to March), light fills the region, yet heat is absent. Glaciers flow from the icy plateau, coalescing into massive ice shelves; the largest of these, the Ross Ice Shelf, is the size of France.

Antarctica's ice cap holds some 70 percent of the Earth's fresh water. Yet despite all this ice and water, the Antarctic interior averages only two inches (five centimeters) of precipitation a year, making it the largest desert in the world. The little snow that does fall, however, almost never melts. The immensely heavy ice sheet, averaging over 1 mile (1.6 kilometers) thick, compresses the land surface over most of the continent to below sea level. The weight actually deforms the South Pole, creating a slightly pear-shaped Earth.

Beneath the ice exists a continent of valleys, lakes, islands, and mountains, little dreamed of until the compilation of more than 2.5 million ice-thickness measurements revealed startling topography below. Ice and sediment cores provide insight into the world's ancient climate and allow for comparison with conditions today. If the ice sheet were to melt, global seas would rise by an estimated 200 feet (61 meters), inundating many oceanic islands and gravely altering the world's coastlines.

Antarctica's animal life has adapted extremely well to the harsh climate. Seasonal feeding and energy storage in fat exemplify this specialization. Well-known animals of the far south include seals, whales, and distinctive birds such as flightless penguins, albatrosses, terns, and petrels.

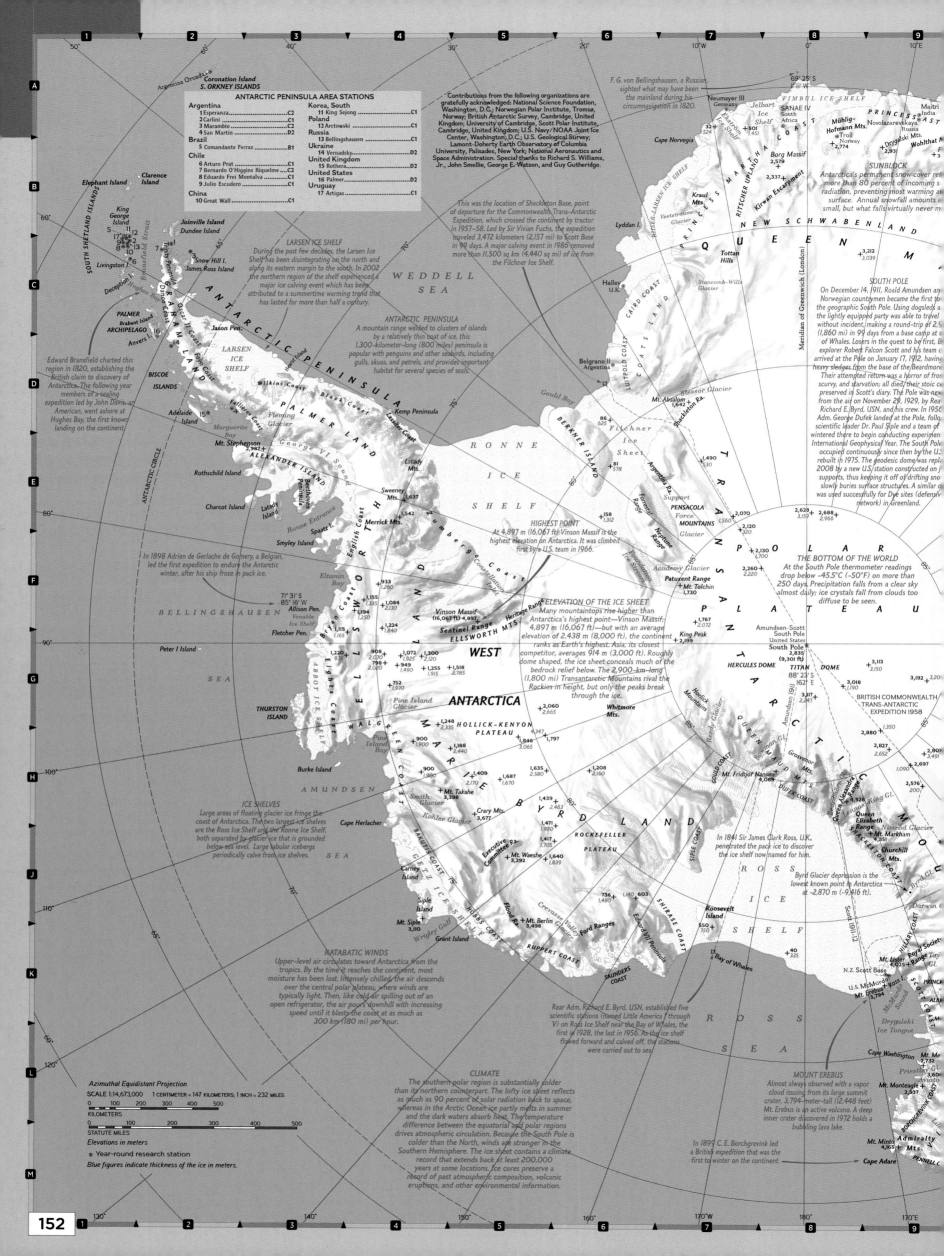

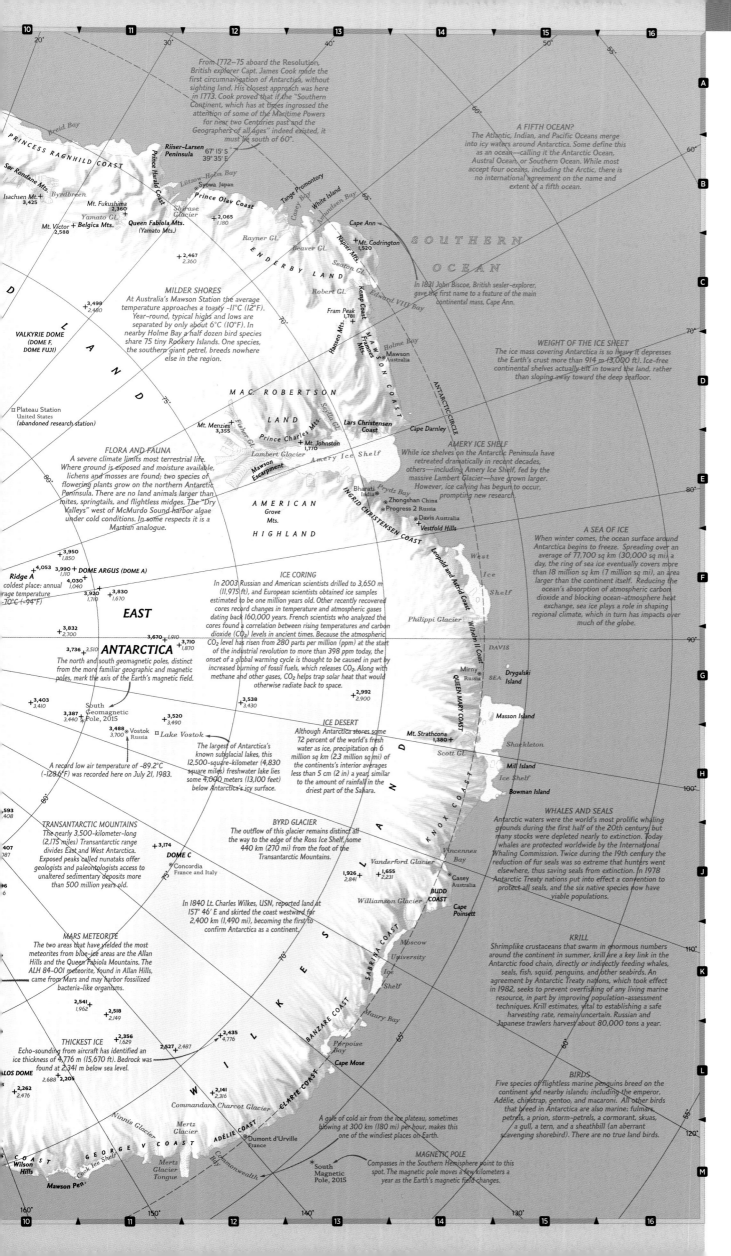

Antarctica
Physical

Continental Data

Area: 13,209,000 sq km
(5,100,000 sq mi)

Greatest extent:
5,500 km (3,400 mi),
from Trinity Peninsula to
Cape Poinsett

Highest point:
Vinson Massif 4,897 m (16,066 ft)

Lowest point:
Byrd Glacier
-2,870 m (-9,416 ft)

Lowest recorded temperature:
Vostok -89.2°C (-128.6°F),
July 21, 1983

Highest recorded temperature:
Vanda Station, N.Z. (closed),
Scott Coast
15°C (59°F), January 5, 1974

**Earth's extremes located
in Antarctica:**
- Coldest Place on Earth:
  Ridge A, annual average
  temperature -74°C (-94°F)
- Coldest Recorded Temperature
  on Earth:
  Vostok -89.2°C (-128.6°F),
  July 21, 1983

Space

IN THE FIRST DECADES OF THE NEW MILLENNIUM, astronomers are conducting extensive surveys of new frontiers in space, registering millions of galaxies, each composed of billions of stars. New orbiters and surface rovers are exploring Mars, confirming the presence of liquid water in its distant past and detecting methane in its atmosphere. A probe descended through the atmosphere of Titan, a moon of Saturn, and returned the first pictures from its surface, showing a strange, cold new world complete with flowing hydrocarbon rivers and extensive lakes. A capsule traveling through space returned samples of the sun, and another spacecraft is now studying Pluto and its neighbors. Meanwhile, a copper "cannonball" deployed from a spacecraft created the first human-made impact crater on a comet and another returned comet dust to Earth.

Wherever we look, we see evidence of cataclysmic events, indicating that we live in a 13-billion-year-old universe that is still evolving. Some suns, their atmospheres curiously enriched with telltale elements, may be "death stars" that swallowed whole planets long ago. The universe began with a big bang and has been expanding ever since. A mysterious "dark energy" that exceeds all known forms of energy is thought to cause this expansion; space is also pervaded by unseen "dark matter," the dominant component of the universe. In laboratories on Earth and on the drawing boards of aerospace engineers, we are preparing to explore the next frontier of astronomical observation, looking for gravitational waves that may disturb the very fabric of space and time.

155

The Moon

Near Side

North Pole

South Pole

YOUNG EARTH HAD NO MOON. At some point in Earth's early history (certainly within the first 100 million years), an object roughly the size of Mars struck Earth a great, glancing blow. Instantly, most of the rogue body and a sizable chunk of Earth were vaporized. The ensuing cloud rose to above 14,000 miles (22,500 kilometers) altitude, where it condensed into innumerable solid particles that orbited Earth as they aggregated into ever larger moonlets, eventually forming the moon. This "giant impact" hypothesis of the moon's origin is based on computer simulations and on laboratory analyses of lunar rocks gathered by Apollo astronauts. It also fits with data on the lunar topography and environment recorded by the United States' Clementine, Lunar Prospector, and Lunar Reconnaissance Orbiter probes.

The airless lunar surface bakes in the sun at up to 243°F (117°C) for two weeks at a time. All the while, it is sprayed with the solar wind of subatomic particles. Then, for an equal period, the same spot is in the dark, cooling to about minus 272°F (-169°C). Day and night, the moon is bombarded by micrometeoroids and larger space rocks. Orbiting at an average distance of 239,000 miles (385,000 kilometers), the moon has a rotation that is synchronized with its orbital period in such a way that it is gravitationally locked, meaning it always shows the same face, the near side, to Earth. The far side can never be seen from Earth and has been photographed only from spacecraft.

Recently, NASA scientists used Earth-based radio telescopes to produce detailed radar maps of the southern polar region, revealing

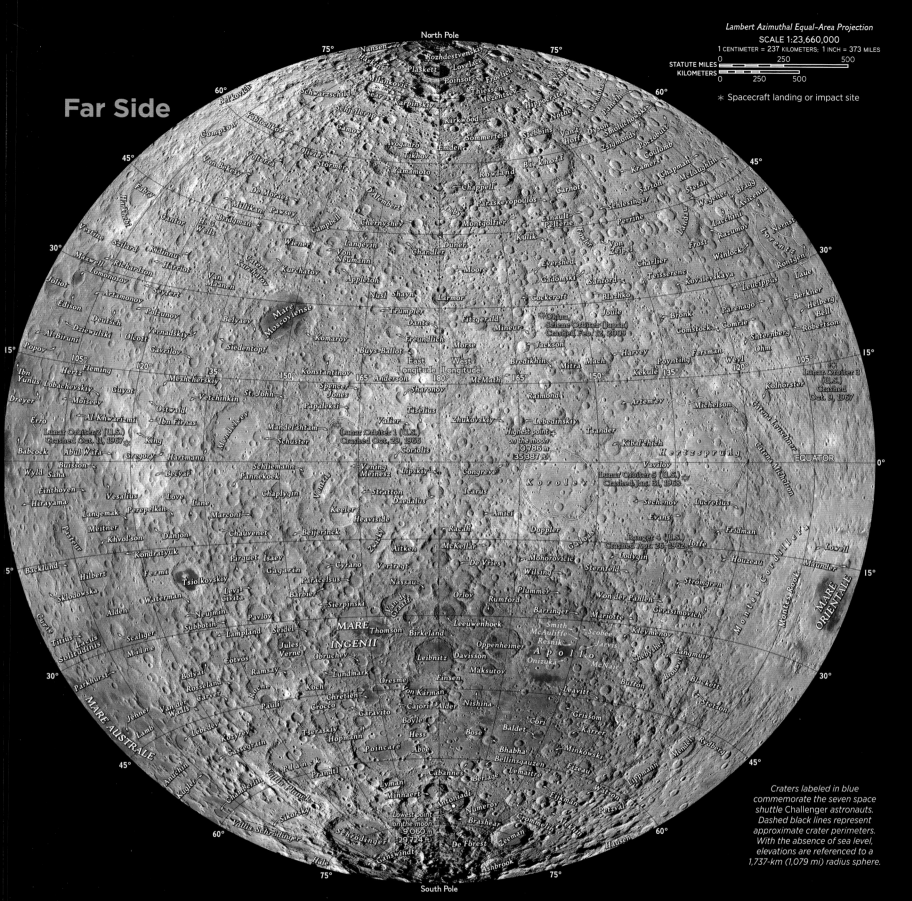

Far Side

Lambert Azimuthal Equal-Area Projection
SCALE 1:23,660,000
1 CENTIMETER = 237 KILOMETERS; 1 INCH = 373 MILES
STATUTE MILES
KILOMETERS
0　250　500
0　250　500

＊ Spacecraft landing or impact site

Craters labeled in blue commemorate the seven space shuttle Challenger *astronauts. Dashed black lines represent approximate crater perimeters. With the absence of sea level, elevations are referenced to a 1,737-km (1,079 mi) radius sphere.*

that the terrain is much more rugged than had been thought. The south pole has been considered as a possible landing site for a future manned mission to the moon. It remains attractive because the deep craters in this region may contain water ice, deposited there by previous comet impacts. The ice is a potential source of liquid water for drinking, as well as hydrogen and oxygen for fuel. If future missions to the moon are able to use local resources, they will not be as reliant on new supplies from Earth. The rocks and materials brought back by the Apollo missions are extremely dry; the moon has no indigenous water. However, it is bombarded by water-rich comets and meteoroids. Most of this water is lost to space, but some is trapped and frozen in permanently shadowed areas near the moon's poles.

To the unaided eye, the bright lunar highlands and the dark maria (Latin for "seas") make up the "man in the moon." A telescope shows that they consist of a great variety of impact features, scars left by objects that struck the moon long ago. The largest scars are the impact basins, ranging up to about 1,500 miles (2,400 kilometers) across. The dark lava flows that flooded the basins are what the eye discerns as maria. Wrinkled ridges, domed hills, and fissures mark the maria, all familiar aspects of volcanic landscapes. Young craters are centers of radial patterns of bright ejecta, material thrown from the impacts that made them. Because the force of gravity is weaker on the moon (only about one-sixth that on Earth), blocks of rock hurled from impacts travel farther than they would on Earth.

OUR SOLAR SYSTEM is mostly the sun. Not in area, perhaps: Measured to its ultimate boundary, the region suffused by solar energy may be 46 billion kilometers (30 billion mi) across, while the diameter of the star itself is just 1.4 million kilometers (865,000 mi). But the sun accounts for about 99.9 percent of the solar system's mass. Everything else—the planets, asteroids, meteoroids, comets, and floating dust and gas—could be considered leftovers from the formation of a medium-size star about 4.6 billion years ago.

The orbits of the inner planets take them from the scorching temperatures of Mercury to the deep winter chill of Mars. Swift Mercury races around the sun, its hemispheres burning and freezing. Torrid Venus bakes under an atmosphere that holds in most of the sun's energy, the greenhouse effect writ large. Uniquely sited, Earth is in the habitable zone, where water can exist as a liquid. Frigid Mars offers tantalizing evidence of a warmer, wetter past. Well studied in the space age, each terrestrial planet has been visited and mapped in detail by spacecraft.

Mercury's speed orbiting the sun—it circles every 88 days on a highly elliptical path—prompted the ancient Romans to name it after the winged messenger of the gods. The planet is densely cratered with a surface like the moon's. Daytime temperatures can reach 465°C (869°F), while readings fall to minus 180°C (−292°F) at night. A nearly vertical axis means relatively little sunlight touches polar regions, where radar reveals hints of water ice at the bottoms of craters.

MERCURY

Average distance from the sun:	57,900,000 km
Perihelion:	46,000,000 km
Aphelion:	69,820,000 km
Revolution period:	88 days
Average orbital speed:	47.9 km/s
Average temperature:	167°C
Rotation period:	58.7 days
Equatorial diameter:	4,879 km
Mass (Earth=1):	0.055
Density:	5.43 g/cm³
Surface gravity (Earth=1):	0.38
Known satellites:	none

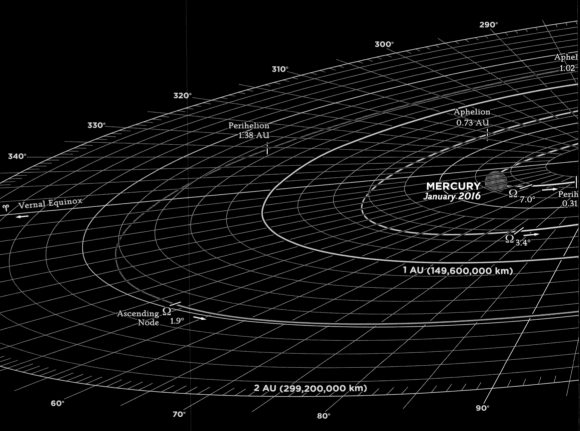

Mapping the Solar System

In this view of the inner reaches of the solar system, the circular grids represent the plane of Earth's orbit around the sun, called the ecliptic. Concentric blue rings show distance from the sun in astronomical units. (One AU is the distance from sun to Earth, about 150 million kilometers or 93 million miles.) Radial lines show degrees of longitude around the sun, and 0° is the vernal equinox. The orbital paths of other planets and dwarf planets are shown in relation to Earth's ecliptic. Above it, they are ascending, with their paths shown as a solid line. Below it, they are descending, with broken lines. Perihelion is the orbital point nearest to the sun; aphelion is the farthest.

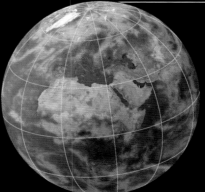

EARTH

Average distance from the sun:	149,600,000 km
Perihelion:	147,090,000 km
Aphelion:	152,100,000 km
Revolution period:	365.26 days
Average orbital speed:	29.8 km/s
Average temperature:	15°C
Rotation period:	23.9 hours
Equatorial diameter:	12,756 km
Mass:	5,973,600,000,000,000,000,000 metric tons
Density:	5.52 g/cm³
Surface gravity:	9.78 m/s²
Known satellites:	1
Largest satellite:	Earth's moon

Earth is the only planet known to support life, and perhaps the sole place the primary necessity of life—liquid water—is abundant, covering most of the planet. It's also the most geologically active of the rocky planets, and movements of sections of Earth's crust, called plates, constantly reshape the planet's surface. Its heavy iron core creates a strong magnetic field, providing a shield against the constant bombardment of high-energy particles ejected by the sun.

Venus is almost Earth's twin in size, but its thick atmosphere of mostly carbon dioxide soaks up far more of the sun's energy. This so-called greenhouse effect raises surface temperatures to 475°C (887°F)—making it the hottest planet in the solar system. The surface has rolling plains and mountainous regions, and intense volcanism has buried many impact craters. Above it all, dense sulfuric acid clouds block our direct view of the sweltering surface.

Sizing Up the Terrestrial Planets

EQUATORIAL DIAMETERS
in kilometers (miles)

Earth	12,756	(7,926)
Venus	12,104	(7,521)
Mars	6,792	(4,220)
Mercury	4,879	(3,032)

Earth · Venus · Mars · Mercury

The inner planets are shown above in proportionate size to one another. Dwarf planets are less than 3,000 kilometers (1,865 mi) in diameter—much smaller than Mercury.

VENUS

Average distance from the sun:	108,200,000 km
Perihelion:	107,480,000 km
Aphelion:	108,940,000 km
Revolution period:	224.7 days
Average orbital speed:	35 km/s
Average temperature:	464°C
Rotation period:	243 days
Equatorial diameter:	12,104 km
Mass (Earth=1):	0.816
Density:	5.24 g/cm³
Surface gravity (Earth=1):	0.91
Known satellites:	none

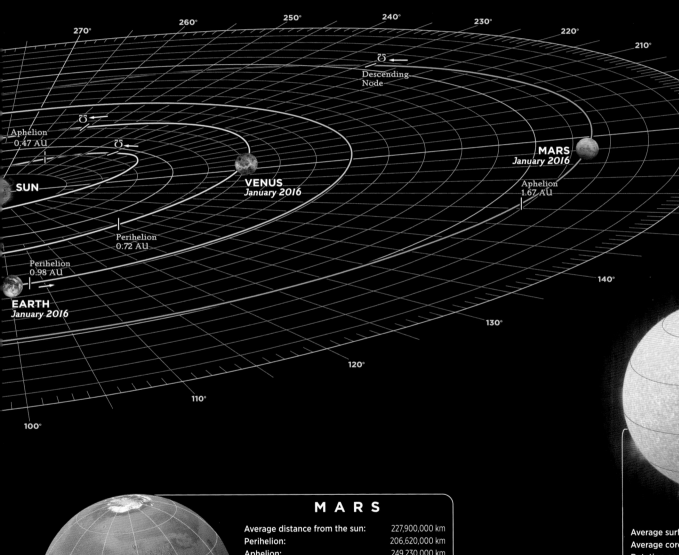

MARS

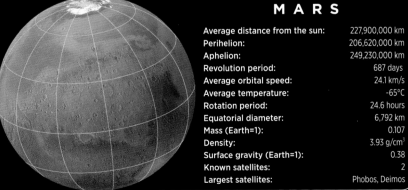

Average distance from the sun:	227,900,000 km
Perihelion:	206,620,000 km
Aphelion:	249,230,000 km
Revolution period:	687 days
Average orbital speed:	24.1 km/s
Average temperature:	-65°C
Rotation period:	24.6 hours
Equatorial diameter:	6,792 km
Mass (Earth=1):	0.107
Density:	3.93 g/cm³
Surface gravity (Earth=1):	0.38
Known satellites:	2
Largest satellites:	Phobos, Deimos

This outermost of the terrestrial planets bears witness to giant floods, but liquid water vanished three billion years ago. Today, its barren surface is swept by global dust storms that can shroud it in a reddish haze for weeks. Southern latitudes are rugged and heavily cratered, while giant volcanoes rise above plains to the north. Despite a cold climate and thin atmosphere, Mars is more like Earth than any other solar system planet, and it could potentially harbor traces of life.

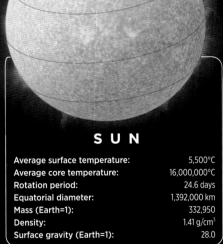

SUN

Average surface temperature:	5,500°C
Average core temperature:	16,000,000°C
Rotation period:	24.6 days
Equatorial diameter:	1,392,000 km
Mass (Earth=1):	332,950
Density:	1.41 g/cm³
Surface gravity (Earth=1):	28.0

The main actor in our solar system, the sun is scientifically classed as an average star—in the mid-range for temperature, energy output, and size. Its energy is the driving force of weather on every planet and moon with an atmosphere, bringing seasonal variation as orbits progress.

Outer Solar System

OUR SOLAR SYSTEM has two classes of planets. Terrestrial planets are small with solid surfaces and mean densities that suggest an iron core surrounded by a rocky, partially molten mantle. The outer Jovian planets are very large, consisting primarily of hydrogen and helium in gas and liquid states with no solid surface. In the past two decades, a large number of rocky, icy bodies have been discovered beyond the orbit of Neptune, in a region known as the Kuiper belt. Some of these objects are comparable to Pluto. One of them, Eris, is slightly larger and has a moon, Dysnomia. The Kuiper belt can thus be considered an icy, distant analog of the asteroid belt between Mars and Jupiter.

In 2006, the International Astronomical Union (IAU), an organization of professional astronomers that provides oversight of the naming and classification of features and bodies in space, decided to redesignate Pluto as a "dwarf planet." Eris and Ceres also share that designation. Large enough to be roughly spherical, they are not of sufficient mass to produce a gravitational field strong enough to clear smaller objects out of their orbital regions.

Saturn's ring system is one of the solar system's most majestic sights. Composed of intricately interacting water ice particles, they are vast in diameter but less than 1.6 kilometers (1 mi) thick. In other respects, Saturn is like a slightly smaller Jupiter, with a comparably fast rotational spin of 10.7 hours, and a similar composition. The planet's atmosphere is banded like Jupiter's but not as dramatic in color, Winds can reach 1,800 kilometers an hour (1,100 mph).

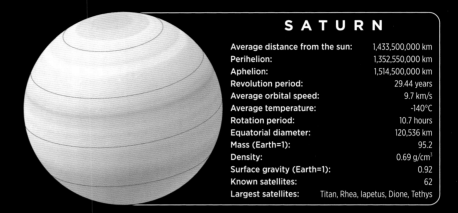

SATURN

Average distance from the sun:	1,433,500,000 km
Perihelion:	1,352,550,000 km
Aphelion:	1,514,500,000 km
Revolution period:	29.44 years
Average orbital speed:	9.7 km/s
Average temperature:	-140°C
Rotation period:	10.7 hours
Equatorial diameter:	120,536 km
Mass (Earth=1):	95.2
Density:	0.69 g/cm³
Surface gravity (Earth=1):	0.92
Known satellites:	62
Largest satellites:	Titan, Rhea, Iapetus, Dione, Tethys

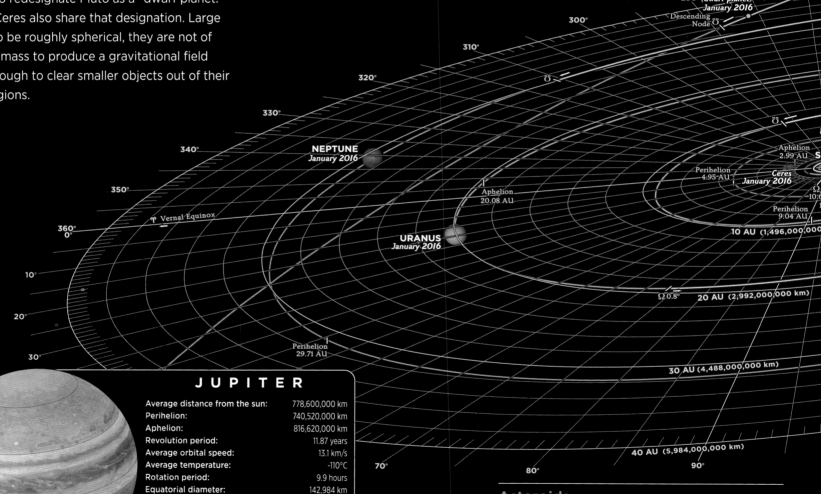

JUPITER

Average distance from the sun:	778,600,000 km
Perihelion:	740,520,000 km
Aphelion:	816,620,000 km
Revolution period:	11.87 years
Average orbital speed:	13.1 km/s
Average temperature:	-110°C
Rotation period:	9.9 hours
Equatorial diameter:	142,984 km
Mass (Earth=1):	317.8
Density:	1.33 g/cm³
Surface gravity (Earth=1):	2.36
Known satellites:	67
Largest satellites:	Ganymede, Callisto, Io, Europa

The striking cloud bands encircling the solar system's largest planet are caused by alternating east-west winds. Light cloud areas are called zones, while darker regions are belts. The famous Great Red Spot is an intense storm wide enough to swallow several Earths. It has raged for the past 300 years. Jupiter has a hydrogen-helium atmosphere and it is thought to have a rocky center. Its 67 moons are the most of any planet in the solar system; the four largest so-called Galilean moons, Io, Europa, Ganymede, and Callisto, were among Galileo's first telescopic discoveries.

Asteroids

Asteroids are rocky remnants left over from the age of planetary formation. They range from gravel-size to gigantic: Ceres, at 950 kilometers (590 mi) in diameter, is classified as a dwarf planet. The greatest concentration is in the asteroid belt between Mars and Jupiter, where Jupiter's gravity prevented them from accreting into a planet. Infrared observation of the belt indicates it could contain well over 1.2 million asteroids with diameters over 1 kilometer (0.62 mi). Concentrations of asteroids known as Trojans also exist in the orbital Lagrange points—islands of gravitational stability—of Earth, Mars, Jupiter, Uranus, and Neptune. A few in orbit near Earth pose a theoretical threat to the planet, though the likelihood of collision is low.

The discovery of Uranus in 1781 was the first planetary find since classical times. A long-ago collision with an Earth-size object may be the reason Uranus "rolls" on its side around the sun, with its rings more or less perpendicular to those of the other gas giants. Unlike the other outer planets, Uranus absorbs more heat from the sun than it generates. The planet's teal green surface is composed of clouds of methane gas; deeper down could be an ocean of superheated liquid water spiked with ammonia and methane. Like Neptune, it is thought to have a rock and ice core.

URANUS

Average distance from the sun:	2,872,500,000 km
Perihelion:	2,741,300,000 km
Aphelion:	3,003,620,000 km
Revolution period:	83.81 years
Average orbital speed:	6.8 km/s
Average temperature:	-195°C
Rotation period:	17.2 hours
Equatorial diameter:	51,118 km
Mass (Earth=1):	14.5
Density:	1.27 g/cm³
Surface gravity (Earth=1):	0.89
Known satellites:	27
Largest satellites:	Titania, Oberon, Umbriel, Ariel

Planetary Comparison

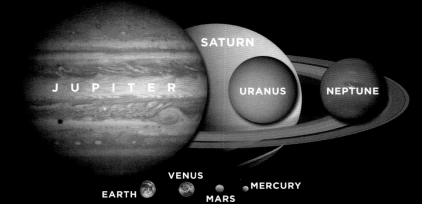

From Jupiter to Mercury, here's how the eight planets of the solar system stack up. The outer gas planets are giants when compared to the inner worlds. Each has a constellation of moons, some even large enough to qualify as planets if they orbited the sun.

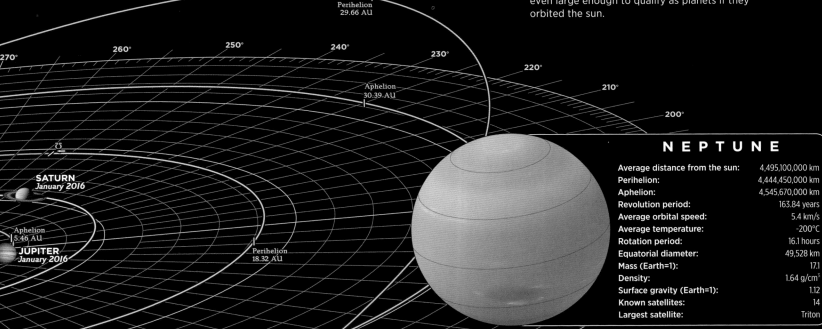

Perihelion 29.66 AU

Aphelion 30.39 AU

270° 260° 250° 240° 230° 220° 210° 200°

SATURN January 2016

ASTEROID BELT

Aphelion 5.46 AU

Perihelion 2.55 AU

JUPITER January 2016

Aphelion 18.32 AU

Perihelion

Ω 2.5°

Ω 1.8°

130°

120°

17.2° Ω
Ascending Node
110°

100°

NEPTUNE

Average distance from the sun:	4,495,100,000 km
Perihelion:	4,444,450,000 km
Aphelion:	4,545,670,000 km
Revolution period:	163.84 years
Average orbital speed:	5.4 km/s
Average temperature:	-200°C
Rotation period:	16.1 hours
Equatorial diameter:	49,528 km
Mass (Earth=1):	17.1
Density:	1.64 g/cm³
Surface gravity (Earth=1):	1.12
Known satellites:	14
Largest satellite:	Triton

Neptune is the outermost of the eight planets and smallest of the gas giants, orbiting 30 times farther away from the sun than Earth does. Active weather systems stir a hydrogen-helium atmosphere with unusual easterly winds, opposite the planet's rotation. A faint ring system surrounds Neptune, while the depths of the planet are ammonia, methane, water ice, and rock.

Comets

Comets are masses of water ice, dust, and rock that mainly orbit far beyond the inner solar system. When they approach the sun, ice begins to vaporize, creating a coma, or atmosphere, around them. The characteristic comet's tail is created when energy from the sun sweeps dust and gas from the coma in a direction opposite our star. Comets travel on widely varying elliptical orbits, usually highly inclined to Earth's ecliptic. They spend most of their time in a comet-filled region outside the Kuiper belt known as the Oort cloud.

PLUTO (Dwarf planet)

Average distance from the sun:	5,906,380,000 km
Perihelion:	4,436,820,000 km
Aphelion:	7,375,930,000 km
Revolution period:	247.94 years
Average orbital speed:	4.7 km/s
Average temperature:	-225°C
Rotation period:	153.28 hours
Equatorial diameter:	2,370 km
Mass (Earth=1):	0.002
Density:	1.86 g/cm³
Surface gravity (Earth=1):	0.06
Known satellites:	5
Largest satellites:	Charon, Nix, Hydra, Kerberos, Styx

For decades after its discovery in 1930, Pluto was considered the ninth planet from the Sun. As astronomers delved into the Kuiper Belt, a frigid band of icy objects on the periphery of the solar system, they discovered many objects of similar size and character. Pluto was reclassified as a dwarf planet. NASA's New Horizon spacecraft made an historic flyby of the world, revealing unexpected topographic details and the possibility of active geologic processes.

The Universe

Looking Back in Time for Origins

Colorful and diverse, an array of galaxies spans a section of sky combining ten years of Hubble data to capture the deepest ever images of the earliest galaxies. They're barely visible in this background image—small bluish blobs of stars one-twentieth the diameter of the Milky Way. Because they are so distant, our current view shows how they existed more than 13 billion years ago, when the universe was perhaps 600 million years old. In the eons following, galaxies combined and grew into larger, more complex structures, with their shapes—whether elliptical like the earliest ones, or spiral like our own—likely determined by the invisible yet massive halos of dark matter surrounding them.

2 million light-years

1 million

Leo II

Leo I

Draco

Ursa Minor — Sextans

MILKY WAY — Sagittarius

Large Magellanic Cloud — Small Magellanic Cloud

Carina

Sculptor

NGC 6822

IC 10

And VII

NGC 185

NGC 147

And V

Andromeda (M31)

NGC 205

And II

M32

And III

And I

Fornax

DDO 210

Triangulum (M33)

And VI

Phoenix

LGS 3

Pegasus

1 million

IC 1613

2 million light-years

NGC 5

NGC 4945

NGC 253

Local Group
(Milky Way)

NGC 628

NGC

NGC 1566

250,000 light-years

200,000

150,000

100,000

50,000

Sagittarius Dwarf

Small Magellanic Cloud

Sculptor Dwarf

MILKY WAY

Orion Spur

Canis Major Dwarf

Magellanic Stream

Large Magellanic Cloud

Ursa Minor Dwarf

50,000

100,000

150,000

200,000

250,000 light-years

Our Local Galaxy Group

Some of the 30 or so galaxies that make up the Local Group are visible from Earth with the naked eye. The spiral Andromeda galaxy is the largest of the group, and also the most distant object visible without a telescope. Its small companion galaxies, M32 and NGC 205, are easily seen through amateur telescopes. Second in size is the Milky Way, followed by the smaller spiral Triangulum galaxy. Both Andromeda and the Milky Way have many small satellite galaxies arrayed around them, giving the Local Group a binary structure around four million light-years across. The group's center of gravity lies between the two great galaxies, which are being pulled inexorably toward each other. They are expected to collide in four or five billion years, perhaps ending as one massive galaxy.

Local Supercluster

The local supercluster, often called the Virgo supercluster, is a massive group of galaxy clusters 100 million light-years or more across. The Milky Way floats on its periphery. At the center of the supercluster is the smaller Virgo cluster, with a diameter of about 15 million light-years. Among its galaxies, the spiral M100 (as it is known in the Messier Catalogue) is one of the brightest. Meanwhile, M87 may be the dominant galaxy of the cluster—a giant ball of stars larger in diameter than the Milky Way. It is believed to have a black hole at its center 6.4 billion times as massive as the sun. Though the local supercluster has a mass of about a thousand trillion suns, 95 percent of its volume is galaxy-free zones called cosmic voids. This supercluster is still only a tiny speck in relation to the entire universe, which measures many billions of light-years across.

◀ **Our Sun's Neighborhood**

The closest stars to the sun make up our solar neighborhood, ranging out to about 20 light-years away. The region is located in the spiral Orion Spur of the Milky Way some 25,000 light-years from the galaxy center. Within the neighborhood confines is Sirius, the brightest star in the night sky, located about 8.6 light-years from Earth. By contrast, the second brightest star from Earth, Canopus, is located far outside the solar neighborhood, some 300 light-years away. In terms of wattage of energy output, Canopus is the far brighter star. Most stars in the solar neighborhood are too dim to see with the naked eye—including tiny Proxima Centauri, the closest star to Earth at 4.2 light-years away.

Galaxy Companions

...galaxies go, the Milky Way ranks as a giant, ...nning nearly 100,000 light-years with its spiral disk. ...ts thrall are several far smaller galaxies that orbit ...The recently discovered Canis Major and Sagittarius ...arf galaxies are the closest, and others include the ...a Minor and Sculptor dwarf galaxies. The Large and ...all Magellanic Clouds, two of the most prominent ...tures of the southern sky, have also long been ...ught to be satellites of the Milky Way. Recent ...search, however, indicates they are passersby, and ...t gravitationally bound.

Our Solar System ▶

On the scale of galaxy clusters and superclusters, our solar system is but a grain of sand in the Sahara at best. In human terms, it is still unmanageably large. ...ne problem that space agencies face as they contem- plate human exploration of the nearby planet, Mars, is whether astronauts can safely undertake a round-trip ...paceflight of more than a year. A human journey past ...e most distant point of Pluto's orbit—50 astronomical ...nits (AU) away, or 50 times the distance from the sun to Earth—for now is unthinkable.

Diagram labels:

75 million light-years
50 million
25 million

NGC 5907
NGC 5248
NGC 5195
NGC 5194
NGC 5457
NGC 4656
NGC 4565
NGC 4631
NGC 4826
NGC 5055
NGC 4594
NGC 4571
M87
M100
Virgo
Virgo III
NGC 3031
NGC 3628
NGC 3593
NGC 4038
NGC 2903
946
236

25 million
50 million
75 million light-years

20 light-years
15
10
5

WX Ursae Majoris
Lalande 21258
Wolf 424 A, B
Groombridge 1618
AD Leonis
GI 687
GI 570 A, B, C
GI 702 A, B
Lalande 21185
Ross 128
GJ 1245 A, B, C
GI 628
Wolf 359
Barnard's Star
Kruger 60 A, B
Eta Cassiopei A, B
Proxima Centauri
Procyon A, B
SOLAR SYSTEM
61 Cygni A, B
Altair
GI 663 A, B
GI 664
Luyten's Star
Alpha Centauri A
Ross 154
Groombridge 34 A, B
Alpha Centauri B
GI 674
Ross 614 A, B
LHS 288
GI 440
Sirius A, B
GI 65 A
EZ Aquarii A, B, C
Epsilon Eridani
AX Microscopium
UV Ceti
Lacaille 9352
Kapteyn's Star
Ross 248
Epsilon Indi
GI 783 A, B
GI 166 A, B, C
Tau Ceti
YZ Ceti
GJ 1002
GI 876 and planet
Delta Pavonis
GI 1
LP 944-20
5
10
15
20 light-years

KUIPER BELT
Pluto (dwarf planet)
NEPTUNE
URANUS
JUPITER
MERCURY
SUN
MARS
VENUS
EARTH
ASTEROID BELT
SATURN

Appendix
Map and Index Abbreviations

A

A.	Arroyo, Arroyo
A.C.T.	Australian Capital Territory
A.O.	Autonomous Oblast
A. Okr.	Autonomous Okrug
Adm.	Administrative
Af.	Africa
Afghan.	Afghanistan
Agr.	Agriculture
Ala.	Alabama
Alas.	Alaska
Alban.	Albania
Alg.	Algeria
Alta.	Alberta
Amer.	America-n
Amzns.	Amazonas
Anch.	Anchorage
And. & Nic.	Andaman and Nicobar Islands
Ant.	Antilles
Arch.	Archipelago, Archipiélago
Arg.	Argentina
Ariz.	Arizona
Ark.	Arkansas
Arkh.	Arkhangel'sk
Arm.	Armenia
Astrak.	Astrakhan'
Atl. Oc.	Atlantic Ocean
Aust.	Austria
Austral.	Australia
Auton.	Autonomous
Azerb.	Azerbaijan

B

B.	Baai, Baía, Baie, Bahía,Bay, Bugt-en, Buḥayrat
B. Aires	Buenos Aires
B.C.	British Columbia
B. Qazaq.	Batys Qazaqstan
Bashk.	Bashkortostan
Belg.	Belgium
Bol.	Bolivia
Bol.	Bol'sh-oy, -aya, -oye
Bosn. & Herzg.	Bosnia and Herzegovina
Br.	Branch
Braz.	Brazil
Bulg.	Bulgaria
Burya.	Buryatiya

C

C.	Cabo, Cap, Cape, Capo
C.H.	Court House
C.P.	Conservation Park
C.R.	Costa Rica
C.S.I. Terr.	Coral Sea Islands Territory
Cach.	Cachoeira
Calif.	California
Can.	Canada
Cap.	Capitán
Catam.	Catamarca
Cd.	Ciudad
Cen. Af. Rep.	Central African Republic
Cga.	Ciénaga
Chan.	Channel
Chap.	Chapada
Chech.	Chechnya
Chely.	Chelyabinsk
Chongq.	Chongqing Shi
Chuk.	Chukotskiy
Chuv.	Chuvashiya
Chyrv.	Chyrvony, -aya, -aye
Cmte.	Comandante
Cnel.	Coronel
Co.-s.	Cerro-s
Col.	Colombia
Colo.	Colorado
Conn.	Connecticut
Cord.	Cordillera
Corr.	Corrientes
Cr.	Creek, Crique
Croat.	Croatia

D

D.	Danau
D.C.	District of Columbia
D.F.	Distrito Federal
D.R.C.	Democratic Republic of the Congo
Del.	Delaware
Dem.	Democratic
Den.	Denmark
Dist.	District, Distrito
Dom. Rep.	Dominican Republic
Dr.	Doctor
Dz.	Dzong

E

E.	East-ern
E. Ríos	Entre Ríos
E. Santo	Espírito Santo
Ea.	Estancia
Ecua.	Ecuador
El Salv.	El Salvador
Emb.	Embalse
Eng.	England
Ens.	Ensenada
Entr.	Entrance
Eq.	Equatorial
Esc.	Escarpment
Est.	Estación
Est.	Estonia
Ét.	Étang
Eth.	Ethiopia
Eur.	Europe
Exp.	Exports
Ez.	Ezers

F

F.	Fiume
F.S.M.	Federated States of Micronesia
Falk. Is.	Falkland Islands
Fd.	Fiord, Fiordo, Fjord
Fed.	Federal, Federation
Fin.	Finland
Fk.	Fork
Fla.	Florida
Fn.	Fortín
Fr.	France, French
ft	feet
Ft.	Fort
Fy.	Ferry
F.Z.	Fracture zone

G

G.	Golfe, Golfo, Gulf
G. Altay	Gorno-Altay
G.R.	Game Reserve
Ga.	Georgia
Geb.	Gebergte, Gebirge
Gen.	General
Ger.	Germany
Gez.	Gezîra-t, Gezîret
Gezr.	Gezâir
Gl.	Glacier, Gletscher
Gob.	Gobernador
Gr.	Greece, Greek
Gr.	Gross-er
Gral.	General
Gt.	Great-er
Guang.	Guangdong

H

H.K.	Hong Kong
Hbr.	Harbor, Harbour
Hdqrs.	Headquarters
Heilong.	Heilongjiang
Hist.	Historic, -al
Hond.	Honduras
Hts.	Heights
Hung.	Hungary

Hwy.	Highway

I

I.H.S.	International Historic Site
I.-s.	Île-s, Ilha-s, Isla-s, Island-s, Isle, Isol-a, -e
Ice.	Iceland
Ig.	Igarapé
Igr.	Ingeniero
Ill.	Illinois
Ind.	Indiana
Ind.	Industry
Ind. Oc.	Indian Ocean
Ingush.	Ingushetiya
Intl.	International
Ire.	Ireland
It.	Italy

J

J.	Järvi, Joki
J.A.R.	Jewish Autonomous Region
Jab., Jeb.	Jabal, Jebel
Jam.	Jamaica
Jap.	Japan
Jct.	Jonction, Junction
Jez.	Jezero, Jezioro

K

K.	Kanal
Kalin.	Kaliningrad
Kalmy.	Kalmykiya
Kamchat.	Kamchatka
Kans.	Kansas
Karna.	Karnataka
Kaz.	Kazakhstan
Kemer.	Kemerovo
Kep.	Kepulauan
Kh.	Khor
Khabar.	Khabarovsk
Khak.	Khakasiya
Khr.	Khrebet
Km.	Kilómetro
Kól.	Kólpos
Kör.	Körfez,-i
Kos.	Kosovo
Kr.	Krasn-yy, -aya, -oye
Krasnod.	Krasnodar
Krasnoy.	Krasnoyarsk
Ky.	Kentucky
Kyrg.	Kyrgyzstan

L

L.	Lac, Lago, Lake, Límni, Loch, Lough
La.	Louisiana
Lab.	Labrador
Lag.	Laguna
Lakshad.	Lakshadweep
Latv.	Latvia
Ldg.	Landing
Leb.	Lebanon
Lib.	Libya
Liech.	Liechtenstein
Lith.	Lithuania
Lux.	Luxembourg

M

m	meters
M.N.M.	Marine National Monument
M. Gerais	Minas Gerais
M. Grosso	Mato Grosso
M. Grosso S.	Mato Grosso do Sul
Maced.	Macedonia
Madag.	Madagascar
Mahar.	Maharashtra
Mal.	Mal-y-y, -aya, -aye
Man.	Manitoba
Maran.	Maranhão
Maurit.	Mauritius

Mass.	Massachusetts
Md.	Maryland
Me.	Maine
Medit. Sea	Mediterranean Sea
Mex.	Mexico
Mgne.	Montagne
Mich.	Michigan
Minn.	Minnesota
Miss.	Mississippi
Mo.	Missouri
Mold.	Moldova
Mon.	Monument
Mont.	Montana
Mont.	Montenegro
Mor.	Morocco
Mt.-s.	Mont-s, Mount-ain-s
Mte.-s.	Monte-s
Mti., Mtii.	Munţi-i
Mun.	Municipal
Murm.	Murmansk

N

N.	North-ern
NA	Not available Not applicable
N.B.	New Brunswick
N.B.P.	National Battlefield Park
N.B.S.	National Battlefield Site
N.C.	North Carolina
N. Dak.	North Dakota
N.E.	North East
N.H.	New Hampshire
N. Ire.	Northern Ireland
N.J.	New Jersey
N.M.	National Monument
N. Mex.	New Mexico
N. Mongol	Nei Mongol
N.M.P.	National Military Park
N.M.S.	National Marine Sanctuary
N.P.	National Park
N.S.	Nova Scotia
N.S.W.	New South Wales
N.T.	Northern Territory
N.V.M.	National Volcanic Monument
N.W.T.	Northwest Territories
N.Y.	New York
N.Z.	New Zealand
Nat.	National
Nat. Mem.	National Memorial
Nat. Mon.	National Monument
Nebr.	Nebraska
Neth.	Netherlands
Nev.	Nevada, Nevado
Nfld. & Lab.	Newfoundland and Labrador
Nicar.	Nicaragua
Nig.	Nigeria
Niz. Nov.	Nizhniy Novgorod
Nizh.	Nizhn-iy, -yaya, -eye
Nor.	Norway
Nov.	Nov-yy, -aya, -aye, -oye
Novg.	Novgorod
Novo.	Novosibirsk
Nr.	Nørre

O

O.	Ostrov, Oued
Oc.	Ocean
Of.	Oficina
Okla.	Oklahoma
Ont.	Ontario
Ør.	Øster
Oreg.	Oregon
Orenb.	Orenburg
Oz.	Ozero

P

P.	Paso, Pass, Passo
P.E.I.	Prince Edward Island
P.N.G.	Papua New Guinea
P.R.	Puerto Rico

Pa.	Pennsylvania
Pac. Oc.	Pacific Ocean
Pak.	Pakistan
Pan.	Panama
Pant.	Pantano
Para.	Paraguay
Pass.	Passage
Peg.	Pegunungan
Pen.	Peninsula, Península, Péninsule
Per.	Pereval
Pk.	Peak
Pl.	Planina
Plat.	Plateau
Pol.	Poland
Pol.	Poluostrov
Port.	Portugal
Pres.	Presidente
Prov.	Province, Provincial
Pt.-e.	Point-e
Pta.	Ponta, Punta, Puntan
Pto.	Puerto
Pul.	Pulau

Q

Q.	Quebrada
Qnsld.	Queensland
Que.	Quebec
Qyzyl.	Qyzylorda

R

R.	Río, River, Rivière
R.R.	Railroad
R. Gr. Norte	Rio Grande do Norte
R. Gr. Sul	Rio Grande do Sul
R.I.	Rhode Island
R. Jan.	Rio de Janeiro
R. Negro	Río Negro
Ra.-s.	Range-s
Rec.	Recreation
Reg.	Region
Rep.	Republic
Res.	Reservoir, Reserve, Reservatório
Rk.	Rock
Rom.	Romania
Russ.	Russia

S

S.	South-ern
S.A.R.	Special Administrative Region
S. Af.	South Africa
S. Aust.	South Australia
S.C.	South Carolina
S. Dak.	South Dakota
S. Estero	Santiago del Estero
S. Ossetia	South Ossetia
S. Paulo	São Paulo
S.W.	Southwest
Sa.-s.	Serra, Sierra-s
Sal.	Salar, Salina
Sask.	Saskatchewan
Scot.	Scotland
Sd.	Sound, Sund
Sel.	Selat
Ser.	Serranía
Serb.	Serbia
Sev.	Severn-yy, -aya, -oye
Sgt.	Sargento
Shand.	Shandong
Sk.	Shankou
Slov.	Slovenia
Slovak.	Slovakia
Smt.-s	Seamount-s
Sp.	Spain, Spanish
Spr.-s.	Spring-s
Sq.	Square
Sr.	Sønder
St.-e.	Saint-e, Sankt, Sint
St. Peter.	Saint Petersburg
Sta., Sto.	Santa, Station, Santo

Sta. Cata.	Santa Catarina
Sta. Cruz.	Santa Cruz
Stavr.	Stavropol'
Str.-s.	Straat, Strait-s
Sv.	Svyat-oy, -aya, -oye
Sverd.	Sverdlovsk
Sw.	Sweden
Switz.	Switzerland
Syr.	Syria

T

T. Fuego	Tierra del Fuego
Taj.	Tajikistan
Tas.	Tasmania
Tel.	Teluk
Tenn.	Tennessee
Terr.	Territory
Tex.	Texas
Tg.	Tanjung
Thai.	Thailand
Tmt.-s	Tablemount-s
Tocant.	Tocantins
Trin.	Trinidad
Tun.	Tunisia
Turk.	Turkey
Turkm.	Turkmenistan

U

U.A.E.	United Arab Emirates
U.K.	United Kingdom
U.N.	United Nations
U.S.	United States
Ukr.	Ukraine
Ulyan.	Ul'yanovsk
Uru.	Uruguay
Uzb.	Uzbekistan

V

V.I.	Virgin Islands
Va.	Virginia
Val.	Valley
Vdkhr.	Vodokhranil-ishche
Vdskh.	Vodoskhovy-shche
Venez.	Venezuela
Verkh.	Verkhn-iy, -yaya, -eye
Vic.	Victoria
Viet.	Vietnam
Vol.	Volcán, Volcano
Volg.	Volgograd
Voz.	Vozyera, -yero, -yera
Vozv.	Vozvyshennost'
Vr.	Vester
Vt.	Vermont
Vyal.	Vyaliki, -ikaya,-ikaye

W

W.	Wadi, Wâdi, Wādī, Webi
W.	West-ern
W. Aust.	Western Australia
W.H.	Water Hole
W. Va.	West Virginia
Wash.	Washington
Wis.	Wisconsin
Wyo.	Wyoming

Y

Yar.	Yarımadası
Yaro.	Yaroslavl'
Yu.	Yuzhn-yy, -aya, -oye

Z

Zakh.	Zakhod-ni, -nyaya, -nye
Zal.	Zaliv
Zap.	Zapadn-yy, -aya, -oye
Zimb.	Zimbabwe

Metric Conversions

CONVERSION CHART FOR METRIC TO ENGLISH CONVERSION**

| 1 METER | 1 METER = 100 CENTIMETERS |
| 1 FOOT | 1 FOOT = 12 INCHES |

| 1 KILOMETER | 1 KILOMETER = 1,000 METERS |
| 1 MILE | 1 MILE = 5,280 FEET |

METERS	1	10	20	50	100	200	500	1,000	2,000	5,000	10,000
FEET	3.28084	32.8084	65.6168	164.042	328.084	656.168	1,640.42	3,280.84	6,561.68	16,404.2	32,808.4
KILOMETERS	1	10	20	50	100	200	500	1,000	2,000	5,000	10,000
MILES	0.621371	6.21371	12.42742	31.06855	62.1371	124.2742	310.6855	621.371	1,242.742	3,106.855	6,213.71

CONVERSION FROM METRIC MEASURES

SYMBOL	WHEN YOU KNOW	MULTIPLY BY	TO FIND	SYMBOL
LENGTH				
cm	centimeters	0.393701	inches	in
m	meters	3.280840	feet	ft
m	meters	1.093613	yards	yd
km	kilometers	0.621371	miles	mi
AREA				
cm^2	square centimeters	0.155000	square inches	in^2
m^2	square meters	10.76391	square feet	ft^2
m^2	square meters	1.195990	square yards	yd^2
km^2	square kilometers	0.386102	square miles	mi^2
ha	hectares	2.471054	acres	--
MASS				
g	grams	0.035274	ounces	oz
kg	kilograms	2.204623	pounds	lb
t	metric tons	1.102311	short tons	--
VOLUME				
mL	milliliters	0.061024	cubic inches	in^3
mL	milliliters	0.033814	liquid ounces	liq oz
L	liters	2.113376	pints	pt
L	liters	1.056688	quarts	qt
L	liters	0.264172	gallons	gal
m^3	cubic meters	35.31467	cubic feet	ft^3
m^3	cubic meters	1.307951	cubic yards	yd^3
TEMPERATURE				
°C	degrees Celsius (centigrade)	9/5 (or 1.8) then add 32	degrees Fahrenheit	°F

CONVERSION TO METRIC MEASURES

SYMBOL	WHEN YOU KNOW	MULTIPLY BY	TO FIND	SYMBOL
LENGTH				
in	inches	2.54	centimeters	cm
ft	feet	0.3048	meters	m
yd	yards	0.9144	meters	m
mi	miles	1.609344	kilometers	km
AREA				
in^2	square inches	6.4516	square centimeters	cm^2
ft^2	square feet	0.092903	square meters	m^2
yd^2	square yards	0.836127	square meters	m^2
mi^2	square miles	2.589988	square kilometers	km^2
--	acres	0.404686	hectares	ha
MASS				
oz	ounces	28.349523	grams	g
lb	pounds	0.453592	kilograms	kg
--	short tons	0.907185	metric tons	t
VOLUME				
in^3	cubic inches	16.387064	milliliters	mL
liq oz	liquid ounces	29.57353	milliliters	mL
pt	pints	0.473176	liters	L
qt	quarts	0.946353	liters	L
gal	gallons	3.785412	liters	L
ft^3	cubic feet	0.028317	cubic meters	m^3
yd^3	cubic yards	0.764555	cubic meters	m^3
TEMPERATURE				
°F	degrees Fahrenheit	5/9 (or 0.55556) after subtracting 32	degrees Celsius (centigrade)	°C

Appendix • Abbreviations and Metric Conversions **165**

Foreign Terms

A

Aaglet — *well*
Aain — *spring*
Aauinat — *spring*
Āb — *river, water*
Ache — *stream*
Açude — *reservoir*
Ada,-sı — *island*
Adrar — *mountain-s, plateau*
Ágios — *saint*
Aguada — *dry lake bed*
Aguelt — *water hole, well*
'Ain, Aïn — *spring, well*
Aïoun-et — *spring-s, well*
Aivi — *mountain*
Akra, Akrotírio — *cape, promontory*
Alb — *mountain, ridge*
Alföld — *plain*
Alin' — *mountain range*
Alpe-n, -s — *mountain-s*
Altiplanicie — *high plain, plateau*
Alto — *hill-s, mountain-s, ridge*
Älv-en — *river*
Āmba — *hill, mountain*
Anou — *well*
Anse — *bay, inlet*
Ao — *bay, cove, estuary*
Ap — *cape, point*
Archipel, Archipiélago — *archipelago*
Arcipelago, Arkhipelag — *archipelago*
Arquipélago — *archipelago*
Arrecife-s — *reef-s*
Arroio, Arroyo — *brook, gully, rivulet, stream*
Ås — *ridge*
Ava — *channel*
Aylagy — *gulf*
'Ayn — *spring, well*

B

Ba — *intermittent stream, river*
Baai — *bay, cove, lagoon*
Bab — *gate, strait*
Badia — *bay*
Bælt — *strait*
Bagh — *bay*
Bahar — *drainage basin*
Bahía — *bay*
Bahr, Baḥr — *bay, lake, river, sea, wadi*
Baía, Baie — *bay*
Bajo-s — *shoal-s*
Ban — *village*
Bañado-s — *flooded area, swamp-s*
Banc, Banco-s — *bank-s, sandbank-s, shoal-s*
Band — *dam, lake*
Bandao — *peninsula*
Baño-s — *hot spring-s, spa*
Baraj-ı — *dam, reservoir*
Barra — *bar, sandbank*
Barrage, Barragem — *dam, lake, reservoir*
Barranca — *gorge, ravine*
Bazar — *marketplace*
Belentligi — *plateau*
Ben, Beinn — *mountain*
Belt — *strait*
Bereg — *bank, coast, shore*
Berg,-e — *mountain-s*
Bil — *lake*
Biq'at — *plain, valley*
Bir, Bîr, Bi'r — *spring, well*
Birket — *lake, pool, swamp*
Bjerg-e — *mountain-s, range*
Boca, Bocca — *channel, river, mouth*
Bocht — *bay*
Bodden — *bay*
Bœng — *pond*
Boğaz, -ı — *strait*
Bögeni — *reservoir*
Boka — *gulf, mouth*
Bol'sh-oy, -aya, -oye — *big*
Bolsón — *inland basin*
Boubairet — *lagoon, lake*
Bras — *arm, branch of a stream*
Braţ, -ul — *arm, branch of a stream*
Bræ-er — *glacier*
Bre, -en — *glacier, ice cap*
Bredning — *bay, broad water*

Bruch — *marsh*
Bucht — *bay*
Bugt-en — *bay*
Buḥayrat, Buheirat — *lagoon, lake, marsh*
Bukhta, Bukta, Bukt-en — *bay*
Bulak, Bulaq — *spring*
Bum — *hill, mountain*
Burnu, Burun — *cape, point*
Busen — *gulf*
Buuraha — *hill-s, mountain-s*
Büyük — *big, large*

C

Cabeza-s — *head-s, summit-s*
Cabo — *cape*
Cachoeira — *rapids, waterfall*
Cal — *hill, peak*
Caleta — *cove, inlet*
Campo-s — *field-s, flat country*
Canal — *canal, channel, strait*
Caño — *channel, stream*
Cao Nguyên — *plateau*
Cap, Capo — *cape*
Capitán — *captain*
Càrn — *mountain*
Castillo — *castle, fort*
Catarata-s — *cataract-s, waterfall-s*
Causse — *upland*
Çay — *brook, stream*
Cay-s, Cayo-s — *island-s, key-s, shoal-s*
Cerro-s — *hill-s, peak-s*
Chaîne, Chaînons — *mountain chain, range*
Chapada-s — *plateau, upland-s*
Chedo — *archipelago*
Chenal — *river channel*
Chersónisos — *peninsula*
Chhung — *bay*
Chi — *lake*
Chiang — *bay*
Chiao — *cape, point, rock*
Ch'ih — *lake*
Chink — *escarpment*
Chott — *intermittent salt lake, salt marsh*
Chou — *island*
Chroüy — *point*
Ch'ü — *canal*
Ch'üntao — *archipelago, islands*
Chuŏr Phnum — *mountains*
Chute-s — *cataract-s, waterfall-s*
Chyrvony, -aya, -aye — *red*
Ciénaga — *marsh*
Cima — *mountain, peak, summit*
Ciudad — *city*
Co — *lake*
Col — *pass*
Collina, Colline — *hill, mountains*
Con — *island*
Cordillera — *mountain chain*
Corno — *mountain, peak*
Coronel — *colonel*
Corredeira — *cascade, rapids*
Costa — *coast*
Côte — *coast, slope*
Coxilha, Cuchilla — *range of low hills*
Crique — *creek, stream*
Csatorna — *canal, channel*
Cù Lao — *island*
Cul de Sac — *bay, inlet*

D

Da — *great, greater*
Daban — *pass*
Dağ, -ı, Dagh — *mountain*
Dağlar, -ı — *mountains*
Dahr — *cliff, mesa*
Dake — *mountain, peak*
Dal-en — *valley*
Dala — *steppe*
Dan — *cape, point*
Danau — *lake*
Dao — *island*
Đảo — *island*
Dar'ya — *lake, river*
Daryācheh — *lake, marshy lake*
Dasht — *desert, plain*
Dawan — *pass*
Dawḥat — *bay, cove, inlet*

Deniz, -i — *sea*
Dent-s — *peak-s*
Deo — *pass*
Deryache — *lake*
Desēt — *hummock, island, land-tied island*
Desierto — *desert*
Détroit — *channel, strait*
Dhar — *hills, ridge, tableland*
Ding — *mountain*
Distrito — *district*
Djebel — *mountain, range*
Do — *island-s, rock-s*
Doi — *hill, mountain*
Dome — *ice dome*
Dong — *village*
Dooxo — *floodplain*
Dzong — *castle, fortress*

E

Eiland-en — *island-s*
Eilean — *island*
Ejland — *island-s*
Elv — *river*
Embalse — *lake, reservoir*
Emi — *mountain, rock*
Enseada, Ensenada — *bay, cove*
Ér — *rivulet, stream*
Erg — *sand dune region*
Est — *east*
Estación — *railroad station*
Estany — *lagoon, lake*
Estero — *estuary, inlet, lagoon, marsh*
Estrecho — *strait*
Étang — *lake, pond*
Eylandt — *island*
Eżeras — *lake*
Ezers — *lake*

F

Falaise — *cliff, escarpment*
Farvand-et — *channel, sound*
Fell — *mountain*
Feng — *mount, peak*
Fiord-o — *inlet, sound*
Firn — *snowfield*
Fiume — *river*
Fjäll-et — *mountain*
Fjällen — *mountains*
Fjärd-en — *fjord*
Fjarðar, Fjörður — *fjord*
Fjeld-e — *mountain-s, nunatak-s*
Fjell-ene — *mountain-s*
Fjöll — *mountain-s*
Fjord-en — *inlet, fjord*
Fleuve — *river*
Fljót — *large river*
Flói — *bay, marshland*
Foci — *river mouths*
Főcsatorna — *principal canal*
Foko — *point*
Förde — *fjord, gulf, inlet*
Forsen — *rapids, waterfall*
Fortaleza — *fort, fortress*
Fortín — *fortified post*
Foss-en — *waterfall*
Foum — *pass, passage*
Foz — *mouth of a river*
Fuerte — *fort, fortress*
Fwafwate — *waterfalls*

G

Gacan-ka — *hill, peak*
Gal — *pond, spring, water hole, well*
Gang — *harbor*
Gangri — *peak, range*
Gaoyuan — *plateau*
Garaet, Gara'et — *lake, lake bed, salt lake*
Gardaneh — *pass*
Garet — *hill, mountain*
Gat — *channel*
Gata — *bay, inlet, lake*
Gattet — *channel, strait*
Gaud — *depression, saline tract*
Gave — *mountain stream*
Gebel — *mountain-s, range*
Gebergte — *mountain range*
Gebirge — *mountains, range*

Geçidi — *mountain pass, passage*
Geçit — *mountain pass, passage*
Gezâir — *islands*
Gezîra-t, Gezîret — *island, peninsula*
Ghats — *mountain range*
Ghubb-at, -et — *bay, gulf*
Giri — *mountain*
Gjiri — *bay*
Gletscher — *glacier*
Gobernador — *governor*
Gobi — *desert*
Gol — *river, stream*
Göl, -ü — *lake*
Golets — *mountain, peak*
Golf, -e, -o — *gulf*
Gor-a, -y, Gór-a, -y — *mountain,-s*
Got — *point*
Gowd — *depression*
Goz — *sand ridge*
Gran, -de — *great, large*
Gryada — *mountains, ridge*
Guan — *pass*
Guba — *bay, gulf*
Guelta — *well*
Guntō — *archipelago*
Gunung — *mountain*
Gura — *mouth, passage*
Guyot — *table mount*

H

Haḍabat — *plateau*
Haehyŏp — *strait*
Haff — *lagoon*
Hai — *lake, sea*
Haihsia — *strait*
Haixia — *channel, strait*
Hakau — *reef, rock*
Hakuchi — *anchorage*
Halvø, Halvøy-a — *peninsula*
Hama — *beach*
Hamada, Ḥammādah — *rocky desert*
Hamn — *harbor, port*
Hāmūn, Hamun — *depression, lake*
Hana — *cape, point*
Hantō — *peninsula*
Har — *hill, mound, mountain*
Ḥarrat — *lava field*
Hasi, Hassi — *spring, well*
Hauteur — *elevation, height*
Hav-et — *sea*
Havn, Havre — *harbor, port*
Hawr — *lake, marsh*
Hāyk' — *lake, reservoir*
He — *canal, lake, river*
Hegy, -ség — *mountain, -s, range*
Heiau — *temple*
Ho — *lake, reservoir*
Hoek — *hook, point*
Hög-en — *high, hill*
Höhe, -n — *height, high*
Høj — *height, hill*
Holm, -e, Holmene — *island-s, islet -s*
Holot — *dunes*
Hòn — *island-s*
Hor-a, -y — *mountain, -s*
Horn — *horn, peak*
Houma — *point*
Hoved — *headland, peninsula, point*
Hraun — *lava field*
Hsü — *island*
Hu — *lake, reservoir*
Huk — *cape, point*
Hüyük — *hill, mound*

I

Idehan — *sand dunes*
Igarapé — *creek, stream*
Île-s, Ilha-s, Illa-s, Îlot-s — *island-s, islet-s*
Îlet, Ilhéu-s — *islet, -s*
Irhil — *mountain-s, range*
'Irq — *sand dune-s*
Isblink — *glacier, ice field*
Is-en — *glacier*
Isebræ — *glacier*
Isfjord — *ice fjord*
Iskappe — *ice cap*
Isla-s, Islote — *island-s, islet*
Isol-a, -e — *island, -s*

Isstrøm — *glacier, ice field*
Istmo — *isthmus*
Iwa — *island, islet, rock*

J

Jabal, Jebel — *mountain-s, range*
Jahīl — *lake*
Järv, -i, Jaure, Javrre — *lake*
Jazā'ir, Jazīrat, Jazīreh — *island-s*
Jehīl — *lake*
Jezero, Jezioro — *lake*
Jiang — *river, stream*
Jiao — *cape*
Jibāl — *hill, mountain, ridge*
Jima — *island-s, rock-s*
Jøkel, Jökull — *glacier, ice cap*
Joki, Jokka — *river*
Jökulsá — *river from a glacier*
Jŏsuji — *lake, reservoir*
Jūn — *bay*

K

Kaap — *cape*
Kafr — *village*
Kaikyō — *channel, strait*
Kaise — *mountain*
Kaiwan — *bay, gulf, sea*
Kanal — *canal, channel*
Kangerlua — *fjord*
Kangri — *mountain-s, peak*
Kaôh — *island*
Kap, Kapp — *cape*
Kavīr — *salt desert*
Kefar — *village*
Kênet' — *lagoon, lake*
Kep — *cape, point*
Kepulauan — *archipelago, islands*
Khalīg, Khalīj — *bay, gulf*
Khirb-at, -et — *ancient site, ruins*
Khrebet — *mountain range*
Kinh — *canal*
Klint — *bluff, cliff*
Kō — *bay, cove, harbor*
Ko — *island, lake*
Kōh — *mountain*
Koh — *island, mountain, range*
Köl-i — *lake*
Kólpos — *gulf*
Kong — *king, mountain*
Körfez, -i — *bay, gulf*
Kosa — *spit of land*
Kōtal — *pass*
Kou — *estuary, river mouth*
Kowtal-e — *pass*
Kronprince — *crown prince*
Krasn-yy, -aya, -oye — *red*
Kryazh — *mountain range, ridge*
Kuala — *estuary, river mouth*
Kuan — *mountain pass*
Kūh, Kūhhā — *mountain-s, range*
Kul', Kuli — *lake*
Kum — *sandy desert*
Kundo — *archipelago*
Kuppe — *hill-s, mountain-s*
Kust — *coast, shore*
Kyst — *coast*
Kyun — *island*

L

La — *pass*
Lac, Lac-ul, -us — *lake*
Lae — *cape, point*
Lago, -a — *lagoon, lake*
Lagoen, Lagune — *lagoon*
Laguna-s — *lagoon-s, lake-s*
Laht — *bay, gulf, harbor*
Laje — *reef, rock ledge*
Laut — *sea*
Lednik — *glacier*
Leida — *channel*
Lhari — *mountain*
Li — *village*
Liedao — *archipelago, islands*
Liehtao — *archipelago, islands*
Lille — *little, small*
Liman-ı — *bay, estuary*
Límni — *lake*
Ling — *mountain-s, range*
Linn — *pool, waterfall*

Lintasan	passage
Liqen	lake
Llano-s	plain-s
Loch, Lough	lake, arm of the sea
Loma-s	hill-s, knoll-s

M

Mal	mountain, range
Mal-yy, -aya, -oye	little, small
Mamarr	pass, path
Man	bay
Mar, Mare	large lake, sea
Marsa, Marsá	bay, inlet
Masabb	mouth of river
Massif	mountain-s
Mauna	mountain
Mēda	plain
Meer	lake, sea
Melkosopochnik	undulating plain
Mesa, Meseta	plateau, tableland
Mierzeja	sandspit
Minami	south
Mios	island
Misaki	cape, peninsula, point
Mochun	passage
Molsron	harbor
Mong	town, village
Mont-e, -i, -ii, -s	mount, –ain, –s
Montagne, -s	mount, –ain, –s
Montaña, -s	mountain, –s
More	sea
Morne	hill, peak
Morro	bluff, headland, hill
Motu, -s	islands
Mouïet	well
Mouillage	anchorage
Muang	town, village
Mūi	cape, point
Mull	headland, promontory
Munkhafad	depression
Munte	mountain
Munţi-i	mountains
Muong	town, village
Mynydd	mountain
Mys	cape

N

Nacional	national
Nada	gulf, sea
Næs, Näs	cape, point
Nafūd	area of dunes, desert
Nagor'ye	mountain range, plateau
Nahar, Nahr	river, stream
Nakhon	town
Namakzār	salt waste
Ne	island, reef, rock-s
Neem	cape, point, promontory
Nes, Ness	peninsula, point
Nevado-s	snowcapped mountain-s
Nez	cape, promontory
Ni	village
Nísi, Nísia, Nisís, Nísoi	island-s, islet-s
Nisídhes	islets
Nizhn-iy, -yaya, -eye	lower
Nizmennost'	low country
Noord	north
Nord-re	north–ern
Nørre	north–ern
Nos	cape, nose, point
Nosy	island, reef, rock
Nov-yy, -aya, -aye, -oye	new
Nudo	mountain
Núi	mountains
Numa	lake
Nunaa	area, region
Nunaat	area, island
Nunatak, -s, -ker	peak-s surrounded by ice cap
Nur	lake, salt lake
Nuruu	mountain range, ridge
Nut-en	peak
Nuur	lake

O

O-n, Ø-er	island-s
Oblast	administrative division, province, region
Oceanus	ocean
Odde-n	cape, point

Øer-ne	islands
Oglat	group of wells
Oguilet	well
Ór-os, -i	mountain, -s
Órmos	bay, port
Ort	place, point
Øst-er	east
Ostrov, -a, Ostrv-o, -a	island, -s
Otoci, Otok	islands, island
Ouadi, Oued	river, watercourse
Ovalığı	plain
Øy-a	island
Øyane	islands
Ozer-o, -a	lake, -s

P

Pää	mountain, point
Palus	marsh
Pampa-s	grassy plain-s
Pantà	lake, reservoir
Pantanal	marsh, swamp
Pao, P'ao	lake
Parbat	mountain
Parque	park
Pas, -ul	pass
Paso, Passo	pass
Passe	channel, pass
Pasul	pass
Pedra	rock
Pegunungan	mountain range
Pellg	bay, bight
Peña	cliff, rock
Pendi	basin
Penedo-s	rock-s
Péninsule	peninsula
Peñón	point, rock
Pereval	mountain pass
Pertuis	strait
Peski	sands, sandy region
Phnom	hill, mountain, range
Phou	mountain range
Phouphiang	plateau
Phu	mountain
Piana-o	plain
Pic, Pik, Piz	peak
Picacho	mountain, peak
Pico-s	peak-s
Pistyll	waterfall
Piton-s	peak-s
Pivdennyy	southern
Plaja, Playa	beach, inlet, shore
Planalto, Plato	plateau
Planina	mountain, plateau
Plassen	lake
Ploskogor'ye	plateau, upland
Pointe	point
Polder	reclaimed land
Poluostrov	peninsula
Pongo	water gap
Ponta, -I	cape, point
Ponte	bridge
Poolsaar	peninsula
Portezuelo	pass
Porto	port
Poulo	island-s
Praia	beach, seashore
Presa	reservoir
Presidente	president
Presqu'île	peninsula
Prins	prince
Prinsesse	princess
Prokhod	pass
Proliv	strait
Promontorio	promontory
Průsmyk	mountain pass
Przylądek	cape
Puerto	bay, pass, port
Pulao	island-s
Pulau, Pulo	island
Puncak	peak, summit, top
Punt, Punta, -n	point, -s
Pun	peak
Pu'u	hill, mountain
Puy	peak

Q

Qā'	depression, marsh, mud flat
Qal'at	fort
Qal'eh	castle, fort
Qanâ	canal

Qārat	hill-s, mountain-s
Qaşr	castle, fort, hill
Qila	fort
Qiryat	settlement, suburb
Qolleh	peak
Qooriga	anchorage, bay
Qoz	dunes, sand ridge
Qu	canal
Quầ'n Đảo	islands
Quebrada	ravine, stream
Qullai	peak, summit
Qum-y	desert, sand
Qundao	archipelago, islands
Qurayyāt	hills

R

Raas	cape, point
Rabt	hill
Rada	roadstead
Rade	anchorage, roadstead
Rags	point
Ramat	hill, mountain
Rand	ridge of hills
Rann	swamp
Raqaba	wadi, watercourse
Ras, Râs, Ra's	cape
Ravnina	plain
Récif-s	reef-s
Regreg	marsh
Represa	reservoir
Reservatório	reservoir
Restinga	barrier, sand area
Rettō	chain of islands
Ri	mountain range, village
Ría	estuary
Ribeirão	stream
Río, Rio	river
Rivière	river
Roca-s	cliff, rock-s
Roche-r, -s	rock-s
Rosh	mountain, point
Rt	cape, point
Rubha	headland
Rupes	scarp

S

Saar	island
Saari, Sari	island
Sabkha-t, Sabkhet	lagoon, marsh, salt lake
Sagar	lake, sea
Sahara, Şahrā'	desert
Sahl	plain
Saki	cape, point
Salar	salt flat
Salina	salt pan
Salin-as, -es	salt flat-s, salt marsh-es
Salto	waterfall
Sammyaku	mountain range
San	hill, mountain
San, -ta, -to	saint
Sandur	sandy area
Sankt	saint
Sanmaek	mountain range
São	saint
Sarīr	gravel desert
Sasso	mountain, stone
Savane	savanna
Scoglio	reef, rock
Se	reef, rock-s, shoal-s
Sebjet	salt lake, salt marsh
Sebkha	salt lake, salt marsh
Sebkhet	lagoon, salt lake
See	lake, sea
Selat	strait
Selkä	lake, ridge
Semenanjung	peninsula
Sen	mountain
Seno	bay, gulf
Sermeq	glacier
Sermia	glacier
Serra, Serranía	range of hills or mountains
Severn-ye, -yy, -aya, -oye	northern
Sgùrr	peak
Sha	island, shoal
Sha'īb	ravine, watercourse
Shamo	desert
Shan	island-s, mountain-s, range
Shankou	mountain pass

Shanmo	mountain range
Sharm	cove, creek, harbor
Shatt, Shaţţ	large river
Shi	administrative division, municipality
Shima	island-s, rock-s
Shō	island, reef, rock
Shotō	archipelago
Shott	intermittent salt lake
Shuiku	reservoir
Shuitao	channel
Shyghanaghy	bay, gulf
Sierra	mountain range
Silsilesi	mountain chain, ridge
Sint	saint
Sinus	bay, sea
Sjö-n	lake
Skarv-et	barren mountain
Skerry	rock
Slieve	mountain
Sø-er	lake-s
Sønder, Søndre	south-ern
Sopka	conical mountain, volcano
Sor	lake, salt lake
Sør, Sör	south-ern
Sory	salt lake, salt marsh
Spitz-e	peak, point, top
Sredn-iy, -yaya, -eye	central, middle
Stagno	lake, pond
Stantsiya	station
Stausee	reservoir
Stenón	channel, strait
Step'-i	steppe-s
Štít	summit, top
Stor-e	big, great
Straat	strait
Straum-en	current-s
Strelka	spit of land
Stretet, Stretto	strait
Su	reef, river, rock, stream
Su Anbarı	reservoir
Sud	south
Sudo	channel, strait
Suidō	channel, strait
Şummān	rocky desert
Sund	sound, strait
Sunden	channel, inlet, sound
Svyat-oy, -aya, -oye	holy, saint
Sziget	island

T

Tagh	mountain-s
Tai	coast, tide
Tall	hill, mound
T'an	lake
Tanezrouft	desert
Tang	plain, steppe
Tangi	peninsula, point
Tanjong, Tanjung	cape, point
Tao	island-s
Tarso	hill-s, mountain-s
Tassili	plateau, upland
Tau	mountain-s, range
Taūy	hills, mountains
Tchabal	mountain-s
Te Ava	tidal flat
Tel-l	hill, mound
Telok, Teluk	bay
Tepe, -si	hill, peak
Tepuí	mesa, mountain
Terara	hill, mountain, peak
Testa	bluff, head
Thale	lake
Thang	plain, steppe
Tien	lake
Tierra	land, region
Ting	hill, mountain
Tir'at	canal
Tó	lake, pool
To, Tō	island-s, rock-s
Tonle	lake
Tope	hill, mountain, peak
Top-pen	peninsula
Träsk	bog, lake
Tso	lake
Tsui	cape, point
Tübegi	peninsula
Tulu	hill, mountain
Tunturi-t	hill-s, mountain-s

U

Uad	wadi, watercourse
Udde-m	point
Ujong, Ujung	cape, point
Umi	bay, lagoon, lake
Ura	bay, inlet, lake
'Urūq	dune area
Uul, Uula	mountain, range
'Uyûn	springs

V

Vaara	mountain
Vaart	canal
Vær	fishing station
Vaïn	channel, strait
Valle, Vallée	valley, wadi
Vallen	waterfall
Valli	lagoon, lake
Vallis	valley
Vanua	land
Varre	mountain
Vatn, Vatten, Vatnet	lake, water
Veld	grassland, plain
Verkhn-iy, -yaya, -eye	higher, upper
Vesi	lake, water
Vest-er	west
Via	road
Vidda	plateau
Vig, Vík, Vik, -en	bay, cove
Vinh	bay
Vodokhranilishche	reservoir
Vodoskhovyshche	reservoir
Volcan, Volcán	volcano
Vostochn-yy, -aya, -oye	eastern
Vötn	stream
Vozvyshennost'	plateau, upland
Vozyera, -yero, -yera	lake-s
Vrchovina	mountains
Vrch-y	mountain-s
Vrh	hill, mountain
Vrükh	mountain
Vūng	bay
Vyaliki, -ikaya, -ikaye	big, large
Vysočina	highland

W

Wabē	stream
Wadi, Wâdi, Wādī	valley, watercourse
Wâhât, Wāḩat	oasis
Wald	forest, wood
Wan	bay, gulf
Water	harbor
Webi	stream
Wiek	cove, inlet

X

Xia	gorge, strait
Xiao	lesser, little

Y

Yanchi	salt lake
Yang	ocean
Yarımadası	peninsula
Yazovir	reservoir
Yŏlto	island group
Yoma	mountain range
Yü	island
Yumco	lake
Yunhe	canal
Yuzhn-yy, -aya, -oye	southern

Z

Zaki	cape, point
Zaliv	bay, gulf
Zan	mountain, ridge
Zangbo	river, stream
Zapadn-yy, -aya, -oye	western
Zatoka	bay, gulf
Zee	bay, sea
Zemlya	land
Zhotasy	mountains

Glossary of Geographic Terms

A

abyssal plain a flat, relatively featureless region of the deep ocean floor extending from the mid-ocean ridge to a continental rise or deep-sea trench

acculturation the process of losing the traits of one cultural group while assimilating with another cultural group

alloy a substance that is a mixture of two metals or a metal and a nonmetal

alluvial fan a depositional, fan-shaped feature found where a stream or channel gradient levels out at the base of a mountain

antipode a point that lies diametrically opposite any given point on the surface of the Earth

Archaean (Archean) eon the second eon of Earth's geologic history, ending around 2,500 million years ago

archipelago an associated group of scattered islands in a large body of water

asthenosphere the uppermost zone of Earth's mantle; it consists of rocks in a "plastic" state, immediately below the lithosphere

atmosphere the thin envelope of gases surrounding the solid Earth and comprising mostly nitrogen, oxygen, and various trace gases

atoll a circular coral reef enclosing a lagoon

B

barrier island a low-lying, sandy island parallel to a shoreline but separated from the mainland by a lagoon

basin a low-lying depression in the Earth's surface; some basins are filled with water and sediment, while others are dry most of the time

bathymetry the measurement of depth within bodies of water or the information gathered from such measurements

bay an area of a sea or other body of water bordered on three sides by a curved stretch of coastline but usually smaller than a gulf

biodiversity a broad concept that refers to the variety and range of species (flora and fauna) present in an ecosystem

biogeography the study of the distribution patterns of plants and animals and the processes that produce those patterns

biological weapon a weapon that uses an organism or toxin, such as a bacteria or virus, to harm individuals

biome a very large ecosystem made up of specific plant and animal communities interacting with the physical environment (climate and soil)

biosphere the realm of Earth that includes all plant and animal life-forms

bluff a steep slope or wall of consolidated sediment adjacent to a river or its floodplain

bog soft, spongy, waterlogged ground consisting chiefly of partially decayed plant matter (peat)

breakwater a stone or concrete structure built near a shore to prevent damage to watercraft or construction

butte a tall, steep-sided, flat-topped tower of rock that is a remnant of extensive erosional processes

C

caldera a large, crater-like feature with steep, circular walls and a central depression resulting from the explosion and collapse of a volcano

canal an artificially made channel of water used for navigation or irrigation

canopy the ceiling-like layer of branches and leaves that forms the uppermost layer of a forest

capitalism an economic system characterized by resource allocation primarily through market mechanisms; means of production are privately owned (by either individuals or corporations), and production is organized around profit maximization

capture fishery all of the variables involved in the activities to harvest a given fish (e.g., location, target resource, technology used, social characteristic, purpose, season)

carbon cycle one of the several geochemical cycles by which matter is recirculated through the lithosphere, hydrosphere, atmosphere, and biosphere

carbon neutral process a process resulting in zero net change in the balance between emission and absorption of carbon

carrying capacity the maximum number of animals and/or people a given area can support at a given time under specified levels of consumption

cartogram a map designed to present statistical information in a diagrammatic way, usually not to scale

cartographer a person who interprets, designs, and creates maps and other modes of geographic representation

chemical weapon a weapon that uses toxic properties of chemical substances to harm individuals

chlorofluorocarbon a molecule of industrial origin containing chlorine, fluorine, and carbon atoms; causes severe ozone destruction

civilization a cultural concept suggesting substantial development in the form of agriculture, cities, food and labor surplus, labor specialization, social stratification, and state organization

climate the long-term behavior of the atmosphere; it includes measures of average weather conditions (e.g., temperature, humidity, precipitation, and pressure), as well as trends, cycles, and extremes

colonialism the political, social, or economic domination of a state over another state or people

commodity an economic good or product that can be traded, bought, or sold

composite image a product of combining two or more images

coniferous trees and shrubs with thin leaves and producing cones; also a forest or wood composed of these trees

continental drift a theory that suggests the continents were at one time all part of a prehistoric supercontinent that broke apart; according to the theory, the continents slowly "drifted" across the Earth's surface to their present positions

continental shelf the submerged, offshore extension of a continent

continental slope the steeply graded seafloor connecting the edge of the continental shelf to the deep-ocean floor

convection the transfer of heat within a gas or solid of nonuniform temperature from mass movement or circulatory motion due to gravity and uneven density within the substance

convergent boundary where tectonic plates move toward each other along their common boundary, causing subduction

core the dense, innermost layer of Earth; the outer core is liquid, while the inner core is solid

Coriolis effect the deflection of wind systems and ocean currents (as well as freely moving objects not in contact with the solid Earth) to the right in the Northern Hemisphere and to the left in the Southern Hemisphere as a consequence of the Earth's rotation

crust the rocky, relatively low density, outermost layer of Earth

cultural diffusion the spread of cultural elements from one group to another

culture the "way of life" for a group; it is transmitted from generation to generation and involves a shared system of meanings, beliefs, values, and social relations; it also includes language, religion, clothing, music, laws, and entertainment

D

dead zone oxygen-starved areas in oceans and lakes where marine life cannot be supported, often linked to runoff of excess nutrients

deciduous trees and shrubs that shed their leaves seasonally; also a forest or wood mostly composed of these trees

deformation general term for folding and faulting of rocks due to natural shearing, compression, and extension forces

delta a flat, low-lying, often fan-shaped region at the mouth of a river; it is composed of sediment deposited by a river entering a lake, an ocean, or another large body of water

demography the study of population statistics, changes, and trends based on various measures of fertility, mortality, and migration

denudation the overall effect of weathering, mass wasting, and erosion, which ultimately wears down and lowers the continental surface

desert a region that has little or no vegetation and averages less than ten inches (25 cm) of precipitation a year

desertification the spread of desert conditions in arid and semiarid regions; desertification results from a combination of climatic changes and increasing human pressures in the form of overgrazing, removal of natural vegetation, and cultivation of marginal land

developed country general term for an industrialized country with a diversified and self-sustaining economy, strong infrastructure, and high standard of living

developing country general term for a nonindustrialized country with a weak economy, little modern infrastructure, and low standard of living

dialect a regional variation of one language, with differences in vocabulary, accent, pronunciation, and syntax

diffuse plate boundary a zone of faulting and earthquakes extending to either side of a plate boundary

digital elevation model (DEM) a digital representation of Earth's topography in which data points representing altitude are assigned coordinates and viewed spatially; sometimes called a digital terrain model (DTM)

disconformity a discontinuity in sedimentary rocks in which the rock beds remain parallel

divide a ridge separating watersheds

dormant volcano an active volcano that is temporarily in repose but expected to erupt in the future

E

earthquake vibrations and shock waves caused by volcanic eruptions or the sudden movement of Earth's crustal rocks along fracture zones called faults

easterlies regular winds that blow from the east

ecosystem a group of organisms and the environment with which they interact

elevation the height of a point or place above an established datum, sometimes mean sea level

El Niño a pronounced warming of the surface waters along the coast of Peru and the equatorial region of the east Pacific Ocean; it is caused by weakening (sometimes reversal) of the trade winds, with accompanying changes in ocean circulation (including cessation of upwelling in coastal waters)

emigrant a person migrating away from a country or area; an out-migrant

endangered species a species at immediate risk of extinction

endemic typical of or native to a particular area, people, or environment

endogenous introduced from or originating within a given organism or system

environment the sum of the conditions and stimuli that influence an organism

eon the largest time unit on the geologic time scale; consists of several shorter units called eras

Equator latitude 0°; an imaginary line running east and west around Earth and dividing it into two equal parts known as the Northern and Southern Hemispheres; the Equator always has 12 hours of daylight and 12 hours of darkness

equinox the time of year (usually September 22–23 and March 21–22) when the length of night and day are about equal and the sun is directly overhead at the Equator

era a major subdivision of time on the geologic time scale; consists of several shorter units called periods

erosion the general term for the removal of surface rocks and sediment by the action of water, air, ice, or gravity

escarpment a cliff or steep rock face that separates two comparatively level land surfaces

estuary a broadened seaward end or extension of a river (usually a drowned river mouth), characterized by tidal influences and the mixing of fresh and saline water

ethnic group minority group with a collective self-identity within a larger host population

ethnocentrism a belief in the inherent superiority of one's own ethnic group and culture; a tendency to view all other groups or cultures in terms of one's own

eutrophication the process that occurs when large amounts of nutrients from fertilizers or animal wastes enter a water body and bacteria break down the nutrients; the bacterial action causes depletion of dissolved oxygen

Exclusive Economic Zone (EEZ) an oceanic zone extending up to 200 nautical miles (370 km) from a shoreline, within which a coastal state claims jurisdiction over fishing, mineral exploration, and other economically important activities

exogenous introduced from or originating outside a given organism or system

external debt debt owed to nonresidents; repayable in foreign currency, goods, or services

F

fault a fracture or break in rock where the opposite sides are displaced relative to each other

fjord a coastal inlet that is narrow and deep and reaches far inland; it is usually formed by the sea filling in a glacially scoured valley or trough

flood basalt a huge lava flow that produces thick accumulations of basalt layers over a large area

floodplain a wide, relatively flat area adjacent to a stream or river and subject to flooding and sedimentation; it is the most preferred land area for human settlement and agriculture

food chain the feeding pattern of organisms in an ecosystem, through which energy from food passes from one level to the next in a sequence

fork the place where a river separates into branches; also may refer to one of those branches

fossil fuel fuel in the form of coal, petroleum, or natural gas derived from the remains of ancient plants and animals trapped and preserved in sedimentary rocks

G

galaxy a collection of stars, gas, and dust bound together by gravity; there are billions of galaxies in the universe, and the Earth is in the Milky Way galaxy

genocide the intentional destruction, in whole or in part, of a national, ethnic, racial, or religious group

genome the complete set of genetic material of an organism

geochemistry a branch of geology focusing on the chemical composition of earth materials

geographic information system (GIS) an integrated hardware-software system used to store, organize, analyze, manipulate, model, and display geographic information or data

geography literally means "Earth description"; as a modern academic discipline, geography is concerned with the explanation of the physical and human characteristics and patterns of Earth's surface

geomorphology the study of planetary surface features, especially the processes of landform evolution on Earth

geopolitics the study of how factors such as geography, economics, and demography affect the power and foreign policy of a state

glaciation a period of glacial advancement through the growth of continental ice sheets and/or mountain glaciers

glacier a large, natural accumulation of ice that spreads outward on the land or moves slowly down a slope or valley

global positioning system (GPS) a system of artificial satellites that provides information on three-dimensional position and velocity to users at or near the Earth's surface

global warming the warming of Earth's average global temperature due to a buildup of "greenhouse gases" (e.g., carbon dioxide and methane) released by human activities; increased levels of these gases cause enhanced heat absorption by the atmosphere

globe a scale model of the Earth that correctly represents not only the area, relative size, and shape of physical features but also the distance between points and true compass directions

great circle the largest circle that can be drawn around a sphere such as a globe; a great circle route is the shortest route between two points on the surface of a sphere

greenhouse effect an enhanced near-surface warming that is due to certain atmospheric gases absorbing and re-radiating long-wave radiation that might otherwise have escaped to space had those gases not been present in the atmosphere

gross domestic product (GDP) the total market value of goods and services produced by a nation's economy in a given year using global currency exchange rates

gross national income (GNI) the income derived from the capital and income belonging to nationals employed domestically or abroad

gravitational waves ripples in the fabric of space and time, usually caused by the interaction of two or more large masses

gulf a very large area of an ocean or a sea bordered by coastline on three sides

gyre a large, semicontinuous system of major ocean currents flowing around the outer margins of every major ocean basin

H

habitat the natural environment (including controlling physical factors) in which a plant or animal is usually found or prefers to exist

hemisphere half a sphere; cartographers and geographers, by convention, divide the Earth into the Northern and Southern Hemispheres at the Equator and the Eastern and Western Hemispheres at the prime meridian (longitude 0°) and 180° meridian

herbaceous a type of plant lacking woody tissue, and usually with a life of just one growing season

hot spot a localized and intensely hot region or mantle plume beneath the lithosphere; it tends to stay relatively fixed geographically as a lithospheric plate migrates over it

human geography one of the two major divisions of systematic geography; it is concerned with the spatial analysis of human population, cultures, and social, political, and economic activities

hurricane a large, rotating storm system that forms over tropical waters, with very low atmospheric pressure in the central region and winds in excess of 74 mph (119 km/h); it is called a typhoon over the western Pacific Ocean and a cyclone over the northern Indian Ocean

hydrologic cycle the continuous recirculation of water from the oceans, through the atmosphere, to the continents, through the biosphere and lithosphere, and back to the sea

hydrosphere all of the water found on, under, or over Earth's surface

hypsometry the measurement of contours and elevation of land above sea level

I

ice age a period of pronounced glaciation usually associated with worldwide cooling, a greater proportion of global precipitation falling as snow, and a shorter seasonal snowmelt period

igneous the rock type formed from solidified molten rock (magma) that originates deep within Earth; the chemical composition of the magma and its cooling rate determine the final rock type

immigrant a person migrating into a particular country or area; an in-migrant

impact crater a circular depression on the surface of a planet or moon caused by the collision of another body, such as an asteroid or comet

indigenous native to or occurring naturally in a specific area or environment

industrial metabolism a concept that describes the process of converting raw materials into a final product and waste through energy and labor

infrastructure transportation and communications networks that allow goods, people, and information to flow across space

inorganic not relating to or being derived from living things

interdependence mutual reliance among beings or processes

internally displaced person a person who flees his/her home, to escape danger or persecution, but does not leave the country

International Date Line an imaginary line that roughly follows the 180° meridian in the Pacific Ocean; immediately west of the date line the calendar date is one day ahead of the calendar date east of the line; people crossing the date line in a westward direction lose one calendar day, while those crossing eastward gain one calendar day

intertropical convergence zone (ITCZ) a zone of low atmospheric pressure created by intense solar heating, thereby leading to rising air and horizontal convergence of northeast and southeast trade winds; over the oceans, the ITCZ is usually found between 10° N and 10° S, and over continents the seasonal excursion of the ITCZ is much greater

isthmus a relatively narrow strip of land with water on both sides and connecting two larger land areas

J

jet stream a high-speed west-to-east wind current; jet streams flow in narrow corridors within upper-air westerlies, usually at the interface of polar and tropical air

K

karst a region underlain by limestone and characterized by extensive solution features such as sinkholes, underground streams, and caves

L

lagoon a shallow, narrow water body located between a barrier island and the mainland, with freshwater contributions from streams and saltwater exchange through tidal inlets or breaches throughout the barrier system

La Niña the pronounced cooling of equatorial waters in the eastern Pacific Ocean

latitude the distance north or south of the Equator; lines of latitude, called parallels, are evenly spaced from the Equator to the North and South Poles (from 0° to 90° N and S latitude); latitude and longitude (see below) are measured in terms of the 360 degrees of a circle and are expressed in degrees, minutes, and seconds

leeward the side away from or sheltered by the wind

lingua franca a language used beyond its native speaker population as a common or commercial language

lithosphere the rigid outer layer of the Earth, located above the asthenosphere and comprising the outer crust and the upper, rigid portion of the mantle

longitude the distance measured in degrees east or west of the prime meridian (0° longitude) up to 180°; lines of longitude are called meridians (compare with latitude, above)

M

macroscopic concerned with or considered in large units

magma molten, pressurized rock in the mantle that is occasionally intruded into the lithosphere or extruded to the surface of the Earth by volcanic activity

magnetic poles the points at Earth's surface at which the geomagnetic field is vertical; the location of these points constantly changes

mantle the dense layer of Earth below the crust; the upper mantle is solid, and with the crust forms the lithosphere, the zone containing tectonic plates; the lower mantle is partially molten, making it the pliable base upon which the lithosphere "floats"

map projection the geometric system of transferring information about a round object, such as a globe, to a flat piece of paper or other surface for the purpose of producing a map with known properties and quantifiable distortion

maria volcanic plains on the moon's surface that appear to the naked eye as smooth, dark areas

meridian a north-south line of longitude used to reference distance east or west of the prime meridian (longitude 0°)

mesa a broad, flat-topped hill or mountain with marginal cliffs and/or steep slopes formed by progressive erosion of horizontally bedded sedimentary rocks

metamorphic the rock type formed from preexisting rocks that have been substantially changed from their original igneous, sedimentary, or earlier metamorphic form; catalysts of this change include high heat, high pressure, hot and mineral-rich fluids, or, more commonly, some combination of these

metric ton (tonne) unit of weight equal to 1,000 kilograms or 2,205 pounds

micrometeoroids a tiny particle of rock or dust in space, usually weighing less than a gram

microscopic considered in or concerned with small units

migration the movement of people across a specified boundary for the purpose of establishing a new place of residence

mineral an inorganic solid with a distinctive chemical composition and a specific crystal structure that affect its physical characteristics

moment magnitude scale a measure of the total energy released by an earthquake; preferred to the Richter scale because it more accurately measures strong earthquakes and can be used with data for distant earthquakes

monsoon a seasonal reversal of prevailing wind patterns, often associated with pronounced changes in moisture

N

nation a cultural concept for a group of people bound together by a strong sense of shared values and cultural characteristics, including language, religion, and common history

nebula a cloud of interstellar gas and dust

node a point where distinct lines or objects intersect

Normalized Difference Vegetation Index (NDVI) a measurement of plant growth density over an area of the Earth's surface, measured on a scale of 0.1 to 0.8 (low to high vegetation)

North Pole the most northerly geographic point on the Earth; the northern end of the Earth's axis of rotation; 90° N

nuclear weapon a weapon that utilizes nuclear chain reactions to derive destructive force

O

oasis a fertile area with water and vegetation in a desert

ocean current the regular and persistent flow of water in the oceans, usually driven by atmospheric wind and pressure systems or by regional differences in water density (temperature, salinity)

offshoring relocating business processes to another country, where they are performed by either another branch of the parent company or an external contractor (international outsourcing)

organic relating to or derived from living things

Glossary of Geographic Terms

outsourcing delegating noncore processes from within a business to an external entity such as a subcontractor

oxbow lake a crescent-shaped lake or swamp occupying a channel abandoned by a meandering river

ozone a bluish gas composed of three oxygen atoms and harmful to breathe

ozone layer region of Earth's atmosphere where ozone concentration is relatively high; the ozone layer absorbs harmful ultraviolet rays from the sun

P

paleo-geographic map a map depicting the past positions of the continents, developed from historic magnetic, biological, climatological, and geologic evidence

Pangaea the supercontinent from which today's continents are thought to have originated

peninsula a long piece of land jutting out from a larger piece of land into a body of water

period a basic unit of time on the geologic time scale, generally 35 to 70 million years in duration; a subdivision of an era

Phanerozoic eon an eon of Earth's geologic history that comprises the Paleozoic, Mesozoic, and Cenozoic eras

photosynthesis process by which plants convert carbon dioxide and water to oxygen and carbohydrates

physical geography one of the two major divisions of systematic geography; the spatial analysis of the structure, process, and location of Earth's natural phenomena, such as climate, soil, plants, animals, water, and topography

pilgrimage a typically long and difficult journey to a special place, often of religious importance

plain an extensive flat-lying area characterized generally by the absence of local relief features

planetary nebula an interstellar cloud of gas and dust formed when a star runs out of central nuclear fuel, finally ejecting its outer layers in a gaseous shell

plate tectonics the theory that Earth's lithospheric plates slide or shift slowly over the asthenosphere and that their interactions cause earthquakes, volcanic eruptions, movement of landmasses, and other geologic events

plateau a landform feature characterized by high elevation and gentle upland slopes

point a sharp prominence or headland on the coast that juts out into a body of water

politicide the intentional destruction, in whole or in part, of a group of people based on their political or ideological beliefs

pollution a direct or indirect process resulting from human activity; part of the environment is made potentially or actually unsafe or hazardous to the welfare of the organisms that live in it

porphyry an igneous rock characterized by large crystals within a matrix of much finer crystals

primary energy energy sources as they are found naturally—i.e., before they have been processed or transformed into secondary sources

prime meridian the line of 0° longitude that runs through Greenwich, England, and separates the Eastern and Western Hemispheres

Priscoan eon the earliest eon of Earth's geologic history; also known as the Hadean eon

proliferation the process of growing rapidly and suddenly

Proterozoic eon the eon of geologic time that includes the interval between the Archaean and Phanerozoic eons and is marked by rocks that contain fossils indicating the first appearance of eukaryotic organisms (such as algae)

protogalaxy a cloud of gas, possibly consisting of dark matter, hydrogen, and helium, that is forming into a galaxy

purchasing power parity (PPP) a method of measuring gross domestic product that compares the relative value of currencies based on what each currency will buy in its country of origin; PPP provides a good comparison between national economies and is a decent indicator of living standards

R

rain shadow the dry region on the downwind (leeward) side of a mountain range

raster data spatial data represented as a unified grid of equal-area cells, each with a single numerical value; best suited for contiguous data such as elevation

red dwarf a relatively small, cool, and faint star with a very long estimated life span; the most common type of star

reef a strip of rocks or sand either at or just below the surface of water

refugee a person who flees his/her country of origin to escape danger or persecution for reasons of, for example, race, religion, or political opinion

regolith a layer of disintegrated or partly decomposed rock overlying unweathered parent materials; regolith is usually found in areas of low relief where the physical transport of debris is weak

remote sensing the measurement of some property of an object or terrain by means other than direct contact, usually from aircraft or satellites

renewable resource a resource that can be regenerated or maintained if used at rates that do not exceed natural replenishment

Richter scale a logarithmic scale devised to represent the relative amount of energy released by an earthquake; moment magnitude has superseded the Richter scale as the preferred measurement of earthquake magnitude

rift a long, narrow trough created by plate movement at a divergent boundary

rift valley a long, structural valley formed by the lowering of a block between two parallel faults

Ring of Fire (also Rim of Fire) an arc of volcanoes and tectonic activity along the perimeter of the Pacific Ocean

S

salinization the accumulation of salts in soil

satellite data information collected by a vehicle orbiting a celestial body

savanna a tropical grassland with widely spaced trees; it experiences distinct wet and dry seasons

seamount a submerged volcano rising from the ocean floor

sedimentary the rock type formed from preexisting rocks or pieces of once living organisms; deposits accumulate on Earth's surface, generally with distinctive layering or bedding

solar radiation energy emitted by the sun

solar wind the stream of atoms and ions moving outward from the solar corona at 300 to 500 kilometers per second

solstice a celestial event that occurs twice a year (usually June 20–21 and December 21–22), when the sun appears directly overhead to observers at the Tropic of Cancer or the Tropic of Capricorn

sound a broad channel or passage of water connecting two larger bodies of water or separating an island from the mainland

South Pole the most southerly geographic point on the Earth; the southern end of the Earth's axis of rotation; 90° S

spatial resolution a measure of the smallest distinguishable separation between two objects

spectral resolution a measure of the ability of a sensing system to distinguish electromagnetic radiation of different frequencies

spit beach extension that forms along a shoreline with bays and other indentations

spreading boundary where plates move apart along their common boundary, creating a crack in the Earth's crust (typically at the mid-ocean ridge), which is then filled with upwelling molten rock; also called a divergent boundary

state an area with defined and internationally acknowledged boundaries; a political unit

steppe semiarid, relatively flat, treeless region getting between 10 and 20 inches (25 and 51 cm) of precipitation yearly

strait a narrow passage of water that connects two larger bodies of water

subatomic particle a part of an atom, such as a proton, neutron, or electron

subduction the tectonic process by which the down-bent edge of one lithospheric plate is forced underneath another plate

T

tariff a surcharge on imports levied by a state; a form of protectionism designed to increase imports' market price and thus inhibit their consumption

tectonic plate (also lithospheric or crustal plate) a section of the Earth's rigid outer layer that moves as a distinct unit upon the plastic-like mantle materials in the asthenosphere

temperate mild or moderate

temporal resolution a measure of the frequency with which a sensing system gathers data

terrestrial radiation natural sources of radiation found in earth materials

threatened species species at some, but not immediate, risk of extinction

tide the regular rise and fall of the ocean, caused by the mutual gravitational attraction between the Earth, moon, and sun, as well as the rotation of the Earth-moon system around its center of gravity

ton a unit of weight equal to 2,000 pounds in the U.S. or 2,240 pounds inthe U.K.

tonne (see metric ton)

topography the relief features that are evident on a planetary surface

tornado a violently rotating, funnel-shaped column of air characterized by extremely low atmospheric pressures and exceptional wind speeds generated within intense thunderstorms

tradewind a wind blowing persistently from the same direction; particularly from the subtropical high-pressure centers toward the equatorial low-pressure zone

transgenic an organism artificially or naturally containing one or more genes from a different type of organism

tributary a river or stream flowing into a larger river or stream

tropical warm and moist; occurring in or characteristic of the Tropics

Tropic of Cancer latitude 23.5° N; the farthest northerly excursion of the sun when it is directly overhead

Tropic of Capricorn latitude 23.5° S; the farthest southerly excursion of the sun when it is directly overhead

tsunami a series of ocean waves, often very destructive along coasts, caused by the vertical displacement of the seafloor during an earthquake, submarine landslide, or volcanic eruption

tundra a zone in cold, polar regions (mostly in the Northern Hemisphere) that is transitional between the zone of polar ice and the limit of tree growth; it is usually characterized by low-lying vegetation, with extensive permafrost and waterlogged soils

U

unconformity a discontinuity in sedimentary rocks caused by erosion or nondeposition

uplift the slow, upward movement of Earth's crust

upwelling the process by which water rich in nutrients rises from depth toward the ocean surface; it is usually the result of diverging surface waters

urban agglomeration a group of several cities and/or towns and their suburbs

urbanization a process in which there is an increase in the percentage of people living and working in urban places compared with rural places; a process of change from a rural to urban lifestyle

V

vector data spatial data represented as nodes and connectors identified by geographic coordinates, and related to one another to symbolize geographic features; best suited for geographic features that can be represented as points, lines, or polygons

volcanism the upward movement and expulsion of molten (melted) material and gases from within the Earth's mantle onto the surface, where it cools and hardens, producing characteristic terrain

W

watershed the drainage area of a river and its tributaries

weathering the processes or actions that cause the physical disintegration and chemical decomposition of rock and minerals

westerlies a regular wind that blows from the west

wetland an area of land covered by water or saturated by water sufficiently enough to support vegetation adapted to wet conditions

wilderness a natural environment that has remained essentially undisturbed by human activities and, increasingly, is protected by government or nongovernment organizations

windward the side toward or unsheltered from the wind

X

xerophyte a plant that thrives in a dry environment

Y

yazoo a tributary stream that runs parallel to the main river for some distance

Z

zenith the point in the sky that is immediately overhead; also the highest point above the observer's horizon obtained by a celestial body

zoning the process of subdividing urban areas as a basis for land-use planning and policy

Place-Name Index

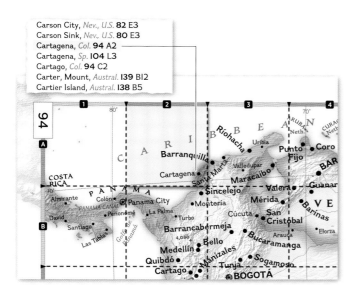

Carson City, *Nev., U.S.* **82** E3
Carson Sink, *Nev., U.S.* **80** E3
Cartagena, *Col.* **94** A2
Cartagena, *Sp.* **104** L3
Cartago, *Col.* **94** C2
Carter, Mount, *Austral.* **139** B12
Cartier Island, *Austral.* **138** B5

The following system is used to locate a place on a map in the *National Geographic Concise Atlas of the World*. The boldface type after an entry refers to the page on which the map is found. The letter-number combination refers to the grid on which the particular place-name is located. The edge of each map is marked horizontally with numbers and vertically with letters. In between, at equally spaced intervals, are index markers (▼). If these markers were connected with lines, each page would be divided into a grid. Take Cartagena, Colombia, for example. The index entry reads "**Cartagena**, *Col.* **94** A2." On page 94, Cartagena is located within the grid square where row A and column 2 intersect (example at left).

A place-name may appear on several maps, but the index lists only the best presentation. Usually, this means that a feature is indexed to the largest-scale map on which it appears in its entirety. (Note: Rivers are often labeled multiple times even on a single map. In such cases, the rivers are indexed to labels that are closest to their mouths.) The name of the country or continent in which a feature lies is shown in italic type and is usually abbreviated. (A full list of abbreviations appears on page 164.)

The index lists more than proper names. Some entries include a description, as in "**Corsica**, island, *Fr.* **102** K5" and "**Danube**, river, *Eur.* **102** J9." In languages other than English, the description of a physical feature may be part of the name; e.g., the "'Erg" in "**Chech, 'Erg**, *Af.* **126** E3," means "sand dune region." The glossary of Foreign Terms on pages 166–167 translates such terms into English.

When a feature or place can be referred to by more than one name, both may appear in the index with cross-references. For example, the entry for Cairo, Egypt, reads "**Cairo** *see* El Qâhira, *Egypt* **128** D9." That entry is "**El Qâhira (Cairo)**, *Egypt* **128** D9."

A

Aarhus, *Den.* **104** F6
Abaco Island, *Bahamas* **75** M9
Abaetetuba, *Braz.* **94** D9
Abaí, *Parag.* **94** J7
Abaiang, island, *Kiribati* **142** E6
Abancay, *Peru* **94** G3
Ābaya, Lake, *Eth.* **126** H10
Abaza, *Russ.* **116** E9
Abbot Ice Shelf, *Antarctica* **152** G3
Abéché, *Chad* **128** F7
Abemama, island, *Kiribati* **142** E6
Aberdeen, *Scot., U.K.* **104** E4
Aberdeen, *Wash., U.S.* **82** B2
Aberdeen, *S. Dak., U.S.* **82** C9
Aberdeen Lake, *Nunavut, Can.* **76** E5
Abidjan, *Côte d'Ivoire* **128** H2
Abilene, *Tex., U.S.* **82** H9
Abitibi, Lake, *Ont., Can.* **74** H8
Abkhazia, disputed territory *Rep. of Georgia* **105** J13
Abminga, *Austral.* **140** G9
Abra Pampa, *Arg.* **94** J5
Absalom, Mount, *Antarctica* **152** D6
Absaroka Range, *Mont., U.S.* **80** C6
Abu Dhabi *see* Abū Ẓaby, *U.A.E.* **116** H5
Abu Hamed, *Sudan* **128** E9
Abuja, *Nigeria* **128** G5
Abū Ẓaby (Abu Dhabi), *U.A.E.* **116** H5
Abyad, El Bahr el *see* White Nile, river, *Af.* **126** G9
Academy Glacier, *Antarctica* **152** F6
Acapulco, *Mex.* **77** P4
Accra, *Ghana* **128** H3
Achinsk, *Russ.* **116** E9
Acklins Island, *Bahamas* **75** N9
Aconcagua, Cerro, *Arg.* **93** L4
Açores (Azores), islands, *Port.* **128** B1
A Coruña, *Sp.* **104** H1
Acraman, Lake, *Austral.* **138** J9
Açu, *Braz.* **94** E11
Ada, *Okla., U.S.* **82** G9
Adair, Cape, *Nunavut, Can.* **74** D8
Adak, island, *Alas., U.S.* **75** R2
Adamawa, region, *Af.* **126** H5
Adam's Bridge, *Asia* **114** K8
Adams, Mount, *Wash., U.S.* **80** B3
'Adan, *Yemen* **116** J4
Adana, *Turk.* **116** F4
Adare, Cape, *Antarctica* **152** M9
Adavale, *Austral.* **141** G12
Ad Dahnā' *Asia, 114* **G4**

Ad Dakhla, *W. Sahara* **128** D1
Ad Dammām, *Saudi Arabia* **116** G4
Ad Dawḩah (Doha), *Qatar* **116** G4
Adelaide, *Austral.* **141** K10
Adelaide, river, *Austral.* **140** B8
Adelaide Island, *Antarctica* **152** D2
Adélie Coast, *Antarctica* **153** M12
Aden, Gulf of, *Indian Oc.* **126** G11
Adieu, Cape, *Austral.* **138** J8
Adirondack Mountains, *N.Y., U.S.* **81** C15
Ādīs Ābeba (Addis Ababa), *Eth.* **128** G9
Admiralty Gulf, *Austral.* **138** B5
Admiralty Island, *Alas., U.S.* **80** L5
Admiralty Islands, *P.N.G.* **142** E3
Admiralty Mountains, *Antarctica* **152** M9
Adriatic Sea, *Atlantic Oc.* **102** K7
Aegean Sea, *Atlantic Oc.* **102** L9
Afghanistan, *Asia* **116** G6
Afognak Island, *Alas., U.S.* **80** M3
Africa **128–129**
Agadez, *Niger* **128** F5
Agadir, *Mor.* **128** C2
Agana *see* Hagåtña, *Guam, U.S.* **142** D3
Agattu, island, *Alas., U.S.* **75** R1
Agnew, *Austral.* **140** H4
Agrakhan Peninsula, *Eur.* **103** H14
Agrihan, island, *N. Mariana Is., U.S.* **142** C3
Agrínio, *Gr.* **104** L8
Agryz, *Russ.* **105** D13
Aguascalientes, *Mex.* **77** N4
Aguja Point, *Peru* **92** E1
Agulhas, Cape, *S. Af.* **127** Q7
Ahaggar Mountains, *Alg.* **126** E5
Ahmadabad (Ahmedabad), *India* **116** J6
Ahmedabad *see* Ahmadabad, *India* **116** J6
Aiken, *S.C., U.S.* **83** H14
Ailinglapalap Atoll, *Marshall Is.* **142** D5
Ailuk Atoll, *Marshall Is.* **142** D6
Ainsworth, *Nebr., U.S.* **82** D8
Aïr Massif, *Niger* **126** F5
Aitutaki Atoll, *Cook Is., N.Z.* **142** G9
Ajaccio, *Fr.* **104** K5
Ajajú, river, *Col.* **92** C3
Ajdābiyā, *Libya* **128** D7
Ajo, *Ariz., U.S.* **82** H4
Akchâr, region, *Mauritania* **126** E1
Akhḍar, Jabal al, *Af.* **126** C7
Akimiski Island, *Nunavut, Can.* **74** G7

Akita, *Japan* **117** E14
Akjoujt, *Mauritania* **128** E1
Akobo, *S. Sudan* **128** G9
Akpatok Island, *Nunavut, Can.* **74** F9
Akranes, *Ice.* **104** A2
Akron, *Ohio, U.S.* **83** E13
Aksu, *China* **116** G8
Alabama, river, *U.S.* **81** J12
Alabama, *U.S.* **83** H13
Alacant *see* Alicante, *Sp.* **104** L3
Alagoinhas, *Braz.* **94** F11
Alakanuk, *Alas., U.S.* **82** K1
Alaköl, lake, *Asia* **114** F9
Alamagan, island *N. Mariana Is., U.S.* **142** C3
Alamogordo, *N. Mex., U.S.* **82** H6
Alamosa, *Colo., U.S.* **82** F6
Åland Islands, *Eur.* **102** D8
Alaska, *U.S.* **82** K2
Alaska, Gulf of, *Alas., U.S.* **80** M3
Alaska Peninsula, *Alas., U.S.* **80** M1
Alaska Range, *Alas., U.S.* **80** L2
Albacete, *Sp.* **104** K2
Albania, *Eur.* **104** K8
Albany, *Austral.* **140** L4
Albany, river, *Ont., Can.* **74** H7
Albany, *Oreg., U.S.* **82** C2
Albany, *Ga., U.S.* **83** H13
Albany, *N.Y., U.S.* **83** D15
Al Baṣrah (Basra), *Iraq* **116** G4
Albatross Bay, *Austral.* **139** B11
Albemarle Sound, *N.C., U.S.* **81** F16
Alberta, *Can.* **76** G4
Albert, Lake, *Dem. Rep. of the Congo–Uganda* **126** H8
Albert, Lake, *Austral.* **139** L10
Albert Lea, *Minn., U.S.* **83** D10
Albert Nile, river, *Af.* **126** H9
Albina Point, *Af.* **127** L5
Albion Downs, *Austral.* **141** E12
Alborán Sea, *Atlantic Oc.* **102** L2
Ålborg, *Den.* **104** E6
Albuquerque, *N. Mex., U.S.* **82** G6
Albury, *Austral.* **141** L13
Alcoota, *Austral.* **140** F9
Aldabra Islands, *Af.* **127** K11
Aldan, river, *Asia* **115** D12
Alegrete, *Braz.* **95** K7
Alejandro Selkirk Island, *S. Amer.* **93** M2
Aleksandrov, *Russ.* **105** E11
Aleksandrovsk Sakhalinskiy, *Russ.* **117** D13
Alenquer, *Braz.* **94** D7
'Alenuihāhā Channel, *Hawai'i, U.S.* **81** M12
Alert, *Nunavut, Can.* **76** B7

Ålesund, *Nor.* **104** C6
Aleutian Islands, *Alas., U.S.* **115** B14
Aleutian Islands, *Alas., U.S.* **75** R2
Aleutian Peninsula, *Alas., U.S.* **80** M2
Aleutian Range, *Alas., U.S.* **75** Q5
Alexander Archipelago, *Alas., U.S.* **74** E2
Alexander Bay, *S. Af.* **129** P6
Alexander Island, *Antarctica* **152** E3
Alexandria, *La., U.S.* **83** J10
Alexandria, *Va., U.S.* **83** F15
Alexandria *see* El Iskandarîya, *Egypt* **128** D8
Alexandrina, Lake, *Austral.* **139** L11
Al Farciya, *W. Sahara* **128** D2
Alger (Algiers), *Alg.* **128** B5
Algeria, *Af.* **128** D3
Algeria, *Af.* **104** M4
Alghiena, *Eritrea* **128** F10
Algiers *see* Alger, *Alg.* **128** B5
Algoa Bay, *S. Af.* **127** P8
Al Ḩarūjal Aswad, range, *Libya* **126** D6
Al Ḩijāz, region, *Saudi Arabia* **116** G3
Al Ḩillah, *Iraq* **116** H4
Alicante (Alacant), *Sp.* **104** L3
Alice, *Austral.* **141** F13
Alice, *Tex., U.S.* **82** K9
Alice Springs, *Austral.* **140** F9
Al Jawf, *Libya* **128** E8
Al Kuwayt (Kuwait City), *Kuwait* **116** G5
Allahabad, *India* **116** J8
Allakaket, *Alas., U.S.* **82** J2
Allan Hills, *Antarctica* **152** K9
Allegheny, river, *Pa., U.S.* **81** D14
Allegheny Mountains, *U.S.* **81** F14
Alliance, *Nebr., U.S.* **82** E8
Allison Peninsula, *Antarctica* **152** F3
Almaden, *Austral.* **141** D13
Al Madīnah (Medina), *Saudi Arabia* **116** G4
Al Manāmah (Manama), *Bahrain* **116** G4
Almaty, *Kaz.* **116** F8
Al Mawşil, *Iraq* **116** F5
Almería, *Sp.* **104** L3
Almirante, *Pan.* **77** Q8
Al Mukallā, *Yemen* **116** J4
Alor, island, *Indonesia* **115** M14
Alotau, *P.N.G.* **141** A15
Aloysius, Mount, *Austral.* **138** G7
Alpena, *Mich., U.S.* **83** C13
Alpha, *Austral.* **141** F13

Alpine, *Tex., U.S.* **82** J7
Alps, *Eur.* **102** J5
Al Quds *see* Jerusalem, *Israel* **116** H4
Alroy Downs, *Austral.* **141** D10
Alta, *Nor.* **104** A8
Altamaha, river, *Ga., U.S.* **81** H14
Altamira, *Braz.* **94** D8
Altar Desert, *Mex.–U.S.* **75** L3
Altay, *China* **116** F9
Altay, *Mongolia* **117** F10
Altay Mountains, *Asia* **114** F9
Altiplano, region, *S. Amer.* **92** G4
Alto Araguaia, *Braz.* **94** G7
Alton, *Ill., U.S.* **83** F11
Altoona, *Pa., U.S.* **83** E14
Alto Purús, river, *S. Amer.* **92** F3
Altun Shan, *Asia* **114** G9
Al' Uwaynat *see* 'Uweinat, Jebel, *Libya* **126** E7
Alvorada, *Braz.* **94** F8
Al Wajh, *Saudi Arabia* **116** G3
Alyangula, *Austral.* **141** B10
Amadeus Depression, *Austral.* **138** F7
Amadeus, Lake, *Austral.* **138** F8
Amadjuak Lake, *Nunavut, Can.* **76** E8
Amamapare, *Indonesia* **117** L15
Amami, island, *Asia* **115** G13
Amami Ōshima, island, *Japan* **142** B1
Amapá, *Braz.* **94** C8
Amarante, *Braz.* **94** E10
Amarillo, *Tex., U.S.* **82** G8
Amata, *Austral.* **140** G8
Amazon, Mouths of the, *S. Amer.* **92** C8
Amazon (Amazonas, Solimões), river, *S. Amer.* **92** D5
Amazonas, river *see* Amazon, river, *S. Amer.* **92** D5
Amazon Basin, *S. Amer.* **92** D4
Ambarchik, *Russ.* **117** B12
Ambargasta, Salinas de, *Arg.* **93** K5
Ambato, *Ecua.* **94** D1
Ambon, *Indonesia* **117** L15
Ambre, Cap d', *Madagascar,* **127** L12
Ambriz, *Angola* **129** K6
Amchitka, island, *Alas., U.S.* **75** R2
American Falls Reservoir *Idaho, U.S.* **80** D5
American Highland, *Antarctica* **153** E12
American Samoa, *U.S., Pac. Oc.* **142** G8

Bakhta, *Russ.* **116** D9
Baki (Baku), *Azerb.* **116** F6
Bakony, range, *Hung.* **102** J7
Baku *see* Baki, *Azerb.* **116** F6
Bakutis Coast, *Antarctica* **152** J4
Balabac, *Malaysia* **115** K13
Balabac Strait, *Philippines* **115** K13
Balakovo, *Russ.* **116** E6
Balaton, lake, *Hung.* **102** J7
Balbina Reservoir (Balbina, Represa da), *Braz.* **92** D6
Bald Mountain, *Nev., U.S.* **80** F4
Baldy Peak, *Ariz., U.S.* **80** G5
Balearic Islands, *Sp.* **102** L4
Balearic Sea, *Atlantic Oc.* **102** K4
Baleia Point (Baleia, Ponta da), *Braz.* **92** H11
Balfour Downs, *Austral.* **140** F4
Balgo, *Austral.* **140** E7
Bali, *India* **115** M13
Balikpapan, *Indonesia* **117** L12
Balkan Mountains, *Eur.* **102** K9
Balkan Peninsula, *Eur.* **102** K8
Balkhash, Lake, *Kaz.* **114** F7
Balladonia, *Austral.* **140** K5
Ballantyne Strait, *N.W.T., Can.* **76** B5
Ballarat, *Austral.* **141** M12
Ballard, Lake, *Austral.* **138** J4
Ballenero Bay (Ballenero, Bahía), *Chile* **93** R4
Ballina, *Austral.* **141** J15
Ball's Pyramid, island, *Austral.* **142** J5
Balonne, river, *Austral.* **139** H14
Balqash, *Kaz.* **116** F8
Balqash Köli *see* Balkhash, Lake, *Kaz.* **114** F7
Balranald, *Austral.* **141** K12
Balsas, river, *Mex.* **75** N4
Balsas, *Braz.* **94** E9
Bălţi, *Mold.* **105** H10
Baltic Plains, *Eur.* **102** F9
Baltic Sea, *Atlantic Oc.* **102** F8
Baltimore, *Md., U.S.* **83** E15
Bam, *Iran* **116** H6
Bamaga, *Austral.* **141** A12
Bamako, *Mali* **128** G2
Bambari, *Cen. Af. Rep.* **128** H7
Bamboo, *Austral.* **140** E4
Bamenda, *Cameroon* **128** H5
Banaba (Ocean Island), *Kiribati* **142** E6
Bañados del Izozog, *Bol.* **92** H6
Bananal Island, *Braz.* **92** F8
Banaras *see* Varanasi, *India* **116** J8
Banâs, Râs, *Egypt* **126** E9
Banat, region, *Rom.–Serb.* **102** J8
Banda Aceh, *Philippines* **117** L10
Bandar-e 'Abbās, *Iran* **116** H5
Bandar Lampung, *Indonesia* **117** M11
Bandar Seri Begawan, *Brunei* **117** L12
Banda Sea, *Pacific Oc.* **115** M14
Bandeirante, *Braz.* **94** G8
Banderas Bay, *Mex.* **75** N3
Bandundu, *Dem. Rep. of the Congo* **128** J6
Bandung, *Indonesia* **117** M11
Banff, *Alta., Can.* **76** G4
Bangalore *see* Bengaluru, *India* **116** K8
Bangassou, *Cen. Af. Rep.* **128** H7
Banggi, island, *Malaysia* **115** K13
Banghāzī (Benghazi), *Libya* **128** C7
Bangka, island, *Indonesia* **115** M12
Bangkok *see* Krung Thep, *Thai.* **117** K10
Bangladesh, *Asia* **116** J9
Bangor, *Me., U.S.* **83** B17
Bangui, *Cen. Af. Rep.* **128** H7
Bangweulu, Lake, *Zambia* **127** L9
Bani, river, *Mali* **126** F3
Banja Luka, *Bosn. & Herzg.* **104** J7
Banjarmasin, *Indonesia* **117** M13
Banjul, *Gambia* **128** F1
Banks Island, *N.W.T., Can.* **74** C5
Banks Islands, *Vanuatu* **142** G6
Banks Strait, *Austral.* **138** L8
Banzare Coast, *Antarctica* **153** L13
Baotou, *China* **117** F11
Baqên, *China* **117** H10
Baraawe, *Somalia* **128** J11
Barahona, *Dom. Rep.* **77** P10
Baraka, river, *Af.* **126** F10
Baranavichy, *Belarus* **104** G9
Baranof Island, *Alas., U.S.* **76** E2
Barataria Bay, *La., U.S.* **81** K12
Barbados, *N. Amer.* **77** P12
Barbados, island, *N. Amer.* **92** A6
Barcaldine, *Austral.* **141** F12
Barcelona, *Sp.* **104** K4
Barcelona, *Venez.* **94** A5
Barcelos, *Braz.* **94** D5
Barcoo, river, *Austral.* **139** F12
Barents Sea, *Arctic Oc.* **103** A10
Bargaal, *Somalia* **128** G12
Bari, *It.* **104** K7
Barinas, *Venez.* **94** B4
Barisan Mountains, *Asia* **115** M11
Barito, river, *Asia* **115** L13
Barkley, Lake, *Ky., U.S.* **81** F12
Barkly Tableland, *Austral.* **138** D9
Barlee, Lake, *Austral.* **138** H4
Barnaul, *Russ.* **116** E8
Barquisimeto, *Venez.* **94** A4
Barra, *Braz.* **94** F10
Barra do Corda, *Braz.* **94** E10
Barra do Garças, *Braz.* **94** G7
Barra do São Manuel, *Braz.* **94** E7
Barrancabermeja, *Col.* **94** B2
Barranquilla, *Col.* **94** A2
Barra Point, *Mozambique* **127** N10
Barreiras, *Braz.* **94** F10
Barreirinhas, *Braz.* **94** D10
Barretos, *Braz.* **94** H9
Barrow, *Alas., U.S.* **82** H2
Barrow Creek, *Austral.* **140** E8
Barrow Island, *Austral.* **138** E2
Barrow, Point, *Alas., U.S.* **80** H2
Bartica, *Guyana* **94** B6
Bartle Frere (South Peak) *Austral.* **139** D13
Bartlesville, *Okla., U.S.* **83** G10
Baruun-Urt, *Mongolia* **117** F11
Barwon, river, *Austral.* **139** J14
Basankusu, *Dem. Rep. of the Congo* **128** J7
Bascuñán, Cape (Bascuñán, Cabo), *Chile* **93** K3
Bashi Channel, *Taiwan, China* **115** H13
Basilan, island, *Philippines* **115** K14
Basra (Al Başrah), *Iraq* **116** G4
Basseterre, *St. Kitts and Nevis* **77** N11
Bass, Îlots de *see* Marotiri *Fr. Polynesia, Fr.* **143** H11
Bass Strait, *Austral.* **139** M12
Bastia, *Fr.* **104** K6
Bata, *Eq. Guinea* **128** H5
Batabanó, Golfo de, *Cuba* **77** N8
Batangas City, *Philippines* **117** K13
Batan Islands, *Philippines* **115** H13
Batemans Bay, *Austral.* **141** L14
Bathurst, *N.B., Can.* **76** H10
Bathurst Inlet, *Nunavut, Can.* **74** E5
Bathurst Island, *Austral.* **138** A7
Bathurst Island, *Nunavut, Can.* **74** C6
Batna, *Alg.* **128** C5
Baton Rouge, *La., U.S.* **83** J11
Battle Harbour, *Nfdl. & Lab., Can.* **76** G10
Baubau, *Indonesia* **117** M14
Baudó, Serranía de, *S. Amer.* **92** B2
Bawku, *Ghana* **128** G4
Bayamo, *Cuba* **77** N9
Bayan Har Shan, *China* **115** G10
Bayanhongor, *Mongolia* **117** F10
Bay City, *Tex., U.S.* **83** K10
Bay City, *Mich., U.S.* **83** D13
Bay Islands, *Hond.* **75** P7
Baykal, Ozero *see* Baikal, Lake, *Russ.* **117** E11
Baykonur, *Kaz.* **116** F7
Plenty, Bay of, *N.Z.* **142** K6
Baytown, *Tex., U.S.* **83** J10
Bazaruto Island, *Af.* **127** M10
Beachport, *Austral.* **141** L11
Beagle Bay, *Austral.* **138** C4
Beagle Bay, *Austral.* **140** D4
Beagle Gulf, *Austral.* **138** A7
Beardmore Glacier, *Antarctica* **152** H8
Bear Paw Mountains, *Alas., U.S.* **80** B6
Bear River Range, *Idaho, U.S.* **80** D5
Beatrice, *Nebr., U.S.* **82** E9
Beatty, *Nev., U.S.* **82** F3
Beaufort, *S.C., U.S.* **83** H14
Beaufort Sea, *Arctic Oc.* **80** H3
Beaumont, *Tex., U.S.* **83** J10
Beaver, *Alas., U.S.* **82** K3
Beaver Glacier, *Antarctica* **153** C13
Béchar, *Alg.* **128** C4
Beckley, *W. Va., U.S.* **83** F14
Beddouza, Cape, *Mor.* **126** C2
Bedford, Cape, *Austral.* **139** C13
Bedford Downs, *Austral.* **140** C6
Bedourie, *Austral.* **141** F10
Beechey Group *see* Chichi Rettō, islands, *Japan* **142** B3
Beenleigh, *Austral.* **141** H15
Beethoven Peninsula, *Antarctica* **152** E3
Beeville, *Tex., U.S.* **82** K9
Bega, *Austral.* **141** L14
Behchokọ̀, *N.W.T., Can.* **76** E4
Beijing (Peking), *China* **117** F12
Beira, *Mozambique* **129** M10
Beirut *see* Beyrouth, *Leb.* **116** F4
Bei Shan, *China* **115** G10
Bejaïa, Gulf of, *Alg.* **126** B4
Bekily, *Madagascar* **129** N11
Belagavi (Belgaum), *India* **116** K7
Belarus, *Eur.* **104** F9
Bela Vista, *Braz.* **94** H7
Belaya, river, *Eur.* **103** D14
Belcher Islands, *Nunavut, Can.* **74** G7
Belele, *Austral.* **140** G3
Belém, *Braz.* **94** D9
Belen, *N. Mex., U.S.* **82** G6
Bélep, Îles, *New Caledonia, Fr.* **142** G5
Belfast, *N. Ire., U.K.* **104** E3
Belgaum *see* Belagavi, *India* **116** K7
Belgica Mountains, *Antarctica* **153** B11
Belgium, *Eur.* **104** G5
Belgorod, *Russ.* **105** G11
Belgrade *see* Beograd, *Serb.* **104** J8
Belgrano II, station, *Antarctica* **152** D6
Belize, *N. Amer.* **77** P7
Belize City, *Belize* **77** P7
Belle Fourche, river *S. Dak.–Wyo., U.S.* **80** D7
Belle Fourche, *S. Dak., U.S.* **82** D8
Belle Isle, Strait of *Nfdl. & Lab., Can.* **74** G10
Belleville, *Ill., U.S.* **83** F11
Bellingham, *Wash., U.S.* **82** A3
Bellinghausen Sea, *Pacific Oc.* **152** F2
Bellingshausen, station, *Antarctica* **152** B3
Bello, *Col.* **94** B2
Belluno, *It.* **104** J6
Belmonte, *Braz.* **94** G11
Belmopan, *Belize* **77** P6
Belo-Tsiribihina, *Madagascar* **129** M11
Belo Horizonte, *Braz.* **94** H10
Beloretsk, *Russ.* **105** D15
Beloyarskiy, *Russ.* **105** A14
Beloye, Lake (Beloye Ozero), *Russ.* **103** D11
Beloye More (White Sea) *Arctic Oc.* **105** B10
Belukha, peak, *Asia* **114** F9
Belyando, river, *Austral.* **139** F13
Belyy Island, *Asia* **114** C9
Bemaraha Plateau, *Af.* **127** M11
Bembe, *Angola* **129** K6
Bemidji, *Minn., U.S.* **83** C10
Benadir, region, *Af.* **126** J11
Bendigo, *Austral.* **141** L12
Bengal, Bay of, *Indian Oc.* **114** K9
Bengaluru (Bangalore), *India* **116** K8
Benghazi *see* Banghāzī, *Libya* **128** C7
Bengkulu, *Indonesia* **117** M11
Bengo Bay, *Ang.* **127** K5
Benguela, *Angola* **129** L6
Beni, river, *Bol.* **92** G4
Beni Abbes, *Alg.* **128** C4
Benin, *Af.* **128** G4
Benin, Bight of, *Af.* **126** H4
Benlidi, *Austral.* **141** G13
Bennett, Lake, *Austral.* **138** F7
Ben Nevis, peak, *Scot., U.K.* **102** E4
Benson, *Ariz., U.S.* **82** H5
Bentinck Island, *Austral.* **139** D11
Benue, river, *Nigeria* **128** G5
Beograd (Belgrade), *Serb.* **104** J8
Berbera, *Somalia* **128** G11
Berbérati, *Cen. Af. Rep.* **128** H6
Berdyans'k, *Ukr.* **105** H12
Berens River, *Man., Can.* **76** G6
Berezniki, *Russ.* **105** C13
Berezovo, *Russ.* **105** A14
Bergen, *Nor.* **104** D6
Bering Island (Bering, Ostrov), *Russ.* **75** Q1
Beringovskiy, *Russ.* **117** A13
Bering Sea, *Pac. Oc.* **75** Q2
Bering Strait, *Russ.–U.S.* **74** B1
Berkner Island, *Antarctica* **152** D6
Berlin, *Ger.* **104** G6
Berlin, Mount, *Antarctica* **152** J5
Bermejo, river, *Arg.* **92** J6
Bermuda Islands, *N. Amer.* **75** L11
Bern, *Switz.* **104** H5
Bernardo O'Higgins Riquelme, station, *Antarctica* **152** B2
Bernier Island, *Austral.* **138** G1
Berri, *Austral.* **141** K11
Berry, *Eur.* **102** H4
Bertholet, Cape, *Austral.* **138** D4
Beru, island, *Kiribati* **142** E6
Bessarabia, region, *Mold.* **103** H10
Bessemer, *Ala., U.S.* **83** H12
Beswick, *Austral.* **140** B8
Bethel, *Alas., U.S.* **82** L1
Betoota, *Austral.* **141** G11
Betpaqdala, desert, *Kaz.* **114** F7
Beyla, *Guinea* **128** G2
Beyneu, *Kaz.* **116** E6
Beyrouth (Beirut), *Leb.* **116** F4
Bharati, station, *Antarctica* **153** E13
Bhopal, *India* **116** J8
Bhutan, *Asia* **116** H9
Biak, island, *Indonesia* **115** K16
Białowieża Forest, *Eur.* **102** G9
Białystok, *Pol.* **104** G8
Biarritz, *Fr.* **104** J3
Bielefeld, *Ger.* **104** G6
Bienville, Lac, *Que., Can.* **74** G8
Bié Plateau, *Af.* **127** L6
Big Delta, *Alas., U.S.* **82** K3
Big Falls, *Minn., U.S.* **83** B10
Biggenden, *Austral.* **141** G15
Bighorn, river, *Mont., U.S.* **80** C6
Bighorn Mountains, *Mont., U.S.* **80** C6
Big Spring, *Tex., U.S.* **82** H8
Big Trout Lake, *Ont., Can.* **76** G7
Bikini Atoll, *Marshall Is.* **142** D5
Bila Tserkva, *Ukr.* **105** H10
Bilbao, *Sp.* **104** J3
Billilla, *Austral.* **141** J12
Billiluna, *Austral.* **140** D6
Billings, *Mont., U.S.* **82** C6
Billiton, *Indonesia* **115** M12
Bilma, *Niger* **128** F6
Biloela, *Austral.* **141** G15
Biloxi, *Miss., U.S.* **83** J12
Biltine, *Chad* **128** F7
Bilwi, *Nicar.* **77** P8
Bimberi Peak, *Austral.* **139** L13
Bingham, *Me., U.S.* **83** B16
Binghamton, *N.Y., U.S.* **83** D15
Binjai, *Indonesia* **117** L10
Bioko, island, *Eq. Guinea* **126** H5
Birao, *Cen. Af. Rep.* **128** G8
Birch Mountains, *Alta., Can.* **74** F4
Birdsville, *Austral.* **141** G10
Bīrjand, *Iran* **116** G6
Birmingham, *Eng., U.K.* **104** F4
Birmingham, *Ala., U.S.* **83** H13
Bir Mogreïn (Fort Trinquet), *Mauritania* **128** D2
Birnie Island, *Kiribati* **142** E8
Birrindudu, *Austral.* **140** D7
Birsk, *Russ.* **105** D14
Bisbee, *Ariz., U.S.* **82** H5
Biscay, Bay of, *Atlantic Oc.* **102** H3
Biscayne Bay, *Fla., U.S.* **81** K15
Biscoe Islands, *Antarctica* **152** D2
Bishkek, *Kyrg.* **116** F8
Bishop, *Calif., U.S.* **82** F3
Biskra, *Alg.* **128** C5
Bismarck, *N. Dak., U.S.* **82** C8
Bismarck Archipelago, *P.N.G.* **142** F3
Bismarck Sea, *P.N.G.* **142** F3
Bissagos Islands, *Af.* **126** G1
Bissau, *Guinea-Bissau* **128** G1
Bitola, *Maced.* **104** K8
Bitterroot Range *Idaho–Mont., U.S.* **80** B4
Biya, river, *Asia* **114** E9
Bizerte, *Tun.* **128** B5
Bjargtangar, *Ice.* **102** A2
Black, river, *Ark., U.S.* **81** G11
Blackall, *Austral.* **141** F13
Black Belt, region, *U.S.* **81** H12
Blackburn, Mount, *Alas., U.S.* **80** L4
Black Coast, *Antarctica* **152** D3
Blackdown, *Austral.* **141** D12
Blackfoot, *Idaho, U.S.* **82** D5
Black Forest, *Ger.* **102** H6
Black Hills, *S. Dak., U.S.* **80** D7
Black Irtysh, river, *Asia* **114** F9
Black Mesa, *Okla., U.S.* **80** G8
Black Mountain, *Ky., U.S.* **81** F13
Black Mountains, *Ariz., U.S.* **80** G4
Black Range, *N. Mex., U.S.* **80** H6
Black Rock Desert, *Nev., U.S.* **80** D3
Black Sea, *Atlantic Oc.* **103** K11
Black Sea Lowland, *Eur.* **103** H10
Black Volta, river, *Af.* **126** G3
Blackwater, *Austral.* **141** F14
Blackwood, river, *Austral.* **138** L3
Blagoveshchensk, *Russ.* **117** E12
Blanc, Mont, *Fr.–It.* **102** J5
Blanca Bay (Blanca, Bahía) *S. Amer.* **93** M6
Blanca Peak, *Colo., U.S.* **80** F7
Blanc, Cape, *Mauritania* **126** E1
Blanc, Cape, *Tun.* **126** B5
Blanche, Lake, *Austral.* **139** H11
Blanco, Cape, *Oreg., U.S.* **80** C2
Blantyre, *Malawi* **129** L9
Blåvands Point, *Eur.* **102** F6
Blaze, Point, *Austral.* **138** B7

Blinman, Austral. 141 J10
Bloemfontein, S. Af. 129 P7
Blönduós, Ice. 104 A3
Bloomington, Ill., U.S. 83 E11
Bluefield, W. Va., U.S. 83 F14
Bluefields, Nicar. 77 Q8
Blue Mountains, Austral. 139 K14
Blue Mountains, Oreg.–Wash., U.S. 80 C4
Blue Mud Bay, Austral. 139 B10
Blue Nile see Azraq, El Bahr el, river, Af. 128 G9
Blue Ridge, U.S. 81 G14
Bluff Knoll, Austral. 138 K3
Bluff Point, Austral. 138 H2
Blumenau, Braz. 95 K8
Boa Vista, Braz. 94 C6
Bobo Dioulasso, Burkina Faso 128 G3
Boca do Acre, Braz. 94 F4
Boca Grande, Venez. 92 B6
Bodaybo, Russ. 117 D11
Bodele Depression, Af. 126 F6
Bodø, Nor. 104 B7
Bogalusa, La., U.S. 83 J12
Bogan, river, Austral. 139 J13
Bogantungan, Austral. 141 F13
Bogda Feng, peak, Asia 114 F9
Bogda Shan, China 114 F9
Bogong, Mount, Austral. 139 L13
Bogotá, Col. 94 C3
Bo Hai, bay, China 115 F12
Bohemian Forest, Ger. 102 G6
Bohol Sea, Philippines 115 K14
Bois, river, S. Amer. 92 G8
Boise, Idaho, U.S. 82 C4
Bojeador, Cape, Asia 115 J13
Boké, Guinea 128 G1
Boknafjorden, bay, Nor. 102 D5
Bolinao, Cape, Asia 115 J13
Bolivia, S. Amer. 94 G5
Bollon, Austral. 141 H13
Bologna, It. 104 J6
Bologoye, Russ. 105 E10
Bol'sheretsk, Russ. 117 D13
Bol'shevik Island (Bol'shevik, Ostrov), Russ. 115 B10
Bol'shezemel'skaya Tundra, Russ. 103 A12
Boma, Dem. Rep. of the Congo 129 K6
Bomba, Gulf of, Libya 126 C7
Bombala, Austral. 141 L13
Bombay see Mumbai, India 116 J7
Bomu, river, Af. 126 H7
Bonaire, island, Neth., Lesser Antilles 77 P11
Bonaire, N. Amer. 94 A4
Bonaire, island, N. Amer. 92 A4
Bonaparte Archipelago, Austral. 138 B5
Bonavista Bay, Nfdl. & Lab., Can. 74 G11
Bondo, Dem. Rep. of the Congo 128 H8
Bone, Gulf of, Pac. Oc. 115 L14
Bongo Lava, Af. 127 M11
Bongos, Chaîne des, Cen. Af. Rep. 126 H7
Bonifacio, Strait of, Fr. 102 K5
Bonin Islands (Ogasawara Islands), Japan 115 G15
Bonners Ferry, Idaho, U.S. 82 B5
Bonnie Rock, Austral. 140 J4
Bonshaw, Austral. 141 H14
Booligal, Austral. 141 K12
Boonderoo, Austral. 141 E13
Boorabbin, Austral. 140 J4
Booroondara, Mount, Austral. 139 J12
Boosaaso (Bosaso), Somalia 128 G12
Boothia, Gulf of, Nunavut, Can. 74 D6
Boothia Peninsula, Nunavut, Can. 74 D6
Bopeechee, Austral. 141 H10
Bor, S. Sudan 128 H9
Bora-Bora, island, Fr. Polynesia, Fr. 143 G10
Borah Peak, Idaho, U.S. 80 C5
Borba, Braz. 94 E6
Borborema Plateau, Braz. 92 F11
Borchgrevink Coast, Antarctica 152 M9
Bordeaux, Fr. 104 J3
Borden Island, N.W.T., Can. 74 B6
Borden Peninsula, Nunavut, Can. 74 D7
Bordertown, Austral. 141 L11
Borger, Tex., U.S. 82 G8
Borg Massif, Antarctica 152 B8
Borisoglebsk, Russ. 105 G12
Borkou, region, Chad 128 F7
Borneo, Indonesia 115 L12
Bornholm, island, Den. 102 F7
Borroloola, Austral. 141 C10
Borzya, Russ. 117 E11
Bosaso see Boosaaso, Somalia 128 G12
Bosnia and Herzgegovina, Eur. 104 J7
Bosporus see İstanbul Boğazı, strait, Turk. 105 K10
Bossangoa, Cen. Af. Rep. 128 H7
Bossut, Cape, Austral. 138 D4
Boston, Mass., U.S. 83 D16
Boston Mountains, Ark., U.S. 81 G10
Botany Bay, Austral. 139 L14
Bothnia, Gulf of, Atlantic Oc. 102 D8
Botswana, Af. 129 N7
Bouaké, Côte d'Ivoire 128 G3
Bouar, Cen. Af. Rep. 128 H6
Boû Djébéha, Mali 128 F3
Bougainville, Cape, Austral. 138 B5
Bougainville, island, P.N.G. 142 F4
Boujdour, Cape, Af. 126 D1
Boulder, Colo., U.S. 82 E7
Boulder City, Nev., U.S. 82 F4
Boulia, Austral. 141 F11
Boundary Peak, Nev., U.S. 80 F3
Bounty Islands, N.Z. 142 L7
Bourke, Austral. 141 J13
Bowen, Austral. 141 E14
Bowling Green, Ky., U.S. 83 F13
Bowling Green Bay, Austral. 139 E14
Bowman Glacier, Antarctica 152 H7
Bowman Island, Antarctica 153 H15
Boyarka, Russ. 117 C10
Boyoma Falls, Dem. Rep. of the Congo 126 J8
Bozashchy Peninsula (Bozashchy Tubegi), Kaz. 103 H15
Bozeman, Mont., U.S. 82 C5
Brabant, Eur. 102 G5
Brabant Island, Antarctica 152 C1
Bradenton, Fla., U.S. 83 K14
Bradford, Pa., U.S. 83 D14
Braga, Port. 104 J1
Brahmapur, India 116 J9
Brahmaputra, river, Asia 115 H10
Brăila, Rom. 105 J10
Brainerd, Minn., U.S. 83 C10
Bramwell, Austral. 141 B12
Branco, Cape, S. Amer. 92 E12
Branco, river, Braz. 92 D6
Brandberg, peak, Af. 127 M6
Brandenburg, region, Ger. 102 G7
Brandon, Man., Can. 76 H5
Bransby, Austral. 141 H12
Bransfield Strait, Antarctica 152 C2
Brasilelro, Planalto, Braz. 94 G9
Brasília, Braz. 94 G9
Braşov, Rom. 104 J9
Brasstown Bald, peak, Ga., U.S. 81 G13
Bratislava, Slovakia 104 H8
Bratsk, Russ. 117 E10
Bratsk Reservoir, Asia 115 E10
Braunschweig see Brunswick, Ger. 104 G6
Brazil, S. Amer. 94 F7
Brazilian Highlands, S. Amer. 92 G9
Brazos, river, Tex., U.S. 80 H9
Brazzaville, Congo 128 J5
Bredy, Russ. 105 E15
Breiðafjörður, Ice. 102 A2
Breid Bay, Antarctica 153 B10
Brejo, Braz. 94 D10
Bremen, Ger. 104 F6
Bremerton, Wash., U.S. 82 A3
Brest, Belarus 104 G9
Brest, Fr. 104 G3
Breton Sound, La., U.S. 81 J12
Brewarrina, Austral. 141 J13
Bria, Cen. Af. Rep. 128 H7
Bridgeport, Conn., U.S. 83 D16
Bridgman, Cape (Bridgman, Kap), Greenland, Den. 74 A7
Brisbane, Austral. 141 H15
Bristol, Eng., U.K. 104 F4
Bristol, Tenn., U.S. 83 F13
Bristol Bay, Alas., U.S. 80 M2
Bristol Channel, Eng.–Wales, U.K. 102 F3
British Columbia, Can. 76 F3
British Isles, Eur. 102 D3
British Mountains, Alas., U.S. 80 J4
Brittany, region, Fr. 102 G3
Brive, Fr. 104 J4
Brno, Czech Rep. 104 H7
Broad, river, S.C., U.S. 81 G14
Broad Sound, Austral. 139 F14
Brochet, Man., Can. 76 F5
Brock Island, N.W.T., Can. 76 B5
Brodeur Peninsula, Nunavut, Can. 74 D7
Broken Bay, Austral. 139 K14
Broken Hill, Austral. 141 J11
Brokopondo, Suriname 94 B7
Brønnøysund, Nor. 104 C7
Brookings, S. Dak., U.S. 82 D9
Brooks, Alta., Can. 76 G4
Brooks Range, Alas., U.S. 80 J2
Broome, Austral. 140 D4
Broughton Islands, Austral. 139 K15
Brownfield, Tex., U.S. 82 H8
Brownsville, Tex., U.S. 82 L9
Brownwood, Tex., U.S. 82 J8
Browse Island, Austral. 138 B5
Bruce, Mount, Austral. 138 F3
Bruce Rock, Austral. 140 K4
Brunei, Asia 117 L13
Brunette Downs, Austral. 141 D10
Brunswick, Ga., U.S. 83 H14
Brunswick (Braunschweig), Ger. 104 G6
Brussel see Bruxelles, Belg. 104 G4
Brüssel see Bruxelles, Belg. 104 G4
Brussels see Bruxelles, Belg. 104 G4
Bruxelles (Brussels, Brüssel, Brussel), Belg. 104 G4
Bryan, Tex., U.S. 82 J9
Bryan Coast, Antarctica 152 G3
Bryansk, Russ. 105 F11
Bucaramanga, Col. 94 B3
Buccaneer Archipelago, Austral. 138 C5
Buchanan, Liberia 128 H2
Buchan Gulf, Nunavut, Can. 76 D8
Bucharest see Bucureşti, Rom. 104 J9
Buchon, Point, Calif., U.S. 80 F2
Buckalow, Austral. 141 K11
Buckingham Bay, Austral. 139 A10
Buckland Tableland, Austral. 139 G13
Bucureşti (Bucharest), Rom. 104 J9
Budapest, Hung. 104 H7
Bud Coast, Antarctica 153 J14
Buenaventura, Mex. 77 L4
Buenaventura, Col. 94 C1
Buenaventura Bay, S. Amer. 92 C1
Buenos Aires, Arg. 95 M6
Buenos Aires, Lake, Arg.–Chile 93 P4
Buffalo, Wyo., U.S. 82 D6
Buffalo, N.Y., U.S. 83 D14
Buffalo Hump, peak, Idaho, U.S. 80 C4
Bug, river, Eur. 102 G9
Buir Nur, lake, Asia 115 F11
Bujumbura, Burundi 128 J9
Bukavu, Dem. Rep. of the Congo 128 J8
Bukhta Dezhneva, Russ. 77 P2
Bulahdelah, Austral. 141 K15
Bulawayo, Zimb. 129 M8
Bulgan, Mongolia 117 F10
Bulgaria, Eur. 104 K9
Bulimba, Austral. 141 C12
Bulloo Downs, Austral. 140 G3
Bulloo Downs, Austral. 141 H12
Bullo River, Austral. 140 C7
Bull Shoals Lake, Ark.–Mo., U.S. 81 G11
Bulpunga, Austral. 141 K11
Bumba, Dem. Rep. of the Congo 128 H7
Bunbury, Austral. 140 K3
Bundarra, Austral. 141 J15
Bungo Strait, Pac. Oc. 115 G14
Bunia, Dem. Rep. of the Congo 128 J9
Bura, Kenya 128 J10
Burakin, Austral. 140 J3
Burdekin, river, Austral. 139 E13
Burgas, Bulg. 105 K10
Burgas Bay, Eur. 103 K10
Burgos, Sp. 104 J2
Burgundy, region, Fr. 102 H5
Burica Point, Pan. 75 R8
Burke Island, Antarctica 152 H3
Burketown, Austral. 141 D11
Burkina Faso, Af. 128 F3
Burley, Idaho, U.S. 82 D5
Burlington, Iowa, U.S. 83 E11
Burlington, Vt., U.S. 83 C15
Burma see Myanmar, Asia 117 J10
Burnie, Austral. 140 L7
Burns, Oreg., U.S. 82 C3
Burnside, Lake, Austral. 138 G5
Burra, Austral. 141 K10
Burragorang, Lake, Austral. 139 K14
Burrendong Reservoir, Austral. 139 K13
Bursa, Turk. 116 E4
Bûr Sa'îd (Port Said), Egypt 128 C8
Buru, island, Indonesia 115 L14
Burundi, Af. 128 J9
Busan (Pusan), S. Korea 117 G13
Busanga Swamp, Zambia 127 L8
Busselton, Austral. 140 K3
Buta, Dem. Rep. of the Congo 128 H8
Butaritari, island, Kiribati 142 E6
Butembo, Dem. Rep. of the Congo 128 J8
Buton, island, Indonesia 115 L14
Butte, Mont., U.S. 82 C5
Buxoro, Uzb. 116 F7
Bydgoszcz, Pol. 104 F7
Bylot Island, Nunavut, Can. 74 D7
Byrdbreen, Antarctica 153 B10
Byrd Glacier, Antarctica 152 J9
Byrock, Austral. 141 J13
Byron, Cape, Austral. 139 H15

C

Caazapá, Parag. 94 J7
Caballo Reservoir, N. Mex., U.S. 80 H6
Cabinda, Angola 129 K5
Cabinda, Af. 129 K5
Caboolture, Austral. 141 H15
Cabo San Lucas, Mex. 77 M2
Cabot Strait, N.S., Can. 74 H10
Cabrobó, Braz. 94 F11
Cáceres, Sp. 104 K2
Cachimbo, Braz. 94 F7
Cachoeira do Sul, Braz. 95 K7
Cachoeiro do Itapemirim, Braz. 94 H10
Cacolo, Angola 129 L7
Caçu, Braz. 94 H8
Cacuri, Venez. 94 B5
Cadale, Somalia 128 H12
Cadillac, Mich., U.S. 83 D12
Cádiz, Sp. 104 L1
Caerdydd see Cardiff, Wales, U.K. 104 F3
Cagayan de Oro, Philippines 117 K14
Cagliari, It. 104 L5
Cagliari, Gulf of, It. 102 L5
Cahora Bassa, Lago de, Mozambique 127 L8
Caicó, Braz. 94 E11
Caicos Islands, Turks & Caicos Is. 75 N10
Caird Coast, Antarctica 152 C6
Cairns, Austral. 141 D13
Cairo, Ill., U.S. 83 F11
Cairo see El Qâhira, Egypt 128 D9
Cajamarca, Peru 94 E1
Calabozo, Venez. 94 B4
Calabria, Eur. 102 L7
Calais, Fr. 104 G5
Calais, Me., U.S. 83 B17
Calama, Braz. 94 E5
Calama, Chile 94 J4
Calamar, Col. 94 C3
Calcanhar, Point (Calcanhar, Ponta do), Braz. 92 E12
Calçoene, Braz. 94 C8
Calcutta see Kolkata, India 116 J9
Caldera, Chile 95 K4
Caldwell, Idaho, U.S. 82 C4
Caledon Bay, Austral. 139 B10
Calgary, Alta., Can. 76 G4
Cali, Col. 94 C2
Caliente, Nev., U.S. 82 F4
California, U.S. 82 D2
California, Gulf of, Mex. 75 L3
Callabonna, Lake, Austral. 139 H11
Callao, Peru 94 G2
Calliope Range, Austral. 139 G15
Calulo, Angola 129 L6
Calvert Hills, Austral. 141 D10
Calvinia, S. Af. 129 P7
Camagüey, Cuba 77 N9
Camapuã, Braz. 94 H7
Camargo, Bol. 94 H5
Camarón, Cape, Hond. 75 P8
Camarones, Arg. 95 P5
Camarones Bay (Camarones, Bahía), Arg. 93 P5
Camballin, Austral. 140 D5
Cambodia, Asia 117 K11
Cambrian Mountains, Wales, U.K. 102 F4
Cambridge Bay, Nunavut, Can. 76 D6
Cambridge Gulf, Austral. 138 C6
Camden, Ark., U.S. 83 H11
Camden Bay, Alas., U.S. 80 J3
Cameroon, Af. 128 H5
Camiri, Bol. 94 H5
Camocim, Braz. 94 D11
Camooweal, Austral. 141 E10
Campania, Eur. 102 K7
Campbell Hill, Ohio, U.S. 81 E13
Campbell Island (Motu Ihupuku), N.Z. 142 M6
Campbell River, B.C., Can. 76 G2
Campbell Town, Austral. 140 L8
Campeche, Mex. 77 N6
Campina Grande, Braz. 94 E11
Campinas, Braz. 94 J8

Estância, *Braz.* **94** F11
Este, Punta del, *S. Amer.* **93** L7
Estevan, *Sask., Can.* **76** H5
Estonia, *Eur.* **104** E9
Etadunna, *Austral.* **141** H10
Ethiopia, *Af.* **128** H10
Ethiopian Highlands, *Af.* **126** G9
Etna, peak, *It.* **102** L7
Etosha Pan, *Namibia* **127** M6
Euboea, *Gr.* **102** L9
Eucla, *Austral.* **140** J7
Eucla Basin, *Austral.* **138** K5
Eucumbene, Lake, *Austral.* **139** L13
Eudunda, *Austral.* **141** K10
Eufaula Lake, *Okla., U.S.* **81** G10
Eugene, *Oreg., U.S.* **82** C2
Eugenia Point (Eugenia, Punta), *Mex.* **75** L2
Eulo, *Austral.* **141** H13
Euphrates, river, *Asia* **114** F4
Eurardy, *Austral.* **140** H2
Eureka, *Nunavut, Can.* **76** B6
Eureka, *Calif., U.S.* **82** D2
Europa, Île, *Fr.* **127** N10
Europe *104–105*
Eva Downs, *Austral.* **140** D9
Evanston, *Wyo., U.S.* **82** E5
Evanston, *Ill., U.S.* **83** E12
Evansville, *Ind., U.S.* **83** F12
Everard, Lake, *Austral.* **138** J9
Everard Park, *Austral.* **140** G8
Everest, Mount, *China–Nepal,* **114** H9
Everett, *Wash., U.S.* **82** B3
Everglades, The, *Fla., U.S.* **81** L15
Executive Committee Range, *Antarctica* **152** J5
Exeter, *Eng., U.K.* **104** G3
Exmouth, *Austral.* **140** F1
Exmouth Gulf , *Austral.* **138** F1
Extremadura, *Eur.* **102** K2
Eyasi, Lake, *Af.* **126** J9
Eyjafjörður, bay, *Arctic Oc.* **102** A3
Eyl, *Somalia* **128** G12
Eyrarbakki, *Ice.* **104** B3
Eyre, Lake, *Austral.* **139** H10
Eyre North, Lake, *Austral.* **139** H10
Eyre Peninsula, *Austral.* **138** K9
Eyre South, Lake, *Austral.* **139** H10

F

Fada, *Chad* **128** F7
Fairbanks, *Alas., U.S.* **82** K3
Fairweather, Mount, *Alas., U.S.–B.C., Can.* **80** L4
Faisalabad, *Pak.* **116** G7
Fais, island, *F.S.M.* **142** D3
Faith, *S. Dak., U.S.* **82** C8
Fakaofo, island, *Kiribati* **142** F8
Fakfak, *Indonesia* **117** L15
Falcon Reservoir, *U.S.–Mex.* **80** K9
Falfurrias, *Tex., U.S.* **82** K9
Falkland Islands, *S. Amer.* **93** Q6
Falkland Sound, *Falk. Is., U.K.* **93** Q6
Fallières Coast, *Antarctica* **152** D2
False Bay, *S. Af.* **127** Q7
False Cape (Falso, Cabo), *Mex.* **75** N3
Falun, *Sw.* **104** D7
Famagusta (Ammóchostos, Gazimağusa), *Cyprus* **105** M12
Fanning Island *see* Tabuaeran, *Kiribati* **142** E9
Farallon de Pajaros, island, *N. Mariana Is., U.S.* **142** C3
Farallon Islands, *Calif., U.S.* **80** E1
Farewell, *Alas., U.S.* **82** L3
Farewell, Cape, *Greenland, Den.* **74** E11
Farewell, Cape, *N.Z.* **142** K6
Fargo, *N. Dak., U.S.* **82** C9
Faribault, *Minn., U.S.* **83** D10
Farmington, *N. Mex., U.S.* **82** F6
Faro, *Port.* **104** L1
Faroe Islands, *Den.* **102** C4
Fartak, Ra's, *Yemen* **114** J5
Fataka (Mitre Island), *Solomon Is.* **142** G6
Fatu Hiva, island, *Fr. Polynesia, Fr.* **143** F11
Faxaflói, bay, *Ice.* **102** A2
Faya-Largeau, *Chad* **128** F6
Fayetteville, *Ark., U.S.* **83** G10
Fayetteville, *N.C., U.S.* **83** G15
Fdérik, *Mauritania* **128** E2
Fear, Cape, *N.C., U.S.* **81** G15
Cape Fear, river, *N.C., U.S.* **81** G15
Federated States of Micronesia, *Pac. Oc.* **142** E2
Feijó, *Braz.* **94** E4
Feira de Santana, *Braz.* **94** G10
Ferkéssédougou, *Côte d'Ivoire* **128** G3
Fernandina, Isla, *Galápagos Is., Ecua.* **143** E16
Fès (Fez), *Mor.* **128** C3
Fezzan, region, *Libya* **128** D6
Fianarantsoa, *Madagascar* **129** M12
Fields Find, *Austral.* **140** H3
Fiji, *Pac. Oc.* **142** G7
Filadelfia, *Parag.* **94** J6
Filchner Ice Sheet, *Antarctica* **152** D6
Fillmore, *Utah, U.S.* **82** E5
Fimbul Ice Shelf, *Antarctica* **152** A8
Finger Lakes, *N.Y., U.S.* **81** D15
Finisterre, Cape, *Eur.* **102** H1
Finke, *Austral.* **140** G9
Finke, river, *Austral.* **138** G9
Finland, *Eur.* **104** C9
Finland, Gulf of, *Atlantic Oc.* **102** E9
Finlay, river, *B.C., Can.* **76** F3
Finnmark Plateau, *Eur.* **102** A8
Firenze (Florence), *It.* **104** K6
Firth of Forth, *Atl. Oc.* **102** E4
Fisher Glacier, *Antarctica* **153** D12
Fiskenæsset *see* Qeqertarsuatsiaat, *Greenland, Den.* **76** E9
Fitzgerald, *Ga., U.S.* **83** H14
Fitzroy Crossing, *Austral.* **140** D5
Fitzroy, river, *Austral.* **138** D5
Fitzroy, river, *Austral.* **139** F14
Flagstaff, *Ariz., U.S.* **82** G5
Flaming Gorge Reservoir, *Utah–Wyo., U.S.* **80** E6
Flanders, region, *Belg.–Fr.* **102** G5
Flat, *Alas., U.S.* **82** K2
Flathead Lake, *Mont., U.S.* **80** B5
Flattery, Cape, *Austral.* **139** C13
Flattery, Cape, *Wash., U.S.* **80** A2
Fleetwood, *Austral.* **141** F13
Flekkefjord, *Nor.* **104** E5
Fleming Glacier, *Antarctica* **152** D3
Fletcher Peninsula, *Antarctica* **152** G3
Flinders Island, *Austral.* **138** L8
Flinders Ranges, *Austral.* **139** K10
Flinders, river, *Austral.* **139** D11
Flin Flon, *Man., Can.* **76** G5
Flint, river, *Ga., U.S.* **81** H13
Flint, *Mich., U.S.* **83** D13
Flint Hills, *Kans., U.S.* **80** F9
Flint Island, *Kiribati* **143** F10
Flood Range, *Antarctica* **152** J5
Florence, *Ala., U.S.* **83** G12
Florence, *S.C., U.S.* **83** G15
Florence *see* Firenze, *It.* **104** K6
Florencia, *Col.* **94** C2
Flores, *Azores, Port.* **115** M14
Flores, *Guatemala* **77** P7
Floriano, *Braz.* **94** E10
Florianópolis, *Braz.* **95** K9
Florida, *U.S.* **83** J13
Florida Bay, *Fla., U.S.* **81** L15
Florida Keys, *Fla., U.S.* **81** L15
Florida, Straits of, *Cuba–Bahamas–U.S.* **81** L14
Florø, *Nor.* **104** D6
Focşani, *Rom.* **105** J10
Fog Bay, *Austral.* **138** B7
Foggia, *It.* **104** K7
Folda, bay, *Nor.* **102** C7
Fonseca, Gulf of, *El Salv.–Hond.–Nicar.* **75** Q6
Forbes, *Austral.* **141** K13
Ford, Cape, *Austral.* **138** B7
Ford Ranges, *Antarctica* **152** K6
Forel, Mount, *Greenland, Den.* **74** C10
Forest Lakes, *Austral.* **138** H7
Formosa, *Arg.* **94** J7
Formosa, Serra, *Braz.* **92** F7
Føroyar *see* Faroe Islands, *Den.* **102** C4
Forrest, *Austral.* **140** J7
Forrestal Range, *Antarctica* **152** E6
Forrest River, *Austral.* **140** C7
Forsayth, *Austral.* **141** D12
Forster-Tuncurry, *Austral.* **141** K15
Forsyth, *Mont., U.S.* **82** C7
Fort Albany, *Ont., Can.* **76** H7
Fortaleza, *Braz.* **94** E11
Fort Benton, *Mont., U.S.* **82** B6
Fort Bragg, *Calif., U.S.* **82** D2
Fort Chipewyan, *Alta., Can.* **76** F4
Fort Collins, *Colo., U.S.* **82** E7
Fort Dodge, *Iowa, U.S.* **83** D10
Fortescue, river, *Austral.* **138** F3
Fort Fraser, *B.C., Can.* **76** F2
Fort Good Hope, *N.W.T., Can.* **76** D4
Fort Hope, *Ont., Can.* **76** H6
Fortín Infante Rivarola, *Parag.* **94** H5
Fort Lauderdale, *Fla., U.S.* **83** K15
Fort Liard, *N.W.T., Can.* **76** E3
Fort McMurray, *Alta., Can.* **76** F4
Fort McPherson, *N.W.T., Can.* **76** D3
Fort Morgan, *Colo., U.S.* **82** E7
Fort Myers, *Fla., U.S.* **83** K15
Fort Nelson, *B.C., Can.* **76** F3
Fort Peck Lake, *Mont., U.S.* **80** B7
Fort Pierce, *Fla., U.S.* **77** M8
Fort Pierce, *Fla., U.S.* **83** K15
Fort Providence, *N.W.T., Can.* **76** E4
Fort Resolution, *N.W.T., Can.* **76** F4
Fort Severn, *Ont., Can.* **76** G7
Fort Simpson, *N.W.T., Can.* **76** E4
Fort Smith, *Ark., U.S.* **77** L5
Fort Smith, *N.W.T., Can.* **76** F4
Fort Smith, *Ark., U.S.* **83** G10
Fort Stockton, *Tex., U.S.* **82** J7
Fort Sumner, *N. Mex., U.S.* **82** H7
Fort Trinquet *see* Bir Mogreïn, *Mauritania* **128** D2
Fort Vermilion, *Alta., Can.* **76** F4
Fort Wayne, *Ind., U.S.* **83** E12
Fort Worth, *Tex., U.S.* **82** H9
Fort Yates, *N. Dak., U.S.* **82** C8
Fort Yukon, *Alas., U.S.* **82** J3
Fossil Downs, *Austral.* **140** D6
Foster, *Austral.* **141** M12
Foster Bay (Foster Bugt), *Greenland, Den.* **74** B10
Foundation Ice Stream, *Antarctica* **152** F6
Fourcroy, Cape, *Austral.* **138** A7
Fouta Djallon, region, *Guinea* **126** G1
Foveaux Strait, *N.Z.* **142** L5
Fowlers Bay, *Austral.* **138** K8
Fowlers Bay, *Austral.* **140** J8
Fox, river, *Ill., U.S.* **81** E12
Fox, river, *Wis., U.S.* **81** D12
Foxe Basin, *Arctic Oc.* **74** E7
Foxe Peninsula, *Nunavut, Can.* **74** E8
Fox Islands, *Alas., U.S.* **75** R4
Foyn Coast, *Antarctica* **152** D2
Foz do Cunene, *Angola* **129** M5
Foz do Iguaçu, *Braz.* **94** J7
Framnes Mountains, *Antarctica* **153** D13
Fram Peak, *Antarctica* **153** C13
Franca, *Braz.* **94** H9
France, *Eur.* **104** H4
Franceville, *Gabon* **128** J5
Francis Case, Lake, *S. Dak., U.S.* **80** D8
Francistown, *Botswana* **129** M8
Frankfort, *Ky., U.S.* **83** F13
Frankfurt, *Ger.* **104** G6
Franklin Bay, *N.W.T., Can.* **74** C4
Franklin Mountains, *N.W.T., Can.* **74** E4
Frantsa Iosifa, Zemlya *see* Franz Josef Land, *Russ.* **114** B8
Franz Josef Land, *Russ.* **114** B8
Fraser Island (Great Sandy Island), *Austral.* **139** G15
Fraser, Mount, *Austral.* **138** G3
Fraser Range, *Austral.* **140** J5
Fraser, river, *B.C., Can.* **74** G3
Frederick, Mount, *Austral.* **138** D7
Fredericton, *N.B., Can.* **76** H10
Frederikshåb *see* Paamiut, *Greenland, Den.* **76** E10
Freeport, *Tex., U.S.* **83** K10
Freetown, *Sierra Leone* **128** G1
Freiburg, *Ger.* **104** H6
Fremont, *Nebr., U.S.* **82** E9
French Guiana, *S. Amer.* **94** C8
French Polynesia, *Pac. Oc.* **143** G10
Fresno, *Calif., U.S.* **82** F2
Frewena, *Austral.* **140** D9
Fridtjof Nansen, Mount, *Antarctica* **152** H7
Frio, Cabo, *S. Amer.* **92** J10
Frisian Islands, *Eur.* **102** F5
Frissell, Mount, *Conn., U.S.* **81** D16
Frobisher Bay, *Nunavut, Can.* **74** E8
Frolovo, *Russ.* **105** G12
Frome, Lake, *Austral.* **139** J11
Front Range, *Colo., U.S.* **80** E7
Fuerte Olimpo, *Parag.* **94** H6
Fuerteventura, island, *Sp.* **126** D2
Fuhai, *China* **116** F9
Fuji, peak, *Japan* **115** F14
Fukuoka, *Japan* **117** G13
Fukushima, Mount, *Antarctica* **153** B11
Funafuti Island, *Tuvalu* **142** F7
Fundy, Bay of, *Can.–U.S.* **81** B17
Furnas Reservoir, *S. Amer.* **92** H9
Furneaux Group, *Austral.* **138** L8
Fushun, *China* **117** F12
Futuna, island, *Vanuatu* **142** G6
Fuzhou, *China* **117** H13
Fyn, island, *Den.* **102** F6

G

Gabes, *Tun.* **128** C6
Gabes, Gulf of, *Tun.* **126** C6
Gabon, *Af.* **128** J5
Gaborone, *S. Af.* **129** N8
Gabras, *Sudan* **128** G8
Gadsden, *Ala., U.S.* **83** H12
Gaferut, island, *F.S.M.* **142** D3
Gagnoa, *Côte d'Ivoire* **128** H2
Gainesville, *Fla., U.S.* **83** J14
Gairdner, Lake, *Austral.* **138** J9
Galápagos Islands (Archipiélago de Colón), *Ecua.* **143** E16
Galdhøpiggen, peak, *Nor.* **102** D6
Galena, *Alas., U.S.* **82** K2
Galera Point, *Chile* **93** N3
Galera Point (Galera, Punta), *Ecua.* **92** D1
Galilee, Lake, *Austral.* **139** F13
Galina Mine, *Austral.* **140** H2
Galiwinku, *Austral.* **140** A9
Gallegos, river, *S. Amer.* **93** Q4
Gallipoli, *Austral.* **141** D10
Gällivare, *Sw.* **104** B8
Gallup, *N. Mex., U.S.* **82** G6
Galveston, *Tex., U.S.* **83** K10
Galveston Bay, *Tex., U.S.* **81** K10
Gambell, *Alas., U.S.* **82** K1
Gambia, *Af.* **128** F1
Gambia, river, *Af.* **126** F1
Gambier, Îles, *Fr. Polynesia, Fr.* **143** H11
Gamet, *N.W.T., Can.* **76** E4
Gander, *Nfld. & Lab., Can.* **76** G11
Ganges, river, *Bangladesh–India* **114** H8
Ganges Plain, *Asia* **114** H8
Ganges River Delta, *Asia* **114** J9
Ganhe, *China* **117** E12
Gannett Peak, *Wyo., U.S.* **80** D6
Gantheaume Bay, *Austral.* **138** H1
Gao, *Mali* **128** F4
Garabogaz Bay, *Asia* **114** F6
Garagum, *Turkm.* **114** F6
Garanhuns, *Braz.* **94** F12
Garda, Lake, *Eur.* **102** J6
Garden City, *Kans., U.S.* **82** F8
Gardner Pinnacles, *Hawai'i, U.S.* **142** B8
Garies, *S. Af.* **129** P7
Garonne, river, *Fr.* **102** J4
Garoua, *Cameroon* **128** G6
Garoua Boulaï, *Cameroon* **128** H6
Gary, *Ind., U.S.* **83** E12
Gascony, region, *Fr.* **102** J3
Gascoyne Junction, *Austral.* **140** G2
Gascoyne, river, *Austral.* **138** G3
Gaspé, *Que., Can.* **76** H9
Gaspé Peninsula, *Que., Can.* **74** H9
Gastonia, *N.C., U.S.* **83** G14
Gastre, *Arg.* **95** N5
Gata, Cape, *Cyprus* **102** L3
Gautheaume Point, *Austral.* **138** D4
Gävle, *Sw.* **104** D8
Gawler, *Austral.* **141** K10
Gawler Ranges, *Austral.* **138** J9
Gayny, *Russ.* **116** D7
Gazimağusa *see* Famagusta, *Cyprus* **105** M12
Gdańsk, *Pol.* **104** F8
Gdańsk, Gulf of, *Pol.–Russ.* **102** F8
Gedaref, *Sudan* **128** F9
Geelong, *Austral.* **141** M12
Geelvink Channel, *Austral.* **138** H2
Geeveston, *Austral.* **140** M7
Gefara, region, *Af.* **126** C6
Gejiu, *China* **117** J11
Gemena, *Dem. Rep. of the Congo* **128** H7
Gemsa, *Egypt* **128** D9
General Alvear, *Arg.* **95** L5
General Guido, *Arg.* **95** M7
General San Martín, *Arg.* **95** P4
General Santos, *Philippines* **117** K14
Geneva, Lake, *Fr.* **102** H5
Geneva *see* Genève, *Switz.* **104** J5
Genève (Geneva), *Switz.* **104** J5
Genoa *see* Genova, *It.* **104** J5
Genova (Genoa), *It.* **104** J5
Geographe Bay, *Austral.* **138** K2
Geographe Channel, *Austral.* **138** G1
George, *S. Af.* **129** P7
George, Lake, *Austral.* **138** F5
George, Lake, *Austral.* **139** L14
George Land (George, Zemlya), *Asia* **114** B8
George, river, *Que., Can.* **74** F9
George Town, *Malaysia* **117** L10
Georgetown, *Austral.* **141** D12
George Town, *Austral.* **140** L8
Georgetown, *Guyana* **94** B7
Georgetown, *S.C., U.S.* **83** H15
George V Coast, *Antarctica* **153** M11
George VI Sound, *Antarctica* **152** E3
Georgia, *Asia–Eur.* **105** J13
Georgia, *U.S.* **83** H13
Georgian Bay, *Ont., Can.* **81** C14
Georgia, Strait of, *Can.–U.S.* **80** A3

Georgina, river, *Austral.* **139** E10
Geral, Serra, *S. Amer.* **92** J8
Geral de Goiás, Serra, *Braz.* **94** G9
Geraldton, *Austral.* **140** J2
Gerdine, Mount, *Alas., U.S.* **80** L3
Gerlach, peak, *Eur.* **102** H8
Germania Land, *Greenland, Den.* **74** A9
Germany, *Eur.* **104** G6
Gerpir, *Eur.* **102** B4
Getz Ice Shelf, *Antarctica* **152** J4
Ghadāmis, *Libya* **128** D5
Ghana, *Af.* **128** G3
Ghardaïa, *Alg.* **128** C4
Ghāt, *Solomon Is.* **128** E5
Ghazal, Bahr el, *Chad* **126** H8
Gibb River, *Austral.* **140** C6
Gibraltar, *U.K.* **128** B3
Gibraltar, *Eur.* **104** L2
Gibraltar, Strait of, *Af.–Eur.* **102** L1
Gibson Desert, *Austral.* **138** F6
Gijón, *Sp.* **104** J2
Gila Bend, *Ariz., U.S.* **82** H4
Gila, river, *Ariz., U.S.* **80** H4
Gilbert Islands, *Kiribati* **142** E6
Gilbert, river, *Austral.* **139** D12
Gilbués, *Braz.* **94** F9
Gilgandra, *Austral.* **141** J14
Gillam, *Man., Can.* **76** G6
Gillen, Lake, *Austral.* **138** G6
Gilles, Lake, *Austral.* **139** K10
Gillette, *Wyo., U.S.* **82** D7
Gilmore Hut, *Austral.* **141** G12
Gilpeppee, *Austral.* **141** G11
Gimli, *Man., Can.* **76** H6
Gingin, *Austral.* **140** J3
Gippsland, *Austral.* **139** M13
Giurgiu, *Rom.* **104** K9
Gjoa Haven, *Nunavut, Can.* **76** E6
Gladstone, *Austral.* **141** F15
Glåma, river, *Nor.* **102** D7
Glasgow, *Scot., U.K.* **104** E4
Glasgow, *Mont., U.S.* **82** B7
Glenayle, *Austral.* **140** G4
Glendale, *Calif., U.S.* **82** G3
Glendive, *Mont., U.S.* **82** C7
Glenelg, river, *Austral.* **139** L11
Glengyle, *Austral.* **141** F10
Glen Innes, *Austral.* **141** J15
Glenmorgan, *Austral.* **141** H14
Glenwood Springs, *Colo., U.S.* **82** E6
Globe, *Ariz., U.S.* **82** H5
Gloucester, *Austral.* **141** K14
Goba, *Eth.* **128** H10
Gobabis, *Namibia* **129** N7
Gobernador Gregores, *Chile* **95** Q4
Gobi, desert, *China–Mongolia* **115** F11
Godhavn *see* Qeqertarsuaq, *Greenland, Den.* **76** D8
Gods Lake, *Man., Can.* **76** G6
Godwin Austen *see* K2, peak, *China–Pak.* **114** G7
Gogebic Range, *Mich.–Wis., U.S.* **81** C11
Goiânia, *Braz.* **94** G8
Goiás, *Braz.* **94** G8
Gold Coast, *Af.* **126** H3
Gold Coast, *Austral.* **141** H15
Goldfield, *Nev., U.S.* **82** F3
Goldsboro, *N.C., U.S.* **83** G15
Goldsworthy, *Austral.* **140** E3
Golmud, *China* **117** G10
Golovin, *Alas., U.S.* **82** K1
Goma, *Dem. Rep. of the Congo* **128** J8
Gomera, island, *Sp.* **126** D1
Gonaïves, *Haiti* **77** N9
Gonâve, Gulf of, *Haiti* **75** N9
Gonder, *Eth.* **128** G10
Good Hope, Cape of, *S. Af.* **127** Q6
Goodland, *Kans., U.S.* **82** F8
Goodnews Bay, *Alas., U.S.* **82** L1
Goodparla, *Austral.* **140** B8
Goomalling, *Austral.* **140** J3
Goondiwindi, *Austral.* **141** H14
Goongarrie, Lake, *Austral.* **138** J4
Goose Lake, *Calif.–Oreg., U.S.* **80** D3
Gora Mus Khaya, peak, *Asia* **115** C12
Gordon Downs, *Austral.* **140** D7
Gordon, Lake, *Austral.* **138** M7
Gorki, *Russ.* **105** A14
Gor'kiy Reservoir, *Eur.* **103** E12
Gorzów Wielkopolski, *Pol.* **104** G7
Gosford, *Austral.* **141** K14
Götaland, *Eur.* **102** E7
Göteborg, *Sw.* **104** E7
Gotland, island, *Sw.* **102** E8
Gouin, Réservoir, *Que., Can.* **74** H8
Goulburn, *Austral.* **141** L14
Gould Bay, *Antarctica* **152** D5
Gould Coast, *Antarctica* **152** H7
Goulimine, *Mor.* **128** D2
Gourma, region, *Af.* **126** G4
Gove Peninsula, *Austral.* **139** B10
Governador Valadares, *Braz.* **94** H10
Govorovo, *Russ.* **117** C11
Goya, *Arg.* **95** K6
Gracias a Dios, Cape (Gracias a Dios, Cabo), *Hond.–Nicar.* **75** P8
Grafton, *Austral.* **141** J15
Grafton, *N. Dak., U.S.* **82** B9
Graham Bell Island (Graham Bell, Ostrov), *Asia* **114** B9
Graham Island, *B.C., Can.* **76** F2
Graham Island, *Nunavut, Can.* **76** C6
Graham Land, region, *Antarctica* **152** C2
Grain Coast, *Af.* **126** H2
Grajaú, *Braz.* **94** E9
Grajaú, river, *S. Amer.* **92** E9
Grampian Mountains, *Scot., U.K.* **102** E4
Granada, *Sp.* **104** L2
Gran Canaria, island, *Sp.* **126** D1
Gran Chaco, region, *S. Amer.* **92** J6
Grand, river, *Mich., U.S.* **81** D12
Grand, river, *S. Dak., U.S.* **80** C8
Grand Canyon, *Ariz., U.S.* **80** G4
Grand Canyon, *Ariz., U.S.* **82** G5
Grand Cayman, *Cayman Is., U.K.* **75** P8
Grande, Bahía, *Arg.* **95** Q5
Grande, Cuchilla, *Uru.* **93** L7
Grande, river, *Bol.* **92** G6
Grande, river, *Braz.* **92** H9
Grande Bay, *Arg.* **93** Q5
Grande Comore *see* Njazidja, *Comoros* **127** L11
Grande Prairie, *Alta., Can.* **76** F4
Grand Erg Occidental, *Alg.* **128** D4
Grand Erg Oriental, *Alg.* **128** D5
Grandes, Salinas, *Arg.* **93** K5
Grand Forks, *N. Dak., U.S.* **82** B9
Grand Island, *Braz.* **92** J9
Grand Island, *Nebr., U.S.* **82** E8
Grand Island Bay, *S. Amer.* **92** J9
Grand Isle, *La., U.S.* **83** K11
Grand Junction, *Colo., U.S.* **82** F6
Grand Marais, *Minn., U.S.* **83** B11
Grand Rapids, *Mich., U.S.* **83** D12
Grand Teton, *Alta., Can.* **80** D5
Granite Peak, *Mont., U.S.* **80** C6
Granite Peak, *Nev., U.S.* **80** D4
Grant Island, *Antarctica* **152** K4
Grants, *N. Mex., U.S.* **82** G6
Grants Pass, *Oreg., U.S.* **82** C2
Grass Patch, *Austral.* **140** K5
Graz, *Aust.* **104** J7
Great Artesian Basin, *Austral.* **139** F11
Great Australian Bight, *Indian Oc.* **138** K7
Great Barrier Island (Aotea Island), *N.Z.* **142** J6
Great Barrier Reef, *Austral.* **139** C13
Great Basin, *U.S.* **80** E3
Great Bear Lake, *N.W.T., Can.* **74** D4
Great Belt, *Atl. Oc.* **102** F6
Great Bend, *Kans., U.S.* **82** F8
Great Britain, *U.K.* **102** E4
Great Channel, *India–Indonesia* **115** L10
Great Dismal Swamp, *N.C.–Va., U.S.* **81** F15
Great Divide Basin, *Wyo., U.S.* **80** D6
Great Dividing Range, *Austral.* **139** C12, L13
Greater Antilles, *N. Amer.* **75** N8
Greater Khingan Range, *Asia* **115** F12
Greater Sudbury, *Ont., Can.* **76** H8
Greater Sunda Islands, *Indonesia* **115** M12
Great Exuma, *Bahamas* **75** N9
Great Falls, *Mont., U.S.* **82** B5
Great Hungarian Plain, *Eur.* **102** J8
Great Inagua Island, *Bahamas* **75** N10
Great Indian Desert, *India–Pak.* **114** H7
Great Karoo, region, *Af.* **127** P7
Great Lake, *Austral.* **138** L8
Great Miami, river, *Ohio, U.S.* **81** E13
Great Namaland, region, *Namibia* **127** N6
Great Oyster Bay, *Austral.* **138** M8
Great Pee Dee, river, *N.C.–S.C., U.S.* **81** G14
Great Plains, *Can.–U.S.* **74** G4
Great Rift Valley, *Af.* **126** J10
Great Ruaha, river, *Tanzania* **127** K9
Great Salt Lake, *Utah, U.S.* **80** D4
Great Salt Lake Desert, *Utah, U.S.* **80** E5
Great Sandy Desert, *Austral.* **138** E5
Great Sandy Desert, *Oreg., U.S.* **80** C3
Great Sandy Island *see* Fraser Island, *Austral.* **139** G15
Great Slave Lake, *N.W.T., Can.* **74** E4
Great Smoky Mountains, *N.C.–Tenn., U.S.* **81** G13
Great Victoria Desert, *Austral.* **138** H6
Great Wall, station, *Antarctica* **152** B2
Great Western Erg, *Alg.* **126** D4
Great Western Tiers, *Austral.* **138** L7
Greece, *Eur.* **104** L8
Greeley, *Colo., U.S.* **82** E7
Green Bay, *Wis., U.S.* **81** C12
Green Bay, *Wis., U.S.* **83** C12
Green Cape, *Austral.* **139** M14
Green Head, *Austral.* **138** J2
Green Islands, *P.N.G.* **142** F4
Greenland (Kalaallit Nunaat), *N. Amer.* **76** B8
Greenland Sea, *Arctic Oc.* **74** A9
Green Mountains, *Vt., U.S.* **81** C16
Green, river, *Ky., U.S.* **81** F13
Green, river, *Utah–Wyo., U.S.* **80** F6
Greensboro, *N.C., U.S.* **83** F14
Greenville, *Liberia* **128** H2
Greenville, *Miss., U.S.* **83** H11
Greenville, *S.C., U.S.* **83** G14
Gregory Lake, *Austral.* **138** E6
Gregory, Lake, *Austral.* **138** G4
Gregory, Lake, *Austral.* **139** H11
Gregory Range, *Austral.* **139** D12
Gregory, river, *Austral.* **139** D11
Grenada, *N. Amer.* **77** P12
Grenville, Cape, *Austral.* **139** B12
Grey, Cape, *Austral.* **139** B10
Greylock, Mount, *Mass., U.S.* **81** D15
Grey, Mount, *Austral.* **138** J3
Grey Range, *Austral.* **139** H12
Griffith, *Austral.* **141** K12
Grim, Cape, *Austral.* **138** L7
Grinnell Peninsula, *Nunavut, Can.* **76** C6
Grise Fiord, *Nunavut, Can.* **76** C7
Groningen, *Neth.* **104** F5
Groote Eylandt, *Austral.* **139** B10
Grootfontein, *Namibia* **129** M6
Groot Vloer, *Af.* **127** P7
Grossglockner, peak, *Eur.* **102** H7
Grosvenor Mountains, *Antarctica* **152** H8
Grove Mountains, *Antarctica* **153** E12
Groznyy, *Russ.* **105** J14
Guacanayabo, Gulf of (Guacanayabo, Golfo de), *Cuba* **75** P8
Guadalajara, *Mex.* **77** N4
Guadalcanal, island, *Solomon Is.* **142** F4
Guadalquivir, river, *Sp.* **102** K2
Guadalupe, river, *Tex., U.S.* **80** J9
Guadalupe Island (Guadalupe, Isla), *Mex.* **75** L2
Guadalupe Mountains, *N. Mex.–Tex., U.S.* **80** H7
Guadalupe Peak, *Tex., U.S.* **80** H6
Guadeloupe, *Fr., Lesser Antilles,* **77** N12
Guadiana, river, *Sp.* **102** K1
Guafo, Boca del, *Chile* **95** P3
Guainia, river, *Col.* **92** C4
Guaíra, *Braz.* **94** J7
Guajará-Mirim, *Braz.* **94** F5
Guajira Peninsula, *N. Amer.* **92** A3
Guam, island, *Guam, U.S.* **142** D3
Guanabara Bay, *S. Amer.* **92** J10
Guanambi, *Braz.* **94** G10
Guanare, *Venez.* **94** B4
Guandacol, *Arg.* **95** K4
Guane, *Cuba* **77** N7
Guangyuan, *China* **117** H10
Guangzhou (Canton), *China* **117** H12
Guantánamo, *Cuba* **77** N9
Guaporé, river, *S. Amer.* **92** F5
Guatemala, *N. Amer.* **77** P6
Guatemala City, *Guatemala* **77** Q6
Guaviare, river, *Col.* **92** C3
Guayaquil, *Ecua.* **94** D1
Guayaquil, Gulf of (Guayaquil, Golfo de), *Ecua.* **92** E1
Guaymas, *Mex.* **77** L3
Guban, region, *Af.* **126** G11
Gubkin, *Russ.* **105** G11
Güeppí, *Peru* **94** D2
Guera Massif, peak, *Af.* **126** G6
Guiana Highlands, *S. Amer.* **92** C5
Guienne, region, *Fr.* **102** J4
Guinea, *Af.* **128** G1
Guinea-Bissau, *Af.* **128** G1
Guinea, Gulf of, *Atlantic Oc.* **126** H4
Guiyang, *China* **117** H11
Gujranwala, *Pak.* **116** G7
Gulfport, *Miss., U.S.* **83** J12
Gulkana, *Alas., U.S.* **82** L3
Gulu, *Uganda* **128** H9
Gunnbjørn Fjeld, *Greenland, Den.* **74** C10
Gunnedah, *Austral.* **141** J14
Gunnison, *Colo., U.S.* **82** F6
Gurupá, *Braz.* **94** D8
Gurupá Island, *S. Amer.* **92** D8
Gurupi, Cape, *Braz.* **92** D9
Gurupi, river, *Braz.* **92** D9
Gusau, *Nigeria* **128** G5
Gustavus, *Alas., U.S.* **82** L4
Gutha, *Austral.* **140** H3
Guwahati, *India* **116** H9
Guyana, *S. Amer.* **94** B6
Guymon, *Okla., U.S.* **82** G8
Gwabegar, *Austral.* **141** J13
Gwardafuy, Cape, *Af.* **126** G12
Gwydir, river, *Austral.* **139** J14
Gyda, *Russ.* **116** C9
Gydanskiy Poluostrov *see* Gyda Peninsula, *Russ.* **114** C9
Gyda Peninsula, *Asia* **114** C9
Gyêgu, *China* **117** H10
Gympie, *Austral.* **141** G15

H

Ha'apai Group, islands, *Tonga* **142** G7
Hachijō Jima, island, *Japan* **142** A3
Hachinohe, *Japan* **117** E14
Ḩadd, Ra's al, *Oman* **114** H6
Hadejia, river, *Af.* **126** G5
Hadhramaut, *Asia* **114** J4
Hadībоh, *Yemen* **116** J5
Hadley Bay, *Nunavut, Can.* **76** C5
Haedo, Cuchilla de, *Uru.* **93** L7
Hagåtña (Agana), *Guam, U.S.* **142** D3
Hagemeister, island, *Alas., U.S.* **75** Q4
Hagerstown, *Md., U.S.* **83** E15
Hahajima Rettō (Baily Group or Coffin Group), *Japan* **142** B3
Haida Gwaii (Queen Charlotte Islands) , *B.C., Can.* **74** F2
Haig, *Austral.* **140** J6
Haikou, *China* **117** J11
Hailar, *China* **117** E11
Hainan, island, *China* **115** J12
Haines, *Alas., U.S.* **82** L5
Haines Junction, *Yukon, Can.* **76** E2
Haiti, *N. Amer.* **77** N10
Haïtien, Cap-, *Haiti* **77** N10
Hakodate, *Japan* **117** E14
Ḩalab, *Syr.* **116** F4
Halayeb, *Egypt* **128** E10
Hale'iwa, *Hawai'i, U.S.* **83** L12
Halfa, Wadi, *Sudan* **128** E9
Halifax, *Austral.* **141** D13
Halifax, *N.S., Can.* **76** H10
Halifax Bay, *Austral.* **139** D13
Hall Beach, *Nunavut, Can.* **76** D7
Halley, station, *Antarctica* **152** C6
Hall Islands, *F.S.M.* **142** D4
Hall Peninsula, *Nunavut, Can.* **74** E8
Halls Creek, *Austral.* **140** D7
Halmahera, island, *Indonesia* **115** L15
Halmahera Sea, *Indonesia* **115** L15
Halmstad, *Sw.* **104** E7
Hamadān, *Iran* **116** F5
Hamamet, Gulf of, *Tun.* **126** C6
Hamar, *Nor.* **104** D6
Hamburg, *Ger.* **104** F6
Hamelin, *Austral.* **140** H2
Hamelin Pool, *Austral.* **138** H2
Hamersley Range, *Austral.* **138** F3
Hamhŭng, *N. Korea* **117** F13
Hami, *China* **117** G10
Hamilton, *Austral.* **141** M11
Hamilton, *Ont., Can.* **76** J8
Hammerfest, *Nor.* **104** A8
Hampton Tableland, *Austral.* **138** J6
Hāna, *Hawai'i, U.S.* **83** L13
Hancock, *Mich., U.S.* **83** C11
Hanggin Houqi, *China* **117** G10
Hangzhou, *China* **117** G13
Hangzhou Bay, *Pac. Oc.* **115** G13
Hann, Mount, *Austral.* **138** C5
Hannover, *Ger.* **104** F6
Hà Nội (Hanoi), *Vietnam* **117** J11
Hanoi *see* Hà Nội, *Vietnam* **117** J11
Hansen Mountains, *Antarctica* **153** D13
Hao, island, *Fr. Polynesia, Fr.* **143** G11

L

Melbourne, Fla., U.S. 83 K15
Melbourne, Mount, Antarctica 152 L9
Melekeok, Palau 142 D2
Melfort, Sask., Can. 76 G5
Melilla, Sp. 128 C4
Melitopol', Ukr. 105 H11
Melo, Uru. 95 L7
Melrhir, Chott, Alg. 126 C5
Melrose, Austral. 141 K10
Melut, S. Sudan 128 G9
Melville Bay, Austral. 139 A10
Melville, Cape, Austral. 139 B13
Melville Hills, Nunavut–N.W.T., Can. 74 D4
Melville Island, Austral. 138 A8
Melville Island, Nunavut, Can. 74 C5
Melville Peninsula, Nunavut, Can. 74 E7
Memphis, Tenn., U.S. 83 G12
Ménaka, Mali 128 F4
Mendebo Mountains, Af. 126 H10
Mendocino, Cape, Calif., U.S. 80 D1
Mendoza, Arg. 95 L5
Menindee, Austral. 141 K12
Menominee, river, Mich.–Wis., U.S. 81 C12
Menongue, Angola 129 L7
Menorca, island see Minorca, Sp. 102 K4
Mentawai Islands, Asia 115 M10
Menzies, Austral. 140 J4
Menzies, Mount, Antarctica 153 D12
Meramangye, Lake, Austral. 138 H8
Merauke, Indonesia 117 L16
Merca (Marka), Somalia 128 H11
Mercedes, Arg. 95 K7
Mercedes, Uru. 95 L7
Mercedes, Arg. 95 L5
Mercy, Cape, Nunavut, Can. 74 E9
Meredith, Lake, Tex., U.S. 80 G7
Mereeg, Somalia 128 H12
Mérida, Mex. 77 N6
Mérida, Venez. 94 B3
Mérida, Cordillera de , Venez. 92 B3
Meridian, Miss., U.S. 83 H12
Meringur, Austral. 141 K11
Merir, island, Palau 142 E2
Mermaid Reef, Austral. 138 D3
Merolia, Austral. 140 H5
Merowe, Sudan 128 F9
Merredin, Austral. 140 J3
Merrick Mountains, Antarctica 152 E4
Merrimack, river, N.H., U.S. 81 C16
Merritt Island, Fla., U.S. 83 J15
Mertz Glacier, Antarctica 153 M11
Mertz Glacier Tongue, Antarctica 153 M11
Mesa, Ariz., U.S. 82 H5
Mesabi Range, Minn., U.S. 81 C10
Meseta, Eur. 102 K2
Mesopotamia, region, Asia 114 F4
Messina, It. 104 L7
Messina, Strait of (Messina, Stretto di), It. 102 L7
Messinia, Gulf of, Gr. 102 M8
Meta, river, S. Amer. 92 C3
Meta Incognita Peninsula, Nunavut, Can. 74 E8
Metán, Arg. 94 J5
Metlakatla, Alas., U.S. 76 F2
Meuse, river, Belg.–Fr. 102 H5
Mexicali, Mex. 77 L2
Mexico, N. Amer. 77 N5
Mexico City, Mex. 77 P4
Mexico, Gulf of, Pacific Oc. 75 N6
Mezen', Russ. 105 B11
Mezen' Bay, Arctic Oc. 103 B11
Mezen', river, Russ. 103 B12
Miami, Fla., U.S. 83 K15
Miami Beach, Fla., U.S. 83 K15
Miass, Russ. 116 E7
Michigan, U.S. 83 C12
Michigan, Lake, U.S. 81 D12
Michipicoten, Ont., Can. 76 H7
Michurinsk, Russ. 105 F11
Micronesia, islands, Pac. Oc. 142 D3
Middlesbrough, Eng., U.K. 104 F4
Middleton, Austral. 141 F11
Middleton Ponds, Austral. 140 F8
Midland, Tex., U.S. 82 H7
Midway Islands, Hawai'i, U.S. 142 B7
Mikhaylovka, Russ. 105 G12
Milagro, Ecua. 94 D2
Milano (Milan), It. 104 J6
Milan see Milano, It. 104 J6
Milbank, S. Dak., U.S. 82 C9
Miles, Austral. 141 H14
Miles City, Mont., U.S. 82 C7
Milgun, Austral. 140 G3
Mili Atoll, Marshall Is. 142 E6
Milikapiti, Austral. 140 A8
Milingimbi, Austral. 140 A9
Milk, river, Can.–U.S. 80 B6
Milk, Wadi el, Sudan 126 F8
Mille Lacs Lake, Minn., U.S. 81 C10
Millennium Island see Caroline Island, Kiribati 143 F10
Mill Island, Antarctica 153 H15
Millmerran, Austral. 141 H15
Millungera, Austral. 141 E12
Milly Milly, Austral. 140 G3
Milparinka, Austral. 141 H11
Milwaukee, Wis., U.S. 83 D11
Minamiiō Jima, island, Japan 142 C3
Minamitori Shima (Marcus Island), Japan 142 B4
Mindanao, island, Philippines 115 K14
Mindoro, island, Philippines 115 K13
Mingäçevir Reservoir, Azerb. 103 J14
Mingenew, Austral. 140 J3
Minigwal, Lake, Austral. 138 J5
Minilya, Austral. 140 G2
Minneapolis, Minn., U.S. 83 D10
Minnesota, U.S. 83 C10
Minnesota, river, Minn., U.S. 81 D10
Minorca, Sp. 102 K4
Minot, N. Dak., U.S. 82 B8
Minsk, Belarus 104 F9
Minto, Lac, Que., Can. 76 F8
Minto, Mount, Antarctica 152 M9
Minxian, China 117 G11
Miraflores, Col. 94 C3
Miranda, Braz. 94 H7
Miriam Vale, Austral. 141 G15
Mirim Lagoon (Mirim, Lagoa), Uru. 93 L8
Mirny, station, Antarctica 153 G14
Mirnyy, Russ. 117 D11
Misima, island, P.N.G. 139 A16
Misool, island, Indonesia 115 L15
Mişrātah, Libya 128 C6
Mississippi, U.S. 83 J12
Mississippi, river, U.S. 81 H11
Mississippi River Delta, La., U.S. 81 J12
Mississippi Sound, Miss., U.S. 81 J12
Missoula, Mont., U.S. 82 B5
Missouri, U.S. 83 F10
Missouri, river, U.S. 80 D9
Mistassini, Lac, Que., Can. 74 G8
Mistissini, Que., Can. 76 H8
Misurata, Cape, Af. 126 C6
Mitchell, Austral. 141 G13
Mitchell, S. Dak., U.S. 82 D9
Mitchell, Mount, N.C., U.S. 81 G14
Mitchell, river, Austral. 139 C12
Mitiaro, island, Cook Is., N.Z. 142 G9
Mitre Island see Fataka, Solomon Is. 142 G6
Mitú, Col. 94 C4
Mitumba Mountains, Dem. Rep. of the Congo 127 L8
Mjøsa, lake, Nor. 102 D6
Mmabatho, S. Af. 129 N8
Moab, Utah, U.S. 82 F6
Moa Island, Austral. 139 A12
Mobile, Ala., U.S. 83 J12
Mobile Bay, Ala., U.S. 81 J12
Mobridge, S. Dak., U.S. 82 C8
Mocajuba, Braz. 94 D9
Moçambique, Ilha de, Mozambique 129 L11
Mocha Island (Mocha, Isla), Chile 93 M3
Môco, Morro de, Af. 127 L6
Modesto, Calif., U.S. 82 F2
Moe, Austral. 141 M13
Moengo, Suriname 94 B7
Mogadishu see Muqdisho, Somalia 128 H11
Mogocha, Russ. 117 E11
Mogollon Rim, Ariz., U.S. 80 G5
Mogotes Point, Arg. 93 M7
Mohéli see Mwali, Comoros 127 L11
Mohotani (Motane), island, Fr. Polynesia, Fr. 143 F11
Mo i Rana, Nor. 104 B7
Mojave, Calif., U.S. 82 G3
Mojave Desert, U.S. 80 F4
Moldavia, region, Rom. 103 H10
Moldova, Eur. 105 H10
Mollendo, Peru 94 H3
Moloka'I, island, Hawai'i, U.S. 81 L12
Molopo, river, Af. 127 N7
Moluccas, islands, Indonesia 115 L14
Molucca Sea, Indonesia 115 L14
Moma, Mozambique 129 M10
Mombasa, Kenya 128 J10
Monaco, Eur. 104 J5
Mona Passage, Dom. Rep.–P.R., U.S. 75 N11
Monchegorsk, Russ. 105 B10
Monclova, Mex. 77 M5
Moncton, N.B., Can. 76 H10
Mondego, Cape, Eur. 102 J1
Mongers Lake, Austral. 138 J3
Mongolia, Asia 117 F10
Mongolian Plateau, Asia 115 F10
Mongu, Zambia 129 L8
Monitor Range, Nev., U.S. 80 E4
Monkira, Austral. 141 F11
Mono Lake, Calif., U.S. 80 E3
Mono Point (Monkey Point), Nicar. 75 Q8
Monroe, La., U.S. 83 H11
Monrovia, Liberia 128 H1
Montague Island, Alas., U.S. 80 L3
Montana, U.S. 82 B5
Monteagle, Mount, Antarctica 152 L9
Monte Alegre, Braz. 94 D7
Monte Bello Islands, Austral. 138 E2
Montego Bay, Jam. 77 P8
Montejinni, Austral. 140 C8
Montemayor, Meseta de, Arg. 93 P5
Montenegro, Eur. 104 K7
Monterey, Calif., U.S. 82 F2
Monterey Bay, Calif., U.S. 80 F1
Montería, Col. 94 B2
Montes Claros, Braz. 94 G9
Montevideo, Uru. 95 L7
Montgomery, Ala., U.S. 83 H12
Monticello, Utah, U.S. 82 F5
Monto, Austral. 141 G15
Montpelier, Idaho, U.S. 82 D5
Montpelier, Vt., U.S. 83 C16
Montréal, Que., Can. 76 H8
Montrose, Colo., U.S. 82 F6
Monywa, Myanmar 117 J10
Mooloogool, Austral. 140 G3
Moora, Austral. 140 J3
Moorea, island, Fr. Polynesia, Fr. 143 G10
Moore, Lake, Austral. 138 J3
Moorhead, Minn., U.S. 82 C9
Moosehead Lake, Me., U.S. 81 B16
Moose Jaw, Sask., Can. 76 H4
Moose Lake, Minn., U.S. 83 C10
Moosonee, Ont., Can. 76 H7
Mootwingee, Austral. 141 J11
Mopti, Mali 128 F3
Moquegua, Peru 94 G4
Moraleda Channel, Chile 93 P4
Morane, island, Fr. Polynesia, Fr. 143 H11
Morava, river, Czech Rep. 102 J8
Moravia, region, Czech Rep. 102 H7
Morawhanna, Guyana 94 B6
Moray Firth, Scot., U.K. 102 D4
Moreau, river, S. Dak., U.S. 80 C8
Moree, Austral. 141 J14
Morelia, Mex. 77 N4
Morella, Austral. 141 F12
Morenci, Ariz., U.S. 82 H5
Moreno Bay, S. Amer. 92 J4
Moresby Island, B.C., Can. 76 F2
Moreton, Austral. 141 B12
Moreton Bay, Austral. 139 H15
Moreton Island, Austral. 139 H15
Morgan, Austral. 141 K11
Moriah, Mount, Nev., U.S. 80 E4
Morioka, Japan 117 E14
Mornington, Austral. 141 C11
Mornington Island, Austral. 139 C11
Morocco, Af. 128 D3
Morogoro, Tanzania 129 K10
Moro Gulf, Philippines 115 K14
Morombe, Madagascar 129 M11
Mörön, Mongolia 117 F10
Moroni, Comoros 129 L11
Morotai, island, Indonesia 115 K15
Morris Jesup, Cape (Morris Jesup, Kap), Greenland, Den. 74 A7
Morro Point, Chile 93 K4
Morrosquillo, Gulf of, Col. 92 A2
Morshansk, Russ. 105 F12
Mortlock Islands, F.S.M. 142 E4
Moruroa, island, Fr. Polynesia, Fr. 143 H11
Morven, Austral. 141 G13
Moscow, river, Russ. 103 E11
Moscow see Moskva, Russ. 105 E11
Moscow University Ice Shelf, Antarctica 153 K13
Mose, Cape, Antarctica 153 L13
Moselle, river, Eur. 102 G5
Moshi, Tanzania 128 J10
Mosjøen, Nor. 104 C7
Moskva (Moscow), Russ. 105 E11
Mosquito Cays, Nicar. 75 P8
Mosquito Coast, Nicar. 75 Q8
Mosquitos, Gulf of, Pan. 75 Q8
Mossaka, Congo 128 J6
Mossel Bay, S. Af. 127 Q7
Mossel Bay, S. Af. 129 Q7
Mossman, Austral. 141 C13
Mossoró, Braz. 94 E11
Mostar, Bosn. & Herzg. 104 K8
Motane see Mohotani, island, Fr. Polynesia, Fr. 143 F11
Mott, N. Dak., U.S. 82 C8
Motu Ihupuku see Campbell Island, N.Z. 142 M6
Motul, Mex. 77 N7
Motu One, island, Solomon Is. 142 G9
Moulamein, Austral. 141 L12
Mould Bay, N.W.T., Can. 76 C5
Moultrie, Lake, S.C., U.S. 81 H14
Moulyinning, Austral. 140 K4
Moundou, Chad 128 G6
Mountain Home, Idaho, U.S. 82 D4
Mountain Nile, river, Af. 126 H9
Mountain Village, Alas., U.S. 82 K1
Mount Arrowsmith, Austral. 141 J11
Mount Barker, Austral. 140 L4
Mount Barnett, Austral. 140 C6
Mount Coolon, Austral. 141 E13
Mount Desert Island, Me., U.S. 81 C17
Mount Eba, Austral. 140 H9
Mount Elsie, Austral. 141 E13
Mount Gambier, Austral. 141 M10
Mount Hope, Austral. 141 K13
Mount Howitt, Austral. 141 G11
Mount Ida, Austral. 140 H4
Mount Isa, Austral. 141 E10
Mount Keith, Austral. 140 H4
Mount Lofty Ranges, Austral. 139 K10
Mount Magnet, Austral. 140 H3
Mount Mulgrave, Austral. 141 C13
Mountnorris Bay, Austral. 138 A8
Mount Sandiman, Austral. 140 G2
Mount Surprise, Austral. 141 D12
Mount Vernon, Austral. 140 G3
Moura, Braz. 94 D6
Mouroubra, Austral. 140 J3
Moyale, Kenya 128 H10
Moyobamba, Peru 94 E2
Moyynqum, Kaz. 114 F7
Mozambique, Af. 129 N9
Mozambique Channel, Indian Oc. 127 N10
Mpika, Zambia 129 L9
Mthatha, S. Af. 129 P8
Mtwara, Tanzania 129 L11
Mubi, Nigeria 128 G6
Muchea, Austral. 140 K3
Muchinga Mountains, Zambia 127 L9
Muckety, Austral. 140 D8
Muhammad, Râs, Egypt 126 D9
Mühlig-Hofmann Mountains, Antarctica 152 A8
Mukhomornoye, Russ. 117 A12
Mukinbudin, Austral. 140 J3
Muko Rettō (Parry Group), islands, Japan 142 B2
Mulanie Mountains, Af. 127 L10
Mulgathing, Austral. 140 J9
Mulgrave Island see Badu Island, Austral. 141 A11
Mulhacén, peak, Sp. 102 L2
Mullewa, Austral. 140 H3
Multan, Pak. 116 H7
Mumbai (Bombay), India 116 J7
Mumra, Russ. 105 H14
Muna, island, Indonesia 115 M14
Munburra, Austral. 141 C13
München (Munich), Ger. 104 H6
Muncie, Ind., U.S. 83 E13
Mundabullangana, Austral. 140 E3
Mundiwindi, Austral. 140 F4
Mundo Novo, Braz. 94 F11
Mundrabilla, Austral. 140 J7
Mungindi, Austral. 141 H14
Munguba, Braz. 94 D8
Munich see München, Ger. 104 H6
Münster, Ger. 104 G5
Muonio, Fin. 104 B9
Muqdisho (Mogadishu), Somalia 128 H11
Muralag Island see Prince of Wales Island, Austral. 141 A11
Murashi, Russ. 105 D13
Murchison Downs, Austral. 140 H4
Murchison Falls, Af. 126 H9
Murchison, river, Austral. 138 H2
Murcia, Sp. 104 L3
Murcia, region, Sp. 102 L3
Murcuripe Point, Braz. 92 E11
Mureş, river, Rom. 102 J8
Murfreesboro, Tenn., U.S. 83 G13
Murgon, Austral. 141 G15
Murgoo, Austral. 140 H3
Murman Coast, Eur. 103 A10

Murmansk, Russ. 105 A10
Murnpeowie, Austral. 141 H11
Murra Murra, Austral. 141 H13
Murray Bridge, Austral. 141 L10
Murray, river, Austral. 139 K11
Murray River Basin, Austral. 139 K11
Murrayville, Austral. 141 L11
Murrenja Hill, Austral. 138 B7
Murrumbidgee, river, Austral. 139 K12
Murwillumbah, Austral. 141 H15
Muscat see Masqaţ, Oman, 116 H6
Musgrave Ranges, Austral. 138 G8
Muskegon, river, Mich., U.S. 81 D12
Muskegon, Mich., U.S. 83 D12
Muskingum, river, Ohio, U.S. 81 E14
Muskogee, Okla., U.S. 83 G10
Mussau Islands, P.N.G. 142 E4
Musselshell, river, Mont., U.S. 80 C6
Mussuma, Angola 129 L7
Mûţ, Egypt 128 E8
Mutarara, Mozambique 129 M9
Mutare, Mozambique 129 M9
Muting, Indonesia 117 L16
Mutoray, Russ. 117 D10
Muttaburra, Austral. 141 F13
Mŭynoq, Uzb. 116 F7
Muzhi, Russ. 105 A13
Muztag, peak, China 114 G9
Mwali (Mohéli), Comoros 127 L11
Mweka, Dem. Rep. of the Congo 129 K7
Mwene-Ditu, Dem. Rep. of the Congo 129 K8
Mweru, Lake, Dem. Rep. of the Congo–Zambia 127 K8
Myanmar (Burma), Asia 117 J10
Myitkyinā, Myanmar 117 J10
Myrtle Beach, S.C., U.S. 83 G15
Mysore see Mysuru, India 116 K7
Mysuru (Mysore), India 116 K7
Mytilíni, Gr. 105 L10

N

Nā'ālehu, Hawai'i, U.S. 83 M13
Nabire, Indonesia 117 L16
Nacogdoches, Tex., U.S. 83 J10
Nadym, Russ. 116 D8
Nafūsah, Jabal, Libya 126 C6
Nagasaki, Japan 117 G13
Nagēlē, Eth. 128 H10
Nagorno-Karabakh, disputed territory, Azerb. 105 K14
Nagor'ye Koryakskoye, Russ. 76 A1
Nagoya, Japan 117 F14
Nagpur, India 116 J8
Naha, Japan 117 H13
Nain, Nfld. & Lab., Can. 76 F9
Nairobi, Kenya 128 J10
Najd, region, Saudi Arabia 116 G4
Nakhodka, Russ. 117 E13
Nakhon Ratchasima, Thai. 117 K11
Naknek, Alas., U.S. 82 L2
Nal'chik, Russ. 105 J13
Namib Desert, Namibia 127 M6
Namibe, Angola 129 L5
Namibia, Af. 129 M6
Namoi, river, Austral. 139 J14
Namonuito Atoll, F.S.M. 142 D4
Namorik Atoll, Marshall Is. 142 E5
Nampa, Idaho, U.S. 82 D4
Nampo Islands (Nampo Shotō), Asia 115 F14
Nampula, Mozambique 129 L10
Namsos, Nor. 104 C7
Namtu, Myanmar 117 J10
Nanchang, China 117 H12
Nancy, Fr. 104 H5
Nanjing, China 117 G12
Nannine, Austral. 140 H3
Nanning, China 117 J11
Nanortalik (Ilivileq), Greenland, Den. 76 E10
Nansei Shotō see Ryukyu Islands, Japan 115 H14
Nantes, Fr. 104 H3
Nantucket Island, Mass., U.S. 81 D17
Nānu'alele Point, Hawai'i, U.S. 81 L13
Nanumanga, island, Tuvalu, 142 F6
Nanumea, island, Tuvalu 142 F6
Nanuque, Braz. 94 H10
Nanutarra, Austral. 140 F2
Nao, Cape, Eur. 102 L3
Napasoq, Greenland, Den. 76 D9
Napier Downs, Austral. 140 D5
Napier Mountains, Antarctica 153 C13
Naples see Napoli, It. 104 K6
Napo, river, S. Amer. 92 D3
Napoli (Naples), It. 104 K6
Napuka, island, Fr. Polynesia, Fr. 143 G11
Nara, Mali 128 F2
Naracoorte, Austral. 141 L11
Narbonne, Fr. 104 J4
Narinda Bay, Madagascar 127 L11
Narmada, river, India 114 J7
Narndee, Austral. 140 H3
Narodnaya, peak, Russ. 103 A13
Narooma, Austral. 141 L14
Narrabri, Austral. 141 J14
Narrandera, Austral. 141 L13
Narran Lake, Austral. 139 J13
Narrogin, Austral. 140 K3
Narsarsuaq, Greenland, Den. 76 E10
Narva, Est. 104 E9
Narvik, Nor. 104 B8
Narwietooma, Austral. 140 F8
Nar'yan Mar, Russ. 105 A12
Naryn Qum, desert, Kaz. 103 G14
Nasca, Peru 94 G3
Nashua, N.H., U.S. 83 C16
Nashville, Tenn., U.S. 83 G12
Näsijärvi, lake, Fin. 102 D8
Nassau, Bahamas 77 M8
Nassau Bay, Chile 93 R5
Nassau, island, Cook Is., N.Z. 142 G8
Nasser, Lake, Egypt 126 E9
Natal, Braz. 94 E12
Natashquan, Que., Can. 76 G9
Natchez, Miss., U.S. 83 J11
Natchitoches, La., U.S. 83 J10
National City, Calif., U.S. 82 H3
Natron, Lake, Af. 126 J10
Natuna Islands, Asia 115 L12
Naturaliste, Cape, Austral. 138 K2
Nauiyu (Daly River), Austral. 140 B7
Nauru, Pac. Oc. 142 E5
Nauta, Peru 94 E3
Navarin, Cape (Navarin, Mys), Asia 115 A13
Navarre, Eur. 102 J3
Naxçivan, Azerb. 105 K14
Nay, Cape, Asia 115 K12
Nay Pyi Taw, Myanmar 117 J10
Nazyvayevsk, Russ. 105 C16
Ndélé, Cen. Af. Rep. 128 G7
N'Djamena, Chad 128 G6
Ndogo Lagoon, Gabon 126 J5
Ndola, Zambia 129 L9
Neagh, Lake, Eur. 102 E3
Neale, Lake, Austral. 138 F7
Near Islands, Alas., U.S. 75 R1
Nebine Creek, Austral. 139 H13
Neblina, Pico da, Braz.–Venez. 92 C5
Nebraska, U.S. 82 E8
Neches, river, Tex., U.S. 81 J10
Neckarboo Range, Austral. 139 K12
Necker Island, Hawai'i, U.S. 142 C8
Necochea, Arg. 95 M6
Needles, Calif., U.S. 82 G4
Neftçala, Azerb. 116 F5
Negomano, Mozambique 129 L10
Negra, Punta, Peru 94 E1
Negro, river, Arg. 93 N5
Negro, river, Braz. 92 D6
Negro, river, Uru. 93 L7
Negro Bay, Somalia 126 G12
Negros, island, Philippines 115 K13
Nehe, China 117 E12
Neiva, Col. 94 C3
Nelson, river, Man., Can. 74 G6
Nelson, B.C., Can. 76 G3
Nelson, Cape, Austral. 139 M11
Néma, Mauritania 128 F2
Neman, river, Eur. 102 F8
Nemiscau, Que., Can. 76 H8
Nenana, Alas., U.S. 82 K3
Nendö (Ndeni Island), Solomon Is. 142 F5
Neosho, river, Kan.–Nebr., U.S. 81 F10
Nepal, Asia 116 H8
Nephi, Utah, U.S. 82 E5
Neptune Range, Antarctica 152 F6
Nerrima, Austral. 140 D5
Netherdale, Austral. 141 F14
Netherlands, Eur. 104 F5
Nettilling Lake, Nunavut, Can. 76 E8
Netzahualcóyotl, Mex. 77 P4
Neumayer III, station, Antarctica 152 A7
Neuquén, Arg. 95 N4
Neuse, river, N.C., U.S. 81 G15
Neusiedler Lake, Eur. 102 H7
Nevada, U.S. 82 E3
Nevada, Sierra, Calif., U.S. 80 E3
New Albany, Ind., U.S. 83 F12
New Amsterdam, Guyana 94 B7
Newark, N.J., U.S. 83 D15
New Bedford, Mass., U.S. 83 D17
New Bern, N.C., U.S. 83 G15
New Braunfels, Tex., U.S. 82 J9
New Britain, island, P.N.G. 142 F4
New Brunswick, Can. 76 H9
Newburgh, N.Y., U.S. 83 D16
New Caledonia, New Caledonia, Fr. 142 H5
New Castile, Eur. 102 K3
Newcastle, Austral. 141 K15
Newcastle, Eng., U.K. 104 E4
Newcastle, Wyo., U.S. 82 D7
Newcastle Bay, Austral. 139 A12
Newcastle Waters, Austral. 140 D8
Newdegate, Austral. 140 K4
New Delhi, India 116 H7
New England Range, Austral. 139 J15
Newenham, Cape, Alas., U.S. 80 L1
Newfoundland and Labrador, Can. 76 F9
Newfoundland, Island of, Nfdl. & Lab., Can. 74 G10
New Georgia, island, Solomon Is. 142 F4
New Guinea, island, Indonesia 115 L16
Newhalen, Alas., U.S. 82 L2
New Hampshire, U.S. 83 C16
New Hanover, island, P.N.G. 142 E4
New Haven, Conn., U.S. 83 D16
New Hazelton, B.C., Can. 76 F3
New Iberia, La., U.S. 83 J11
New Ireland, island, P.N.G. 142 F4
New Jersey, U.S. 83 E16
New Liskeard, Ont., Can. 76 H8
Newman, Austral. 140 F4
New Mexico, U.S. 82 G6
New Norfolk, Austral. 140 M8
New Orleans, La., U.S. 83 J12
Newport, Oreg., U.S. 82 C2
Newport News, Va., U.S. 83 F15
New Schwabenland, region, Antarctica 152 B7
New Siberian Islands, Russ. 115 B10
New South Wales, Austral. 141 J12
Newton, Kans., U.S. 82 F9
New York, N.Y., U.S. 83 D16
New York, U.S. 83 D15
New Zealand, Pac. Oc. 142 L6
Nganglong Kangri, China 114 H8
Ngatik Atoll, F.S.M. 142 E4
Ngoko, river, Cameroon–Congo 126 H6
Nguigmi, Niger 128 F6
Nguiu, Austral. 140 A8
Ngukurr, Austral. 140 B9
Ngulu Atoll, F.S.M. 142 D2
Nha Trang, Vietnam 117 K12
Nhulunbuy, Austral. 141 B10
Ni'ihau, island, Hawai'i, U.S. 81 L10
Niagara Falls, Can.–U.S. 81 D14
Niamey, Niger 128 F4
Nias, island, Indonesia 115 L10
Nicaragua, N. Amer. 77 Q7
Nicaragua, Lake (Nicaragua, Lago de), Nicar. 75 Q7
Nice, Fr. 104 J5
Nicholson Range, Austral. 138 H3
Nickavilla, Austral. 141 G12
Nickol Bay, Austral. 138 E3
Nicobar Islands, India 115 L10
Nicosia (Lefkoşa, Lefkosía), Cyprus 105 M11
Nicoya Peninsula (Nicoya, Península de), C.R. 75 Q7
Nieuw Nickerie, Suriname 94 B7
Niger, Af. 128 F5
Nigeria, Af. 128 G5
Niger, river, Af. 126 H5
Niger River Delta, Nigeria 126 H4
Nihoa, Hawai'i, U.S. 142 C9
Ni'ihau, island, Hawai'i, U.S. 142 C9
Nikolayevsk na Amure, Russ. 117 D12
Nikol'sk, Russ. 105 D12
Nikšić, Montenegro 104 K8
Nikumaroro, island, Kiribati 142 F7
Nile, river, Af. 126 D9
Nile River Delta, Egypt 126 D9
Nimba Mountains, Côte d'Ivoire 126 G2
Nîmes, Fr. 104 J4
Nimrod Glacier, Antarctica 152 J9
Ningaloo, Austral. 140 F1
Ningbo, China 117 G13
Ninnis Glacier, Antarctica 153 L11
Ninty Mile Beach, Austral. 139 M13
Niobrara, river, Nebr., U.S. 80 D8
Nioro du Sahel, Mali 128 F2
Nipigon, Ont., Can. 76 H7
Nipigon, Lake, Ont., Can. 74 H7
Niquelândia, Braz. 94 G9
Niš, Serb. 104 K8
Niterói, Braz. 94 J10
Niuafo'ou, island, Tonga 142 G7
Niuatoputapu, island, Tonga 142 G7
Niue, island, Pac. Oc. 142 G8
Niulakita, island, Tuvalu 142 F7
Niutao, island, Tuvalu 142 F7
Nizhnaya Tunguska, river, Russ. 115 D10
Nizhnevartovsk, Russ. 105 A15
Nizhniy Novgorod, Russ. 105 E12
Nizhniy Tagil, Russ. 116 D7
Njazidja (Grande Comore), Comoros 127 L11
Nkomi Lagoon, Gabon 126 J5
Noatak, river, Alas., U.S. 80 J2
Noatak, Alas., U.S. 82 J2
Nogales, Mex. 77 L3
Nogales, Ariz., U.S. 82 H5
Noginsk, Russ. 116 D9
Nola, Cen. Af. Rep. 128 H6
Nome, Alas., U.S. 82 K1
Nonda, Austral. 141 E12
Nonouti, island, Kiribati 142 E6
Noondoo, Austral. 141 H13
Noosa Head, Austral. 139 H15
Nordaustlandet, Nor. 116 A8
Nordfjord, Atl. Oc. 102 D6
Nordkinn Peninsula, Nor. 114 B7
Noreena Downs, Austral. 140 F4
Norfolk, Nebr., U.S. 82 E9
Norfolk, Va., U.S. 83 F15
Norfolk Island, Austral. 142 H5
Noril'sk, Russ. 116 C9
Normanby Island, P.N.G. 139 A15
Normandy, region, Fr. 102 G4
Norman, river, Austral. 139 D12
Normanton, Austral. 141 D11
Norman Wells, N.W.T., Can. 76 D4
Nornalup, Austral. 140 L3
Ñorquincó, Arg. 95 N4
Norrköping, Sw. 104 E7
Norrland, Eur. 102 C7
Norseman, Austral. 140 K5
Norte, Canal do, Braz. 94 C8
Norte, Punta (North Point), Arg. 95 M7
Nortelândia, Braz. 94 G7
North America, 76-77
Northampton, Austral. 140 H2
North Aral Sea, Kaz. 114 E6
North Atlantic Ocean, Atlantic Oc. 23
North Battleford, Sask., Can. 76 G4
North Bend, Oreg., U.S. 82 C2
North Canadian, river, Okla., U.S. 80 G9
North Cape, Ice. 102 A3
North Cape, Nor. 102 A8
North Cape (Otou), N.Z. 142 J6
North Carolina, U.S. 83 G14
North Channel, Ire., U.K. 102 E3
North China Plain, Asia 115 G12
Northcliffe, Austral. 140 L3
North Dakota, U.S. 82 C8
North East Land, Nor. 114 A8
Northern Cyprus, disputed territory, Cyprus 105 M11
Northern Dvina, river, Eur. 103 C11
Northern European Plain, Eur. 102 G5
Northern Ireland, U.K. 104 E3
Northern Mariana Islands, Pac. Oc. 142 C3
Northern Sos'va, river, Russ. 103 B14
Northern Sporades, Gr. 102 L9
Northern Territory, Austral. 140 D8
Northern Uvals, Eur. 103 D12
North Island (Te Ika-a-Māui), N.Z. 142 K6
North Korea, Asia 117 F13
North Land, Russ. 115 B10
North Magnetic Pole, Arctic Oc. 74 A5
North Pacific Ocean, Pacific Oc. 22-23
North Platte, Nebr., U.S. 82 E8
North Platte, river, Colo.–Nebr., U.S. 80 E8
North Point (Norte, Punta), Arg. 93 M7
North Pole, Arctic Oc. 74 A7
North Saskatchewan, river, Alta.–Sask., Can. 74 G4
North Sea, Atlantic Oc. 102 E5
North Siberian Lowland, Asia 115 C10
North Slope, Alas., U.S. 80 J2
North Stradbroke Island, Austral. 139 H15
Northumberland, Cape, Austral. 139 M10
Northumberland Islands, Austral. 139 E14
Northway, Alas., U.S. 82 K4

Prince Regent Inlet, *Nunavut, Can.* **76** D7
Prince Rupert, *B.C., Can.* **76** F2
Princess Astrid Coast, *Antarctica* **152** A9
Princess Charlotte Bay, *Austral.* **139** B13
Princess Martha Coast, *Antarctica* **152** C7
Princess Ragnhild Coast, *Antarctica* **153** B10
Prince William Sound, *Alas., U.S.* **80** L3
Príncipe da Beira, *Braz.* **94** F5
Príncipe, island, *Sao Tome and Principe* **126** H5
Pristina, *Kos.* **104** K8
Privolzhskaya Vozvyshennost', *Russ.* **105** G13
Prizren, *Kos.* **104** K8
Progress 2, station, *Antarctica* **153** E13
Propriá, *Braz.* **94** F11
Proserpine, *Austral.* **141** E14
Provence, region, *Fr.* **102** J5
Providence, *R.I., U.S.* **83** D16
Providencia Island (Providencia, Isla de), *Col.* **75** Q8
Provideniya, *Russ.* **77** P3
Provo, *Utah, U.S.* **82** E5
Prudhoe Bay, *Alas., U.S.* **82** J3
Prut, river, *Mold.–Rom.* **103** H10
Prydz Bay, *Antarctica* **153** E13
Prypyats', river, *Eur.* **103** G10
Pskov, *Russ.* **104** E9
Pskov, Lake, *Eur.* **102** E9
Puán, *Arg.* **95** M6
Pucallpa, *Peru* **94** F3
Puducherry (Pondicherry), *India* **116** K8
Puebla, *Mex.* **77** P5
Pueblo, *Colo., U.S.* **82** F7
Puerto Aisén, *Chile* **95** P4
Puerto Ángel, *Mex.* **77** P5
Puerto Armuelles, *Pan.* **77** R7
Puerto Ayacucho, *Venez.* **94** B4
Puerto Coig, *Arg.* **95** Q5
Puerto Deseado, *Arg.* **95** P5
Puerto Leguízamo, *Col.* **94** D3
Puerto Libertad, *Mex.* **77** L3
Puerto Madryn, *Arg.* **95** N5
Puerto Maldonado, *Peru* **94** F4
Puerto Natales, *Chile* **95** Q4
Puerto Páez, *Venez.* **94** B4
Puerto Plata, *Dom. Rep.* **77** N10
Puerto Princesa, *Philippines* **117** K13
Puerto Rico, *U.S.* **77** N11
Puerto Rico, island, *U.S., Greater Antilles* **75** N11
Puerto San Carlos, *Chile* **95** P4
Puerto San Julián, *Arg.* **95** Q5
Puerto Santa Cruz, *Arg.* **95** Q5
Puerto Williams, *Chile* **95** R5
Puget Sound, *Wash., U.S.* **80** B3
Pukapuka Atoll, *Cook Is., N.Z.* **142** F8
Pukapuka, island, *Fr. Polynesia, Fr.* **143** G11
Pulap Atoll, *F.S.M.* **142** D4
Pullman, *Wash., U.S.* **82** B4
Pulo Anna, island, *Palau* **142** E2
Pulog, Mount, *Philippines* **115** J13
Pulusuk, island, *F.S.M.* **142** E4
Puluwat Atoll, *F.S.M.* **142** E3
Pune, *India* **116** J7
Punta Alta, *Arg.* **95** M6
Punta Arenas, *Chile* **95** Q4
Punta Delgada, *Arg.* **95** N6
Punta Prieta, *Mex.* **77** L2
Puntarenas, *C.R.* **77** Q7
Puntland, region, *Somalia* **128** G12
Punto Fijo, *Venez.* **94** A3
Purus, river, *Braz.* **92** E6
Pusan *see* Busan, *S. Korea* **117** G13
Putorana Plateau, *Asia* **114** C9
Pu'uwai, *Hawai'i, U.S.* **83** L10
Puy de Sancy, peak, *Fr.* **102** H4
Puysegur Point, *N.Z.* **142** L5
Pweto, *Dem. Rep. of the Congo* **129** K9
Pya, Lake, *Eur.* **102** B9
Pyay, *Myanmar* **117** J10
P'yŏngyang (Pyongyang), *N. Korea* **117** F12
Pyramid Lake, *Nev., U.S.* **80** E3
Pyrenees, range, *Eur.* **102** J3
Pýrgos, *Gr.* **104** M8
Pyu, *Myanmar* **117** J10

Q

Qaanaaq (Thule), *Greenland, Den.* **76** C7
Qaidam Basin, *Asia* **115** G10
Qamar, Ghubbat al, *Yemen* **114** J5
Qaqortoq (Julianehåb), *Greenland, Den.* **76** E10
Qaraghandy, *Kaz.* **116** F8
Qarataū, *Kaz.* **114** F7
Qardho, *Somalia* **128** G12
Qasigiannguit (Christianshåb), *Greenland, Den.* **76** D9
Qatar, *Asia* **116** H5
Qattara Depression, *Egypt* **126** D8
Qazaly, *Kaz.* **116** F7
Qeqertarsuaq (Disko), island, *Greenland, Den.* **74** D8
Qeqertarsuaq (Godhavn), *Greenland, Den.* **76** D8
Qeqertarsuup Tunua, bay, *Greenland, Den.* **74** D9
Qiemo, *China* **116** G9
Qikiqtarjuaq, *Greenland, Den.* **76** D8
Qilian Shan, *China* **115** G10
Qimusseriarsuaq, bay, *Greenland, Den.* **76** C7
Qingdao, *China* **117** G12
Qinghai Hu, *China* **115** G10
Qing Zang Gaoyuan, *China* **116** H9
Qin Lin, *Asia* **115** G11
Qiongzhou Strait, *Pac. Oc.* **115** J12
Qiqihar, *China* **117** E12
Qishn, *Yemen* **116** J4
Qizilqum, *Uzb.* **114** F7
Qom, *Iran* **116** G5
Quanzhou, *China* **117** H12
Quartz Hill, *Austral.* **140** F9
Quebec, *Can.* **76** H8
Québec, *Que., Can.* **76** H9
Queen Adelaida Archipelago, *S. Amer.* **93** Q4
Queen Alexandra Range, *Antarctica* **152** H8
Queen Charlotte Sound, *B.C., Can.* **74** G2
Queen Elizabeth Islands, *Nunavut, Can.* **74** C6
Queen Elizabeth Range, *Antarctica* **152** H8
Queen Fabiola Mountains (Yamato Mountains), *Antarctica* **153** C11
Queen Mary Coast, *Antarctica* **153** G14
Queen Maud Gulf, *Nunavut, Can.* **74** D6
Queen Maud Land, region, *Antarctica* **152** C7
Queen Maud Mountains, *Antarctica* **152** G7
Queens Channel, *Austral.* **138** C7
Queensland, *Austral.* **141** E11
Queenstown, *S. Af.* **129** P8
Queenstown, *Austral.* **140** L7
Quelimane, *Mozambique* **129** M10
Querétaro, *Mex.* **77** N4
Quesnel, *B.C., Can.* **76** G3
Quetta, *Pak.* **116** H6
Quetzaltenango, *Guatemala* **77** Q6
Quezon City, *Philippines* **117** J13
Quibdó, *Col.* **94** B2
Quilpie, *Austral.* **141** G12
Quince Mil, *Peru* **94** G4
Quincy, *Ill., U.S.* **83** E11
Quinhagak, *Alas., U.S.* **82** L1
Quito, *Ecua.* **94** D1
Quixadá, *Braz.* **94** E11
Qullai Somoniyon (Communism Peak), *Asia* **114** G7
Qulsary, *Kaz.* **116** E6
Quobba, *Austral.* **140** G2
Quorn, *Austral.* **141** J10
Qusmuryn Köli, *Kaz.* **105** D16
Quy Nhơn, *Vietnam* **117** K12
Qyzylorda, *Kaz.* **116** F7

R

Rabat, *Mor.* **128** C3
Rabaul, *P.N.G.* **142** F4
Rābigh, *Saudi Arabia* **116** G3
Race, Cape, *Nfld. & Lab., Can.* **74** H11
Racine, *Wis., U.S.* **83** D12
Raeside, Lake, *Austral.* **138** H4
Raga, *S. Sudan* **128** G8
Ragged, Mount, *Austral.* **138** K5
Raiatea, island, *Fr. Polynesia, Fr.* **143** G10
Rainbow, *Austral.* **141** L11
Rainier, Mount, *Wash., U.S.* **80** B3
Rainy Lake, *Can.–U.S.* **81** B10
Raipur, *India* **116** J8
Raivavae (Vavitu), island, *Fr. Polynesia, Fr.* **143** H10
Rajkot, *India* **116** J7
Rajshahi, *Bangladesh* **116** J9
Rakahanga Atoll, *Cook Is., N.Z.* **142** F9
Rakiura *see* Stewart Island, *N.Z.* **142** L6
Raleigh, *N.C., U.S.* **83** F15
Ralik Chain, islands, *Marshall Is.* **142** D5
Rampart, *Alas., U.S.* **82** K3
Rancagua, *Chile* **95** L4
Ranco, Lake (Ranco, Lago), *Chile* **93** N4
Rangiauria *see* Pitt Island, *N.Z.* **142** L7
Rangiroa, Atoll, *Fr. Polynesia, Fr.* **143** G10
Rangoon *see* Yangon, *Myanmar* **117** K10
Rankin Inlet, *Nunavut, Can.* **76** F6
Rannes, *Austral.* **141** G14
Rann of Kutch, *India* **114** H7
Raoul Island (Sunday, island), *Kermadec Is., N.Z.* **142** H7
Rapa, island, *Fr. Polynesia, Fr.* **143** H10
Rapa Nui *see* Easter Island, *Chile, Pac. Oc.* **143** H14
Rapid City, *S. Dak., U.S.* **82** D8
Rarotonga, island, *Cook Is., N.Z.* **142** H9
Ras Dejen, *Eth.* **114** H3
Rasht, *Iran* **116** F5
Rason, Lake, *Austral.* **138** H6
Ratak Chain, islands, *Marshall Is.* **142** D6
Rat Islands, *Alas., U.S.* **75** R2
Raton, *N. Mex., U.S.* **82** G7
Rattray Head, *Eur.* **102** E4
Raufarhöfn, *Ice.* **104** A4
Ravenshoe, *Austral.* **141** D13
Ravensthorpe, *Austral.* **140** K4
Rawaki, island, *Kiribati* **142** F8
Rawalpindi, *Pak.* **116** G8
Rawlinna, *Austral.* **140** J6
Rawlins, *Wyo., U.S.* **82** E6
Rawson, *Arg.* **95** N5
Raymondville, *Tex., U.S.* **82** K9
Ray Mountains, *Alas., U.S.* **80** K3
Rayner Glacier, *Antarctica* **153** C12
Reading, *Pa., U.S.* **83** E15
Realicó, *Arg.* **95** L5
Rebecca, Lake, *Austral.* **138** J5
Rebiana Sand Sea, *Af.* **126** E7
Recherche, Archipelago of the, *Austral.* **138** K5
Recife, *Braz.* **94** F12
Recife, Cape, *S. Af.* **127** Q8
Red, river, *U.S.* **80** H9
Red, river, *China–Vietnam* **115** J11
Red Bluff, *Calif., U.S.* **82** D2
Red Bluff Lake, *Tex., U.S.* **80** H7
Redcliffe, Mount, *Austral.* **138** H4
Red Deer, *Alta., Can.* **76** G4
Red Devil, *Alas., U.S.* **82** L2
Redding, *Calif., U.S.* **82** D2
Red Hills, *Kans., U.S.* **80** G8
Red Lake, *Minn., U.S.* **76** H6
Red River of the North, river, *Can.–U.S.* **80** B9
Red Rocks Point, *Austral.* **138** J7
Red Sea, *Indian Oc.* **126** E10
Reedy Glacier, *Antarctica* **152** H7
Regência Point, *Braz.* **92** H11
Reggio di Calabria, *It.* **104** L7
Regina, *Sask., Can.* **76** H5
Rehoboth, *Namibia* **129** N7
Reid River, *Austral.* **141** E13
Reims, *Fr.* **104** H5
Reina Adelaida, Archipiélago, *Chile* **95** R3
Reindeer Lake, *Sask.–Man., Can.* **74** F5
Reliance, *N.W.T., Can.* **76** E5
Remanso, *Braz.* **94** F10
Renk, *S. Sudan* **128** G9
Rennell, island, *Solomon Is.* **142** G4
Rennes, *Fr.* **104** G3
Rennick Glacier, *Antarctica* **153** L10
Reno, *Nev., U.S.* **82** E3
Republican, river, *U.S.* **80** E9
Repulse Bay, *Austral.* **139** E14
Repulse Bay, *Nunavut, Can.* **76** E6
Requena, *Peru* **94** E3
Resistencia, *Arg.* **95** K6
Resolute, *Nunavut, Can.* **76** C6
Resolution Island, *Nunavut, Can.* **74** E9
Reval *see* Tallinn, *Est.* **104** E9
Revillagigedo Island, *Alas., U.S.* **80** M5
Revillagigedo Islands (Revillagigedo, Islas), *Mex.* **75** N2
Reyes, Point, *Calif., U.S.* **80** E1
Reykjanes, *Eur.* **102** A2
Reykjavík, *Ice.* **104** A3
Rēzekne, *Latv.* **104** E9
Rhine, river, *Switz.* **102** G5
Rhinelander, *Wis., U.S.* **83** C11
Rhir, Cape, *Af.* **126** C2
Rhode Island, *U.S.* **83** D16
Rhodes (Rodos), island, *Gr.* **103** M10
Rhodope Mountains, *Bulg.–Gr.* **102** K9
Rhône, river, *Fr.–Switz.* **102** J5
Ribeirão Preto, *Braz.* **94** H9
Riberalta, *Bol.* **94** F5
Richards Bay, *S. Af.* **127** P9
RichardsonMountains, *N.W.T.–Yukon, Can.* **74** D3
Richfield, *Utah, U.S.* **82** F5
Richland, *Wash., U.S.* **82** B4
Richmond, *Austral.* **141** E12
Richmond, *Austral.* **141** K14
Richmond, *Va., U.S.* **83** F15
Ridge A, *Antarctica* **153** F10
Ridgecrest, *Calif., U.S.* **82** F3
Rifstangi, *Eur.* **102** A4
Rīga, *Latv.* **104** E9
Riga, Gulf of, *Est.–Latv.* **102** E8
Riiser-Larsen Ice Shelf, *Antarctica* **152** B6
Riiser-Larsen Peninsula, *Antarctica* **153** B11
Rijeka, *Croatia* **104** J7
Rimatara, island, *Fr. Polynesia, Fr.* **143** H10
Rimouski, *Que., Can.* **76** H9
Rincón del Bonete, Lake, *Uru.* **93** L7
Riobamba, *Ecua.* **94** D2
Rio Branco, *Braz.* **94** F4
Río Cuarto, *Arg.* **95** L5
Rio das Mortes, river, *Braz.* **92** G8
Rio de Janeiro, *Braz.* **94** J10
Río de la Plata, river *see* River Plate, *Arg.–Uru.* **93** L7
Río Gallegos, *Arg.* **95** Q5
Río Grande, *Arg.* **95** R5
Rio Grande, *Braz.* **95** L8
Rio Grande, river, *Mex.–U.S.* **80** K8
Ríohacha, *Col.* **94** A3
Río Muni, region, *Eq. Guinea* **128** J5
Rio Verde, *Braz.* **94** H8
Ritscher Upland, *Antarctica* **152** B7
Rivas, *Nicar.* **77** Q7
Rivera, *Uru.* **95** K7
Riverina, region, *Austral.* **139** L12
Riverina, *Austral.* **140** J4
River Plate, river, *Arg.–Uru.* **93** L7
Riverside, *Calif., U.S.* **82** G3
Riversleigh, *Austral.* **141** D10
Riverton, *Wyo., U.S.* **82** D6
Riviera, *Fr.–It.* **102** J5
Riyadh *see* Ar Riyāḍ, *Saudi Arabia* **116** G4
Roan Cliffs, *Utah, U.S.* **80** E5
Roanoke, *Va., U.S.* **83** F14
Roanoke, river, *N.C.–Va., U.S.* **81** F15
Robe, *Austral.* **141** L10
Robert Glacier, *Antarctica* **153** C13
Roberts Butte, *Antarctica* **153** L10
Roberts Mountain, *Alas., U.S.* **80** L1
Robertsport, *Liberia* **128** G1
Róbinson Crusoe, Island (Róbinson Crusoe, Isla), *Chile* **93** L3
Robinson Range, *Austral.* **138** G3
Robinson River, *Austral.* **141** C10
Robinvale, *Austral.* **141** K11
Roboré, *Bol.* **94** H6
Robson, Mount, *B.C., Can.* **74** G3
Roca, Cape, *Eur.* **102** K1
Roca Partida, Isla, *Mex.* **143** C14
Rocas Alijos, islands, *Mex.* **143** B13
Rocha, *Uru.* **95** L7
Rochedo, *Braz.* **94** H7
Rochester, *Minn., U.S.* **83** D10
Rochester, *N.Y., U.S.* **83** D14
Rock, river, *Ill.–Wis., U.S.* **81** E11
Rockefeller Plateau, *Antarctica* **152** J6
Rockford, *Ill., U.S.* **83** D11
Rockhampton, *Austral.* **141** F15
Rockingham, *Austral.* **140** K2
Rockingham Bay, *Austral.* **139** D13
Rock Island, *Ill., U.S.* **83** E11
Rock Springs, *Wyo., U.S.* **82** E6
Rocky Mountains, *Can.–U.S.* **74** F3
Ródos, *Gr.* **105** M10
Ródos (Rhodes), island, *Gr.* **105** M10
Roebuck Bay, *Austral.* **138** D4
Rogers, Mount, *Va., U.S.* **81** F14
Rojo, Cape, *Mex.* **75** N5
Rolla, *Mo., U.S.* **83** F11
Rollingstone, *Austral.* **141** D13
Roma, *Austral.* **141** G14
Roma (Rome), *It.* **104** K6
Romania, *Eur.* **104** J9
Romano, Cape, *Fla., U.S.* **81** K14
Romanzof, Cape, *Alas., U.S.* **80** K1
Rome, *Ga., U.S.* **83** G13
Rome *see* Roma, *It.* **104** K6
Roncador, Serra de, *Braz.* **92** G8
Rondonópolis, *Braz.* **94** G7
Rongelap Atoll, *Marshall Is.* **142** D5

Santa Maria, *Braz.* **95** K7
Santa Maria, *Calif., U.S.* **82** F2
Santa Maria, Cape, *Angola* **127** L5
Santa Maria da Vitória, *Braz.* **94** G9
Santa María, Isla, *Galápagos Is., Ecua.* **143** F16
Santa Marta, *Col.* **94** A2
Santa Marta Grande, Cape, *Braz.* **93** K8
Santana, *Braz.* **94** G9
Santander, *Sp.* **104** J2
Santarém, *Braz.* **94** D7
Santa Rosa, *Arg.* **95** M5
Santa Rosa, *Calif., U.S.* **82** E2
Santa Rosa, island, *Calif., U.S.* **80** G2
Santa Teresa, *Austral.* **140** F9
Santa Vitória do Palmar, *Braz.* **95** L7
Santee, river, *S.C., U.S.* **81** G15
Santiago, *Pan.* **77** R8
Santiago, *Chile* **95** L4
Santiago de Compostela, *Sp.* **104** H1
Santiago del Estero, *Arg.* **95** K5
Santo Domingo, *Dom. Rep.* **77** N10
Santos, *Braz.* **94** J9
San Valentín, Cerro, *Chile* **93** Q4
San Valentín, Monte, *Chile* **95** Q4
San Vito, Cape, *Eur.* **102** L6
Sanya, *China* **117** J12
São Borja, *Braz.* **95** K7
São Carlos, *Braz.* **94** H8
São Félix do Xingu, *Braz.* **94** E8
São Francisco, river, *Braz.* **92** F11
São Francisco Island, *Braz.* **93** K9
São Gabriel da Cachoeira, *Braz.* **94** D4
São José Bay (São José, Baía de), *Braz.* **92** D10
São José do Rio Preto, *Braz.* **94** H8
São José dos Campos, *Braz.* **94** J9
São Leopoldo, *Braz.* **95** K8
São Luís, *Braz.* **94** D9
São Marcos Bay (São Marcos, Baía de), *Braz.* **92** D10
Saône, river, *Eur.* **102** H5
São Paulo, *Braz.* **94** J8
São Paulo de Olivença, *Braz.* **94** D4
São Raimundo Nonato, *Braz.* **94** F10
São Romão, *Braz.* **94** E4
São Sebastião, Cape, *Mozambique* **127** N10
São Sebastião Island, *Braz.* **92** J9
São Tomé, *Sao Tome and Principe* **128** J4
São Tomé, Cape (São Tomé, Cabo de), *Braz.* **92** J10
Sao Tome and Principe, *Af.* **128** J4
São Tomé, island, *Sao Tome and Principe* **126** J4
Sapporo, *Japan* **117** E14
Sapri, *It.* **104** L7
Sarajevo, *Bosn. & Herzg.* **104** J7
Saraji, *Austral.* **141** F14
Saraktash, *Russ.* **105** E15
Saranac Lake, *N.Y., U.S.* **83** C15
Saransk, *Russ.* **105** F12
Sarasota, *Fla., U.S.* **83** K14
Saratov, *Russ.* **105** F13
Sardinia, island, *It.* **102** K5
Sarh, *Chad* **128** G7
Sarigan, island, *N. Mariana Is., U.S.* **142** C3
Sarina, *Austral.* **141** E14
Sarīr Calanscio, *Libya* **126** D7
Sarīr Tibasti, region, *Libya* **128** E6
Sarmi, *Indonesia* **117** K16
Särna, *Sw.* **104** D7
Sarny, *Ukr.* **104** G9
Saryesik-Atyrau Desert, *Asia* **114** F8
Saskatchewan, river, *Can.* **74** G5
Saskatchewan, *Can.* **76** G4
Saskatoon, *Sask., Can.* **76** G4
Sassafras Mountain, *S.C., U.S.* **81** G14
Sassari, *It.* **104** K5
Satawal, island, *F.S.M.* **142** D3
Satka, *Russ.* **105** D14
Satpura Range, *India* **114** J7
Satu Mare, *Rom.* **104** H9
Sauðárkrókur, *Ice.* **104** A3
Saudi Arabia, *Asia* **116** H4
Sault Ste. Marie, *Mich., U.S.* **83** C12
Saunders Coast, *Antarctica* **152** K6
Saurimo, *Angola* **129** K7
Sava, river, *Bosn. & Herzg.–Croatia* **102** J7
Savai'i, island, *Samoa* **142** G7
Savannah, river, *Ga.–S.C., U.S.* **81** H14
Savannah, *Ga., U.S.* **83** H14
Save, river, *Mozambique* **127** M9
Savissivik, *Greenland, Den.* **76** C8
Savonlinna, *Fin.* **104** D9
Savoonga, *Alas., U.S.* **82** K1
Savu Sea, *Indonesia* **115** M14
Sawdā', Jabal as, *Libya* **126** D6
Sawu, island, *Indonesia* **138** A4
Saxby Downs, *Austral.* **141** E12
Saxony, region, *Ger.* **102** G6
Sayḩūt, *Yemen* **116** J4
Scandinavia, *Eur.* **102** D7
Schefferville, *Que., Can.* **76** G9
Schell Creek Range, *Nev., U.S.* **80** E4
Schenectady, *N.Y., U.S.* **83** C15
Schleswig, *Ger.* **102** F6
Scioto, river, *Ohio, U.S.* **81** E13
Scoresby Land, *Greenland, Den.* **74** B10
Scoresbysund *see* Ittoqqortoormiit, *Greenland, Den.* **76** B10
Scotland, *U.K.* **104** E4
Scott Base, station, *Antarctica* **152** K8
Scott Coast, *Antarctica* **152** K9
Scott Glacier, *Antarctica* **153** H14
Scottsbluff, *Nebr., U.S.* **82** E7
Scottsdale, *Austral.* **140** L8
Scottsdale, *Ariz., U.S.* **82** H5
Scranton, *Pa., U.S.* **83** D15
Scrubby Creek, *Austral.* **141** B12
Sea Islands, *Ga.–S.C., U.S.* **81** H14
Seal, Cape, *S. Af.* **127** Q7
Seaton Glacier, *Antarctica* **153** C13
Seattle, *Wash., U.S.* **82** B3
Sebastián Vizcaíno Bay, *Mex.* **75** L2
Sebring, *Fla., U.S.* **83** K14
Sechura Bay, *Peru* **92** E1
Sechura Desert, *S. Amer.* **92** E1
Seemore Downs, *Austral.* **140** J6
Seg, Lake, *Eur.* **103** C10
Segezha, *Russ.* **105** C10
Ségou, *Mali* **128** F3
Seguam, island, *Alas., U.S.* **75** R3
Seine, river, *Fr.* **102** G4
Sekondi-Takoradi, *Ghana* **128** H3
Selawik, *Alas., U.S.* **82** J2
Selawik Lake, *Alas., U.S.* **80** J2
Seldovia, *Alas., U.S.* **82** L2
Selenge, river, *Mongolia* **115** F10
Selinde, *Russ.* **117** D12
Selkirk, *Man., Can.* **76** H6
Selkirk Mountains, *Can.–U.S.* **74** G3
Selma, *Ala., U.S.* **83** H12
Selvas, region, *S. Amer.* **92** E4
Selwyn Mountains, *Yukon, Can.* **74** D3
Semarang, *Indonesia* **117** M12
Semey, *Kaz.* **116** F9
Seminole, Lake, *Fla.–Ga., U.S.* **81** J13
Semisopochnoi, island, *Alas., U.S.* **75** R2
Sena Madureira, *Braz.* **94** F4
Sendai, *Japan* **117** F14
Senegal, *Af.* **128** F1
Sénégal, river, *Af.* **126** F1
Senhor do Bonfim, *Braz.* **94** F11
Sennar, *Sudan* **128** F9
Sentinel Range, *Antarctica* **152** G4
Senyavin Islands, *F.S.M.* **142** D4
Seoul, *S. Korea* **117** F13
Sept-Îles, *Que., Can.* **76** H9
Serbia, *Eur.* **104** K8
Serdobsk, *Russ.* **105** F13
Serengeti Plain, *Tanzania* **126** J9
Sergino, *Russ.* **105** B14
Sermilik, *Greenland, Den.* **74** D10
Serov, *Russ.* **105** C14
Serpentine Lakes, *Austral.* **138** H7
Serpent's Mouth, *Venez.* **92** A6
Serra do Navio, *Braz.* **94** C7
Sérres, *Gr.* **104** K9
Sertão, region, *S. Amer.* **92** F10
Sesfontein, *Namibia* **129** M6
Sete Lagoas, *Braz.* **94** H10
Sete Quedas Falls, *Braz.–Parag.* **92** J7
Sétif, *Alg.* **128** C5
Setté Cama, *Gabon* **128** J5
Setúbal, *Port.* **104** K1
Sevan, Lake, *Arm.* **103** K14
Sevastopol', *Ukr.* **105** J11
Severn, river, *Ont., Can.* **74** G6
Severnaya Dvina, river, *Russ.* **105** C11
Severnaya Zemlya *see* North Land, *Russ.* **115** B10
Severnyye Uvaly, *Russ.* **105** D12
Severobaykal'sk, *Russ.* **117** E11
Severodvinsk, *Russ.* **105** C10
Severoural'sk, *Russ.* **116** D7
Severo Yeniseyskiy, *Russ.* **116** D9
Sevier Lake, *Utah, U.S.* **80** E5
Sevilla, *Sp.* **104** L2
Seward, *Alas., U.S.* **82** L3
Seward Peninsula, *Alas., U.S.* **80** K1
Seychelles, *Af.* **129** K12
Seyðisfjörður, *Ice.* **104** B4
Seylla Glacier, *Antarctica* **153** D13
Seymour, *Austral.* **141** L12
Sfax, *Tun.* **128** C5
Shackleton Coast, *Antarctica* **152** J8
Shackleton Ice Shelf, *Antarctica* **153** H15
Shackleton Range, *Antarctica* **152** D7
Shaḩḩāt, *Libya* **128** C7
Shakhty, *Russ.* **105** H12
Shalqar, *Kaz.* **116** E7
Shamattawa, *Man., Can.* **76** G6
Shanghai, *China* **117** G13
Shannon, river, *Ire.* **102** F3
Shannon (Sionainn), *Ire.* **104** F3
Shannon Ø, *Greenland, Den.* **74** B9
Shantar Islands, *Asia* **115** D12
Shantou (Swatow), *China* **117** H12
Sharbatāt, Ra's ash, *Oman* **114** J5
Shark Bay , *Austral.* **138** G2
Sharpe, Lake, *S. Dak., U.S.* **80** D8
Shar'ya, *Russ.* **105** D12
Shasta, Mount, *Calif., U.S.* **80** D2
Shawnee, *Okla., U.S.* **82** G9
Shay Gap, *Austral.* **140** E4
Shebelē, river, *Af.* **126** H11
Shebelē, Wabē, *Af.* **128** H11
Sheboygan, *Wis., U.S.* **83** D11
Shed Lakes, *Austral.* **138** H7
Sheffield, *Eng., U.K.* **104** F4
Shelburne Bay, *Austral.* **139** A12
Shelby, *Mont., U.S.* **82** B6
Shelikhova, Zaliv, *Russ.* **117** C13
Shelikhov Gulf, *Pac. Oc.* **115** C13
Shelikof Strait, *Alas., U.S.* **80** M2
Shell Beach, *Guyana* **92** B6
Shendi, *Sudan* **128** F9
Shenkursk, *Russ.* **105** C11
Shenton, Mount, *Austral.* **138** H5
Shenyang, *China* **117** F12
Shepparton, *Austral.* **141** L12
Sherbro Island, *Sierra Leone,* **126** G1
Sherbrooke, *Que., Can.* **76** H9
Sheridan, *Wyo., U.S.* **82** C7
Sheridan, Cape, *Nunavut, Can.* **76** B7
Sherman, *Tex., U.S.* **82** H9
Sherman Peak, *Idaho, U.S.* **80** D5
Shetland Islands, *Scot., U.K.* **102** D4
Sheyenne, river, *N. Dak., U.S.* **80** B9
Shihezi, *China* **116** F9
Shijiazhuang, *China* **117** G11
Shikoku, island, *Japan* **115** F14
Shirase Coast, *Antarctica* **152** J7
Shirase Glacier, *Antarctica* **153** B11
Shīrāz, *Iran* **116** G5
Shire, river, *Malawi* **127** L10
Shishaldin Volcano, *Alas., U.S.* **75** R3
Shishmaref, *Alas., U.S.* **82** J1
Shizuishan, *China* **117** G10
Shmidta, Mys (East Cape), *Russ.* **76** A2
Shoalhaven Bight, *Austral.* **139** L14
Shoalwater Bay, *Austral.* **139** F15
Sholapur, *India* **116** J8
Shoshone Falls, *Idaho, U.S.* **80** D5
Shoshone Mountains, *Nev., U.S.* **80** E3
Shostka, *Ukr.* **105** G11
Shoyna, *Russ.* **105** A11
Shreveport, *La., U.S.* **83** H10
Shumagin Islands, *Alas., U.S.* **75** R4
Shungnak, *Alas., U.S.* **82** J2
Shuryshkary, *Russ.* **105** A13
Shymkent, *Kaz.* **116** F7
Siberia, region, *Asia* **103** B15
Siberia, region, *Asia* **114** D8
Sibiu, *Rom.* **104** J9
Sibu, *Malaysia* **117** L12
Sibut, *Cen. Af. Rep.* **128** H7
Siccus, river, *Austral.* **139** J11
Sichuan Basin, *Pac. Oc.* **115** H11
Sicily, island, *It.* **102** M6
Sicily, Strait of, *It.* **102** L6
Sidmouth, Cape, *Austral.* **139** B12
Sidney, *Mont., U.S.* **82** B7
Sidney, *Nebr., U.S.* **82** E7
Sidra, Gulf of, *Libya* **126** C6
Sierra Blanca Peak, *N. Mex., U.S.* **80** H7
Sierra Leone, *Af.* **128** G1
Sierra Madre del Sur, *Mex.* **75** P4
Sierra Madre Occidental, *Mex.* **75** L3
Sierra Madre Oriental, *Mex.* **75** M4
Sierra Morena, *Sp.* **104** K2
Sigguup Nunaa, *Greenland, Den.* **76** D8
Siglufjörður, *Ice.* **104** A3
Signal Hill, *Austral.* **139** E11
Sikasso, *Mali* **128** G2
Sikhote Alin' Range, *Asia* **115** E13
Silesia, region, *Pol.* **102** G7
Silet, *Alg.* **128** E4
Siletitengi, Lake, *Asia* **114** E7
Silver Bay, *Minn., U.S.* **76** H6
Silver City, *N. Mex., U.S.* **82** H6
Silverton, *Colo., U.S.* **82** F6
Simeulue, island, *Indonesia* **115** L10
Simferopol', *Ukr.* **105** J11
Simpson Desert, *Austral.* **139** F10
Sinai, peninsula, *Egypt* **126** D9
Sincelejo, *Col.* **94** B3
Singapore, *Asia* **117** L11
Singleton, *Austral.* **141** K14
Sinkiang, region, *China* **116** G8
Sinop, *Braz.* **94** F7
Sionainn *see* Shannon, *Ire.* **104** F3
Sioux City, *Iowa, U.S.* **82** D9
Sioux Falls, *S. Dak., U.S.* **82** D9
Sioux Lookout, *Ont., Can.* **76** H6
Siple Coast, *Antarctica* **152** J7
Siple Island, *Antarctica* **152** J4
Siple, Mount, *Antarctica* **152** J4
Siracusa, *It.* **104** M7
Sir Edward Pellew Group, *Austral.* **139** C10
Sir Thomas, Mount, *Austral.* **138** G7
Sisimiut (Holsteinborg), *Greenland, Den.* **76** D9
Sitka, *Alas., U.S.* **82** M5
Sittwe, *Myanmar* **117** J10
Sivers'kyy Donets', river, *Russ.–Ukr.* **105** G11
Sīwa, *Egypt* **128** D8
Skagerrak, strait, *Atlantic Oc.* **102** E6
Skagway, *Alas., U.S.* **82** L5
Skåne, *Eur.* **102** F7
Skeleton Coast, *Af.* **127** M6
Skien, *Nor.* **104** E6
Skirmish Point, *Austral.* **138** A9
Sklad, *Russ.* **117** C10
Skopje, *Maced.* **104** K8
Skovorodino, *Russ.* **117** E12
Skwentna, *Alas., U.S.* **82** L2
Slave Coast, *Af.* **126** H4
Sleaford Bay, *Austral.* **138** L9
Slessor Glacier, *Antarctica* **152** D7
Slide Mountain, *N.Y., U.S.* **81** D15
Slovakia, *Eur.* **104** H8
Slovenia, *Eur.* **104** J7
Slyudyanka, *Russ.* **117** E10
Smallwood Reservoir, *Nfld. & Lab., Can.* **74** G9
Smeïda *see* Taoudenni, *Mali* **128** E3
Smith Bay, *Nunavut, Can.* **74** C7
Smith Bay, *Alas., U.S.* **80** H3
Smith Glacier, *Antarctica* **152** H4
Smith Island *see* Sumisu, *Japan* **142** B3
Smith River, *B.C., Can.* **76** E3
Smithton, *Austral.* **140** L7
Smokey Hill, river, *Kan., U.S.* **80** F8
Smoky Bay, *Austral.* **140** J9
Smoky Hills, *Kan., U.S.* **80** F9
Smolensk, *Russ.* **105** F10
Smolensk-Moscow Upland, *Eur.* **103** F10
Smyley Island, *Antarctica* **152** F3
Snake, river, *U.S.* **80** D4
Snake River Plain, *Idaho, U.S.* **80** D5
Snares Islands (Tini Heke), *N.Z.* **142** L5
Snowdon, peak, *Wales, U.K.* **102** F4
Snow Hill Island, *Antarctica* **152** C2
Snowy Mountains, *Austral.* **139** L13
Snowy, river, *Austral.* **139** M13
Snyder, *Tex., U.S.* **82** H8
Sobradinho Reservoir (Sobradinho, Represa da), *Braz.* **92** F10
Sobral, *Braz.* **94** D10
Sochi, *Russ.* **105** J12
Socompa, *Chile* **94** J4
Socorro, *N. Mex., U.S.* **82** H6
Socorro Island (Socorro, Isla), *Mex.* **75** N3
Söderhamn, *Sw.* **104** D8
Sofia *see* Sofiya, *Bulg.* **104** K9
Sofiya (Sofia), *Bulg.* **104** K9
Sogamoso, *Col.* **94** B3
Sognefjorden, bay, *Nor.* **102** D6
Sokol, *Russ.* **105** D11
Sokoto, *Nigeria* **128** G5
Sokoto, river, *Nigeria* **126** G4
Solikamsk, *Russ.* **105** C14
Solimões, river *see* Amazon, river, *S. Amer.* **92** D5
Solitary Islands, *Austral.* **139** J15
Sologne, *Eur.* **102** H4
Solomon Islands, *Pac. Oc.* **142** F5
Solomon, river, *Kans., U.S.* **80** F9
Solomon Sea, *P.N.G.* **142** F4
Somalia, *Af.* **128** H11

Moon Index

Latin Equivalents

Catena, catenae	*chain of craters*
Crater, craters	*circular depression*
Dorsum, dorsa	*ridge*
Lacus	*lake; small plain; small, dark area with discrete, sharp edges*
Mare, maria	*sea; large, circular plain*
Mons, montes	*mountain*
Oceanus, oceani	*very large, dark area*
Palus, paludes	*swamp; small plain*
Rima, rimae	*fissure*
Rupes, Rupii	*scarp*
Sinus	*bay; small plain*
Vallis, valles	*valley*

Features

Note: Entries without a generic descriptor are craters.

Abbe, *Far Side,* **197** H14
Abel, *Near Side,* **196** H8
Abul Wáfa, *Far Side,* **197** E11
Adams, *Near Side,* **196** G8
Aestuum, Sinus, *Near Side,* **196** E5
Aitken, *Far Side,* **197** F14
Al-Biruni, *Far Side,* **197** D10
Al-Khwarizmi, *Far Side,* **197** E10
Albategnius, *Near Side,* **196** F5
Alden, *Far Side,* **197** G11
Alder, *Far Side,* **197** H14
Alekhin, *Far Side,* **197** J15
Alexander, *Near Side,* **196** C6
Aliacensis, *Near Side,* **196** G5
Alpes, Montes, *Near Side,* **196** C5
Alphonsus, *Near Side,* **196** F5
Altai, Rupes, *Near Side,* **196** G6
Amici, *Far Side,* **197** F14
Amundsen, *Near Side,* **196** J5
Anaximander, *Near Side,* **196** B4
Anaximenes, *Near Side,* **196** B4
Anderson, *Far Side,* **197** D13
Anguis, Mare, *Near Side,* **196** D8
Ansgarius, *Near Side,* **196** F9
Antoniadi, *Far Side,* **197** J14
Anuchin, *Far Side,* **197** H11
Apenninus, Montes, *Near Side,* **196** D5
Apianus, *Near Side,* **196** G5
Apollo, *Far Side,* **197** G15
Appleton, *Far Side,* **197** C13
Archimedes, *Near Side,* **196** D5
Aristarchus, *Near Side,* **196** D3
Aristillus, *Near Side,* **196** C5
Aristoteles, *Near Side,* **196** C6
Arnold, *Near Side,* **196** B6
Artamonov, *Far Side,* **197** D11
Artem'ev, *Far Side,* **197** E16
Arzachel, *Near Side,* **196** F5
Ashbrook, *Far Side,* **197** J14
Asperitatis, Sinus, *Near Side,* **196** F6
Atlas, *Near Side,* **196** C7
Australe, Mare, *Far Side,* **197** H11
Autumni, Lacus , *Near Side,* **196** F1
Avicenna, *Far Side,* **197** C17
Avogadro, *Far Side,* **197** B13

Baade, *Near Side,* **196** H2
Baade, Vallis, *Near Side,* **196** H2
Babbage, *Near Side,* **196** B3
Babcock, *Far Side,* **197** E10
Backlund, *Far Side,* **197** F10
Baco, *Near Side,* **196** H6
Baillaud, *Near Side,* **196** B6
Bailly, *Near Side,* **196** J4
Balboa, *Near Side,* **196** D1
Baldet, *Far Side,* **197** H15
Balmer, *Near Side,* **196** G8
Barbier, *Far Side,* **197** G13
Barnard, *Near Side,* **196** G9
Barocius, *Near Side,* **196** H6
Barringer, *Far Side,* **197** G15
Barrow, *Near Side,* **196** B5
Beaumont, *Near Side,* **196** F7
Bečvář, *Far Side,* **197** E11
Behaim, *Near Side,* **196** F9
Beijerinck, *Far Side,* **197** F12
Bel'kovich, *Near Side,* **196** B7
Bel'kovich, *Far Side,* **197** B12
Bell, *Far Side,* **197** D18
Bellinsgauzen , *Far Side,* **197** H14
Belyaev, *Far Side,* **197** D12
Berkner, *Far Side,* **197** D17
Berlage, *Far Side,* **197** H14
Berosus, *Near Side,* **196** C8
Bettinus, *Near Side,* **196** J4
Bhabha, *Far Side,* **197** H14
Biela, *Near Side,* **196** H7
Birkeland, *Far Side,* **197** G14
Birkhoff, *Far Side,* **197** B15
Birmingham, *Near Side,* **196** B5
Blackett, *Far Side,* **197** G16
Blancanus, *Near Side,* **196** H4
Blanchinus, *Near Side,* **196** G5
Blazhko, *Far Side,* **197** D15
Bohr, *Near Side,* **196** D1
Bolyai, *Far Side,* **197** G12
Boole, *Near Side,* **196** A3
Bose, *Far Side,* **197** H14
Boussingault, *Near Side,* **196** J6
Bouvard, Vallis, *Near Side,* **196** H2
Boyle, *Far Side,* **197** H14
Bragg, *Far Side,* **197** C17
Brashear, *Far Side,* **197** J14
Bredikhin, *Far Side,* **197** D15
Brianchon, *Near Side,* **196** A4
Bridgman, *Far Side,* **197** C12
Bronk, *Far Side,* **197** D16
Brouwer, *Far Side,* **197** G16
Buckland, Dorsum, *Near Side,* **196** D6
Buffon, *Far Side,* **197** G16
Buisson, *Far Side,* **197** E11
Bullialdus, *Near Side,* **196** F4
Bunsen, *Near Side,* **196** B2
Buys-Ballot, *Far Side,* **197** D14
Byrd, *Near Side,* **196** A5
Byrgius, *Near Side,* **196** G2

Cabannes, *Far Side,* **197** H14
Cajori, *Far Side,* **197** H13
Campbell, *Far Side,* **197** C13
Cantor, *Far Side,* **197** C11
Cardanus, Rima, *Near Side,* **196** E2
Carnot, *Far Side,* **197** C15
Carpatus, Montes, *Near Side,* **196** D4
Carver, *Far Side,* **197** H12
Cassegrain, *Far Side,* **197** H12
Cassini, *Near Side,* **196** C5
Catharina, *Near Side,* **196** F6
Caucasus, Montes, *Near Side,* **196** C5
Challis, *Near Side,* **196** A5
Chamberlin, *Far Side,* **197** J12
Chandler, *Far Side,* **197** C14
Chaplygin, *Far Side,* **197** F12
Chapman, *Far Side,* **197** B16
Chappell, *Far Side,* **197** B14
Charlier, *Far Side,* **197** C16
Chauvenet, *Far Side,* **197** F12
Chebyshev, *Far Side,* **197** G16
Chernyshev, *Far Side,* **197** C14
Chrétien, *Far Side,* **197** H13
Clairaut, *Near Side,* **196** H6
Clavius, *Near Side,* **196** H5
Cleomedes, *Near Side,* **196** D8
Cockcroft, *Far Side,* **197** D15
Cognitum, Mare, *Near Side,* **196** F4
Compton, *Far Side,* **197** B12
Comrie, *Far Side,* **197** D17
Comstock, *Far Side,* **197** D17
Condorcet, *Near Side,* **196** D8
Congreve, *Far Side,* **197** E15
Copernicus, *Near Side,* **196** E4
Cordillera, Montes, *Near Side, Far Side* **196, 197** F2, G17
Cori, *Far Side,* **197** H15
Coriolis, *Far Side,* **197** E13
Coulomb, *Far Side,* **197** B16
Cremona, *Far Side,* **197** A16
Crisium, Mare, *Near Side,* **196** D8
Crocco, *Far Side,* **197** H13
Crommelin, *Far Side,* **197** J15
Crüger, *Near Side,* **196** F2
Curie, *Far Side,* **197** G10
Curtius, *Near Side,* **196** J5
Cusanus, *Near Side,* **196** A6
Cuvier, *Near Side,* **196** H5
Cyrano, *Far Side,* **197** F13
Cyrillus, *Near Side,* **196** F6

D'Alembert, *Far Side,* **197** C13
Daedalus, *Far Side,* **197** F14
Danjon, *Far Side,* **197** F11
Dante, *Far Side,* **197** D14
Darwin, *Near Side,* **196** G2
Davisson, *Far Side,* **197** G14
De Forest, *Far Side,* **197** J14
De La Rue, *Near Side,* **196** B7
De Moraes, *Far Side,* **197** C13
De Sitter, *Near Side,* **196** A6
De Vries, *Far Side,* **197** F14
Debye, *Far Side,* **197** C14
Demonax, *Near Side,* **196** J6
Desargues, *Near Side,* **196** A4
Deslandres, *Near Side,* **196** G5
Deutsch, *Far Side,* **197** D11
Doppelmayer, *Near Side,* **196** G3
Doppler, *Far Side,* **197** F15
Dreyer, *Far Side,* **197** E10
Drygalski, *Near Side,* **196** J4
Dunér, *Far Side,* **197** C14
Dyson, *Far Side,* **197** B15
Dziewulski, *Far Side,* **197** D10

Edison, *Far Side,* **197** D10
Eijkman, *Far Side,* **197** J15
Einstein, *Near Side,* **196** D1
Einthoven, *Far Side,* **197** F10
Emden, *Far Side,* **197** B14
Endymion, *Near Side,* **196** B7
Eötvös, *Far Side,* **197** G12
Epidemiarum, Palus, *Near Side,* **196** G4
Epigenes, *Near Side,* **196** B5
Eratosthenes, *Near Side,* **196** E4
Erro, *Far Side,* **197** E10
Esnault-Pelterie, *Far Side,* **197** C15
Eudoxus, *Near Side,* **196** C6
Evans, *Far Side,* **197** F16
Evershed, *Far Side,* **197** C15
Excellentiae, Lacus, *Near Side,* **196** G3

Fabricius, *Near Side,* **196** H7
Fabry, *Far Side,* **197** C11
Faraday, *Near Side,* **196** G5
Fecunditatis, Mare, *Near Side,* **196** F8
Fermi, *Far Side,* **197** F11
Fernelius, *Near Side,* **196** G5
Fersman, *Far Side,* **197** D16
Finsen, *Far Side,* **197** G14
Firmicus, *Near Side,* **196** E8
Fitzgerald, *Far Side,* **197** D14
Fizeau, *Far Side,* **197** H15
Fleming, *Far Side,* **197** D11
Fourier, *Near Side,* **196** G3
Fowler, *Far Side,* **197** C15
Fra Mauro, *Near Side,* **196** F4
Fracastorius, *Near Side,* **196** F7
Franklin, *Near Side,* **196** C7
Freundlich, *Far Side,* **197** D13
Fridman, *Far Side,* **197** F17
Frigoris, Mare, *Near Side,* **196** B5
Froelich, *Far Side,* **197** A15
Frost, *Far Side,* **197** C16
Furnerius, *Near Side,* **196** G8

Gadomski, *Far Side,* **197** C15
Gagarin, *Far Side,* **197** F12
Galois, *Far Side,* **197** F15
Galvani, *Near Side,* **196** B2
Gamow, *Far Side,* **197** B13
Ganswindt, *Far Side,* **197** J13
Garavito, *Far Side,* **197** H13
Gärtner, *Near Side,* **196** B6
Gassendi, *Near Side,* **196** F3
Gauss, *Near Side,* **196** C8
Gavrilov, *Far Side,* **197** D12
Geminus, *Near Side,* **196** C7
Gerard, *Near Side,* **196** B2
Gerasimovich, *Far Side,* **197** G16
Gibbs, *Near Side,* **196** G9
Gilbert, *Near Side,* **196** E9
Gill, *Near Side,* **196** J7
Goddard, *Near Side,* **196** D9
Goldschmidt, *Near Side,* **196** B5
Gregory, *Far Side,* **197** E11
Grimaldi, *Near Side,* **196** F2
Grissom, *Far Side,* **197** H15
Gruemberger, *Near Side,* **196** J5
Gum, *Near Side,* **196** H8
Gutenberg, *Near Side,* **196** F7
Gutenberg, Rimae, *Near Side,* **196** F7
Guyot, *Far Side,* **197** E11

H. G. Wells, *Far Side,* **197** C12
Haemus, Montes, *Near Side,* **196** D6
Hagecius, *Near Side,* **196** H6
Hahn, *Near Side,* **196** C8
Hainzel, *Near Side,* **196** G4
Hale, *Far Side,* **197** J13
Hamilton, *Near Side,* **196** H8
Hanno, *Near Side,* **196** J7
Harkhebi, *Far Side,* **197** C11
Harlan, *Near Side,* **196** H8
Harriot, *Far Side,* **197** C11
Hartmann, *Far Side,* **197** E12
Hartwig, *Near Side,* **196** F1
Harvey, *Far Side,* **197** D16
Haskin, *Far Side,* **197** A13
Hausen, *Near Side,* **196** J3
Hausen, *Far Side,* **197** J16
Hayn, *Near Side,* **196** A7
Heaviside, *Far Side,* **197** F13
Hecataeus, *Near Side,* **196** G9
Helberg, *Far Side,* **197** D17
Helmholtz, *Near Side,* **196** J6
Hercules, *Near Side,* **196** C7
Herodotus, *Near Side,* **196** D3
Hertz, *Far Side,* **197** D10
Hertzsprung, *Far Side,* **197** E16
Hess, *Far Side,* **197** H14
Hevelius, *Near Side,* **196** E2
Hilbert, *Far Side,* **197** F11
Hippalus, *Near Side,* **196** G4
Hipparchus, *Near Side,* **196** F5
Hippocrates, *Far Side,* **197** B15
Hirayama, *Far Side,* **197** F10
Hommel, *Near Side,* **196** H6
Hopmann, *Far Side,* **197** H13
Houzeau, *Far Side,* **197** F17
Hubble, *Near Side,* **196** D9
Humboldt, *Near Side,* **196** G9
Humboldtianum, Mare, *Near Side,* **196** B7
Humorum, Mare, *Near Side,* **196** G3

Ibn Firnas, *Far Side,* **197** E11
Ibn Yunus, *Far Side,* **197** D10
Icarus, *Far Side,* **197** F14
Imbrium, Mare, *Near Side,* **196** C4
Ingenii, Mare, *Far Side,* **197** G13
Inghirami, *Near Side,* **196** H3
Inghirami, Vallis, *Near Side,* **196** H2
Insularum, Mare, *Near Side,* **196** E3
Ioffe, *Far Side,* **197** F16
Iridum, Sinus, *Near Side,* **196** C4
Isaev, *Far Side,* **197** F12

J. Herschel, *Near Side,* **196** B4
Jackson, *Far Side,* **197** D15
Jacobi, *Near Side,* **196** H5
Jansky, *Near Side,* **196** E9
Janssen, *Near Side,* **196** H7
Jarvis, *Far Side,* **197** G15
Jenner, *Far Side,* **197** H11
Joliot, *Far Side,* **197** C10
Joule, *Far Side,* **197** D16
Jules Verne, *Far Side,* **197** G12
Julius Caesar, *Near Side,* **196** E6
Jura, Montes, *Near Side,* **196** C4

Kane, *Near Side,* **196** B6
Karpinskiy, *Far Side,* **197** B14
Karrer, *Far Side,* **197** H15
Kästner, *Near Side,* **196** F9
Keeler, *Far Side,* **197** F13
Kekulé, *Far Side,* **197** D16
Kepler, *Near Side,* **196** E3
Khvol'son, *Far Side,* **197** F11
Kibal'chich, *Far Side,* **197** E16
Kidinnu, *Far Side,* **197** C12
Kiess, *Near Side,* **196** F9
King, *Far Side,* **197** E11
Kircher, *Near Side,* **196** J4
Kirkwood, *Far Side,* **197** B14
Klaproth, *Near Side,* **196** J5
Kleymenov, *Far Side,* **197** G16
Koch, *Far Side,* **197** H13
Kolhörster, *Far Side,* **197** E17
Komarov, *Far Side,* **197** D13
Kondratyuk, *Far Side,* **197** F11
Konstantinov, *Far Side,* **197** D13
Korolev, *Far Side,* **197** E15
Kovalevskaya, *Far Side,* **197** C16
Kozyrev, *Far Side,* **197** H12
Krafft, *Near Side,* **196** D2
Kramers, *Far Side,* **197** B16
Kugler, *Far Side,* **197** H12
Kulik, *Far Side,* **197** C15
Kurchatov, *Far Side,* **197** C12
Kurchatov, Catena, *Far Side,* **197** C12

La Pérouse, *Near Side,* **196** F9
Lacchini, *Far Side,* **197** C17
Lagrange, *Near Side,* **196** G2
Lamarck, *Near Side,* **196** G2
Lamb, *Far Side,* **197** H11
Lamé, *Near Side,* **196** F8
Lampland, *Far Side,* **197** G12
Landau, *Far Side,* **197** C16
Lane, *Far Side,* **197** F12
Langemak, *Far Side,* **197** F11
Langevin, *Far Side,* **197** C13
Langmuir, *Far Side,* **197** G16
Langrenus, *Near Side,* **196** F8
Larmor, *Far Side,* **197** D14
Laue, *Far Side,* **197** C17
Lavoisier, *Near Side,* **196** C2
Le Gentil, *Near Side,* **196** J4
Leavitt, *Far Side,* **197** H15
Lebedev, *Far Side,* **197** H11
Lebedinskiy, *Far Side,* **197** E15
Leeuwenhoek, *Far Side,* **197** G14
Legendre, *Near Side,* **196** G8
Lehmann, *Near Side,* **196** H3
Leibnitz, *Far Side,* **197** G14
Lemaître, *Far Side,* **197** H15
Leucippus, *Far Side,* **197** C17
Leuschner, Catena, *Far Side,* **197** E17

Moon Landing Sites

NEAR SIDE

Apollo 11 (U.S.)—Tranquillity Base Landed July 20, 1969 **E6**
Apollo 12 (U.S.)—Landed Nov. 19, 1969 **E4**
Apollo 14 (U.S.)—Landed Feb. 5, 1971 **E4**
Apollo 15 (U.S.)—Landed July 30, 1971 **D5**
Apollo 16 (U.S.)—Landed April 21, 1972 **F6**
Apollo 17 (U.S.)—Landed Dec. 11, 1972 **D7**
Chandrayaan-1 Moon Impact Probe(India)— Crashed Nov. 14, 2008 **J5**
Chang'e 3 (China)—Landed Dec. 14, 2013 **C4**
GRAIL A (Ebb) (U.S.)—Crashed Dec. 17 2012 **B12**
GRAIL B (Flow) (U.S.)—Crashed Dec. 17 2012 **B12**
Hiten (Japan)—Crashed April 10, 1993 **B4**
LCROSS, Centaur Impactor (U.S.)— Crashed Oct. 9, 2009 **J5**
Luna 13 (U.S.S.R.)—Landed Dec. 24, 1966 **D2**
Luna 15 (U.S.S.R.)—Crashed July 21, 1969 **D8**

Luna 16 (U.S.S.R.)—Landed Sept. 20, 1970 **E8**
Luna 17 (U.S.S.R.)—Landed Nov. 17 1970 **C4**
Luna 2 (U.S.S.R.)—Crashed Sept. 14, 1959 **D5**
Luna 5 (U.S.S.R.)—Crashed May 10, 1965 **E4**
Luna 7 (U.S.S.R.)—Crashed Oct. 7 1965 **E3**
Luna 8 (U.S.S.R.)—Crashed Dec. 6 1965 **E2**
Luna 9 (U.S.S.R.)—Crashed Feb. 3, 1966 **E2**
Luna 18 (U.S.S.R.)—Landed Sept. 11, 1971 **E8**
Luna 20 (U.S.S.R.)—Landed Feb. 21, 1972 **E8**
Luna 21 (U.S.S.R.)—Landed Jan. 15, 1973 **D7**
Luna 23 (U.S.S.R.)—Landed Nov. 6 1974 **E8**
Luna 24 (U.S.S.R.)—Landed Aug. 18, 1976 **D8**
Lunar Prospector (U.S.)—Crashed July 31, 1999 **J5**
Ranger 6 (U.S.)—Crashed Feb. 2, 1964 **E6**
Ranger 7 (U.S.)—Crashed July 31, 1964 **F4**
Ranger 8 (U.S.)—Crashed Feb. 20, 1965 **E6**
Ranger 9 (U.S.)—Crashed Mar. 24, 1965 **F5**

Selene/Kaguya (Japan)—Crashed June 10, 2009 **J7**
SMART-1 (ESA)—Crashed Sept. 3, 2006 **G3**
Surveyor 1 (U.S.)—Landed June 2, 1966 **E3**
Surveyor 2 (U.S.)—Crashed Sept. 22, 1966 **E5**
Surveyor 3 (U.S.)—Landed Apr. 20, 1967 **E4**
Surveyor 4 (U.S.)—Crashed July 17 1967 **E5**
Surveyor 5 (U.S.)—Landed Sept. 11, 1967 **E6**
Surveyor 6 (U.S.)—Landed Nov. 10, 1967 **E5**
Surveyor 7 (U.S.)—Landed Jan. 10, 1968 **G5**

FAR SIDE

Lunar Orbiter 1 (U.S.)—Crashed Oct. 29, 1966 **E13**
Lunar Orbiter 2 (U.S.)—Crashed Oct. 11, 1967 **E11**
Lunar Orbiter 3 (U.S.)—Crashed Oct. 9, 1967 **D18**
Lunar Orbiter 5 (U.S.)—Crashed Jan. 31, 1968 **E16**
Okina, Selene Orbiter (Japan)—Crashed Feb. 12, 2009 **D15**
Ranger 4 (U.S.)—Crashed Apr. 26 1962 **F16**

Acknowledgments

COVER, FULL TITLE PAGE AND INTRODUCTION

IMAGE: Félix Pharand-Deschênes / Globaïa. globaia.org

DATA SOURCES: *Paved and unpaved roads, pipelines, railways, and transmission lines:* VMap0, National Geospatial-Intelligence Agency, Sept. 2000; *Shipping lanes:* NOAA's SEAS BBXX database, from Oct. 2004 to Oct. 2005. *Air networks:* International Civil Aviation Organization statistics. *Urban areas:* naturalearthdata.com; *Submarine cables:* Greg Mahlknecht's Cable Map; *Earth texture:* VMAP0; NOAA's SEAS BBXX database; Tom Patterson/Natural Earth: naturalearthdata.com

WORLD THEMATIC OPENER GLOBES

IMAGE AND DATA SOURCES: Blue Marble Next Generation, NASA's Earth Observatory; Population density data: Landscan 2014 Population Dataset created by UT-Battelle, LLC, the management and operating contractor of the Oak Ridge National Laboratory acting on behalf of the U.S. Department of Energy under Contract No. DE-AC05-00OR22725. Distributed by East View Geospatial: geospatial.com and East View Information Services: eastview.com/online/landscan

WORLD THEMATICS

Satellite World   pp. 14–15
IMAGE: Blue Marble Next Generation, NASA's Earth Observatory

Limits of the Oceans and Seas   pp. 22–23
Data derived from *International Hydrographic Organization Publication S-23 Limits of Oceans and Seas Draft 4th Edition 2002*

Paleogeography   pp. 26–27
GRAPHICS

CONTINENTS ADRIFT IN TIME: Ron Blakey, © Colorado Geosystems, Inc. cpgeosystems.com

GEOLOGIC TIME: International Commission on Stratigraphy. *International Chronostratigraphic Chart*, v2014/10. stratigraphy.org

Structure of the Earth   pp. 28–29
GRAPHICS

PLATE TECTONICS: *Earthquake data:* USGS Earthquake Hazards Program and USGS National Earthquake Information Center (NEIC). earthquake.usgs.gov. *Volcanism data:* Smithsonian Institution, Global Volcanism Program. volcano.si.edu; USGS and the International Association of Volcanology and Chemistry of the Earth's Interior. vulcan.wr.usgs.gov

INTERIOR OF THE EARTH: Tibor G. Tóth

TECTONIC BLOCK DIAGRAMS: Chuck Carter

Landforms   pp. 30–33
LANDFORMS MAP AND TEXT

Deniz Karagülle, Charlie Frye, Sean Breyer, Peter Aniello, Randy Vaughan, Dawn Wright Environmental Systems Research Institute (ESRI)

Roger Sayre
U.S. Geological Survey (USGS)

GRAPHICS

RIVER, GLACIAL, AND FICTIONAL LANDFORMS: Chuck Carter

DUNES: Lawson Parker

Land Cover   pp. 34–35
GRAPHICS

GLOBAL LAND COVER COMPOSITION: Boston University Department of Geography and Environment Global Land Cover Project. Source data provided by NASA's Moderate Resolution Imaging Spectraradiometer

Freshwater   pp. 36–37
GRAPHICS

WORLD OF RIVERS: *National Geographic*, 2010. Water: A Special Issue. Sources: World Wildlife Fund; Igor A. Shiklomanov, State Hydrological Institute, Russia; USGS; University of Kassel Center for Environmental Systems Research, Germany; National Snow and Ice Data Center, University of Colorado

WATER WITHDRAWALS, BY SECTOR: UNESCO. *Managing Water under Uncertainty and Risk, The United Nations World Water Development Report 4.* 2012, p. 443

MAPPING IRRIGATION: Food and Agricultural Organization of the United Nations (FAO), 2008

RENEWABLE FRESHWATER RESOURCES: United Nations Statistics Division. *Renewable Freshwater Resources per Capita: Long Term Annual Average.* unstats.un.org (accessed Oct. 2014)

SAFE DRINKING WATER: WHO / UNICEF Joint Monitoring Programme (JMP) for Water Supply and Sanitation. wssinfo.org (accessed Oct. 2014)

Climate   pp. 38–41
GRAPHICS

TAKING THE PLANET'S RISING TEMPERATURE: Steven Mosher and Robert Rohde, Berkeley Earth

RISING TEMPERATURES AND CO₂: NCDC/NOAA: "The Global Surface Temperature Is Rising." ncdc.noaa.gov/indicators/

SHRINKING POLAR ICE: National Snow and Ice Data Center. nsidc.org/data/seaice_index

SATELLITE IMAGES

Images originally created for the GLOBE program by NOAA's National Geophysical Data Center, Boulder, Colorado, U.S.A.

CLOUD COVER: International Satellite Cloud Climatology Project (ISCCP); National Aeronautics and Space Administration (NASA); Goddard Institute for Space Studies (GISS)

PRECIPITATION: Global Precipitation Climatology Project (GPCP); International Satellite Land Surface Climatology Project (ISLSCP)

SOLAR ENERGY: Earth Radiation Budget Experiment (ERBE); Greenhouse Effect Detection Experiment (GEDEX)

TEMPERATURE: National Center for Environmental Prediction (NCEP); National Center for Atmospheric Research (NCAR); National Weather Service (NWS)

Biodiversity   pp. 42–43
GENERAL REFERENCE

Catalogue of Life: catalogueoflife.org

GRAPHICS

THE NATURAL WORLD, SPECIES DIVERSITY: *Biodiversity*. NG Maps for *National Geographic* magazine, February 1999

BIODIVERSITY HOTSPOTS: Conservation International. conservation.org

THREATENED SPECIES: International Union for Conservation of Nature and Natural Resources (IUCN): iucnredlist.org

CONSERVATION STATUS OF TERRESTRIAL ECOREGIONS: World Wildlife Fund. wwf.panda.org

Human Influences   pp. 44–45
GRAPHICS

ANTHROMES, HUMAN INFLUENCES OVER TIME: Ellis, E. C., K. Klein Goldewijk, S. Siebert, D. Lightman, and N. Ramankutty. 2010. "Anthropogenic transformation of the biomes, 1700 to 2000." *Global Ecology and Biogeography* 19(5):589–606

HUMAN INFLUENCE INDEX, LAST OF THE WILD: Wildlife Conservation Society—WCS, and Center for International Earth Science Information Network—CIESIN—Columbia University. 2005. Last of the Wild Project, Version 2, 2005 (LWP-2): Global Human Influence Index (HII) Dataset (IGHP). Palisades, NY: NASA Socioeconomic Data and Applications Center (SEDAC). sedac.ciesin.columbia.edu/data/set/wildareas-v2-human-influence-index-ighp

Population   pp. 46–49
GENERAL REFERENCES

CIA. *The World Factbook.* cia.gov (accessed 2014); United Nations Department of Economic and Social Affairs Population Division. *World Urbanization Prospects: The 2014 Revision*; *World Population Prospects: The 2012 Revision*; and *Trends in International Migrant Stock: The 2013 Revision*

GRAPHICS

POPULATION PYRAMIDS: U.S. Census Bureau

POPULATION DENSITY: See World Thematic Opener Globes above

Languages   pp. 50–51
GRAPHICS

LANGUAGE FAMILIES: Global Mapping International (GMI) and SIL International. World Language Mapping System, version 3.2.1

EVOLUTION OF LANGUAGES: *National Geographic Almanac of Geography.* Washington, D.C.: National Geographic Society, 2005

HOW MANY SPEAK WHAT: Loh, Jonathan, and Dave Harmon. 2013. Data from Gordon, R.G. (ed.), 2005. *Ethnologue: Languages of the World*, Fifteenth edition. Dallas, TX.: SIL International

MAPPING LANGUAGE DIVERSITY: Ethnologue (2016 data). ethnologue.com

VANISHING LANGUAGES: Living Tongues Institute for Endangered Languages/ National Geographic. *Language Hotspots map.* travel.nationalgeographic.com/travel/enduring-voices

Religions   pp. 52–53
GRAPHICS

DOMINANT RELIGION: Johnson, Todd M., and Brian J. Grim, eds. World Religion Database: worldreligiondatabase.org. Leiden/ Boston: Brill (accessed 2014)

BY THE NUMBERS: World Religion Database; Pew Research Center, pewforum.org (accessed 2013)

Health and Education   pp. 54–55
GRAPHICS

HEALTH CARE AVAILABILITY: World Health Organization. *World Health Statistics 2012.* who.org

INCOME LEVELS: World Bank. data.worldbank.org

ACCESS TO IMPROVED SANITATION: UNICEF. *2014 Update: Progress on Drinking Water and Sanitation.* unicef.org

NUTRITION: Food and Agriculture Organization. *The State of Food Insecurity in the World*, 2014. fao.org

HIV: UNAIDS. unaids.org

GLOBAL DISEASE BURDEN: World Health Organization. WHO Mortality Database; Mortality and Global Burden of Disease (GBD), 2012

UNDER-FIVE MORTALITY: United Nations Statistics Division. Millennium Development Goals Indicators. mdgs.un.org

MATERNAL MORTALITY: World Bank, with WHO, UNICEF, UNFPA, and UN Population Division. who.int

EDUCATION AND LITERACY: CIA. *The World Factbook.* cia.gov (accessed Oct. 2014)

SCHOOL ENROLLMENT FOR GIRLS: UNICEF. *The State of the World's Children 2015.* unicef.org

DEVELOPING HUMAN CAPITAL: Adapted from Human Capital Projections developed by Education Policy and Data Center. epdc.org

Economy   pp. 56–57
GRAPHICS

DOMINANT ECONOMIC SECTOR: CIA. *The World Factbook.* cia.gov (accessed Sept. 2014); "Value added, by activity" data from *OECD Factbook 2013: Economic, Environmental and Social Statistics.* oecd.org

HUMAN DEVELOPMENT INDEX: United Nations Development Programme. *UNDP 2015 Human Development Report.* undp.org

TOP GDP GROWTH RATES: World Bank. data.worldbank.org (accessed Feb. 2016)

THE WORLD'S RICHEST AND POOREST COUNTRIES, GROSS DOMESTIC PRODUCT: International Monetary Fund. imf.org (accessed Feb. 2016)

GLOBAL INNOVATION INDEX: The Global Innovation Index 2015. globalinnovationindex.org

MAJOR EXPORTERS: World Trade Organization. *International Trade Statistics 2015.* wto.org

Trade   pp. 58–59
GRAPHICS

WORLD ECONOMIES: World Bank. data.worldbank.org (accessed Oct. 2014)

SINGLE-COMMODITY-DEPENDENT ECONOMIES: International Trade Centre. intracen.org (accessed Oct. 2014)

STOCK EXCHANGES: World Federation of Exchanges. world-exchanges.org (accessed Oct. 2014)

WORLD MERCHANDISE TRADE, GROWTH OF WORLD TRADE, MERCHANDISE EXPORTS, MAIN TRADING NATIONS, TRADE FLOW; FUELS: World Trade Organization. *International Trade Statistics 2013*

WORLD DEBT: CIA. *The World Factbook.* cia.gov (accessed Oct. 2014)

TRADE BLOCS: APEC (apec.org), ASEAN (asean.org), COMESA (about.comesa.int), ECOWAS (comm.ecowas.int), EU (europa.eu), MERCOSUR (mercosur.int), NAFTA (ustr.gov), SAFTA (saarc-sec.org)

Food   pp. 60–63
GENERAL REFERENCES

Foley, Jonathan. "A Five-Step Plan to Feed the World." *National Geographic*, May 2014. Available online at nationalgeographic.com/foodfeatures/feeding-9-billion/

Food and Agriculture Organization of the United Nations (FAO). *FAO Statistical Yearbook 2013.* Available online at fao.org/docrep/018/i3107e/i3107e.PDF

GRAPHICS

AGRICULTURE'S FOOTPRINT, WHERE CROP YIELDS COULD IMPROVE, HOW OUR CROPS ARE USED: Global Landscapes Initiative, Institute on the Environment, University of Minnesota

AGRICULTURE'S FOOTPRINT: "Land Transformation by Humans: A Review." Roger LeB. Hooke, José F. Martín-Duque. *GSA Today*, Volume 22, Issue 12

DISTRIBUTION OF MAJOR CROPS AND LIVESTOCK, FISHING AND AQUACULTURE, FOOD SECURITY: Food and Agriculture Organization of the United Nations Statistics Division (FAOSTAT). *FAO Statistical Yearbook 2013*

WORLD FOOD PRODUCTION: FAOSTAT. faostat.fao.org (accessed Oct. 2014)

GENETICALLY MODIFIED CROPS: International Service for the Acquisition of Agri-Biotech Applications. isaaa.org (accessed Oct. 2014)

CALORIC SUPPLY: FAOSTAT Food Balance Sheets. faostat.fao.org (accessed Oct. 2014)

Energy pp. 64–65

GRAPHICS

ENERGY CONSUMPTION BY LEADING SOURCE: Energy Information Administration, U.S. Department of Energy. eia.gov (accessed Oct. 2013)

ENERGY PRODUCTION BY FUEL TYPE, ENERGY PRODUCTION BY REGION: International Energy Agency. *2014 Key World Energy Statistics*

BALANCING CONSUMPTION AND PRODUCTION: Energy Information Administration, U.S. Department of Energy. eia.gov

RENEWABLE RESOURCES, RENEWABLE LEADERS: Renewable Energy Policy Network for the 21st Century (REN21). *Renewables 2014 Global Status Report*. Paris: REN21, 2015. ren21.net

Environmental Stresses pp. 66–67

GRAPHICS

LAND DEGRADATION AND DESERTIFICATION, DEFORESTATION HOT SPOTS: *Millennium Ecosystem Assessment*. Ecosystems and Human Well-Being, Synthesis

AIR POLLUTION: van Donkelaar, A., R.V. Martin, M. Brauer, R. Kahn, R. Levy, C. Verduzco, and P.J. Villeneuve. "Global estimates of exposure to fine particulate matter concentrations from satellite-based aerosol optical depth." *Environ. Health Perspec.*, doi:10.1289/ehp.0901623, 118(6), 2010

WATER SCARCITY: International Water Management Institute. waterdata.iwmi.org

SATELLITE IMAGERY

DEPLETION OF THE OZONE LAYER: NASA. Ozone Hole Watch. ozonewatch.gsfc.nasa.gov/monthly/ (accessed Feb. 2016)

CONTINENTAL AND U.S. THEMATICS

NORTH AMERICA, PAGES 78–79
SOUTH AMERICA, PAGES 96–97
EUROPE, PAGES 106–107
ASIA, PAGES 118–119
AFRICA, PAGES 130–131
AUSTRALIA AND OCEANIA, PAGES 144–145

CHAPTER OPENERS: Land cover data: Tom Patterson/Natural Earth: naturalearthdata.com; Topographic relief: SRTM 30m, U.S. Geological Survey (USGS); Population density data: See World Thematic Opener Globes p. 198.

POPULATION DENSITY: See World Thematic Opener Globes p. 198.

ENERGY CONSUMPTION: EIA (U.S. Energy Administration)

LAND COVER: Boston University Department of Geography and Environment Global Land Cover Project. Source data provided by NASA's Moderate Resolution Imaging Spectraradiometer.

CLIMATE ZONES: H. J. de Blij, P. O. Muller, and John Wiley & Sons, Inc.

NATURAL HAZARDS (TECTONIC EVENTS): USGS Earthquake Hazard Program; Global Volcanism Program, Smithsonian Institution; National Geophysical Data Center/World Data Center (NGDC/WDC) Historical Tsunami Database

WATER AVAILABILITY: Aaron Wolf, Oregon State University.

PROTECTED AREAS: IUCN and UNEP-WCMC (2016), The World Database on Protected Areas (WDPA) Online (accessed January 2016), Cambridge, UK: UNEP-WCMC. Available at: www.protectedplanet.net

UNITED STATES, PAGES 84–85:

TEMPERATURE AND PRECIPITATION: National Oceanic and Atmospheric Administration (NOAA), U.S. Department of Commerce

LAND USE AND LAND COVER: Boston University Department of Geography and Environment Global Land Cover Project. Source data provided by NASA's Moderate Resolution Imaging Spectraradiometer

POPULATION: LandScan 2014 Global Population Database. Developed by Oak Ridge National Laboratory (ORNL). Distributed by East View Geospatial: geospatial.com and East View Information Services: eastview.com/online/landscan

NATIONAL PARK SERVICE LANDS: National Park Service, U.S. Department of the Interior.

SPACE

Introduction pp. 154–155

IMAGE

VEIL NEBULA, NGC 6960: NASA, ESA, and the Hubble Heritage Team (STScI/AURA)

Moon pp. 156–157

DATA SOURCES

PHYSICAL FEATURE NAMES: Gazetteer of Planetary Nomenclature. Planetary Geomatics Group of the USGS (United States Geological Survey) Astrogeology Science Center. planetarynames.wr.usgs.gov (accessed Aug. 2014)

TERRAIN, MAIN MAP GLOBAL MOSAICS: Lunar Reconnaissance Orbiter (LRO); NASA; Arizona State University

PHASES OF THE MOON, LUNAR INFLUENCE ON TIDES: National Geographic Society, Lunar Reconnaissance Orbiter (LRO); NASA

Inner Solar System pp. 158–159

IMAGES

NASA/JPL-Caltech, Johns Hopkins University Applied Physics Laboratory, Carnegie Institution of Washington.

Outer Solar System pp. 160–161

IMAGES

NASA/JPL-Caltech, Johns Hopkins University Applied Physics Laboratory, Carnegie Institution of Washington

Universe pp. 162–163

ARTWORK

Ken Eward, National Geographic Society

IMAGES

LOOKING BACK IN TIME FOR ORIGINS (BACKGROUND): Hubble Ultra Deep Field 2012; NASA, ESA, R. Ellis (Caltech), and the UDF 2012 Team

PHOTOGRAPHS (BY PAGE)

PAGE 30 (LE), James P. Blair/National Geographic Creative; 30 (CT UP), iStock.com/martinhosmart; 30 (CT LO), iStock.com/MBRubin; 30 (RT), iStock.com/wsfurlan; 31 (LE), iStock.com/paule858; 31 (CT LE), iStock.com/mangosage; 31 (CT RT), iStock.com/Stephan Hoerold; 31 (RT), Irina Solatges/Shutterstock; 32 (LE), iStock.com/kavram; 32 (CTR), iStock.com/SPrada; 32 (RT), iStock.com/kongxinzhu; 33 (UP LE), NASA image created by Jesse Allen, using data provided by the University of Maryland's Global Land Cover Facility; 33 (UP CTR), iStock.com/Bernhard Richter; 33 (UP RT), iStock.com/KingWu; 33 (LO LE), iStock.com/Art Wager; 33 (LO RT), Natalia Davidovich/Shutterstock; 34 (UP LE), iStock.com/Pgiam; 34 (UP RT), iStock.com/tzooka; 34 (LO-A), iStock.com/EvgeniiAnd; 34 (LO-B), iStock.com/Clarissa Painter; 34 (LO-C), iStock.com/oei1; 34 (LO-D), iStock.com/Achim Prill; 34 (LO-E), iStock.com/Gleb_Ivanov; 34 (LO-F), iStock.com/tella_db; 34 (LO-G), iStock.com/Totajla; 35 (A), iStock.com/stevegeer; 35 (B), iStock.com/brytta; 35 (C), iStock.com/Richard Gillard; 35 (D), Jon Bilous/Shutterstock; 35 (E), iStock.com/allgord; 35 (F), iStock.com/Halstenbach; 35 (G), iStock.com/Lingbeek; 39 (LE), iStock.com/alacatr; 39 (RT), iStock.com/TasfotoNL; 45 (UP LE), iStock.com/piccaya; 45 (UP CTR), iStock.com/StratosGiannikos; 45 (UP RT), iStock.com/Wildnerdpix; 45 (LO LE), iStock.com/mathess; 45 (LO CTR), iStock.com/Jonathan Eastland; 45 (LO RT), iStock.com/disorderly; 52 (LE), iStock.com/wastesoul; 52 (CTR), Zurijeta/Shutterstock; 52 (RT), iStock.com/Tarzan9280; 53 (UP), iStock.com/belizar73; 53 (CTR), iStock.com/Michele Alfieri; 53 (LO), iStock.com/Claudiad

Key to Flags and Facts

The National Geographic Society, whose cartographic policy is to recognize de facto countries, counted 195 independent nations at the end of 2011. At the end of each chapter of the Concise Atlas of the World there is a fact box for every independent nation and for most dependencies located on the continent or region covered in that chapter. Each box includes the flag of a political entity, as well as important statistical data. Boxes for some dependencies show two flags—a local one and the sovereign flag of the administering country. Dependencies are nonindependent political entities associated in some way with a particular independent nation.

The statistical data provide highlights of geography, demography, and economy. These details offer a brief overview of each political entity; they present general characteristics and are not intended to be comprehensive studies. The structured nature of the text results in some generic collective or umbrella terms. The industry category, for instance, includes services in addition to traditional manufacturing sectors. Space limitations dictate the amount of information included. For example, the only languages listed for the U.S. are English and Spanish, although many others are spoken. The North America chapter also includes concise fact boxes for U.S. states, showing the state flag, population, and capital.

Fact boxes are arranged alphabetically by the conventional short forms of the country or dependency names. Country and dependency boxes are grouped separately. The conventional long forms of names appear below the conventional short form; if there are no long forms, the short forms are repeated. Except where otherwise noted, all demographic data are derived from the CIA *World Factbook*.

AREA accounts for the total area of a country or dependency, including all land and inland water delimited by international boundaries, intranational boundaries, or coastlines. Figures in square kilometers are from the CIA *World Factbook*. Square miles were calculated by using the conversion factor of 0.3861 square mile to 1 square kilometer.

POPULATION figures for independent nations and dependencies are July 2012 estimates from the CIA *World Factbook*. Next to CAPITAL is the name of the seat of government, followed by the city's population. Capital city populations for both independent nations and dependencies are from World Urbanization Prospects: The 2009 Revision, and represent the populations of metropolitan areas. In the POPULATION category, the figures for U.S. state populations are 2011 U.S. Census estimates. POPULATION figures for countries, dependencies, and U.S. states are rounded to the nearest thousand.

Under RELIGION, the most widely practiced faith appears first. "Traditional" or "indigenous" connotes beliefs of important local sects, such as the Maya in Middle America. Under LANGUAGE, if a country has an official language, it is listed first. Often, a country may list more than one official language. Otherwise both RELIGION and LANGUAGE are in rank ordering.

LITERACY generally indicates the percentage of the population above the age of 15 who can read and write. There are no universal standards of literacy, so these estimates are based on the most common definition available for a nation.

LIFE EXPECTANCY represents the average number of years a group of infants born in the same year can be expected to live if the mortality rate at each age remains constant in the future. (Data from the CIA *World Factbook*.)

GDP PER CAPITA is Gross Domestic Product divided by midyear population estimates. GDP estimates for independent nations and dependencies use the purchasing power parity (PPP) conversion factor designed to equalize the purchasing powers of different currencies.

Individual income estimates such as GDP PER CAPITA are among the many indicators used to assess a nation's well-being. As statistical averages, they hide extremes of poverty and wealth. Furthermore, they take no account of factors that affect quality of life, such as environmental degradation, educational opportunities, and health care.

ECONOMY information for the independent nations and dependencies is divided into three general categories: Industry, Agriculture, and Exports. Because of structural limitations, only the primary industries (Ind), agricultural commodities (Agr), and exports (Exp) are reported. Agriculture serves as an umbrella term not only for crops but also for livestock, products, and fish. In the interest of conciseness, agriculture for the independent nations presents, when applicable, four major crops, followed respectively by leading entries for livestock, products, and fish.

NA indicates that data are not available.

NATIONAL GEOGRAPHIC

Concise
Atlas of the World

FOURTH EDITION

Published by National Geographic Partners, LLC

Copyright © 2016 National Geographic Partners, LLC. All rights reserved.
Reproduction of the whole or any part of the contents without written permission from the publisher is prohibited.

NATIONAL GEOGRAPHIC and Yellow Border Design are trademarks of the National Geographic Society, used under license.

ISBN: 978-1-4262-1660-2

The Library of Congress has cataloged the second edition as follows:
National Geographic
concise atlas of the world -- 2nd ed.
p.cm.
ISBN 978-1-4262-0196-7 (alk. paper)
1. Atlases.
G1021.C76.N43   2007
912--dc22
2007630027

First Edition 2003
Second Edition 2008
Third Edition 2012
Fourth Edition 2016

Since 1888, the National Geographic Society has funded more than 12,000 research, exploration, and preservation projects around the world. National Geographic Partners distributes a portion of the funds it receives from your purchase to National Geographic Society to support programs including the conservation of animals and their habitats.

National Geographic Partners, LLC
1145 17th Street NW
Washington, DC 20036-4688 USA

Become a member of National Geographic and activate your benefits today at natgeo.com/jointoday.

For information about special discounts for bulk purchases, please contact National Geographic Books Special Sales: ngspecsales@ngs.org

For rights or permissions inquiries, please contact National Geographic Books Subsidiary Rights: ngbookrights@ngs.org

Printed in Hong Kong

16/THK/1